The Tactical Edge

I like the edge, the challenge. I get a high off it. You're out there in the concrete jungle or the cornfield jungle. You know the guy you're up against has no regard for authority or society. He doesn't care about you. But he knows he's got to go, and you've got to get him.

I like the element of danger. It makes me feel *alive*. But I don't expose myself to danger blatantly. I'm not going to give anybody the opportunity to get even just a little bit of me if I can help it. Going up against danger and coming out whole because I'm prepared tactically, that's what the rush comes from.

My dad used to say there are no new frontiers...they've all been explored. But in our society, there's still one: the street. It's the only place you can be that has any edge to it....

—*Sgt. Dean Ray, Savannah, Georgia,
survivor of an armed confrontation
with a mentally deranged suspect
who had slashed a man's chest open
with a razor.*

The Tactical Edge

Surviving High-Risk Patrol

by
CHARLES REMSBERG
author of STREET SURVIVAL:
Tactics for Armed Encounters

photography and design by
DENNIS ANDERSON

Calibre Press · Northbrook, IL

Copyright © 1986 by Calibre Press, Inc.
First printing: January, 1986
Second printing: May, 1986
Third printing: December, 1986

Published by:
CALIBRE PRESS, INC.
666 Dundee Road
Suite 1607
Northbrook, Illinois 60062
(312) 498-5680
1-800-323-0037

Library of Congress Catalog Card Number: 85-73162
ISBN Number: 0-935878-05-X

Printed in the United States of America

**For those officers
who want to win**

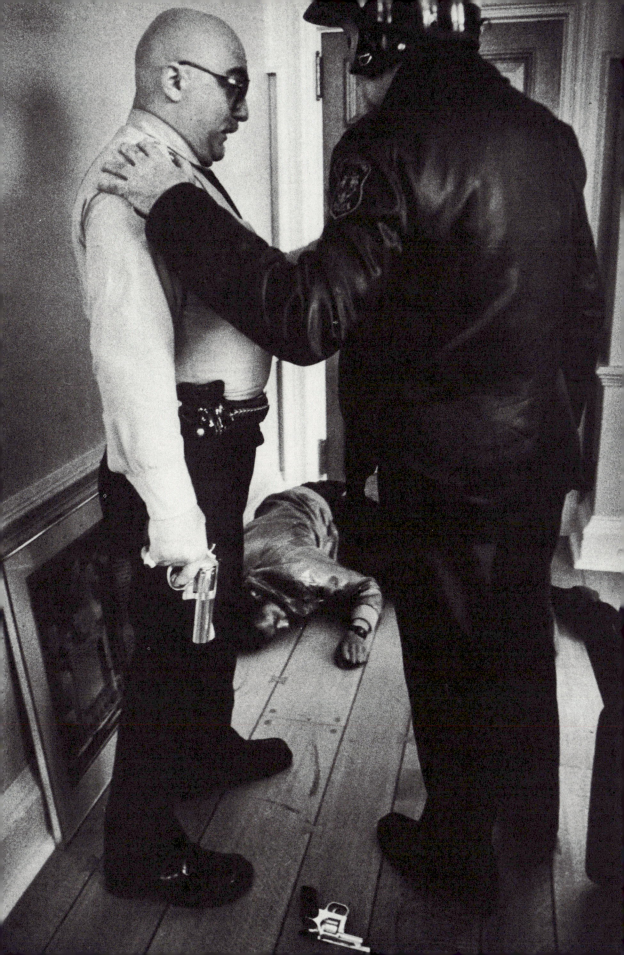

CONTENTS

ACKNOWLEDGMENTS

The thinking and experiences of hundreds of individuals have helped to shape the content of this book. Most have had extensive first-hand involvement with high-risk situations. All are dedicated to the advancement of law enforcement training, and particularly the cause of officer survival.

Research for **The Tactical Edge** began in 1980 after the publication and enthusiastic reception of the book, *Street Survival: Tactics for Armed Encounters* and the creation of the Street Survival® Seminar. Assured that whatever they shared would be used strictly within the law enforcement family in an on-going effort to save lives, officers, trainers, administrators and other interested professionals from throughout the world graciously responded with an inundation of letters, lesson plans, clippings, case reports, photographs, sketches, tapes, phone calls, demonstrations, Seminar questionnaire replies, invitations to training sessions and probing personal interviews. Overflowing files quickly expanded far beyond any initial anticipation...and so did the challenge of distilling the tactical wisdom from all those sources into some manageable and useful form. The last two years have been devoted intensely to that demanding task.

Some of those who helped have asked to remain anonymous. Also, anonymity has been granted to the officers and agencies involved in the case histories used to underscore tactical concepts. This is done in respect for privacy, not because the incidents are without documentation. To all these unnamed collaborators, including those who have lost their lives for lack of effective survival options—and to all others whose valuable assistance should be but inadvertently is not acknowledged—goes my deep appreciation.

Special thanks is due **Dave Tracy,** formerly a survival trainer and special-weapons team leader with the Baltimore County (MD) Police Department. His original concepts formed the foundation for the chapters on Tactical Thinking and hostage officers, and his tactical knowledge contributed heavily to several other chapters, including those on building searches, barricaded subjects and vehicle stops. His ability to analyze problem situations and articulate options was relied upon for answers to many thorny issues throughout the text.

Sergeant **Dave Smith,** proficiency skills supervisor with the Arizona Law Enforcement Training Academy, also had important input on multiple subjects, including vehicle stops, building searches, physical control and especially mental conditioning. His efforts in applying athletic performance techniques to the psychological conditioning of officers was a significant contribution.

Patrolman **David Lendzian,** a seasoned street officer with the New York City Police Department, prepared a series of specially commissioned manuscripts and research reports that supplied fresh ideas about survival attitudes, armed robbery responses, domestic disturbance calls, hand-to-hand combat and firearms proficiency. He also reviewed **The Tactical Edge** in manuscript form and offered numerous valuable suggestions for improvement.

Seven other reviewers also critiqued this book in full before its final editing, in some cases spending more than 100 hours detailing recommended alterations. They were selected for their long-standing commitment to officer survival and their breadth of knowledge about high-risk patrol tactics. Some were also interviewed at length on subjects ranging from chemical agent delivery to control of barroom brawls. The reviewers are:

Sergeant **Larry Hahn** of the Waterloo (IA) Police Department;

Sergeant **Wayne Corcoran** of the Phoenix (AZ) Police Department;

Sergeant **Steve Gibbs** of the Marion County (IN) Sheriff's Department;

Sergeant **A. C. Hart** of the Minneapolis (MN) Police Department;

Captain **Mark Stephens,** assistant provost marshal operations officer for law enforcement activity, United States Army, Fort Polk, LA;

Deputy **Brian Stover** of the Los Angeles County (CA) Sheriff's Department, and

Bill Groce, supervisor of firearms and tactical operations for the Ohio Peace Officer Training Academy.

Certain individuals served as major sources of specialized information, and in some cases they, too, reviewed portions of the manuscript. The special consultants include:

Psychologist **William J. Lewinski,** assistant professor in the law enforcement program at Mankato (MN) State University, who offered perceptive insights about body language, negotiation and mediation skills, the motivations and manipulation of barricaded subjects and the dynamics of domestic disturbances;

Kevin Parsons, director of the Justice System Training Association and one of the nation's foremost expert witnesses, who contributed stimulating ideas on the use of force and many innovative concepts from his R.I.S.C. Management System of Defensive Tactics;

Sergeant **Gary T. Klugiewicz,** defensive tactics coordinator for the Milwaukee County (WI) Sheriff's Department and world-class competitor in "knock-down" karate, whose development of Countermeasures and several new verbalization concepts and enthusiastic demonstrations of other realistic defensive tactics provided the foundation for much of the chapter on physical control;

Psychologist **Roger Solomon** of the Colorado Springs (CO) Police Department, whose shared his vast knowledge of officer stress, post-shooting effects, relaxation techniques and mental imagery and his original concept, the Survival Resource;

Bruce Siddle, special program coordinator, Greater St. Louis (MO) Police Academy, whose exhaustive investigation of the human nervous system and its vulnerability to pain and dysfunction undergirds the description of Pressure Point control;

Social Psychologist **F. Barry Schreiber,** associate professor in the Department of Criminal Justice at St. Cloud (MN) State University, and **Donald W. Rabon,** instructor/coordinator at the North Carolina Justice Academy, who helped formulate key tactical and verbal considerations for safely controlling domestic disturbances;

W. Fred Pickler, of Wilmington, North Carolina, a specialist in high-risk patrol tactics and chemical munitions, whose unsurpassed knowledge of chemical agents served to clarify many points of confusion and contradiction about that complex topic;

Gerald M. Smith, training coordinator, Smith & Wesson Academy, Springfield, Massachusetts, and Undersheriff **David Sikes** of the Clear Creek County (CO) Sheriff's Department, who offered important observations on body language and verbal skills related to physical control;

Dr. **William G. Farlow, Jr.,** of Rochester, New York, whose knowledge about the effects of high-powered rifle rounds on the human anatomy made an invaluable contribution to the understanding of proper sniper tactics;

James Lindell, supervisor of physical training for the Kansas City (MO) Police Department Regional Training Academy, whose dogged physiological research is reflected in the description of proper neck restraints;

Sergeant **Dean Ray** of the Chatham County (GA) Sheriff's Department, who generously shared the lessons of control he has learned from dealing with thousands of violent mental patients;

Officer **Jim Marsh,** coordinator of defensive tactics for the Chicago Police Department, who supplied valuable information related to the physical stamina of officers and to the improvement of handcuffing techniques, and

Special Agent **John C. Desmedt,** supervisor of defensive measures for the United States Secret Service, whose theories on tactical positioning, principles of physical control and management of resistant subjects were helpful in properly describing certain control techniques.

For additional research help, in some cases spanning several years, I wish to express my profound gratitude to: **Harvey Goldstein,** director of psychological services for the Prince George's County (MD) Police Department; Officer **Marvin Klepper,** remedial training officer, Los Angeles (CA) City Housing Authority Police; Lieutenant **Curtis McGee,** Detroit (MI) Police Department Training Academy; Security Director **Don Waterfill,** Jewish Hospital, Louisville, Kentucky; Sergeant **W. W. Wilson,** training coordinator, Valley Brook (OK) Police Department; Rangemaster **Maury Baitx,** Anaheim (CA) Police Department; Coordinator/Instructor **Charles Brown,** Oklahoma Council on Law Enforcement Education and Training; Police Officer **Steve May,** Modesto (CA) Police Department; **Larry Frahm,** commnications skills consultant, Lincoln, Nebraska; Sergeant **John R. Brooks,** Marion County (IN) Sheriff's Department; Commander **Gary Stryker,** Deerfield (IL) Police Department; **Debi Lebeda,** formerly a patrol officer with the Cedar Rapids (IA) Police Department; Officer **David D. Blood** of the Norfolk (VA) Police Department; Chief **Mike Nordin,** Sturgeon Bay (WI) Police Department; **Daniel Vega,** executive director of the Catalyst Counseling Center, Milwaukee, Wisconsin; Patrolman **James G. Smith,** Milwaukee (WI) Police Department; Patrolman **Robert C. Willis,** New Berlin (WI) Police Department; Reserve Deputy **Jeffery G. Cobb,** East Baton Rouge (LA) Parish Sheriff's Office; Sergeant **John Hyland,** president of the New York City Auxiliary Police Benevolent Association; Officer **John H. Pride,** firearms instructor, and former Captain **Mike Nielsen** (ret.), of the Los Angeles (CA) Police Department; Officer **Michael W. Quinn,** chemical agents instructor, Minneapolis (MN) Police Department; Sergeant **Robert Givan,** Indianapolis (IN) Police Department; **Herb Cohen,** Power Negotiations Institute, Northbrook, Illinois; Attorney **Joseph E. Scuro, Jr.,** San Antonio, Texas; Chief **Martin E. Strones,** Training Branch, Transportation Safeguards Division, United States Department of Energy; Trooper **David H. Miller,** North Carolina State Patrol; Training Officers **Larry E. Scott** and **Gary Berry,** Ohio Peace Officer Training Academy; Deputy **Emlyn Cassman,** Baton Rouge Parish (LA) Sheriff's Office; Training Sergeant **Richard Lee,** Shawnee County (KS) Sheriff's Department; Sergeant **James Vizza,** New York City Police Academy; Reserve Sergeant **J. Howard Cooper,** Struthers (OH) Police Department; Statistical Assistant **Patricia A. Lee,** Federal Bureau of Investigation; **Edward Nowicki,** police training coordinator, Milwaukee (WI) Area Technical College; Trooper **Shayne Slovacek,** Oklahoma Highway Patrol; Inspector **Les C. Smith,** United States Marshals Service; Lieutenant **Rich Wemmer,** Los Angeles (CA) Police Department; **Massad Ayoob** and **Ray Chapman,** instructors for the Advanced Officer Survival Seminar, and **John S. Farnam,** Defense Training, Inc., Niwot, Colorado.

For special consideration that made possible continued progress on this book at several key points, I thank Colonel **Ralph T. Milstead,** director of the Arizona Department of Public Safety.

I wish also to express my appreciation to **Dennis Anderson,** co-founder of Calibre Press, Inc. His dynamic creativity and tireless efforts helped in innumerable ways to push this long project across the finish line. My thanks, too, to the employees and professional consultants of Calibre Press, Inc., who contributed in their individual ways to make this book possible.

And finally, I want to thank my wife, **Colleen,** who was there through the good days and the sleepless nights alike and whose resourceful and inspiring support never wavered. My debt to her is beyond words.

Charles Remsberg
Northbrook, Illinois

INTRODUCTION

Back before officer survival got the attention it does today, four California Highway Patrolmen were gunned down one night during a traffic stop involving two ex-convicts with bank robbery on their minds. Later the offender who started the shooting reflected on the first victim: "He got careless, so I wasted him."

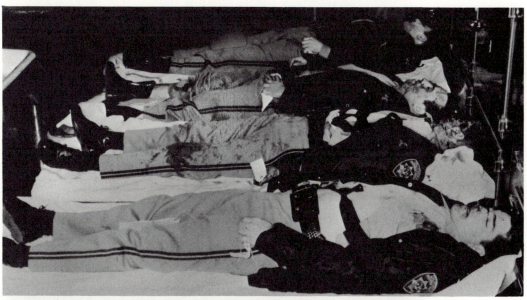

There's a lot less "wasting" now. More officers understand that despite the high risks they encounter on patrol, whether they come home at the end of their shifts can be determined by more than just chance. They know that fatalistically believing "When your number's up, it's up" or "If someone really wants to take you, there's nothing you can do about it" is obsolete thinking. They are no longer content to operate on the old police attributes of nerve, luck and raw courage.

They are committed to **winning by design,** even against long odds.

This commitment is paying off. In 1973, 134 law enforcement officers were killed in the line of duty in the United States. Since then, the toll has *dropped significantly,* in some years reaching the *lowest* levels since federal authorities began compiling these figures in 1971. But this welcome improvement is not because today's offender is any less violent than those in the past. Indeed, the consensus is that there is a *greater* capacity for violence on the street today than ever before.

What's making the difference is that officers now are more aware of the adversary's ways and will...and more dedicated to the mental attitudes and tactical maneuvers that can defeat his violent intent.

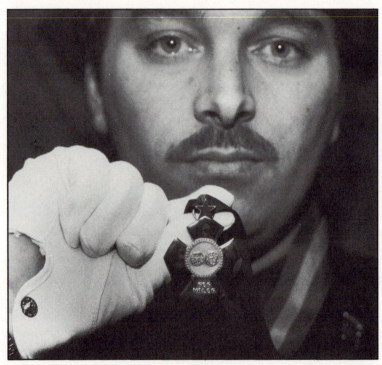

This Medal of Honor was awarded for a single-handed capture of two suspects. The first suspect rushed his car and fired. The officer rolled out, took cover and wounded the suspect. A second occupant went for his gun, and was wrestled to the ground.

The first book in this series, *Street Survival: Tactics for Armed Encounters* and the two-day Seminar that grew out of it helped foster that dedication. The goal of **The Tactical Edge** is to expand and advance it.

This is not a revision of *Street Survival* nor a substitute for it. The two books should be regarded as distinct but complementary works. *Street Survival* offers you the *core considerations* for surviving and winning an armed confrontation. **The Tactical Edge** shows you how to use those fundamentals in *tactical strategies* of thinking and deployment at a wide variety of high-risk calls. If you regard *Street Survival* as being about climbing, **The Tactical Edge** is about mountaineering. One book builds on the other; together they constitute the most comprehensive treatment of what it takes to stay alive in law enforcement ever published.

Besides enhancing your personal skills, this volume can provide a wealth of information for updating and improving your academy and in-service training. In some needy quarters, hopefully, it may stimulate action for the first time. For despite the gains of recent years, some administrators still dismiss officer survival as "militaristic bullshit." One survey of more than 250 departments, in fact, revealed that *47% did not conduct officer survival training.* Of those that did, 70% did so only in their basic academies.[1]

Such departments are missing a documented opportunity to serve not only their own officers but their public, as well. One major East Coast agency, for example, has overhauled its entire firearms program to reflect officer survival principles. It has eliminated old-fashioned bullseye targets and instituted moving and multiple targets...close-combat shooting...dim-light firing...cover and concealment exercises... qualification for off-duty weapons...guidelines for verbal challenges...and practical, stressful, decision-making role-playing in a tactical "fun house."

The result:
• armed confrontations down 45%
• officers wounded or killed down 56%
• offenders wounded or killed down 51%.

Yet felony contacts by that agency (many of which *could* have resulted in shootings) have increased 28% and felony arrests are up 10%. In short, more policing, fewer injuries and casualties. Rather than breed a kind of reckless vigilantism, as some administrators seem to fear, survival training fosters *conservative* control measures.

Courts are increasingly supporting such efforts by holding administrators legally liable for negligence if an officer or someone else is injured because they have failed to provide contemporary, realistic, job-related training. Administrators who continue to ignore their training obligation do so today at their own peril.

Yet even the most conscientious department is—and will be— hampered in its training efforts by budget constraints, manpower constraints, time constraints, political constraints, creativity constraints and a host of other very real limitations that can easily sabotage a *willingness* to train. Formal training by many agencies *is* vastly improving, but: *Compared to what is needed or desired, training in most departments will ALWAYS fall short.*

Which leaves a cold, hard bottom line:

THE GAP BETWEEN THE TRAINING YOU GET SPOON-FED AND WHAT YOU NEED TO SURVIVE ON THE STREET IS LEFT UP TO *YOU* TO FILL. That gap does not have to be very wide to make you vulnerable. Just wide enough for an offender to fire a bullet through.

This book will help you help yourself. Its content examines in detail tactics and techniques for controlling the situations you encounter on patrol that are most likely to expose you to life-threatening assault.

---

[1]Nielsen and Eskridge, "Police Shooting Incidents," *Law and Order*, March, 1982.

Some information will help you *prevent* attacks by would-be assailants. Other will help you successfully *overcome* attacks that still occur despite your best efforts. Still other will improve your insights into your *adversary's thoughts and actions* so you can be better prepared to anticipate and counter them.

Tactical *options* are presented, recognizing that the same approach does not always work best for every officer or in every situation. These options are *evaluated* where appropriate, so you can better judge which choice is likeliest to protect you effectively, given the circumstances you face. Although most of these options are explained in the context of specific calls— hostage barricades, vehicle stops, domestic disturbances, etc.—keep in mind that the *principles* that underlie them are usually applicable across the board in safely managing *any* high-risk situation.

In some cases, the options given may contradict the "right" ways you learned in the past. This is a *positive* development. It shows that police tactics are undergoing an appropriate evolution as more thought is focused on them, more field testing is being conducted under street conditions...and as offenders continue to change and strengthen their tools and methods of operation. *Your tactics should never remain static,* because the world in which you need to perform is constantly in flux. Indeed, as you experiment with what you find here you undoubtedly will discover ways of your own to improve further on what are believed to be the best protective measures currently available.

In most chapters, *procedures* are referenced, as well as tactics and techniques. Although it is accurately said that the true test of a police department's effectiveness is the manner in which it deals with high-risk situations, many (if not most) law enforcement agencies lack any kind of policy-and-procedural guide for high-risk calls. Officers are left on their own to develop response plans. Commonly they end up doing whatever comes to mind; often what one officer tries conflicts with what another is attempting. If this is the case in your jursidiction, the structures outlined for getting through dangerous calls can be invaluable aids to strengthen your tactical maneuvers and those of your fellow officers. They can also serve as a guideline for written departmental policies.

Firearms, of course, are positioned throughout as an important part of your tactical response. Your gun, after all, is your ultimate defense for your life, and your skill in using it may in some situations be the only edge you'll have against a violent assailant. Yet you should emerge from this book with a fresh appreciation of how much *more* there is to officer survival than mere firearms proficiency. As you read, remain aware of how:

1. **Mental Conditioning** can prepare you for a crisis encounter before it happens and help you cope with stress hazards during and after its occurrence;

2. **Tactical Thinking** helps you safely and confidently approach not only the high-risk situations you may confront every day but also the ultra-dangerous rarity you may face only once in your career;

3. **Verbal Manipulation** can enable you to prevent a volatile confrontation from escalating and let you nonviolently defuse a situation that is already near its flashpoint;

4. **Physical Skills** may keep you alive and in many cases injury-free when you cannot resort to deadly force;

5. **Attitude** is essential in gaining the tactical edge...and keeping it until the day you retire. More than anything else, high-risk calls are "attitude" calls.

A key component of a survival attitude is the willingness to *practice* what you read about BEFORE you need to use it on the street. Repeated "rehearsal" in a safe setting not only improves your retention but can instill a sense of having "been there before," which will underscore your self-confidence and performance when you are confronting real danger. Remember, though, that the old saying, "practice makes perfect," is not entirely accurate. It's *perfect* practice that makes perfect. Otherwise, you are simply creating and imprinting new bad habits.

Some material that follows will refresh and reinforce what experience or common sense have already taught you. Other concepts and methods will be new to you. Incorporating them into your patrol behavior may require that you break old habits and carefully develop new ones. You can minimize your risk of becoming discouraged and bolster your will to persevere if you remember this Stairway to Survival.

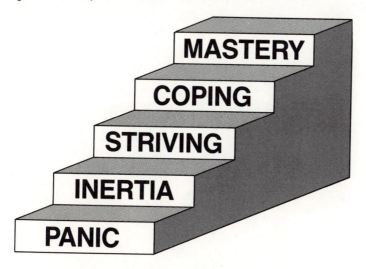

It is *normal* when confronting new challenges to experience mild *panic.* You may question your ability to solve the tactical problems you face, and you may feel frustrated, confused, uncertain, depressed. This may be followed by *inertia,* where you feel hopeless and lack initiative, perhaps feel sorry for yourself. Here you may be tempted to decide, "Aw, shit, I'll just take my chances." But if you consciously recommit yourself to surviving, you will then find yourself *striving* with serious effort and energy to improve. As you gain proficiency with new tactics, you'll build confidence by *coping* with more and more problems. Finally, you will achieve *mastery,* where your survival practices have become a way of life…where you have an unshakable belief in yourself and your ability to win…where *YOU ARE IN CONTROL OF YOUR FATE.*

As you revise and expand your survival skills in the years ahead, you may have to scale these steps many times. If there comes a time when you doubt whether mastery is worth all it takes, just reread the next 14 paragraphs. They highlight major social trends that impact your job. And they are only part of what could be mentioned.

• The U.S. prison population is now at a record high, up more than 40% since 1980. After incarceration averaging four years or less even for serious violent crimes, most convicts will be back on the street, better schooled legally, better conditioned physically and better equipped tactically.

Expectations when you're inside: Relaxation…Exercise…Escape.

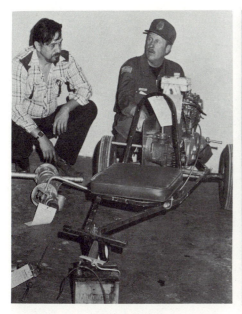

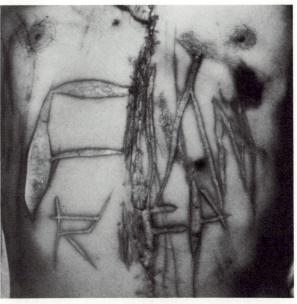

Corrections personnel look over a homemade, one-man helicopter found inside a maximum security prison.

The chest of an inmate who was murdered during a recent major prison riot. While still alive and held down, his body was mutilated with gang graffiti.

A disturbing phenomenon. Early release for inmates to ease an overcrowded prison.

• Low bail or no bail is being set by judges in many jurisdictions to keep down the populations of overcrowded jails. Offenders in record numbers are jumping bail, remaining at large beyond their trial dates.

• More than half the population growth in this country in the next 20 years will come from ethnic minority groups, which have the highest ratio of law enforcement contact and are disproportionately associated with criminal violence.

• Arsenals of deadly weapons are being stockpiled by private armies associated with the so-called "survivalist" movement. These fast-growing paramilitary groups are training thousands of members with machine guns, antitank cannons, rocket launchers and even antiaircraft artillery. Some advocate that member households keep on hand from 12 to over 100 guns per person.

A member of the Invisible Empire, Knights of the Ku Klux Klan takes part in a "special forces" maneuver.

Armed with a special gun which shoots paint pellets, a survivalist captures the "enemy flag" during a game called Strategy Plus.

Outlaw motorcycle gangs pose an increasing threat to you. There are over 900 gangs in the United States alone with estimates of over 10,000 members. Their past criminal activity has included the execution of police officers.

A member of the "peacekeeping force" for a major West Coast religious cult whose members are heavily armed.

• More than 10 million people in this country are trained to some degree in the martial arts, giving them a fighting skill that most police officers lack.

• Among the U. S. population generally, there are now nearly four times as many machine guns and assault rifles in the hands of private citizens as in the hands of police officers.

• Among inner-city teen-agers, the current status symbols are fully automatic weapons, rifles and sawed-off shotguns. An epidemic of black-market guns has made them as easy as drugs for kids as young as 10 to obtain.

• Social scientists and street cops alike point to "a shifting nature of crime," with robbery, especially, becoming increasingly vicious. "We are dealing with individuals who are using more guns than ever before, and the individuals who are using them have less regard for human life than they did in the past," says one chief of detectives. Middle- and upper-class offenders are showing up more frequently.

• New evidence is confirming that violence on television has a significant effect in producing violence in real life, especially among young people. Television viewing, meanwhile, has reached a new level in U. S. households—more than seven hours a day.

• Pre-schoolers left in day-care centers are 15 times more aggressive than other youngsters, according to one study. Their behavior is not just more assertive but involves physical violence, verbal abuse and resistance to authority. The public schools, meantime, report growing numbers of "a new kind of child," with "different values" and profound problems that our schools are ill-equipped to handle. During a recent 30-year span, serious crime by youngsters under 15 years of age multiplied by 110 times.

Teenager uses detective's car for a trampoline while being cheered by a companion. Retaliation for a drug bust.

Outside a bar two youths brutally assault and rob this man for $31.

• Some sociologists argue that our population will get less violent as it grows older. Yet serious offenses—including criminal violence—are increasing at a more furious rate among the elderly than among the population generally. Almost 30% of the crime committed by aged offenders is violent, and the problem is expected to worsen as the number of people over 65 doubles by the end of the century.

• In 1948 there were three times as many police officers as violent crimes. Now there are twice as many violent crimes as there are police.

• Experts consider it "a definite possibility" that today's typical officer will experience at least one armed encounter during his career. "People are no longer hesitant to respond violently to an armed policeman," says the executive director of a major crime commission. "It used to be that whatever you do, you don't kill a cop. People don't have that block any more."

Some officers construct for themselves what psychologists call a "personal fable." This is a fantasy of being special and not subject to the natural laws which pertain to others. The "story" these officers tell themselves about themselves is that nothing bad is ever going to happen to them. Or because they just never happen to run into the wrong situation at the wrong time, they believe the poor tactics they use are really satisfactory. This gives rise to the "veteran hairbag," the sarcastic locker room commando who criticizes, maligns and questions survival-oriented officers as if they were court jesters.

A bit of graffito scrawled in the squad room of one police station tells the truth:

"This ain't the movies
and you ain't John Wayne."

On the street you will meet the human beings, the weapons, the mentalities behind the dismal facts above. They are waiting for you. Either you or they will have the edge.

I

THE
MENTAL
EDGE

MENTAL CONDITIONING

An off-duty deputy sheriff driving along a California freeway was picked at random by members of an outlaw motorcycle gang for torment and intimidation. Their traffic harassment escalated quickly to a road-side confrontation. Then, amidst their verbal abuse, the bikers suddenly flashed guns, and shooting erupted. Facing six armed assailants, the deputy shot two, then ran to a nearby auto repair shop and called police. As the others closed in, blasting away at his position, he stayed on the line, giving a running account of the action and reporting his name, badge number, exact location, even the name and phone number of his watch commander. Sporadically, he interrupted himself to shout out warnings and to fire back at his attackers. Two more went down, one so close that the dispatcher could hear his body hit the ground. Yet throughout the battle, the deputy's voice stayed calm, authoritative and articulate, no more emotional than if he were running a license check. Each of his four shots scored a solid hit, and he avoided any personal injury. He was just 17 days out of his academy....

In Florida, an officer was caught by surprise while investigating a possible break-in at a convenience mart and was shot at belt level with a .22 round that "felt like being hit with a baseball bat." Even as he was falling backward, he drew his gun and fired back, ending the assault before more serious injury occurred and sending the attacker fleeing. Then, despite concern about his wound, he helped the dispatcher direct the response. He requested only one unit, to minimize confusion at the scene, and methodically outlined the safest approach route for that officer, in light of the gunman's line of flight. He commented on the radio that there was no need for anyone else to get injured and urged responding officers to drive safely....

Another Southern officer, responding to a rape-in-progress in a car, took six hits from the armed offender before incapacitating him with a shotgun. One of the first bullets smashed into the officer's mouth and destroyed a large part of his tongue. When he tried to radio for help, the dispatcher could not decipher his mumbles, so the officer showed the near-hysterical rape victim how to use his radio. Then, bleeding profusely, he comforted her and tended his wounds until help came. When responding officers arrived, they found him standing alert and ready to help in any way he could. By this time, more than half his uniform was drenched in his own blood.

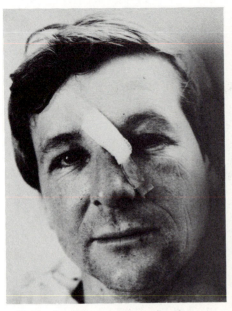

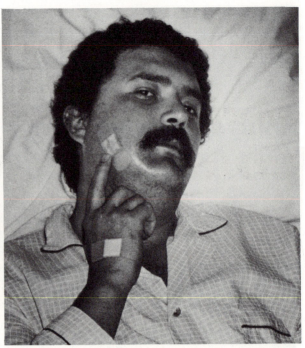

A bullet fired by one of two bank robbers ricocheted off this deputy's patrol car and struck him between the eyes. After being shot, he pursued the men 3 miles and aided in their capture. Only then did he allow himself to be taken to a hospital.

An excellent example of mental conditioning, this chief was shot in the cheek, swallowed the bullet and then proceeded to incapacitate the offender.

If Academy Awards were given for performances under stress, officers like these would walk away with Oscars. And yet other officers, with comparable experience and professional training and in circumstances of no greater pressure, react in ways that are barely functional.

For instance, an Oklahoma detective team hunting two prison escapees on a murder spree spotted the fugitives standing beside their stolen truck in a residential driveway a few miles from where they had just gunned down two state troopers. The detectives were nearly a block away, but the driver sped their unit directly to the mouth of the driveway and *stopped*, only feet from the killers. His maneuver placed his partner directly in the assailants' line of fire. One of them promptly blew off the top of the partner's head...In Illinois, officers trying to control a hostage-taker at a roadblock completely surrounded his vehicle, oblivious to their blatant cross-fire exposure. Although the suspect had a revolver in hand, one officer walked up within inches of him, with no cover and with his own semi-automatic holstered, to negotiate. When talking failed and shooting broke out, officers *left* cover positions to rush closer. In a barrage of bullets, the offender was killed—with his hands extended out his open door, trying to surrender...During the nighttime pursuit of an armed robber who was fleeing from a shootout with police, an officer in the Southwest within minutes: fired two shotgun blasts from his speeding patrol car at the suspect's vehicle without any idea where the rounds hit, ran *toward* the suspect on foot after the gunman stopped his car and fired two shots at the officer, took off in foot pursuit without advising his location and with no radio or flashlight, kept going despite losing sight of the suspect, and then ran past his hiding places and through his line of fire three times without seeing him. Later the officer had such poor recall of the incident that he could not remember that he and his partner had totaled their vehicle at the end of the car chase....

What accounts for these radical contrasts in response? How can some officers exhibit calm and control against incredible challenges, yet others be so overwhelmed with fear, anger, excitement or panic that they make themselves—or fellow officers—easy candidates for stretchers or body bags?

An interesting response to a subject's verbal threats. The officer (top photo) elected to place his gunbelt and baton on the sidewalk, out of camera view, to deal with the situation! After the subject left, the officer walked away toting his gear. He was suspended from duty for having disarmed himself before dealing with the threat.

The answer is not necessarily that those who fail to perform well are just ignorant or contemptuous of survival principles. Some, through reading and role-playing, are actively striving for survival mastery, but still fall drastically short when the chips are down.

The explanation lies with the orphan child of officer survival training: *mental* preparedness.

The first three officers cited, either through deliberate study or by trial and error, have hit upon the psychological secrets of maintaining composure even under enormous stress. Their mental control allowed them to select and apply appropriate tactical options without emotional disruption. *Everyone* has that capability. Yet thousands of officers, like those others described above, are failing to tap it.

From *Street Survival: Tactics for Armed Encounters*, you'll recall that mental/physical preparation, along with tactics and shooting skill, comprise the essential elements of the "survival triangle," a figurative shield from harm. From what is *now* known about officer survival, the mental/physical component should occupy the triangle's *foundation*, connoting key importance. Yet survival training tends to focus almost exclusively on improving tactics and firearms proficiency, with heavy emphasis on equipment considerations. Lately, physical fitness is beginning to draw some attention, too. But the concept of preparing *mentally* for survival—a *core* concept—remains, for the most part, either sadly slighted or misunderstood. Trainers and street cops alike either don't really know *how* to prepare mentally, or they don't fully appreciate the remarkable degree to which you can actually *program* your mind and body to carry you successfully through a violent confrontation. The consequence of this neglect is a shallow approach to survival...and needless tragedy.

Your mind is the most dangerous weapon you carry on patrol. The extent to which it is prepared for a high-risk, high-stress encounter determines for *whom* it is dangerous. *Properly* prepared, it can be a paralyzing threat to your adversary. *UN*prepared, it can prove devastating to *you* or to your fellow officers because of its capacity, under stress, to mercilessly sabotage your performance.

If you approach high-risk situations without the proper mental preparation, the strongest force in deciding your destiny is going to be *luck*. In fact, after studying dozens of shootings, one trainer has assigned this relative weighting to the factors that tend to determine whether *UN*prepared officers survive:

> Mental Skill.............. 5%
> Physical Skill............ 5%
> Shooting Skill 15%
> LUCK 75%

With such a small reservoir of mental skills to draw upon, these officers' responses to a crisis situation tend to be *strong in uncontrolled emotions, weak in disciplined tactics.* Stress overwhelms their thought processes, often with results few would ever have predicted. For example, two officers stopped a young suspect who was driving a stolen vehicle. As one officer approached the vehicle, the suspect suddenly produced a snub-nose .38 and without speaking a word cranked off five fast rounds, hitting the officer in the face. The victim's partner reacted by drawing her service revolver and, after firing once and missing, reportedly *threw* it toward the offender. She then turned and ran. He shot her in the lower back. Luck saved her life, but her partner's luck was not so good; he died.

(Top) The hat of an officer who was shot twice as he attempted to arrest three men. This badge, shot off the hat, saved the officer's life. (left) This officer narrowly escaped death when an offender's bullet penetrated his notebook and bounced off a metal pen in his jacket pocket.

Officers are sometimes asked by civilian friends: "Who are you most scared of out on the street?" The officer who's unprepared mentally *should* answer, without hesitation: "Me."

Instead of going on patrol feeling confident because he is *competent*, this type of officer operates either with a lurking *fear* of what might happen or with an immobilizing *insecurity* about his ability or with a cocky *denial* that anything might arise that he couldn't control. When such officers—or partners who are depending on them—are killed, "failure to be effective in the face of a threat" should be listed as a contributing cause of death.

In truth, most threats *can* be successfully defeated or out-maneuvered. Luck—good or bad—can probably never be eliminated entirely as an element in staying alive. But its ranking on your survival scale can be dramatically *reordered*. What *truly prepared* officers can depend on for winning violent clashes is this:

> MENTAL SKILL......... 75%
> Shooting Skill 15%
> Physical Skill............. 5%
> Luck.................... 5%

On their chart, not chance but the factors that they can *control* predominate. And mental preparedness, because of its crucial role in conquering stress and directing tactics, heads the list.

One way mental preparation has been given short shrift, even by conscientious officers, is by being regarded too superficially. Commonly it's equated only with staying aware of possible dangers and "psyching up" a "will to win" against any assailant who takes you on. These ingredients—alertness and commitment—*are* vital. But to prepare yourself mentally *to the fullest extent possible* you need to delve much deeper than that.

In this chapter, you can learn proven techniques for developing a *thoroughly prepared* survival mind. With them, you can *condition* yourself mentally so that your mind will be *predisposed* to helping you survive a crisis on the street. This mental training will *automatically* and *reliably* enable you to:

1. minimize the perilous stress overload inherent in any life-or-death situation;
2. select your best tactical options for controlling threats and for counter-assaulting;
3. better perform any physical moves demanded by these tactics, and
4. maximize your chances of surviving if you are injured.

Honing your mind to this level requires practice long before the moment of need. You cannot just *read* about the regimen involved now and expect it to save you six months or six years from now when you're staring down the barrel of an offender's gun. That's "magical thinking," a co-conspirator of luck in destroying police lives. Once you've intellectually absorbed the techniques that follow, you need to begin *working* on a *conditioning program* that features them. By *regularly* repeating easy-to-learn, easy-to-do mental exercises, you will quickly improve your mental capability, much as physical exercises improve your muscle capability.

Just "trying harder" to stay calm and perform well on hazardous calls is not enough. That approach may, in fact, prove *counter* productive, by actually *increasing* your anxiety and thus further impeding your performance. What works better is a more sophisticated *system* for mental self-conditioning that is increasingly being used by Olympic and professional athletes to sharpen their performances in stressful competition. The United States military also has begun training command personnel in these methods to enhance their tactical decision-making during combat. Here, the system that helps these people win against their adversaries has been adapted specifically to *your* needs as a law enforcement officer. *This system works* because it takes into account and *positively* exploits the way in which the human body reacts to stress and threat.

THE MORE YOU MASTER THE MENTAL EXERCISES PRESCRIBED, THE BETTER YOU WILL BE ABLE TO USE THE TACTICS FOR CONTROLLING HIGH-RISK ENCOUNTERS DESCRIBED IN THE REMAINDER OF THIS BOOK.

Your mental preparation begins with understanding a fundamental phenomenon of physiology....

The Mind/Body Partnership

Many people think of the mind and the body as separate entities, but in reality they operate much like a police partnership. When you and another officer respond to a call, what each of you does or experiences necessarily affects the other, in blatant or subtle ways. A similar interplay carries messages and reactions back and forth between your mind and your body and your body and your mind, so that the influence of each registers unavoidably on the other. There are physiological manifestations of what is on your mind and psychological manifestations of what happens to you physically.

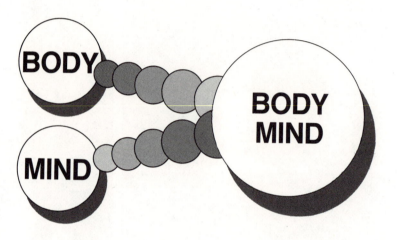

This *unified* relationship is what makes it possible for you to control stress and to improve your decision-making and physical performance through mental conditioning.

You can document the two-way connection with two quick experiments. Trying them both now will help you better understand and have confidence in the exercises suggested for managing stress and preparing mentally for patrol.

First, to demonstrate how your body—and your physical moves—can affect you mentally, *frown* as you would if you wished to display anger or displeasure. Don't consciously try to *feel* that way; just contract your facial muscles as if you did. If you hold that expression, you will find your mind flooding with negative thoughts and emotions within a few seconds. Similarly, adopt the posture of depression—hanging your head, slumping your shoulders, looking "down in the mouth," etc. Soon you'll have a mental state to match. Your body is stimulating your mind to react via physical cues. Researchers in fact have documented a body-mind-body "feedback loop." Subjects who mimic facial expressions of anger, fear, sadness, disgust, surprise and happiness not only quickly begin to *feel* those emotions but also soon experience *measurable changes* in heart rate, hand temperature, skin resistance and muscle tension. Their minds, reacting to physical in-put, relay back "mood messages" to their bodies, causing more profound physiological change. Indeed, some researchers now contend that subjects can control the physical changes measured by polygraphs just by controlling their facial expressions.

A good example of mind and body working together to perform a unique feat. This body builder is lifting two trucks with a combined weight of eight tons. His mind told his body he could succeed at his goal, and he did.

To confirm that your mental processes can directly generate physical reactions beyond your conscious control, make a pendulum by tying about 10 inches of string or thread to a small, light object, like a paper clip, finger ring or steel washer. With your elbow resting on a stable surface and bent at about 45° hold the string gently between your thumb and forefinger, letting the weight dangle. Without moving your arm or fingers, think to yourself: "Yes...yes...yes...," over and over again. *Concentrate* on that thought. With most people, the pendulum soon will begin a definite movement, either in a circle or along an axis. If you change your thought to "No...no...no...," the pendulum's motion will change, too. Do not try to anticipate or direct the movement; the weight will consistently activate on its own.

This may seem like a séance trick, but it actually results from tiny muscle contractions you cannot see or feel. Your mind is transmitting subconscious communications, and your body is responding.

The principles involved can be put to serious practical purpose on your behalf on the street. The easiest and most immediate application is in coping with stress.

Stress Response

Stress is the strain placed on your internal systems by anything that disturbs or makes a demand of you. Being under some degree of stress is a natural part of being alive and reacting to stimuli from your environment. Your body can accommodate some stress without undue wear and tear. But your inner reactions to a *major* disturbance—like the acute crisis of a shooting, a fight, a high-speed chase or some other violence-laden event—quickly can tax or surpass your ability to adapt, *unless* your mental conditioning has equipped you with good stress-control skills. If an elevated level of stress *sustains* for a long period of time and becomes *chronic*, the effects on your health and lifestyle can be profound.

In a high-intensity episode, your mind/body circuitry is more alive with action than a pinball board. As your brain interprets incoming stimuli as threatening, it broadcasts urgent messages of arousal along your nerve network.

Adrenalin (sometimes called epinephrine), cortisol, aldosterone and other hormones pour into your bloodstream, mixing a "chemical cocktail" of alarm that reinforces and prolongs the stress reaction. Certain blood vessels tighten down and others expand as your circulatory system diverts blood away from your skin surface, your extremities and your digestive organs and channels it to the large muscle groups most closely related to strength and speed. Your heart and lungs work harder and faster to rush fresh nutrients to these tissues and clear away waste. Your spleen discharges more red blood cells into your bloodstream to increase your oxygen supply. Your liver releases stored sugar to hype your energy. Your blood pressure leaps. Your muscles tense, especially in your lower back, neck and shoulders, staying near the threshold of action in anticipation of movement. Your sweat glands kick in as your body tries to cool itself. And so on.

Uncomfortable feelings spawned by these physical changes are detected by your brain as *psychologically alarming.* These internal signals increase your *mental* distress which, in turn, prompts even more *physical* reaction. Before long, the stress "feedback loop" is racing in high gear.

Eons ago, when human biology first emerged, cavemen experienced identical psycho-physiological reactions when they confronted dangerous wild animals. The arousal syndrome quickly prepared them either to *fight* the threat or take *flight* from it. In that context, stress responses were crucial to survival; the diversion of blood to large muscle groups, for instance, prepared the arms for swinging and the legs for running, both potentially life-saving movements.

Today, the equipment you carry is more sophisticated than the clubs of your Neanderthal ancestors and the *responses* that are appropriate or even possible for you to make to threats are often much more complex than their brute reactions. Your internal response to stress has endured as your legacy from prehistoric times. But because your response options now must usually be so different from mere fight or flight, acute stress in *your* environment may endanger—or *terminate*—your survival rather than help it.

Extra blood nourishment for your large muscles means less for your small muscles involved in, say, finger dexterity and eye-hand coordination. Thus fine motor movements that ordinarily are easy may become impossible. Firing your sidearm accurately and smoothly or reloading quickly without fumbling will be much harder than if you were calm. With your digestive processes disrupted, you may experience nausea that is distracting or disabling. Your tightened muscles may affect your voice, making effective verbal challenges difficult...or your eyes, causing excessive watering and blurring your vision...or your breathing, making you choke or gasp and robbing you of stamina…or your flexibility, leaving you unable to perform important physical moves with the right fluidity and limberness.

Under high-stress bombardment, your brain is so busy devouring input and spewing out responses that other mental functions are necessarily sacrificed. The part of your brain responsible for large muscle control (essential for fighting or fleeing) gets priority at the expense of the part of your brain responsible for abstract thought. Your ability to *concentrate* is disrupted; the risk increases that you will select improper stimuli to focus your attention on. Your *judgment* suffers; your decisions are less likely to be appropriate to the demands of the situation, and indeed may be wildly inappropriate. Your *analytical thinking* is hampered; it's much tougher to reason clearly and logically about strategy and tactics, and harder to retrieve options from your memory. Your *creative capacity* shrinks; your hope of improvising good maneuvers on the spot virtually evaporates. In short, *anxiety overcomes function.* During what may prove to be critical moments, you may be overwhelmed by emotion, and in confusion and fear you may set up in your response the very errors that you desperately want and need to avoid.

Officers who've survived shootings and police psychologists who've later analyzed their behavior at the peak of those incidents point out several phenomena that commonly result from sudden super stress on the mind and body.[1] If you are like many other officers, at the moment your life is in greatest jeopardy you may have to contend not only with the adversary who's trying to kill you, but with your own:

Startle Response: This refers to the animal instinct to *jump* or

[1]Solomon and Horn, *Post-Shooting Traumatic Reactions*, 1984.

make other involuntary movement in reflex to a sudden fright, such as the sight or sound of a firearm. The more you are caught by surprise, the more startle reaction you'll have and the greater will be your lag time in responding to counter the threat. Even when gunfire is anticipated, such as in an extended barricaded suspect incident, the first shot by either side usually startles officers at the scene. One patrolman, assigned to the inner perimeter at a barricade site in the Southwest, was standing in a concealed position with his shotgun on his hip when the suspect fired the initial round. The officer jumped at the noise and his finger pulled the trigger, sending a round blasting into the air. This not only jeopardized fellow officers, but gave away his position, allowing the assailant to aim his next shots directly at the officer's location. Another officer, in Nevada, was startled when his partner fired at an armed offender. He spun to look in the direction of the sound. A bullet from the adversary's gun that otherwise would have whizzed past his head caught him in his profiled face. Often an initial shot fired by a startled officer creates the "domino effect;" other officers reflexively begin to shoot, even though they may have no justifiable target. The end result is complete loss of fire control.

Thought Distraction: At the moment you need to focus your concentration on the threat, uninvited thoughts may jam your mind and divert your attention. Often these "racing" intrusions are doubtful questions or negative conclusions that you may "hear" phrased in your own voice: "Hey, can I really shoot this guy?" "If I shoot, I'll be sued!" "What's my sergeant gonna say?" "Is my line of fire clear?" "If I take him out, I'll be writing reports for two weeks," etc. Sometimes a fantasy of the confrontation is played out to the very end; one officer even "read" newspaper headlines of the outcome in his head as his assailant's bullets were flying around him. One study of survivors suggests that nearly 60% of the officers involved in shootings experience distracting thoughts at the height of their encounters. Their distraction is often compounded by their wondering, with aggravation, "Why on earth am I thinking about this at a time like *now*?"

Physical Distress: Your stress may express itself in ways that are even more upsetting or distracting. On the scene immediately before, during or after a high-risk episode, some officers vomit, some faint, a few

Patrolman sits in his car following a shootout. Paramedics in the background treat the offender who tried to kill the officer.

urinate or defecate beyond their control, and many suffer discomforts such as dry mouths, sweaty palms, aching muscles or throbbing chests. One officer who had just fatally wounded an assailant insisted to other officers that he could hear another offender in the vicinity. What he really heard were his own knees knocking. Again, surprise tends to be a factor in this phenomenon. Where assaults are unexpected, an estimated 60 to 75% of officers will have one or more noticeable physiological manifestations of stress.

After shots were fired into this bank robber's car, officers rushed up—unaware of crossfire problems.

Sensory Distortion: The odds are extremely high that during your stress crisis you will perceive the action unrealistically, in terms of what you see or hear or the amount of time the event appears to take. Often a variety of perceptual distortions occur. About half the officers in shootings suffer *visual* tricks. Your eyes may tunnel in on just a fragment of the bigger picture, blocking out what's above, below or to the sides of it like a television camera's zoom lens. In one Western state, an officer and an offender were wrestling when the officer's partner drew his gun. From then until he finished firing three shots, the partner admitted later, he saw nothing but the spot on the offender's back where he was aiming. Visually, the other officer simply did not register with him—so he never considered the possibility that his bullets might bore right through the suspect and strike that officer, who was clinched in the struggle. Fortunately, the suspect's backbone stopped or sufficiently slowed all the rounds. For some officers, size is distorted ("The asshole's derringer looked like a *cannon!*"); some experience exceptional acuity ("I could see the bullets in his chamber from 20 yards"); some see mental flash pictures of their families just before they shoot; a few hallucinate that an offender has already fired at them before the attack actually begins, or that they have fired back when they really haven't. Where *sounds* are concerned, nearly 65% of officers under peak stress experience distortions. *Auditory blocking*—hearing important sounds only faintly or not at all ("I did not hear any of the five shots fired by myself and my partner")—is most common. In fact, one prominent trainer claims that "as a general rule in an actual gunfight, you will fire three to five *times* as many rounds as you think you have." In a minority of cases, noise is intensified rather than diminished, and some officers hear a mixture ("The sniper's gun went '*BOOM*,' mine went 'pop'"). The sensation most frequently distorted is *time*. More than 80% of officers involved in shootings or other high-stress incidents perceive them occurring either much faster or much *slower* than they actually do. By far the more common distortion is a sense of slowness. The action may seem to unfold before you in slow motion, like one fluid, continuous movement, and you may feel impatient or alarmed because your responses appear unalterably slow, too.

Awareness Lapse: On rare occasions, you may mentally block out part of the stressful episode, not just after it's over but while the event is actually taking place. In a Western state, an outlaw biker tried to run over an officer with his motorcycle. As the officer leaped clear, he thought: "Someone ought to shoot this guy!" Seconds later, the biker toppled to the ground. The officer thought: "Great! Somebody shot him!" Then he looked down at his hand...and saw his smoking service revolver. He had no conscious awareness of having drawn and fired it. In California, two officers approached a mentally disturbed subject who was chopping down a telephone pole with an axe. Challenged, he knocked one officer to the ground and raised the axe over his head to swing it down on him. The partner saw this...and then the next thing he was conscious of was someone slapping him on the shoulder, saying, "Good shot!" In the interim, blanked out, he had drawn his gun, shot the axe-wielder and saved his fellow officer.

These stress phenomena are especially likely to occur the FIRST TIME you are involved in a shooting or some other critical incident. Some officers report that they *diminish* somewhat on repeat exposure. But if the first incident leaves deep emotional scars on you or leaves you plagued with unresolved fear, they may actually *intensify* the next time around.

Under the stress of seeing a dead officer lying on the sidewalk (left), the uniformed officer's response was to keep his sidearm holstered. The shootout involved two men who were being served an eviction notice. The plainclothes officer stayed low with his sidearm ready.

These phenomena and other aspects of the stress response can prove *fatal* if you are *unprepared* for their effects, because they can interfere with your ability to function at optimum capacity or at any capacity at all. Officers who respond inadequately in high-risk encounters are believed by psychologists in many cases to "freak out," freeze up or become dangerously distracted by these occurrences. They do not expect them and do not realize that for many officers they are *normal reactions to abnormal situations* at moments of peak stress. If you don't hear your rounds going off and don't understand sensory distortion, you may think your gun isn't working and stop trying to shoot...or you may continue to "fire" an empty weapon. You may fail to hear warnings shouted out by fellow officers or fail to see signs of danger that they pick up on. If your startle response to hearing gunfire is to look around wondering "What was *that?*" instead of diving for cover instantly, you may leave yourself vulnerable to attack precious seconds longer than necessary. If you experience the slow-motion effect but don't know that this can happen and do not understand that you are not *really* slowed down, you may frantically wonder, *"My God, why can't I move faster!"* and become so unnerved that you fail to function.

(On the other hand, you may be able to *use* some of these stress phenomena to your *advantage* if you expect them and thus are not alarmed by them. Two officers in Colorado were pursuing an armed robber when the suspect suddenly stopped his car, bailed out and started shooting. As the passenger officer started to roll out with a rifle, "Everything went slow motion." He perceived this distortion as an *aid,* telling himself, "Wow, I have *all the time I need* to steady myself, take aim and take this guy out." And that's exactly what he did. If you sense the action slowing down in a crisis, tell yourself, "This is one time I can deal with more things than ever before in my life." Don't consider it a limitation and stop. Keep going!)

Besides affecting your survival on the job, the impact of stress can have serious ramifications regarding your *courtroom* survival. In postshooting reports, you're expected to recall an armed encounter in detail. But sensory distortions or awareness lapses may cause you to report different "facts" than what forensic evidence or the statements of witnesses substantiate. Discrepancies may occur about the number of shots fired...how you handled your firearm...the distances between you and your assailants...the sequencing and timing of events...the presence of other persons at the scene...the nature of the threat, and so on. If other officers have lived through the same high-intensity event with you, you may *each* remember a different version of what happened. Then in the legal arena, you can end up looking unreliable or, worse, like you are trying to color or cover up the truth.

The more stress you are already under as you go into a high-risk situation, the more a surge of stress associated with a sudden crisis is likely to overwhelm you. And a *chronically high* level of stress is pandemic in law enforcement, compared to many other segments of the population.

Your day-by-day—sometimes minute-by-minute—contact with criminals, complainants and citizens alike who are crying, cursing, bleeding, puking, yelling, spitting, biting, fighting, lying, dying, dead, drunk, doped, dirty, scared, scarred, angry, vengeful, irrational, evasive, outlandish, grieving, manipulative, taunting, demanding, defiant, cruel, neurotic, hopeless and just plain crazy subjects your system to repeated onslaughts of disturbance. Laboratory observations indicate that just talking to strangers, arguing or being criticized—guaranteed staples of your day—can raise blood pressure *as high as 40 to 50%* above resting levels. Unless you know how to rid your mind and body of stress, each call leaves a residue that continues to smoulder after the original stimulus is gone and that builds cumulatively through your shift, although you may not be consciously aware of it. Even quiet periods are not necessarily restorative; *boredom* often can be almost as stressful as excitement. And back at the station, you may be forced to deal with supervisors and administrators whose personalities and/or policies compound the tension you feel from the street. Off the job, you may face marital problems, offspring problems, financial problems, second-job problems, house problems, car problems, medical problems, digestive problems, sex problems, sleep problems and other unpleasant stimuli that hammer you with pressure of their own.

Your mind and body cannot distinguish between these symbolic *emotional* "threats" to you and actual *physical* threats. Your brain relays the same alarm alert and your body gears up the same hormonal and cardiovascular fight-or-flight responses internally. The extent to which this occurs depends only upon the degree of anxiety you feel from these pressures.

Usually you do *not* fight or flee in these situations. Indeed, you may have to consciously *suppress* those impulses in order to behave professionally and legally. Therefore, the extra energy generated by the biochemical arousal is not exhausted. Consequently, the overmobilization of your body is, on at least some level, sustained and perpetuated. The stress by-products continue to circulate through your system until they can eventually be reabsorbed or otherwise used up.

Even in the midst of offering support to a wounded officer, the tactical officer still maintains a controlled reaction to a continuing hazard. Notice the barrel does not extend over the top of the wall.

You may become so accustomed to chronic stress that you are no longer conscious of it. Even so, it tends in time to fatigue your organs and your immunological response system. Eventually, the wear and tear of its insidious strain may provoke chronic tiredness, heart trouble, ulcers, cancer, migraine headaches, arthritis or other stress-related disorders. Some of these, in fact, end up killing far more officers every year than do hostile assaults.

Meanwhile, this inveterate stress makes you more prone to injury on the job. You are more likely to get hurt accidentally when you are tired and tense, because of your poorer coordination, your diminished mental alertness and your lessened commitment to caution. Moreover, *your stress burden sets you up to become a victim in a crisis:* it consumes reserves that might otherwise be available to help you absorb acute stress without overt, adverse reactions. In other words, if you're already close to being "stressed out" when you're thrust into a life-threatening confrontation, the urgent acute stress load, layered on top of the psychological stress you're already under, can hopelessly compound your mental and physical performance problems. Among other things, it can erode your reaction time to the point that you can't respond quickly enough to defend yourself even if you try to.

Because stress responses occur automatically, many people assume that little can be done to prevent or regulate them. True, you cannot always eliminate them entirely, but *with the proper techniques you can exert far more control over your reactions than you may imagine.* You do not have to be a victim of your own stress response.

As part of your mental conditioning, you can learn to:
1. *relax your mind and body* so that stress is minimized as you approach a potentially high-risk situation;
2. *control your reactions in a crisis* so that the occurrence and effects of stress threats to your survival are forestalled or vastly diminished;
3. *recover your equilibrium faster* after a high-intensity event, and
4. *reduce any chronic stress* before it reaches a dangerous level.

One of many experiments proving this is possible involved eight world-class pistol shooters.[2] Each was injected with a dose of adrenalin that would have completely overloaded the average person. Yet when these shooters then engaged targets, only two shot significantly less accurately than normal. The others all had developed strategies that were so efficient in controlling stress that they could counter even this mammoth upheaval of their nervous systems.

Your key to achieving this kind of control is breaking into the stress feedback loop. Just as the interplay between your mind and your body can *aggravate* stress, so can it also be used to *combat* stress if the proper signals are injected into the cycle. If either your mind or your body can be made to relax, it will message its partner that the alarm alert is no longer necessary, and a quieting effect will begin to spread by chain reaction throughout your whole system. *If your body relaxes, your mind must follow, and vice versa, because of the effect the signals have on the other.*

A multitude of proven stress management techniques are available. These include self-hypnosis, meditation, biofeedback, aerobic exercise, progressive muscle release and a variety of other methods designed to induce the relaxation response.

---

[2]Yagoda, "Relaxation," *Esquire*, May, 1984.

But the simplest and the most practical for law enforcement involves an easy task you already perform 20,000 times a day without conscious thought: *breathing.*

Relaxation Response

The type of breathing associated with stress is fast and shallow. So to break the stress cycle you want to breathe in just the opposite way, *slow* and *deep.* Most officers have to *learn* this breathing pattern because even during non-stressful parts of their day they tend to breathe poorly. Once you've mastered how to breathe to relax, you can use it as an antidote to both acute and chronic stress on the job and also as an essential *first step* in your mental conditioning for survival.

One option is to *"belly breathe,"* a method used with concentration to completely fill and flush out your lungs so that your body expels carbon dioxide waste and replenishes itself with fresh oxygen at a spaced, rhythmic rate. The effect is to reverse the alarm response, restore your psychological sense of self-control and return your body to a naturally balanced state.

Especially at first, practice this technique in a private, quiet, softly lighted place where you can stretch out in a reclining chair, on a bed or on the floor. Take the phone off the hook and ask your family not to disturb you.

Close your eyes and place your hands on your abdomen, just above your pubic area. To a slow count of 4, *inhale* steadily and deeply. Let the air first fill and expand your belly, moving your hands. Then let it fill the lowest portions of your lungs...the middle portions...and finally your chest, so that your shoulders move up slightly. *Feel* and *visualize* this filling, from your beltline to your collarbone.

Now *hold* your breath through another slow count of 4. During this period, work gently to empty your mind of troubling thoughts. You might picture it as a scribbled blackboard being wiped clean or as a rough pond over which the wind is gradually dying, leaving it placid and smooth.

For the next slow count of 4, *exhale.* Let the air escape through your mouth, unhurriedly. Push out as much as you can, all the way down into your belly. As the air is expelled, imagine tension flowing out of your body with it.

The most peaceful point in breathing is during the pause between exhalation and inhalation. Through another slow count of 4, become conscious of the stillness of that moment and let its quiet further pacify your mind. Then slowly begin inhaling again.

Repeat this four-stage cycle for at least 15 minutes. The slow, rhythmic drum beat of your breathing will begin to feel natural. Air will seem to come in and out of its own accord. Soon your heart beat will slow, your blood pressure will drop, your muscles will stretch and loosen.

An alternative breathing style is to exhale twice as long as you inhale. Inhale to a count of 3, exhale to a count of 6.

With either method, you can deepen your positive altered state by adding some *"directed mental activity"* as you breathe. Through a process called *"autogenics,"* you can willfully raise the temperature of your hands and feet by *imagining* that they are getting warm and heavy.

Fix on each one and *calmly* tell yourself this change is taking place. Perhaps you can visualize each hand and foot immersed in a bucket of hot water or exposed to heat radiating from a fireplace. The power of your mind will actually stimulate improved blood circulation there and further counteract the stress response, which restricts the flow of blood to your extremities and leaves them cold. As these areas feel warmer, imagine the same warmth and heaviness radiating into each muscle, one at a time. Take your time, to let the feeling sink in.

In your mind you can also picture a large magnifying glass lazily scrutinizing each segment of your body, from toes to scalp. As each muscle comes into focus under the glass, concentrate on how it feels. Give it "permission" to relax still more, and imagine the last vestige of tension seeping out as the glass glides on. Or envision a vat of "magic potion" being spilled over your head. The liquid is Relaxation in fluid form. As this warm substance oozes down your body, slowly covering every inch, feel all your nerves and muscles completely let go. Along with the release of tension, you will gradually experience increased energy and a sense of well-being.

If you have difficulty capturing this imagery at first, don't worry. Other soothing fantasies may be easier for you to conjure. All take practice. *Don't try to force them;* that will only create stress. Concentrate instead on your deep breathing. The visualizations will develop at a point that's right for you.

As your breathing and imagination relax your body, your mind, too, will be freed of tension and stress and be more quiet and orderly. Remember, an anxious mind cannot exist within a relaxed body. Become aware of how you feel now compared to how you felt before you began the exercise. Developing enough mind/body awareness to distinguish the difference will help you detect *when* you are feeling *stressed* and, equally important, when you have successfully created a state of *relaxation*.

You can use this same technique inside your patrol car. Instead of pausing for coffee and a doughnut to "relax" (the caffeine and sugar in which will only stimulate more of the chemical stress response in your body), consider taking a *"breathing break."* A few minutes of deep breathing and perhaps some visualization will drain away at least some of the stress build-up you may be experiencing from your shift and send you back to work more relaxed and re-energized.

As you become proficient with this exercise, you'll be able to quicken the relaxation response. Eventually, just a few cycles of belly breathing or focused thoughts about your extremities growing warm and heavy will trigger calming signals in your mind and body, and you can relax yourself completely in one or two minutes. Then you can use an abbreviated form of exaggerated breathing throughout your tour of duty. Enroute to a call—particularly one that may become a high-risk encounter—*allow yourself time for several slow, deep breaths before you leave your patrol car.* This will counter unproductive stress and anxiety that may already be building up in anticipation of the contact and put you in a better mental and physical state for coping with the challenges you may confront.

Like some other officers, you may find that you are not conscious of stress *during* a high-risk call, but afterwards experience a pronounced stress "rush" that can leave you shaking, weak-kneed and mentally overwhelmed. Officers often misinterpret this as a belated *fear* response, when actually it stems from the body trying to readjust itself. Here you can use slow deep breathing, perhaps while walking, as a *"cool down"* device to help neutralize the stress chemicals in your body as quickly as possible. *Cooling down is as important to you after a stressful confrontation as it is to athletes after physical exertion.* It will clear your mind and help minimize wear and tear on your heart and other organs by emphatically signalling that the alarm stage is over and your body can return to normal.

"Quick fixes" of deep breathing can really be taken any time they seem comfortable or needed during your shift. They're a way of beating the game you're forced by your vocation to play. You can't in most cases alter your *environment* to be less stressful, but with this technique you *can* alter *yourself* to feel better in it.

Longer sessions—before or after work, at bedtime or whenever is convenient—should be scheduled into your life at least once, preferably twice, *daily.* They allow you a total separation from your stress world, during which you can repair and recharge yourself for the next go-round.

Remember: STRESS HAMPERS PERFORMANCE...RELAXATION ENHANCES IT...AND *BREATHING* IS THE GATEWAY TO RELAXATION.

Positive "Self-Talk"

The relaxed state you achieve through deep breathing is the state you need to be in to program yourself mentally to survive. Basically, this mental conditioning consists of implanting psychological and physical suggestions in your conscious and subconscious minds which will work automatically toward your protection in any high-risk encounter.

This can be done on various levels of complexity. The simplest involves generating and reinforcing *positive concepts* about yourself and your job that will help you deliver a winning performance under stress.

This goes beyond mere "positive thinking." In reality, that is often just *wishful* thinking, because it is anchored more in blind hope for good luck than in skills that really *warrant* optimism and self-confidence.

The kind of mental messages or *"self-talk"* you give yourself here should be rooted in the practice and mastery of the street tactics and techniques discussed throughout this book. With that background, positive mental monologues about yourself and your actions in critical situations will help banish *false* doubts and *irrational* negative expectations, which can intrude on your mind and erode performance.

Positive thinking *without a foundation of professional competence* is an exercise in self-delusion. Positive self-talk *grounded in survival proficiency* is an active ingredient of mental preparation, one means of giving yourself the *will* to match your *skill*.

With seclusion and without the pressure of time, once your mind is cleared and your body calmed by concentrated deep breathing, take a few moments with your eyes still closed to think about the possibility of needing to use *deadly force.*

This is a core consideration in survival that many officers won't— or at least don't—let themselves ponder—until one day with an awful suddenness, their lives or others are in jeopardy and a decision to shoot or not shoot must be made *instantly.* Officers who've not thought beforehand about this issue frequently *hesitate* when milliseconds count. Or they *over-react* to the threat and pull the trigger when lesser alternatives still are viable. Or—very common—they experience extreme anguish *afterwards* in adjusting to having shot and ended or altered another human life.

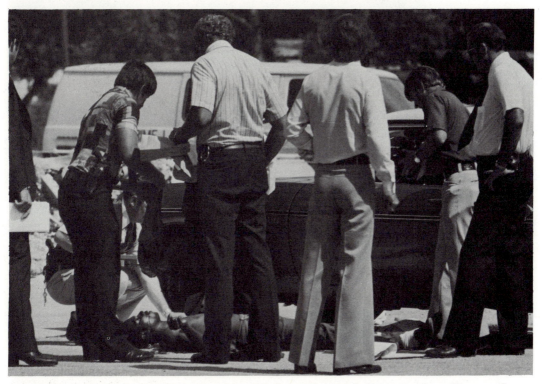

Lying fatally shot is the body of a man who killed an officer and shot two other officers and a woman.

Making deadly force decisions *appropriately*, without faltering and without crippling afterburn, requires *emotional preparation*. You need to raise and resolve questions that may require some soul-searching *before* they actually impact on your life. For instance:

Are your religious and philosophical beliefs on the use of deadly force at least as liberal as the legal provisions in your state? As a police officer, the law clearly gives you the right to take a human life under certain circumstances. Can you accept that, or does the possibility even of a righteous shooting still stir moral doubts in your mind? Only you can decide the answer, and you owe it to yourself and others to be honest in your assessment.

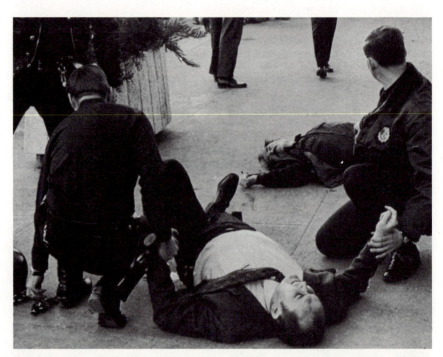

Detective in foreground receives aid from fellow officers after being seriously wounded in a bloody shoot-out. The suspect (background) was an escaped convict serving a life sentence for murder. How do you think you would react inside if you were at this scene?

Are you ready for the nitty-gritty of lethal force? The vast majority of armed encounters occur at close range, many within touching distance of your adversary. This means you may see your opponent's eyes when you pull the trigger...or hear his last breath...or get some of his blood or brains splattered on your uniform. Unanticipated, such occurrences can be dangerously distracting during the action and haunt your memories afterwards. Anticipated, however, their effect is much less likely to be crippling.

Have you considered that the person you need to shoot may not fit your stereotype of an armed adversary? Officers commonly imagine that they'll be up against a "typical dirtbag"—a repulsive, defiant, adult male of another race who's in the process of committing a violent felony. It's relatively easy to be in the position of a Connecticut officer whose target was a hopped up doper who'd just disemboweled his pregnant girlfriend on a public sidewalk and was still chopping at her body when the officer confronted and shot him. But what if your assailant turns out to be a young kid of your own ethnic background who's scared and shaking when he points a gun in your direction...or a middle-aged woman who reminds you of Mom? Is he or she going to be as easy to shoot, even if the threat is the same?

Have you thought about how you will respond if you are shot? Many officers just fall to the ground and give up even though they are not truly incapacitated or fatally wounded. Offenders, on the other hand, may advance, determined to kill. Do you have the will to keep fighting? Do you understand that even in wartime combat, where heavier weapons are generally involved than those you'll confront on the street, only 10% of people shot actually die? And do you know that most of those who do die do so within a few seconds of impact? If you live long enough to comprehend that you have been hit, the odds are great that *you will survive*, provided you are mentally conditioned *not to give up.*

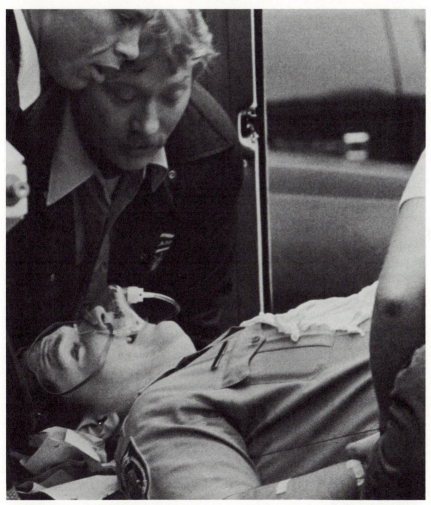

Paramedics talk softly to a wounded officer after a shooting which left one dead and three wounded inside a courthouse. What thoughts have you given to coping if this had been you?

Explore your *honest* feelings about these and other pertinent questions as you rest alone in your relaxed state. It will be more candidly and productively done then than at a bar with other off-duty "soul searchers."

You may conclude, all things considered, that you *cannot* deliver deadly force. Others have reached that decision. Until they were discovered and fired, two officers on a major West Coast department habitually went on patrol with *empty guns* because they had decided they were incapable of shooting anyone regardless of circumstances and did not want to risk violating their conviction. If your conscience cannot accept deadly force as one of your professional options, there is no shame in that. *But admit it*...and LEAVE LAW ENFORCEMENT *IMMEDIATELY!* With that attitude you are dangerous to your fellow officers, to the citizens you are sworn to protect and, most important, to yourself. *To remain on the street without a complete range of options for responding to threats is suicidal.*

Assuming you *do* accept the full responsibilities and obligations of being armed, it's advisable as part of your mental conditioning to reflect on these questions and their implications periodically. And as a *regular* part of your preparation, you will want to underscore your commitment to using whatever legal options are necessary to survive.

That's done by programming your self-talk, the silent language with which you speak to yourself, with phrases of *support*. Repeating such phrases while you are relaxed imprints them on your mind. With continual reinforcement, they can have great influence. It's well known in psychology that your thoughts *do* become your reality—you *are* what you *think*—through the power of your subconscious mind to respond to suggestion and *shape your behavior in line with your expectations.* Assuming that your talents and training permit, your subconscious will tend to *guide* you in the direction that you *tell* it to.

It's best if you construct "auto-suggestions" in your own words. Here are the kinds of messages to concentrate on. They'll help you *approach* a high-risk situation...actually *confront* the stressful circumstances...and cope with the *fear* involved. With your eyes still closed, repeat each message at least 3 times. Concentrate on hearing your inner voice slowly say the words and absorb what they mean. Also visualize them in printed form for extra emphasis. In your relaxed mental and physical state, you can concentrate on each concept to the exclusion of other thoughts and sensations.

> On any high-risk call, I will survive.
> I have succeeded on dangerous calls before.
> I know the tactics I need.
> I know how to make the physical moves I need.
> I am skilled with my firearms.
> I can stay focused on what I have to do.
> I can take care of myself.
> I have options for controlling any problem.
> I can take each call step by step, without rushing.
> I can breathe deeply to control stress any time I start
>   feeling tense.
> I can keep any situation within limits I can handle.
> I can decide not to be afraid.
> I can defeat any threat against me.
> I can use deadly force to save my life or the life of someone else.
> I can survive and keep going, no matter what, even if I am hit.

All suggestions should be direct and *positive.* Avoid negative wording, like "I won't give up," because it suggests the *possibility* of negative behavior. *Permissive* suggestions ("I *can* feel relaxed") tend to meet less resistance from your subconscious mind than *orders* ("I *will* feel relaxed"). Change the suggestions occasionally as they seem to lose their power. *NEVER USE THE WORD "TRY" IN ANY SUGGESTION.* That implies doubt and the possibility of failure.

Until you've memorized the statements that are most meaningful to you, you may want to tape record a series to play as a guide during the exercise. Record each message in a quiet, authoritative voice, and allow enough time on the tape after each suggestion for you to repeat it to yourself and absorb it.

Also consider writing out your self-talk list and posting it on your bathroom mirror, inside your closet or some other place where you can review it privately every day. As they are "psyching up" for work, some officers like to review the list to the background of motivational, "up" music, like the theme songs to such motion pictures as *Rocky, Superman, Wild Geese, Star Wars* and *Patton.*

Every day before going to work, the officer who wrote this list opens his dresser and reads *each* concept.

As you approach a potentially high-risk call, repeat these phrases in your *conscious* mind. That will help calm you and build your confidence by reinforcing what already is embedded and active in your *subconscious* mind.

Any time you complete a high-risk call, use self-talk then to *congratulate* yourself. That will reinforce your success. Forget the superstition that you'll tempt fate by indulging in self-praise. Actually, if you don't credit *yourself* for how things turn out, you are really saying that luck and other factors outside your control are responsible for your survival. *So acknowledge each achievement, no matter how small.* Take a few deep breaths to relax and clear your mind, then concentrate on messages like these:

I did it!

I did well.

I dealt successfully with some tough problems.

I can feel more comfortable and work even more smoothly next time.

I can control violent situations.

Now I can really relax for a bit.

One officer who used this kind of mental preparation was hit in the face, chest and arm one night by pellets from a sawed-off shotgun during a gunfight with a gas station robber. The officer fell to the ground but kept shooting. The suspect was hit three times but refused to drop. Suddenly, the officer felt a surge of energy and a conscious conviction that he was *going to win* no matter what. Although blood was streaming down his face, he got back on his feet, tackled the suspect, and subdued him enough to handcuff.

His mental preparation, the officer said later, had conditioned him "never to give up even if hit" and to finish successfully whatever an assailant started. "I couldn't see because of blood in my eyes, but I kept telling myself it was no big deal...I was okay...and I was going to be just fine." And in the end, he was.

Crisis Rehearsal

The next step beyond self-talk is an advanced form of positive reinforcement called *Crisis Rehearsal.*

Here, instead of internal verbal messages, you use *"mental movies"* to develop appropriate reactions to street confrontations. By repeatedly imagining yourself in a crisis where you successfully defeat a threat on your life, you "pre-set" yourself to respond with the same proficiency in a real encounter. Your fantasy practicing of proper tactics, physical movements and firearms skills "programs" your nerves and muscles to respond automatically as they need to to let you win and lessens your susceptibility to stress interference.

Crisis rehearsal is not idle daydreaming. It is a *purposeful* drill. You are *instructing* yourself through visual imagery. Like other aspects of mental conditioning, it capitalizes on the mind/body partnership.

In sports, this type of mental preparation is known as "playing the game in your head," and it has been polished to a fine science. Alone in a quiet, private place, with his eyes closed, an athlete imagines himself going through a competitive experience in vivid detail from start to finish. An Olympic downhill skier visualizes every bump and every turn on the hill he'll be running and fantasizes the precise physical movements he'll have to make to successfully maneuver each one. A pro football player methodically conjures up all the plays he is likely to see in an upcoming game and then mentally rehearses his responses to them. A professional golfer envisions himself teeing off and then experiences in his mind's eye every fairway swing and every putt for every hole on through to the clubhouse. The same process is used by outstanding tennis players, basketball stars, diving champions, weightlifters, boxers, skeet- and trapshooters and countless others who want to correct bad habits, improve speed and strengthen their performing style. One American serviceman in Vietnam used this form of mental conditioning to practice his golf game while he was a prisoner of war. Every day he mentally played 36 holes on his favorite course. When he finally came home, he found that he performed better than ever in an actual game, even though he had not really held a club for seven years!

Athletes face somewhat the same stress problem you do. In the midst of the game when tension is high, they can't think clearly and creatively about movement and strategy. Their full attention needs to be on the action. Their responses have to be automatic, and in order to win, they must be *desirable.* Mental rehearsal is a method of making desirable patterns automatic and habitual. In all, more than 75 scientific investigations have supported its value in sports training.

There's just no stopping Dave Cowens of the Boston Celtics. While other players relax, Cowens loosens up and uses mental rehearsal to gear his performance to another victory.

You can adapt this technique to improve your "game" on the street, where the outcome of "competition" is infinitely more important than on any sports field. And it can work for you for the same reasons it works for athletes:

1. mental rehearsal helps you *"overlearn"* tactics and techniques so they become second nature to you;
2. by familiarizing you with the look and feel of crisis situations, it *defuses* the impact of the stress-shock phenomena, and
3. it *imprints* learned response patterns on your system so that under pressure they guide your physical actions instantly and successfully without conscious thought.

In short, this powerful psycho-physiological tool will allow you to turn what you would most *like* to do when your life is in jeopardy into what you will most *likely* do.

You can Crisis Rehearse as an extension of your positive self-talk. You use the same relaxed state, induced by deep breathing, because your mind is most susceptible then to visual suggestions, just as it is to your inner verbal suggestions; tension and emotional distractions tend to block the success of this technique. Also avoid doing this exercise within two hours of a heavy meal, because digestion will interfere with your ability to remain relaxed and alert.

Eyes closed, body in a comfortable position, mind cleared of extraneous thoughts, imagine yourself on patrol. You're in your vehicle, driving down a specific street or road on your beat, passing by familiar buildings and other landmarks. On your mental movie screen, you want to recreate the whole environment—sights, sounds, smells, tactile sensations, people, weather conditions, time of day—as realistically as possible. At first, you may be able to visualize clearly only certain elements of the scene, but with practice you'll learn to "dress" it with details.

Once you have the sense of being there, envision yourself in some patrol function that escalates into a crisis. Say you initiate a vehicle stop, pull the violator over and approach his car. Just as you reach the rear fender, he whips around in his seat with a gun in his hand. You want to see this happen in vivid detail, as true to life as you can imagine it. Visualize yourself, the vehicle, the offender, his weapon and his movements as exactly as possible.

Now consider what options you have for protecting yourself. Select a response *that is effective and that you can perform*, and imagine yourself doing it. Perhaps you decide to leap to your right out of the line of fire, roll over the trunk and land on your feet behind the opposite fender. There you draw down on your would-be assailant. You are mentally and physically ready to shoot, but in this case you manage to control his threat through verbal commands. As you create that reaction in your mind, see yourself making *ALL the precise physical moves* that would be necessary. Also, hear yourself barking out orders and note the offender's verbal and physical responses. By forming the image thoroughly, in detail, you are making a clear mental statement of the behavior you want to accomplish. (This presupposes, of course, that you *know* good tactics and techniques for responding. You can't *make* a good choice if you don't *know* a good choice.)

The first time through, you may need to start and stop the action as you create the "plot" of your scenario. Next time, see your physical movements taking place in *slow motion*. This will allow you to carefully observe each element of the move, where your feet are, what your hands are doing, how your body is postured, etc. As you repeat the scene again and again, gradually speed it up until it is taking place in "real time" and your physical responses are smooth and without interruption. *Always* imagine yourself responding deliberately, with CALM CONTROL. *Always carry the rehearsal to the point that your protective reaction is made INSTANTANEOUSLY once you perceive a threat.* And always have your imagery include the *follow through* that is necessary to maintain control of the situation after the main action has taken place.

As you become familiar with Crisis Rehearsal, it's important to do more than just *watch* yourself in a high-risk situation. Try actually to *experience* what being there *feels* like. *Get into the action*, let the episode touch each of your senses, so that what happens happens to *you*, without emotional or physical separation. This will imprint the rehearsal and its benefits more lastingly.

When you rehearse mentally, the visual images actually have a *training effect* on you. As you carry your mind through various physical movements, your body responds similar to the way it would if you were having the experience for real. Brain signals traveling along your nerve network initiate motor responses that are below your threshold of conscious awareness. Your muscles faintly but measurably tense and contract as they would if they were actually making the moves you are imagining. This gives them practice and coordination, a physical feeling for the right moves, which makes those movements easier and quicker to perform correctly in reality. In effect, you are establishing a *"muscle memory"* of proper responses. These responses will kick in under pressure because they are the most familiar and compelling ones your body knows. If someone confronts you on the street with a gun after extensive Crisis Rehearsal, you don't have to *think* how to move; your mind and body *know* how to move because they have been through the proper reaction perhaps hundreds of times in your imagination. With visualization, you have used *conscious suggestion* (a mental picture of desired behavior) to affect *unconscious processes*.

By the same token, your *stress* will be diminished in a real confrontation. This is just as important as the extra development of your motor skills. An effective way for you to *desensitize* yourself to emotional situations is to imagine being in them over and over again until you are able to envision them without stressful feelings. By repeatedly imagining yourself *calmly* controlling street crises, you defuse them. When you encounter an actual threat, you've "been there before," in effect, so the stress impact is lessened. You are not overwhelmed by anxiety and panic or by the interference of the stress-shock phenomena. The mental repetition has conditioned your mind to *expect* a calm reaction, and the signals that it sends to your body *support* that expectation.

Of course, on the street you will never confront *exactly* the same scenario as any you arrange in your head. But the *principles* of the survival reactions that you rehearse will carry over and apply.

Understand, however, that MENTAL REHEARSAL IS *NOT* A *SUBSTITUTE* FOR ACTUAL PHYSICAL PRACTICE AND ROLE-PLAYING. You *must* know how to correctly perform the physical, tactical and firearms skills *before* you imagine using them. Otherwise you will not know how to carry yourself properly through the mental scenarios. Remember: *your rehearsal, like your street performance, can only be as good as the tactics you know.* Crisis Rehearsal is intended to *complement* and *enhance* other training, not replace it. Through a *unified* approach—overlearning through *both* mental and physical practice—you can cement important survival skills in your mind and body so they become instinctive to you. *Overlearning prevents underplaying.*

For effectiveness, you'll need to Crisis Rehearse at least 3 times a week, about 20 minutes each session. In a given period, you can play out from one to three different vignettes, experiencing each in slow motion maybe five times and at true speed 10 times. Vary the setting, the suspect(s) and the threat(s) presented in each so that you also are forced to vary the responses that are appropriate. This will help train you in rapid decision-making based on *the nature of the threat* rather than lock you into one standard reaction in every case. Think in terms of *multiple* options. In some scenarios, you may be searching a building…or trying to deal with a barricaded subject…or working an undercover drug buy…or responding to a silent alarm at a bank…or driving in a high-speed pursuit…or trying to arrest an emotionally disturbed individual or facing an unruly crowd when the threat occurs. The threat may be a physical attack with feet or fists or a knife…a firearms assault…an ambush by multiple assailants…an attempted disarming…or any other format by which offenders may try to hurt you. Your responses may include the tactical use of cover and deployment to prevent or escape attack...the use of "empty hand" control systems...the use of equipment, such as your baton...the use of deadly force—the whole spectrum of options, depending on what would work best to resolve each threat you create. This is an ideal opportunity to play the "what if" game. You can invent innumerable "what ifs" and imagine how you'd cope with them—the more the better.

Whatever threats and control tactics you select, *always* envision yourself performing *correctly* and *successfully.* DO NOT IMAGINE FAILURE OR REHEARSE SOMETHING THE WRONG WAY OR YOU WILL REINFORCE THOSE RESPONSES. Concentrating on what you should *not* do may actually prepare your body to make the very actions under stress that you want to avoid. Psychologists working with athletes find that those without an image of high performance have a difficult time producing high performance. So you want to practice as you wish to perform. In real life, you'll find that success becomes an additional stress-reducer, not to mention a life-saver. Successfully completing any task, including a physical movement, more swiftly reduces muscle tension than does failing at the task.

In your visualization, *congratulate* yourself for defeating the threat, just as you do with positive self-talk after resolving a high-risk incident on the street. Imagine fellow officers, family members and citizens from the community praising you for your good performance. If you've used

The payoff for mental rehearsal is embodied in these officers who were fired upon by a sniper outside a housing project. They were writing tickets when the shooting started. The officer on the left reacted by drawing his gun and diving for cover. The female officer ducked into her patrol car and called for back-up while releasing the trunk lid which flipped up and offered concealment from the sniper's fire. It worked.

deadly force as your response option, it is especially important to believe that you acted as a representative of good and of justice on behalf of every officer in your agency and the law-abiding citizens of your community and with their full support. Remind yourself that society has a right to defend itself from evil, and in this incident you happened to be the instrument chosen to make that defense. Such an orientation in real life will help you perform with more conviction in threat situations and adjust more easily to the emotional impact afterwards if you do need to shoot someone.

The luckiest cop alive. The role that the mind and body play together can never be taken for granted.

Some officers are skeptical about Crisis Rehearsal. Some reject outright the idea that physical responses can be preconditioned to the point of becoming reflexive. But a federal immigration agent who advocates mental conditioning offers defensive driving as a parallel:

"A defensive driver constantly observes his surroundings, identifies and evaluates potential threats, formulates an effective response and prepares to execute that response. If a threat materializes, he is primed to act, with minimal lag time.

"After a period of defensive driving, the driver will begin to recognize recurring threat patterns and standardized responses to them. It is at that point that his reactions are almost fully conditioned and reflexive.

"Similarly, a defensive officer will constantly evaluate his surroundings for threats (potential as well as real), formulate a basic response and prepare mentally to execute it. Initially, conscious thought is required to set the pattern of observation, evaluation, formulation and response in the mind. Eventually, the action of evaluation becomes unconscious and continuous, and the responses reflexive."

Crisis Rehearsal is one powerful form of conscious thought that can advance that goal. "The degree to which an officer believes in it," the agent adds, "will have a strong effect on how quickly it works."

Besides exercising with it in relaxed seclusion, some officers use a modified version of Crisis Rehearsal on patrol to further reinforce good responses. Every time one Miami officer gets a call, for example, he thinks of it "as old-time radio." He tries to visualize what the scene might be like and what might happen there. He always envisions at least two possible courses of action by the suspect.

"With a robbery in progress, for instance, three alternatives immediately come to mind:
"1. the bad guy books with his gun down;
"2. he has his gun up shooting or in a shooting position;
"3. he surrenders.
"Before I physically get there, I put in my mind what I'm going to do in each of those cases. I'm not deciding on what *he's* going to do, just what *I'm* going to do. In any situation, I can control only *my response* in an attempt to influence the outcome. If his gun comes out and is a threat, I'm going to take care of business."

You can also use visual imagery to rehearse new physical skills or polish old ones. This will shorten the learning time you need to become proficient. Without envisioning a specific setting or a threat, just imagine yourself going through the proper movements of the skill, whether it's handcuffing, shooting, use of the baton, whatever. Be sure to *feel* yourself doing it. By slowing down the action and internalizing the *correct* way to execute each component of the procedure, you can lay the foundation for mastering it. As your confidence builds and the rhythm of the moves begins to feel natural, accelerate the action and then incorporate the skill into your threat scenarios. Building self-assurance through many mental repetitions will help relax you when you need to use the skill for real. Your anxiety about errors will be minimized. In recent studies, researchers have documented that when your confidence level increases, your blood chemistry changes.[3] Fewer of the stress-related hormones are active in your blood stream then than when you are fearful

---

[3]"The Chemistry of Confidence," *American Health Magazine*, March-April, 1984.

or uncertain. Consequently, you feel fewer stress effects.

Over time, *all the tactics and techniques in your survival repertoire should be repeatedly rehearsed.* If Crisis Rehearsal seems difficult at first, don't be discouraged. A month or more may be required before you can easily construct the right mental images and notice *significant* improvement in your performance. Mental conditioning is a gradual process that requires steady, faithful nurturing, just like physical conditioning.

You may hear the opinion that Crisis Rehearsal will promote paranoia and encourage the hair-trigger use of deadly force in unwarranted circumstances. This will not be a problem if: 1) you rehearse responding to *various* levels of threat with *various* levels of force, and 2) you rehearse *only* force that is appropriate, necessary and within departmental policy to resolve each scenario. Rather than foster irresponsibility, Crisis Rehearsal will *sharpen* your ability to assess a situation *accurately* and make a valid decision about how to best control it. It is officers who are *not* mentally and physically conditioned in *multiple* tactical and skill options who are most likely to resort, out of fear, panic, over-reaction, loss of control or confusion, to inappropriate gunfire. Or they just surrender themselves to armed aggressors through inaction, saying, in effect: "Kill me."

Your Survival Resource

When you're in a relaxed state, reinforcing positive self-talk or rehearsing crisis responses, you can also practice another mental technique, this one to help you control the *fear* you may experience in some street situations.

Although this subject is not commonly discussed among officers, you are virtually certain sometimes to feel fear or at least extreme anxiety because of your vulnerability to danger. The answer is not to *deny* it, which will only increase the stress you feel, or to give in to it, which will allow you to be overwhelmed with terror. The answer is to *cope* with that emotion, to *use* it as a spark to *mobilize* yourself.

Feeling fear does not mean you are helpless. On the contrary, you can get stronger and have your response capability enhanced during a time of fear. Indeed, you can actually *train* yourself to consciously find *strength* in fear, by tapping into what's called your *Survival Resource.*

With your body relaxed and your mind clear, think back to some time when you were scared, but you *responded* to deal with the threat. (Response, incidentally, does not necessarily mean *action.* You may have chosen to stay still in an encounter where an offender had the drop on you and it was dangerously inappropriate to move.) Whatever the situation, remember what you felt like then: did you feel *strong*…or weak? Was your strength *calm*…or agitated? Were your thoughts *clear*…or confused?

What you want to focus on is a vivid, fearful experience with which you attempted to cope and, for at least a fleeting moment, you felt *strong, controlled and clearheaded* in your response. If the incident you remember was somewhat complicated or extended over a period of time, you may need to recall different aspects of it other than the image you initially conjure up in order to find this moment. In other words, move forward (or backward) in the incident until you remember yourself responding as described. Somewhere in your memory that response is there; everyone has experienced such a moment at least once in the face of fear, although they may not have been consciously aware of it at the time.

When you isolate that moment, "jump into" the action in your mind. See the incident as you saw it then...hear it as you heard it then...feel it as you felt it then. When the experience seems once again to be real to you, go "beneath" the fear and *feel* the part of you that was *able to respond* strongly, clearheadedly and with control. Initially, you may have had a sense of dread or helplessness as you recognized the threat you were up against, but at the *best moment of your response*, feelings of weakness, confusion and agitation gave way at least momentarily to a sense of strength and control.

Recapture that feeling of excellent performance fully. This is your *"resource state"* frame of mind. It reflects an optimal, functional *core strength* that makes you *able* to survive. The more intense your fear was, the more intense this Survival Resource had to be to carry you through the experience.

What you want to develop for the future is the ability to consciously *access* that state of mind at will, because it represents the very best that is in you and it is the foundation of your capability to overcome even the most formidable odds.

When you have recaptured this feeling, use deep breathing to clear your mind of other sensations and concentrate on it. Acknowledge that you have drawn upon this Resource in the past, that it is still an innate part of you and that it will always be there for you to call upon whenever you need it. Tell yourself that whenever you resolve that it is time to respond in the face of fear, this Survival Resource will click in and fuel your response capability.

Practice calling up this mental state in the context of your Crisis Rehearsals. Develop an association with some *cue* so that you can summon this state in "real world" environments, too. When you experience the Resource feeling in a period of relaxation, for example, say a special word to yourself and as you say it, let the word become associated with that frame of mind. Keep repeating the word and deepening the association until merely by saying the word you can feel the state being there. Other cues can also be used, if you prefer, such as touching the thumb and forefinger of your non-gun hand together or imagining some visual image that will call up the Resource feeling.

Practice this technique two or three times a day in the beginning, later once a day. After considerable practice, you should be able to use it automatically on the street. Whenever you approach a high-stress situation—or are in a circumstance where you feel fear or anxiety—use the cue to go beneath your negative emotions to bring forth the state of mind that will enable you to react with maximum confidence, effectiveness and control.

Any time you handle a tense situation *well*, reinforce the feeling of excellence you have to strengthen your Survival Resource. And if there is a time when you think you performed *poorly*, recreate the situation in your mind during a relaxation period later and imagine how you could have handled the circumstances *differently*, supported this time by your Resource state. Then imagine yourself actually reliving the incident with that response in order to reinforce the better option(s).

There may be times when all that will keep you alive will be your ability to tap into your Survival Resource. One officer, for example, got into a fight with a suspect who was much bigger and stronger than he was. At a point of exhaustion, the officer was disarmed. The offender stood over him with the service revolver, leering, while the officer begged for his life. In slow motion, the officer saw the suspect start to pull back the trigger. At that instant, the officer remembered a line from a piece of prose called "The Police Officer's Code," which he had learned to associate with the Resource state of mind. Suddenly energized, he sprang up, seized the gun and shot the suspect twice in an ensuing struggle. Getting in touch with his Survival Resource gave him the strength and control to turn the tables.

Awareness Spectrum

On the street, as you respond to a high-risk call or otherwise approach what could be a crisis situation, you'll be at one of several possible levels of alertness, depending on your anticipation of danger. The better conditioned you are mentally, the more likely you will: 1) be operating at the *proper* level of awareness relative to the degree of readiness you need; 2) be able to detect early *warning* signs of a risk or threat and 3) manage to jump to a higher plane of alertness and readiness in an *appropriate* fashion if necessary. These factors can be decisive in how you come out. Certainly, the *state of alertness* with which you approach a confrontation will usually prove much more decisive than the equipment you carry in determining the outcome.

Colors can be used to mark the different levels of awareness, anticipation, concentration and self-control that constitute your mind-set:

Condition White: This is a state of *environmental unawareness*. You are oblivious to what's going on around you, because you are daydreaming...tired...preoccupied with distractions...or assuming there is no possibility of trouble and thus no cause for alarm. As one trooper puts it, "Your thinker is out of gear, even though your patrol car isn't." There is *no* readiness for a threat confrontation in this mental state.

Condition Yellow: You are *relaxed but alert*, cautious but not tense. You maintain an easy but steady 360° surveillance of the people, places, things and action around you. You are not specifically expecting a hostile act, but you are aware that aggression is possible. Because you are constantly perceiving and evaluating your environment, you are attuned to any signal that may suggest a threat potential. Your alertness is a preliminary step to action.

Condition Orange: This is a state of *alarm*. You know there is trouble, and you're concentrating on evaluating it further and resolving it. Based on your training, experience, education and common sense, you have a tactical plan in mind that you begin following, including the calling of backup...the use of cover...and the identification of an adversary who may present a threat. There's reason to believe that a confrontation is likely. You are cognizant of the provocations that would demand that you use deadly force. The situation is volatile; you guard against over-reaction, but you think in term of controlling a threat with gunfire if necessary. Your being surprised is now impossible.

Condition Red: What looks wrong is wrong. Instant reaction is mandatory. You *focus in on your threat* and act to control it, with verbal force, physical force or deadly force, as circumstances warrant. All systems are GO, totally committed to the defense of yourself or someone else. Despite the urgency, the decisions you make are not knee-jerk reactions, but *rational*, based on the threat.

An officer rolls in to buy cigarettes, oblivious to a robbery-in-progress. What is the officer's mental state?

Scene of a major disturbance. What mental state would you say the dog and the arrestee are experiencing?

The officer on the right leaves the chambers of a county judge. What mental state is he in?

An officer exits and sees three occupants on a low-risk stop exit at the same
time. What should your mental state be here? Answers: (top of page 48)
Condition White. (bottom left, page 48) Condition Red. (bottom right, page 48)
Condition Yellow. (top) Condition Orange.

All of us pass at least part of our lives in "mindless" Condition
White, but unfortunately many officers permit themselves to drift into
this state while they are *on duty* and even when they are in the midst of
situations that are virtually clanging with warning bells. The color
suggests street virginity—pure innocence and naivete; the white belt in
the martial arts symbolizes no knowledge. Yet veteran officers as often as
rookies—sometimes *more* often than rookies—spend their working
hours wrapped in White. A patrolman in Connecticut with 34 years on
the job went for nearly three days without carrying his gun because his
holster was torn. He didn't think it was "worth" getting repaired
immediately. In addition to *his* mental White-out, only one out of more
than 100 fellow officers—and *not* his partner—noticed the absence of his
weapon. In Wisconsin, several officers were conducting a building
search. As one started up a flight of stairs, another appeared in a doorway
at the top and said, "Come on up, it's clear." As he spoke, he winked
repeatedly and made exaggerated facial expressions. Also his holster was
empty. But the advancing officer noticed none of this and hurried
upstairs—where he was taken hostage by an offender who had disarmed
and was hiding behind the first officer.

Officers like these are on fertile ground for fatal surprise. Condition
White may actually *encourage* attack, even on what seem to be "safe"
assignments. On the Western desert, a deputy pulled into a highway rest
stop to check a minor traffic mishap; a car had run off the highway into a
ditch nearby. The driver, quiet and dazed, was slumped in a chair at a
campsite with a blanket wrapped around him. Tourist families were
milling about. The deputy took the man's license, turned his back and

bent over the hood of his patrol car to fill out his report. The driver jumped from his chair and shot the deputy in the head with a .22 he had concealed under the blanket. He had seemed to be an unremarkable accident victim, but he was in fact an ex-convict wanted for questioning in two murders in another state.

The officers in this scene are looking for gunmen who moments earlier shot a homicide investigator. Notice the different levels of caution used by these officers.

If officers attacked in White ever realize the crisis that is upon them before they are injured or killed, they realize it too late. After eonic lag time from the startle response, they try in one giant leap to escalate from White to Red to defend themselves. But the mental and physical adjustments required are too enormous. Massive, unexpected stress is deluging their systems, and under this emergency ultra-mobilization they fail to land in Red. Instead, they shoot off the color spectrum into:

Condition Black: Panic...misdirected frenzy...paralysis. It's called Black because your mind is *blacked out* and because it symbolizes the ultimate black moment: *Lights out for you.*

In Condition Black, your eyes may fixate on the threat...you may point at the assailant, as if your finger is a magic ray gun...you may hit, kick or grapple ineffectually or shoot wildly...you may fearfully back away or turn and run in desperation...you may fall to the ground in defeat...you may be immobilized. One version of Black was experienced by a transit officer in Ohio who was fired on twice without provocation while on patrol one night. He bailed out of his car, an initial good reaction. But then he froze, unable to take action while the assailant leisurely blasted away at him with three more rounds. The officer's mind was swimming with disbelief ("That motherfucker's really trying to *kill me!*") instead of commanding a response.

Conditions Orange and Red can be held as states of mind for only brief periods of time. If you try to operate continually at these advanced levels of awareness, you will quickly become exhausted or psychotic. But Condition Yellow can be sustained *indefinitely* without undue nervous strain.

Yellow is the state of mind you should be operating in all the time you are on patrol, prior to the actual detection of a potential threat. Seldom are officers hurt by something they could not have anticipated or seen and moved to avoid or control had their antennae been up for danger signals. Alertness and the tactical edge it offers actually *discourage* attack. It's ironic but true that the officer who is habitually prepared to defend himself *rarely has to.* In a lesser state of alertness, you are more likely to be made as an easy mark, and any tactical knowledge and skills you have will be lost irretrievably in the White "fog."

Condition Yellow is not a *guarantee* of protection, but it gives you the best odds for reading danger cues and moving in proper sequence and in a controlled manner up to Orange and on to Red if necessary. Anticipating danger and thinking and planning ahead will reduce your startle response if danger does explode. If an *immediate* escalation to Red is required, the jump from Yellow is much easier to accommodate than from White, because the springboard of alertness is already there. You can see the problem, decide what to do and then begin doing it—all within a split second.

Consider an incident in the East in which officers were searching an abandoned apartment for an armed suspect believed to be hiding there. One officer entered the kitchen, glanced around casually, then passed on to another room. Just behind him, a second officer entered—and noticed shelves from a refrigerator scattered on the floor. This registered on his Yellow mental state as a possible warning. Maybe the shelves had been thrown there by a previous tenant—or maybe the suspect had tossed them out to make a hiding place inside! The officer shifted to Orange, took cover and prepared to challenge the refrigerator at gunpoint. His verbal commands were delivered in Condition Red. If the door had been flung open and a threat presented, he could have reacted without hesitation. The suspect *was* inside but surrendered meekly. Only luck had guarded the first officer, who had wandered through the suspect's potential kill zone in Condition White.

The need for heightened awareness on the street is documented by an extensive analysis of police shooting incidents.[4] The study reveals how quickly violence develops. In over half the shootings involving police officers, shots are fired within *60 seconds* of an officer's arrival on the scene. In a significant number of cases (45%), the shootings occur while the officer is alone, before any backup arrives to support him.

Given those limitations, *your only reliable ally is going to be yourself*, with your mind conditioned and in a state of readiness for defense.

[4] Nielsen and Eskridge, "Police Shooting Incidents," *Law and Order*, March, 1982.

An incredible sequence of an officer's ability to shift from one mental state to the next higher and finally to the use of deadly force. The off-duty officer (striped shirt) stands at the counter to conduct a personal transaction (Condition White). Suddenly the offender in the white cap announces a stick-up. Look at how the officer shifts to Condition Yellow immediately. In Condition Orange he slowly bends down to decrease his vulnerability. In the bottom photo the officer assumes a kneeling position in Condition Red and incapacitates the offender with multiple rounds. Back in Condition Orange, he then positions himself in a non-threatening manner so responding officers will not rush in, thinking he's the robber.

TACTICAL THINKING

One of the saddest truths of the police world is that officers who exhibit no survival thinking whatsoever so often end up lionized. They're downright reckless in approaching high-risk situations, but they're trumpeted by the media, their community, their administrators, even their fellow officers, as heroes who demonstrate "the stuff good cops are made of."

Example: A plainclothes sergeant in the Midwest, responding to a silent alarm at a shoe store, looked through the front window and saw one armed robber rifling a cash register, another herding customers and employees at gunpoint into a rear storage room. Outnumbered, without waiting for backup and without his own gun drawn, the sergeant strode right through the front door. He managed to surprise the first gunman and disarm him. The second surrendered after other officers arrived.

It was then discovered that the sergeant had been targeted for easy killing just seconds after he penetrated the scene. From a hiding place in back, the second robber had squeezed the trigger on him six times. Every round in his revolver bore a heavy dent from the firing pin—but none had gone off.

That miracle alone prevented a probable officer death, the devastation of a police family, a major escalation of the incident and a potentially tragic compounding of danger to other police and civilian lives. Yet the sergeant drew his department's highest award for valor, the state chiefs' association's highest medal for honor and the praise of the press for "meritorious service." His administrators held his behavior up to his fellow officers as the kind of professional skill and thought "for which we all strive." They specifically *commended* his "total disregard for his own safety."

When foolhardiness is equated with professionalism, somebody doesn't understand professionalism. One survival-conscious officer jotted down his feeling on the subject in a note to his trainer: "The Deman of The SeRvice, and The imporTence of The Job. Are Never so Great that you can noT Take Time To do The Job SafEly". His spelling's not so hot, but his thinking's right on. And what's ironic is that by thinking *self-protectively* you *still* can resolve volatile situations favorably, not only with less risk to yourself but to citizens you may be trying to defend.

Good self-protective thinking means good *Tactical* Thinking: not just rushing in, flaunting your machismo and hoping for the best, but *analyzing* the situation you're up against...*anticipating* what problems you might encounter...and deciding what you say and do as *part of a plan* for controlling the action.

Failing to understand that all this *can* be done is what leads some officers to react emotionally with ill-advised "heroics." Failing to understand how it *should* be done leads others to tactical failures. They may talk a good show about survival, but they're not able to actually apply survival principles in a meaningful way on the street.

Some, for example, rigidly compartmentalize their thinking. They memorize and try to apply one set of prescribed procedures for responding to all silent alarms...another for conducting all building searches...another for making all vehicle stops.

Other officers are conditioned into poor tactical thinking by their range training. Even some "stress-combat" courses, supposedly teaching "survival shooting," still ingrain bad habits; they just do it under more pressure. A top marksman recently ran the gauntlet on one such course, featuring remote-controlled turning targets. He consistently delivered fast, center-mass shots, but his performance was tactically illiterate. Near the start, he jumped up from behind a wall to shoot a target 6 feet away. When three targets turned on him simultaneously, he stood his ground in the open and shot his pistol dry—only to have another "assailant" spin around as he was reloading, also without cover. In moving from one target station to the next, he ran exposed along an open trail. He would doubtless have been a victim many times over in an actual gunfight. Yet he was scored highly on the basis of time and accuracy. On the same course, another shooter, tactically more astute, just raised his pistol with one hand and shot over the wall at the first target, without exposing his head or torso. Instead of running down the trail, he zig-zagged along a brushy creek bed that paralleled the course. He scoped out targets from cover, patiently waited out their turning and moved on only when each "adversary" had been eliminated. The instructor was furious when this shooter finished because he'd "acted silly" and "done it wrong" by going outside the course boundary!

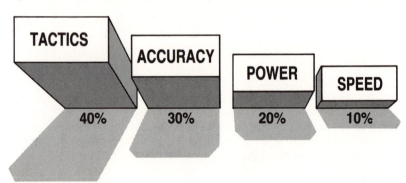

One way to remember the importance of tactics and tactical thinking is to arrange in the order of importance the four considerations involved in a shooting. The acronym TAPS and what it means should be reflected in your qualification course as well. Note how speed is rated of least importance in a shooting, yet so important on most ranges. Why?

Tactical Thinking that *works* involves a simple formula: you match options for defense and control to the type of threat you're facing. Obviously, that's easier said than done. But it is *easier done* than a lot of officers imagine. The key is *the way you think.* That's going to be more important to your survival than the kind of firearm you carry, the kind of ammunition it's loaded with or the kind of scores you pull down in "practical" shooting.

Good Tactical Thinking begins with assessing your potential dangers. And *that* begins with your recognizing that despite their infinite variety of detail, high-risk situations share some *universal* characteristics. People and places can present threats to you in *only certain ways.*

Once you understand those ways, it is then possible for you to readily evaluate the threat potential in *any* situation you confront, including one that's entirely new to you. And once you've identified your true hazard in a given situation, you're then in a position to apply the appropriate measures to overcome it.

Achieving all this involves only a few cardinal concepts, but they can revolutionize your street behavior. As you grasp the principles of Tactical Thinking, you may discover that some tactics you've been taught or have used in the past are *wrong* for the situations they're *supposed* to help you control. You'll see what's *really* needed to do the job and *why.* New tactics and techniques you read about in this book or hear about elsewhere will be easier for you to evaluate and use. You'll have guidelines for creating your own tactical maneuvers. And you'll be able to judge your tactical capability *before* it's put to the acid test at the end of an assailant's gun.

Threat Assessment

When you answer any call or approach any street situation, three terms—*the triad of Tactical Thinking*—should be at the forefront of your conscious thought:

- Problem Area
- Area of Responsibility
- Focus Point

These are touchstone concepts that will help you *assess the risk* you may be facing and *react* to it. You can use them as a "sorting out" mechanism for reducing confusion and properly directing your attention under stress. They'll help you:

1. categorize different elements of the scene you're approaching
2. establish priorities for control
3. formulate a tactical plan
4. monitor your safety as you progress through the call, and
5. effectively neutralize threats you may encounter.

These concepts are also important to incorporate in your Crisis Rehearsal scenarios. Practicing applying them there will help make them automatic to you in the field.

A **Problem Area** is *any PERSON, OBJECT or SITE that may produce a HAZARD to you.* Besides human beings, Problem Areas commonly include dogs, buildings, vehicles, fields, woods, alleyways, excavations, dumpsters, booby traps—anything at a scene that could harbor a threat, even though the threat is not immediately visible or known.

Often you have more than one Problem Area to contend with. If you stop a suspect for a field interrogation and he has companions with him, each constitutes a separate Problem Area. On a "shots fired" or "man with a gun" call at a residence, you may find a house, a garage, a storage shed, a couple of cars, shrubbery, fences, large trees—an abundance of potential threat locations. On a traffic stop, if the driver and passengers get out, you then have multiple mobile Problem Areas, plus the vehicle itself with its hidden unknowns.

Problem Areas require *prompt* identification. And as soon as you see one, you want to "grab a little A.S.S." In this case, that means Assess Situation and Structure. You need to determine what is going on right now...what threat(s) this action is currently presenting, if any... and what threat potential could develop a few seconds or a few moments (in some cases, maybe a few hours) from now. In particular, what you're looking for as you assess the Problem Areas are "Areas of Responsibility."

An **Area of Responsibility** is *an EXACT LOCATION within a Problem Area from which an ATTACK could emanate.* Some portions of any Problem Area are "hot spots," the places that have the greatest possibility for producing threats. On a human being, they're the hands, the feet and the head. An attack by a person will emanate from one or more of those spots because they can either hold or be used as assault weapons (a subject can butt with his head). With a car, any threat will come through a window or an open door or from the trunk. With a building, exterior threats will generate from the rooftop or around corners, while doors and windows are the likeliest outlets for an attack from inside. Each of these is an Area of Responsibility. (Technically, shooting out through the walls of a building is also a possibility, but in real life this can be difficult to do and few offenders actually attempt it. Don't forget *upper* windows, though. Assailants *can* climb steps, and with that high-ground advantage some have picked off officers several hundred yards away.)

Emotionally disturbed gunman threatening he won't be taken alive. Because of available information, the newsman is not regarded as a Problem Area at this point. The subject for sure is the Problem Area. The Areas of Responsibility are the hands and the gun. Officer uses appropriate tactics from behind cover.

Your responsibility regarding any Area of Responsibility is two-fold: 1) to *detect* and 2) to *control* any threat that emanates from it. Areas of Responsibility demand your *immediate* attention. *They must become the framework that shapes your tactical planning.* Even if an Area of Responsibility reveals no *present* evidence of threat (an empty hand, for instance), it still warrants continued *awareness*, at least peripherally.

As you progress through a call, ask yourself *three key questions* as precautions against overlooking Areas of Responsibility or rushing into situations that you don't understand or that may be more complex than you initially assumed:

1. *Where are my potential hazards in this situation?* Say you're approaching a residence on a domestic and a female comes out to meet you on the front walkway. Consider: Where are the doors and windows from which you could be seen and shot by someone still inside...What other locations could harbor an unseen assailant...Is the woman herself a potential threat?

2. *Do I control those hazards?* At the scene described, there are threat locations you do *not* control. Any threat that may be *hidden*—like someone who can see you through a window but whom you cannot see— is *automatically* uncontrolled. The unknown is always high-risk. Standing on the walkway exposed to such Areas of Responsibility at the front of the residence increases your potential danger.

3. *If I don't currently control my hazards, how can I do so?* In this case, consider the nearby cover possibilities: a large tree, a porch support, a car parked in the driveway. Direct the female to a cover position for questioning and stand so you face the residence and her back is to it. Periodically check from around your cover to assess the scene. And remain aware of the woman as an additional threat potential.

Inside this bar is a hostage-taker who has fallen asleep. Three of four officers shown here prepare to make entry. The officer on the right controls his Area of Responsibility (doorway) and the officer on the left controls his (the window) but failed to use cover. The third officer is now safe for entry without a crossfire problem.

When danger does erupt from an Area of Responsibility, you then have a "Focus Point."

A **Focus Point** is *a CLEAR and PRESENT THREAT that* must *be immediately CONTROLLED to protect you or another innocent party.* You concentrate (Focus) your attention, your energy and your skill against it, either in defensive moves or in counterattack. This is the moment when you will be under maximum stress, and in that condition you will *have* to Focus in order to function.

Exactly *where* you Focus your response can be tricky. To be most effective, you need to Focus in some cases on the *weapon* as your true hazard, in other cases on the *person* wielding the weapon. Time and distance can make the difference.

Classic example of officers overextending their position. Without cover they key in on only the gun, not knowing that both hands as well as the gun are Areas of Responsibility. The hidden hand is an unknown hazard. Better to have suspect place gun on window ledge and exit building.

Say you're in the open, far from cover, and a suspect gets the drop on you but you're within *touching distance* of his gun. If you try to quick-draw and shoot him, time is against you; his gun is already out and pointed at you. If you physically attack his head or some other part of his body in an effort to control him, he can still get a round off. Your *proper* Focus Point in this case is the *gun. That* is your true hazard and you *can* control *it* immediately, with a *disarming* move. Controlling *him* then can be done with subsequent maneuvers.

On the other hand, if you are *farther away* and you already have your firearm in a ready position when the threat is made, your proper Focus Point is the *person.* At that distance, you must control the person to control the gun, so *he* becomes your true hazard. Deadly force directed center mass is likely your best hope of stopping his lethal threat quickly. (Of course, in most jurisdictions before legally using deadly force you must reasonably believe that the gun constitutes an imminent, severe threat to you or someone else. You cannot shoot a person *just* because he is armed.)

Two California officers were called to deal with a man who was lounging against the entryway of a hotel with a cocked revolver in his hand. The officers drew down on him from several yards away. The suspect, who was standing in profile to them, lowered the gun to arm's length on his far side, then slowly began to turn the barrel toward one of the officers, who had not yet reached cover. The gun was well below the offender's waist and the officer was able to watch it in his peripheral vision. But the Focus Point was the offender's upper torso. As the gun barrel moved up, the officer incapacitated the suspect instantly with multiple shots.

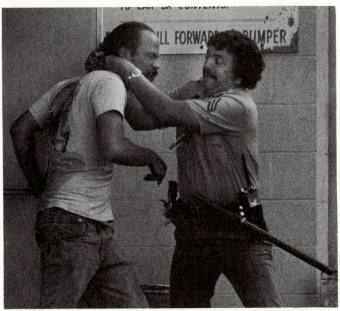

Areas of Responsibility include burglary suspect's hands, feet, and the officer's own weapons. The officer chose to focus on the head and neck, rather than apply a tactic which controlled hands and feet.

It seems logical enough on the printed page, but under stress officers time and again misperceive their true hazard and proper Focus Point. In South Dakota, a patrolman walked up to the driver's open window on a nighttime traffic stop and found himself staring down a gun barrel. He selected the offender's *neck* as his Focus Point and tried to choke him with a hammer lock, ignoring the hand with the gun. The offender, his gun hand unrestrained, fired and almost killed the officer. In a similar case in a Great Lakes state, a prisoner disarmed an officer inside a police station and pointed the sidearm at another officer who was just touching distance away. That officer, too, lunged for the suspect's head—and was easily shot and killed. On the other hand, if you examine targets with realistic figures used on stress firearms courses, you'll notice that bullet

holes often are grouped around the target figure's gun; officers have fixated on the weapon as their Focus Point, although shots at a gun rarely will prevent the subject holding it from pulling its trigger. Such inappropriate Focus may well be a factor in why officers have such poor track records for hitting center mass in gunfights. They often do better on the range shooting silhouette targets, where nothing competes with the printed 10-ring for their Focus Point attention.

In some situations, time and distance may be so loaded against you that you cannot realistically Focus on *either* the weapon or the person presenting the threat. In that case, your only chance to control it may be immediate tactical retreat—exiting the danger area by leaping or diving to cover, ducking to a place of concealment, or running like hell. Then what you want to Focus on is the place you're *moving toward*.

You can relate these concepts in the threat assessment triad to the awareness color codes. As you approach a Problem Area and begin analyzing it, your *mental state* should be Yellow—alert, evaluating what you see, conscious that danger may be present. As you identify and assess your Areas of Responsibility, you may escalate to Orange, the alarm state. In the California incident mentioned above, as soon as the officers saw the revolver in the subject's hand (their prime Area of Responsibility), they readied themselves mentally and physically for action. The suspect's movement of his gun barrel toward one officer was almost imperceptible; a videotape of the incident filmed by a television crew later had to be slowed down and magnified to confirm it. But in his ultra-attentive Orange state, the officer noticed the subtle but heightened threat from that Area of Responsibility. When he opened fire on the Focus Point, he was in Condition Red, as you also need to be when you act against a point of Focus to defend yourself. Otherwise you remain in Orange or below, not the level of mental intensity required.

Controlling a Focus Point is difficult and laden with risk, even if you have devoted a lot of time to Crisis Rehearsal and role-playing and have outstanding firearms skills. Consequently, your goal on the street is to *prevent* any situation from escalating to that point. You want to resolve calls *without* the necessity of moving to Condition Red and having to act immediately to save your life. *The better you identify and work to control Problem Areas and Areas of Responsibility, the better your chances of avoiding threat confrontations.* Yet many officers do not take these concepts into consideration *at all* when deploying.

Inside a residence during a disturbance call in Massachusetts, a deputy chief was shot in the chest with a .45 and gravely wounded. His assailant remained free and still armed inside the two-story house. Officers who surrounded the place knew the circumstances, yet none paid the slightest heed to the Areas of Responsibility within that Problem Area. They disembarked from their patrol cars right in front of the house, in full view and easy firing range of upper and lower windows...Some casually stood, guns holstered, on the front porch in front of windows and a partially glass door...Some stood in the street without cover with their backs to the house. Although there was a lot of weaponry and personnel outside eventually, including a special weapons team, the *assailant* controlled that scene without even knowing it. Only his decision not to attack again protected those very vulnerable officers, *not* their tactical "thinking."

Location of the Massachusetts Incident.

Similarly, a suburban officer in Illinois making an all-too-typical vehicle stop recently placed his fate solely with the violator he had pulled over. The officer stopped a teenager driving a junker with no plates. He parked his patrol car only a foot behind his Problem Area (the violator car), shortening his time and distance for observation and assessment. Then as he made his approach, he permitted the driver to step out, thereby creating another, ambulatory area of potential threat. Both the driver's hands (two of the officer's Areas of Responsibility) were in his jacket pockets. The officer made no effort to get them visible...he walked past two other Areas of Responsibility, the windows on the driver's side, without checking inside...and he stood in front of the windshield to write a ticket, with the violator, hands still concealed, several feet behind him and out of view. Again, the only control at that scene was the violator's, which in this case turned out to be cooperative.

A California officer was less fortunate when he acted equally oblivious to Tactical Thinking. On patrol about midnight, he spotted two men acting suspiciously around a truck entrance to a warehouse. The entry's overhead door was open, the interior dark—clearly an Area of Responsibility that could be hiding an unseen threat who might already be prepared to attack. By definition, Areas of Responsibility demand *immediate* attention. But the officer ignored the doorway. Indeed, he parked at an angle to the front of it (that is, in front of a potential threat source that he did not control), put his high beams on the two suspects, ordered them to stop and then stepped out to question them. The officer had misinterpreted his hazards by assuming that these suspects were his only true threats. From the darkened doorway a third offender hit him in the chest with a blast of 00 buck from a sawed-off 12 ga. shotgun. The officer returned fire and missed. One of the visible suspects then pulled a .38 cal. revolver and shot the fallen officer once. A second round impacted his portable radio.

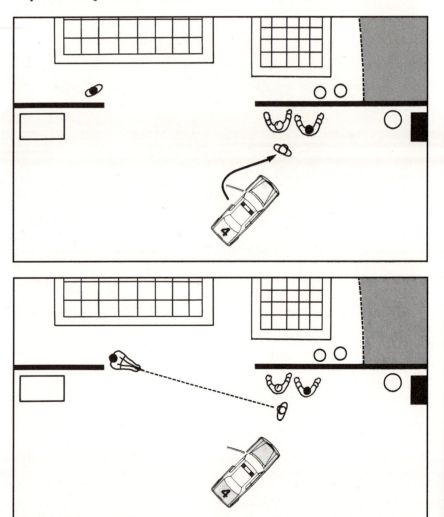

Had he understood the concept of Area of Responsibility, the officer could have deployed more astutely. At the very least, he could have shined his spotlight into the doorway to illuminate the shadowed interior and then have exited on the other side of his patrol car, using it as concealment and possibly some cover between himself and that potential threat location. And facing alone so many Problem Areas (the building and each visible suspect) and Areas of Responsibility (at least five, counting the open doorway and each suspect's hands), he could have summoned aid for better control. Backup was available 3 minutes away, but never called.

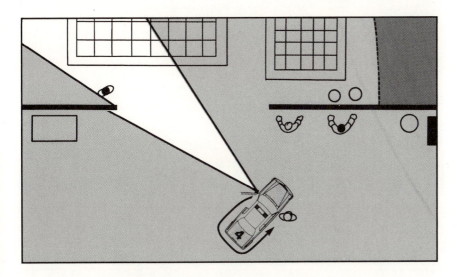

Sometimes officers initiate action in situations without seeming to realize that they face *more* potential threat locations than they can possibly control. A lieutenant with an Eastern housing authority police department, for instance, was off-duty and in civilian clothes in a tavern when three armed robbers invaded the place. Even though he was clearly outnumbered and was not himself in any immediate threat, he drew his handgun and tried to control the offenders. In an exchange of gunfire, he was shot in the chest at close range and killed. If he had analyzed the scene on the basis of Problem Areas and Areas of Responsibility, he might have better comprehended that he was up against more hazards than he could successfully defend against. Whenever this is the case, it is ALWAYS a signal to lie low, back off or summon aid, unless you are *forced* to defend yourself as best you can against imminent or active assault.

Where backup is used, you want to divide Problem Areas and Areas of Responsibility between you so that no one officer is overloaded. Taking on more such Areas than can effectively be controlled is probably the most common tactical pitfall. From a Tactical Thinking standpoint, it's usually absurd for just two officers (and certainly for one) to be expected to safely search a large building or control a large group of suspects. There are more Problem Areas and Areas of Responsibility in those circumstances than can ever be watched and managed effectively with such limited manpower. Rarely is the ideal possible: one officer assigned to each Area of Responsibility. But the ratio should be such that if violence erupts from one or more potential threat locations, you will not be automatically overwhelmed.

Again, time and distance will help determine your limitations.

The greater the distance between you and your Areas of Responsibility and the more reaction time you can build for yourself (through invisible deployment, use of cover, weapon readiness, the use of restraining devices, etc.), the better your chances for controlling several threat locations simultaneously.

There is a deployment problem here. But why? Officer with shotgun is attempting to control multiple Areas of Responsibility (hands, feet, window). Three officers control one Area of Responsibility (doorway). A cover officer and arrest officer could control the suspect, while the third officer covers the door, and the fourth officer covers the window.

Be careful when dividing Areas of Responsibility that *all* get covered. Sometimes several officers concentrate on only one or two, leaving others unmonitored. Three West Coast detectives, for example, arrested a band of five religious terrorists and proned them out in a parking lot. They constituted five Problem Areas. Their feet were probably useless for assault in that position, but their hands still were potential threat locations. Yet with five Problem Areas and at least ten Areas of Responsibility to cover, all three detectives concentrated their gaze on only one place during most of the arrest process: the semi-automatic rifle. Because of its close proximity and high threat level, the .30 calibre carbine could be considered an eleventh. Had one of the terrorists made a sudden movement for *another* gun in a waistband or a pocket, his action *might* have been noticed in time. But extremist groups, especially, tend to be trained in the art of "subtle movement"— moving so slowly and in such small increments that the action can't normally be detected in peripheral vision. With all the officers' attention elsewhere, one of the other Areas of Responsibility could conceivably have been able to inch gradually to a hidden gun and become transformed into a Focus Point without the officers having even been aware of it.

The Problem Areas in the terrorist arrest incident are identified by number. The officers who responded are noted by letters. A better approach to consider: officer A maintains cover of suspects 2 thru 5. Officer B removes the carbine as he directs his primary attention to suspect 1's hands. Officer C directs his attention away from the carbine, and assists Officer A with control of suspects 2 thru 5. Officers E and F should then move in and assign themselves to one of the remaining suspects for control. Officer D could either assign himself a suspect or work inner perimeter control.

Deliberate *distraction* from your Area of Responsibility is another problem you need to guard against. One officer stopped a subject for a field interview and told him to approach her location. At first, she properly kept her eyes on his hands, but as he got close he began making subtle glances over his shoulder. The officer shifted her gaze to see what he was looking at—and in that instant, the abandoned Area of Responsibility (the suspect's hand) drew a gun and shot her. In a domestic disturbance, a husband who'd been threatening his wife with a revolver raised his hands and said he wanted to surrender when an officer arrived. His gun was dangling from his index finger, upside down and apparently in no position to fire. The officer commanded him to lay the weapon on the floor. The man started to lean down, but he continued to look directly at the officer and to talk a blue streak. Something he said caused the officer to glance away from his hand and into his eyes. Of course, the offender knew how to fire without putting the gun fully into his hand—and he did, with fatal results.

Eye contact is one of your greatest distraction risks. From childhood on, most of us are told to "look people in the eye" as a mark of respect and sincerity. Even in threat situations, this is a tough habit to overcome. Experiments with recruits have shown that often they notice a handgun in a suspect's hand *only* when he and the gun are positioned in profile to them. Facing a gunman head-on, they tend to look at his *eyes* and miss the weapon altogether. Remember: eyes may "spit fire" in cheap novels, but they don't spit bullets on the street. *Eyes are never an Area of Responsibility.*

If a threat does occur from an Area of Responsibility despite your best efforts, your ability to understand and apply the Focus Point principle of Tactical Thinking will then be pivotal to your survival. Two important considerations:

1. *Do not confuse the channeling of concentration involved in Focusing with "tunnel vision."* Proper Focus directs your attention and the full force of your energy when and where they *need* to go to stop the threat—and for only a very *limited* amount of time, measured sometimes in mere fractions of a second. If you don't Focus, you weaken the response you deliver or you fail to respond at all. Tunnel vision, on the other hand, is a form of Condition Black. In a sense, it is *inappropriate Focus:* you lock your attention in too soon...too late...too long...on the wrong stimulus...or for no defensive or offensive purpose. You may, for example, stare transfixed at your assailant's gun. In that or any other tunnel mode, you cannot react properly to your true hazard.

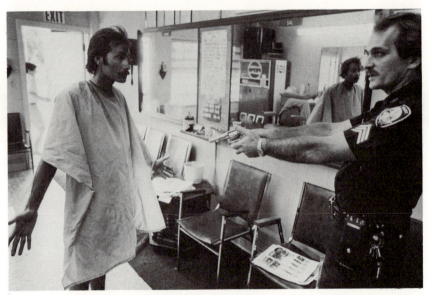

An eerie example of how easy it is to lose control of your Problem Area. Officer went into this barbershop to arrest this bank robber. Note how vulnerable the officer is to being disarmed.

2. *Do not separate your Focus.* Depending upon time and distance, you may be able to monitor more than one Problem Area or Area of Responsibility simultaneously, but you *cannot* successfully control more than one Focus Point at a time. This may seem mandatory to do if you are under attack by multiple adversaries. But think in bird-hunting terms. When a covey of quail flies up, the novice usually tries to blast away at the whole group and hits nothing. The experienced hunter aims at the lead bird and shoots it, then beads on another. He deals with one Focus

Point at a time. If three attackers assault you at once and you try to shoot all simultaneously, they will overwhelm you. Condition Red demands *all* your attention at *one* location, *undivided,* at least briefly. Try to determine your most *immediate* and *serious* threat and deal with it as your first Focus Point. When you eliminate it, you have decreased the group's ability to assault you by one-third. When you stop the second threat, you've knocked out half the remaining assault force. Then you deal with your final Focus Point. Between each adversary, your mind may flicker for a split-second back to Orange, allowing you to evaluate any change in the situation.

Survival has to do with *probability of risk,* preparing for threats as they are *most likely* to occur. You can't erase *all* hazard; no law enforcement officer can. But by using the principles of Tactical Thinking, you *can* substantially reduce your risk and increase the odds on your side.

Can you believe this?

Thought Processes

As part of your tactical strategy for avoiding a direct threat, you need to understand the Thought Processes involved in an assault. That is, the *mental steps* an adversary must go through to *harm* you—and the steps you must complete to *defend* yourself. As with other Tactical Thinking concepts, Thought Processes apply to unarmed as well as armed situations, but they're especially important where deadly force is a possibility on either side.

To assault with any reasonable hope of success, an offender must LOCATE you by sight, sound, intuition or some other of his senses. He must REACT; that is, *prepare* for aggression, as by cocking his fist or pointing his gun. And he must actually ATTACK, *delivering* the act of aggression for which he has primed.

Usually these steps occur in that sequence, but not always. Say you're searching a storage area on a burglary-in-progress call and the suspect is hiding behind a packing crate. He hears you coming, but before he can either Locate or Attack you, he first has to React, by popping up from behind or around his cover to get a visual.

Whatever the order, a would-be assailant has only those three Thought Processes to accommodate. Which puts you at a distinct disadvantage—because *you* have *four* that are necessary to respond to his threat.

You, too, must *Locate* him...prepare to *React* with defensive or offensive moves of your own...and try to *control* the threat, by actually delivering a counterattack with deadly force, by performing a physical defense measure (such as disarming) or by tactically retreating. But somewhere along the way, *you must also IDENTIFY that the offender is indeed initiating an assault.* This may occur before you prepare to respond to his threat or after such preparation.

If you skip this Thought Process, you could find yourself in hot legal soup. You may Locate an armed burglar in a storage area, for instance, and React by drawing down on him. But before you can actually squeeze the trigger justifiably, you need to Identify that an attack from him is imminent or already underway. In high-risk situations, you may repeatedly reach the React step in your Thought Processes, but unless you have already Identified an urgent threat or do so as your next step, you will have to abort your counterattack.

The officer takes a position where the suspect can't see him, thereby interfering with suspect's Thought Processes.

Officers conduct door-to-door search for six jail escapees. Absence of a tactical plan makes it easy for suspects to locate these officers. They have also eliminated the possibility of interfering with the suspects' Thought Processes. Is this really searching?

What this extra Process means for you is a certain built-in *lag time*. Even with top mental conditioning and the keenest anticipation of danger working on your behalf, to Identify (comprehend) that an act of aggression is taking place will require about ³/₁₀ to ½ second. That's how much longer it will take you, at a minimum, to *respond* to an attack than it takes an assailant to *make* one. This is not because of negligence on your part; it's because of nature…and it represents a real limitation.

The tactical way to overcome this disadvantage is to *compensate* for it by understanding and manipulating Thought Processes.

As one simple example, say you're attempting to arrest an offender who has a gun in his hand. You've drawn down on him but you're not behind cover. *So long as he is facing you, even if his hands are in a surrender position, he can shoot before you can respond if he decides to Attack and moves fast.* Role-play this with cap guns or blanks if you're skeptical. He knows when he's going to act; you don't. He has already Located you, so he has only *two* Thought Processes left before he can harm you: 1) React and 2) Attack. You've Located him, too, but you still have your other *three* Processes to accommodate before you can stop him, and the minimum ³/₁₀ second it takes you to Identify his aggressive movement will invariably leave you lagging.

To compensate, *turn the gunman around* so he's facing *away* from you, then move silently to a different position, behind cover if possible. By turning him, you've added back a Thought Process to his roster— Locate; he now has to move (turn) to *find* you before he can Attack you. Because you still can see him, you've already completed your Locate Process. So with this simple maneuver, turning him, you've evened things up. In fact, you've probably gained an edge on him. In most cases, it will take him longer to Locate you than for you to Identify his aggressive movement to do so. You've bought yourself *time with which to stop him.*

As you plan tactically for handling high-risk situations, *five broad, key concepts* will help you compensate for your disadvantage by interfering with a suspect's Thought Processes:

1. *Invisible deployment.* If the suspect does not know you are present or at least does not know exactly where you are, he will not be able to Locate you for assault. He may shoot or strike out randomly in a blind effort to hit you, but then he is depending on luck rather than true target acquisition, and luck may be no more dependable for him than for you.

2. *Surprise.* If you can deploy or move in an unexpected way, the suspect will have greater difficulty either Locating you or Reacting to your presence with a plan of assault. Surprise, by definition, goes hand-in-hand with invisible deployment.

3. *Distance.* Generally speaking, the farther you can stay from a potential adversary, the longer it will take him to React and Attack. Certainly where physical assault is concerned, the more distance he has to cover to reach you, the slower his attack must be, and the more time you'll have to Identify the threat, React and Control his aggression. It's well documented that the closer you get to a suspect, the greater your chance of injury. You're safest, of course, when you can remain beyond the effective range of whatever weapon he has.

4. *Restraint.* In an eagerness to get the job done, officers often short-cut good tactics or rush into territory controlled by a potentially hostile subject. If you take your time and make him come to a position you control, you are likelier to interfere with all his Thought Processes.

One of the major problems with this hostage-taker and arresting officer is that the suspect has not been placed at a disadvantage. Better to have turned him around (making it harder to locate you) then select a search position, and then approach from a point of cover. If the suspect had weapons inside his cap, could he have defeated the officer at this point?

Two suspects took an officer's revolver when their car was pulled over. Later, this arrest of one took place. Suspect should have been turned around, brought away from the vehicle to eliminate cover for him, and far greater distance maintained.

5. *Cover.* Undoubtedly the most important compensation of all. If you can position yourself behind something that will truly stop bullets and when you move, move from one cover location to another, a suspect cannot successfully attack. Cover also gives you more time to Identify any threat he may pose. Where a physical assault is concerned, even putting some kind of *physical barrier* that doesn't qualify as true cover between yourself and a suspect can be helpful. A hedge, a mailbox, your patrol car or some other object separating you will slow down his Attack Process.

As these concepts suggest, your goal always is to *maximize* or *lengthen* the Thought Processes for the *offender* while, where possible, *minimizing* and *shortening* your *own.* Too often, however, officers' actions tend to conveniently *remove* Processes for their opponents, so an attack by a suspect can be made *even faster.* One night, two veteran Indiana officers spotted a subject walking hurriedly in a darkened part of town a few blocks from where a service station had been robbed shortly before. They approached from behind and ordered him to stop and put his hands up. Then, while standing only 8 feet away without cover, they commanded him to turn and face them. That order—a "gift" which cut his Thought Processes down to two—set them up. In the poor light, they had failed to see a small semi-automatic in the suspect's right hand. When he turned, he whipped his arm down, fired, and hit one of the officers.

Understanding Thought Processes can help you evaluate Areas of Responsibility to establish your tactical priorities where deployment is concerned. Say you've entered a living room where a gunman may be hiding. In front of you is a sofa and off to the side is a darkened closet with the door ajar. Which is your most *severe* hazard, demanding your most *immediate* attention?

Considering the Thought Processes needed to harm you, you know it is the *closet*. An assault from behind the sofa will necessitate someone moving to look over or around it and pointing a gun at you (Locating and Reacting) before Attacking. But in the darkened confines of the closet, an unseen offender may *already* have Located you and Reacted (positioned himself) to shoot through the opening. If so, he has completed two-thirds of the Thought Processes needed to hurt you. All he has left to do, unless he is defended against immediately, is to fire.

Your first act should be to remove yourself from the line of fire from the closet or seek cover that protects you from it. Before allowing yourself to become exposed to that location again, you must be certain it is safe. Remember: the *unknown* hazard is often the hazard that kills. This was vividly illustrated late one night when a veteran patrolman, responding to a prowler call, approached a man carrying a white canvas laundry bag outside a New Jersey apartment house. The officer asked about the bag's contents, and the suspect reached inside it. At that instant, a primary Area of Responsibility (the man's hand) disappeared from the officer's view. Inside the bag, unknown to the officer, the suspect gripped a 12 ga. sawed-off shotgun. He fired through the canvas and killed the officer. Because the threat was a hidden one, the officer had no chance to Identify it or Control it to defend himself. Nothing interfered with the assailant's Thought Processes, however. He was able to Locate the officer, React and Attack with ease.

In some cases, knowledge about Thought Processes may help you escape from situations that seem to be no-win. One example is when you are held at close quarters at gunpoint. The circumstances then cause the Thought Processes that you and the suspect normally have to be switched. If you are close enough to attempt a disarming, *you* now will know in advance when you are going to move and *you* will have the minimum number of Processes to go through to complete your Control of him. On the other hand, *he* will be stuck with the extra Process of Identifying your aggressive action, and *he* will experience the lag time that comes with it. Before he can respond, you can defeat him and free yourself, if you are skilled in a valid disarming technique.

Understanding Thought Processes hopefully will help you *avoid* reaching the point where you have to take such desperate action to save your life. As you assess your Problem Areas and Areas of Responsibility in dealing with potential threat situations, ask yourself where, at any given moment, a would-be assailant might be on his scale of mental steps leading to Attack...and know where you are in your ability to respond.

Analyzing a Tactic

As long as you're on the job, you'll get a lot of advice about survival tactics. Some of what you hear may indeed prove life-saving. But a lot, though well-intentioned, is really life-*threatening*. The wrong tactic tried at the wrong time in the wrong situation can leave you on the wrong end of a violent encounter.

An important part of your Tactical Thinking is your ability to analyze what you hear and read about and what you invent on your own, to be certain it can work for you when you need it.

It's a given that your tactics should be *simple* and *direct*. The stress of a high-risk situation dictates that the demands on both your memory and your physical performance be kept as minimal as possible.

Beyond that, any tactic, whether it's a physical defense technique or a deployment strategy, should be tested against four criteria:

1. *Can you really conduct the move under stress?* Some officers may be able to employ tactics that you cannot, because of differences in their physical strength and agility, mental and emotional makeup, memories, equipment, administrative policies, state laws, experience, amount of practice, and so on. We all have individual capabilities and, as the

This officer is attempting to control protestors. But under stress, he chose an inappropriate control option without understanding his limitations. Could he really shoot in this situation?

preeminent police philosopher, Dirty Harry, has observed: "A good man always knows his limitations." If you don't, you may *think* you can pull off a tactical maneuver which, when your life is on the line, you can't. On the other hand, *under*estimating your abilities can be dangerous, too. If you assume, without diligent practice attempts, that you can't perform a tactic that is new and requires training, you are denying yourself a tool that might someday help you gain a vital edge over a high-risk offender.

Even if you personally cannot accomplish a given tactic, that does not necessarily mean you can't gain the benefits of it. Perhaps your *partner* has capabilities that fill in some of your weak spots and vice versa. By *working together* and understanding your individual and joint range of talents you can strengthen your tactical approach as a team. On the other hand, if a tactic or technique *depends* on a partner doing it with you and you are paired with someone who can't—or won't—perform as needed, the tactic is obviously of much less value to you. Besides knowing *your* capabilities and motivation, you need to consider those of your *fellow officers*, too.

Keep in mind that "knowing" a tactic, in the sense of having seen or heard about it and "learned" it intellectually, is not necessarily the same as being able to actually *do* it. And being able to do it in a non-threatening training environment is not the same as being able to perform it under *high stress*. Likewise, being able to do it at one point in your career does not necessarily mean it is within your capability forever. *Continual practice* in the forms of *realistic* role-playing and mental rehearsal is ESSENTIAL to *your* maintaining control over the tactics and techniques you want to use to control others. The more familiar you are with a tactic, the more relaxed you will be when using it, and this will add to your ability to do it. With thousands of repetitions, it will become so embedded in your memory that you will call on it reflexively, without conscious thought. But if a tactic is *not* one you are willing to practice regularly, then it is not one you can really count among your options.

2. *Does the tactic take into account probable responses?* Officers and suspects alike have certain "natural" reactions to stimuli that you must allow for in developing successful street control. If a certain tactic requires that you fall face down on the ground, for example, it must presuppose that you will move to shield your face as you fall, an instinctive reaction dictated by nature to protect the eyes. If this movement is not accommodated for in the successful application of the tactic, then the maneuver won't work when you try to use it in the field.

Similarly, if you're approaching a suspect on foot from behind and he may be armed, his probable reaction should be part of your tactical decision about where best to stand or walk. *Most* people who are right handed (which is the vast majority) will turn to their right to attack, if standing. In doing so, they then hit what they're shooting at about 85% of the time, according to tests. This compares to only 15% hits if they go against the "natural" reaction and spin around to the left. *You can't reduce your risk to zero*, but you can *improve* your odds, then, by keeping to a suspect's left rear, in lieu of a good cover position. A tactic that would not accommodate this probable response should be carefully questioned. Studying people and role-playing reactions will help you identify other probable responses that are important to keep in mind for tactical analysis.

Thought Processes are included in probable responses. Tactics like shining light into a subject's rear view mirrors on a nighttime vehicle stop, approaching buildings with invisible deployment, proning out suspects for searching to slow their mobility are all tactics that *meet the test* because they acknowledge a would-be attacker's Thought Processes and influence them to your advantage. Tactics that ignore or contradict Thought Processes have serious—possibly fatal—flaws.

3. *Does the tactic, once executed, control the offender's movements?* Where physical techniques are concerned, this involves considerations like body mechanics...the element of surprise...positioning superiority...and a tactic's defeatability, all of which must be weighted in your favor for a maneuver to be desirable. Thus, grabbing a suspect by the shoulder, which is predictable and gives you no leverage against him, is not an effective means of control, whereas a proper wrist lock that may catch him off-guard and from which he cannot wrench free may be.

Officers often fail to understand that once you touch an individual, you *must* control him. If he has not already Located you, he now has an excellent idea just where you are, and if he is big, fast, drugged beyond the point of pain compliance or skilled in the martial arts, he's in an excellent position to control *you*—and hurt you badly—unless you control him first.

Tactics that offer control for some officers may not do so for others. You'll have much greater success with some techniques if you're tall and brawny and your suspect is smaller than if you're short and slightly built, up against a bigger, stronger suspect. The body mechanics of trying to maintain an arm-bar hold on some suspects, for example, may work more for the suspect's *defeating* control than for you *achieving* it, unless your strength and stature give you clear superiority.

Physical tactics must be evaluated, *not* in terms of what works for *most* officers or *some* officers, but for *what works for YOU*. The tactics that are good for *you* are the good tactics.

Where deployment strategy is concerned, your tactics may not always immediately control a suspect physically. But they should always be designed to *limit* his ability to hurt you, and they should contribute to your gaining an advantage over him that ultimately will lead to control. In that context, maneuvers that give you a high-ground advantage, better cover and concealment than he has or improved time and distance for dealing with him are control-oriented measures that foster your positioning superiority.

4. *Does the tactic allow for a follow-through?* A good tactic helps you finish what you start. Yet so much of what officers are taught ends like a freeze frame in the middle of the action.

Some gun-retention techniques, for example, show you how to keep your gun in your holster, but nothing beyond that. Unless the suspect meekly says, "Okay, you've retained your gun, so I surrender," what do you do *after* you've protected your weapon? With some techniques, you're more vulnerable to physical attack after retention than you were before, because of the position you end up in in relation to your attacker.

Tactics should culminate in control. If more than one step is required, each should flow smoothly to the next without causing you to lose ground. A good deployment strategy for high-risk vehicle stops, for example, helps you get the offender car stopped safely, but it also guides you in getting the suspects out of the car and into your custody. If your tactics are only half measures and lack follow through, they'll create *new* problems for you instead of helping you move the incident closer to a favorable conclusion.

The more tactics you can *successfully* test against these criteria and integrate into your street performance, the better equipped you'll be for surviving high-risk situations. If you have only a small "trick bag" of tactics, you are adding to your limitations. If a tactic you're depending on does not work, or you're injured and can't perform it, or the situation is such that it simply is not the most appropriate option, you may be in serious trouble if you don't have other options to call upon. With *multiple choices* and the versatility to use them, your ability to apply the *best* tactics to the street problems you face is dramatically enhanced.

One purpose of this book is to broaden your options, to introduce you to tactical skills that you may not previously have heard of or known how to master. With the principles of mental conditioning and Tactical Thinking in mind, let's look now at specific threat situations and explore valid techniques that can help you control them.

An off-duty sergeant is confronted by a man wielding two bottles. Here all four of the evaluation criteria for the use of a tactic are working toward a successful response. The sergeant's analysis of his tactical skills told him he could control this offender without resorting to deadly force. Notice the expression of confidence on the sergeant's face.

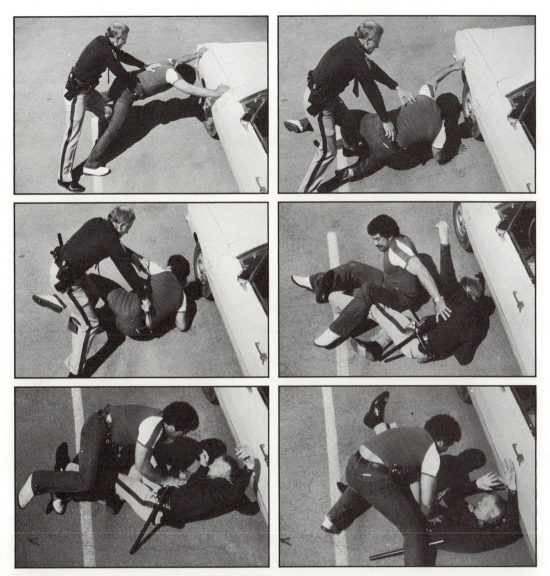

One of the most widely taught control and arrest tactics is the wall position. It has been adapted for searching and handcuffing against a car for years. But how frequently does an accepted tactic like this one get taken for granted as being highly effective. As you can see, it not only can be defeated, it can lead to your being easily disarmed (bottom right photo). Offenders in prison practice the very same arrest defeat. Now the question for you becomes this: What tactical option do you know that will work better for *you* in this situation?

II

THE
TACTICAL
EDGE

Building searches offer a maze of variables both for you...and the offender.

3

BUILDING SEARCHES

In any high-risk situation, there are two aspects of your tactical competence:

1. the *physical mechanics* of the movements you make, and much more important,
2. the *decision making* (Tactical Thinking) that initiates them.

Where survival often goes on-line is when an officer doesn't know how to do the former and/or does the latter too late…or not at all.

In searching a building for one or more suspects who may be primed to attack you, you'd better have *both* aspects down pat—plus the timing to make them effective. For a building search can be one of the toughest assignments in law enforcement.

Your greatest hazard always is the ability of the suspect(s) to hide and lie in wait for you in an almost limitless number of places. Within the maze of stairways, hallways, doorways, furnishings, fixtures, closets, attics, basements, false ceilings, nooks, crannies and other lairs of concealment in a building, the natural odds overwhelmingly favor the hunted over the hunter.

Yet despite the infinite variables presented by the commercial and residential buildings on your beat, you *can* be tactical in approaching any of them. True, there is no "standard" building. But there are standard *movements* that can be adapted to the multitude of architectural configurations you encounter. Indeed, there are few assignments on which the principles of Tactical Thinking and the movements that support them can be better applied.

Whether you're a special-weapons team member handling a known emergency or a street officer responding to your third breaking-and-entering call of your shift, you'll need to make some of the same movements and employ similar thinking. The difference is that a special weapons team may take four hours to negotiate an area that you as a patrol officer will move through in 15 minutes. In a very real sense, the patrol function is harder. The special weapons team *knows* a threat exists and often exactly where it could emanate from. Patrol officers may or may not be pursuing an actual danger…probably won't know its exact location…and yet are expected to do the job faster, while still using caution and tactical savvy.

You should never feel completely safe searching any building. If you do, you're tempting fate with complacency, and complacency is fate's favorite bait. *Always think attack, expect attack.* And then base your actions on tactics that will discourage or counter it.

Keep in mind that no tactical concept is perfect. Each involves a trade-off—sacrificing something to gain something else. When facing choices, take the *best* that a given tactic offers, weigh it against the *worst*, and see where the advantage lies—with you or with your adversary.

Think your choices through. What seems obvious is not always so. For example, some officers believe that to minimize the problem of being silhouetted in hallways they should prone out or low-crawl through them. They are so focused on the *silhouette* threat that they are ignoring a far greater menace that this tactic creates, particularly on concrete and other hard surfaces: *ricochet fire.* In sound Tactical Thinking, you don't *decrease* yourself as a target (from silhouetting) by *increasing* yourself as a target (from ricochet fire).

If a procedure won't work *predominantly* in your favor, then you need to keep searching for something better. In your evaluation, however:

DO NOT fall victim to "what-if paralysis." With all the variables buildings present, you can conjecture about extraordinary attack situations forever. But trying to adjust good tactics to fit every potentiality will only weaken them. Accept that you cannot achieve total immunity from risk, yet still employ the proven techniques that will guard you from the *most* risk.

DO remain flexible. Remember: rigidity kills. As you approach each new problem on your search, assess the threat potential it presents and select the tactical techniques that buy you the greatest safety in that location at that time. *Let the building tell you what to do.* It's design should shape your strategy. You can't just memorize arbitrary rules. You have to *think* about the situation you're moving into, even if your evaluation takes only a split second. And you have to *continue* your evaluation AFTER you're inside. As you progress, you may encounter things there that will necessitate changing your plans completely, on the spot.

Enter...or Wait?

Any time you enter a building that may be offender-occupied, you increase your risk of injury. So *if there is any other reasonable option, DO NOT GO IN.* Especially wait outside if you have good evidence that one or more suspects actually *are* inside. You may get more help, including a K-9, to locate, isolate and control the suspect(s) as time passes. If you set up an "invisible perimeter" around the place, they may come out on their own and unwittingly run into your trap. Or they may be talked out or bluffed out (as with threats to "send in the dogs" if they don't surrender). One search team, after threatening to use tear gas, discharged a fire extinguisher through the transom of a room where a suspect was hiding. Thinking he was being subjected to chemical agents, he quickly emerged.

Some assignments—raids, serving warrants, hunting for welfare cheats—*presume* your going in. But even when you feel *forced* to enter and/or search, *ALWAYS* EVALUATE WHETHER YOU ARE GOING TOO FAR. No call is really important enough to justify your plunging into a building and then discovering that you have overextended yourself into a no-win situation. And just because you've committed yourself to *one* step in a building search does not necessarily mean you have to commit to the next.

Consequences of premature entry. Seeing a suspect just inside door, officer starts in after him (center). He shoots, and officer runs from steps, shot in head (right).

Before automatically launching a search, ask yourself:

1. *Do I have enough backup?* A minimum of two officers are required to clear most buildings with any degree of safety. A large area or complicated structural design will likely require more. A department store or underground garage, for instance, can never be searched *safely* by just two officers. In any large building, will you be able to maintain communication with your fellow officers?

Size aside, some experts say you need three officers for every suspect believed to be inside. However, it can be just as dangerous to get too many searchers involved as too few, because of problems with cross fire, identity, tracking and coordination. For most buildings, *five,* working together as a team, is probably the *maximum* that's feasible.

NEVER TRY TO SEARCH A BUILDING ALONE. *Any structure that has to be entered to be adequately cleared offers far too many Problem Areas and Areas of Responsibility for one officer to control.* If there turn out to be multiple suspects scattered in different parts of the building, how are you going to control them (perhaps with only one set of handcuffs for five offenders) even if you *do* find them?

Early one winter morning, four officers responded to a silent alarm at a Michigan party shop and saw a shadowy figure moving inside. A patrolman volunteered to climb through a broken window and investigate. He quickly captured and handcuffed a teen-age burglar, then, still without backup inside, continued searching for others. Unable to control doorways properly by himself, he did the best he could. But when he opened a rest room door, an intruder hiding inside blasted him with a .38. The bullet penetrated the officer's side between the panels of his vest and struck his heart.

Scarcely a year later, a sergeant on the same department repeated essentially the same blunder—overextension. While children were filing past to school, he entered a video arcade being burglarized by two suspects. Searching without support, he was overpowered and disarmed, then shot in the back of the head with a .357 Magnum while being marched down a rear hallway.

2. *Do I have the right equipment?* The type of building involved will largely determine what's proper. A shotgun may be appropriate if you're searching a warehouse, but could be a hindrance in most residences, unless the weapon has a pistol grip or folding stock. It's cumbersome while searching or handcuffing, and is vulnerable to disarming in close quarters. Between you and a partner, only one of you at most should carry a shotgun. Similarly, a baton can add noise and awkwardness in tight places, although where space is ample it can come in handy as a tool for propping open doors.

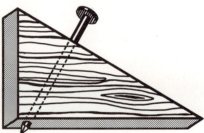

A side-handle baton is used as a wedge between the door and frame to hold door completely open for other entry members. (Above) A nail driven through a wooden wedge so the nail tip protrudes can also be useful. Under pressure from the door, the wedge is made secure.

Door wedges (preferably rubber to hold better on slick floors, but possibly wood cut to different thicknesses from scrap) and a wad of nylon cord for tying door knobs can be tucked in pockets. Or you can carry them in a "search bag" that might also include bungee cords, a mirror or two, distractors, gas grenades, a gas mask, extra handcuffs, a listening device for detecting human sounds through walls, a spare flashlight bulb and other aids for securing rooms or suspects. If you're taking a portable with you, wear an ear plug to eliminate radio noise. Some officers also insert ear plug hearing protectors, so if a shot is fired they will not experience any momentary deafness.

One of the biggest mistakes officers make is going in with an inadequate light source—or none at all. An Indiana patrolman searching a house known to be occupied by an armed suspect ended up trying to clear a dark basement by lighting a *piece of paper.* He was lucky enough only to be shot in the hand. A high-intensity flashlight throwing out at least 20,000 candlepower is *essential* on any search. On raids, this blinding beam (*not* the flashlight handle!) can make an effective stunning device as well as a valuable search aid. Even during daylight hours there'll inevitably be closets, storerooms, attics, basements or other interior spaces you can't properly clear of darkness or shadows with less than a high-intensity light. A *low*-powered light can only aid your adversary; it will glow enough to target *you* when you hold it, but may not illuminate your *adversary.* A Maryland officer shined his feeble "regulation" flashlight directly on a suspect lying atop some overhead pipes in a basement, but the weak beam failed to distinguish his human form sharply enough for the officer to detect. The officer was surprised at not finding the man there because that was exactly where he'd expected him to hide. Then when he turned to search elsewhere, he discovered that his poor light had betrayed him. The suspect attacked from the very spot the weak flashlight had just "cleared."

As backup to your flashlight, consider carrying a *penlight.* This can provide an emergency light source in case your main bulb burns out and may also be appropriate for finding switches in light panels where a strong light is unnecessary.

If you don't have the equipment you need, another source may. When deputies from an Eastern department assembled one night outside a rural home where a bank robber had possibly holed up, they discovered that their 500,000-candlepower power pack was kaput. Rather than attempt such a high-risk search with just flashlights, they called the nearest fire department and borrowed *its* high-intensity power pack.

3. *Am I free of civilian interference?* In an Eastern county, an officer was properly waiting for backup and a K-9 outside a furniture warehouse that had been broken into when the manager showed up. Dressed in a tuxedo, he was impatient to get to a banquet and threatened to enter the building alone unless the officer searched it immediately. Just then an unarmed guard from an alarm company arrived and offered to accompany the officer inside. Under the manager's mounting harangue, the officer gave in. All three went in. All three were shot to death by two burglars hiding inside.

STEADFASTLY RESIST REQUESTS FROM CIVILIANS TO "HELP" YOU SEARCH, AS WELL AS PRESSURE FROM THEM TO MAKE ENTRY WHEN YOU FEEL IT'S INADVISABLE. Their lack of training and tactical sophistication can boomerang against you. This was the case with a Midwestern trooper who permitted a tenant to help him search an apartment building. The civilian spotted two burglars hiding on a terrace and rapped on a window to "scare" them. In their flight, they gunned down the trooper who happened to be in the path of their escape.

Early on, innocent civilians associated with the building should be relocated to a safe place, such as a neighbor's home or perhaps your patrol car, out of the kill zone and beyond the point where they might be taken hostage. If they insist upon entering the building and searching it themselves, warn them of the danger to their safety and discourage that action. If they still insist, advise them: "This building is the scene of an on-going criminal investigation and is off-limits to all civilians. Please wait until it has been secured." If they ignore your lawful order not to enter, you technically can arrest them for failing to obey. Better to deal with potential complaints about that than to be put on the spot later for *not* having restrained them, if they do go inside and get injured or killed. Above all, do NOT give in to pressure or demands and go in with them.

If you and other officers choose to make entry yourselves, *instruct concerned civilians not to come in after you at any point.* Two officers in the Baltimore area kicked open a bedroom door while checking a house after a burglary. The female victim had followed them in and was waiting in the living room. She heard the door slam against the wall and screamed, thinking it was the burglar making noise. The officers spun around, assuming she was being attacked...and exposed their backs to the uncleared bedroom. Fortunately, the burglar had fled before the search began, or the woman's next screams might have been over the distracted officers being shot from behind.

4. *What intelligence is available?* Someone familiar with the building may be able quickly to sketch its floor plan, highlighting any unusual features or fixtures. On a drug raid, you'll want to know in advance where the toilets are, because that's where the suspects will go. In apartment complexes, hotels and motels, and some residential subdivisions, you may get permission to view other premises nearby with the same layout as those you're considering searching. You may also be able to find out where light switches are and what they turn on...and where are the most likely hiding places.

Metal gate is removed as a small part of the $2,500 worth of gate and door protection reinforced within this apartment. The location prior to being raided was a major drug operation in the East.

86

The kind of building it is may affect your entry decision. Is it a PCP lab, where you may become dangerously contaminated by touching things barehanded and where the risk of explosion is high? A biker clubhouse, which may have hard-to-penetrate fortifications? A jewelry store, which typically will be hit by a large group of professionals, who may still be inside? A warehouse, stacked with munitions? Try to learn the *exact spots* where any combustible or hazardous materials are stored inside. Materials in some environments present fatal risks in case of a gunfight. With airborne particles of grain or flour inside a mill, for instance, gunfire can touch off a major explosion.

Certain building types—biker hangouts, the headquarters or "safe houses" of extremist groups, the homes of emotionally disturbed subjects, among others—may be mined with booby traps. An electrician wanted in Wyoming for contempt of court in connection with a tax case rigged his house with 19 destructive devices made of shotgun shells, smokeless powder and shot pellets, just waiting for federal agents to enter and search for him. The devices could have been tripped by hidden wires. Other locations have been booby trapped with light bulbs filled with gunpowder and buckshot. These explode when you flip the switch to light a room. Rattlesnakes were hidden in boxes and drawers inside a biker clubhouse in Florida. Elsewhere, an officer searching a tenement where radicals allegedly had stockpiled weapons leaped through a doorway—and felt the floor give way when he landed. Some boards had been cut to collapse while others popped up to impale his groin with four 6-inch nails. Ordinary items, such as plastic soft drink bottles, clothes pins, mouse traps, shoe boxes, cigaret packs, beer cans, tape recorder cassettes, brief cases, etc., can be transformed into deadly weapons that are rarely obvious or easily avoided. The booby trap risk is highest when a suspect has had access to a location for some time and is anticipating an eventual confrontation with law enforcement. When you're dealing with a location that may have been "worked on," you're safest to back off and let specialized experts handle it.

Intelligence gathering may also give you a fix on the probable number of suspects inside, their location and their state of mind. Your decision about entering a school that has likely been broken into by unarmed juvenile vandals will probably be much different than about entering a small trailer house occupied by a drunk or disturbed individual who's firing shots. Amazingly, however, in-service training exercises reveal that many experienced officers *approach* a building cautiously—but then make entry *immediately* when they hear shots fired inside. Instead of backing off, taking cover and using an option like chemical agents, they burst right into the kill zone, as if learning that there's a suspect inside prepared to shoot them is a signal for making entry! This irrational compulsion to enter can apply to *rooms* as well as buildings. On a major northern department, an officer searching a house where a subject had been found shot in the living room came to a dimly lighted bedroom. Inside, he saw a man sitting in a chair, holding a gun in his lap. The officer's reaction was to vault *into the doorway* in a "classic combat shooting stance." When he shouted, "Freeze!" and the gunman didn't move, the officer then *holstered his weapon and walked up to the chair*. Only when he got within touching distance did he discover that the subject—luckily—was dead.

If the presence of firearms isn't obvious, ask about them, including any kept in desks or personal areas. You'll want to know if your risk of being attacked has been increased by the availability of weapons inside the building—and how your firepower stacks up against what's in there. Also inquire where valuables are kept. A suspect may have been near those sites when forced to hide. And find out if any dogs are in the place and whether they can be called out before you go in. Good searching requires the application of Focus, and unnecessary diversions like a dog attack that may separate your Focus are unnecessary dangers.

5. *Is there a safe point of entry?* If you can't even get into the place without incurring high risk, that alone may abort your search.

With most buildings, doors and windows are your only options. A door almost always is preferred. Ideally, you want one on the side of the building with the least number of windows, to reduce your chances of being seen. Also try for one as far as possible from the suspect's apparent point of entry. He may anticipate your entering where he did, plus he'll likely leave the same way he came in and he may be heading toward his exit as you start in. Even if you have to use a door the suspect used, though, it'll likely be safer than a window. Windows slow, silhouette and cramp you...rob you of movement that's coordinated with other officers... make you almost impossible to cover...and require contortions that keep you from covering yourself.

Avoid windows as a point of entry, especially a window this narrow. Tactical officers search for a suspect who wounded an officer the day before. Who is most vulnerable here?

Securing a safe entry point may take time...time to get a key to a door or find one whose security you can breach (back doors usually are less secured by locks)...time to set up a distraction at the opposite end of the building to divert the suspect at the moment you make entry. *Cherish*

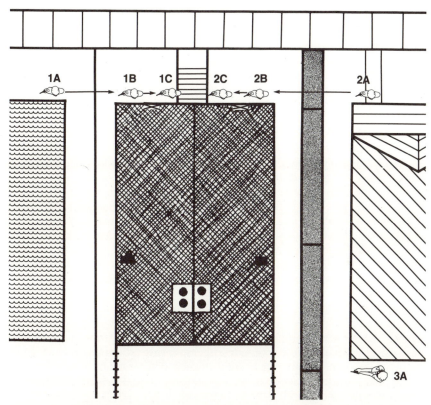

Here three officers are involved in the response. As Officers 1 and 2 move into position with the front door as their point of entry, they pass below windows and avoid crossfires. Officer 3 covers the rear of the house and stays back to avoid detection. Each officer can control designated Areas of Responsibility.

One important principle in building entries is to initially deploy to avoid detection (see art above). In this incident, two of the three officers could be detected by someone in the house because of either weapon or body positioning.

time. With information, equipment, manpower and tactics, it should be the bedrock of your search.

Unless you are conducting a raid, you and all other officers should consider entering only through one place, to reduce the risk of cross fire. Officers staying *outside*, as well as those going in, should know this point of entry, and *neither entry nor exit should be made except through there.* A young plainclothesman gave chase to two suspects he flushed out during the search of a "dope flat." When they leaped out a window, he started to climb through after them—and was shot by an officer outside who logically assumed he was a third fleeing felon.

Consider more than just your risks from the suspect in assessing the safety of an entry point. A Michigan sergeant who was preparing to make entry through the back door of a dwelling was injured when decayed wooden steps on the back porch collapsed under him.

As you approach a building that may require penetration, you can always come up with reasons why you *should* go in. With this checklist, play devil's advocate and argue why you *shouldn't.* You may wisely be persuaded not to.

As you make your evaluation about entering, stay *behind cover.* A Tennessee patrolman was shot in the head and killed with a single round from a .30-30 rifle while standing on the sidewalk in front of a home he and other officers were considering entering. A gunfight had been reported in a back room, out of sight of their deliberations. But unknown to the officers, the suspect had come outside and hidden himself where he could watch—and attack—them before they arrived.

If you do decide to enter, your penetration must be as tactically sound as any subsequent movement inside. Your search moves begin at the outer wall of the structure. In your mind, the suspect should always be waiting just on the other side. *Always expect the unexpected.* If someone's in there, you're now in *his* territory.

Principles of Movement

Nothing is more important to your surviving building searches than the *principles of movement* that can minimize your risk. They can help you construct a systematic plan of action rather than relying just on random movement. Yet, ironically, in the searches you conduct you often will not be able to apply many—sometimes even *most*—of these tactical gospels because of the constraints of manpower, the impulses of human nature or the realities of architectural design.

Think of these principles, then, as you do the moral principles of your personal life: appreciate their value, try to adhere to them as often as you can and understand that there will be times when you have to compromise them because of forces you cannot control. At least be aware when you are violating them...and why.

Not all authorities agree on all these fundamentals. With these, as with other tactics, there tend to be regional and individual preferences. You will need to weigh the pros and cons and, based on your experience, ability and *role-playing*, choose what seems most likely to work best for you and your fellow officers in your circumstances.

During any search, key considerations to keep in mind include:

Verbal challenge. While you want your actual entry to be as discreet as possible, sometime before you move to enter address the suspect(s) who may be inside. From *behind cover*, yell something like: "Police! You inside… make your presence known and *come out*. Walk out *backwards*…with your *hands up*. If you do not come out NOW, you will be considered armed and dangerous. YOU MAY BE SHOT!" This may evoke a voluntary surrender…or it may prevent a tragedy.

Even if your warning fails to prompt an innocent party or a harmless suspect to emerge, if you *do* end up shooting an unarmed occupant inadvertently, you will be in a stronger legal and disciplinary position having issued a challenge before entering, making clear the risks to anyone who stays inside. C.Y.A.: challenge your area…cover your ass. That's precisely what two officers in Illinois did before entering a suburban home that neighbors believed was being burglarized. Inside, a shadowy figure suddenly banged open a basement door, surprised an officer standing nearby and was shot. The victim turned out to be an 18-year-old who lived there. He'd forgotten his key and had crawled through a window to get inside. The officers' repeated warnings before entering, however, contributed to their being cleared of criminal wrong-doing and departmental violations in the investigation that followed.

Remember, of course, that not everyone who claims to have a legitimate connection with a building necessarily does. When two Virginia officers approached a house on a burglary call, a teen-ager inside raised the window as if he lived there and indignantly demanded to know, "What's going on out there?" He proved to be an offender; his partner was found hiding under a bed.

Search pattern. It's said about building searches that the higher you enter, the better; "search from the top down." For some exquisitely choreographed special-weapons operations, that may be valid. But for the average officer facing a search that may or may not produce an armed confrontation, how practical is it? Will you have a helicopter or fire department snorkel to hoist you above ground level? Responding to a possible breaking-and-entering at the average home, would you climb up a rain spout to break through the roof…or rappel down to crash through an upper bedroom window? In truth, you'd probably have to go up stairways to reach the top, so to some degree at least you'd have to search *up* in order to start searching *down*.

Even if you could magically appear on the top floor, the supposed "high-ground advantage" of searching down tends to be more question-able on patrol assignments than in the military. Unable to fire ahead or toss hand grenades to clear a path, coming *down* most stairways is one of the highest-risk aspects of searching, because of your limited visibility compared to what someone hiding below can see of you and because of the physical difficulties of returning effective fire. That's why searching basements is so justifiably scary to most officers. You can easily be targeted and assaulted before you even perceive the threat, simply because your eyes are not at the ends of your toes.

When you have no fix on the suspect's location (or even whether he's in there), you're generally safer tactically to work your way *up*. In a typical house, search the first floor first. Then if manpower permits, leave an officer or officers behind to secure access points to the upstairs and basement while you and the rest of the search party move up and search the upper floor(s) and attic. The basement is searched last. *Do not attempt searching more than one floor at a time.*

As you move up or down stairways, along hallways and through rooms, *keep your back toward but slightly away from the wall.* Although offenders may be able to shoot through some walls, a wall generally will be the closest thing to cover available for your backside. Without your back exposed, you'll feel more comfortable concentrating on the Areas of Responsibility toward which you are advancing. Your potential threat locations are ahead of you, and you are constructed physically to do your best fighting forward. If you feel the need to look in the opposite direction, you can do so easily with a slight glance toward your trailing shoulder instead of having to turn your head fully as you would if you were moving perpendicular to the wall. If you find yourself in a hallway or a room where you feel your back isn't covered, *reevaluate.* Chances are high that you have failed to do something earlier that you should have.

Take care not to rub against walls as you advance or to crash into them when you run from one spot to another. Not only may the noise be a give-away but in some positions against hard surfaces you may also be exposing yourself to the risks of ricochet fire.

Moving, think continually about your cover and the suspect's *field of view.* In other words, could the offender be hidden in a spot from which he could see—and more important, *shoot*—you where you are now or where you intend to move?

Field of view. Ideally *you should NEVER move into an adversary's potential field of view that you personally cannot cover;* that is, where you could not readily meet force with force. As a tactical minimum, NEVER enter a field of view that at least your *partner* cannot cover.

The officer killed in this room search violated both principles:

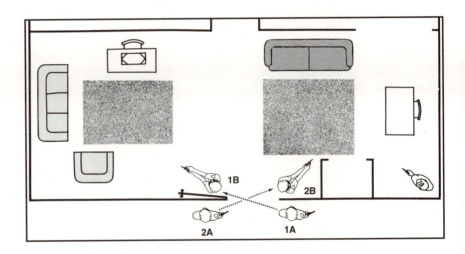

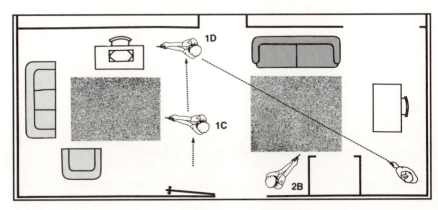

As he moved out from the doorway, his back was toward the suspect's hiding place in a part of the room that had not been searched. Neither he nor his partner was in position to detect the suspect's presence or to defend the officer once he entered the offender's field of view. He was shot in the back without ever realizing he had made himself an easy victim. Had he moved around the room to his left upon entering, with his back to the wall, conscious of possible hiding places and what might be seen from them, he would have been in a much stronger position to anticipate the attack and either thwart or respond to it.

Any movement that does not permit you to face the danger area and maintain target acquisition while moving is likely to be a bad movement technique.

Light control. One means of expanding your own field of view and diminishing the suspect's is through the *manipulation of light* in darkened locations. Use it *for* you and your partners, *against* the subject you're searching for.

Where you have varied or controllable lighting, you want if possible to move from dark areas into lighted ones, never the reverse. Also avoid searching in the dark unless you have extensive training and experience with a special-weapons team. Darkness tends to disorient most people, and because you can't effectively clear an area when it's dark, you won't be able to see the potential hazards you face. Lighting up a room places a suspect at a tactical disadvantage. It shows you clearly where your potential threat locations are...it may deprive him of concealment by illuminating him, silhouetting him or causing him to cast a shadow... and it may temporarily affect his vision if his eyes have grown accustomed to the dark.

Light switches for most rooms are about 48 inches off the floor (chest height), but don't linger there once you've flipped one on. The suspect may know the switch location, too. Where you have light panels to work with, as you might in a warehouse, try to light the building up from the rear forward. You may be able to expose the suspect while you are still concealed in darkness.

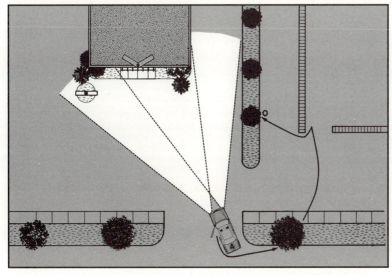

You may be able to position your patrol car so that its headlights shine into the area. After the spotlight is aimed at the entrance, quickly flank out to cover where an adversary will not expect you to be located.

Fight the temptation to turn room lights on if you have to move without tactical soundness in order to do it. There are undoubtedly other light sources. A high-intensity beam bounced off the ceiling from behind a doorway may do the trick. This can be especially effective in illuminating someone hiding behind a shower curtain, for example. Your flashlight can even be made to "bend" around corners. Just shine your light into a convex mirror with about a 3-inch surface diameter that you hold in your hand or have attached to a small wooden paddle or a piece of flexible conduit.

In using your flashlight and other lighting sources, your principal danger will be silhouetting yourself. In addition to obvious sources of back-lighting, remember as you move down a lighted hallway, for instance, that a suspect hiding in a darkened room may be able to see your feet silhouetted under the door and learn your location. When light is behind you and you are nearing a corner, your shadow will be cast ahead and may give away your presence prematurely. In their search bags, some officers carry a water pistol that can be used to squirt on naked hallway light bulbs to break them.

In searching, two types of silhouetting may present risks: *primary* silhouettes, such as windows, and *secondary* silhouettes, areas of wall and floor where light coming through a window is cast. You may be able to move *under* primary silhouettes, but this may prove impossible with secondary ones because of the angle and extent of the light splash. Here speed is probably your best ally: don't *creep* through any silhouette.

If you come into an area that is more dimly lit than one you've just left (like coming indoors in daytime), blink your eyes several times. This will stimulate your night vision. Also, avoid searching while wearing glasses with photograde lenses. The lens density changes too slowly for your eyes to adjust to changes in light level as fast as you need to. Amber lensed *shooting glasses*, however, will help your eyes gather light in low-light level.

Relative positioning. Regardless of the illumination you create, *before you pass any corner or enter any doorway, you want to see what (or who) might be waiting on the other side.* One option is to use a mirror. Another surveillance move is the quick peek technique. Done fast enough and with the proper limited exposure, a lurking suspect may not even detect this move. You don't need to poke your head out far enough to see with both eyes; *one* will do the job.

Just as you remain conscious of where you are relative to where the suspect might be, also *stay aware of your position relative to that of your partner(s).*

Getting into each other's *cross fire* is a major risk, especially in close quarters and where high stress tends to keep you engrossed in the searching process. Indeed, on many searches your biggest threat is likely to be the officer with you. Sometimes cross fire can be avoided by adjusting your relative heights, getting low while your partner remains upright, so if he is forced to fire at a suspect beyond you his bullets will go over your head. Your partner should always tell you ("Stop!") when you are about to cross his line of fire and vice versa. Try then to adjust your positions. At times, though, you may have to accept that, at least for a split second, either you or your partner will not be able to fire because of the risk of hitting the other. Just be certain you are not *both* in this position simultaneously, so that neither of you can shoot.

Avoid the *bunching effect*, the strong tendency to cluster together in the illusion of safety from closeness as you prepare for entry, move or search. The closer together you are, the easier it will be for a suspect to shoot both of you with just a fractional shift in his aim. Plus, you are dangerous to each other. Five officers sent to deal with a drunk who was threatening suicide were clustered together on the subject's front porch when he suddenly appeared in the doorway with a rifle. Officers spun out and away from the doorway, all drawing their service revolvers and firing at the same time. One officer was shot to death, taking close-quarters rounds from three of his colleagues.

Another consideration in relative positioning is the fact that an offender's feet usually stick out farther than the rest of his body. If you glance down as you peek, you might see him before he can see you. (below) The bunching of officers can create an easy target for an offender who needs to concentrate his assault in only one area to jeopardize multiple officers.

Tactical separation buys you time for proper reaction. In Chicago, two officers were searching a wholesale grocery warehouse after an alarm when one of them was overwhelmed and disarmed by four gunmen. His partner was far enough behind that he could dive for cover behind a van. When the robbers fired at both officers, the protected partner was able to return fire, providing some protection for himself and the first officer until the assailants finally fled. However, you don't want your distance apart to reach the point where you cannot keep in visual contact. For example, don't search by having everyone on your team go to separate rooms. Again, with only momentary exceptions in the most extreme circumstances, *you should be able to see your partner and all other officers in your search party at all times.* Not being able to see each other invites shooting each other... or not being able to warn one another of danger.

Strive for the *principle of triangulation,* which will promote separation, minimize cross fire and bunching and maximize the impact of your defensive fire by directing it to a central point. Think of each of the potential hiding places (Areas of Responsibility) in your field of view as being at the apex of a triangle. You and your partner ideally should be positioned so that figuratively you form the other two corners of a triangle relative to each of these spots. If a threat presents itself, you're then able to direct fire at it from different angles, while the suspect will be forced to separate his firepower in order to hit both of you.

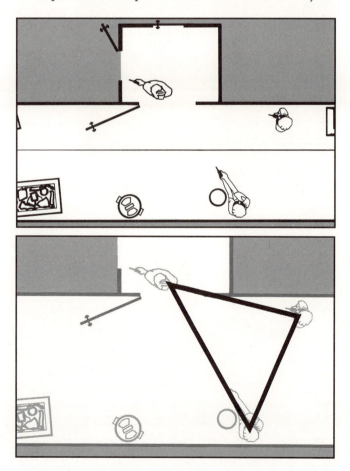

As you move and clear Areas of Responsibility, your partner may need to shift his relative position in order for triangulation to be maintained on new potential threat locations. If more than two officers are involved in your search, the triangulation concept still holds.

During a search, *only one officer should move at a time.* One of you covers...one moves. Moving and shooting simultaneously is difficult if not impossible to do with accuracy. So this principle assures that someone is always maintaining control and is prepared to provide reliable defense.

Two movement styles that accommodate this principle are:

1. *follow-the-leader* (sometimes called "the traveling overwatch"), where one officer moves and stops, then the second positions himself in the vicinity of the first but with some separation between them. This generally is the appropriate method for maneuvering stairways, for example. The main risk here is that the second officer will stop so close behind the first that an offender can pin them down with a single line of fire. Adequate separation not only precludes this, but also prevents collisions during quick movement and assures that the two officers maintain at least slightly different fields of view. Besides being responsi-

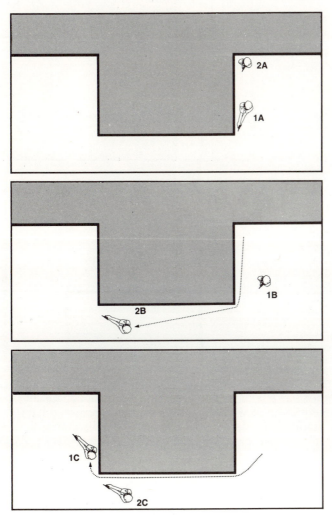

ble for keeping the separation, the second officer also has rear-guard responsibilities.

2. *leapfrog* (also called "the bounding overwatch"), where one officer searches an area and signals when it's secured, then the second goes past him into a new area and searches and secures it. They keep switching back and forth as the search progresses. This method is usually the faster and is appropriate when the officers have equal firepower.

However, either style of movement can be tactically sound, and both can be used interchangeably during a particular search. The environment will determine which is more appropriate at any given moment.

If you have a partner who insists on wandering through a search in a careless manner, *you* become the officer who remains stationary and covers. *Don't be lured into joining him or her in untactical movements.* By staying behind you'll be able at least to call on the radio if that officer gets shot.

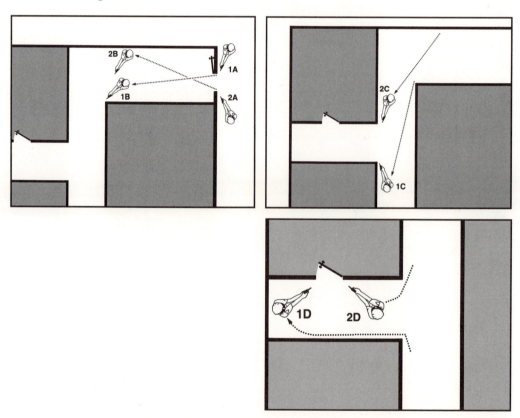

Gun positioning. *Search with your gun in hand,* even if you believe the offender has left the premises. You'll be at enough disadvantage if he does present a threat without slowing your response by having to draw. As you stand or move, however, avoid the "Starsky and Hutch Syndrome." That's holding your gun up beside your head like you see tv cops do. In Hollywood, that's great because it allows close-ups of an actor's face with his gun framed in the picture. But in real life, it's a good way to lose your two most important senses (sight and hearing) on at least one side of your head if, because of stress or as a startle reaction to a sudden threat, you pull the trigger without lowering the gun. During a raid on an apartment house for traffic warrants in Indiana, an undercover trooper trying to force a rear door accidentally discharged his .45 while holding it up. The round entered under his chin and tore through the roof of his mouth into his brain.

(above left) Conducting searches with the barrel of a handgun pointed up is common but that doesn't make it safe. At least one officer has died because of a handgun position like you see here. (above) A one- or two-hand hold pointed downward is far safer and reduces crossfire problems when moving. (lower left) Belt tuck technique as an example of "the third-eye concept."

Besides that risk, if you thrust your gun from a high position into an Isosceles or Weaver stance under intense stress, there's a tendency for the force of your move to point the barrel toward the ground, sabotaging your aim at a distance. In one test, this loss of control caused rounds to hit the floor about 12 feet in front of the shooter. In addition, of course, having to bring the gun down increases the time necessary for target acquisition.

On the other hand, if you keep your sidearm down alongside your leg, beware the tendency to let it point backward—toward your backup's toes or toward a hard surface where it could ricochet into him.

Consider moving most of the time with your gun pulled back snugly in a two-hand hold against your waist *just above your belt buckle* (not off to the side over your hip), with the muzzle pointed straight out or slightly down. This "belt tuck" position provides good stability, standing or squatting, even if you have to release one hand to open doors or move furniture. It's safer for you and the officer(s) behind you...it keeps you from "leading" with your sidearm in your outstretched arm and giving away your position around corners or through doorways...and it's less tiring than trying to sustain an Isosceles or Weaver stance all the time you're searching. Yet in case of trouble or when you're challenging a potential threat location, you can thrust your sidearm up to those postures in an instant...or fire in place from the beltline with accuracy, if you have to. If the threat comes from either side by surprise, you're just half a turn from being on target.

This position accommodates the *"third-eye concept."* As your body turns toward a threat, your sidearm, lined up in the center, turns, too...it "sees" (and targets) what your eyes see. This is the essence of instinct shooting: what your gun "sees" like a third eye, it can hit. Extensive testing, especially with officers who are average-to-poor shots, indicates that the belt tuck can remarkably increase accuracy without exceptional practice or training. Shooting from the beltline, you won't necessarily get 3-inch groups. But you will do better than if you shoot one-handed with your gun on your hip to the side. In the belt tuck position, you have good support for controlling your weapon if fatigue sets in and are better able to retain it and return fire if you get shot and go down.

Thoroughness. When you're searching for the whereabouts or existence of a suspect (in contrast to when you are moving toward an area where you are *certain* he is located), you'll want to observe this principle: *avoid passing any potential hiding place without first checking and securing it.* Convince yourself it is *safe* to pass. Don't forget to look up...and don't dismiss any place as "too small" or "too far-fetched." Motivated by fear of detection, human beings can squeeze into amazing spots. Officers repeatedly searched a house in Ohio over several months looking for a man and his pregnant companion who were wanted on federal warrants. To check under a bed, they rolled a flashlight along the floor and watched to see if the beam was interrupted as it showed through onto an opposite wall. Every time the officers searched, the couple were hiding under the bed but were not detected because they pulled themselves up off the floor by hanging onto the springs. They were caught finally when the woman's pregnancy advanced to the point that she couldn't get off the floor far enough to avoid the light. Other times, suspects have been known to hide inside stereo speaker cabinets, inside dressers, in cardboard boxes, on top of elevator cars, inside the trunks of automobiles parked inside the building being searched and other unlikely places. One rape suspect hid in a tiny hole dug through the floorboards and into the foundation of his house beneath his living room sofa. He eluded everyone who looked for him for eight years!

Any time you check an area or even an entire building without finding anyone, keep your senses sharp by thinking, "I was unable to locate anyone"—*not* "There's nobody in there." Michigan officers "thoroughly" searched a large church one night after its alarm went off, discovered no one and left. An hour later, the alarm rang again. Suspects who'd eluded the first search had now made off with several thousand dollars worth of goods. The next time the church's intrusion device detonated, a sergeant ordered it reset, loudly instructed his troops to withdraw—but left three officers secreted behind with shotguns. Forty-five minutes later, four burglars confidently emerged from hiding places to ransack the church offices...but this time they were arrested. Less fortunate was a Minnesota officer who searched an office building one night after an employee working late noticed that one of the suites had been broken into. Finding no one, the officer returned to his vehicle. Meanwhile, the burglar emerged from a hiding place inside and seized the complainant as a hostage. In a bid for escape, he fired two shots into the idling patrol car and killed the officer, who was caught by surprise behind the wheel with his sidearm in its holster.

Noise control. *Be conscious of the noise you make.* Chances are the suspect will know you are there, especially once you enter the room where he's hiding. Your breathing alone may be enough to alert him. But don't tip your hand unnecessarily or help him know *exactly* where you are. Get rid of jangling keys, rattling coins (leave them on the floor if you have to and retrieve them later), squawky radios, watches with alarms. Five officers made entry in California one night and precisely at 10 o'clock, while they were still searching, the wristwatches of all five started buzzing. In New York, an officer who was sneaking up behind an armed robber in an apartment house stairwell was betrayed by his portable radio, which suddenly blurted out a transmission. The robber spun around...shots were fired back and forth...the officer grappled for the suspect's gun and soon found himself tumbling down the stairway, wounded in the hand, while the offender escaped.

To eliminate noise from leather soles and heels on uncarpeted floors, some officers search in stocking feet or wear tennis shoes. Getting quiet neoprene soles on your duty shoes is the minimum you should consider. You can further minimize foot noise by using the sides of your feet. Lightly "feel" the floor by rolling forward with the whole length of the outer edge of your foot before putting any weight on it. This allows you a warning of objects in your path so you can nudge them out of the way before you crunch down on them, and also avoids creating the pounding noise usually made when a foot strikes the floor.

As you move around inside, remain aware of how your environment may betray you with noise. In video arcades, for example, some machines are designed to start "talking" when you walk in front of them.

Also consider eliminating visual "noise" like hats with protruding brims before the search begins. At least turn your hat around. Besides announcing your presence in maneuvers like the quick peek, a hat bill will restrict your peripheral vision when looking around furniture and may discourage you from looking *up*, an important but frequently neglected part of searching. Get rid of the "loudness" of unnecessary odors, too. The scent of cologne or perfume can give away your location as easily as being heard. You're better off saving it for after work, when its "fatal attraction" will be more to your liking.

Communication. *The sounds you make in communicating with* *your partner should be soft,* too. Instead of speaking out loud (a "hard" sound that can be easily pinpointed), *whisper* (a "soft" sound whose precise location cannot be so easily placed by a suspect who overhears it)...instead of snapping your fingers (hard sound), briskly rub your pants leg or sleeve (soft sound) to signal or attract attention.

Obviously, if a threat is imminent, shout out *loud,* so there's no doubt the warning will be heard. For instance, if you see that your partner is moving into a hazard area that he does not perceive, you might yell: "You! Behind the refrigerator! Don't move! We've got you covered!" etc. This tells your partner where the hazard is and challenges a potential subject simultaneously.

Simple non-verbal signals can easily be communicated without losing visual control of your hazard.

The risk of not communicating was gravely illustrated during a Midwestern building search where a suspect was cornered inside a bedroom. An officer outside a window spotted him and shot, believing he had a gun. Actually, he was unarmed, but two officers about to make entry through the bedroom doorway thought the suspect was firing at them. They killed him and, in the process, shot the outside officer. He had failed to communicate his position and they had no idea until he was hit that he was in their cross fire.

As you move through the interior, keep in mind that your partner may not always hear and see what you do, even though it may seem impossible that he wouldn't. However, *be sure your communication does not require that your partner look away from his Area of Responsibility.* Hand and head signals should be used ONLY if they can be seen in direct or peripheral vision while surveillance is kept on the potential threat location. In other words, you can signal safely only if the officer you're signaling is at least slightly *behind* you. If that officer is ahead of you, though, whisper; the sound will project forward and he won't have to turn and look.

As you *give* a signal, don't take *your* eyes off *your* Area of Responsibility, either. Likewise, resist the impulse to turn and look at your partner when you whisper to him or to confirm that he has followed a signal from you. When either of you receives a directive from the other, whisper back or rub your pants leg in confirmation, then repeat that return signal when you have followed through on the command.

All signals should be *simple* or they are certain to be forgotten or confused under stress. Develop and practice them *in advance* with your partner. As an Ohio trainer puts it, "When you work with a partner, you have to *work* with a partner."

Listening. As you search, pause frequently and just LISTEN. *Listening is your safest option for determining whether a suspect is waiting in the area you're about to enter.* Absorb the sound around you. Remember, the suspect is excited and under stress, too. He's also experiencing bodily reactions that he may not be able to control, like fast, audible breathing. His bodily functions do not cease just because he is in a tactical situation. He may fart, belch, cough because his throat is dry, he may shuffle his feet because of a muscle cramp. Often through quiet vigilance, you can gain the edge by hearing *his* noise. Take your time. Just because your mind is accelerating under stress does not mean you have to accelerate your movements to match.

In Arizona, an officer responded to a malicious mischief call at a vacant apartment, expecting to encounter juvenile vandals. Instead, he was confronted by a crazy adult with a .357 Magnum, who opened fire as the officer made entry. The officer wisely did not pursue the suspect as he disappeared toward the far bedrooms, but instead took cover in the living room...and waited.

The floor plan was such that the gunman could have tried to attack from either the front or the rear. By keeping his own noise quiet and *listening,* the officer could hear which way he was coming, even though the offender moved with great stealth. He tried to come from behind, but the officer was ready—and shot him dead.

Stairways

One Problem Area inside buildings that's a veritable seedbed for impatience is stairways. Officers know what death traps stairs can be, so the desire to short-cut or circumvent them is understandable. Sometimes, though, they choose alternatives that are even worse. Elevators, for one.

In a scenario familiar in the chronicles of police assaults, a sergeant and three officers crowded into a single elevator to reach the floor of an apartment building where a recent prison releasee had fired shots through a door in a squabble with his girlfriend. When the elevator whooshed open, the gunman was standing directly in front of it. He shoved a .22 revolver at the sergeant's face and fired twice. The sergeant saved himself by diving to the floor, but still he was temporarily deafened. Worse damage was prevented only because one of the officers had drawn his gun before the door opened and was able to shoot back before the assailant got off another round. He hit the suspect in the arm, causing him to drop the gun and flee down a stairway.

Because elevators offer no visibility out and no cover within and announce your arrival in advance, you're usually safer with stairs, *provided* you use good tactical movements. In low-rise buildings, bring all elevators to the first floor, lock them in place so they can't be activated by a suspect...and start climbing.

A full stairway ascent in a high-rise building is not realistic (especially considering the heart attack risk for some officers). But when you have an approximate fix on your trouble location, you can at least exit the elevator a floor or two *below* the level you're going to and use the stairs from there. (Be sure, however, that you can exit from the stairwell. Fire stairs in some buildings permit exit only at the ground level.) *NEVER take an elevator to a floor where there's suspicion or evidence of trouble until the hallway outside it has been cleared and secured.* Even then, have your sidearm in the ready position when the doors open...so you can "open up," too, if necessary.

One recommendation for climbing stairs has been for two officers to ascend together back-to-back. One climbs forward, his sidearm ready for an assault from the top, the other walks up backward, guarding the rear. Besides being awkward to do, especially under stress, this tactic exemplifies the bunching effect and makes both officers vulnerable to a single line of fire. Even if they climb up shoulder-to-shoulder (facing opposite directions), they are still both essentially cover men, neither in a protected position. If there is an assault, they're likely to knock each other over trying to flee or, at best, return random fire that may be hampered by the fact that both of them are moving.

Bunching together makes you fair game for any hidden suspect.

Separating yourselves and dividing the Areas of Responsibility are as important on stairs as in other parts of your search. Unless you *know* the area is safe and your top priority is speed, you or your partner should try to maintain a barricade cover position at the bottom of the flight while the other climbs. Once the moving officer reaches a landing, then the other can reposition to provide the best possible cover for the next section.

As the ascending officer you may be exposed to some threats that your partner can't directly cover you against, in order to maintain the integrity of his own position. So your movements need to be ones that not only yield you the best field of view for searching but also provide you the best opportunity to defend yourself. *Don't make the most common mistake on stairways: staring at your feet as you move.* You must maintain a visual on your Area of Responsibility at all times.

Some officers claim you shouldn't walk in the center of (wooden) stairs because they're most likely to creak there. Others say you *should* walk in the middle in order to keep off walls and avoid ricochet shots. What's *really* important about where you climb is the *advantage of angle* that a given position affords you.

Considering what appears to be above and to your sides, calculate the likely hiding places and climb along the portion of the stairs that will give you your earliest revealing view of those spots. Quick peeks can be made *up* with slight springs of your toes to survey landings or adjacent

(top) Notice one officer stays back as the cover officer while the advancing officer ascends, keeping his body away from touching the wall. (below) On a narrower stairway, this officer elects to advance with a lower body positioning. Bunching in either case is not a problem.

staircases. At other times, you may want to use a mirror or stay low, almost crawling up the stairs in a sideways squat, for different perspectives. As you near the landing, consider stepping onto it on your *knees*, keeping at an unexpected low height until you can check the next flight up. Remember: you do not have to see the entire person to know someone is there. A tuft of hair, a protruding toe, the slightest part of a human being or his clothing is all that's necessary.

As you move, your firearm should *always* be ready to fire, pointed at the most probable point of attack. Use the "foot drag" method of climbing: advance quietly to the next step with one foot and pull the other up to that level, then advance again without crossing your feet over one another. This keeps you from tripping and losing balance. If you need to shoot, you can drop to the knee of your uppermost leg. In this braced "star" position, you can steady yourself better than if you are standing upright on two different levels. (The foot drag or shuffle method is often recommended for getting across rooms, too, when you have to move more or less sideways. But there you may find it too slow and awkward. Assuming you have an adequate sense of balance, you should be able to cross over your lead leg with your trailing leg as you move, for a faster, more fluid, and possibly less noisy walk. Bend your legs to keep your center of gravity low for the best stability. Some officers feel more comfortable with this cross-over climb for stairs, as well. Practice is important. Discover what works best for you and stick with it.)

The "Star position." Notice he also uses "the third-eye concept."

On some staircases, there will be an overhanging balcony, hallway or landing that you have to pass under as you climb up. Here, to guard against becoming a target from behind, an option is to ascend *on your back*. With your head pointed toward the next landing, use your feet and seat to wiggle yourself up. This allows you to keep your firearm trained on the overhang, which will be your primary Area of Responsibility. You do have limited mobility, but you are covering the suspect's potential field of view as you enter it. Your partner, staying below to avoid bunching, covers the landing toward which you are advancing and any exposed areas to the sides. Depending on the length of the flight, he may eventually need to move up a few steps from the bottom to keep you clear of his cross fire; with this ascent, as with others, it's important that you maintain your relative heights. If someone attacks from the overhang, you can meet force with force and/or push yourself off and bounce down the stairs out of his line of fire.

A variation is to go up in a *sitting* position, again advancing one stair at a time, your eyes and firearm up to cover yourself as you move.

The tactic for ascending on your back (wearing body armor) is to maintain a visual on the top of the landing as you move. This is your Area of Responsibility. Your cover officer can either stay at the foot of the stairs for awhile (out of camera view), or approach (right photo) to clear his Area of Responsibility.

108

As you ascend and round a corner, both of you should position yourselves so you can effectively cover existing Areas of Responsibility.

Your risks *descending* stairs, as into a basement, can be even greater than going up. If one or both sides of the stairway are open, you are potentially exposed in a fatal funnel for the whole length of your body until your field of view clears the side wall(s) and edge of the staircase ceiling and you get a full look at what's below. Consequently, *you want to exhaust every other possible option before making a physical descent.*

With a basement, you may be able to turn the light on at the top of the stairs or shine your flashlight down, then have another officer check all or significant portions of it by quick peeking through its windows from outside. (At night, you can take longer looks in without being seen, provided you stay back about 18 inches from the window and are not silhouetted by an outside light.) Or consider sending a dog down first or using chemical agents. In one case, Montana officers who felt certain a potential assailant was hiding in a basement panicked him into submission by having the local fire department pump billows of foam down the stairway.

If as a last resort you decide you *must* descend, first try to quick peek through the open side(s) from a proned-out position on the landing.

In an effort to get off the stairs as fast as possible (a *commendable* goal), some officers take a flying leap to the bottom, then dart to the nearest cover upon landing. This may offer an element of surprise, but the risks of ankle injury and of jumping into an unperceived threat zone are high.

Where one side of the stairs is open, an option for hastening a good field of view is to scoot down on your *seat*, like kids do. Except you keep a shotgun or your handgun pointed toward the open side as you bounce down, ready to react. The trade-off here is that this move is noisy, slow and potentially painful. An alternative is to descend in a low crouch.

Probably safest is to use a mirror on the end of an extendable wand to scope out the basement from the safety of a landing or from behind the wall of an enclosed staircase. This will allow you to see under stairs as well as into other areas.

 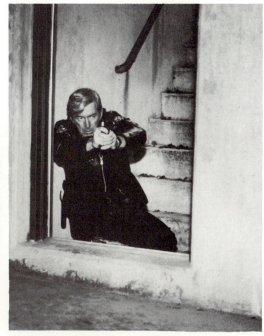

In descending exterior stairs consider advancing low to avoid silhouetting your body against the sky or casting shadows. At the bottom, the officer still maintains a low position.

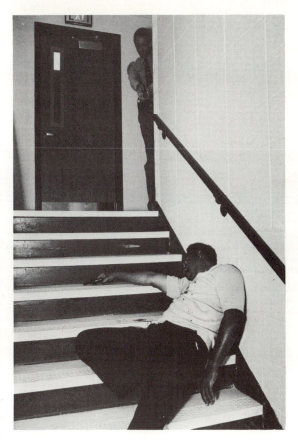

How would you approach this downed subject? Is it safer for you to descend from a position of cover, or would it be safer for a back-up to ascend from the stairway below while you cover? It would be safer to check visually for vital signs and then descend. Coming from above, you'll be at a more difficult angle for the offender to shoot, if he's still functional. Back-up approaching from below can be more readily targeted.

Hallways

Approaching any hallway during your search, you'll have one of two objectives. Either to:

1. move *through* it to reach a more distant area that you intend to enter and search, or
2. position yourself *in* the hallway to enter a room or other area that opens off of it.

In either case, the hallway itself may become an area to search. Your entry into it must be cautious. It's always possible the suspect has changed locations from where you *think* he is and is waiting with hostile intent just around the corner. Indeed, hallways are ready-made for an ambush.

If silently pausing and *carefully listening* reveal no clues that anyone's there, you should minimally make a quick peek to "clear" the hallway before you enter it. A high peek gives you the greatest speed and does not subject your vital areas to the risk of bullets bouncing off the floor. However, a high peek is more likely to be anticipated by a suspect, and he may even have his gun up and ready for it. A low peek is less likely to be seen. Indeed, if the suspect is in certain shooting stances, his arms may block out some of his vision downward. If he does see you, he'll have to lower his aim to target you, thus creating more lag time.

Instead of automatically positioning yourself in the conventional location for a quick peek (right at the corner you want to see around), consider moving to the opposite wall, then peeking out. If someone *is* just past the corner, this maximizes your distance from him.

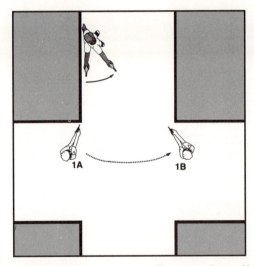

To surveil from the opposite wall means the wall *behind* you, not moving across the hallway laterally as shown here where you are totally vulnerable to attack.

Ideally in building searches, the quick peek should be performed with two officers. You peek while your partner covers you. If an offender sees you and moves to assault before you can get into position to control him, your partner is prepared to deal with him.

If that's not possible and you see an immediate threat, *follow through*. Either prepare for or activate a confrontation or, much better, *withdraw* to a position of cover. If you just pull your head back and wait by the corner to see what's going to happen next, the offender has a golden opportunity to charge around or just stick his arm around and shoot you, or fire through the wall to your position.

If the hallway seems empty, take another peek from a *different* elevation to solidify your identification of other Problem Areas and Areas of Responsibility, so you know what challenges you'll face once you enter. In a darkened hall, this can be done with your flashlight held high above your head and pointed slightly down (as can your initial peek, of course). *Check particularly for doors that are ajar or open.* These likely will be your highest-hazard areas. Many times a high-intensity flashlight will reveal them when the hallway's ambient lighting does not.

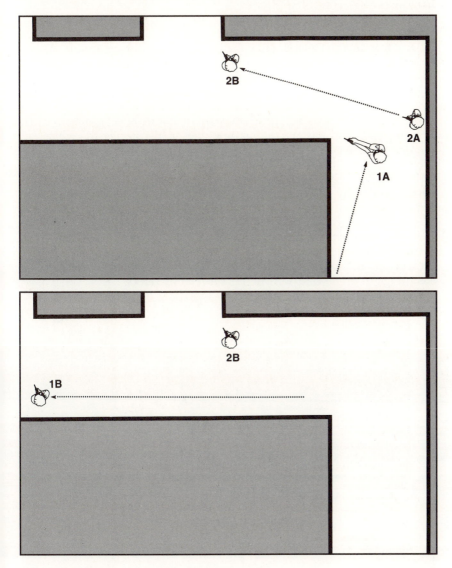

If you're approaching a hallway that extends both to your right and your left, as at a "T" intersection, you and your partner can *simultaneously* quick peek in opposite directions from opposite corners. True, you

113

are somewhat bunched together at the intersection and you do momentarily sacrifice firepower readiness because your guns will not be in a shooting position during the quick peeks. But you gain a comprehensive view of the hall and its possible threats in both directions with essentially one fast movement. (If you try to keep your sidearm ready, you are likely either to expose its barrel before your head bobs out or dangerously slow down your out-and-back movement.)

When you want to exercise greater caution and present a higher degree of readiness as you enter, use a *security* move, either in place of or in addition to a surveillance move. Here you move around a corner with your sidearm ready to meet resistance with resistance. It takes longer than quick surveillance and requires greater body movement, but it heightens your control.

One option is called *"slicing the pie."* It's appropriate not only for entering hallways, but any time you need to move around a corner or other cover and feel a threat may be imminent on the other side. As you near the corner, carefully move out from the wall 3 feet or so, assuming space permits. Face the corner with your body straight, your feet and legs together. Your sidearm should be out in a two-hand hold, but keep your elbows close together, pulled back and tucked in toward the center of your body. This steadies your sidearm in a third-eye position while keeping your body as narrow as possible. It also tends to reduce the tendency to "lead" with your sidearm, exposing it around the corner prematurely. By shuffling your feet to the side a little bit at a time, tightly following one with the other, you can move in little slices toward the corner, gradually increasing your field of view around it. If someone is hiding there, chances are that you'll be able to pick up his protruding feet or shoulder *before* he can see you.

You may have to fight an impulse to hug up close against the wall because it is hard material. What you're fighting, really, is a *false* sense of protection. By swinging out in this slow fashion, you can gain an advantage of angle that will better serve your safety.

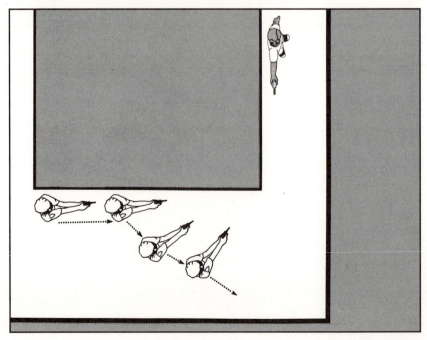

If the hallway is dark, consider placing your flashlight into it to light it up. But when you slice the pie, be sure the light is located well ahead of you so you are not silhouetted by the splash-back.

Again, at some "T" intersections, you and your partner can slice the pie simultaneously, covering opposite directions by standing back-to-back. Most hallways are not wide enough to accommodate this technique, and it does create a bunching risk. But where it's possible, it's likely to be better tactically than having one officer conduct a move in which he faces only the potential threat(s) in one direction without having his back covered.

Once you decide to enter, only one officer should enter the hallway at a time. Again, one moves…one provides as much cover as possible. One may want to maintain a standing barricade cover position at the corner, ready to shoot, while the other moves down the hall, staying low and going down the side opposite the cover officer or down the middle to minimize the cross-fire risk. This way if shooting erupts, both officers are not in the hall scrambling to escape; the officer at the corner has *some* hope of concentrating fully on returning fire.

Both you and your partner may eventually be in the hallway simultaneously (if you're going to make a room entry from there, this will be mandatory), but you still want to stay a distance apart, probably on opposite sides, one farther back than the other. Try to apply the principle of triangulation as you approach doorways and other Areas of Responsibility. But that does NOT mean moving shoulder to shoulder, side by side, down the hall.

This corridor advance illustrates proper positioning for triangulation as well as good separation. A suspect would have difficulty assaulting both officers at the same time.

If you are moving *through* a hallway to another location rather than searching each room along it, it usually won't be practical to check every closed door as you pass. In an apartment building or hotel, if you twist or rattle each doorknob to see if it's locked, as is often recommended, you may alarm innocent people inside. They may shout at you, creating a commotion, or pop out behind you as you move on to see what's going on…and thereby present additional Problem Areas. In certain environments, these occupants, who otherwise might remain unaware of your presence, may become fresh sources of hostility and danger. You may be safer in the long run to get out of the hallway with as little time and disturbance as possible and get on to your destination. Manpower permitting, you can leave an officer behind to maintain security.

In some settings, especially if there's no one available to leave behind, you may want to secure or "alarm" the doors you pass, even though you don't try to open them. Doorknobs can be tied together with pieces of nylon cord, your pants belt or bungee cords (although the elasticized nature of the latter tend to make them the least satisfactory). Wedges will block doors that open out into the hall. So will furniture shoved against them. To secure doors that open into rooms or closets, some officers use a piece of plywood in which a keyhole shape has been cut. This slips down over the doorknob and is wide enough to overlap the frame, preventing the door from being pulled open from the inside. Another option is to connect doorknobs that are across the hall from each other with a strap or cord so neither can be opened in.

To "alarm" doors, rig them so you can hear if one behind you is opened. Lean something against it (a broom, for example) that will clatter when it falls or is knocked down by the door moving. Or balance an item on the doorknob or jam it between the door and the frame so it will crash to the floor if disturbed.

Even without special alarming, you can hear most doors open. Remember, it take some *time* for an offender to get a door open, locate and try to shoot you—and at the first sound, you can be moving to return fire or reach cover.

As you move down the hallway, particularly if it is a long one or you plan to stay in it long enough to make a room entry, try to establish a place to which you can rapidly retreat if trouble explodes. This "escape oasis" may be an alcove, an elevator whose doors you can lock open, a utility closet or an open room you have cleared—some place where you can take cover and regroup so that you do not have to defend yourself out in the open.

Doorways

Everyone knows that because of the penetrability of most doors and the gut instincts of violent subjects, the most dangerous place you can be outside a closed door is right in front of it. But many officers fail to consider another important doorway characteristic: the *second* chanciest place to stand is on the hinged side if the hinges are *not* visible and on the knob side if they *are*. When the door opens and you're there, you risk being in the immediate field of view—and direct field of fire—of a suspect waiting in the area you're preparing to enter.

To make entry, either into a building or into a room inside, you or your partner may eventually need to position yourself in this hot spot. But be aware that if you're "it" and your partner is on the other side of the doorway, he can offer you little effective cover fire there initially. You'll have to control your field of view *yourself* as the door opens. So get low and get ready, with your sidearm in a firing position.

The "fatal funnel" concept connected with doorways is usually

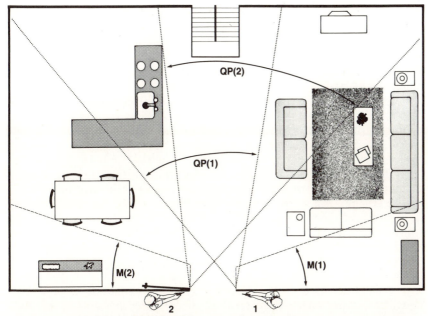

These two drawings show the comparative fields of view you can establish with different visual techniques before entering a room. If you use a mirror, you can surveil the area designated by M(1). With a proper quick peek, your field of view will be roughly within the QP(1) area. Your partner's vantage point permits him views M(2) and QP(2) respectively.

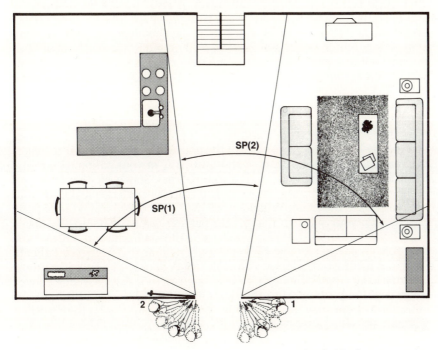

A security move like "slicing the pie" gives you a wider field of view inside the room than either of the two surveillance moves illustrated in the first drawing. Plus you are able to control the area with firearms readiness as you observe it.

thought of only in terms of standing *in* or going *through* the opening. But if a suspect is hiding along the wall that the door is on, his angle of sight through the opening door may be such that he can see (and shoot) you even if you are standing to the side of the actual doorway. Even if he's on the hinge side of a door that opens in, he may be able to see through the crack. He'll have greater difficulty angling his gun just right to *shoot* through the slit, but it can be done, as a sergeant in Texas learned when he was shot to death through the crack with a .38 as he and three plain-clothes officers were trying to execute a narcotics search warrant at a motel. To truly be clear of the fatal funnel, you will need to stand well back from the doorway, if possible, while the door is being opened.

These and other considerations make it important that you *analyze* the door you're dealing with *before* you get into position around it. When you're trying for a swift, smooth, coordinated entry, you don't want to have to rearrange your intended pattern of movement to compensate for miscalculations you made about getting the door open. The more times you have to cross back and forth in front of the door and the more time you have to spend in other vulnerable spots, the higher risk your entry becomes.

Any time you *do* cross a doorway, especially when the door is *open*, consider *leaping* rather than striding or crawling. It's noisier, but as a faster-moving target, you'll be harder to sight and shoot before you clear the other side, even if a suspect has his gun trained on the doorway. Be sure you start and end your leap well to the sides of the frame. For certain, don't mimic some television "cops" by swinging into the center of an open doorway with your sidearm pointed into the room, then pivot to the other side. That slow move prolongs your exposure to the fatal funnel and effectively Locates you for the adversary. It also violates the dictum: "If you're going to move, *move*, if you're going to shoot, *shoot.*" Don't try to accommodate *both* with the same tactic. If the door is *closed*, you can step across, which is quieter. Start at a 90° angle to the wall, move your outside foot first and pivot on your other foot as you move. This will turn you so you are properly positioned for defense when you reach the other side.

The risks of getting a closed door open in order to make entry can be eased by you and your partner working together.

If the door is *unlocked* and opens *out*, one method is for the two of you to stay low on opposite sides of the doorway. Assuming you're nearer the knob, loop a piece of cord, a shotgun sling or your pants belt around the knob and toss the loose end to your partner. Stay back along the wall as far as possible from the doorway and reach out the full length of your arm to release the latch. When you've then pulled back even farther and have gotten your sidearm ready, your partner pulls the door fully open.

If you have nothing with which to rig the knob, you can "throw" the door to your partner and he can reach out and grab it. That keeps either of you from having to risk total vulnerability. A door with a heavy spring or automatic closing device can be held open with a sturdy wedge shoved underneath or jammed into the crack between the door and frame. (An automatic closer may be signaled by a hook or coupling on the door that you can see when assessing its characteristics.)

If the door opens *in* and you're on the *knob* side, you should try to throw it back against the wall by yourself because your partner will be in the most vulnerable field of view. First open the door about an inch, back away from the doorway and *listen* for a moment. Then try to shove the door open with enough force to strike the wall or anyone hiding behind the door. At most, your partner should reach his fingers out at arm's length while staying close to the wall to press the door through the final part of its arc if it's too heavy to move fully from your throw alone. As the door swings, you should be able to get a partial visual through the crack.

Using a rope to open the door, the officer limits exposure to a possible threat inside. Once the door is open he surveils his Area of Responsibility.

Some doors that open in will have screens that open out. When you "throw" the screen to your partner, he may be able to unhook the spring, engage a stop or prop the outer door back against the wall with his foot while you deal with the main door. If the screen does not open back fully, he can hook the toe of his shoe under it and hold it open for you without tying up his hands.

When you find a door already *ajar*, you can push it all the way open (*hard*, so it hits the wall behind it) with your flashlight without exposing vital parts of your body.

How you open a *locked* door may depend on your mission. In raid or special weapons situations, where there's access to special equipment and time for planning, your options include: a two- or four-officer battering ram (much better than a sledge hammer)...primer cord wrapped around the knob and ignited to blow it off...a knob cutter (available from most fire departments)...a maul with a V-shaped head to splinter the door...or a prying device, operated by crank or hydraulic power, designed to force the door open by spreading it apart from the frame, releasing any locks and bolts. With a door that opens *out*, a prying wedge may be essential to your forcing it open successfully.

(left) Early morning drug raid. Officer forced to stand directly in front of door in order to use sledge hammer. (right) This officer demonstrates a home-made battering ram made from eight inch steel sewer pipe which only required one swing to pop this dead-bolted door. Note that contact is made off to the side which allows mobility.

As a patrol officer dealing with a door that opens *in*, your *foot* is probably going to be the "key" that does the unlocking. And when you use it, your risk rockets. When you're kicking (or knocking, in less urgent situations), a suspect inside may then think he knows where you are, and *that's* when he's likeliest to try to shoot what he can't see by firing through the door.

In terms of body mechanics, the *lower* you can make your kick the *stronger* it will be. Of course, you want to avoid standing in front of the door to kick it, but if you're left no other choice, then give a *sideways* thrust as close to the knob as possible, immediately drop to the floor and roll away. Or perform the kick on your back (which will be well below the height your adversary probably expects), your sidearm pointed toward the doorway, then roll after kicking.

A preferred alternative is the "fireman's" or "mule" kick. You and your partner are both positioned on the knob side of the door. As kicker, you're nearer the knob, away from the wall a bit, facing out. You lean forward and your partner supports you with his hand on your chest for balance. Then you raise your knee and drive your heel back into the door. This can deliver amazing power. Try to hit to the side of the knob that's away from the frame, yet not in the dead center where your foot's likeliest to go *through* the door and hang you up. Hitting the knob itself or between the knob and frame can break your ankle or trap your foot. You kick the *door*, but it's generally the *frame* that gives.

If the door resists because it is reinforced with a deadbolt or other supplementary locks on the inside, try kicking the *hinged* side. This is often the weakest part of the door, but is frequently overlooked. Yet hinges are almost *never* reinforced. Or, probably better yet, use a ram.

Just because no one fires at you when the door flies open, don't assume no one's in there. You may be dealing with a more sophisticated offender than the average junkie you can spook. Once you've opened or forced the door, WAIT a bit, unless there's an urgent need to enter or your mission requires an immediate, dynamic assault.

You may want to throw a distractor into the room to see if you can provoke a response before making entry. With some exceptions, *sound* distractors generally seem less successful in drawing a hidden offender's

The "fireman's kick" affords a surprising degree of control, even when used alone.

fire, exposing his position and causing him to deplete his ammunition than do distractors that are *light*-oriented. One exception is the "flash bang" or stun grenade. Its loud explosion and smoke tend to disorient anyone confined in the typical room, giving you several seconds in which to capitalize on his lag time. A cherry bomb can accomplish a similar effect. But throwing in non-explosive items (brooms, cans, lightbulbs, etc.) in hopes their clatter will divert an offender from the doorway usually proves futile.

Light distractors generally are more effective because of the eyes' natural tendency to be attracted automatically to light, especially in darkness. Thus a strobing light, a Cyalume "glow stick" or some improvised light source tossed from behind cover to a spot in a room away from where you plan to enter may prompt an offender to reveal his presence or at least cause him to look away from your location at the crucial moment. Two officers responding to a burglary-in-progress at a record shop saw a suspect inside when they looked through a broken window. From behind cover, they tossed in a strobing device attached to a fish line. The startled suspect fired at it five times with armor-piercing .357 Magnum rounds. He said later that he thought it was an officer's flashlight. While he was distracted, the officers deployed safely to positions where they had the drop on him, forcing him to surrender with no one hurt. If the distractor is bright enough, it may also assist in lighting a darkened room for a safer entry, but by themselves most devices are not adequate to search by.

The principles which have been shared on doorways so far have a special significance in approaching exterior, multiple doorways adjacent to glass. Here is such a situation in which officers conducted a door-to-door search for a gunman who was alleged to have killed five people. A number of things here bear some thought: the choice of searching with a lever-action deer rifle, two officers standing in a doorway at the same time, everyone positioned so close together. If shooting were to erupt, what would the officer lying on his side do?

Tactical officers look for a man who shot two FBI agents. One room has been cleared, the adjacent one is now their Problem Area. The officer on the far right is positioned inappropriately in front of the window. The officer crouched with the cut-down Ithica shotgun has advanced as far forward as he should, but appears to be a cover officer rather than a point man. Proning out reduces mobility for a possible retreat with others potentially in the line of fire. What might be an alternative approach to this mission, using fewer officers and more control? Turn the page.

Here is a re-creation of the typical motel scene. The offender is believed to be hiding in one of the rooms. Officer 1 is the only one in the doorway which has been wedged with a knife. From the hall behind, Officers 2 and 3 are concealed. Officer 1 advances using a low position which is both quiet and affords Officer 2 (shotgun) the opportunity to cover Officer 1. Officer 1 passes underneath the wide window. After he quickly glances into the room through the open curtain, he signals Officer 2 as to the room condition (empty from what he can see.) Officer 2 now advances to cover Officer 1's entry to the first room. Officer 3 is signalled to advance his position to the first window to provide cover, especially since the curtains are open. Officer 1 makes entry to the second room as Officer 2 again provides cover. Note how Officer 2 stands so Officer 1 has an escape route if needed. In the sixth sequence, bunching is avoided. Officer 1, using the third eye concept, attempts to see into the third room past the curtains. Once Officer 4 opens the door to the third room, he can move back inside for cover, should shooting erupt. All movements are made swiftly and with a limited number of officers, all with pre-assigned duties.

This portable strobe can be an effective distractor with a hidden subject.

When you do make entry, strive for the "Five S's": *speed...surprise ...simplicity...safety* and...*superiority* of manpower and firepower. Quick peek before you move. Then get in...get low...get your back protected...and get your Areas of Responsibility established and under control as quickly as possible.

How you go through a doorway will be influenced by its structure, by the configuration of your "launching pad" area outside, by the size and shape of the room you're entering and by what you can see of the room before you go in. Remember, for entering doorways as with other aspects of building searches, DESIGN DICTATES.

Don't dally in the doorway; don't just stand there and look in or saunter through, as some officers do. For speed, move *high;* that is, in nothing lower than a crouch. If you go *low* (squatting, with knees radically bent) you'll have to go *slow.* Moving at or near your top speed will then be virtually impossible.

Use a pattern, an organized way of entering in minimum time with minimum exposure. Patterns are not absolutes, and getting in fast is usually more important than executing a perfect entry movement. Nonetheless, here are some of the "classic" methods you may find handy to have among your options. (Although these patterns are described as if both you and your partner are making entry, where the environment demands a one-officer penetration, these movements for the most part can be adapted. If only you go in, your partner takes as secure a position as possible outside the doorway and provides you as much protection as he can. As a rule, he should *not* enter unless the position he would take in the room offers him at least as much cover, concealment and visibility as he can get from his security cover position outside. Few rooms, especially in residences, will permit more than two officers inside without serious cross-fire problems. Additional searching officers can remain outside the room for doorway and/or hallway security.)

(left) Prior to making entry you should be aware of your body and firearm positioning, and concealment. Officer (right) is not touching the wall and has his long gun pointed up for mobility. His gaze is toward his Area of Responsibility. Back-up officer has a similar degree of awareness and is operating in Condition Orange as he prepares to enter. He, too, is away from the corner and has his hat bill turned around to avoid detection.

The Wrap-Around or "button hook" most often starts with you and your partner on the same side of the doorway, perhaps because a wall or some other barrier inside or outside prevents your taking opposite sides initially. Ideally, you want to perform this move *opposite* the hinged side so you won't have the door itself to contend with. One at a time, keeping your backs close to the frame, you "wrap" yourselves around it to the other side of the wall. Practicing your foot placement so you can move in a continuous, fluid motion without pausing in the doorway is the secret to making this technique successful.

Either your partner enters immediately after you or he moves to the position you just left and waits a bit, meantime covering the field of view he has of the room. Either method can be tactically sound. If both of you enter nearly simultaneously and there's only one suspect inside, right off you have him outnumbered. If your partner delays and you happen to get shot at, your partner's still in a somewhat protected position.

Drawbacks of this pattern are that it's relatively slow and unless you space yourselves properly after entering, you may tend to bunch near the door. (Where doorway characteristics permit, the Wrap-Around can also be done with you and your partner starting on opposite sides of the doorway. You wrap around simultaneously and cover each other's position as you move. This is only appropriate with *wide* doorways, however, lest you bump into each other in the entrance.)

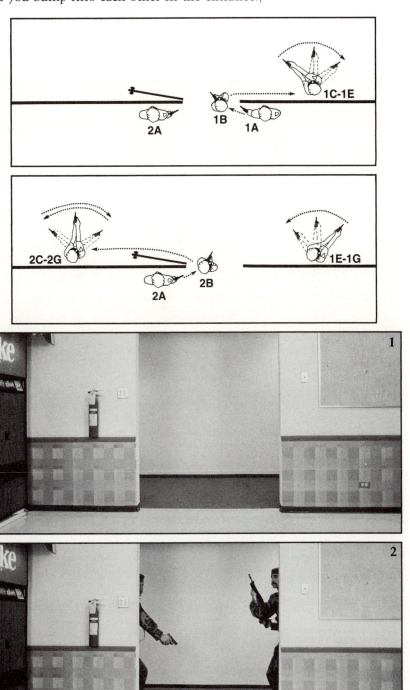

Sequence illustrates the Wrap-Around as a quick series of movements. Notice at the point both officers move through the doorway, there are no crossfires. Movement has not compromised weapon positioning. Both move simultaneously inside to a position away from the door opening. As you can see, the officer on the right has not as yet reached his final inside position since he has farther to move than his partner.

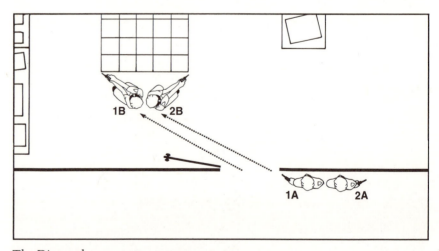

The Diagonal room entry pattern.

The Diagonal is now regaining popularity, especially among special weapons teams, because of its speed. With both you and your partner on the same side of the doorway, you simultaneously rush crosswise through the entrance, ideally to some position(s) of cover inside the room. An offender may expect you to remain near the doorway once you've entered, so ending up in less obvious positions not only can be fast but also *unanticipated*. The Diagonal works best *if* there are cover opportunities near the doorway...*if* what you're running to is adequate cover...and *if* it's not cover that the adversary himself has chosen. The Diagonal takes planning and assessment *before* movement. It's not just charging blindly into a room and hoping you will somehow end up behind something that can stop bullets.

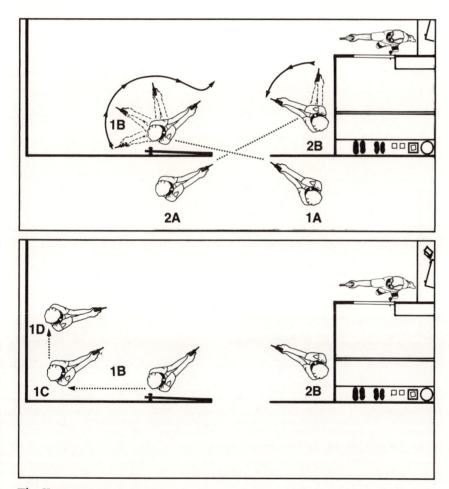

The X room entry pattern.

The X is the entry pattern of choice for many officers. Deploying from both sides of the doorway, you and your partner enter in crisscross fashion. This allows you to readily subdivide the room and split the Areas of Responsibility once you are inside. To avoid colliding in the doorway, develop and *practice* a count system: beginning simultaneously

129

and counting to yourselves, the officer on the right initiates his move on the count of 3, the officer on the left moves one beat later on 4.

When you can use it, the X Pattern will tend to separate a suspect's focus and create lag time while he decides which potential target to concentrate on first. However, a drawback of the X is that few homes have rooms and/or doorways whose size or design can support its use. Furniture near the door may also limit it. Plus, if the suspect decides to charge toward the doorway to escape or attack, you and your partner may find yourselves in a cross-fire position as he nears or crosses the threshold.

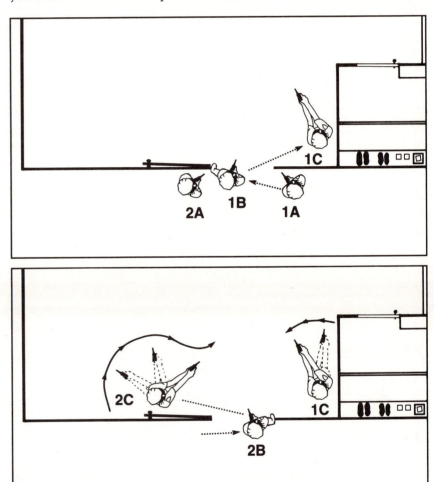

The Reverse X room entry pattern.

The Reverse X starts like the conventional X, with you and your partner on opposite sides of the doorway, but here you don't enter on diagonal lines. Instead, as you're going in you step against the bottom of the door frame opposite where you started and spring off of it. You come back across the entrance so that you land in the room just around the frame from the location where you began. Your partner follows suit. He starts moving when your foot touches the frame. Sometimes a suspect, especially if he has military training, will try to "lead" your position with his firearm, following you like a hunter as you go through the doorway. The Reverse X can throw him off. The disadvantage is that his lag time may leave his gun positioned so that your partner now leaps into his line of fire. Also, although the movement can be very fast if practiced sufficiently, each officer in fact must cross the open doorway twice to complete the pattern, and this may leave both of you in the fatal funnel too long.

All entry patterns, while infinitely better than impulsively rushing the room, are tricky to perform and are freighted with risk. They require enough practice with your partner for you to be able to conduct them smoothly and confidently, knowing what each of you is going to do. Without practice, you are likely to stop cold to think and ask yourself, "What do I do next?" While you're wondering, the offender's Thought Processes can reach the point of Attacking. And you cannot *think* faster than an assailant can *act*.

Once you and your partner are across the threshold and inside the room, *get down and get away* from the doorway. You may be tempted to stay close for escape but, if too near it, you can still be silhouetted from certain angles inside the room. Immediately establish your respective Problem Areas and Areas of Responsibility, with the officer on the left taking the left side of the room, the one on the right the right side.

The moment you are out of the doorway and at your new position, squat low and *"sweep"* your half of the room. With your sidearm up in the ready position, you quickly move it in a flat arc from the outside of the room toward the middle. Your partner does the same. Different from a wild swing, the sweep is a *systematic* movement that really is the finish of your fluid motion of entry. It allows you to assess the room fully in no more than 1 to 1½ seconds while prepared to control or counter any threat.

"Softening" Rooms

Having established your Areas of Responsibility, your challenge now is to clear them, to "soften" the room, with the same amount of safety you used to enter. Threat locations typically include under beds, behind sofas and other large pieces of furniture, in closets, or around corners within the room. Look especially for furniture that sits out more than 8 or 10 inches from the wall, doors that are open and doorways that lead to adjoining rooms, and scan the floor under drapes to check for feet.

Considering a suspect's Thought Processes, your *primary* Area of Responsibility will be that spot which, if someone's hiding there, would give him the greatest opportunity to Locate *and* effectively Attack you. An offender may be able to Locate you with equal ease from under a bed or from inside a closet with the door ajar. But an attack from the closet would likely be more grave because that location may permit a center mass chest hit, while from under the bed an assailant will likely be able only to shoot at your feet or legs. Also it's more likely that someone will hide in the typical closet than under the typical bed because of space considerations. The closet thus becomes your primary Area of Responsibility. In a majority of residential rooms, closets with doors open or ajar *will* prove in fact to be your most hazardous sites.

Sometimes in order to approach and check your *primary* Area of Responsibility, you have to first clear one or more *secondary* hazard areas to make cover for yourself or create a pathway for safe movement. You cannot always approach your greatest threat potential *directly*. Also, your top concern may *change* as portions of the room are cleared and potential threat locations are eliminated. Typically, you'll have to monitor more than one Area at a time. So resist the temptation to tunnel in solely on just one trouble-spot, or you may exclude other valid threat locations. Because these locations will differ from room to room, you will *not* be able to follow any rigidly prescribed search pattern, such as "always search all rooms clockwise or counterclockwise" or "always start at one wall and go to the opposite wall." *Your positioning relative to your threat location(s) will determine your pattern of search.*

Don't help a would-be attacker Locate you by being careless around mirrors and other reflective objects (even shiny chrome on bathroom fixtures may reflect your image)...by turning off radios or tv sets before you've cleared the entire room (the suspect may know their location and thus know where you'd have to be to touch them)...by becoming silhouetted against doors or windows...by turning your back to unsearched areas...or by succumbing to impatience and abandoning cover or concealment to rush a potential high-risk site.

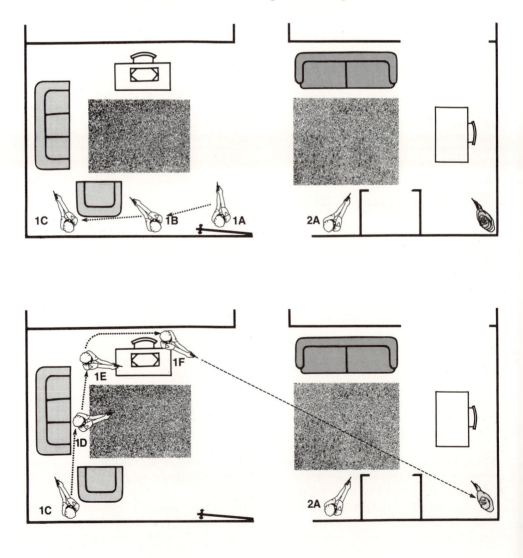

The "rules" of building searches say you should always move around the *perimeters* of rooms, your back to the wall. In real life, furnishings or other obstacles often prevent this, but in large open rooms (like warehouse areas and auditoriums) it's tactically sound for lessening the chance that you'll unwittingly expose your back to a suspect's field of view. Stay low to reduce yourself as a target. At your standing height, a suspect looking up from behind cover may be able to see you before you can see him because of your different angles of observation. Low, you're not only better protected from his view but you also may be better able to see under furniture to spot him.

In large spaces that require time and distance to search, a *"duck walk"* or a *"crab walk"* will be more comfortable for moving than an ordinary crouching crawl. The duck walk is a forward movement, initiated from a squatting position. Push off and alternately let one knee down to the floor while the other is raised. By letting each knee descend all the way down in turn, you allow your leg muscles alternating moments of relaxation as you move. With practice, you can move quickly, while still keeping your gun in a third-eye position. The crab walk or "side shuffle," which also offers those advantages, is a lateral movement. From a kneeling position, you take steps sideways in the direction you want to move. If fatigue sets in, you are able to rest on one knee, still with your firearm ready.

Whether you and your partner choose to negotiate the same side of the room or along opposite sides or whether your partner remains outside the room, *only one of you should move at a time,* just as with halls and stairways. The other provides security. Ironically, it's the *stationary* officer who often ends up doing the "searching." As the moving officer, you may be able to open closet doors or raise bedcovers so he can see into such potential hiding places and clear them from his more distant vantage point.

For opening a door, say to a closet, don't just fork your fingers over the knob and gently pull it open. Someone inside who decides to force his way out can hit the door hard enough to break your fingers and knock it out of your control. *Grip* from under the knob with your fist, thumb side up, and *yank.* Then if there's sudden pressure from the other side, you have the power to shove the door back against him with force.

Generally you'll gain little by moving furniture, unless to temporarily block doors from being opened. Ramming a piece of furniture against a door may startle a suspect and cause him to give his position away. But officers sometimes become obsessed with shoving sofas and chairs around, believing they afford cover when actually their soft material can easily be penetrated by even modest ammunition.

Be careful about randomly or automatically moving other items, too. This is where officers generally run into problems with improvised explosives encountered during searches. Their curiosity proves stronger than their critical thinking. One searcher canvassing a restaurant that had been bombed found a shopping bag on the roof. He might have regarded that as something that didn't quite fit right, but instead he unthinkingly picked it up. It proved to be a second bomb, rigged to explode from motion, and it blew off his hand. Luckier, but no less careless, was an officer in the Southwest who picked up a piece of pipe he encountered during a search and curiously unscrewed the cap on one end. Black powder cascaded out. The cap and threads on the other end of this homemade bomb had been packed with match heads. Had the officer twisted *that* end ¼ inch, he would have touched off a blast.

The "duck walk" movement.

134

When turning the knob, maintain proper handgun placement.

The rule is: *move yourself, not other things.* If you *do* encounter something that seems out of place or suspicious, DON'T TOUCH IT. Follow the bomb squad philosophy: Don't do anything unless you know *for certain* the reaction that's going to follow. Back out by *retracing your path* and get someone with bomb disposal experience on the scene to advise you. As you search, be conscious of what you *smell*, as well. An odor of flammables may alert you to a trap an offender has left behind—or to a home-brew weapon that is in his hands as he waits for you. Be alert also for any *ticking* sounds. These may be coming from the clock-work timing mechanism of an explosive device.

As you move, your sidearm should be ready to meet with force any movement or sound that you believe presents an imminent deadly threat. *Commit yourself to the idea that resistance is met with resistance.* Noises or motions you can't identify should be forcefully challenged from your nearest cover. "You in the closet! I want to see your hands! *Hands first!*" Command the cause of your concern *to come to you.* Don't you approach what may prove to be an armed suspect lying in wait.

If a suspect is captured, stop searching until he's dealt with. Move him to a secured area and, while another officer covers, handcuff and search him for hidden weapons. Be sure *you* pick the spot for this search, not him. If he's allowed to choose, he may select a site where he has weapons hidden within reach. If more than two officers are present, one can remain to guard the suspect while others resume the building search. Or the offender can be removed from the building via a pathway that has previously been cleared.

If only two of you are involved in the search and parts of the building have not yet been cleared, the safest procedure is for both of you to exit the premises with the suspect. If your partner is left inside alone, he may be ambushed and overpowered or may get antsy and decide to continue the search by himself, changing to a location unknown to you. If one of you *does* stay inside, hold a position that gives you maximum security and observation and that allows you to provide a protected pathway for your partner to rejoin you. If both of you go out, then reenter and *re-search* the building back to your previous position, after back-up has taken control of the subject. Finding one suspect, of course, should be regarded like finding one concealed weapon: assume *more*.

Anyone you encounter during a building search should at least be detained and thoroughly interrogated and preferably be arrested, handcuffed and searched pending further information. Had this principle been followed in Dallas when President John F. Kennedy was assassinated, considerable public hysteria and the death of a police officer would have been prevented. Less than two minutes after the motorcade attack, a motor officer rushed inside the Texas School Book Depository to search for the assailant—and on the second floor came face to face with Lee Harvey Oswald. Oswald was allowed to pass on out of the building when a civilian identified him as an employee. As you recall, the next police contact with Oswald involved his killing Officer J. D. Tippit.

After you've cleared a room, be sure all doors behind you are closed and *locked* if possible, before you move on. Even if the doors are

unsecured, a suspect will have to expend time and noise to get them open, and these can constitute an early warning system. If you're moving out of earshot or beyond surveillance range, wedge or tie them for peace of mind. When you pass these doors again on your way out, collect your wedges or cords—and be sure none has been disturbed.

Attics and ceiling crawl spaces are commonly the last places searched on upper floors before dealing with the basement. To minimize your exposure, use a broom handle or like device to push open the trap door or panel covering the opening. One option then is to bounce a high-intensity flashlight beam off a mirror to scope out the area from below. (If the mirror is angled properly, the light won't bounce back and blind you.) Or, on the access ladder or a stool, take quick peeks into the area, tilting your head so you peek with only your top eye. This risks less of your head above the opening. If you need to place a light source on the attic floor for illumination, consider using a strobing device rather than your flashlight to more effectively disorient a hidden suspect. Keep other officers away from you. If you're fired upon, you'll want to leap down instantly and dart to cover, without colliding with them or being caught in their impulsive cross fire.

Real World Adaptations

How can you adapt these principles to actual field situations?

Consider the tactical decision-making of two officers responding recently to a daylight residential break-in in a middle-class suburb. Their movements do not represent the *only* desirable way the building involved could have been searched. Nor do they reflect the meticulous ultra wariness a special-weapons team might display. But they *do* demonstrate *planned action*, not impulse, indifference or indecision. Unlike SWAT-

team members, who *assume* an assailant is lying in wait, the officers weren't anticipating a shootout. But they were aware that in any building search, *anything can happen*...and they wanted to be ready. Their choices played off the environment they faced and were shaped by tactical caution and a continual reassessment of potential threat.

Given their circumstances, see how *your* Tactical Thinking would compare with theirs. And, just as important, understanding the *reasoning* behind the choices that were made.

The scene is a two-story brick house, whose occupants are out of town. A neighbor returning from shopping notices a second-story window over the attached garage smashed in, the front door open wide. Having never been in the house, she cannot advise on its layout. In a quick canvass of the exterior, the officers find side and rear doors, locked. Quick peeks in garage windows show it clear. They shout commands for anyone in the house to exit. No response. Additional manpower is unavailable. They decide to make entry through the front door, which opens from a small stone porch into a narrow foyer and hallway.

From flanking positions outside the arched stone doorway, the officers between them can see this much:

View from right side of front door.　　View from left side.

First objective: establish a security position in the house.

Officer 1, crouched to the right of the doorway, throws the screen door to his partner, who holds it open with his toe. Officer 1's goal is to wind up on the *lower steps* that parallel the hallway.

There, he reasons, he'll be offset enough from the hall to be out of the fatal funnel. That is, not directly silhouetted in the front doorway for an assailant who might shoot down the corridor from the kitchen. And at the moment, that's what he considers his *primary* threat. Because the lower steps are also offset somewhat from the rest of the stairs, the position additionally affords some protection from the stairtop. To Locate and shoot him, an attacker would have to jump from the upstairs hallway onto the upper landing: stumbling, awkward, resulting likely in inaccurate fire. Officer 1 feels he'd have more time on the lower steps to react to that threat than he would to an attack from the kitchen if he were positioned in the hallway. He knows the two closed doors down the hall both open to his advantage; he can see the hinges on his side. Anyone attacking from behind them will first have to swing them open, then reveal himself in the hall, giving Officer 1 time to react. From the steps, even an assault from the living room could be met with force.

It's not a place he'll want to stay long. But it can serve as a starting point for searching the first floor.

As Officer 1 prepares to enter, Officer 2 assumes a barricade position on his side of the doorway, his sidearm pointed toward the upper landing, the potential threat location he can best observe. Moving low with sidearm in hand, Officer 1 wraps around onto the threshold and initiates a rapid series of quick peeks at different heights to clear a path to the steps. After each he pulls back to his cover position outside rather than stay steadily in the doorway. First from the threshold he yanks back the closet door and quick peeks around it to clear the interior. Then with a low, giant step he ducks forward to clear the lower corner of the staircase that neither he nor his partner can see from outside. A quick glance up while he's low clears the blind spot on the upper landing. With a final peek in, he checks slightly more of the living room. All this takes just seconds. Then he moves, his sidearm in the belt-tuck position.

With Officer 1 in position, Officer 2 braces the screen door open with its stop accessory and leaps across the doorway to his partner's former position.

The choice now: soften the kitchen...or the living room.

From the steps, Officer 1 can see in the reflective surface of the dishwasher that the right-hand portion of the kitchen is clear. Through the distant doorway at the kitchen's left rear, he sees about the same thin slice of the family room or den at the back of the house as he saw from the front porch. One big section of the kitchen is still blind to him.

By bobbing to different angles on the steps and by taking one fast, low, springing step with one foot across the hall and back to peek into the right corner past the living room arch, he's able quickly to piece together this visual of the living room:

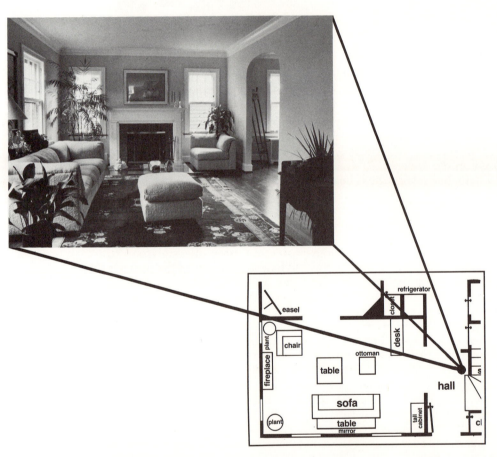

Officer 1 identifies several potential threat locations here: around the corner of the tall cabinet...inside it...behind the sofa...behind the large chair...and at the far archway (from hidden regions of the dining room).

To try to reach the kitchen, Officer 1 reasons, he'd have to make himself vulnerable to the risk of cross fire; if shooting starts while he's in the hallway, his partner will either be helpless to defend him or, if Officer

2 does shoot, that will itself become a threat to Officer 1. The narrow hallway will drastically restrict Officer 1's mobility. He'll have to open and check both doors along it; he'd not feel safe passing and exposing his back to them, especially since once he was past them, they'd open to his disadvantage. And the whole time, he'd be silhouetted in the fatal funnel of the front doorway.

He opts for the *living room*, believing its risks are the ones he can best control. None of its contents provides true cover for an offender, as the officer could likely shoot through any of the furniture if he perceived an imminent threat behind it.

His objective now is to reach a position at the *far archway*, from which he can make entry to the dining room.

To begin systematically eliminating his Areas of Responsibility, Officer 1 moves from the steps to the end of the cabinet. A low quick peek around it confirms no one's hiding on its front side and that it extends too close to the wall to shield anyone behind its other end. Its doors are closed tight.

The officer then steps across to the other side of the entry arch, behind the writing desk. He feels least control—and thus most apprehension—over the dining room. But with the officer in the corner by the desk, an offender will have to reveal more of himself around the dining room arch to Locate him than anywhere else in the room, buying the officer more reaction time. Here he can monitor all the Areas of Responsibility he has yet to clear, while Officer 2, on signal, moves with his sidearm ready to Officer 1's former position on the lower steps.

Squatting with his feet on different steps and his back braced against the wall, Officer 2 can maintain that position comfortably for some time. His primary responsibilities are: the upper stairway landing...the kitchen door...and through it, the family room door. This requires an undesirable separation of focus, but at that Officer 1 prefers having him stay there rather than having both of them in the living room with no security on these potential threat locations. With Officer 2 on the steps, the officers can still provide triangulation of fire to a large portion of the living room, including the worrisome dining room arch.

As Officer 2 moves, Officer 1 clears another Area of Responsibility in the living room—without himself moving an inch. His angle of view into the mirror over the sofa shows him no one's hiding behind the large chair at the other end of the room. As for the sofa, Officer 1 decides, the long table behind it limits its risk as a threat location. Anyone trying to rise up from behind will have to raise the table with them. Far likelier, an assailant would try to come out from under one of the ends of the table and attack around the sofa. Earlier surveillance by Officer 1 when he was checking around the cabinet has revealed no one near the end closest to the officers.

The instant Officer 2 is in position, Officer 1 rounds the writing desk and moves with his back against the wall toward the dining room arch. His principal focus is on the mirror, in which he can see some of the dining room...while maintaining peripheral vision on the unexplored end of the sofa and on the closed doors of the tall cabinet. As his angle of view to the sofa changes as he moves, the chance of anyone being concealed at its end evaporates. The only possibility left is behind it, under the table. Also step by step, more of the dining room unfolds on the mirror's surface. At one point, the officer discovers that in the back wall of that room is a doorway to the family room, separate from the one in the kitchen. He knows the mirror constitutes no threat to him. The nature of angulation dictates that no one can see him in it without him being able to see them.

Near the dining room arch, Officer 1 stops, listens for sounds from the dining room. Quiet. Now Officer 1 quick peeks around the dining room arch to clear what he hasn't seen of that room. No evident danger.

Two quick chores now complete his softening of the living room. First, on his signal, Officer 2 moves to the end of the cabinet. Keeping his back to the cabinet so he can quickly cover the stairs or hall if he hears anything, he reaches around and gently flips open one of its doors. Officer 1, sidearm ready, can see inside from across the room. Shelves top to bottom...no hiding place. Now Officer 2 moves in front of the cabinet and quick peeks behind the sofa. No one's there. After quick peeking back in the hallway toward the kitchen, Officer 2 resumes his security position on the steps.

Back at the archway, Officer 1 knows the dining room looks like this:

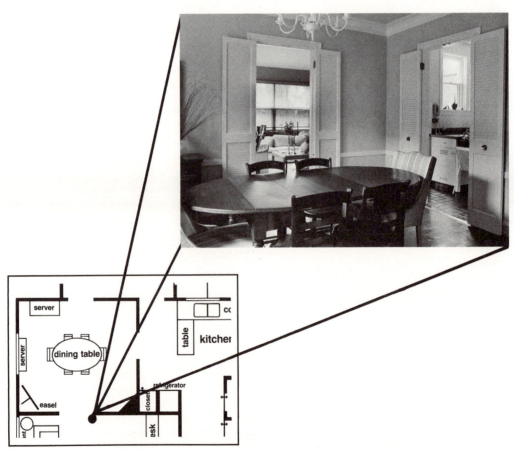

Since it has been visually cleared already, it's now just space to traverse in order to soften the family room and the kitchen.

Choice: move clockwise...or counterclockwise.

Officer 1's first impulse is to advance counterclockwise, toward the corner china cabinet. It's the shortest route to the kitchen (certainly an area critical to search), and it "feels" as if it would offer less exposure than moving across the end of the dining room. He can, for example, wrap around the dining room arch rather than cross its full width and also can avoid having to put his back to the room's windows.

Yet thinking tactically, he chooses the *clockwise* route.

The windows, he decides, present the very least probability of risk. Why would a breaking-and-entering suspect who's outside, with no obstacle to escaping, want to shoot in? More important, as Officer 1 thinks ahead like a good chess player about how each move sets him up for the next, he realizes he'll walk into a control nightmare going counterclockwise. There he'll face *three* known Areas of Responsibility. A hazard could present itself in: the doorway to the kitchen…the doorway from the kitchen to the family room…or the doorway from the dining room to the family room, and he'd be in the field of view of each. Moreover, what does he do when he reaches the kitchen doorway? To make entry or even to quick peek from that position to either the kitchen or the family room will require that he turn his back on some potentially hazardous field of view. His partner, still back near the front hallway, can't cover him, and his own control goes down the tubes.

Clockwise, he figures he'll *reduce* his Areas of Responsibility. As he moves, he'll pass out of the field of view from the kitchen-family room doorway. And he'll be able to control both fields of view he's moving in. On either route, he and his partner will lose sight of each other. But they consider that an acceptable trade-off for Officer 2 continuing his vital security on the hallway and stairs. Clockwise, at least they can maintain visual contact longer. And if sudden retreat becomes necessary, Officer 1 can move faster from the end of the dining room back into the living room, without exposing his back to hostile fire.

He makes a diagonal entry across the archway to the front of the easel. Meanwhile, Officer 2 changes location slightly. He moves across the front hallway to a high position by the living room cabinet. Because he's right-handed, it's easier for him to cover the stairs and hallway from there, and his concealment from both the kitchen and stairs is better. If his partner needs immediate assistance with an arrest in the dining room or family room, Officer 2 is just that much closer to provide it.

With sidearm still in position, Officer 1 advances to the family room door. After a quick peek into the family room, he sees that the family room couch and bookshelves are too close to the wall to allow anyone behind them. The dead-bolt lock on the door tells him it leads outside…little concern. The room's safe. He moves in, diagonally.

His objective now: eliminate the kitchen and the hallway doors as hazards.

He knows there's a dangerous blind spot in the kitchen—the corner beyond the dining room doorway—that he has not yet cleared. Right now that doorway is out of his sight, blocked by the wall he's standing against.

Problem: suppose a hidden offender sneaks out of the corner and into the dining room, then attacks him through the family room doorway while he's concentrating on the kitchen.

It seems only the remotest possibility. An assailant would need totally silent movement and perfect timing to be effective. But as a precaution, Officer 1 opts to move gradually out from the wall and clear the kitchen by "*slicing the pie.*" If he were to hug the wall and quick peek into the kitchen, he'd be more vulnerable to surprise attack from the dining room. With the pie-slicing security move, he can better keep both Areas of Responsibility (the two doorways into the family room) under observation, and be ready to meet force with force at either.

Slice by slice, this view unfolds:

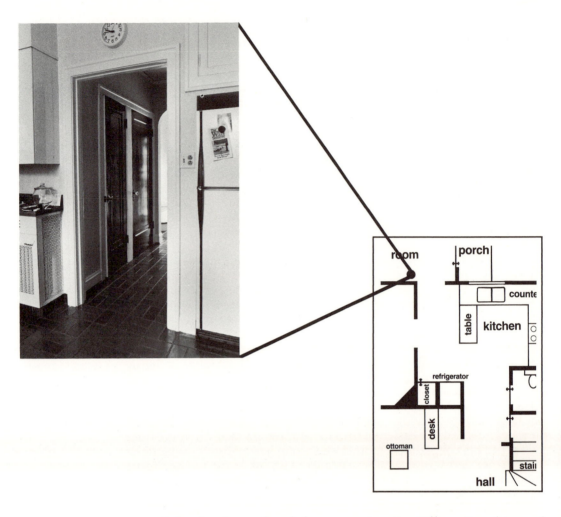

Only the three closed doors remain. On Officer 1's whispered command, Officer 2 moves forward in the hallway and yanks open the first door he reaches so his partner can look inside. It leads to the basement, a few steps visible. After it's closed and blocked with a wedge from Officer 2's pocket, he opens the second door. Powder room. Part of the interior is visible to Officer 1, the rest to Officer 2 as he looks through the door crack. Cleared, it's closed, and Officer 2 pulls back to his security position on the steps. Finally, Officer 1 moves into the kitchen until by stretching at arm's length he can reach the knob on the pantry door. As he throws it open, he dodges into the dining room to buy some protection while checking its interior. Empty.

After 8 tense minutes, floor 1 is clear.

Ready to leave the kitchen, Officer 1 tells his partner that he's going to come into the hallway. This communication is a safeguard against being shot accidentally.

Choice now: search the basement...or upstairs.

They select *upstairs*, reasoning that the basement door has been secured. For an offender to try to force the door open against the wedge would make noise they'd likely hear upstairs. Whereas the staircase cannot be secured unless the officers split up again and one descends alone into the basement.

144

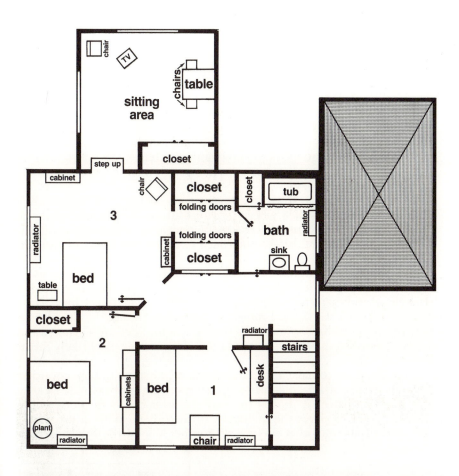

Officer 2 remains below in his security position. Officer 1, sidearm extended in a two-hand hold, ascends the stairs. He keeps close to the wall side and quick peeks up on his toes to get the fullest advantage of angle into the hallway above. This scene develops:

At the landing, Officer 1 is about to commit himself to opening the door on his right when he realizes he's *overextending* himself. Already he sees at least a half-dozen possible threat locations over which he feels his control is questionable at best. There are the three open bedroom doorways...under the beds in the far two rooms...behind the bed in the last one...inside the linen closet in the hall...plus the closed door on his right, probably a bathroom. Opening that door will only compound his problems. So long as it's shut and he does not pass beyond it, its threat is minimized because it opens to his advantage. (Judging from his observations outside, incidentally, that's the room with the broken window, the burglar's point of entry.)

He wants to clear his mind, reassess his strategy. He backs off to a place lower on the stairs where he can still watch the hall while he thinks. However, he continues to keep his sidearm in the ready position.

Decision: he and his partner need to divide the Areas of Responsibility.

Through hand signals, Officer 1 communicates that their roles are now to be reversed. He needs a break from active searching to reduce his stress level and sustain his alertness. *He'll* be the *cover* officer, his *partner* will *search* to clear. Officer 1 moves to the stairtop beside the closed door, Officer 2 to the radiator outside the first bedroom. They are separated and are positioned so they have triangulation of fire on the most likely threat locations.

They'd like to have a third officer to deploy now to help cover the multiple Areas of Responsibility opening off the hallway. But lacking that luxury, Officer 2 moves to clear the first bedroom alone while Officer 1 tries to cover the doorways to the others. With quick peeks, Officer 2 establishes that no one is to either side of the first bedroom doorway. His observations reveal an interior like this:

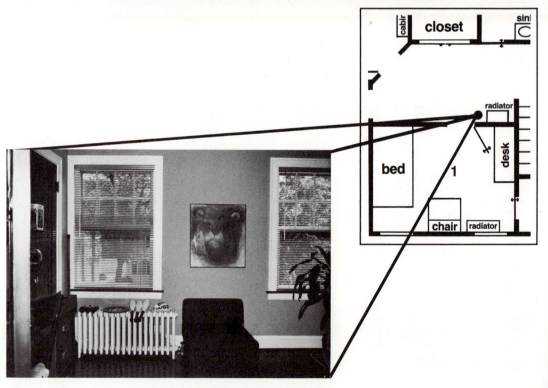

Officer 2 darts diagonally to the far corner and advances along the windowed wall toward the closet, the only portion of the small room not cleared. This movement keeps him out of the immediate field of view should the door open. But aside from that, the room works against him.

He'd like to pull the closet door open and stay behind it, looking through the crack to check the interior. But the radiator prevents that. He could climb up on the radiator and pull the door open by its top to look down inside. This would be unexpected to anyone inside, but he might not be able to see into the nearest corner of the closet without exposing his head over the door, and if someone inside flung the door back against him, he'd be pinned behind it. Effective return fire would be nearly impossible.

So, when he reaches the radiator, he yanks the closet door open in one fast, fluid motion and ducks low across it in a giant stride to the left. As he completes the move, he is positioned down in front of the small desk. His sidearm is on the closet, pointed over the corner of the desk.

It's clear, but in ducking across the doorway, Officer 2 has noticed a ladder leading up a closet wall, apparently to an attic. Later, he'll check that. For now, he secures the door with another wedge.

The officers could now check the bathroom, but their knowledge of offender Thought Processes convinces them to concentrate elsewhere. For a suspect to Attack from the bath so long as that door remains closed would involve a major physical Reaction (getting the door open) in order to Locate them. Attacking through the open bedroom doors at the end of the hall would be much easier.

Conclusion: the bedrooms constitute their most immediate threats. They'll deal with those primary hazards first.

The goal now: using team work, approach and clear the bedrooms —with minimum bunching...minimum risk of cross fire...minimum exposure to potentially lethal fields of view.

The first obstacle blocking safe movement, the linen closet, is cleared quickly. From within the room he's just searched, Officer 2, standing upright near the doorway, takes a bead on the closed bathroom door directly across the hall. Officer 1, staying low to avoid cross fire, crosses that door and opens the first linen closet door, from the bottom. Shelves, as expected. He can see through the crack that they extend behind the other door as well. He retreats quickly, still monitoring the two open bedroom doors in front of him to cover the fields of view to which he's exposed.

Now Officer 2 leaves the first bedroom, closing the door behind him. His back to the wall, he advances along his side of the hall, gradually opening a fuller view into the third bedroom. Sidearm ready, he covers that view as he moves. He sinks almost to his knees as he goes, figuring this is less expected positioning and, more important, safer in case his partner, still in a standing position, needs suddenly to respond to a threat from the second bedroom. His intent is to clear enough of the third bedroom visually to permit him safe entry into the second. But halfway down the hall, the emerging view alters his plan.

The back room, evidently a sitting area, represents a hazard he can't adequately clear from the hall and also can't control when making entry into the second bedroom. There's also the possibility a suspect is hiding around the other end of the tall cabinet.

Question: what now?

Answer: an uneasy *compromise* of ideal building search principles.

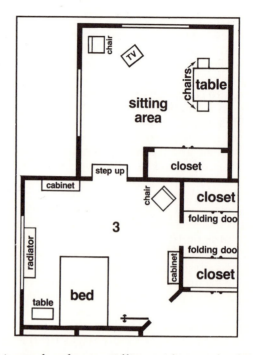

After a whispered exchange, Officer 1 advances to the far end of the linen closet, concentrating his attention and firearm on the second bedroom as he moves. He has to pass beyond the closed bathroom door he has been standing near, and he's now potentially in its field of view should it open. Officer 2 attempts to monitor that Area of Responsibility as well as the doorway to the third bedroom. This is a relatively wide separation of focus, putting him at a disadvantage if he needs to react. He tries to watch the bedroom with his peripheral vision, keeping his sidearm trained on the closed door once Officer 1 is past it, as a cross fire preventative. At least with this positioning, despite its deficiencies, the officers between them manage to keep all their hazard areas in front of them so they can be better monitored.

Combined with the areas of the room he could see earlier while coming upstairs and while standing security at the stairtop, Officer 1's view of the second bedroom from his new position gives him three threat locations: the floor just beyond the bed ... under the bed ... and inside the built-in closet.

The bed frame appears too low to allow anyone under it, so Officer 1 puts it last among his priorities. His primary concern (the area beyond the bed) becomes sufficiently exposed to him as he enters the room, darting to a position at the end of the built-in. After he moves, his partner changes his point of aim and principal concentration from the closed bathroom door to the doorway of the third bedroom, as *his* main Area of Responsibility. Officer 1 then clears the built-in closet as he cleared the linen closet, popping its nearest door from a low position and peeking through the crack.

Checking under the bed takes only a moment more. He moves the small chair to the end of the bed ... climbs up on it ... then bends over and jerks up hard on the dust ruffle pad and mattress at the corner nearest the door. This hikes the ruffle off the floor. From outside the room, his partner now can check under the bed without Officer 1 having to expose his face below the frame. Clear!

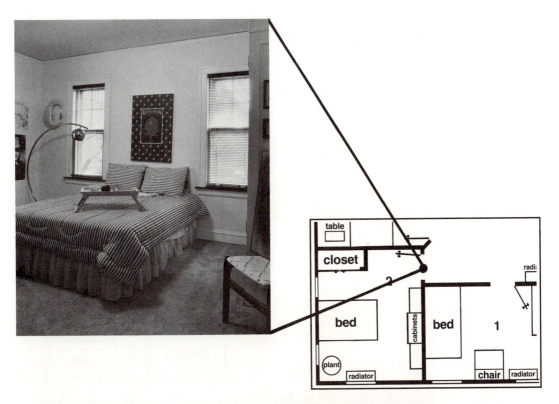

Officer 1 now takes a position against the hallway wall outside the second bedroom where he can monitor the master bedroom, the sitting room and, in his peripheral vision, the closed bathroom door. Officer 2 crosses the hall from the first bedroom and, moving low to avoid cross fire, advances to the end of the tall cabinet in the master bedroom, a bookcase. As he quick peeks out, trying to clear the other end, he adds to their knowledge of the room...and discovers for the first time what appears to be an entrance to a dressing room just beyond the end of the bookcase.

That makes four known Areas of Responsibility, counting the entrance to the sitting room...the blind spot behind the bed...and under the bed. Cramped with furniture, the room allows little mobility. Checking the threat locations will be tough without becoming vulnerable to a field of view that can't be covered. If he pulls his partner in from the hall to help, a lurking suspect could open the unchecked bathroom door and sneak up on them from the rear.

Dilemma: how to advance.

By *retreating*, Officer 2 decides. They'll now get the unchecked door open first and clear that room, then deal with the master bedroom and the Problem Areas branching off of it.

Officer 1 retreats down the hallway to the first bedroom, from which he can cover the bathroom door. Officer 2 pulls the door to the master bedroom shut behind him as he leaves his position by the bookcase. This will restrict the Reaction of any suspect(s) coming through that Area of Responsibility. Then Officer 2 positions himself at the stairtop to open the bathroom door. As he pushes the door open, he can see shards of glass sprinkling the floor inside from the window that has been broken and raised for entry.

Between the two officers, they have this view of the bathroom:

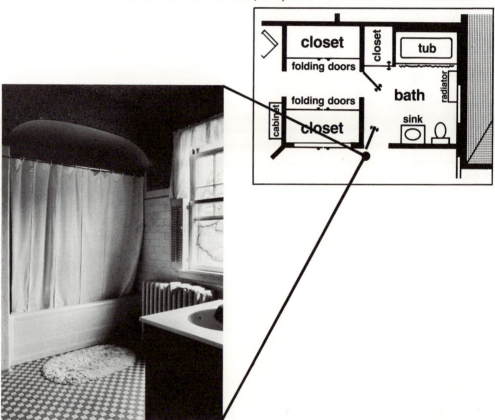

Officer 2, who'll make entry, considers three possible threat locations: in the bathtub behind the shower curtain...in the small closet...and in the dressing area that he now knows connects the bathroom with the master bedroom. The hardest to deal with, he feels, is the bathtub. Someone hiding there may be able to see at least his shadowy image through or around the shower curtain or pick up his reflection in the chrome fixtures. He'll have to move as swiftly and as deceptively as possible.

First he wraps in and slams shut the door to the dressing area to slow down any attack that might come from there. He pushes in the door's knob lock button to make it an even more effective barrier, then quickly pulls back out to the hall so as not to linger in one place. Back in the second time, he deals with the bathtub. Trying for the least expected movement, he advances toward its *far* end, drops low—and simultaneously knocks aside the shower curtain. In his other hand, his sidearm is ready for action...but no one's there. Moving forward along the tub, he now opens the closet door. From across the hall, Officer 1 whispers that it's clear.

Next challenge: approach the sitting room, probably the highest-hazard Area of Responsibility remaining.

On Officer 2's instruction, Officer 1 now moves back to the end of the hall where he can maintain a visual and firearms control through the master bedroom to the sitting room doorway. Dodging out and back from the bathroom, Officer 2 clears the built-in closets that line both sides of the dressing area. Once again, the officers are *separated* from visual contact, but they consider the security provided by Officer 1 and the avoidance of being bunched together in the dressing area worth this sacrifice. In a matter of seconds, they have advanced to the positions they want. Officer 2 is near the bookcase just inside the dressing area. Officer 1 has moved to the master bedroom, quick-peeked over the bed to clear the blind spot behind it and advanced to the dresser, yielding a progressive view of the sitting room.

The officers are triangulated on the sitting room doorway.

As Officer 1 stays high to provide security, Officer 2 wraps around low, through the sitting room doorway to the end of the built-in closet. After a quick peek, he reaches around the closet end and pushes the nearest sliding door open along its track. After a pause, he quick peeks. It's a large closet, so he peeks several times from different heights before he's convinced it, too, is clear.

Before they leave the second floor, the officers return to the first bedroom to check the *attic*. Officer 1 handles the inspection. He finds a hockey stick in the closet that he uses to slide off the hatch, then from the ladder he pops a few tilted-head quick peeks to canvass across the unfloored joists. His flashlight held at eye level provides the illumination he needs. Nothing.

The *basement* in this case is easier. Turning on the light switch and quick peeking on his knees from the basement's upper landing, Officer 1 sees that it's a single, open room, with few apparent places for concealment. He keeps the light on and maintains security there while his partner double checks from outside through the basement windows.

Some cynics might quip that the suspect was found in an obscure basement alcove, having died of *old age* waiting for the officers to get there. Actually, they were on the second floor only about 12 minutes. Their total search, including the basement, took roughly 20 minutes.

Did they regret the time and caution they expended, considering that no threat turned out to exist after all? "No way!" says Officer 2. "It's like a middle-aged man with a family history of heart disease. When he spends time and money to take an EKG, he doesn't regret having done it if it shows he's okay. And he doesn't plan not to take others in the future, either. He's at risk...we're at risk—and it's *unpredictable.*"

Canine Considerations

Some agencies estimate that search time can be cut by half or more through the use of a police K-9. Yet, as a Missouri policeman observes, the effectiveness of a dog is often diminished because "most officers who aren't handlers don't know how to work with or around a K-9 unit." This is important these days because the concept of a handler and his dog searching *alone* has been largely supplanted in some jurisdictions by the tactical understanding that a second officer should always be along.

If a dog's use is anticipated, first officers at the scene should secure the building from the outside, seal off avenues of escape and *not* enter. This will prevent contaminating the interior with scents other than that of the suspect. Before the dog is released, his handler should shout verbal warning into the interior that a K-9 is being sent in. Don't assume, however, that no response means no one's inside. In one study, only six suspects out of 800 who were hiding in buildings surrendered at this point.

Tactical team members prepare to enter a tv station where offender is barricaded. K-9 and handler stand by for support.

The dog should always enter the building first. Handlers sometimes have difficulty accepting this, but better that the dog take the brunt of an immediate assault than an officer. In the Midwest, a patrolman responding to an early hours burglar alarm at a liquor store unleashed his K-9 and ordered him into a hole that had been chopped in the wall. Ordinarily, the officer himself went first, but the hole was so small he paused to remove his gunbelt before climbing through. Seconds later, a shot rang out. Unknown to the officer, the store owner had entered from the front with a gun in hand. The dog's unexpected movement startled him and he wounded it in the face. Had the *officer's* movement been his source of surprise, his reflexive firing could easily have proven fatal. In fact, hitting an officer will generally be easier than hitting a low, fast-moving K-9 at close range, especially if the suspect has a long gun.

A properly trained dog will generally be *unleashed* during the search. The handler should maintain some separation from him, while staying close enough behind him to monitor his activities. The handler should be doubly certain that the K-9 is the first one into all the *blind spots* and any other hinky locations. The handler might want to stay 15 to 30 feet back in a large location, perhaps only 3 feet back in a close-quarters situation. *You* should always stay *behind* the *handler*. Don't get *too* far behind, though, or the dog, in circling around, may take you to be an isolated offender. (If this does happen, remain perfectly motionless until the handler approaches, or the dog may feel your movement is aggressive.) *Always explicitly follow the handler's instructions regarding the dog*, including commands not to pet him.

The success of K-9 use in a building search is based on teamwork between the dog, handler and responding officers. These photos were taken during a garage search for a burglar. (top) Notice the proper distance between the unleashed canine and its handler as the dog advances toward an area of investigation. (bottom) As the handler monitors Problem Areas in the vicinity of the dog, a cover officer provides security over other areas.

As the search progresses, you still employ caution, of course. Indeed, probably the most common mistake officers with dogs make is to feel a false sense of security just because the K-9 is present. Still, some tactical concepts—such as "one officer secures while the other moves"—won't apply because of the compensating factor of the K-9. Instead, you, the handler and the dog for the most part will strive for *fluid, simultaneous movements.* If gunfire starts, the handler should be prepared to go low while you respond from a standing position.

DON'T RELY SOLELY ON THE K-9. True, his sense of smell is infinitely more sensitive than yours, but it's by no means 100% reliable. When he indicates a presence, you hope he has keyed on a human suspect. But it may be a hamster or a rat. Also air currents can diffuse or displace scents and throw the dog off. During cold weather, particularly, scents near the offender's point of entry may be sucked outside. The dog may not be able to pick up on the faint residue, and because officers too often imagine that suspects only lie in wait near their entry point, the searchers may falsely assume the building is clear. In some locations, the K-9 may indicate the presence of a suspect in one room while, in fact, he is hiding in an adjacent one. One experienced handler estimates that at least 20% of the time, suspects turn out to be some place different from what the dog thinks. Sometimes certain fabrics stored in commercial buildings, like nylon, dacron and polyesters, hide or stifle the human scent. During one warehouse search, a burglar hid on top of a stack of cartons. A K-9 sniffed right past him down below.

Remember: *dogs are notoriously poor at picking up VISUAL cues.* 80% of their sensory perception is through *smell,* while 90% of ours is through *sight.* So while the K-9's nose is working, be sure your eyes are.

Some handlers let their dogs bark at will during a search, believing that the noise will make a hidden suspect sweat more and thus give the dog more odor cues. But if the K-9 is making a lot of noise, you'll have a harder time hearing tipoff sounds from the suspect. When the suspect is *located,* though, the animal *should* bark to alert you and the handler and to heighten its intimidation.

If the handler is shot or otherwise injured and unable to give commands, the K-9 in all probability will stand guard over him. DO NOT rush in on the handler or the dog. Try first to call the dog by using an authoritative voice. If that's unsuccessful and time permits, contact another K-9 officer or a member of the injured handler's family, who will be familiar with the dog. Otherwise, get a protective sleeve, muzzle and extra leash from the K-9 vehicle. Let the dog attack the sleeve. Once he grips it, he won't let go and you can then secure him with the leash and muzzle with minimum danger.

A more likely threat to you during a search will be *non-police dogs,* such as pets and specially trained attack animals. In a scenario becoming increasingly common as more homes, businesses and criminal lairs are guarded by watch dogs, a New York detective searching a social club for four drug suspects surprised four other "offenders"—three Doberman pinschers and a German shepherd. The shepherd attacked. Twice the detective shot him point blank, but the savage frenzy of the dog's gnashing jaws didn't let up. By the time the animal finally dropped dead, the officer was chewed on the thigh, forearm and knee. As a Kansas officer who had to kill an attacking 130-pound rottweiler points out: "A vicious dog doesn't really care" about your command presence, your uniform—or in many cases even your gun. In fact, some are trained to attack at sight of a firearm.

A dog's anatomy can offer strong resistance both to firearms and survival knives. His bony, sloping head may deflect or absorb rounds before they reach his small brain. In a large dog, the carotid arteries are buried deep under muscle—hard to cut—and the more easily reached jugular veins won't bleed out in time to keep you from being harmed. To reach his heart, you may need a knife with at least a 6-inch blade, and even then, in the fury of the attack, be able to place it accurately through his ribs or the base of his throat. Sometimes you may be able to improvise. About to be attacked, a California state ranger shoved his portable radio in the dog's mouth.

Your *sidearm* is probably your best defense, despite its handicaps. With large, savage dogs, multiple body shots may be required to be effective. For the fastest-stopping *head* hit, shoot upward into the dog's open mouth, where your slug is likely to penetrate his brain. Another prime target is the area across his eyes. To hit there, though, you'll probably need to wait until he clamps his jaws on you so you'll have a more stationary target. That is, if you can endure the pain involved. The pressure per square inch that the jaws of a large dog can inflict is roughly equivalent to four refrigerators being stacked on top of each other on your arm. If you do shoot under these circumstances, try to contact the dog's

body with your muzzle. This will discharge damaging gases into him as well as lead.

An alternative is your flashlight. Shining a high-intensity light into the eyes of some dogs will scare them off. If the dog attacks, smashing a metal flashlight down on his skull can crush it.

Maybe when he bites, though, it's your gun hand he chomps, or perhaps there's some other reason you can't or won't use deadly force. Your best empty-hand defense against his jaws (your Area of Responsibility) is to get him *off his feet*. This disorients most dogs because it breaks their balance and puts you in control. With both hands (if possible; otherwise, with your free hand), grab a fistful of his hide—not just his fur—along and just under his ears. Hold firmly and lift him up completely off his paws. An *untrained* dog can be easily flung hard against a wall or drop-kicked away from you, buying you time to regroup. An average-strength officer can throw even a 120-pound dog, although you may need to swing him, like a discus thrower, to do it.

A *trained* dog may still hang on with incredible tolerance to pain. Here, if you're able to lift him, kick him *hard* in the testicles, the underbelly or the rib cage. Well-placed kicks will have much the same effect as they would on a man, and may even kill or cripple him. But it may require more and harder kicks to shatter his pain barrier. You may also be able to strike a quick blow to his larynx, which is exposed about like it is on humans...or to attack his eyes. Or stick your finger(s) up his rectum as a distractor. Another possibility is to work your thumb in the side and rear of his mouth. There are no teeth back there. You may be able to press down hard enough to break his jaw...or shove your thumb down his throat. When he gags, a good grip on his hide can wrench him loose. Understand, though, that attack-trained dogs will be *tough* to defeat. Some authorities, for example, estimate that even a black belt martial artist will have only about a 30% chance of overcoming a trained Doberman empty-handed.

If there's warning that the dog is coming at you, try to sidestep his lunge and hammer him with a powerful kick to the ribs as he goes past. With some breeds, you'll need exceptional speed and timing. Dobermans, for instance, are so agile they can literally change direction in mid-air.

Another option is to try to channel the dog's attack so you're in a good position to attack him. Although some may have been taught to go for your throat or crotch, most will seize the nearest target. So if you see him coming, extend your arm. Once he grips it, jerk him up off the floor with it to begin your counterassault. If he does aim for another part of your body, you may at least be able to block him with your out-thrust limb.

On some searches you may encounter the body of a dog's master with the dog standing guard over it. Here you may be able to drive the dog into another room with a fire extinguisher, a road flare or perhaps a garden hose.

Dogs may not be the only guardians of premises you have to deal with. Officers who went to a Nashville residence to search for an elderly man who'd fallen and broken his hip were confronted not only by two guard dogs but were attacked by a huge pet rooster when they kicked in the front door. And in India, a bootlegger trained monkeys to attack police and strip off their clothes when they raided her illegal brewery. After some embarrassing encounters, officers outwitted her—by carrying pocketfuls of diversionary peanuts.

4

BARRICADED SUBJECTS

Two incidents a few months and a few hundred miles apart in a large Eastern state show the extremes in dealing with armed subjects who barricade themselves inside fortified structures.

In one case, two ex-convicts holed up in a public housing apartment after robbing a cabdriver and tying him to a tree. They had shotguns, a box of ammunition, soft body armor and a police scanner with which they monitored the movements of some 100 officers who surrounded the place.

Electricity to the apartment was shut off, but the suspects didn't budge. A K-9 was sent in twice, but he only circled the living room, missing the scents of the gunmen who waited in a back bedroom. With no negotiation attempted, with no chemical agents tried, a five-man SWAT team burst through the apartment's front door.

In the darkness, the officers could see little. As one looked around a corner, the hidden gunmen suddenly opened fire. One hundred rounds flew back and forth in the next 15 minutes. Some officers were cut off from escape. Two were wounded. One dove out a window and was shot in the head by a fellow officer deployed outside.

After the others finally scrambled to safety and the barricaders were alone again, another 13 hours passed before the incident ended. By then, three people, including the leader of the entry team, were dead.

In the other case, two patrol partners responded to a family fight at a suburban home and discovered that the angry husband had barricaded himself on the second floor with the couple's baby and a shotgun.

Based on their knowledge of the neighborhood and on their estimate of the offender's firepower, one officer advised dispatch of the best "safe routes" for responding backup. He directed incoming squads to positions where they could seal off the house from vehicle and pedestrian traffic—yet remain beyond the boundaries of the kill zone. He handled all further communication, keeping the units informed of developments inside the house via his portable.

Meanwhile, after numerous unsuccessful attempts, the other officer finally managed to get the husband engaged in conversation. The officer stood behind cover and talked to him up a stairway. Many times the offender broke off dialogue, but each time the officer, speaking softly and slowly, expressed understanding for the man's plight and concern for his safety and got him talking again.

Barricader aims high-powered rifle at the congregation of a church.
He surrendered after holding 27 people hostage for 3½ hours.

158

After 40 tense minutes, the officer finally persuaded the man to slide the shotgun down the stairs. Now unarmed and standing at the stairtop, the offender promised he'd surrender if the officer would meet him halfway.

With his partner covering him, the officer cautiously climbed up the steps as the man descended. He kept his hand extended until the husband grasped it and collapsed into his arms. No shots were fired. No one was hurt.

The officers in the second incident understood the proper *dynamic balance* for resolving most barricade events with *minimum* risk. The *capability* to use force should be present and tactically deployed to isolate and contain the barricader(s)...ready to assault when and if needed. But the key most likely to *safely* "unlock" the house, the motel room, the office, the car, the train, the restaurant, the mobile home, the bank or wherever else a gunman has chosen to stand off the police is something much subtler. It's *psychology.*

As you confront the Problem Area where the suspect is confined, the principles of physical tactics for protecting yourself and other innocent persons are a paramount concern. But as you work to resolve the situation *with a survival orientation,* one Area of Responsibility that will probably prove pivotal for you to control is one you cannot see: the suspect's *mind.* Managing that requires a different kind of tactics.

Physical assault often is clearly impractical when analyzed with Tactical Thinking (or is unjustifiable from a legal standpoint). Frequently your access to the barricader's location is limited, while he enjoys a wide field of view and good protection on all sides. He may be able to fire high-power weapons and defend his position with virtual impunity. Then *psychological tactics* become the *only* sensible choice, at least for the *first* "assault."

Your overall tactical priority on barricade calls usually will be:
1. **talk** him out
2. **force** him out
3. **take** him out.

Especially at first, when everyone's stress is stratospheric, you may itch for a hard-line showdown. But even tough *verbal* commands are rarely your best option. If you go "hard" against most barricaders, you'll get hard back—or you'll kite their emotional distress to a level that's even more difficult to control.

Trying *"softer"* does not mean being weak or naive. It does not mean taking crazy risks like walking unarmed into a barricade to prove you're a nice guy. It means being manipulative...convincing...conning ...cunning, from a position of strength and street smarts, but under a mantle of empathy and understanding. Remember: *end result*, not macho ego, is the name of the game.

Unlike most street episodes you encounter, a barricade is likely to spark a major law enforcement mobilization. Written policies for "crisis management" may kick in. Multiple agencies may respond. Trained negotiators and tactical teams eventually may come to dominate the scene. But the "star" specialists are rarely on hand when barricades *begin.* Patrol officers or detectives are almost always the first responders. As such, you'll probably make the first contact with the suspect—and with it potentially imprint the whole course of what follows.

Depending on your agency and the circumstances, you may need to hang in only until help arrives. Or you may end up spending hours trying to bring a highly charged confrontation all the way home. In Alaska, for example, a young man armed with two handguns and distraught over a one-sided love affair positioned himself inside a high school hallway and threatened suicide. An extensively trained "crisis intervention" team set up a command post nearby. But a patrolman maintained all contact with the suspect because of the rapport he'd established as the first responding officer. After nearly four hours, he got the youth to lay down his guns and give up. Two California deputies patrolling past a deserted parking lot happened to spot a car wanted in a kidnapping. Inside, a former Explorer Scout had handcuffed his teen-age girlfriend to the steering wheel and was holding her at gunpoint. The deputies spent most of the night working to keep him from killing her. Their sergeant became their intelligence gatherer, scrounging information on the suspect's psychological background, on various sedatives that might be used on him and on the type of gun he had. By the time his surrender was finally maneuvered, the most serious injuries that had occurred were handcuff bruises to his victim's wrists. In other instances, patrol officers have been called to barricade scenes specifically to establish contact with the suspect because they knew the offender involved.

In such roles, you face a complex problem-solving challenge: to solve *your* ultimate problem of getting the suspect—and any hostages he may have—*out* of the barricade, you must first understand *his* problem that got him *in*...then manipulate him into readdressing it in a less dangerous way.

The psychological techniques explored here can also be useful when you're dealing with domestic combatants or emotionally disturbed persons outside of a barricade. The more force-oriented considerations may help guide your response if you double as a tactical team member. Even if you end up stationed on the outer perimeter at a barricade, this hard-earned street wisdom will help you better understand what should be taking place closer up and help you shape your actions for your own survival.

Whatever your function on this call:

ALWAYS ASSUME
1. the subject is dangerous
2. anyone exposed to his line of fire will be injured
3. there is always one more suspect than you know about.

NEVER ASSUME
1. he won't hurt anyone
2. he is alone
3. he is gone
4. he has committed suicide
5. things can't turn sour in a millisecond.

Identifying "the Problem"

Barricading is a subject's *temporary, ineffective attempt to solve a consuming personal problem*...to resolve a *crisis* that he's in. It's created, spontaneously or by planning, to bring about some *outcome*, not as an end in itself.

The standard approach has been to categorize barricaders (especially those with hostages) as criminal...emotionally disturbed...or terroristically fanatic. But a newer and often more useful technique is to determine what *motivates* the suspect's action. The operative motivation, even of terrorists, may vary from barricade to barricade.

Once you identify what the subject is so desperate to accomplish, you can use that as leverage to maneuver him toward a more acceptable way of achieving his goal...and away from the unreasonable and dangerous option he has chosen. You don't need to shrink his head or social work him. But in order to control him you *do* need to *see the world from his perspective and communicate that you do.*

One test is how you approach the brief discussion of barricade psychology that follows. If you're impatient and skip ahead to the portions of the chapter that deal with all-out force tactics, you will probably be impatient with manipulating a barricader in real life, too. And you may, like many impatient officers before you, pay dearly for your unwillingness to adapt your approach to what works *best* against the type of problem you face.

A hand holding a rifle appears in the broken window on the top floor of an office building. At this point, the gunman had fired over 40 shots.

Allowing for some overlapping and occasional contradictions and understanding that the flavor of an incident can change as it evolves, the barricaders you confront as first responder or later as a negotiating specialist will be driven predominately by one of these *basic motivations:*

1. **Attention.** Here, the barricading and possible hostage-taking is a cry for help in resolving some vexing problem the subject cannot solve himself. Usually he wishes to demonstrate some point regarding a plight he's in.

Cases: An off-duty policeman in Illinois was distraught about police salaries, a transfer turn-down and stationhouse harassment. He disarmed two fellow officers at gunpoint in his home, emptied their revolvers into a wall and kept dozens of responding officers at bay with his personal arsenal...A subject whose father died of lung cancer holed up in a West Coast office building and orated against tobacco. He wanted the "whole world" to hear his message against smoking...An unemployed welder was told at a California hospital that there was nothing wrong with the son he has brought there. He took over the hospital cafeteria, threatened occupants and responding officers with a shotgun, and insisted that doctors "won't admit" that the boy had been "poisoned."

2. **Power.** Actively or passively, this subject is using his barricade and/or hostages to say, "I will make you (or someone else) do something" or "I will prevent you (or someone else) from doing something."

Cases: A former philosophy professor, denied tenure at a university in South Carolina, burst into an administrative office with a .38 and a 9mm semi-automatic. He held a student hostage, demanding reinstatement...A bank robber with a sawed-off shotgun pushed past an airport security officer in Nebraska and seized the passengers and crew aboard a commercial airliner. He wanted federal agents to provide $3 million, two submachine guns, two parachutes and the release of his homosexual lover from a Southern jail...A Midwestern farmer chased two deputies off his property with a handgun, then barricaded himself in his house and later opened fire on state troopers with an AR-15. He was resisting a bank's attempt to seize his livestock.

3. **Revenge.** "I'm going to get even for wrongs done against me."

Cases: A drunken Vietnam veteran invaded the village hall in a small Wisconsin town and stood off police and deputies with shots from his 12 ga. He hoped to find and kill the police chief, in resentment over past arrests...An itinerant Rhode Island fisherman, who'd been threatening his ex-wife for having left him, grabbed her and a male friend and forced them into his van, which was later stopped at a roadblock. With a gun in each hand, he insisted that the woman read Bible verses condemning divorce...A white man in Kansas held his mother hostage and shot two policemen answering a disturbance call. He believed himself to be an Indian and felt "people were doing him wrong."

4. **Despair.** The subject has given up on the world, on everyone he knows and on himself. The barricade, usually with no hostages involved, is his stage setting for suicide. He may be planning for "suicide by cop," getting you to do the job for him. (Suicide occurs with other barricaders, too. In fact, some experts think latent suicide may be a factor in most barricades—but not as the *primary* goal.)

Cases: An alcoholic mental patient, who'd lost his legs to a land mine, killed a California patrolman responding to a disturbance call at his home. He pinned down other officers with rifle fire and told a reporter: "I want to die today"...An Illinois father, despondent over being separated from his children, shot a little girl in the hand and stood off responding police with a shotgun and a hunting knife. "I want you to kill me," he yelled to them. As the hours passed, he scraped skin off his arm with the knife.

Barricadings by *terrorists*, who are a growing concern to American law enforcement, tend to fall into the *first three categories*. People with criminal backgrounds or with mental problems, of course, can act from any of the motivations.

The danger level presented by barricaders tends to vary somewhat with what their motivation is. Experience shows that those driven by *power* and *revenge* in particular are extremely dangerous, either for you or other innocent parties. *Despairing* types most often direct the danger toward themselves (although they may try to get you to harm them because of personal sanctions against suicide). *Attention*-seekers— especially those who seem to want the attention of society as a whole— often seem to be presenting danger to hostages they have taken, but they seldom end up presenting much real threat to these individuals.

Yet, so long as any barricader has a gun or other destructive device, the potential for harm, even if accidental, is indisputable.

However you read the motivation, DO NOT ATTEMPT TO ADVANCE ON THE SUSPECT(S). Approaching may seem a show of good faith to you, but to the barricader it may only provide a convenient opportunity to shoot. A New York officer approached a shotgun-toting suspect on a front porch with his arms spread to show he meant no harm. "Don't hurt me," he said. "I just want to talk to you." The suspect fired a blast that sent nearly 100 pellets into the officer's heart and lungs and killed him. Shouting or using your outside P.A. admittedly are lousy means of establishing communications, but they make more sense tactically than going face-to-face if you can't make voice-to-voice contact from behind cover or by phone. Your first responsibility at a barricade, as at any other high-risk call, is *to protect your own life.*

In seeking motivation clues to formulate your best tactics, check your early impressions as you sort out what's going on. Ask yourself: If *I* were the subject in *these circumstances*, what would *I* be trying to accomplish? If a hostage is involved, how is that victim being used by the offender? Why this hostage in this incident? Their relationship may be important (husband and wife, for instance), but how that relationship is being *exploited* right now will tell you more about the barricader's motivation. Is the hostage just a trigger squeeze away from death with a gun to her head, very much the focus of the subject's intensity? Or does she seem more a background figure, almost incidental to the barricade?

As you develop *dialogue* with the subject, try to read his emotional state—and *your own*—for more insights about his goal. With street experience, your *gut* becomes a good diagnostician.

Subjects after **attention** tend to come across as unstable, neurotic, unsure of themselves, ineffective, reflecting strong feelings of inadequacy. Anger seems to be a relatively minor factor with them. They feel frustrated, powerless, weak, *anxious. You* may feel *annoyed.* You may perceive that the barricader is a flake, and his inept handling of his life and "solution" to his problems may bug you.

Anger is likely to be a *predominant* feature, though, of subjects going for **power**. They may seem either cool or distraught, but the angry undercurrent roils around them either way. Their power play will probably provoke *anger* in *you,* too. You sense that the demanding, manipulative subject is out to work you for something, and you resent it.

With **revenge**, the subject's telltale emotions are *anger* at the fury level, combined with *hurt*. Here you're very likely dealing with *homicidal* intensity. Indeed, if someone besides the subject is present, you may have interrupted an intended murder-suicide. The would-be murder victim may have been turned into a hostage simply as a way to stand you off. Up against a vengeful barricader, *you* probably feel *scared.*

With **despair**, the mood is gloomy and passive. An air of *hopelessness* prevails. The subject may be having difficulty putting any purposeful thoughts together. *Your* reaction's likely to be, Boy, is this guy *gone!*

With any motivation except despair, the suspect may pop off a vast range of demands as you talk to him. These can be important clues, too. If the first few times they're mentioned you avoid discussing them and probe instead for the feelings behind them, he'll eventually drop most of them voluntarily. What he *sticks to* and talks about most intensely is what's really important to him—and what you can use to pry him out. A convicted terrorist gunrunner and his wife seized control of a county office building in rural New York with two shotguns, a rifle, some detonators and a box of ammo. During their eight-hour seige, they asked for $4 million, meetings with various television stars, a phone chat with the White House, ad infinitum. But what they kept coming back to was concern for 43 dogs that had been taken from them by humane officials. Troopers finally resolved the incident by tracking down and returning two of their "kidnapped" animals.

A strong psychological tool throughout your manipulation of the subject will be the deep subconscious urge most people have to come together—to *bond* with someone else—in a crisis. In effect, you want to get the barricader to experience the familiar Stockholm Syndrome toward *you*. The dynamics are there, especially with the emotionally fragile attention-seeker. For while the barricader may be holding other people hostage, *you* in a sense are holding *him* hostage, through your containment. (Just be careful, especially when you know the barricader, not to let yourself fall *victim* to this syndrome, so you become emotionally involved with *him*.)

An assistant manager (left) plus two others are held hostage inside a restaurant. The gunman released his prisoners and surrendered after four hours. The key to reading your barricader is not to approach the problem with a preconceived solution to sell, force or defend—but with an open mind to viable options that can resolve the impasse.

In selecting your options, you may need to remind yourself that what's important here is *different* from much police work. You're accustomed to winning most confrontations *absolutely.* You get people to conform to what you want your way, whether they like it or not. But at barricades a *compromise,* with elements acceptable to the offender as well as to yourself, is more realistic. In other words, you calculatedly "give way in order to triumph."

BARRICADED SUBJECT ASSESSMENT INDICATORS OF SUBJECT'S MOTIVATION				
		Subject's Emotional State	Your "Gut" Reaction	Subject's Common Reaction To Your Initial Contact
MOTIVATIONAL POSSIBILITES	**ATTENTION**	Unstable, anxious, frustrated, ineffective; strong feelings of inadequacy.	Annoyance over subject's "flakiness."	Telling you to listen to often-irrational demands or "important" information.
	POWER	Angry, manipulative, demanding, may seem either cool or distraught.	Anger; resentment at being considered a pawn.	Rejection of your intervention or the voicing of immediate demands.
	REVENGE	Angry, possibly homicidal; hurt at being rejected, betrayed or abused.	A sense of fear about subject's intensity.	An indication that it's "too late" to stop his/her intended action.
	DESPAIR	Gloomy, passive, hopeless; suicidal.	A feeling that subject is too far "gone" to save.	Silence or depressive, disjointed comments.

YOUR MOST PROMISING OPTIONS FOR EFFECTIVE MANIPULATION	
ATTENTION	Calming dialogue, focused on compassion and empathy; avoid abrasive, insensitive orders; keep your force capabilities secondary and low-key; stress concern for suspect's safety.
POWER	Calming dialogue, leading to overt negotiation; buy time and gradually induce pressure; keep your force options openly present as part of the negotiation.
REVENGE	Calming, compassionate dialogue, with awareness that the subject may try to buy time to realign the situation in his favor; avoid agreeing that violent revenge is justified; consider prompt intervention with force if the object of his revenge is a hostage.
DESPAIR	Calming, compassionate dialogue with possible self-disclosure that you've "been there," too; avoid trying to unrealistically build subject's optimism and self-confidence; beware that he may try to manipulate you into using force as a means of "suicide."

Manipulation

The "tongue tactics" you use to build rapport and gain control begin with your opening statement to the barricader. DO NOT say: that the subject has a problem (he may flip back: "*I* don't have a problem, asshole, *you* do!")...that he doesn't "want to do this" (at the moment, he *does* want to, which is why he's doing it!)...that you are there to put him in jail or in any way "clean his clock" (not a good solution in his eyes; likely to immediately provoke demands, hostile action or alienation)...or anything that labels, belittles, derides or displays contempt for him.

You'll get farther with a *broad, neutral opening* that gives him a chance to reveal something about himself and the situation.

1. Introduce yourself by your first and last names, *without* referring to your rank or perhaps even to your affiliation with law enforcement. If you're high-ranking, the suspect may insist that you make immediate decisions about his demands. If you reveal a low rank, he may demand someone higher on the echelon and refuse to deal with you. (Given a choice, some agencies feel that sergeant is the best rank for a negotiating officer.)

2. Use his first name. Ask if you don't know it. When one barricader wouldn't give it, the officer involved provoked a response by telling him, "I'm going to *assign* you a first name. It'll make things more personal. May I call you Bill?" You want to get the conversation around to *you and him* as fast as possible.

3. Say something like "I'd like to help." Sounds corny, but it often works even with hardened pros. Alternatives might be: "What's on your mind?" (asked sincerely, not sarcastically) or "Is there something you'd like to talk about?" All these focus attention directly on the subject and immediately communicate your interest in him and his problems.

He may respond with a motivation clue. **Attention**-seekers will very often tell you to *listen*; they have demands or other information they want you to know. This may happen with **power** also, or there you may initially get: "Fuck off! I don't need help!" Responses from **revenge** subjects may reflect: "It's too late...it's all over." With **despair** you may get back...*nothing*; the subject's sense of hopelessness is so profound he won't even speak.

Reinforce your role as helper and problem-solver with your counter-response. "Are you all right?" (displaying concern for the subject). Or: "Is there anyone in there who needs medical attention?" (gathering intelligence on whether there are hostages and what their condition might be). Early on, indicate that it is *safe to surrender*...you *guarantee* he won't be hurt if he comes out peacefully. *Within five minutes of establishing communication, suggest surrender and ask that any hostages be released.* Some officers become so involved in developing rapport that they forget to pursue the primary goal they're there for, yet the suspect may welcome an early resolution and just be too distraught to suggest it himself. If he refuses, you can ask him to explain his resistance as a means of furthering the conversation.

As you work to develop dialogue, to assess risks and to uncover manipulative handles, certain *types* of questions are more likely to stimulate revealing answers from him...and to demonstrate a "genuine" interest on your part. Rather than letting the suspect bail out with a dead-end "yes" or "no," frame inquiries that lure him into being:

DESCRIPTIVE	What's it like in there? What kind of situation is this for you?
HISTORICAL	What happened before you got here?
VALUE-ORIENTED	What do you like (dislike) about what's going on?
PREDICTIVE	If this keeps going on, what will it be like for you?
CREATIVE	How could this situation be better for you? What could be changed?
EXPERIMENTAL	If you try (some alternative), what do you think will happen?

Try to keep his mind occupied with reporting and decision-making as one means of draining his energy and psychologically wearing him down. Be cautious about "Why" questions, though—questions that ask for reasons, causes, interpretations. They're often intimidating and hamper conversation because they call for explanations or insights that the suspect may be unwilling or unable to provide. Always *prescreen* your questions—and comments—to see how they might sound from *his* point of view.

Certain verbal devices will subtly prompt him to talk more. *Echoing* is one, but use it *sparingly*. If he says, "Everyone here ignores me," you might reply, "Ignores you?" as a tactic for getting him to elaborate without asking directly. This also *mirrors* what he has said so he can reevaluate it. If he spews out multiple ideas, you can highlight the one you'd like to focus on by echoing only it. Another technique is to phrase your observations *tentatively:* "You *seem* upset" or, "It seems to me you're upset," rather than "You are upset." Or end your comment with, "Am I wrong?" or, "Could that be?" This lessens the chance he'll feel threatened or judged and makes it easier for him to correct you if you *are* reading things wrong.

Play off what *he* wants to talk about. A state police major in Pennsylvania had little personal interest in religion, but he spent hours discussing it with a cop killer who was barricaded with a shotgun. At one point he even stumbled through reciting the 23rd Psalm with the offender, although he had to keep turning to another officer to ask, "What the hell's the next line?" When the suspect finally got around to wondering "what the Lord would want me to do now," the major had built the rapport necessary to suggest some possibilities.

Generally you should spend most of your time *actively listening*. Take the conversational lead away from the offender only to avoid a topic that may explode him into violence or break off communication. If you shut him off just because he's boring or rambling, you may block important revelations that he's moving toward in an oblique way. Often it's from evaluating the *buried* messages in what he says that you'll pick up the most about his goal, intentions, emotional state, rationality, candor, willingness to barter, and clues for solutions.

DON'T argue the logic or rightness of his position. Especially when he's drunk or drugged, as many will be, being confrontive is likely to escalate things. Anyway, expressing your approval or disapproval shifts the focus to *your* standards of acceptability, which will doubtless be vastly different from his. You can say you *understand* his point of view without endorsing it. To win his confidence in you as a problem-solver and his willingness eventually to respect your advice, UNDERSTAND-ING *is what you must project.*

Not surprisingly, many subjects will greet you with extreme hostility and suspicion early on, firing abusive verbal volleys if not hot lead. One psychological trick for overcoming distrust is to tell the suspect *not* to trust you. Example: "Don't take my word on anything. You evaluate everything I do. If it doesn't check out, you'll be the first to know it." By encouraging suspicion, he'll tend to see you as someone who's not trying to con him—when, in effect, you are…and with this ploy you've just done it!

As the motivation you're up against becomes clearer, you can adapt the "feeling tone" of what you say more specifically to your barricader and his circumstances. Here's where your talent for *acting*, potentially one of your greatest resources on the street, may get sorely tested as you mask your true feelings to project the image that's needed.

While you are carefully applying your verbal skills, remember that a successfully managed response involves both verbal and physical tactics. Here, a negotiator (dark jacket) talks through bullet-resistant glass in the auto teller window to a hostage-taker. At this range, if the gunman fired, glass shards exiting could be potentially lethal projectiles. Control of time and distance is as important for the negotiator as it is the tactical team.

If you read the suspect's goal as **attention**, then use *compassion* and *empathy* for your manipulation. Be gentle, "caring" (without being wimpy so that he doubts you have enough personal strength to help him). Come on as an abrasive, insensitive ballbuster, ordering him around, and you'll just project what he probably faces and resents in the rest of his troubled life.

Force with an attention-seeker should generally be strictly *secondary*, kept well in the background. If he looks out the window of his barricade and sees the SWAT team forming up, the situation may deteriorate fast if he thinks they're there to assault. Fear of being killed by police is the greatest barrier to surrendering for many suspects. Reassure him: "They're not here to hurt you. They just want to keep things *safe*. There are people out here who are very upset. The officers will make sure no one rushes in and hurts you. You're important to me. I want to protect you. The officers can give us the time and the privacy and the security to talk about what's happening to you," etc. In your dialogue, try to avoid using the word "we," referring to yourself and the rest of the police. Keep it "I"...you *alone* relating to him. Your fellow officers, if mentioned, should be "they." The actual use of force against these subjects, incidentally, is seldom necessary.

The **power**-motivated barricader requires different handling. Your listening skills, calming dialogue and empathy are still essential. But here you more overtly *negotiate*. Liken it to a union-management bargaining session, where each side is trying to jockey to a position that's advantageous to its own interests.

At the outset, the barricader feels he has tremendous power. Against his power chips—his armaments and often hostages—you want to indicate that you are powerful, too. Not with emotional threats and a high fear arousal, which will make him feel more anxious, more threatened, more rigid and less receptive to changing his behavior. But perhaps by delivering a *moderate fear* message in a calm and deliberate manner. You can tell him matter-of-factly, once you fix on his power goal: "If you shoot any hostages, you are going to die" (unless, of course, he shows evidence of being suicidal, in which case he may take you up on your offer). With a power suspect, your incoming backup or SWAT response can be acknowledged to underscore your force capability. *Your power is openly present and part of the negotiation.* But at the same time, it's important to communicate what he can do to *avoid* its consequences; e.g., make sure the hostages stay safe.

Your strategy is to gradually reduce his psychological feeling of strength. So you contain his demands by ignoring, delaying or deflating them...You consider ways to make him feel the pressure of confinement and to make his barricade environment intolerable (say by manipulating the heat, water and lights)...And you trade on the fact that he may need food, water or medical care that you are in position to control. What you give, you get back more for. Even your prolonging the negotiation will help generate in the suspect a feeling of helplessness and futility, setting the stage for major concessions or surrender.

By buying time (especially when hostages are involved), you also buy the hope of engineering a major shift of power. While one officer dragged on a telephone conversation with a gunman barricaded in a California eatery, another was able to sneak up to a glass door behind the suspect's back and attract the attention of some of the 15 people he was holding captive. The officer held up a note instructing the hostages to sneak out the back in twos and threes. By the time the barricader realized what had happened, they'd all slipped away—and so had his bargaining strength. Similarly, authorities in Texas confronting a fugitive who held hostages at gunpoint in a bank vault stalled for about 12 hours, until the suspect got hungry. They placed the food he wanted beyond his reach outside the vault. When he came out to get it, the hostages slammed the heavy door behind him, leaving him easy prey for the deputies, troopers, police and federal agents who instantly swooped down.

When **revenge** is a barricader's prime motivation, however, some experts now believe that you may *not* be wise to play for time indefinitely. Indeed, if the offender has the intended target of his revenge as a hostage, he may be willing to relate to you only long enough to *realign the situation* to where he is able to go ahead and commit murder and, possibly, suicide.

In this case, the old axiom that the longer an incident goes on, the safer it becomes may not be true. A classic example occurred in a remote community in Oregon, where a middle-aged man tracked down the woman who'd divorced him after eight children and 30 years of abusive marriage. Armed with a .25 semi-automatic, he confronted her and the boss who'd provided the financial independence for her to leave in the pizza parlor where they worked. An unexpected customer interrupted and called the sheriff. Over more than five hours, a sergeant maintained sporadic telephone contact with the gunman, convinced his talking was saving lives. Officials were so reassured by the offender's claims that he wouldn't harm anyone that they never bothered even to establish control perimeters. Traffic continued to flow by, a nearby grade school was permitted to let out with no warning to its students, and at one point the offender was allowed to step outside with his gun in hand and face the assembled deputies and troopers. During the leisurely negotiations, he managed to murder both his ex-wife and her employer, with shots to their heads. Authorities remained unaware until the suspect finally killed himself. All along, a bewildered undersheriff said later, "We thought we were gaining rapport and control."

If you are *convinced* you are dealing with a revenge situation and your intelligence-gathering indicates the suspect has a violent history...now has weapons...continues to voice angry threats...and has ready access to his would-be target, the most conscientious option may be to try to beat him to the punch with force, rather than wait until he takes provocative action. His hostage(s) risk *great* physical and psychological damage. When hostages are killed in these situations, it's usually when extended negotiation is relied upon as the sole or primary option. Your most realistic verbal goal may be to try to stabilize this situation just long enough for a tactical team or sniper to get ready for urgent action.

It's important that you hear the underlying pain and hurt of the vengeful subject, both to assess him and to *express your compassion*. Work to divert his thinking away from his hostage and his locked-in intent and make *yourself* the chief focus of his mind. You've got to get his anger down. Let him verbally vent his pent-up feelings to you without censure or defensiveness. You may agree he has had a rough deal, but *never* agree with his violent process of resolving it. Indeed, you may mildly chide him that people will see his behavior as "out of character" for him.

Revenge events (which fortunately are probably the rarest you'll encounter) tend to come to abrupt ends. Still, *don't try to "John Wayne" the barricade yourself*. There will be far too many Areas of Responsibility between your location and the suspect's for you to control alone. Your injury or death will help no one.

The barricader who's into **despair** may be the hardest of all to manipulate. He sees no meaning, purpose or hope in life, so there's little to exploit. He's likely to have a heavy history of drug and alcohol abuse, a lifetime of shattered personal relationships, an arm-long sheet of civil and criminal contacts with the law. With whatever remains of his reasoning, he has figured (probably accurately) that his future is as bleak as his past...and he's determined to pull the plug.

You won't build credibility by telling him he's a great guy and the world is full of roses if he'd only open his eyes. Your best bet here is probably *self-disclosure*. If you have ever despaired or considered suicide, share that with him. Certainly, like everyone, you've contemplated at some point whether life is worth living. Your experience *may* extend a branch of hope for him. Perhaps his despair is recent and episodic rather than chronic, in which case you stand better odds of breaking through.

Throughout your contact with *any* barricader, you want to:

• *AVOID providing weapons or additional (or different) hostages.* Meeting these demands can only tip the balance of power more in his favor or complicate your job. Some officers have successfully supplied guns that were inoperative, but if such a ruse is detected, your credibility plummets while his anger surges. If you trade hostages, then you're responsible for those who go in. Before, *he* was responsible. At the very least, this puts you at a psychological disadvantage. Drugs and liquor are usually on the blacklist also—unless you have *reliable* intelligence, say, that the suspect always falls asleep after he swigs a few beers. Otherwise, you're likely only to increase his irrationality, which officers who've negotiated with barricaders agree is the hardest factor of all to deal with.

You can defer a direct "no" to a demand by claiming that your superiors are "working to see what can be done." But if you're pushed, you may have to state, "They won't let me do it." Always add, however, "We can negotiate other areas," to keep the bargaining alive.

Hostage-taker lies wounded at an airport where he took a 13 year old captive. Local police traded the boy for a pilot who was shot to death by this man.

Remember, you want the best deal at the lowest cost. You may be able to get it for something the barricader had not thought he wanted...or had not thought of at all. One hard-nosed subject surrendered meekly when he had to defecate but couldn't find the toilet...while another in Pennsylvania who'd raped a woman, stolen her credit card to buy an Uzi, fired a shotgun at responding officers and insisted he would break out of his barricade to kill celebrities on a "hit list," ended up surrendering for two glasses of water. In New York, it was in exchange for breakfast—after the negotiating officer manipulated the suspect with the aroma of bacon and eggs that he cooked up in the apartment next door and blew down the hall with a fan.

• *AVOID involving civilians in your manipulations.* Spouses, employers and others whom the subject may ask to be brought to the scene may be the very ones who will detonate him into further violence. Where you're dealing with a revenge goal, you may unwittingly provide the very victim he wants by presenting such individuals. Relatives or acquaintances who volunteer that they know him "better than anyone" and can "talk him out of this" may in fact alienate him further by their lack of psychological savvy. Despite careful coaching by officers, a mother permitted to talk to her barricaded son in southern California immediately started ripping him for being "such a pain in the ass" and advised him to kill himself. After that, police let him talk to a public defender. Before *he* was yanked off the phone, he casually mentioned that the suspect probably was looking at 10-to-life if he surrendered. The suspect ultimately killed himself and his hostage wife. If the suspect feels his family and friends are there, witnessing yet another of probably many failures in his life, he may vow *not* to surrender in order to show them a "success." Or he may welcome them as an audience to witness a "vindictive goodbye" as he kills himself or forces you to kill him.

Use these people to gather intelligence for your assessment and dialogue, but keep them in the background, unannounced. One option is to let them make a tape-recorded message that you can play for the suspect—after you've screened and/or edited it.

• *AVOID being pushed against deadlines.* Don't establish any yourself, and deftly circumvent any he tries to invoke, because deadlines close down options. Say he demands a patrol car and clear passage out by 2 o'clock. At about 1:50, start raising questions or problems that will cause the deadline to be passed, while still demonstrating that you are "trying" to resolve the dilemma. This is called the "salami technique"...buying time a little slice at a time. In different contacts, you can ask whether he wants a marked or unmarked vehicle...a radio with a county frequency as well as city, and so on. Once one deadline glides by, it's rare that another will be enforced.

(Clear passage out, especially with hostages along, should be among the *last* things you'd ever agree to, incidentally. When a barricade situation goes mobile, control unravels and risk rockets. Some agencies consider an attempt to flee a barricade with a hostage an automatic go-ahead for police snipers. In California, police negotiated for 14 hours with a revenge subject who'd barricaded himself in an abortion clinic where a doctor allegedly had injured a friend of his. Authorities seemed cooperative by bringing a car he wanted to the scene. The gunman burst out of the clinic with two women hostages tied together and tried to conceal himself by setting a smoke screen with a fire extinguisher. But when he reached the car door, officers without hesitation fired half a dozen shots and killed him.)

• *AVOID telling lies that can trip you up.* If you're setting the suspect up for a controlled shot or a crisis entry, tricking him on a *one-*

time basis may work. But if there's any chance that your falsehood can be detected and that the incident then will *continue on,* you are risking all your credibility and rapport. If he's a Vietnam vet rampaging about Agent Orange, for instance, don't tell him you were slogging through the rice paddies over there, too, if you weren't. Pretty soon he'll start asking about details, and if you don't have the right answers, he may react violently. Don't promise what you can't or won't deliver...and deliver what you do promise.

That's not to say you can't be shrewd. An Illinois officer developed such rapport on the phone with a woman who was firing shots from her barricaded house that she finally told him she'd surrender—*if* she could give him a blow job. His response: "You lay down your gun and come out and *I'll be there.*" As hoped, she inferred from that a promise that he didn't really make.

Other examples of how creatively toying with the truth can strengthen your psychological clout occurred in Canada during a five-day ordeal with a sex killer who'd invaded a doctor's home and taken family members hostage. With plenty of food and drugs on hand, he seemed capable of remaining barricaded indefinitely. The weary police decided to tactically induce stress periodically to keep him from resting, figuring that wearing him out might motivate him to surrender. This required "mind games" to keep him from feeling threatened, where he might break off communication or start abusing his hostages.

Once when he seemed about to fall asleep, the negotiator told him that officers outside were getting sleepy and cold and needed to move around. "But I want you to know exactly what they're doing so you'll feel safe," the negotiator told him by phone. "They'll turn on their lights and sirens as they move, so you can see and hear exactly where each car's going." The noise inside the house was ear-splitting. "The suspect's feet never touched the floor for five minutes as he ran from window to window to watch," the negotiator recalls. "It was three hours before he came down."

At another point, intelligence gathering revealed that the barricader was a hypochondriac. The negotiator used this to orchestrate a major psychological assault. Aware that people in crisis tend to urinate (and sometimes defecate) a lot and eventually become "all peed out," he told the suspect during one call:

"I'm really concerned about your bearing up under all this stress. When was the last time you took a piss?"

Pause. "About four or six hours ago."

"That long? Any blood?"

Longer pause. Then, uncertainly, "No."

"Well, I'm just concerned because under stress sometimes the kidneys break down.

"When was the last time you took a good shit?"

"About a day and a half ago."

The negotiator (softly): "Oh, no!"

Excited talk about the suspect's health then went on for hours. Repeatedly the negotiator referred to ways his system could be "breaking down" under stress and fed him symptoms of serious diseases involving urinary and eliminative problems which other officers obtained from consultants at a medical school. "The idea," explains the negotiator, "is to keep the conversation going and at the same time implant ideas that gnaw away" at the subject.

Scene from one of the longest domestic hostage-takings in history—11 days. Here an inmate hands a fellow inmate a demand note to deliver to negotiators. The back of the correctional officer has been positioned as a target.

Some researchers claim that the average barricading (with hostages) lasts about 12 hours. But with good psychological skills, you *usually* can at least get the talk turned toward alternative solutions to the suspect's problem within *one to three hours*. In that time, people who are very upset typically have drained their emotions enough to deal more rationally with their circumstances. Most can't sustain the level of excitement and intensity necessary to prolong the barricade beyond that, and as they get tired they start looking for ways out.

Aside from the initial confrontation and random stress peaks that may occur unpredictably during the episode, the highest-stress moment you'll face, if your manipulations are successful, will be the suspect's *surrender*. This is a delicate moment, with high risk that clumsy handling will "snatch defeat from the jaws of victory."

Rehearse the surrender with him before he leaves the barricade. In some cases, this has taken up to three hours. Many subjects will not know police procedures and because of their excitement, exhaustion, stress and other factors may not be thinking clearly on their own. Indeed, they are likely to experience some of the same physiological reactions officers suffer in high-stress shooting situations, including visual distortion and auditory blocking. *Be sure the suspect understands EXACTLY what is going to happen...who he will see (officers with guns, tv cameras, crowds, etc.)...and what he is expected to do.*

Psychologically, he'll justify the surrender to himself more easily (and more quickly) if you let him come out with as much "dignity" as possible. The fear of being embarrassed seems almost as strong a factor as the fear of being killed in keeping many barricaders from surrendering sooner. Even small trappings of "respect" help. A suspect in Utah wanted a new suit to replace the Army fatigues he was wearing. One suspect was willing to strip to his shorts before he came out to prove he was unarmed—but he wanted the officer giving him verbal commands by bullhorn to call him "Mister".

Any hostages present should exit first, after the same kind of detailed rehearsal. Until you know better, *handcuff and search them* the same as if they were suspects. One of the "hostages" who proned out on the floor with his hands behind his back during a robbery in Indiana and later ran out holding hands with the others when police resolved the incident turned out to be the backup man for a gunman who had shot and killed two deputies.

Hostages exiting the barricade, from two separate incidents. If you responded to these scenes and didn't have a positive ID on those exiting, would you respond as you see here? Why not maintain control at a greater distance and have subjects exit to your location designation. What about cover? (right photo) This incident involved multiple offenders. The leader was killed later making an escape.

Before the offender emerges, tell him to lay his weapon down or push it out (not throw it out, because of the possibility of accidental discharge) and then to walk out backwards, hands up, palms turned so they can be seen, fingers spread.

As the suspect's tie-line to the outside world, some negotiators feel comfortable being present and involved in the surrender, even if they are not part of the arrest team. If you choose that option, describe yourself so he'll recognize you on sight. Because of the emotional bond likely to have developed between you, you may be a calming influence during his transition into custody.

Other negotiators feel safer not being present. If that's your feeling and the suspect *wants* you present, tell him that you'll meet with him *after* everything is successfully concluded. What you don't have to tell him is that *any* time you go face-to-face with a barricader, even if it's during his surrender, you want it to be on *your* terms.

Escalation of Response

As you try to effect a surrender with your early verbal contact, command personnel and special emergency response teams who've been alerted by your supervisor may begin to assemble. As they plan and execute a comprehensive management of the crisis, they will (among many other things) delineate certain *operational territories*, including: threat perimeters...a command post...and a staging area. Here, certain concerns not always considered in the frenzy of the moment are important to keep in mind.

(top) It's easy to forget that emergency vehicles may need to enter the area or a clear path may be needed for a tactical retreat. (bottom) News media can take over in the absence of perimeter control.

For one, consideration should be given to establishing an *additional threat perimeter*. Normally you think only of *two* concentric areas (more likely of irregular shape than true circles) enclosing the territory around the barricade:

1. the **inner perimeter**, which may range from 25 yards to a quarter-mile around a single location, depending on terrain and other factors. Often underestimated initially, it equates essentially with the area the barricader can control with his weapon(s) (kill zone) and is an area where his activities can be observed and evaluated. It is kept off limits to all but

Here is an example of exceptional inner and outer perimeter control. An entire block was shut down on the inner perimeter where a barricader held 12 people hostage.

tactical personnel, such as scouts, anti-snipers, the gas team and the entry team members.

2. the **outer perimeter**, a protective buffer where some access may be permitted to *selected* officers and civilians. The command post and staging areas are located within this zone. Some agencies permit the news media to operate here, but others keep them farther away on the belief that the best managed barricade incidents are those from which no footage can appear on television. (If footage *is* taped, however, remember that it makes good training material. You'll always see things in reviewing it later that weren't evident to you at the scene.)

Some agencies now also identify a *third* area, *inside the inner perimeter*, called:

3. the **"sterile zone"** or "No Man's Land." This is a region immediately surrounding the barricade which *only* the tactical entry team and its scouts are permitted to enter. With this area officially designated, there's less danger that other officers will intrude and be mistaken for offenders by members of the entry team. Also without having to maneuver around other personnel, the speed and efficiency of this team can be increased. And, of course, close-up exposure to the threat is eliminated for other personnel.

One phenomenon to beware of as a barricading drags on is the *"creep-up" effect.* This is the tendency, in the absence of hostile action, for officers on the various perimeters to move closer and closer to the barricade. Their discipline fails, until suddenly they find themselves in much closer proximity to the suspect than they were originally positioned—and much more vulnerable to his assault. While the passage of time can have a strong positive effect on a barricade situation, it also has negatives that you need to guard against, including exhaustion, boredom and a loss of objectivity and caution.

As these threat perimeters are established, it's usually assumed that all innocent civilians should be evacuated from the inner perimeter. This should not be an *automatic* conclusion, however. *Unless there are exit paths that afford good cover and concealment,* the very process of getting civilians out of the area may actually *increase* their exposure to risk. If they're in houses or apartments that are within the offender's firing range, say, they may be safer if you tell them to stay low in an *inside room* or in the basement, away from doors, windows and other vulnerable points where they may attract attention. One alternative to trying to watch the action is for them to take a nice soapy bath and attempt to relax until the excitement is over. Inside a cast-iron tub, surrounded by water, most of the human body will have excellent protection. At a hostage-taking in New Hampshire, the apartment above the barricade was occupied by an invalid who could not be moved out. Troopers piled four mattresses and a layer of soft body armor under him to protect against shots fired up from below. A trooper stayed with him with two gas masks in case chemical agents were used. In some cases, it is too risky to try even evacuating people who've been wounded at the scene. A computer technician in the South, angered about a neighbor's party, shot one of the guests as she honked her car horn outside his house. Then he shot a responding officer who insisted on running into the kill zone to try to drag her to safety. As it turned out, she was already dead...and he died, too.

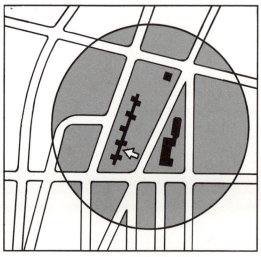

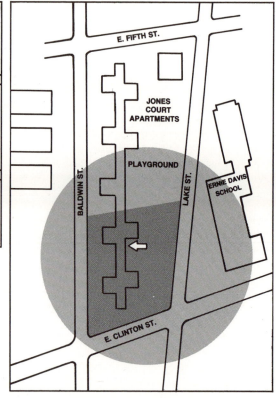

(above) Arrow points to the barricaded gunman's location in an apartment building. The circle represents the approximate boundary of the outer perimeter. Beyond this, traffic control is also essential. (right) Circle represents the inner perimeter and dark shading shows the sterile zone. This is the scene of an actual barricaded incident.

As for the **command post**, authorities sometimes forget to establish it *up-wind* of the barricade. This is important so that this nerve center for the on-scene decision-makers is not in the drift of chemical agents that may be fired. Wind direction should be one of the first factors determined at the barricade scene.

The post should have easy access for personnel...little or no access for the press...ample phone service...and *rest rooms.* It should ALWAYS be located out of the suspect's sight and *outside the kill zone.* At one infamous episode in the South, where a gunman barricaded himself inside a high-rise motel, the command headquarters was set up in the *first floor* restaurant of that same building—even though the suspect was still as highly mobile as he was deadly. Indeed, officers throughout most of the incident thought they were dealing with multiple assailants, none of whom was contained. Confusion and anxiety inside the command post is believed to have contributed in part to the carnage of this incident: three officers and four civilians killed, 15 other officers and civilians seriously wounded. In another case, an offender was able to sneak out of his barricade, invade the command post and kill the commander. Being close enough for up-to-the-second intelligence on new developments is desirable. But if commanders must continually be concerned about their own safety, their stress will never be controlled enough for them to orchestrate the response with solid decisions.

Another common error is to underestimate the number of vehicles that may become part of an extended barricade mobilization. For the efficient maneuvering of equipment trucks, personnel buses (good for keeping evacuees and standby officers warm and dry in bad weather), fire engines, utility vans, ambulances, patrol cars, K-9 transports, mobile canteens, armored personnel carriers and other equipment that may be needed, a **staging area** near the command post should be able to comfortably accommodate from *10 to 20 vehicles*.

Inside the outer perimeter, the tactical unit requires a tactical vehicle. The low-key appearance of this van (which can also double as a tactical command post) reduces the possibility of suspect detection as well as neighborhood interest.

As incoming personnel are deployed to tighten control on the barricader, *intelligence* about the suspect and his circumstances becomes the primary pursuit. As first responding officer, you should be *thoroughly debriefed*—not just summarily relegated to outer perimeter security, as too often happens. It may well be that you know the subject from previous contacts and that you know the interior layout of the barricade, which will be vital information should an entry team be activated.

All intelligence from you and other sources should be channeled to the command personnel and, at their discretion, relayed to the appropriate tactical specialists. This data should include: the suspect's identity and apparent motivation...as complete a description of him as possible, including his clothing...the number and type of his weapons, if known...his current level of violence...his exact location, with changes as they occur...structural details and vulnerabilities of the barricade, with a diagram of the interior...the identities, clothing descriptions and conditions of anyone else inside...their relationship to the barricader...information on any officers or civilians injured in the kill zone or pinned down by hostile fire...the locations of all officers in position...and the safest routes for relieving these officers to avoid cross fire or assault.

As an important part of on-going intelligence gathering, command personnel should also encourage maximum cooperation from the local telephone company. Though telephone representatives may be reluctant to acknowledge their capabilities, they can do a good deal to help control the barricade scene. Electronic switching systems and other modern techniques allow modern phone companies to quickly change the phone number inside the barricade to eliminate in-coming calls from the media. Also, all outgoing calls can be directed exclusively to a phone controlled by the police. Even the normal effect of the barricader's phone receiver being in its cradle can be overridden. In this case, electronic changes that take about an hour to perform in effect convert the receiver into a microphone that can broadcast to officers listening at the other end of the line what is going on inside the barricade. Phone company personnel are often hesitant to perform this service because of concern about the legal ramifications of eavesdropping, but especially where hostages' lives are at stake, cooperation can often be obtained through a formal request to telephone security officers.

As preparations are made for an extended response, you may join the action as a specialist, if you are not already on the scene as an initial responding officer. You may be part of a gas team, a rifle team, an entry team. (On small departments, manpower limitations may dictate that some of these functions be combined, rather than handled separately by full-fledged teams.) Or as a regular patrol officer without extensive special training, you may be assigned these functions because trained groups are delayed or unavailable. The use of specialists on well-honed emergency response teams is ALWAYS the preferred course of action, of course. But in the real world that is not always possible.

Your tactical considerations now will depend, in large part, on the function(s) you are expected to perform.

Team Movement

The core consideration for movement in or near the inner perimeter is *cover*. This applies whether you're aiding evacuation, scouting for intelligence, approaching the barricade to deliver a "throw phone" for communication with the suspect, deploying as anti-sniper or gas personnel or moving to position for physical entry.

Cover in this case means always having another officer ready to return suppressive fire if you're shot at, as well as referring to physical objects that can stop bullets. *Any time you shift position or advance on the barricade, at least one fellow officer should watch over your movement, ready to fire at the suspect.* This "buddy system" means you do not undertake missions alone. If you're sent out to scout and diagram safe routes of approach, for example, another officer should come with you, so you can support each other. As with building searches, he covers while you move, and vice versa. Team movement is covered by one or more anti-snipers.

Unless you are caught in the open by an attack, *NEVER move when you are actively under fire.* The military concept that "cover fire" can be laid down to permit your safe movement against a shooting adversary is bogus for police operations. When bullets are flying, you should be behind protective cover—and *stay there.* If you need to suppress the fire of a barricader shooting out of a window, do it from *the strongest point of cover you have*—not while moving or in preparation to move.

(top) Three officers deploy outside the house of a barricaded gunman, about to make entry. The entry officer on the left has a cover officer to his right. The officer on the far right thinks he has concealment. He doesn't. (below) In contrast, here is an excellent example of the use of cover—not only as a physical barrier, but in providing the scout with a properly positioned cover officer. Notice his hand positioning of the Mini-14. Each officer has a specific objective, yet they work as a team.

For proper exterior movement, you and another officer should avoid bunching up which restricts mobility. A safer deployment in the open is illustrated (middle photo) for exterior movement where you are moving inside the inner perimeter.

One of the common mistakes at corners is for two officers to be aiming their guns in the same direction, standing side-by-side or one behind with his gun aimed into the other officer. What you see to the left is a practical way of positioning your cover officer for maximum control of hazards.

At a safe distance from the threat, you want to be careful how you position yourself relative to cover. (left) Here you have a bad position which offers inadequate concealment. (bottom left) Although this position does not offer total concealment, you are protected as long as your distance from the threat is sufficient to avoid detection. (below) By staying back and away from the cover, you become a slightly smaller target as well.

In selecting cover, don't overestimate its capabilities. Trees and telephone poles, for instance, are often cited as among the "best" protection around. But keep in mind that to either side of their dead-center diameter, their thickness narrows. Away from its mid-line, a pole that is a foot or so in diameter will in fact be much less than that, and its cover potential will dwindle accordingly. Just an inch or so off center, .45 cal. rounds often will rip right through. Likewise, about the only reliable cover afforded by a patrol car or other automobile is its engine block. Yet officers commonly crouch beside the *rear* fenders of cars for "cover." Against the high-powered rifles often wielded by barricaded subjects, even wheel rims (much solider than trunks) have on occasion proven penetrable.

Stay alert for opportunities to improvise. At a barricade scene in Illinois, officers found a bulldozer left by a construction crew. A tactical officer who knew how to run it brought his whole team up behind it. Federal agents storming a fugitive's coverless barricade in rural North Dakota made the same move behind an carrier.

Your soft body armor, of course, will serve as your final cover barrier. If a barricader fires at you with a high-powered rifle, your vest probably won't save you. But many barricaded subjects have only handguns. Then the odds are overwhelming that if you are shot while wearing soft body armor you will not even need surgery.

Cover's companion concept—concealment—means *TOTAL concealment*. If any part or shadow of your body (or the glow from a cigaret) can be seen, a direct center-mass hit can be easily calculated by the barricader. To better their concealment, some tactical teams bring .22 cal. pistols with silencers or pump-up pellet rifles on their calls to shoot out street lights where these cannot be quickly turned off. (With sodium or mercury-vapor lights, the effect will be only to dim rather than to extinguish them completely.) Remember, besides looking for movement itself, an offender will be alert for shape...shine...shadow... silhouette...and smell.

Try to time your movements so their *sound*, as well as sight, can be masked. If muffling noises from traffic, trains, aircraft, thunder, wind or other sources aren't ambient, you may need to *produce* sound out of the line of fire (with bullhorns, sirens, helicopter rotor noise, etc.) to obscure team movement. This is especially important when dry leaves, broken glass and other environmental "alarm systems" have to be crossed near the open windows of the barricade. Eliminate your radio noise by wearing a molded earpiece, available at any hearing aid center. Without it, the suspect may know where you are and what you're doing simply by listening; with a lot of radios blaring, it'll be like a giant amplifier around his barricade. Shutting off electrical power to his location can aid your concealment, too. Then there's little danger that he can be watching your deployment as photographed by television camera crews at the scene.

Where concealment, such as shadows, is available, slow, silent movement may be appropriate to avoid attracting attention. But when cover and concealment are *not* available, speed will be your prime protector. For a barricaded suspect to see movement, bring his gun up and line up a sight picture normally takes about three seconds. So when you have to move from cover to cover across *open space*, whether as an individual or as a team, try to *keep your movement to three seconds or less*. Of course, if he has already targeted your location, anticipates your movement and knows how to "lead" a moving target with his gun, you may have even less time. But the faster you move, the more lead he'll need on you, thereby decreasing his probability of accuracy.

You're fastest with a *rush* (straight, low run) from your starting location to your objective. Just *crouch* and begin running, if you're upright. If you're prone, do a spread-legged push up, bring your stronger leg up under your chest, then thrust off for the most efficient start. If you have a shotgun or rifle, you can use it to push yourself up. Bring the weapon across in front of you, butt angled against the ground on your off (weak) side. With your dominant hand gripping the receiver, grasp *low* on the stock with your off hand and push up from there while pulling up from the receiver, using the butt as leverage. *Do not* clutch the stock at its narrowest part, however; the pressure may snap the wood. Rush with the shotgun at the ready position, stock tucked *under* your arm, not in the ineffectual port-arms carry.

Your best *pattern* for running will depend on the barricader's location. Say you want to move from the tree to behind the garage in the illustration below:

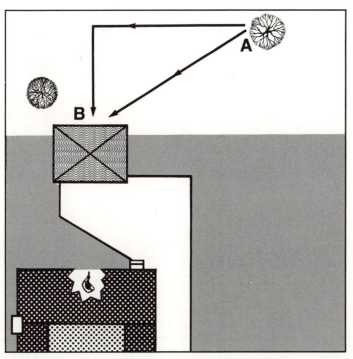

The *shortest* distance between your location ("Point A") and where you're going ("Point B") is along a diagonal path. But it may not be the *safest.* By moving diagonally in relation to the barricader, you are actually *reducing* your angle of movement across his field of fire. That lessens the extent to which he has to "lead" you as a target and increases his probability of hitting. If you run straight across his line of fire and then make an "L" turn to come forward once you're in line with your cover, you *increase* the lead he needs—*plus* you actually get behind your cover sooner. As soon as you get to a point behind the garage where he can't see over it, you are protected by it.

When a *team* is moving, covered by anti-snipers or other inner-perimeter personnel, it generally should move *together,* all members rushing simultaneously. The contrary concept of crossing open areas like streets, alleys, yards and vacant lots one at a time is both obsolete and high-risk. Once the barricader spots the first member moving, he then has time to anticipate and target the moves of others. By the time he can react to your *whole group moving together,* however, you'll probably already have reached your next point of cover, if you keep to the three-second rule. At worst, the group moving together produces a *"covey effect".* If the suspect shoots, he'll tend to fire at the team as a whole rather than at an individual target. This will markedly reduce his shooting efficiency (as bird hunters bitterly know).

Crossing an area he potentially controls, your team is safest moving in a *column* vertical to the suspect's location...*not* in a horizontal *row* that, in effect, requires members to run one at a time across his line of fire. If possible, keep at least 3 feet between yourselves in the column so you're not bunched together. This makes a longer (and harder) field of fire for the barricader and lessens the risk of officers bumping or tripping each other. You still benefit from the covey effect.

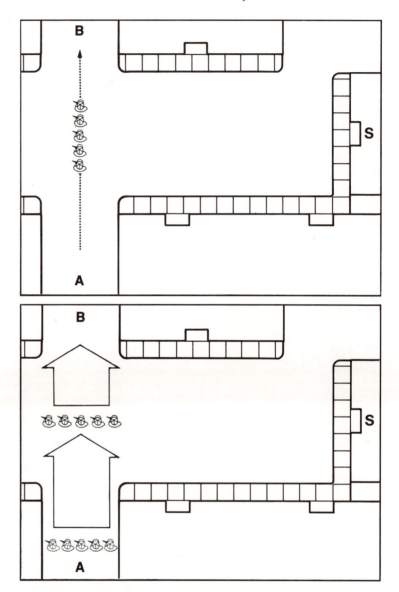

Ideally, you want to start running in your column formation while *still behind cover*, so you're up to speed before you hit the open area. Sometimes you won't have enough space behind your cover to accommodate that. Say, for example, you are behind the cover of a wall in a narrow passageway between buildings. Perhaps all you can get is two officers abreast. In moving a five-officer team in that case, pair off with the remaining officer in front. All start running behind cover, then when you hit the open area, fan out into a column, with one pair going to the left, the other to the right of the lead officer. The pattern is akin to shot blasting out from the end of a shotgun barrel.

In other locations, you may not be able to form multiple officers abreast behind cover without exposing those at the end of the column to the suspect's field of view. In other words, the angle is such from the barricade that if you were to column up perpendicular to the cover (say it's a wall) those farthest out from it could be seen. To minimize that risk, first line up single file, each spaced behind the other, parallel to the wall. The officer at the rear starts running first. As he approaches the next in line, he tugs that officer's arm as a signal to him to take off. That officer does the same to the next in line and so on. Those running try to stay abreast as each new runner is signaled into action. By the time the column is formed out far enough for the outer officers to be seen by the suspect, they are up to speed, making them more difficult targets. All officers on the team are running in column when they enter the open area. (This procedure obviously is involved and to work under stress, it *must* be practiced extensively by a team that trains together on a regular basis.)

Sometimes the cover you're running toward must be reached through a narrow opening or bottleneck (again like a narrow passageway between buildings) so you can't sustain your column formation until you get fully behind it. The most efficient and fastest option then is for the second and third officer in the column (counting out from the barricade) to pull slightly ahead as you near the opening. They go in first and keep running to clear the entrance. As they are pulling forward, the officers to each side of them come together to go in next. The last officer (the one farthest from the barricade) moves behind them and is last in. This pattern allows you to sustain the column as long as possible and avoid an unplanned bunching at the cover opening.

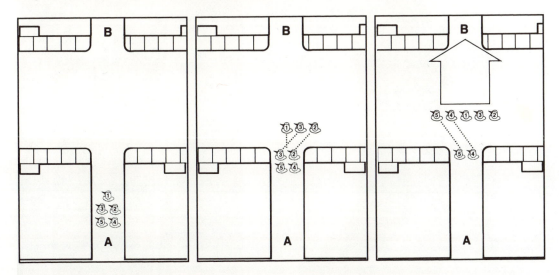

If the area you're crossing is itself too narrow to permit your columning out or the distance from A to B is short, a row formation may be your only practical option. But at least stagger yourself relative to the man ahead of and behind you. This mixes the shooting ranges for the adversary, lets each man run at his own speed and reduces the chances of your stumbling if the officer ahead falls or is shot down.

Before any movement begins, you always need to analyze the cover you're leaving, the cover you're heading for and the area you have to cross. Your movement formation and the means of shaping it will have to be adapted to the circumstances you face.

If a member of your team does go down in any formation, *DO NOT stop to assist.* You need to *train out* that natural reaction. If he has suffered only a minor wound and is left alone, he may be able to play 'possum, but your stopping is likely to draw more fire to him—and yourself. If he's seriously injured or dead, you *really* can't do much to help at that moment, anyway. Perhaps rescue will be possible later. But for right now, keep going...and save yourself and your skills to use to help neutralize the threat. *The most suicidal mistake you can make is to delay while in the open.* (The possibility of debilitating injury, incidentally, is a strong argument for all team members cross-training so they can perform tasks interchangeably.)

Regardless of formation, DO NOT ATTEMPT TO MOVE *IN* ON A BARRICADE FROM THE *FRONT,* that is, head-on to the barricader's known position. Good tactical teams don't make frontal assaults. They approach instead from angles, from around corners, from the rear, from a blind side—wherever they have the *least* vulnerability.

In moving or deploying, you may need to negotiate *physical obstacles,* such as fences, walls, deep ditches, even buildings. You may need to go over or through them rather than around them. To move with minimum risk, noise discipline, cover and concealment will be important considerations. In accommodating these demands, *teamwork* usually makes for the greatest speed and efficiency and the least risk of injury.

Team lifts, for instance, can help you clear a wall...climb to a roof...or reach an upper-level window (which, in *extremely rare* circumstances, might be the most desirable point for reconnaisance or entry to a barricade). They may also be useful in *rescue* work in non-adversary situations. They include:

Before a lift is conducted, you want to make sure you and fellow officers involved in the climb have security.

TWO-OFFICER HOIST. This maneuver can extend your upward reach by about 9 feet. Two of your teammates stand side by side about 30 inches out from the wall you want to scale, their backs to it. Their inner legs slightly overlap, allowing them to brace their feet for solid support while keeping their shoulders close together. Facing the wall, you step into their gloved hands to be lifted. Their fingers should *not* be interlaced. Rather, their hands are cupped so that one lifter grasps the heel and the ball of your right foot, while the other takes similar grips on your left.

As you climb into their hands, grab their shoulders for support. Then as they start to lift, you'll find that their being out from the wall will let you balance yourself against it with your hands (almost in a wall-search position) so you don't pitch backwards. If you're carrying a long gun, secure it on your back with the sling, barrel *up* to protect the lifters. (Climbing, incidentally, is the only time you use your weapon's sling. Whenever else you're moving, you want the firearm ready.)

To be hoisted, put your *full weight* first on your left foot. This lets the other lifter easily raise your right foot to his waist level. Then shift your weight to your right foot, while the other lifter raises your left foot to his chest level. This alternating, progressive hoist allows each lifter less strain and periods of rest.

When you're able, step onto the outermost shoulders of the lifters. Then, one at a time, they will carefully pivot to face the wall. They're then in a good position to use their full upper-body strength to raise you up to their arms' length using the same weight-shifting technique.

You also can be hoisted while standing on a strong pipe, a board or a shotgun held by two teammates. Some officers fear this will damage the weapon, but that risk is really minimal, *provided* it is not held with a flat side up. It should be *cleared first*, then gripped so you can step onto the *top* of the receiver, the strongest part of the gun. Lifting with this method, though, does put more strain on the lifters, and it's hard to hoist to shoulder level or above.

As you crest the rooftop, stay low to avoid silhouetting yourself.

BODY CLIMB. Here the lifter stands with his back directly against the wall, knees bent, hands cupped to receive your foot, as before. With your hands on his shoulders for balance, you seat one foot in his hands. With your full weight on that foot, you then climb to his shoulder with the other. Shift your weight to that foot and let your hands slide up the wall as you straighten up and he hoists your first foot to his other shoulder. If you both are balanced well, he may be able to slowly turn under you and then lift you higher by raising one of your feet and having you shift your weight onto it.

A slight variation in hand positioning for the body climb.

This lift can be awkward, but it does provide an option for a two-officer team. As with the two-officer hoist, the lifter should keep his back *straight* to avoid injury.

All lifting should be done out of the suspect's field of view. If multiple officers need to be lifted, be sure the heaviest in your group are raised first. Then if you need help, more people are still on the ground to assist. The "SWAT grip," similar to the "soul brothers'" handshake, works best for pulling teammates up.

Once two are up, they can help raise others by improvising a rig of flat nylon banding or nylon rope, available at camping equipment stores and easily rolled and carried in your pocket. Knot about a 15- to 20-foot length into a large loop. Tie off two smaller loops that you and a partner can use as "handles." When the rig is lowered, the climber below tucks his hands up under the large loop and clutches its sides. Then as you and your partner pull, he walks up the wall in an L posture, his upper body parallel to the climbing surface. This technique also can be used for descents.

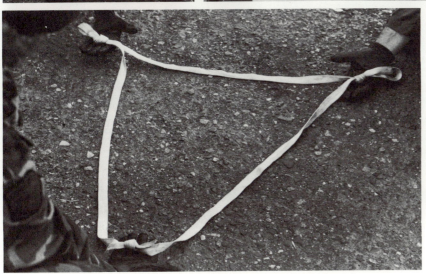

Another descent maneuver is the:

SPIDER DROP. This minimizes your distance to the ground from a wall or roof and lessens the risk of injuring your heels or back in a direct jump. Lying prone atop the obstacle you're leaving, your head pointing in the direction you want to move after you reach the ground, inch your body over the edge and down until you are hanging on only by the fingers of one hand and the toes of one foot. The other hand and foot should hang down toward the ground, your firearm in that hand.

Once you're fully stretched, use your lower hand as a pivot. Release your upper foot and let your body swing down. Your lower elbow braced against your hip and the toes of your trailing foot can be used as brakes to control your swing.

When you're almost perpendicular to the ground, release your grip on the edge and drop. Land on the balls of your feet, with your feet spread shoulder-width, knees bent. *Be careful not to swing too far before dropping*, or you may land painfully on your heels or topple backwards.

These same maneuvers can sometimes be used where a *fence* is the obstacle in your way, although most tactical officers prefer to go *through* fences rather than over them. Cyclone fences, for example, yield easily to bolt cutters or metal clippers, which your team should have along as requisite equipment. One slice cut up 16 or 18 inches from the ground will easily accommodate you and your gear crawling through. Two team members pull the corners of the cut back while the rest of the group sneaks through. Then the corners are pushed through the opening and pulled back by two officers on the other side while the last two come through. Or you can just cut a quick "door" through the metal. With wooden fences, slats or pickets usually can be pried loose to create a passageway.

Any fenced yard should be checked for the presence of a dog and an estimation of its size before you enter. Is there a dog house or dog dung around (how big?)...a dish on the porch...a running path worn around the perimeter? It's difficult to justify shooting neighborhood pets during

Tactics for negotiating a *low* window like this one, present at least two tactical options. On this page you see the officer crossing as he would an open doorway: quickly. If an offender were hiding back inside behind shadows, the officer's speed would make it hard for the offender to assault. Note the officer does not aim his long gun into the window because this would only slow him down. (right page) This approach advocates a crouch, covering the window as he moves around. If shooting were to erupt, the officer could fall backwards and return fire. If an offender is inside and using darkness as concealment, he might see the officer especially if the officer could not see inside because of window glare. If this were you, could you Locate and React to a threat quick enough? Keep in mind that your initial movement in the crouch might give away your position. Which of the two tactics would work best for you? Why?

your deployment. Better to find another route or have the owner call the animal inside. Or, if you're surprised by a dog, consider shining your high-intensity flashlight square in its eyes. One Maryland officer did this just as a snarling dog reached him to attack. The beast stopped dead in its tracks, giving the officer enough time to flee the yard.

Windows may be other obstacles you'll need to out-maneuver, particularly when you're deploying around the barricade itself. Rather than just ducking below a window to get by it, you may want to *crab walk* past it. With your weapon in a ready position, keep facing *toward* the window as you move, so you can monitor it. Crab-walking is slower than just stepping across, but it can keep you from being surprised by an attacker and shot in the back from the opening as you're moving past it. By facing the building, you have good peripheral vision on *both* sides of you. Because you're close in, the barricader will have to duck out of the

window to see and target you, and this would permit your covering forces to take him out.

With team movement, an alternative is to crouch below sill level with your firearm and that of the officer behind you both aimed at the far side of the window. As you move, you shift your point of aim to the side of the window you just left. After you're across, you then cover from that angle until the officer behind you crosses and assumes your cover position so you can advance farther or at least cover to the front.

With either tactic, avoid rubbing or bumping against the wall. With non-brick structures, especially, the sound can radiate inside.

With basement windows, don't go out from the building and around them, making yourself visible from inside. Step over them...but be sure to keep your trailing leg *up* above the window until it has cleared the other side.

Crawls. At times, your movement may have to be in a *prone* or near-prone position, to accommodate low cover or concealment or to negotiate under certain obstacles, like barbed wire fences. For the *low* (prone) *crawl*, lie flat on your stomach. You can keep your head lowest if you propel yourself by bringing one elbow and an opposite knee forward against the ground, then pressing them down firmly as you push your body forward. If you have a long gun, it's laid over your opposite arm, with the receiver resting near the bend of your elbow to protect it and the muzzle from the dirt. Grip the weapon by the front sling swivel. Or you can raise up slightly on both elbows and use them and your feet to pull you forward, cradling your weapon across your arms. This position tends to bring your head higher, however.

The **LOW CRAWL.** This can also be performed on your back and is sometimes used for crawling under low windows. Here your long gun lies lengthwise on your chest, gripped at the front sling swivel. The barrel should be to the right or left of your head, safety on. Unless, of course, you are keeping your gun ready to monitor a window above.

The low crawl.

The **HIGH CRAWL.** A move which is quicker, more comfortable and can be used where your cover or concealment won't quite accommodate a crouch. One version is a hands-and-knees movement, where your weapon lies across the tops of your hands, held by the slings. An alternative is elbows-and-knees, with your weapon cradled in the crooks of your arms.

Beware, with any movement that puts your head or chest close to the ground, that *bullets can ricochet off grass and dirt* as well as hard surfaces. Indeed, tests by one Oklahoma department show the ricochet potential off grass to be *greater* than off a sidewalk.

Also remember the rule of *target expansion.* When you are standing, an assailant generally must shoot you in your upper body or head for fatal results. If you are proned out on a surface that can "bounce" bullets, he can now fire anywhere in a long strip stretching between him and you and still likely strike you with ricochet fire. In effect, you expand his effective target area and make yourself a *larger* target by lying down. That's why you should *only* prone out behind cover or concealment.

The high crawl with the officer's torso raised off the grass. Note weapon positioning and his concealment from possible detection on the other side of the wall.

For crawling, as for other movements, *wear gloves.* Black leather racquetball gloves are thin and form-fitting enough for good dexterity, but still protective. Don't wear handcovering you have to *remove* to fire, however; there may not be time. In cold weather, you can wear mittens over them, slit to permit you fine finger movements when necessary. Another invaluable piece of seasonal equipment, for hot summer nights, is mosquito repellent.

Your skill and safety in moving individually or as a team will depend on your knowledge of appropriate techniques...your capacity for sustained performance...your ability to recover rapidly from exertion...your commitment to completing a designated task...and your confidence in facing hazardous circumstances. THESE CAN BE DEVELOPED *ONLY* THROUGH RIGOROUS, CONSISTENT AND FREQUENT PHYSICAL TRAINING *IN ADVANCE* OF THE BARRICADE EPISODE.

Chemical Agents

Sometimes a hostile crowd adds pressure to your handling of a barricaded subject...or the offender is too emotionally disturbed, violent or uncommunicative for reasoning. When time and talk no longer seem viable options, chemical agents usually are the safest next step for everyone involved. This is especially true if the barricader is alone. If he has hostages, that may limit this option. Gassed, the hostages may try to flee in panic, endangering their lives even more. Or if the chemical agent does not quickly incapacitate the suspect, its use may anger him into violence against them. With hostages in the barricade, you must weigh relative risks, as well as departmental policy. But certainly, if the offender is the only factor in your decision, chemical munitions generally give you superior protection over entering the barricade and trying to capture him.

Chemical agents won't work equally against all people all the time. PCP users and emotionally disturbed people, for example, tend to have high resistance and may be unfazed. But when chemicals fail to provoke surrender, the fault is more likely due to equipment failure, improper application technique, use of outdated chemicals or lack of sufficient concentration of the agent.

An Eastern incident that illustrates several of these shortcomings involved an asphalt worker who killed his neighbor, then fired more than 100 shotgun rounds at over 50 officers who surrounded his house. He refused to answer his phone or to respond to messages shouted through bullhorns. After six hours, police twice lobbed tear gas through his windows. Twice he turned on an electric fan to blow it out, before orders were finally given to shut off his electricity. Then, without replenishing the gas lost, officers attempted entry, smashing down a kitchen door with an axe and a sledge hammer. Just inside, the gunman waited behind a steel plate, unaffected by the faint chemicals. Two blasts from his double-barreled 12 ga. hit an entry officer. After more gunfire back and forth, a third gas assault was launched. This time, the suspect was killed. The chemical agents used set fire to his house, and he died of smoke inhalation.

The proper goal in using chemical agents is to *incapacitate* the barricader. That does not mean to kill him, but to *make him emerge onto your turf wholly incapable of any further assaultive action.* He should be able only to fall down and gasp for air...not even to aim a firearm. If he emerges still able to attack, you have only managed to relocate the threat. If he remains inside, still able to shoot, or if he does not come out because you've set his house afire and he has become a crispy critter, chances are overwhelming that your chemical agent selection or delivery was deficient.

For safest suspect control, you want munitions which ideally meet these requirements:

- **rapid action**
- **prolonged effect**
- **few or no undesirable side effects**
- **simple, accurate delivery**
- **ease of decontamination**

Of course, no perfect agents exist, but two main chemical compounds that are commercially manufactured come closest to meeting these requirements—CN (chloraceteophenone), whose containers are generally color-coded *red*, and CS (orthochlorobenzalmalononitrile), usually color-coded *blue* by manufacturers. *Read the fine print* on the container to know for sure what you are using.

Chemical agents obtained from the military (which are likely to be color-coded *gray*) or from foreign manufacturers are *not* appropriate for law enforcement use. Agencies that use them put themselves in a precarious liability position. One department, for example, recently complained to a manufacturer that their CN grenades were all "flaming out and burning." Investigation revealed that the "malfunctioning" grenades were actually military incendiary grenades, capable of attaining 3,500° F. and burning holes in concrete. The department hadn't understood the symbol "TH" printed on the devices, which indicates a special thermal gas—but went ahead and used them anyway. In another incident, a New York corrections officer supplied a military product labeled "WP" to use as a smoke grenade in a training exercise. WP stands for white phosphorus, which ignites spontaneously upon exposure to air and burns at extremely high temperatures for about 60 seconds. Anything it touches also bursts into flames. The device exploded as a trainee held it, blew apart his hand, virtually obliterated his facial features and roasted more than one-third of his body. He lived, but 19 hospitalizations were required for the painful surgery to construct even a grotesque parody of what he had been.

If any chemical agent is brought forth for your use that is not *commercially* manufactured in the United States, *leave it alone*. If you are uncertain, contact the manufacturer before experimenting.

(left) Ten different chemical agent munitions used by just one department. Know what they are designed to do and know the labels. (below) Here is how the containers look after being used. (l. to r.) Smoke grenade canister, CS canister (outdoor use), CS burning grenade with internal heat absorber, and a liquid 37mm CS cartridge.

CN (best known to officers in the form of Mace®) is primarily a *lachrymator;* i.e., the agent, in concentration, can cause a cascade of tears, a burning sensation on moist skin, "snot that hangs clear down to the belly button" and an inability to control the eyelids. CS is an *irritant.* It does all that CN does, but it also produces a burning in the chest, severe coughing, dizziness, *a reduced capacity for physical action and a panicky feeling of suffocation.* With an adequate dose of CS, a suspect's sole concern becomes escaping the barricade for fresh air. An armed robber, shot in the liver during a liquor store stickup, holed up in a house nearby. He was probably 30 minutes away from bleeding to death when officers filled the place with CS. He forgot all about his wounds. He crawled up a flight of basement steps and out into a foot of snow and told arresting officers, "I can't stand that stuff any more!"

CS is much more powerful and longer lasting than CN; significantly less CS is required to cause incapacitation. Yet it is also far safer, because a much heavier concentration is required to be lethal. CS is unlikely to damage open wounds, and it tends to work against a broader range of people than CN. However, it tends to be *slower* to take effect initially (sometimes requiring up to two minutes). So some officers like to fire a *combination* of agents into a barricade—CN to cause an immediate effect and CS to deepen and prolong the incapacitation. While the effects of CN may wear off within 15 minutes, CS can last for hours.

For barricades, you want the tiny agent particles containerized in *liquid* suspension. Most commonly, this will be in 37mm gas gun shells or 12 ga. shotgun shells. When the thick liquid splats out as the projectile nose breaks on impact with something solid, the irritant particles become airborne on an *invisible* mist.

Generally *avoid* agents that are dispersed by burning or explosion. These *pyrotechnic* or *blast dispersive* munitions can be effective *outdoors*, especially for riot control. But the only time they should be considered for barricades is as a *last-ditch effort* against a highly dangerous, intractable suspect. Besides the fire risk to his life and property from most pyrotechnics, other innocent people may be endangered. In Arkansas, for example, hot canisters ignited a house and fatally burned the suspect's wife, who was being held hostage inside.

At best, the smoke from these devices can create concealment for the offender and seriously hamper officers entering and searching the barricade, if that becomes necessary. When two robbers were believed barricaded in a two-story house in Minnesota, officers fired 30 rounds of liquid CS inside. One bandit crawled out the back door, rolled over on his back and meekly raised his arms over his head. Thinking the second was still inside, a search team went in, tossing two small smoke-producing canisters into a root cellar upon entry to "secure" it. The masked team moved through the CS with excellent visibility and no ill effects. But on the second floor, they encountered the smoky agent filtering up from the cellar. The team had to prone out on the floor in clearer air for 15 minutes before being able to resume their search. Fortunately, the second suspect was not in there to begin with. A dramatic skirting of disaster with incendiaries occurred during a chemical agent assault on a house in North Dakota, where a tax protester who had killed two federal agents was believed barricaded. The assault team fired two 40mm pyrotechnic grenades into the house—despite the fact that 98 loaded long guns and 150,000 rounds of live ammunition were reputed to be inside. Fortunately, the grenades, which can burn at over 950° F., did not ignite.

Again, to avoid misuse of materials, read the fine print on labels.

Take a guess how this barricader's house happened to burn to the ground.

Packaging may be confusing, but phrases like "continuous discharge" or "may cause fires" are signals of generally inappropriate barricade munitions. To pick chemical agents indiscriminately, without regard to the jobs they were designed for, is like randomly selecting ammunition for your firearm.

Where *delivery* is concerned, officers frequently fall short by firing a single round of gas...then waiting, to see what happens. Often, not much does; the barricade—and the threat—continue, sometimes with the suspect more infuriated than ever.

Gas enthusiasts argue that it's safer to go full force with a no-nonsense barrage that has a high likelihood of incapacitating from the outset. Gas officers from one major department in Minnesota with extensive chemical agent experience like to fire *multiple rounds at once,* or as closely sequenced as possible. They initially try to put two 37mm rounds (or sometimes eight 12 ga. and one 37mm) through *each opening* into the barricade structure, including attic and basement windows. If that does not end the action within 10 minutes, they consider a second barrage all around.

That amount far exceeds manufacturers' recommendations, which generally say that one 12 ga. projectile can contaminate the air in the average-size room, with a single 37mm round being capable of contaminating five times that much air space. To fire more, according to manufacturers' representatives, raises the risk of lawsuit liability and also complicates decontamination efforts afterwards. However, gas officers from the Minnesota department argue that considerable agent is *lost* during a typical delivery. Drawn curtains or shades may intercept 75% or more, or a double pane of glass may interfere with proper delivery. Fired through an open window, the agent may stick to a wall or other solid object inside without becoming properly airborne. Or it may penetrate sheetrock and fall to the floor inside a concealed space without ever reaching the suspect. If you get *half* of what you fire dispersed where it counts, you're doing well, according to these officers. Once while trying to roust an emotionally disturbed barricader, they fired *eight* CS rounds into her bedroom where she lay on a bed with a gun by her head—with no apparent effect. They calculated later that only about one-half of one round had actually managed to penetrate her extra-sturdy bevelled-glass window—and most of that stuck on a curtain.

Tactical differences also exist on *where* to deliver gas. Some officers argue that you should try to drive the suspect down and out of the barricade by first gassing openings on the floor *above* where you believe him to be. This will discourage him from moving to higher ground. But you leave a clear passageway ungassed between him and an outside door to encourage and channel his exit.

Others argue, however, that this offers too much risk that he will emerge without having been properly incapacitated. If targets must be prioritized because of limited gas team manpower, this viewpoint says, you first gas *exits*. If the suspect decides to bail out, he'll at least have to go through gas first before he confronts you or other surrounding officers. Next, work to contaminate interior areas he might decide to move to for refuge. If he's on the second floor of a house, then gas the attic, the entire first floor and the basement. Next, do the rooms *around* him. Finally, after all his options for establishing a new location are eliminated, gas *his present location*, perhaps more heavily than the rest. This thorough pattern means more area to decontaminate afterwards, which in some cases may be an impossible task. But it is designed to thwart the kind of incident that occurred in Virginia, where a cop killer was holed up in a house. Officers fired gas through the front windows and door only. Unfazed, the offender burst out the back with a cartridge belt and an extra rifle slung over his back, firing rapidly at tactical officers with an M-1 carbine in his hands.

To make each round you fire count most, you want ideally to penetrate one pane of glass to rupture the container's nose, then ricochet it off the ceiling. This usually means firing through the *tops* of windows.

Puff of smoke on the right is a 37mm cartridge which has just bounced off the glass. Not all glass can be penetrated with munitions.

A barricaded incident where just two rounds were fired into a paneled door. The top hole was made with a 12 ga. Ferret, the other with a 37mm liquid projectile.

Gas guns are considered "second-shot accurate," so you may have to adjust your aim after your first effort before you can penetrate. Some officers feel they get the greatest accuracy from the prone position, because of its stability. But because of your risk from ricochet hostile fire, this position should only be taken from behind cover.

Some officers who work in cold climates believe they need to put liquid projectiles inside their shirts next to their bodies or wear special vests that accommodate them to keep them from freezing. That may have been necessary with old-style munitions, but chemical additives inserted now during the manufacturing process keep them from freezing. In fact, you should *not* wear or carry these projectiles in your chest area. If you are struck by hostile fire, the bullet passing through the gas round and then into your lungs can cause compounded damage.

Even with the fastest-acting agent, the suspect's incapacitation, at best, will not be instantaneous. He will likely have *some* time to react. He may see the hole caused by your 12 ga. chemical agent round or its spent container and think you're firing live shotgun ammunition at him...and fire back. (In fact, in the dark it's easy for *you* to confuse gas shells with regular shotgun shells. One difference is obvious when you shoot: a 12 ga. chemical agent round produces no recoil.)

Offenders who've carefully planned their barricading may have protective masks (late model versions are on sale at nearly every gun show). Or a streetwise subject may be able to defeat what you fire with running water. A barricader who has listened to prison bull sessions on police tactics may know how to get a continuous supply of fresh air by sticking his head in a toilet bowl and repeatedly flushing it or by putting his head in a sink under a towel with the faucet running or by hiding in a closet after sealing the door crack with wet towels. A Chicago barricader stood in his bathtub with the shower on to clear the air after his home

205

(top) An offender who preplanned. His protective mask and heavy clothing help protect against chemical agents being fired. (left) Another offender with a planned response. He clings to a windowsill after fleeing his hotel room where police had just fired in chemical agents. He later fell to the roof below.

was gassed...and was still fully capable of fighting when an entry team reached him. Try to get the water shut off in the barricade *before* you gas it. Even then, if entry is made, don't assume the adversary is out of the game just because all has been quiet since gas was fired. In some barricades, offenders may be able to use an air vent connected to a furnace for a clean air supply.

(top) A 12 ga. shotgun with a scope is an ideal combination for penetrating accurately into small windows, basement air vents, etc. Effective range up to 50 yards. (above) An effective firing position with the 37mm gas gun. Note the weapon is cocked, the officer is behind cover and is wearing a mask. (left) For ease of handling, straighten the pin prior to pulling. Then save it in case it needs to be reinserted.

Female suspect is being led from her home where she had barricaded herself and fired shots. Chemical agents brought her out. Even if you have what you believe to be the suspect, don't let your guard down. Note the entry officer approaching low. In working with chemical agents, remember to wear gloves for your protection.

After a gas assault, keep in mind when you do go in that you may not know for sure where the suspect is or what condition he's in. A Florida deputy discovered this fatally when he approached a fashionable suburban home where a domestic disturbance had turned into a barricading. After a gas barrage, the deputy thought the offender was still inside. Instead, he had escaped and was hiding behind a concrete wall. He opened up with a .223 cal. rifle that penetrated the deputy's flak jacket and protective vest under his arm.

Everyone on the inner perimeter should be masked when gas becomes part of a barricade scene. Munitions can malfunction. Also each time you fire a 12 ga. round, residue builds up in your shotgun barrel. In a heavy siege, it may create enough friction to break open a round upon firing. Your weapon won't be damaged, but seeping vapor may get you full in the face. A long-sleeved shirt or coveralls can help protect other parts of your body.

If you are exposed to gas without a protective mask, get to fresh air immediately and remove any exterior clothing that is contaminated. Face into the wind so the air has a chance to blow the gas particles off your face. If you wear contact lenses, remove them promptly or have someone else do it if your hands have been exposed; particles can penetrate some lenses and get behind others and burn your corneas. *Do not rub your skin.* This will force particles into your pores where they'll be harder to get rid of. Also do not apply first aid creams or ointment to contaminated areas, as these can coat the particles and trap them against your skin. Agents can best be flooded off with a solution of baking soda and water. Water alone has little effect and may actually carry the agent to other parts of the body.

If you are wounded, life-threatening injuries should be treated first;

chemical agent contamination is strictly a secondary concern. There's about one chance in 1,000 that you will experience an allergic reaction, like a bad poison ivy infection. This is most likely to occur if you are allergic to chicken products, such as feathers or eggs, or have experienced allergic reactions to influenza vaccine. In time, an allergic reaction, too, will pass. If you are asthmatic or have a bad cold, chemical agents may have a more serious impact that normal. (This, plus heart conditions and allergies, may also be a consideration where hostages are involved.)

Any police or medical personnel who tend you while you are contaminated should wear protective masks, as particles of agent are easily spread from one person to another. Ideally, the local hospital should be prepared to treat in facilities such as a tent or plastic-sheeted "ready" room to avoid contaminating the full emergency room.

After the barricade incident, your gas gun or shotgun will need "first aid," too. Unburnt residue from discharging the munitions can eat into even stainless steel *overnight*. Use hot water and dispenser hand soap to clean the barrel, blow the last moisture out with an air hose, then treat with solvent and oil as you would any firearm. The action should be totally broken down and cleaned before its next use.

The remains of a 37mm gas gun too corroded to be used again.

Besides the *active* chemical agents used to control suspects, there are *inert* munitions available that simply produce billowy clouds of smoke. These grenade-shaped devices are sometimes used outside a barricade to mask team movements in large open areas. Be sure that you use *only* HC (hexochlorothane; color-coded yellow) for this purpose. NEVER use white phosphorus.

Tactically, HC smoke is tricky to use. Wind moves it around a lot. In one case, an entry team released a thick cloud and was moving through it well-concealed toward a barricaded house. Fifteen feet from the edge of the house, wind coming over the roof sheared the smoke off like a knife, leaving a sudden, dangerous open gap between the officers and their destination. At other scenes, wind currents have thinned the smoke above officers so that they were readily visible to suspects in upper windows when they thought themselves hidden.

Smoke works best in humid, still weather, because then it will hang in a low, thick concentration and last for hours. Fire small canisters first to accurately determine wind direction, then use more than you think you'll need to provide you with concealment. Don't use it only in the area you're moving through, though, or you'll tip the suspect to your location…and potentially draw his hostile fire into the smoke that surrounds you. Your concealment will be more effective if you can cloud an area at least half the size of a football field in two *separate* locations. The subject then may be distracted to the area where you are not concealed. Anything else tells him clearly, "Here we come, from this direction."

Remember that smoke comes in a pyrotechnic container and can start fires on grassy areas. In enclosed areas, it can be toxic. Smoke should never be used indoors.

Sniper Control

As a response escalates, the first group of specialists deployed to position should be the officers who will serve, if needed, as snipers (or *anti*-snipers or marksmen, as they're better referred to for public and courtroom consumption). Their forceful presence helps underpin the gentler work of the negotiator and, usually even more critical, they and their partners serve as *the single most reliable and important sources of information on the operation.* Equipped with high-powered weapons and unique vantage points, they have the capability of "spying" directly on most of the action and passing on critical, detailed information. And, of course, they can take out a barricader with controlled, highly selective fire at the point where it's judged that the only realistic means of eliminating his threat is to eliminate him.

Commonly approved sniper weapons include .223, .270, .308 and .30-06 bolt-action rifles with a 3 x 9 variable scope and a sling. Some snipers prefer semi-automatic to bolt-action weapons, arguing that bolt manipulation may cause head movement off target and slow a second shot, if that is necessary. Sniper guns are different from any long guns carried by the entry team, which are intended to deliver large-volume fire to suppress a close-range assault. As a sniper, you want a rifle *personally assigned to you* that has a high degree of accuracy out to about 3,000 feet, even though that distance would never actually be used in a barricade situation.

Open sights won't do your job reliably. Even a good shooter with open sights will probably stand only about a 50-50 chance of delivering instantly incapacitating rounds at realistic sniper ranges. A small error in adjustment between your front and rear sights can make a *big* difference in where your rounds hit. An alignment that's off just .0067-inch at 25 yards will cause you to miss your intended target by a full inch. And here your objective definitely is *one-shot stopping.*

Your ammunition should be target match quality of a type that is 1) *expansive* and 2) *fragmenting,* to provide the greatest first-hit impact. (Incidentally, never mix even the same caliber and grain bullets from *different* manufacturers in your ammunition supply. All should have the same lot number from the same manufacturer. A slight difference in bullet points and powder charges can make 3 to 4 inches' difference in point of impact at 100 yards.)

Some teams feel a sniper should be assigned automatically to each side of the barricade structure. More likely, though, manpower will permit only *one* or possibly two sniper locations. The first, guided by intelligence from the first responding officer or a scout team, should be where you can best observe and potentially target the suspect at his current location...where some defense can be provided against outright attack on you and the inner perimeter...and where you have at least effective concealment and ideally cover as well. Secondary locations should offer observation and target acquisition where the suspect seems most likely to *move* should he change location. If you can't see the area you need to cover or if the action shifts, be flexible enough to *redeploy*, with command permission, by withdrawing along a protected route.

Stay within 100-200 yards of the barricade. Beyond that, even with a scope, adversary identification will be difficult. In lining up a shot, you won't be able to rely on the barricader's clothing color for identification (he may switch clothes with a hostage). You'll want to be able to distinguish his *facial features*.

(left) Tactical officers prepare to climb to the roof of a store where two hostages are being held. The ascending officer has no cover officer. The point is to gain the high ground advantage from an adjacent building, *not* the one where the incident is occurring. (bottom) If you select a roof top as your marksman location, avoid the errors you see here: no scope, no forward observer, no ability to site in the offender without exposing position, and not being ready.

211

(above) Why deploy on top of a cold roof where you could be seen by the offenders from across the street when you could be inside, warm, and concealed? Also the shotgun is of little value for a marksman. (right) Here the high ground is perceived to be a location without cover and concealment. The news photographer had selected a better location.

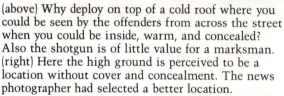

If there are multiple snipers, having each of you positioned higher than the suspect will eliminate the cross-fire risk; you'll shoot *down* rather than across toward each other. If you are all on the same level as the barricader, the primary sniper should be positioned first, with others off-set slightly around the barricade so none is in line with another. Stay aware of *all* officer locations on the inner perimeter to avoid cross-fire tragedies.

One deployment temptation that probably *won't* work is to place two snipers at diagonal corners of a building and expect them to control four sides between them. This is appropriate—and effective—deployment for *surveillance* ONLY. For sniper purposes, it usually will not permit you an effective angle of fire to *any* side. Plus, with high-powered rifle ammunition, you may create a cross-fire threat.

Also, despite the height advantage they may offer, *rooflines* should usually be considered *taboo* as sniper sites. Silhouetting is too easy there—as tragically shown by a Florida barricader who was threatening to blow up his house with explosives. As telephone negotiations were underway, he suddenly said he knew SWAT was outside and to prove it would kill the deputy on the roof across the street. Although the deputy was proned out low, the offender without further warning shot him square in the forehead with a scoped .223 rifle. If you must deploy on a roof, try to get behind a dormer or other projection you can peer and shoot *around*. Some creative snipers have placed a cardboard box on a roof and positioned themselves behind it. At a distance at night, the barricader may mistake the box for duct work or a chimney. But this, of course, is only *concealment*, not true cover.

A better alternative usually will be to gain access to the *inside* of a another building from which you can observe the barricade. In a room in another house in the neighborhood, for example, you'll be protected from the weather, have more overall comfort and probably better cover, have more opportunity to move about without being seen and probably gain some flexibility as to shooting position. (On a roof, its configuration will dictate the position you'll have to take, which will probably be prone.)

Don't assume that distance alone hides you, though. A sergeant was at least 450 feet—roughly a block and a half—away from a barricade in Connecticut, yet came within a hair of being hit by a suspect with a scoped M-1 carbine. *Probably the greatest single mistake made by officers at barricade calls is being in the line of fire and acting as if they are invisible.* Don't bench-rest your weapon on the window sill or stand at the window to look out. Try to *stay back in shadow* where no sunshine or outside light falls on either you or *your gun barrel when it is in position.* You may have to sacrifice some field of view, but you gain concealment. If you can't escape light, having the window lowered may give you some protection because of the reflective nature of glass looking in. (Thoroughly knowing your weapon and ammunition will tell you what compensation you'll have to make, if any, should you need to shoot through the glass.)

Some officers have been able to create a firing port from inside a building by removing a vent cover or, in extreme cases, by punching a hole in the wall. Positioned back from it and aiming through it, such a "mouse hole" gives you a wide view. Yet at a distance from the outside, it looks to the barricader like a black patch. Others have hung a piece of cheesecloth that they've painted grey over the window. They can see out through it, but the barricader can't see in. However, this kind of device may draw the suspect's attention because it will make the window you're behind unique.

Once in position, the shooting stance you select may depend in part on the height of any objects between you and the suspect that you'll have to sight—and shoot—over. Of course, you want to make the best use of your bone and muscle structures for assuming and maintaining any posture. Your options include:

FREE STANDING. The least stable and probably least desirable position, but to increase stability, don't face the target straight on. Bring your dominant leg back about 70°, feet shoulder-width apart. Don't support the rifle with your arm fully extended, as some officers attempt. You'll be able to hold your position longer if you keep your elbow bent. The rigid part (bone side) of your upper arm should be lying against your side. If your shot is angled down, throw your hip out a bit to support your elbow. This can measurably increase your accuracy. So, of course, can the proper use of a *sling*, which should be incorporated any time you intend to place a bullet in a small area at any range.

To check your stance, line up your target with your cheek firmly in position. Don't crunch down to sight; bring the rifle up to you. Now lower it slightly, then raise it back up with your eyes closed. If you're not still on target when you open your eyes, shift your foot back or forward a bit and it'll adjust you properly. If you're off too much one way or the other, you will develop shoulder and muscle strain trying to force the gun to the right alignment.

PREFERRED-SIDE BARRICADE. As a sniper, you *never* shoot from behind a weak-side barricade...*only* from one that accommodates preferred-hand shooting. You can position your support arm or hand against it for better stability, but *never* lay the rifle barrel itself against the barricade (or against a sandbag, either, if one is available). The barrel whips when fired, and if it is touching anything the recoil will distort the flight of the bullet.

If you do brace yourself against a barricade (or sandbag), you want to be able to resume the same position if you move away from it. A small piece of tape on your forearm can mark where it is supposed to touch.

KNEELING. *Upright* kneeling, where one leg is against the floor or ground at a 90° angle and the other is up, bent at the knee, is very unstable. There's too much strain on your back, and you can lose balance easily. Unless you need this position for the height it affords or unless it's the only kneeling position you can assume because you are physically thick and inflexible, try *sitting* on your lowered leg, resting your buttocks back on your heel. If you put the toes of that foot out behind you, you'll be steadier, although perhaps less comfortable.

Keep your elbow *off* your knee cap as you support your rifle. You never want to put bone against bone; it wobbles too much. Lean over enough so your knee cap is just below your triceps, the meaty part of your upper arm. Or, if you're not that flexible, put your elbow behind the knee cap on the meaty part of your leg. Best yet, bring the elbow down on the inside of your knee, with your upper arm braced against your thigh. This tends to be steadiest.

Avoid hunching forward to sight, sometimes a temptation if you've knelt too far behind a barricade and are straining forward to brace against it. This can produce neck stress that constricts blood flow to your brain, causing you to get dizzy, see spots, etc. At best, kneeling is not a long-term position. The way it locks your legs up cuts circulation and fatigues them.

An application of the kneeling position. In this situation, taking the highest ground was not possible. This marksman selected the roof of the next tallest building which necessitated his aim to be elevated. Note his body positioning to minimize detection.

SITTING. A good sitting position is a stable position. Probably the least desirable is to sit with your knees bent, feet spread, heels resting on floor. Here you lean forward with your elbows braced near your knees . . . very clumsy, stressful, unstable. A better option is to turn your body to about a 45° angle to the target and sit cross-legged. Pull your feet up as close as possible to your body and brace your elbows on the meaty part of your legs, just behind your knees. This does not require much flexibility, but if it's difficult for you, try sitting with your legs farther extended, your ankles crossed.

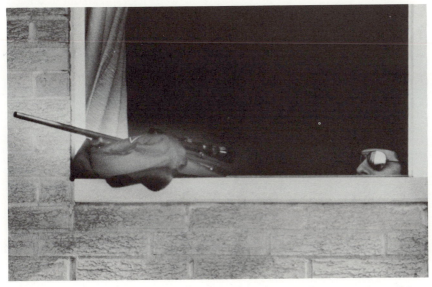

This is *not* the sitting position you want. If a photographer can see you this close, so can the bad guy. Your goal will be to have a concealed position, also avoid resting your rifle on your jacket and wearing reflecting sunglasses.

An alternative is to sit in a straight-back chair and pull another one up in front of you. Tape a pillow or rolled towel across the top of the second chair to use as support for your gun. You can move to the edge of your chair so you straddle the support chair with your knees or you can sit at an angle in your chair. Either way gives you a solid position.

PRONE. Probably your most stable position, if you can get into it, but desirable long-term only if you have a bipod or a bench rest like a sandbag or rolled up jacket. Otherwise, the tension on your neck will reduce your circulation and restrict your breathing, causing blurred vision, trembling and other erosions of accuracy.

Angle your body off to one side with your legs spread out and keep your support arm directly under your rifle as much as possible. Lying flat, your heart beat may cause your muzzle to move up and down faintly. This will be evident in your scope. You can alleviate this somewhat by pulling your right leg up to lift your chest off the ground a little.

An alternate prone position is with your legs straight back, so your whole body is in alignment with your rifle. Here you hold it almost directly in the center of your chest. It's awkward and cricks your neck more, but it does reduce the amount of your body exposed potentially to ricochet fire.

If you're outdoors, try to get some insulation to lie on (an army blanket, a foam mat, a poncho) to protect you from hot or cold surfaces. Knee pads and elbow pads are good, too, especially if you're crawling around on buildings.

Like other tactical officers, you should not operate *alone* as a sniper. A partner should serve as your eyes and ears in monitoring both the barricade and the command post. With binoculars or a spotting scope, this "spotter" can see more than the limited view you have through the rifle scope and can assist in directing your shots. Over his portable, he can relay pertinent intelligence to command and screen feedback so your concentration is not disrupted. And with a weapon of his own capable of long-range, large-volume, rapid fire (like a Mini-14 or AR-15), he can provide cover for you and for personnel in the inner perimeter.

In this incident, officers set up to look for suspects hiding in a field. They're using their van for a high ground view. But what's missing is a spotter using the binoculars. Also turning the hat around eliminates the problem of blocked vision.

His vital role is illustrated by a confrontation in the Baltimore area. A young PCP user shot a civilian, killed one police officer and paralyzed another from the chest down, then barricaded himself in his house with multiple weapons, thousands of rounds of ammunition and a survivalist's supply of canned food. A rifle team was established outside behind a knoll, about 40 yards away. As they were observing, the suspect suddenly came to a window, knocked out the glass and beaded down on something out of the sniper's field of view (later proved to be another police officer).

"Do I have the green light?" the sniper demanded, his eye still glued to his scope. The spotter quickly confirmed it.

Just then, the subject apparently spotted the rifle team and turned in their direction. The sniper squeezed his trigger. He was able to react immediately to the deadly threat, whereas if he'd been handling the radio transmission himself he might not have been able to maintain the necessary concentration on his Area of Responsibility because of separation of focus. Indeed, he might even have taken his eye from the scope momentarily.

His first shot hit a chain link fence and disintegrated. The spotter, watching through binoculars, exclaimed: "He's still up! It's not a hit! *It's not a hit!*"

With that audio confirmation of his own visual, the sniper fired again within two seconds. This time his round struck center mass. The offender went down without getting off a shot.

In communication between you and the spotter and back to command, *sectorizing*—numbering the components of the barricaded building—may conserve words and reduce confusion. Rather than referencing the sides and corners by *direction*, which may be unreliable in an unfamiliar area...at night...or when the building is irregularly shaped or set at an angle, one format is this:

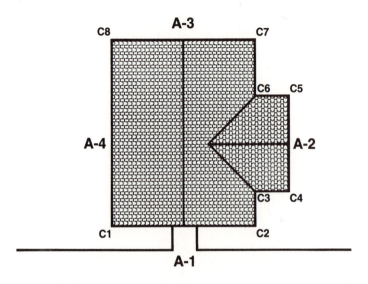

A-1 always refers to the *front* side of the structure; that is, the street or address side. The other sides are then numbered in military-map fashion—*counterclockwise*...to your right as you'd face the building. (With circular buildings, consider dividing the structure into quadrants that would equate to four "sides".) C-1 is always the *left-hand* corner on the A-1 side, with other corners also numbered counterclockwise around the building.

Command personnel as well as tactical officers should have a *sketch* of the building, sectorized. Then if your spotter reports where he observes the subject by number designations, everyone understands immediately where he is. Where appropriate, your spotter can add *landmark references* ("That's the window by the big tree") to double-assure clarity.

As an alternative, some agencies only number the principal corners of a building (C1-4), and some, to keep things simpler, number *clock*wise. Understanding and using a *consistent* system is what's important.

Traditionally, sectorizing has called for *floors* to be numbered from the top of the building *down*. This is intended to prevent mistakes where the ground floor at the back of the building is at a different level than in the front. Like this:

Floor 1 in sectorizing is considered the first level below the roof to which gas can be delivered or from which an offender can fire. Thus, a sealed attic would not normally be considered a floor. (Under stress, this "unnatural" numbering, unless it is thoroughly ingrained, may actually *add* to confusion rather than relieve it. If your community does *not* contain buildings of this configuration, you may be better off to stick with conventional floor designations.)

Openings (windows, doors, etc.) are numbered left to right on each floor along each side of the structure. Thus the sliding glass doors on the structure above could technically be designated as "A-3, Floor 3, Opening 2." Again, however, remember that clarity is the goal. If code makes your communication more complicated, you have defeated your purpose.

(Another code that some departments favor is numbering their sniper teams, rather than referring to the spotters and/or snipers by name. Then if a shot is made and the press or other outsiders are monitoring the radio, the shooter's identity is not revealed.)

As your team's surveillance of the barricader wears on, monotony, boredom and *fatigue* will be among your greatest enemies. You'll be saddled with a lot of "dynamic inactivity," that is, doing nothing and resisting the temptation to "do something." Idealists argue that snipers should be rotated so that each is in service only 20 to 30 minutes every four hours. This is impossible for practically any agency. One study suggests that snipers can be held at full alert for up to an hour before being called upon to fire without a significant effect on accuracy.[1] After that, deterioration of both accuracy and response time tend to set in. There's no doubt, though, that you can't *steadily* look through your rifle scope for very long even during the first hour. Images will get fuzzy, you may begin to hallucinate, headache may develop and certainly you will suffer painful muscle strain.

During lulls in the action, pull off scope occasionally, warning your spotter that you're doing so. The two of you should be capable of interchanging roles (but don't interchange weapons). Rotate your neck.

When the marksman takes a break in the mission, he can still observe the location from behind a position of cover.

Take a series of deep breaths. Exercise your feet, calves, thighs, stomach, chest, arms—one group of body muscles at a time—alternately tensing and relaxing them. You can still maintain your basic shooting position in case you're needed back on scope quickly. Medicinal drops and rotational exercises can refresh your eyes, but don't rub them; that will cause blood vessels to break and increase their irritation. Under stress, you'll get thirsty; chewing gum will help keep your mouth moist. Aspirin will help relieve tired muscles and painful joints, and serve as an anti-inflammatory agent. And have some Band-Aids in your pocket, too. You may nick a hand while climbing to position or accidentally close your finger in your rifle bolt. Nothing is more disconcerting than trying to get a shot sighted with blood on your rifle!

Watching the barricader, your spotter can alert you to *potential danger cues* that should pull you back on scope instantly. Such as:

- the offender grabbing a weapon...or putting a weapon to the head of a hostage...or looking out of a window with one in his hand;
- a sudden change in the offender's movement pattern, especially quick changes of location or quick looking around;
- evidence of heightened anger, reflected in more assertive motions by the offender, or changes in his facial expression.

You'll wonder: What's making him do this? Has the negotiator given him an idea...or taken an idea away from him? What's his intent? And in case it's imminently more deadly than before, *get ready for the ultimate part of your job.*

The old concept of a sniper waiting for a "Green Light" command before using deadly force is now being abandoned by a growing number of experienced teams. This signal has proved fraught with problems, including confusion over the backup code system that usually accompanies it and misinterpretation of what is said because of radio breakup.

What's becoming more current is this approach:

From the beginning of any barricade situation, you and the others at the scene are automatically authorized to use the normal discretion given a police officer by your state law and departmental policy regarding the use of deadly force. Certainly that means you can shoot in self-defense or in defense of another officer or civilian who is in risk of imminent serious bodily injury. That would include situations in which the suspect points a gun at an officer or hostage, or attacks them with any weapon capable of inflicting grave injury. In short, with justification, the decision about when to shoot is up to you.

Beyond this, if the barricader's threat is serious and persistent, some agencies authorize the use of deadly force *at the first clear opportunity,* regardless of whether defense of life is urgently required at that precise moment. For example, they may specify its use if the suspect crosses a "kill point." That's a line, generally outside the barricade, that has been predesignated as a boundary beyond which he can clearly be considered a danger to the public, say if he tries to escape.

As a sniper, your purpose in shooting is to *stop WITH CERTAINTY any further activity by the suspect.* You shoot to kill...with your *first* round.

Top preference: a *head* shot that inflicts instant brain death and severs nerves, thus preventing any further motor function. The suspect collapses upon impact and is still.

Because, unlike a paper target, a living suspect is never perfectly stationary, it may be monumentally difficult, even with a scope, to hit his head precisely where you'd like. Still, you should try for *idealized targets* (preferred aim points) because a bullet that impacts one of these spots and then explodes inside his skull will have the highest guarantee of devastating effect. Practically speaking, an expanding, fragmenting, high-powered rifle round penetrating at some 1,800-2,500 feet per second anywhere within a *2- to 3-inch square* surrounding these spots has an ultra-high probability of ending the incident. Just the traumatic shock effect to the skull cavity will almost certainly be lethal. So don't feel "I don't have a shot" if you can't bead in exactly.

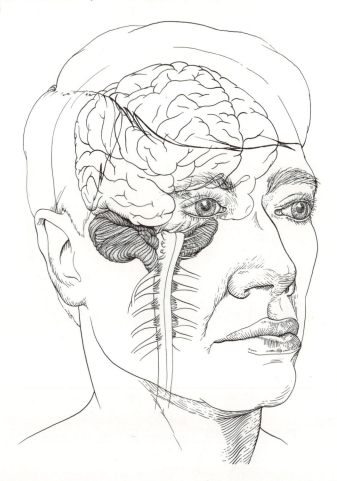

What you're hoping to sever or pulverize is his *brain stem*, the "celery stalk" about an inch in diameter that joins the spinal column to the brain. Nerves that control motor function are channeled through there, and the lower third of the stem (the medulla) controls breathing and heartbeat. Hit here, he won't experience even *reflexive* motor action. His entire body will *instantly* experience what doctors call "flaccid paralysis"; all his muscles will suddenly relax, incapable of any motion of any kind thereafter.

Regardless of how the suspect is positioned relative to you, think in terms of shooting *center mass* to his head. According to a concensus of medical examiners and forensic pathologists who've studied the incapacitating effects of sniper shots to the head, there are different considerations depending on his head positioning. If he's:

221

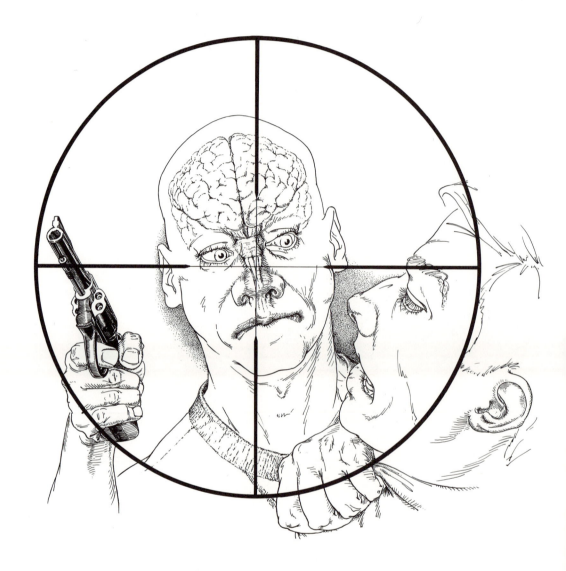

FACING YOU, your best aim points—virtually guaranteed to produce instantaneous death—are the *tip of his nose* or the center of the bridge of his nose. Actually, anywhere slightly to either side of a vertical line running from his nose tip to the top of his eyebrows is excellent, as is the area formed by a triangle between his eyes and nose tip. One advantage of the nose itself is that it's cartilage...penetrable, like tissue paper. If the suspect happens to be looking down, then raise your aim point to his hairline, so the bullet's pathway will be to the center of the back of his neck.

222

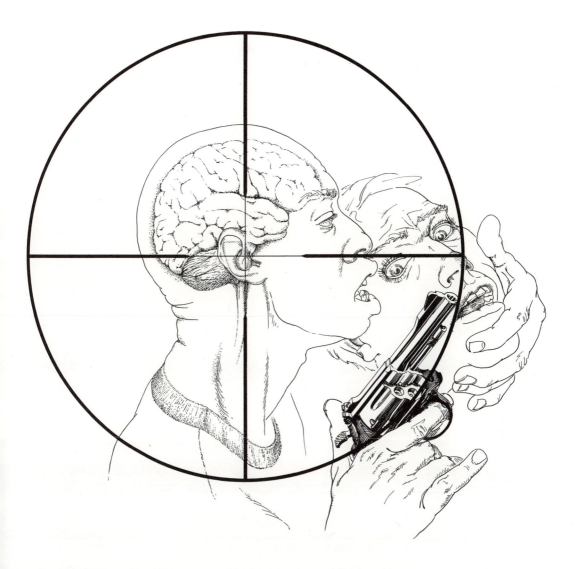

PROFILE, aim for his *ear canal*...or, alternately, his temple. If you hit right, you won't have your bullet "softened" by the muscle tissue that's below the ear lobe or the hard bone behind the ear. Gangsters in the Roaring 'Twenties understood this pathway to the brain when they shoved ice picks in their enemies' ears.

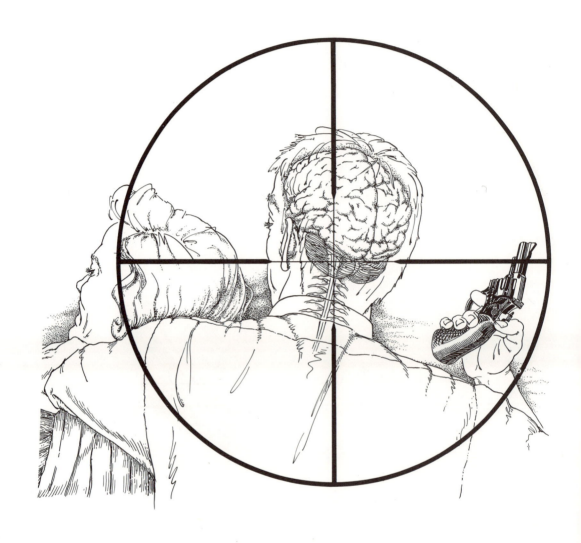

FACING AWAY, the preferred aim point is centered about 1 inch below the *base of his skull*, right where his neck begins. If you shoot above a horizontal center line on the skull, your round may deflect...and be less than incapacitating.

Usually you will have to adjust your aim point to the suspect's stance, but occasionally you may get help from other officers in engineering him into the shot you prefer. In Louisiana, officers had negotiated an escape car for a barricaded bank robber. When he came out, a hostage in tow, everyone in the inner perimeter was silent. Then by prearrangement just as he reached the curb, a patrol car parked down the street sounded a siren yelp. Startled, the gunman turned to look—and presented a clear profile to the sniper, who took him out. So slight was the tolerance for error that the bullet actually creased the hostage's face.

Being at an elevated angle to the suspect, up to about 20 feet above him, should make no difference in your aim point...or in the results. Neither will the suspect's gender; male/female anatomy is the same.

One quick reading on whether your head shot has been successful is how your target falls. If he goes straight down, limp, or pitches forward, you have high assurance of fatality. If he falls to the side, you're likely only to have partially incapacitated him. Almost never with a high-powered rifle round do you see the Hollywood phenomenon of the target being blown backwards. The pattern of kinetic energy being transferred within his skull from your shot just does not produce that result.

Sometimes because of your angle to him, you won't be able to see the barricader's head. Or maybe he's moving too much or is too far away for you to feel confident of controlling a hit there (beyond about 115 feet, accuracy on a head shot diminishes significantly). Then instead of shooting at the *smallest* area with the greatest chance of incapacitating him (his head), shoot for the *biggest:* center mass to his chest.

In Milwaukee, a barricaded subject with an officer as a hostage began firing shots at other police in the inner perimeter, vowing to "take out one of these assholes." He was highly agitated, moving jerkily. The sniper feared he'd miss a head shot and, if he did, that the suspect would then kill the hostage. The sniper blasted him with a .308, center mass in the breastbone at armpit level. The suspect flipped a backward somersault like a circus performer (that *can* happen with chest hits)—and was dead before he hit the ground.

San Ysidro, CA. Barricader killed 21 people, wounded 20 more. Killed by a marksman from the roof across the street with a center mass chest hit.

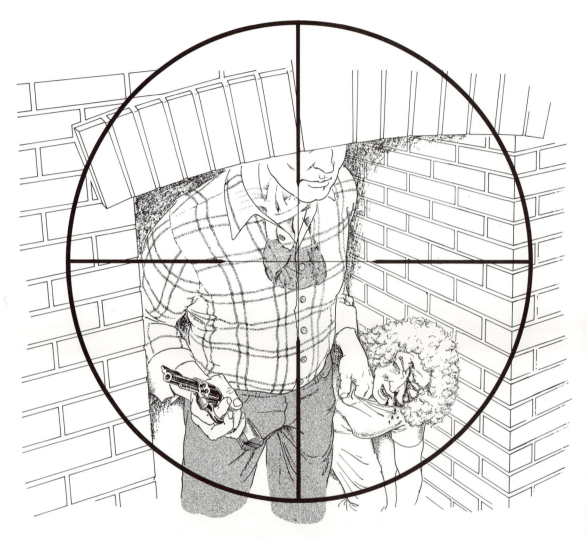

For a chest shot, that was ideally placed—mid-sternum, where the bullet strikes the largest and hardest of the bones overlying the vital organs. If soft-nosed or hollow point, a bullet hitting there expands like a mushroom upon impact, pushing ever larger sections of tissue ahead of it and causing increasingly more damage to structure as it tears through the suspect's body. The slug and fragments of sternum blast through the main sections of his heart and rip both his lungs off at the windpipe. When the bullet strikes and severs his spine, his legs buckle under flaccid paralysis.

His *arms*, however, may not be incapacitated instantly. With a chest shot, even though the suspect may technically be "dead" from the devastation of your round, there *may* be a brief and dangerous delay before he *acts* dead. His blood pressure will plummet, he'll have major tissue damage and hemorrhaging, he'll develop shock and eventually all his body functions will cease from massive bleeding and suffocation. But in the process, his brain may not die for one to two minutes after his heart has ceased to function—even if his heart has been *blown out*—because of a residual supply of blood.

During that time, his brain may command his arms to commit some simple, final act, like shooting. Such "purposeful" activity is *unusual*, but possible. It is most likely to occur in someone who is psychotic or who has no regard whatever for his life or personal injury. In other cases, the suspect may simply twitch "purposelessly" from reflexive nerve action or from a semi-conscious attempt to bring things back under control. If his finger is on a trigger, this movement can bring injury or death to someone else.

(The twitching phenomenon can also occur with head shots, if inappropriate ammunition is used. At a Wisconsin barricade, where a young gunman was holding a police chief hostage in a car, a lieutenant in the inner perimeter fired his .45 semi-automatic pistol and hit the suspect in the head. The slug ricocheted around inside his scalp but never penetrated his skull. He was still able to struggle with the chief before a second head shot, fired from a .38 revolver achieved penetration. The suspect seemed dead, but when officers rushed the car and dragged him out, he still clutched a gun in his right hand... and all his fingers were twitching. To still him, a sergeant pumped five rounds into him as he lay sprawled on the ground—action the ever-suspicious media interpreted as a vengeful, emotional outburst.)

If you have *missed* your mid-sternum target, he may be capable of much broader action. If he moves even slightly as you're firing, your bullet may hit the curved surface of a rib and glance off. Or it may penetrate between two ribs and exit his back without ever touching a vital organ. When sniper fire at a robber barricaded at a Montana airfield missed center mass and hit his upper arm, he instantly pulled the trigger of his .38 and killed a hostage with a shot to the head. Not incapacitated, a barricader remains every bit as dangerous as he wants to be.

Anticipate these possibilities and deliver an immediate second round if the suspect is not fully down and out and anyone is within his sphere of danger.

When you're dealing with *multiple* offenders—say two hostage-takers covered by yourself and another sniper—you will need to *coordinate* with your colleague so you fire *simultaneously*. Taking them out one at a time may allow the second suspect time to harm the hostages. One technique, if you are within earshot or in radio contact with each other on a clear frequency, is for each of you to keep saying aloud in a steady, low voice, "Wait... wait... wait... " so long as you do not have a clear shot. When you *do*, stay silent. Listen for the moment you are *both* silent. Allow a one-second pause, then open fire together.

In some cases, two snipers are assigned to engage a *single* suspect, particularly if he's behind heavy glass and there is fear that shots may be deflected. One option here is for one of you to aim for his head, the other for his chest, and fire simultaneously.

Head or chest or both, delivering effective rounds requires good breath control and trigger squeeze. Some snipers say: After you've lined up your shot and are ready to fire, take *half a breath* and hold it. At about the 8 second count, shoot. If you hold past about 12 to 15, you'll start to tremble slightly from lack of oxygen and move your weapon. Other snipers say: Take a good breath in as you begin to lay back on the trigger and *exhale* half of it as you begin to squeeze. This is said to relax the body and prevent quivering more effectively. Experiment to learn what works best for you. Slowly, steadily *squeeze* with the fingerprint (pad) part of your finger on the center of the trigger. If you use just the tip of your finger, it may slip off or not pull straight back. Your whole finger will move the weapon too much.

If circumstances permit after you fire, hold your rifle and yourself as stable as possible for a bit. This "follow through" assures that the bullet is well out of the barrel before there's movement or a loosened grip that could make its crucial flight erratic.

As a sniper, you want to strive for "minute of angle" accuracy—the ability to fire all your shots into less than a 1-inch circle at 100 yards. On the range, some officers with finely tuned rifles can fire into a ¼-inch circle at that distance—but usually only with ideal weather conditions, a calm mind and careful preparation.

At a barricade scene, these and many other variables are likely to be working against you. In sniper training, you learn tables and formulae for compensating your aim to overcome some interfering factors, such as wind speed, mirage distortion, sudden temperature change, bullet drop, etc. This reference material can be jotted down in abbreviated form and taped to your rifle stock to refresh your memory at the scene. But remember: it is valuable as a *guide* only.

Extensive, year-around practice at least once a month under varying conditions will be your *best* reference. You know intellectually that the first shot you fire through a cold rifle barrel may have a much different point of impact than one fired when the barrel is hot. But are you confident that you know *from experience* how to adjust your aim when you're at a scene covered with snow, your telescopic sights are obscured by frost and your trigger finger is chilled to the bone? Do you know that your gun shoots different dirty than clean? And if you cleaned it after you last sighted it in and have not fired it since, can you compensate adequately for your first shot at the scene? Or do you know how *your* shooting is affected by different *light?* Most officers tend to shoot high on a dull, cloudy day and low when it's bright and clear because of differences in the way their eyes perceive the target. Can you accurately anticipate how your ammunition will be affected by various types and thicknesses of glass? Controlled tests and street experience have shown that different rounds experience vastly different effects from blasting through different types of glass. Depending upon the angle at which it breaks a pane and the character of the glass, a .223 bullet may be off by as much as 7 *inches* by the time it finally hits its target, while the maximum deflection for .308 rounds through a glass window is usually about 1½ inch. Double-pane glass will deflect the bullet twice. Other tests have shown that high-power rounds fired at ranges closer than 9 feet will send shards of glass flying into the room that may in themselves prove lethal to hostages and other innocents. How about your shooting with a gas mask on? Even modern masks without a canister to interfere with your aim can have a *major* negative impact on your sighting a target unless you have learned to compensate for them.

Each time you practice, the prevailing conditions and the adjustments you made to achieve target accuracy should be noted in a personal data book. At a barricade, this becomes your Bible as you note the variables that exist and look back to find a practice session where they were similar, so you know what to do about them when it's time to act.

Entry

Far too many entries into barricades are made by special weapons teams because physical penetration is placed higher on the options scale than it should be. ENTRY INTO A BARRICADE BELIEVED TO BE OCCUPIED SHOULD *ALWAYS* BE ABSOLUTELY THE *LAST RESORT* —*after* waiting...*after* negotiation and manipulation...*after* gassing... *after* sniping all have been considered and rejected as impossible or tried unsuccessfully. *Physical assault should be selected ONLY when there is no other response alternative less likely to result in injury or death.* Think of a SWAT action in the ideal sense as representing "Success Without Assaulting Target." For whenever you go in after a suspect you *know* is armed and who may be able to fix on your location before you can reach his, the potential for losing one or more entry team members is great.

Success will depend on comprehensive intelligence gathering, careful primary and alternative planning, thorough rehearsal, coordinated team movement to the barricade, smooth team action during the assault and good follow-through afterwards.

In *rare* circumstances, the risk and effort may be deemed justified. Say you've got a drunk or drugged barricader who has mellowed out, passed out or gone to sleep, thereby lowering his defenses...or one you believe has killed himself...or one who has begun, or you feel certain is about to begin, killing or torturing hostages and who is unresponsive to less forceful options, such as chemical agents or dogs. Even then, the first rule for your tactical unit should be, IF YOU CAN'T WIN, DON'T GO IN.

Going in, your options are twofold:

1. **tactical entry.** This is a slow, quiet, cautious approach to the barricader's location. You will meet resistance with resistance, but the level of force actually used will be dictated by the suspect's actions. You may end up arresting rather than assaulting him. (This form of entry is appropriate *after* a barricading appears to be over, too. Even if an offender has surrendered, officers eventually will enter the location to look for possible additional suspects, bodies of victims, physical evidence, etc.)

2. **rapid assault.** Here your primary objective usually is to rescue hostages. You're not making entry for a search; you're doing it for *immediate action.* The expectation is that the barricader may very well have to be killed as quickly as possible for the safety of everyone involved. You go in hard and fast, relying on speed, surprise and radical tactics to overcome his resistance. You want the situation to be one where one second there is nothing happening and the next all hell breaks loose and your goal is accomplished before the confused suspect realizes what has happened. That was the case in Tennessee when officers swarmed into a farmhouse where a wanted murderer was holding seven people hostage. "Everyone panicked and started screaming when we came in," one of the officers said later. But even though they had to get past a door blockaded with a sofa, they moved so fast they surprised the suspect in bed with one of his captives and wrestled him to the floor before he could reach a .22 cal. revolver on a bedside table.

These two forms of entry share some important similarities, especially in preparation, but in the actual execution they have decided differences of both technique and risk.

With both, *THOROUGH* INTELLIGENCE GATHERING AND REHEARSAL AHEAD OF TIME IS ESSENTIAL.

First and foremost, your intelligence must include *realistic* information on the barricader's ability to resist you. If he has access to an automatic weapon, particularly a submachine gun, experience suggests a high probability that he has military training and is intimately familiar with tactics of urban guerrilla warfare. Ditto, if he has taken positions back away from access points, where he cannot be seen by your sniper(s). If he has barricaded doors and windows, knocked out glass to clear fields of fire or appears to keep ammunition available at multiple sites, he may well have fortified positions inside. And if he has knocked holes in walls to change room access, he can be expected to move swiftly and decisively to meet your threat from any direction. Any evidence of a paramilitary uniform would suggest the self-discipline and/or political motivation to actively resist. Remember, an increasing number of extremist religious and political groups are providing paramilitary and survival skills training, as well as sophisticated weaponry, to their members. Such information may significantly influence the entry decision.

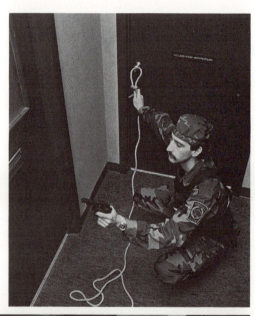

Through intelligence information, you may have the opportunity to limit escape routes for the offender by tying off doors so they won't open. The officer maintains a constant visual of his Area of Responsibility while he quickly loops the rope around the knob of the adjacent door (right) and the door next to it (below). A cover officer stands by (out of camera view).

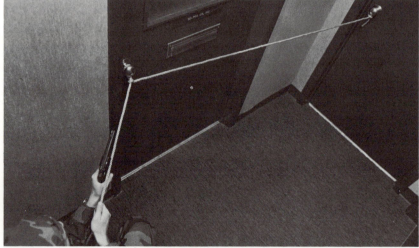

If entry is still considered feasible, information on *where* a suspect is located and the *obstacles* that will be in your path is more valuable as a foundation for entry than money; in a sense, it *is* the currency of a successful barricade entry. From the early stages of the incident, the entry team (among others) should be working to pinpoint this data as precisely as possible; tactical officers in New Jersey dealing with a man who'd shot two in-laws and then barricaded himself with other relatives as hostages even listened through the wall of his apartment with a stethoscope from next door to track his movements. Do not assume if the suspect is on the phone with a negotiator that this necessarily tells you much about where he is. Cordless phones, extensions and long cords today allow much greater mobility than in the past. In building a plan based on known intelligence, *always* "worst case" the matter and assume problems that have not been discovered, such as trapped civilians, booby traps, additional subjects and dead bodies.

The entry should be *rehearsed* continually just before the assault, so that your moves when it's actually made are automatic and even hand signals are unncesssary once you're inside. Find a building of similar design to the barricaded structure or, *out of sight of the media*, draw a life-size diagram of it with chalk or spray paint in a parking lot and practice your entry and movements repeatedly to polish your team's timing and coordination. (In Memphis, before officers stormed a house where barricaded cultists had tortured and killed a patrolman, they conferred extensively with the contractor who built the place and with a carpenter who'd recently remodeled it. In some communities, you can get blueprints, at least of newer structures, from the municipal building and zoning department.) Pile spare tires, cardboard boxes and dairy cases or tape off areas to simulate known obstacles, hiding places and blind spots.

Understand, even then, that there undoubtedly will be obstacles inside that you haven't anticipated. A psycho who barricaded himself in New England, for instance, used a chainsaw to cut away part of the floor near the door he thought an entry team of troopers would rush in. He was ready for them to plunge into the basement, where he waited behind a bunker of concrete blocks with a shotgun, a rifle and a .44 Magnum.

At the *least*, the barricader is likely to have moved furniture to block doors or provide cover for himself. And additions may have been made to the interior that don't show up on blueprints or in "identical" housing units. One team member making a wrap-around entry into a bedroom in a barricaded house collided with an extra cabinet that had been built just inside the door and knocked himself out. Another, making rapid entry, hit an unexpected vanity table so hard at groin level that he dropped his weapon and collapsed, his Focus and hands suddenly diverted to a personal Area of Responsibility.

Once the mock barricade is prepared, room entry techniques, team composition, weapons, special equipment and so on can be *tailored* to fit the physical features anticipated. Cross fires can be "planned out" or minimized, and contingencies such as losing a team member during the assault can be rehearsed. If a tactical entry is planned, all team members should jump up and down during practice, wearing and carrying all equipment they intend to bring on the entry, to be sure nothing will jangle to alert the barricader.

Entry weapons assigned should be as *short* as possible, to increase maneuverability and flexibility. Increasingly, special weapons teams are making entry armed *only* with semi-automatic handguns. Or they are supplementing shotguns with semi-automatic rifles or sound-suppressed machine pistols. If one or more of your members do carry a shotgun, it should be *sawed off* (12 inches is a favored length, if this is legal in your jurisdiction), with a guard near the end of the barrel to keep your hand from slipping off the slide into the line of fire. Some agencies also attach a scatter choke to the shotgun barrel to spray the buck over a wider area. One model turns a normal shotgun spread pattern into one that's about 4 feet wide and 10 inches high at 21 feet.

Practice controlling the *sling* on any long gun you intend to carry. Hanging loose, it may snag on a doorknob, and this has been known to result in unintentional discharges. With a shotgun, pull the sling back taut with your trigger hand and clamp it against the stock beneath your thumb. Your support thumb slips under it as you grip the slide to further prevent it from dangling. *Any long gun you carry should have a sling*, so you can properly secure it without having to hand it to another officer if you need to use both your hands.

(above left and above right) The problem of a sling hanging up as you enter. (right) The simple solution to the problem.

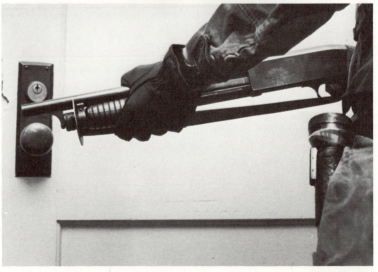

Rehearsals should include a complete equipment check. As for clothing, body armor is an absolute. Some teams now also use a Kevlar "head hood." Otherwise, consider wearing a dark woolen ski-mask. It allows full visibility, is less porous to chemical agents than a billed cap, protects against the cold and better absorbs sweat. Its shock effect can add to a subject's disorientation. It takes only a second to roll up into a cap to make room for a protective mask. Coveralls of a dark, light-weight, porous material are preferable to two-piece uniforms which can gap and let chemical agent crystals get on your bare skin. If you do wear a two-piece uniform, make sure the shirt is tucked in. If it's loose, it, too, can snag a lamp or doorknob. For footwear, high-top black tennis shoes with thick, black corrugated soles are quietest, lightest, and give the best traction on most surfaces. It is extremely easy to slip and fall while doing a fast wrap-around on tile floors in hard-sole combat boots.

During rehearsal, a *launch point* should be selected. This is the point closest to the barricade that a team can move to without being detected. In some cases, that might be immediately outside the room where the subject is barricaded; in others, it might be blocks or miles away from the building he occupies.

Up to and beyond the moment of entry, you will certainly want all possible intelligence from the negotiator, there should be undoubted confidence in his verbal skills before he's alerted that entry is about to be made. Barricaders under stress become extremely sensitive to voice and tone, and a negotiator who knows action is imminent may unwittingly betray it, giving the suspect an edge that could cost lives. On the other hand, if your negotiator is a certified cool actor, he may be able to shift subtly from trying to resolve the incident himself to providing support for your entry. Tactical deputies in California who wanted to penetrate a barricaded ranch house before sunrise to take advantage of darkness and fog asked the negotiator to get the suspect (who'd already shot four officers) into his kitchen, where they figured he'd be most vulnerable to attack and the least threat to them. The negotiator talked him into going there for a cup of coffee. Deputies came in from other locations and captured him without gunfire.

Where that kind of manipulation is not possible, a *diversion* should be used when the team is ready to make entry. A good diversion accomplishes two goals: 1) it *channels* the subject's mental focus, and 2) it *moves* him to a desired location, *both* away from the intended point of entry. Someone can bang on the front door while the team is entering the rear...or a sling shot can be used to break his window...or he can be called on the telephone...or the fire department can be summoned with its lights and sirens; your creativity will invent numerous possibilities. A diversion can be especially important when officers about to make entry are lined up on the same side of the door to be breached. The diversion can help lessen the risk of their obvious bunching problem. But stay away from anything that sounds like gunshots, such as firecrackers. You don't want to precipitate hostile fire.

Once the suspect reacts physically and moves away from the point of entry, the diversion can be followed quickly by a *distraction*. This is something designed to disorient, confuse and delay the subject's physical response capabilities. One of the best devices for this is a "flash bang" (stun grenade) thrown into the barricader's location.

Filled with 1 to 3 ounces of flash powder, this hand grenade simulator explodes after a 1 to 1.5-second delay with a boom that may literally be deafening, a brilliant white-out of light that may cause at least temporary blindness, and a staggering concussion designed to jar and disorient anyone in its vicinity. These effects can last up to 10-15 seconds. (Some flash bang models emit a shrill whistle just before exploding to make the barricader look in their direction so he gets the full dazzling/dazing effect of the blast. Some also throw out rubber projectiles to sting anyone nearby.)

Used properly, the flash bang can forestall meaningful resistance and give you time to get through the fatal funnel and cover considerable ground inside safely. Many teams would not consider making a rapid assault, especially, without this device. But it can have drawbacks. For instance, smoke from one grenade can easily fill a 12 x 12-foot room and will seriously hamper visibility. Fire-setting is a possibility. Hostages near the blast may suffer damage to hearing or sight. There is the risk also that if the suspect perceives what's happening, he may harm them. (However, if he's functional, he'll more likely be most concerned now about his own survival, and any hostages will take second place.) And there's the chance the flash bang strategy will not work as planned, injecting fresh risk into the entry. In Washington state, a grenade expected to stun a barricader with "super-human strength" who'd stabbed a detective to death with a cavalry sword failed to penetrate his apartment and instead exploded outside. A second went off inside just as the entry team was crashing through the front door. This unexpected blast startled the team but didn't faze the suspect. He slashed one officer with the sword and retreated to his bathroom. Officers shot through the door and threw two more grenades before he came out. He still was able to lunge at the officers with his blade and finally was killed with bursts of fire from the team's handguns, a shotgun and an Uzi—action that sparked a major community uproar. Sophisticated barricaders, such as terrorists, who anticipate flash bangs may wear sunglasses and ear plugs to lessen their effect.

This is the proper hand position for a stun grenade, being careful to hold the spoon with the palm rather than holding it with your fingers. (above right) Cutaway of the same device. Inside is a sub-munition to prevent the metal fuse from becoming a projectile. Never attempt to improvise or duplicate such devices. They are more complex in construction than you might think.

To maximize the impact on the suspect, consider throwing *two* flash bangs simultaneously into his location. This is usually done by non-team members coordinating with team movement. The flash bangs should be thrown *hard*, not lobbed, so they will bounce off walls and skitter around more erratically, lessening the chance the subject can kick or throw them back toward officers. Every attempt should be made to place the devices *away* from the intended point of entry to minimize the smoke effect there. If team members are waiting nearby, ear plugs or a blast shield can provide some protection from the blasts.

Detonation of the flash bang(s) can be the signal to begin entry. When the explosion goes off, the team goes in. If a *silent* distractor is used instead, like brilliant halogen spotlights, then a physical signal can be used among the team members. One option when officers are lined up on the same side of the selected entrance is the *"bounce" signal.* Leaning slightly forward, each officer tucks his butt into the stomach of the team member behind him. The first officer in line starts by "bouncing" down about 3 inches. By the time he is back up, everyone knows he has started and is relaying the movement down the line. Three bounces and you're off.

An alternative: When the point man is ready to move, he gives a thumbs-up sign. This is relayed back one officer at a time to the last in line, the rear guard. If he's ready, he starts a return signal—3 *squeezes* (less likely to be misinterpreted than mere taps) on the shoulder of the man ahead of him. When the squeeze code reaches the point man, he takes off as if signaled by a starter pistol, and the others follow.

If you are able to deploy to avoid bunching, you can coordinate entry via hand signals or whispers. Whispering can work even through a gas mask.

Once your team goes in, other officers normally should be prohibited from shooting into the barricade from outside. The only exception is when a sniper gets a clear target that he himself can identify as the suspect and clears shooting with the team via radio communication.

It is from the moment of entry on that the *differences* between tactical entry and rapid assault are most sharply drawn.

With a **tactical entry,** you may need to search the premises enroute to the subject's location, in case the suspect has moved (and he's likely to be moving around a *lot*) or there are other offenders involved whom you're unaware of. With tactical entry, you buy leverage with all the tactical concepts of a building search: field of view, advantage of angle, doorway characteristics, entry patterns, the establishment of Areas of Responsibility, the prioritizing of hazards, the use of mirrors and periscopes, etc. Except now you have more manpower (usually at least five officers) and more fire power, plus the accessibility of chemical agents and other special equipment that you can take with you.

Even with more backup available, there still will be few rooms that can safely accommodate more than two searchers. But your extra team members can be used to expand the stationary positions of security outside rooms. This allows each officer to concentrate on fewer Areas of Responsibility and thus impose superior control over the environment. It also speeds up your search. If an arrest must be made, you'll have enough personnel for three officers to focus solely on the arrest: one handling handcuffing and searching, the others covering him from different angles to avoid bunching.

Some agencies send in *two* teams for tactical entry: the first searches the places that seem likeliest to harbor threats enroute to the

One tactical entry concept is called "limited penetration." The room is cleared with a mirror. Only your arm and eye nearest the doorway penetrate. Now you quickly pass through to the next room.

barricader's location...the second canvasses the areas by-passed. The first team leaves behind patches of tape as signals. A square of red tape on a door indicates a room that was skipped over without searching ("Don't go past the red line"); green means a cleared area...a safe haven.

Be sure that *some* team members make a point of searching all *crawl spaces* in the building, especially if chemical agents have been delivered. Often there is more fresh air in these spots than in main areas. Officers dealing with a Maryland husband and wife who barricaded themselves to escape eviction discovered that they had built false walls and trap doors all through their house—and were equipped with better gas masks than the police had.

Rapid assault is infinitely more dangerous than tactical entry...its use *very limited*. It is most commonly talked about in the context of dealing with hard-core terrorists; indeed, it's modeled on antiterrorist raids conducted by the Israeli military. Special weapons teams that train for it concede that even with extensive practice they're likely to sustain casualties if they ever use it. *This is for the very best of seasoned SWAT teams only.* IT'S DEFINITELY *NOT* SOMETHING THAT A GROUP OF PATROL OFFICERS, THROWN TOGETHER AS AN IMPROMPTU TEAM AT A BARRICADE SITE, CAN PULL OFF WITHOUT SPECIAL TRAINING.

If you don't have EXCEPTIONAL intelligence on the barricader and his exact location, in addition to extensive training, FORGET THIS OPTION. Besides information on the building's layout and furniture placement and on the suspect's position, your research *must* include a photograph of him that will allow instant identification. If you don't go in with 1) a specific destination in mind, 2) a planned route for getting there and 3) a mental visual of the person you intend to assault, YOU ARE SIGNING ON FOR A SUICIDE MISSION.

Once in, *stay low...move fast* with rapid assault. You are giving up noise discipline and compensating with intelligence information and speed. One suburban department in the Midwest claims its rapid assault approach can clear the average house in *8 to 15 seconds.* The department's assault plan works like this:

Before entry, two officers are assigned to each room of the structure; if there are six rooms, 12 officers comprise the entry team. Each partner of each team is assigned a specific portion of the room as his responsibility, so that the room is divided between them. Generally, one covers the right half, the other the left. They always assume that the suspect could be *anywhere* in the room and make certain the *entire room* is covered.

When a stun grenade goes off, the assault team goes in, all through the same point of entry. Split-second timing is required here. Too fast, the team may be affected by the flash bang; too slow, the suspect may have time to recover and the crucial element of surprise may be lost. Leap-frogging past each other, the two-officer units run as fast as they can to their assigned rooms. Their high-capacity, semi-automatic pistols are up in a two-hand hold, and the officers are so close they're almost on top of each other. As they peel off at their rooms, they make immediate entry without stopping. They favor the wrap-around pattern, one officer high, one low.

They sweep, staying near the door. The offender, or anyone else who appears to be a threat, is double-shot, preferably in the head, without delay. (Some agencies specify triple shots—two chest, one head.) Other occupants of the room are ordered down and covered until a search-and-arrest team takes over. If the room is unoccupied, the officers continue to secure it until the team leader relieves them.

There are variations on this rapid-entry approach. One specifies that the first two-officer team(s) always go for the *known* subject(s). The next teams go for the *hostages* and subsequent teams search *throughout* the barricade for other subjects. If manpower permits, a third officer is assigned to each team dealing with suspects. This officer carries a shotgun and covers blind spots, such as closed closets and cabinets and over beds and desks. If one of the team members goes down, he fills in there. Other variations include: sending two-officer teams in simultaneously through multiple points of entry, at different levels...sending a K-9 with the entry teams...or first sending in a remote-controlled robot, with a retractable claw to open doors, a spot-lighted TV camera eye to scope out what's inside, a loud speaker to issue commands and a built-in shotgun.

Whatever your technique, do *not* depend on help from hostages to make rapid entry work. Hostages are likely to be frightened and even angry with you at this point and, especially in a protracted barricade, may even side with the suspect.

With either tactical entry or rapid assault, careful *follow through* after neutralization of the known offender(s) is crucial and should be included in the rehearsal ahead of time. Otherwise, a multitude of secondary hiding places may be overlooked after an entry because there is a tendency to drop back from Condition Red to Condition White after the main action is over. Yet there are numerous examples where additional suspects are discovered during this period.

Despite the special equipment that has been developed and the tactical attention it has received, resolving barricades is still more an art than a science, open to much individual interpretation and adaptation. What works for one agency may not work for another; even what works at one incident won't necessarily work at the next. The concept of an entry team *always* consisting of five officers, for example, is far too rigid for today's needs; better to be able to adjust your team to the structure, the number of suspects and the level of their sophistication.

Whatever numbers, *practice* is still the core of a successful operation. Where entry is concerned, that means focusing heavily, at least once a month, on fast friend-foe distinction, tactical decision-making, coordinated movement and *discipline of assignment*. The latter crops up again and again in training for rapid assault. Without extensive reinforcement, you'll tend to be distracted from concentrating on your Area of Responsibility when something happens in your partner's sphere...or you'll want to rush into a building the first time threatening sounds (which may or may not be gunshots) are heard...or you'll come in as a member of a secondary entry team and drop your guard because you assume the areas you're in have been thoroughly cleared by the first officers. Unless these discipline flaws are trained out, you are substantially at risk at a barricade scene.

Some of what you train in you'll probably never use at an actual barricade. Rappelling is a good example; you're more likely to use it for rescue work than for barricade penetration. But the skills of teamwork, physical control and self-confidence you develop will sharpen your performance of other tasks.

Consider including *paramedical personnel* in your training. Some agencies now send one or two paramedics into buildings with each entry team. That puts someone on hand to administer first aid *immediately*, CPR or treatment of gunshot wounds (including sucking chest wounds and internal bleeding), if needed. The medics do not carry weapons in with them, but are trained so they can protect an injured officer with his weapon. They are certified as reserve officers for liability purposes and are expected to meet the same training requirements as SWAT members, including proficiency in chemical munitions, cover and concealment and Tactical Thinking. If an officer is injured, he can be stabilized on the spot, without depleting the entry force to tend him.

5

ARMED ROBBERY RESPONSE

Every six months the FBI issues a thin report that speaks volumes about the way officers handle armed robberies. Amidst its columns of statistics, the latest casualties from such calls are tallied according to the types of victims involved and the factors that contributed to their deaths and injuries. Attacks on customers and employees of places being robbed typically are blamed on "failure to comply with the perpetrator's demands," "defensive action," or "unprovoked action by the perpetrator." But law officer victims rarely are marked down in those categories.

Overwhelmingly—and in most of these reports, *exclusively*—law enforcement officers are judged to have been hurt or killed because of the way they *responded* to the robberies in progress.

Technically, these tabulations pertain only to robberies at federally insured financial institutions. But the same conclusions can be drawn about the myriad other target locations where cops and robbers come together in what is one of the most hazardous of all calls.

Indeed, officer deaths on robbery calls (which have accounted for 11% to 21% of the annual police toll over the last 10 years)[1] occur predominately because of two "traditional" forms of response:

1. Where *silent alarms* are concerned, victim officers commonly approach in a Condition White cloud of complacency. Because so many of these calls prove unfounded (more than 95% nationally), officers automatically assume that their day is being interrupted by just another pointless run, caused by accidental activation, misjudgment, weather conditions or equipment malfunction. In his response to silent alarms, one officer routinely begins filling out a false alarm form on his clipboard as he walks toward the front door! The manager of a rural gun vault in the Midwest says that when his alarm goes off, he can hear the sirens of responding deputies while they're still over a mile away. "They always stride right in and ask if coffee's ready. If it was a real robbery, we'd all be killed."

Sometimes, despite visible danger cues, this nothing-can-be-wrong presumptiveness continues up to the moment of assault. Walking into a clothing store where an alarm had sounded, a New Jersey patrolman confronted a young black male coming out. He looked "menacing" and kept his right hand hidden. Yet the officer let him advance to within touching distance before hesitantly drawing his sidearm. He still didn't bring the weapon into firing position—until the youth whipped a .22 revolver "out of nowhere" and shot him point-blank in the face. With a bullet lodged close to his jugular, the officer at last took defensive action and shot the robber dead.

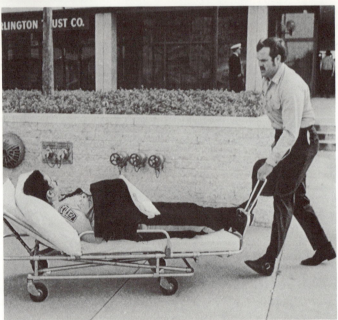

Three gunmen masquerading as telephone company repairmen shot and killed a branch manager and a police officer during a hold-up. Here telephone company personnel examine the manhole outside the bank where telephone cables were cut prior to offenders making entry. The men escaped.

2. In cases in which a robbery is reported by a victim or witness or is otherwise *verified* before an officer arrives at the scene, what's often seen then is the Crime Fighter response: high-profile, gun drawn, charging in with commando (or kamikaze!) zeal. Notified of a confirmed robbery-in-progress at a nearby bank, a Maryland chief ran to the scene on foot without backup, burst through the front door with his 2-inch 5-shot drawn and demanded to know: "Where's the robbery at?" In that case, he'd luckily barged into the wrong bank. But in Washington state a patrolman responding in much the same manner rushed face-to-face into a robber armed with a double-barrelled, sawed-off shotgun, a revolver, an alleged bomb and an alleged bottle of acid. Before that incident was over, the officer was shot several times in the stomach...a second officer narrowly missed being hit by a blast from the shotgun that blew a 6-inch hole through a pane of "bullet-proof" glass...bullets smashed through the front windows of six crowded stores during a sidewalk handgun battle...a bystander who tried to tackle the bandit was shot in the stomach...and a third officer was so frozen with fear that he could not react when the robber jumped up from a hiding place and leveled the shotgun at him. Only the fact that the weapon by then was empty permitted a fourth officer—finally—to make an arrest.

Despite repeated harrowing or disastrous results, officers stick to these response modes with fatalistic commitment. In some cases, they blatantly violate their department's written policies and risk disciplinary action in addition to their lives. More often, claims a New Mexico trainer, they respond dangerously because "most law enforcement agencies do not know how to respond safely." Officers who survive actual encounters under those circumstances are likely to parrot a 25-year veteran officer in Massachusetts. After rushing in on a savings bank holdup and managing to disarm two masked gunmen singlehandedly, he observed: "If they'd been professionals, they could have put me away. But *I know I have to do this stuff.*"

With good tactical planning, of course, you *don't* have to take outrageous risks. And with knowledge of what you're up against on today's robbery scene, you won't likely *want* to, either.

Sophisticated weaponry and careful planning by offenders increasingly are part of today's picture, in all sizes of communities. A recent "Bonnie-and-Clyde" team, specializing in knocking over banks in Texas towns with less than 900 population, armed themselves with shotguns and rifles, wore soft body armor and vowed they would kill without hesitation anyone who challenged them. To rob 70 patrons in an urban pool- and dancehall, another team came equipped with automatic and semi-automatic weapons and more than 100 rounds of extra ammunition. They exchanged more than 70 shots in a battle with police before one was killed and the other surrendered. In a raid on a small bank in California, officers were up against five extremists armed with an AR-15, a .30 cal. carbine, three rifles, two shotguns, four semi-automatic pistols, five revolvers, 5,000 rounds of ammunition and 21 homemade, shotgun-launchable grenades. Not surprisingly, the robbers slew one deputy and wounded eight others. (The deputy who was killed, incidentally, made the fatal error of popping back up in the *same* spot to resume firing after pausing to reload.) More recently, five other male robbers struck a small-town bank in Louisiana on payday for a nearby army base. They were disguised in SWAT-like blue coveralls and police riot helmets, carried military weapons, moved with military precision and arrived and left in a stolen, jet-powered helicopter. And in several states, police have encountered a roving robbery band of refugees from the Cuban "Freedom Flotilla," all with military training, all adept with multiple weapons. As part of their planning, they employ a back-up car whose sole purpose is to intercept responding police units. Says one report: "They favor excessive violence and are not afraid of shooting it out, even in the face of insurmountable police resistance."

An eerie example of the kind of mind that can pull off a robbery. (top) The robber in this case has walked into a bank where the officer with hands extended had previously been sitting, doing paperwork. (The policy of his department is to encourage officers to write reports in public locations for visibility purposes.) The offender walks in and draws down on the officer. (lower left) The offender disarms the officer and places his gun inside the paper bag and withdraws a claw hammer. (lower right) Moments later the offender repeatedly beats the officer with the hammer, almost scalping him. The offender did escape. A miracle the officer wasn't killed.

242

This female robber was part of a team that hit banks in Texas. In addition to being armed with a Colt .45 semi-automatic, she allegedly was wearing soft body armor. Note what she's holding in her left hand.

At the core of such planning is Tactical Thinking, offender style. Example: entries in a crude notebook recovered from a would-be supermarket robber who tried to kill a reserve officer in Nevada. Under "Reminders for Robbery," he noted the importance of choosing a location that cannot be easily surrounded by police...of parking the getaway car where it is least detectable...of "knowing all possible exits and cover opportunities before entering a building"...of remaining "concealed from outdoors" while inside a robbery site...of anticipating "the probable directions of approach" by patrol cars...of making "confusing turns" when fleeing the scene and so on. Also listed, amidst detailed diagrams of robbery targets and tips on taking hostages, were 23 "rules" for winning shootouts with police. Such as:

ambush or surprise attack.

Use cover for protection and also to confuse the opponent as to the next point from which an attack will come.

left If pursueed, make right turn and stop on right side of street, get out quick and use door or parked car for cover.

Predict an opponent's cop move for his gun and beat him to the draw.

A wise fugitive looks for plainclothes cops and recognizes one about as well as the cops recognize him. The first to be convinced has the advantage.

Most robbers, of course, still operate more on impulse and intuition than with elaborate strategy. (Indeed, three-fourths of bank robbers don't even disguise themselves, despite the widespread use of surveillance cameras.) But their motivation and desperation can be just as dangerously high. Nearly half of those robbing financial institutions are narcotics users and about 46% are armed. These proportions are undoubtedly even higher among those you might encounter preying on high-risk retail businesses during nighttime hours.

Robberies usually are over fast. Under two minutes is the rule of thumb, so the robber may well be gone by the time you respond.

But not always. Not dependably.

One study relating response time to apprehension rates indicates that even when you take four minutes to reach the scene, there's a 50-50 chance that the robber(s) will be apprehended.[2] This suggests a high proportion of police-offender confrontations *at the scene.* If you are almost there when you get the call, the odds are even higher. Or, if the thieves are going for big money (like extremist groups conducting bank "take overs") or if they meet resistance inside, they may take 15 minutes or more to pull off the heist, extending the chances of an encounter.

When they come out, even without the influence of drugs, they're on an adrenalin high from stress and excitement. Without doubt, *they* are in Condition Orange.

In making your response to *any* robbery call, your safety is best assured if you assume the robbery is still in progress...and you *anticipate an armed confrontation.*

Approach and Deployment

The basic rule is: *DO NOT ENTER the robbery location initially.* Inside, the odds dramatically favor the offender. In a confrontation there, you must play by his rules on turf he controls.

In terms of Thought Processes, you usually cannot Locate, React and Identify any threat until you are inside, yet the robber may long before have anticipated your probable point of entry and be prepared to shoot while you are passing through that fatal funnel. He has only to key on your uniform, while you may face uncertainties. *Who is the offender?* In convenience store robberies, the stickup man may pretend to be a customer or stand behind the counter posing as a clerk while the true clerk is shaking on the floor out of sight. In Missouri, an officer who entered a jewelry store in response to a silent alarm met a man with a cane coming from behind a display case. He said he was the owner and that he had fallen and tripped the alarm accidentally. In fact, the owner was bound and gagged with his employees in the basement. The imposter was part of a robbery team that shot and killed the officer as soon as he turned away, convinced nothing was amiss. *Where are my other potential threats?* Increasingly, offenders are using one or more unobtrusive back-up men with hidden superior firepower at strategic locations inside. These so-called "tailgunners" often have specific instructions to "eliminate" any officer who interferes. They may initially be hidden from you completely. (One m.o. in supermarket robberies is for a backup gunman

[2]U.S. Senate Subcommittee on Criminal Law, hearings on pharmacy robbery legislation, 1982.

to prone out in a checkout aisle with a shotgun. He has target acquisition on anyone entering, yet he cannot be seen.) Or they may be indistinguishable from customers and other witnesses. Two California officers responding to a holdup alarm at a jewelry store walked right in and directly approached the proprietor. In the presence of several unidentified people whom they took to be bystanders, they asked him if everything was alright. He very quickly raised his hands—and four nearby "customers" drew hidden weapons and started shooting. One officer was wounded and his partner killed, along with two of the gunmen.

Location of the Missouri jewelry store robbery.

How many robbery offenders do you see in this bank surveillance photo? The answer is visualized on the next page.

246

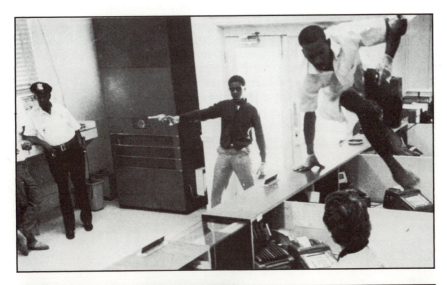

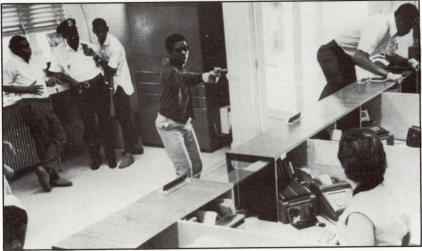

A team of three robbers in action. A fourth waits outside in the getaway car. One offender holds a gun to the head of a security officer. What chances do you think you'd have making entry on this?

The fact is that alone or perhaps aided by another officer, *there are simply too many Problem Areas and Areas of Responsibility for you to control inside a location.* Plus, your control options may be severely limited. A robber in reacting to his threat (you) can use maximum force with only one consideration in mind: escape. Yet in the presence of innocent bystanders occupying a confined space, *your* use of such force may be impossible.

Moreover, in entering some locations you may be mistaken for the robber you've come to apprehend. Responding to an alarm from a doctor's residence early one morning, officers near Baltimore climbed through a glass door that had been broken and forced. They shouted out "Police!" several times to identify themselves. Yet when they tried a bedroom door upstairs, a shot suddenly blasted toward them from the other side. The doctor, huddled in the bedroom, thought they were home invaders and was prepared to stop them with his .357 Magnum.

Instead of rushing in, you can gain the advantage of surprise by waiting *outside* for any bandits who may still be at the scene. There you *buy time* to possibly gather intelligence about the number of offenders, their weaponry and their escape intentions…and you establish *tactical superiority*. Maintaining distance from the location, you diminish your risk of ambush or of being taken hostage. If you *are* assaulted, research has confirmed that the greater the distance between you and your attacker, the greater your chances of surviving. Also, by restricting any challenge of the robbers to the outdoors, you lessen the threat to civilians inside from stray or ricochet rounds should shooting develop; they at least have the outer walls of the building as a shield. If you are seen and the robbers inside seize hostages, the situation even then is almost certainly less threatening to the victims than an immediate shoot-out in their presence. *The more you can slow down the events at an in-progress scene, the better you will be able to contain and control the incident and bring it to a successful conclusion.*

Good deployment begins with a *low-profile approach*. To avoid giving offenders an early warning and unnecessarily drawing curious civilians into the kill zone, your overhead lights and siren should be turned off a sufficient distance from the scene. In the case of your siren, that's at least a mile away in urban settings, perhaps even farther at night or in the country. In some jurisdictions, you'll need to slow down from that point on because state law or department policy requires that your emergency accessories be activated so long as you're driving at emergency speeds. Be sure your radar unit is turned off, too. During some robberies, lookout men are stationed outside with "fuzzbusters."

Another reason for a low profile approach is the possibility of the robbery occurring directly outside the business. Two people are outside. The one on the right is holding up the other man.

Usually only two officers need respond to the immediate scene. Additional patrol cars rushing in to join the excitement will only increase your chances of being made, add to the confusion and set the stage for a tactical "clusterfuck." Extra backup can best serve to control traffic or to patrol side streets which may be used as getaway routes; if the call has been received within 5 minutes of the robbery, the gunmen are probably still well within a 5-mile radius of the scene.

As an assigned responding unit, try to avoid using the street of the incident until the last possible moment. Approaching along a parallel street and then turning onto the street of the robbery at the nearest intersection will maximize surprise if a lookout is watching.

If the robbery location is at GROUND LEVEL:

Where possible, you and your partner or backup want to deploy essentially at diagonal corners of the target building, so that each can monitor the Areas of Responsibility on two sides. At night you can illuminate both sides by parking so your headlights shine on one side and aiming your spotlight on the other. (If you approach the building, however, be sure to turn the lights off.) If you must respond alone, take a position where you can observe the robbers' *most likely exit.* That also should be your destination if you are the first responding officer of a team. Whoever arrives first is considered the primary officer and directs the response from then on.

Deployment should be preplanned and rehearsed. Some departments compile confidential booklets for their patrol personnel, in which sites with a high risk of robbery are diagrammed and the safest observation points for responding officers to position themselves are clearly indicated. The approach path for each officer...recommended cover...and cautionary reminders pertinent to each location are itemized.

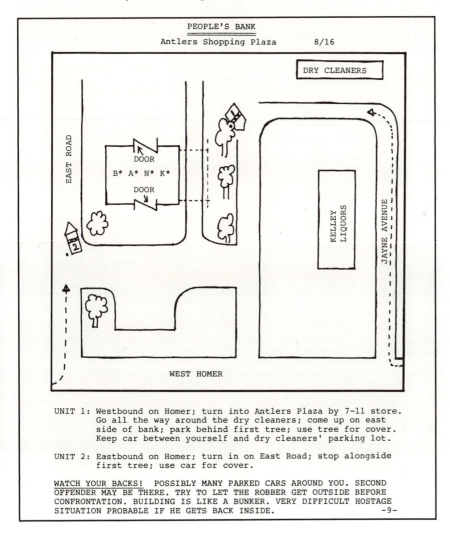

PEOPLE'S BANK
Antlers Shopping Plaza   8/16

UNIT 1: Westbound on Homer; turn into Antlers Plaza by 7-11 store. Go all the way around the dry cleaners; come up on east side of bank; park behind first tree; use tree for cover. Keep car between yourself and dry cleaners' parking lot.

UNIT 2: Eastbound on Homer; turn in on East Road; stop alongside first tree; use car for cover.

WATCH YOUR BACKS! POSSIBLY MANY PARKED CARS AROUND YOU. SECOND OFFENDER MAY BE THERE. TRY TO LET THE ROBBER GET OUTSIDE BEFORE CONFRONTATION. BUILDING IS LIKE A BUNKER. VERY DIFFICULT HOSTAGE SITUATION PROBABLE IF HE GETS BACK INSIDE.   -9-

Advance contact from your agency should be made with the manager of each location, of course, to be certain he understands what you will and won't do in your response and what will be required of him and his employees to mesh with your procedures. If location guidelines are not issued by your agency, you and your partner can develop your own response plans for sites on your beat. These can be incorporated in your Crisis Rehearsal and in the mental games of tactics you play on patrol, as well as in actual role-playing at the scenes in practice runs.

Your deployment, like your approach, should be as undetectable as possible to anyone inside. Most often, robbers make no attempt to use their weapons inside, but if they are aware of your presence they have high motivation to start shooting or to seize hostages. In New York state, an alarm was activated when a suspect tried to take over a loan company with a 12 ga. pump shotgun. The first responding officer pulled alongside the building to look in and was quickly made by the offender, who promptly shot at him and hit him in the hand. A second officer initially approached more cautiously, but before stopping his patrol car, he let go of the steering wheel with both hands to try to free a jammed shotgun lock. His car rolled directly into the line of fire. Even though he exited the vehicle and sought cover behind a wheel, the suspect fired 27 rounds of buckshot and slugs, penetrating the officer's "barricade" and leaving him disabled with multiple hits. In North Carolina, two armed bandits who were still inside a bank gathering up more than $76,000 15 minutes after the robbery started were tipped off to a police presence when an officer walked up first to the locked front door, then to the back door trying to get in. "The robbers never intended to be involved in a hostage situation," a report concluded later. But one was "cinched by the police officer." The robbers fled by surrounding themselves with a human shield of six bank employees. In a stolen station wagon, they led a reckless hostage motorcade at speeds up to 90 miles an hour through heavy nighttime traffic. When a roadblock failed, a federal agent finally climaxed the pursuit by crashing head-on into the hostage vehicle, touching off a shootout that left one agent wounded.

An example of good angle parking to the alarm location at the far right (Convenience Mart).

Overall, it is estimated that nine out of 10 hostage situations that develop out of robberies occur because of a too-visible first responding officer. Your deployment should also be as undetectable as possible to potential criminal backup *outside,* who may be in walkie-talkie communication with the robbers inside.

Two robberies that went sour because of early detection of uniform personnel. (top) One of four gunmen (stocking cap) talks with a negotiator inside a supermarket where 40 clerks and customers were held. Even here there was too much police visibility. (above) The actual robber who was portrayed by Al Pacino in "Dog Day Afternoon".

Besides the obvious considerations of concealing yourself and your vehicle, invisible deployment demands that you be conscious of:

Your sound. Calls blaring from your radio can locate you as easily for the offender as your standing in the open. Turning your car radio low and using an ear plug for your portable can provide you audio "concealment." In some cases, your radio transmissions may be monitored by an offender with a scanner. You can at least avoid revealing your *exact* location by referring to deployment points by the pre-arranged letter designations for buildings, as described in connection with barricaded subjects. (This also gives your partner a shorthand cue to finding the corner that's diagonal to your location for his deployment.)

Your movement. *Never run* from your vehicle to your observation position. Running officers draw civilian rubberneckers who may give away your presence, eliminate your opportunity for surprise, impede your tactics or become inadvertent targets. Also, running heightens your stress reaction, which can hamper your ability to shoot.

Your lighting. At night, roll to your position with headlights and spotlight blacked out, if possible. *Remember the risk of being silhouetted.* A young officer responding to a silent alarm at a Southern military base, for example, stood under a street lamp to wait for his backup! At some convenience stores, the lighting design can aid your deployment. Because of bright lights directly outside the front doors, offenders inside will be unable to see much beyond the entry area. Knowing which potential targets on your beat offer that advantage will increase your positioning options.

Your cover. Some locations, especially all-glass financial institutions set in the middle of parking lots make a safe approach nearly impossible. If you have binoculars or a monocular, you may be able to use cover a considerable distance away and still survey the scene adequately. Or a mailbox, a parking lot light pole, a parked car or your own patrol car may be practical cover closer in. If you deploy in a parking lot, try to keep your visibility to a minimum by parking your car behind a larger vehicle. You may have to give up an undetected arrival. But NEVER GIVE UP COVER OF SOME KIND.

During this initial period, you may be able to discreetly control pedestrian traffic to clear a "free-fire" zone between yourself and the exit, your principal Area of Responsibility. When a Virginia officer responded to a bank alarm recently, a female civilian was sitting in a car parked between his observation point and the location. He quietly advised her to take refuge in a cleaning shop nearby until the call was resolved. This protected her but left her car still in place to provide him additional cover and concealment.

As for pedestrians who may be heading into the location, you'll have to make a difficult judgment call. If you give up your tactical advantage to warn them not to enter, you may motivate a hostage-taking inside if offenders there now realize officers are deployed outside. Plus, you may make yourself vulnerable to assault. On the other hand, if you don't issue a warning and someone unwittingly walks into a dangerous situation and is injured or killed, you may be considered liable. Whatever your decision, be ready to substantiate *why* your best judgment dictated the action you took, based on the factors known to you.

If the robbery location is OTHER THAN GROUND LEVEL:

The same approach-and-deployment considerations apply, although the stickup is reported on an upper or lower floor, say at a bank in a high-rise office building or a pharmacy in a hospital basement.

Your most prudent deployment will still be outdoors, anticipating the robbers' exit. Inside you will be exposed to the risks of moving through hallways, up or down stairwells or elevators and past innumerable possible hiding places to reach the robbery vicinity. You'll face all the dangers of a building search without the time to resolve them systematically, plus the probable presence of civilians at close quarters hampering your response. Even attempting to deploy successfully inside the main building but outside the robbery site will be unnecessarily hazardous.

With robberies reported from inside enclosed shopping malls, the same rule applies: let the robbers come outdoors to you. Don't get sucked into territory they can better control.

Four officers "take position" on the ground floor of an office building in which a major robbery took place above. If you were one of the two robbers and looked out the window, do you think you would have a target?

As you approach and deploy at any location, *be alert to possible backup offenders and getaway cars.* Try to take in the whole scene. *Listen* for sounds that may be signals: whistles, car horns, shouts. *Scrutinize* doorways, shadowed areas, parked vehicles (including under them) in alleys and parking lots. *Watch* for individuals who start walking away...who abruptly change posture; such as stiffening or slumping in a car...or who approach your patrol car, especially if their hands are concealed. *What seems innocent may not be.* A band of robbers that hit a jewelry store in Oklahoma stationed five armed lookouts outside, one of whom stood quietly at a bus stop like a shopper. In Michigan, a backup offender dressed in janitorial coveralls appeared to be assembling a vacuum cleaner in the trunk of his car. The vacuum bag actually contained a sawed-off shotgun. Two officers in New York were killed by a lookout dressed as a nun, who cut loose with a 9mm pistol hidden in her habit.

Stereotyping of either suspects or vehicles can leave you open to unexpected attack. In California, 11 stickups were pulled off by a 15-year-old boy, who rented chauffeurs and limousines to drive him to his target locations and wait outside while he completed his "income transfers." In the Oklahoma jewelry store heist, the getaway vehicle was a cumbersome (but deceptive) motor home, and in another state the getaway car pulled a horse trailer; the robbers just jumped in back. In a Midwest bank robbery, the backup was left behind on a curb in front of the institution as a rear guard. Because he was dressed like an executive, the first responding officer mistook him for a bank official and pulled right up to him. "Come on, get in! Let's go get 'em!" the officer said...and opened the door to his executioner.

Don't wait until you are in your deployment position to be alert for lookouts. One of the last things you want is for a backup offender to be *behind* you with a gun. A young officer in Maryland who tried to approach a jewelry store robber at a shopping center suddenly found himself caught in a cross-fire position between the suspect and a backup gunman who came up from the officer's rear. Both offenders opened fire, and the officer was slain by 9mm and .38 cal. hits to the chest and back.

If you can arrest a backup unobtrusively, particularly the wheelman of a getaway vehicle, and then disable the vehicle, you may save yourself and fellow officers the many risks of a high-speed chase. But be careful that your actions do not alert offenders inside. When a sergeant took a lookout into custody outside a money exchange in Missouri, the robber was watching from just inside the front door. He came from behind, knocked the sergeant down with a blow to the head, then fired two shots at him as both offenders escaped.

If you can't act covertly, you may be safer to summon additional backup of your own, take surveillance positions that will allow you to control the suspect vehicle and anyone approaching it...and wait.

Verification

To verify the status of the call, some agencies at this point still send plainclothes officers into the location. The theory is that they'll be mistaken for customers by any robber(s) and thus can see what's going on without revealing the uniformed presence outside. In other cases, officers outside try to cautiously approach the site for quick peeks within. At some banks, they may attempt a visual through the teller window of an attached drive-in facility, relying on the bullet-resistant glass as cover.

Both these tactics offer a false sense of security.

Quick peeks can easily be detected and even "bullet-proof" glass is not necessarily an effective shield. When high-velocity ammunition hits it, the bullet may indeed be stopped. But the impact can send a chunk of glass about the size and speed of the bullet flying out the opposite side toward you, with potentially lethal results.

Using plainclothes officers for "free" looks naively underestimates the "radar" that seasoned offenders have for officers in *any* garb...fails to take account of the risks involved if the robbery *is* in progress and the officer tries to take action...and leaves little leeway for human error from overconfidence or miscalculation. A detective sergeant in soft clothes responded to a silent alarm in California by walking up to the desk of a bank official who was talking with a seated visitor in a three-piece suit. The sergeant identified himself to inquire about the alarm, and with that, the "safe"-looking "visitor" spun around and shot him dead. He had, in fact, been conducting a robbery, but with such short time and distance involved, the sergeant had no chance to overcome his tactical gaffe. With a multi-agency response or a large department where plainclothes personnel may not be readily recognized by uniformed officers, there's an additional risk of misidentification. When several departments responded to a small-town bank alarm in rural New York, a detective rushed inside from the rear, determined that the alarm was unfounded, then ran out front to announce the good news. Uniformed personnel mistook him for a fleeing felon and cut him down with gunfire.

Where plainclothes officers are involved in the response, they can more safely be used patrolling side streets, alleys or logical escape routes looking for the getaway car or for fleeing suspects.

To initiate verification, rely on the telephone. One option is for you or a fellow officer to call into the location from a nearby phone, preferably one that allows you to maintain your surveillance of the Problem Area. To facilitate this, some officers carry a list of the numbers and the names of the managers of all alarmed locations on their beat.

An alternative is for a dispatcher to make the call (on a non-beeped line), either at your request or in adherence to department policy. If the call indicates that the robbery either is over or never existed in the first place, the manager or some other representative is asked to come outside *alone* and meet you. *You and other officers remain in a cover position* until you confirm his or her identity and feel assured the scene is safe. (When the original report comes from a robbery victim rather than from a witness or a silent alarm, the complaint taker can request at that time that the complainant go outside *alone* and await your arrival. If he's afraid to do so either because of the neighborhood or the possibility that the robbers may still be around, he can be kept on the line and notified when you're in position and the area is secured, then be advised to exit.)

As you study these surveillance photos you could write your own caption. This really reinforces the extreme disadvantage you put yourself into if you enter an alarm location without verification as to status or description. Just think if this had been you entering and the offender had been a lot less cooperative. The important thing here is to learn from the near-misses of others.

On departments where this "calling in/coming out" concept is not standard policy, the assumption often is made that civilians won't cooperate because of inconvenience or a reluctance to "look foolish." But in community after community, survival-oriented agencies are proving that with the right eductional program, cooperation *can* be won. Besides saving lives, having the original contact with police occur outside the robbery site also tends to hasten the broadcast of "wanted" descriptions and to better protect evidence that robbers may have left behind inside.

To camouflage the call into the location, a prearranged code is sometimes used. A binder can be kept in the communications room with the names of persons at each location who know the code. At least three individuals should be listed to cover absences. The dispatcher asks for one personally or calls their direct number. Example:

DISPATCHER: Mr._____ (name of designated person inside location), this is Mr. Hansen's office. Will you be able to keep your appointment tomorrow?
RESPONDENT: No (if alarm is unfounded). Or: Yes (if robbery is in progress).
DISPATCHER: (if answer is "Yes"): Exactly what time can you be here?
RESPONDENT: I think 2 o'clock (hour stated indicates number of offenders believed to be involved).

Another option for a prearranged signal, among many that are used, involves this type of chart, kept in your communications room and also posted near the phone in locations with a high risk of robbery:

	1	2	3	4	5
A	18	25	19	12	29
B	20	11	13	17	27
C	22	24	14	21	30
D	15	16	26	23	28

The dispatcher can say, for example: "This is the accounting office. Can you give me verification on C-4?" The respondent knows to look where column C and column 4 intersect and, if everything is okay, replies: "21." Any other number—or no answer—indicates a robbery-in-progress.

If you call in on your own or if your dispatcher calls but is not equipped with an established code for that location, the initial inquiry still can be kept unrevealing to an offender who may answer or overhear. There's no need to identify yourself outright. You might begin by pretending you're with the telephone company and ask whoever answers, "Are you having a problem with your phone lines?" Because silent alarms travel via telephone lines, this may cue an astute employee to your true identity and prompt him or her to answer "yes" if there's trouble. If not, you can continue probing discreetly, evaluating the other voice for nervousness, evasiveness, deceptiveness or other clues. Gradually, if you feel comfortable doing so, you can make your questioning more direct.

If you're told or have reason to believe a robbery is going on, ask the person you're talking to to discreetly lay the receiver down rather than disconnecting or putting you on hold. What you overhear through the open line may provide additional intelligence about the robbery status and the robbers' intentions.

Some departments have arranged for businesses to place a colored placard in a window to signal officers outside when it's "safe" to enter after a robbery report, but this trick is by now well-known among offenders. You're better off having a representative from the location exit and approach your position for first-hand verification that the coast is clear.

Regardless of what response is given to the initial call in, *continue to operate as if a robbery is in progress.* Before the representative comes out, he should be told what door you want him to use. Select the exit you can most easily control, such as one that opens into a deserted alley rather than into heavy traffic. You should be given a description of him and his clothing, assuming you do not know him personally. If he has picture ID, he should be told to carry it at arm's length ahead of him; you don't want him reaching in a pocket for it outside. He should also be told to walk out *slowly*; if he dashes out excitedly, he may be mistaken for a fleeing bandit. He should be directed to some nearby landmark—a mailbox, a utility pole, a street sign—so that you can observe him for a few seconds without having to reveal your presence. He should *not* be told specifically where you or any other officers are deployed.

Once he's in view and clear of the door and you've made your initial assessment, use your P.A. or your command voice to instruct him, if you're the primary officer. You want his hands visible. Consider asking him to open his jacket so you can see that no weapons are tucked in the lining or in his waistband, if that is necessary to put you at ease. Direct him *slowly* toward the sound of your voice if he seems safe. Ideally, this will place him, with you, out of the kill zone. Reach for his I.D. from behind cover, and be convinced of his identity before you emerge.

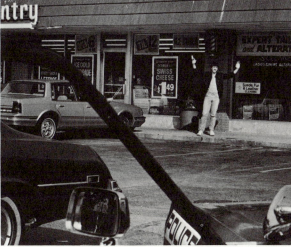

(above) A civilian exits a bank to meet you. In the window is a color-coded placard which signifies "no problem." Do not take this situation for granted. His right hand is not visible nor his identity yet confirmed. These factors justify your remaining cautious. (left) A safer situation with both hands visible. Civilian is commanded to your location with driver's license visible.

Don't be fooled by appearances. An officer deployed in a bank parking lot in New Jersey saw a man dressed in a suit and carrying a briefcase come out. Assuming he was the manager, the officer exposed his position and called out: "Everything okay in the bank?" The individual turned and shot him in the head. Even a uniform can be deceptive, considering the increasing number of offenders dressing as security and police officers to pull stickups.

Most often you can expect the representative to report that an alarm was sounded in error or that the robbers have departed. But occasionally you may encounter someone sent out as an emissary from the bandits. He may deliver hostage demands, then tell you that if he does not return others inside will be killed. Or he may have been instructed to bring you back with him.

If he seeks your advice about what he should do regarding himself, don't assume responsibility for making that decision. You can't possibly offer guarantees either way. His own conscience is as good a guide as any. Under *no* circumstances, however, should you knowingly volunteer to become a hostage yourself. That can only complicate the situation and expose you to a high risk of injury or death.

CAUTION: If no one comes out, *stick with your procedures.* Officers sometimes employ good tactics but if they don't get the response they anticipate, they readily revert back to a bad approach, to the convenience of a more patient adversary. An example occurred in South Carolina, where an officer waited outside a savings and loan for a manager to appear, according to his department's policy. But when no one emerged, the officer then *entered* the building. Three robbers waiting inside overpowered and disarmed him and took him hostage. An alert passerby outside called for help on the patrol car radio. But even with this danger sign, the second responding officer walked right into the bank, too. A fight and several shots later, one suspect was dead and the others had fled—but one officer was shot twice in the process.

Once you've interviewed a representative and feel things are okay inside, you can consider entering to double check the interior or to protect evidence and gather witnesses in the event robbery has occurred. But on the chance he *is* being coerced to lure you in, let him precede you. This may buy you precious milliseconds if you spot danger. If there's no hazard, most representatives will welcome going first because it psychologically allows them to resume a "dominant" leadership role after being under your control. Only one officer should enter initially. He should come out and give an "all clear" before others go in.

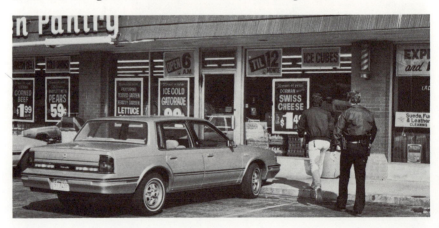

Be conscious of where offenders may be secreted inside. Some officers keep sketches of the interiors of robbery-prone locations on their beats on 3 x 5 cards, with special attention to hiding places that are not immediately in their field of view upon entry. Take advantage of fixtures such as anti-shoplifting mirrors in convenience stores to increase your surveillance capability. Even if an arrest has been made, other offenders may still be present. In one bizarre case in the Los Angeles area, a bank was hit simultaneously by two robbers who did not know each other. When one exited and was apprehended with $10,000 in his briefcase, the second was still inside tucking his $160 loot into his wallet.

Maintain your alertness as you approach and enter, even if you are not the first officer in. An Oklahoma patrolman thought it was safe to leave the cover of his patrol car at a filling station robbery when he saw a fellow officer already inside the cashier's office, walking calmly toward a clerk at the cash register. Not until he was about to stride through the doorway did he see a suspect crouched behind the counter with a shotgun on the clerk. The officer inside had not yet spotted him. When the patrolman shouted out a warning, the suspect jumped up and started firing, hitting them both.

When no call is made into the location to verify status, you are being robbed of important input. (top) This masked robber did pull out the phone and was greeted by a sheriff's deputy who answered the alarm and walked in. He shot and killed the robber. Extreme caution should be exercised (at bottom) in making further entry only after you are assured there are no additional offenders and back-up is present.

If phones have been yanked out...or robbery victims are at gunpoint...or they have been tied up, locked in a refrigerator or vault or seriously injured, a verification call may not be answered. Also, some alarm systems shut down phone communications. When that happens, wait at least 10 minutes more, anticipating a sudden exit by the robbers. During this period, you may be able to get a visual with binoculars through a window. You also can address the location over your P.A., advising a representative to come out or the robbers to surrender. As more officers are available to come to the scene, begin clearing the area and establish a firm inner perimeter. Your first goal is to stabilize and contain the situation, as you would with a hostage barricade. In the absence of new intelligence or new developments, as a *last resort*, you may need to summon or assemble a tactical team to make an extremely cautious emergency entry. You'll want to use a side or back door to which you can obtain a key, if possible, following good entry tactics.

Confrontation

Sometimes the person you'll meet coming out of the location, perhaps even before the verification call is made, is the offender himself. This is particularly likely when your response is especially fast...the robber is especially slow...or you've been assigned to watch a "stop-and-rob" location as part of an outside stakeout team whose purpose is to confront the robber redhanded.

If you're not in a protected position at the moment of confrontation, your first consideration should be tactical retreat to cover. If you are already deployed, your actions then will be determined by a split-second evaluation of the circumstances.

This robber was greeted with a special surprise. Officers outside used tear gas to get the offender to exit. He did, but look at the deployment. A more observant offender would have spotted the pepper fogger as a giveaway that the police were in vulnerable positions.

Do the number of Problem Areas and Areas of Responsibility seem within the ability of you and other officers present to control? If so, shout out: "Police! Don't move!" and get the action stopped from behind cover. You want the offenders facing away from you...their hands up...their visible weapons down on the ground, out of reach. Order them away from entrances and windows to a point where you can control them, then prone them out, secure them, search them and complete your arrest.

Are you outnumbered? Out-gunned? Are innocent bystanders in close proximity? Are hostages involved? Are you at a tactical disadvantage? In these cases, you will not want to risk detonating a gunfight. Your best option may be to let the robbers escape. Radio in descriptions of them, their getaway vehicle(s) and their armaments. Outlying officers may be able to intercept them under more favorable circumstances. Or you may be able to take delayed action yourself. Observing two men running from a service station stick-up, a Baltimore officer working alone followed them until one entered a store. He waited outside until the suspect walked back out. Then, using the element of surprise, placed him under arrest.

Are you, other officers or civilians in imminent danger of serious injury or death from the offender(s)? If so, deadly force may be justified. But before you play that card, be *certain* of your target identification. Not everyone who bursts out of a robbery location is an armed robber, as a rookie officer learned the hard way in Tennessee. When the rookie and her field training officer responded to a stick-up at a drive-in market, three men ran out and ignored commands to halt. The rookie shot all three. Only then did she determine that she'd killed the market manager and wounded two customers. The shotgun-wielding robber was still inside.

Whether gunplay is involved or not, you want any challenge to take place far enough from doorways that the robber is not likely to run back inside and seize hostages. As you maneuver him, keep your ballistic backstop in mind in case shooting does become necessary.

And remember his Thought Processes. Two Missouri detectives on stakeout saw a man enter a fast-food restaurant with a pistol in hand. Because the place was full of customers, they properly waited until he emerged with a bag of money before challenging him. But then one detective conveniently Located himself by stepping from his hiding place to announce his office. The suspect, who still held the pistol, fired instantly and narrowly missed the detective's head. Similarly, a patrolman staking out an adult bookstore and theater in Colorado saw a man in a ski mask run out with a canvas bag. He ordered the suspect to stop and turn *toward* him, which he did—with a .357 Magnum loaded with hollow points in hand. Fortunately, the patrolman fired first, but his risk would have been less if he'd stayed concealed during his initial challenge. Although your voice alone may Locate you to some degree, an offender is less likely to shoot—or shoot accurately—if he can only *hear* you than if he can actually *see* you.

A better performance was turned in by a Detroit narcotics officer. He was approaching a fast-food place where all employees are uniformed when he noticed a man in an Army trench coat standing behind the counter. The officer ducked behind the corner of the brick building and through quick peeks kept track of the action until two robbers emerged, one carrying a handgun, the other walking with one hand in his coat pocket. The officer waited until he had a clear line of fire, then challenged them. As the first subject swung around and pointed his gun toward the officer and the other started to withdraw his hand, the officer instinctively squeezed off two rounds and dropped both offenders. (He waited, incidentally, 20 minutes before the first responding car arrived. During this time, unbeknown to him, the brother of one of the suspects was in the crowd that formed. He had come over from the get-away car parked near the scene.)

During or after a confrontation, ALWAYS ANTICIPATE AT LEAST ONE MORE OFFENDER. Officers who deployed properly outside a Florida bank and effectively captured a robber who came out the front door with a bag of money were handcuffing him when a second offender secretly exited a rear door and crept up behind them. He grabbed one officer around the neck and shot him twice with a .22 before the officer could fight back. One round fatally severed the officer's aorta. His partner was wounded, too, but managed to shoot the suspect in the stomach.

Stay aware also of backup weapons. Some robbers hide extra guns inside the bag or satchel in which they carry their loot, counting on you to concentrate only on visible weapons and to relax your guard.

Know the weapons you have at hand. An officer in Wyoming, trying to deal at close range with an armed robber who was shooting at him, refused to use his shotgun, even though he was *carrying* it. He feared that if he fired, the spread pattern would expose civilians on the periphery to injury. He didn't understand that at such a tight distance, the fanning out

The Wyoming Incident.

262

of buckshot is negligible (about 1 inch per yard). After a small-town bank robbery in California, three deputies were showered with a fusillade from four offenders at the climax of a wild chase along a narrow mountain road. One deputy was unarmed except for an M-16 in his patrol car, which he did not know how to use. He bailed out and tried to crawl under the car, clawing at the dirt with his fingernails to dig enough room to fit. Convinced he was going to die as the attack continued, he tried repeatedly to fire back with the rifle. At first he couldn't keep the magazine from falling out into the dirt. Then he didn't know how to set the selector switch for automatic. He had to fumble with the charging handle until by trial and error he chambered a round. Even though he finally was able to get off semi-automatic shots, his control was so poor that he hit none of the assailants. They, on the other hand, wounded him and killed another deputy before fleeing on foot.

In making your confrontation decision, keep your goals in mind. Your top priorities *always* must be to protect the safety of yourself and your fellow officers and of civilians who may be innocently drawn into the incident. Much *lesser* priorities are to gain information that can be used to apprehend the offenders at a safer time or place…to recover stolen property…or to make an immediate arrest. YOUR HIGHEST PRIORITY SHOULD NEVER BE SACRIFICED TO ACCOMPLISH A LOWER ONE.

Inside Tactics

If you're *inside* a location when a robbery takes place, the *reason* you're there may influence the tactical options you have.

On a stakeout, you're anticipating trouble. You probably have a good cover position out of sight (in a back room, behind a false partition or behind one-way glass) or you're effectively disguised (as an employee, a repairman or a delivery person). If you've planned right, you have manpower (at least two officers inside plus an outside observer)…you're wearing a protective vest…you have communication equipment…you have the right firearms for the job (including a shotgun for both its psychological effect and its firepower)…and you have a pre-planned strategy for action. To a great extent, you can time your moves to maximize surprise and minimize risk.

But if you're working inside in uniform…or you're there as a customer…or you inadvertently walk in on a robbery-in-progress, you're not likely to enjoy these tactical advantages. The strengths of surprise, cover and concealment, fast target identification, fields of fire and superior firepower are likelier to belong to the *suspects* than to you. Besides the threat from obvious offenders, there's the added risk of undetected backup men or women, the same as when you rush inside from outdoors. If you're off-duty especially, you are not likely to have the support of other officers nearby…or radio communications…or a "heavy-duty" firearm that you've practiced with extensively. Members of your family may be with you, and your judgment or reaction may be hampered by the sudden interruption of "normal," non-police activities.

Assuming you or someone else are not jeopardized by imminent or direct assault, *observation without action may be your only sensible option* in such circumstances. In other words, if you can, just be a good witness. Nothing more. One study has shown that persons who actively resist robbers are 14 times more likely to be killed than those who passively let the robbery occur.[3] Officers have pulled off successful confrontations inside, of course. An off-duty highway patrolman in casual clothes was waiting in a West Coast bank line when he noticed a robbery going down at a teller station nearby. He was able to pull a handgun from under his shirttail without being seen. He took cover at the end of the counter, drew an unobstructed bead on the robber and neatly incapacitated him as he vaulted the counter. A Virginia bandit, who selected a Fraternal Order of Police bingo game to rob, was seconds away from grabbing several thousand dollars when a noise distracted him. The split-second diversion gave three off-duty officers a chance to draw guns. They shot him in the chest, legs and buttocks.

But more often, officers inside have gotten themselves and others in trouble with aggressive intervention. In Michigan when an off-duty patrolman standing in a teller line tried to interrupt a bank robbery, a backup man was watching from a desk area 5 feet behind him. He shot the officer, who fell wounded and helpless to the floor. The primary offender then ran over and fired a fatal round into the officer's head, while the victim's 2-year-old son looked on. A Kansas detective working off-duty as uniformed security in a drug store was in a good cover position when a masked robber wanting drugs brandished a gun at a pharmacist. The detective left his cover to shoot. Not atypically, he missed five times in a wild exchange of gunfire. Then when he tried to tackle the robber, he was shot in the neck. In Utah, two federal agents had just completed a banking transaction when an armed robbery took place in their presence. Although they were unarmed (their sidearms were back in their desks), they jumped the gunman. Before that fray was over, one agent was shot and grazed in the head, a woman customer was shot in the stomach and another customer was cut in the neck by flying glass. A

[3]*Bottom Line Personal* Newsletter, June 30, 1985.

If you are off-duty and armed, think carefully about whether or not you have justification to engage the offenders. (left) Here the robbers entered with a revolver and a single-shot 12 ga. Would you take them on? (below) If you have made up your mind already that *your only* action would be to engage, take a good look at what you would be up against here. A .38 revolver vs. a 12 ga. pump shotgun and an Uzi with a scope. Lousy odds for survival.

fatality may have been averted only because one of the robber's rounds failed to fire when the hammer hit it.

Even though you are uniformed and armed as security, an employer should not expect you to interfere with a robbery except in extraordinary circumstances. Your main purpose is to be high profile as a *deterrent*. If robbers decide to hit the place anyway, there's a strong probability they've figured you in their plans. You may be fingered for a hostage-taking or disarming, covered by a backup man or marked for execution if necessary. *The less threat you can appear to pose to them while they are inside, the less threat you are likely to bring to yourself and others.* If you are wearing a security uniform, for example, do not identify yourself as a *police* officer. A robber who perceives you as "only" a guard may not consider you as threatening as he would if he knows you are a cop.

Be certain, however, that you discuss the issue of your response with your employer *before* a robbery occurs. Explore such questions as: are you covered under his insurance (some police agencies won't back you up for private work)...what does he expect of you if a holdup occurs...how will his other employees respond if you're working in "soft" clothes rather than in uniform (will someone shout out, "Do something!" while looking at you, thereby revealing your police status?)...how will you try to capture the robber, if that seems a possibility...and so on. Many moonlighting officers take for granted that a robbery won't happen because "they're there," and many employers never consider any ramifications beyond protecting their property until after the action is over. Make sure you *and your employer* are educated *before* you become involved.

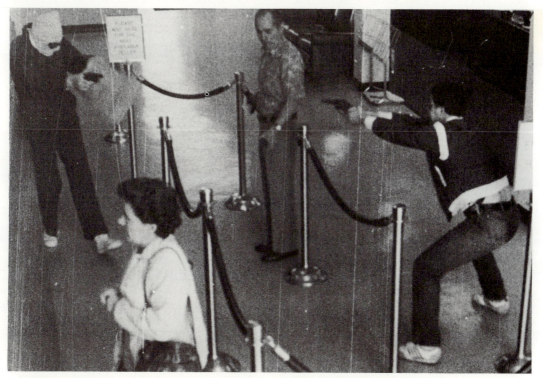

Off-duty transit officer who went inside to make a deposit suddenly finds himself defending his life against a robber who had just hit another bank for $7,200. Notice the superb two-hand hold with a slight crouch.

A decision to stay low-key is *not* an excuse for operating in Condition White. Alert, you may prevent a robbery or initiate an effective police response outside or at least keep yourself from becoming a sitting duck inside. Ideally, position yourself so you can see anyone who enters the location before they can see you. If anyone looks hinky, approach with proper field interrogation tactics or alert the police. In approaching, be conscious of persons who may be behind you and be ready to defeat an attempted disarming from any direction.

As you work, try to station yourself near cover or at least be conscious of where you can move to cover if shooting starts. Avoid standing near doorways, where you may be perceived as blocking an escape. (The risk of not acting promptly while you still have a margin of safety was illustrated in Massachusetts, where a reserve officer was on guard duty at a savings bank. From inside, he noticed two suspects in ski masks pull into the parking lot. At that point, he could have locked the doors, prevented their entry and summoned police. Instead, he waited as they approached, unable to believe they really intended to rob the place, he said later. In a matter of seconds, they were inside...the stick-up was announced...and the officer challenged them. Shooting started, with one robber and the officer firing repeatedly at each other while just 2 feet apart as they crawled around the same column in the lobby on their hands and knees. Several bullets whistled past the officer's head before the robbers finally fled. They took $300. Damage done to the bank's interior totaled over $3,000. And, yes, the officer was praised for his "coolheadedness" by his department and the city government!)

Working inside some locations (hospitals, for example), you may not always be in the vicinity of the most likely robbery sites. Be conscious, though, of where those sites are, and if you are called to those areas, always anticipate serious trouble. An off-duty policeman working security at a Minnesota hospital was summoned to the basement on a complaint that three men were suspiciously whispering in a hallway near the pharmacy. In any hospital, the pharmacy is the most likely place to be robbed, yet instead of taking the stairs and making a cautious approach, the officer took an elevator which opened directly in front of the pharmacy. By the time he got there, an armed robbery was underway. The lookout heard the elevator bell ring, signaling that the doors were about to open. In the brief gun battle that followed, the officer was fatally shot in the forehead.

The same rules of caution apply if you come into a location on police business or as a customer. Just as you want to get a good visual, especially on the areas where money is kept, *before* you enter, maintain one *after* you are inside. A patrolman who ducked into a convenience store to make a telephone call made the mistake of facing the wall rather than facing out while he talked. He didn't see a teen-aged gunman, who shot him in the back.

If you leave the main part of the store temporarily—say to use a washroom in the back—be sure to reestablish a good visual of the interior before reentering the customer area. If you discover that a robbery has started in your absence, consider exiting from the rear (an escape route rarely used by robbers) and take a good position outside. (This may also be an option rather than challenging a robber inside, if a stickup goes down while you are working security.) At the very least, remain concealed inside until the offender has left. Making a mental note of the store's layout and alternative exits as you come in can help you if there's trouble. Be particularly cautious between 1 A.M. and 3

When you enter the rear of a convenience store to use the washroom, stay in Condition Yellow when you exit. There may be a surprise by the counter that you can avoid confronting.

A.M., the prime time of robberies in convenience stores...and carry your portable radio with you.

Perhaps the most common setting in which officers witness robberies from the inside are drinking spots, during their leisure time. And the sad truth is that the vast majority of officers who have been killed or injured in taverns invited attack by *voluntarily* identifying themselves as police and thereby attracting the robbers' special attention. Incredibly, some officers seem to feel that their police status *alone* is enough to defeat an armed offender. Of course, the robbers and their "undercover" back-ups are likely to perceive the officers as "trained killers" who must be eliminated.

Your best tactic is to avoid drinking in taverns. Or at least avoid them in the *early morning hours* or when there are *few other customers.* (Never be the last guy out.) Crowded bars are less likely to be robbed, and cop bars are probably least likely of all. Neighborhood bars where you're known are probably the most dangerous. If a robbery occurs, someone is bound to look at you or call out for you to "do something" and thus "give you up." Avoid wearing a T-shirt, ring, belt buckle or anything else with a police insignia that can give away your profession. Don't throw your keys on the bar if you have a handcuff key on the ring. And be circumspect in your conversations. Some backup men or women enter taverns three hours or more before the intended stickup just to sound out who's there.

If a robbery goes down, resist your natural instinct to reach for your gun, unless your life or someone else's is directly threatened and that seems your only viable option. Your efforts to stay low-key may be foiled if the robbers decide to steal from the customers as well as the cash register. If they force you to remove your wallet and see your badge and police I.D. in there, you may be cornered into a confrontation or shot outright. You can reduce this risk by keeping your badge and police credentials in a carrier separate from your money and credit cards...or carry· them in an elasticized leg wallet...or just leave them behind in your car any time you enter a robbery-prone location. One officer who thought he would be searched put his finger down his throat and threw up on himself. The robbers disgustedly passed him by.

After the robbers have left, *continue to conceal your identity.* Without identifying yourself as an officer, you can still suggest that someone call the police, as any customer might do, and you can suggest that the doors be locked as quickly as possible to prevent the robbers from bursting back in, as they might do if the police are waiting outside. *Do not produce your gun needlessly* or initiate a foot pursuit. Remember: backup offenders usually stay behind waiting for just such developments.

Money Escorts

As a regular assignment or on special occasions, you may be asked to escort bank employees, local merchants, payroll officials or other individuals carrying large sums. Varying your pick-up times and travel routes and informing as few people as possible about this information is your first line of defense against offenders anticipating your movements and targeting you and your escortee for surprise attack.

Some departments believe that high visibility with heavy weaponry will discourage attack. But in fact, this approach may be self-defeating. In the criminal mind, high visibility = big money = worth the risk. It's usually wiser to keep money movements as low-key as possible in hopes of not attracting attention and criminal planning.

If you walk with the person you're escorting, you become easier to ambush. Through the bunching effect, you both are then confined to a tight, easily controlled kill zone. However, if you remain *in your unit,* you increase the area the offender has to control. From outside a kill zone that normal criminal logistics could support, you then provide "reactionary observation" to the escortee, who is on foot or in his own vehicle.

You're safest from being sucked into a set-up if you can start your escort as the person you're protecting leaves his location and end it as he enters his destination, without your having to physically enter either place. If he is going to a bank, say, once he's inside he enjoys the same protection from its cameras and silent alarm procedure as any other customer. Whereas if you're with him, you enter an environment with more Problem Areas and Areas of Responsibility than you can likely control alone, while you become a highly visible subject for assault or hostage-taking. The former is the worst thing that can happen to you personally, and the latter is the worst thing that can happen to you tactically. Either only complicates the situation.

When you arrive for the escort and reach your destination, try in both cases to pick a "non-obvious" spot to park. You'll need to consider not only your observation of the escortee, but also the possible deployment of multiple offenders lying in wait and the probable kill zones they could control. As you follow your escortee, visually "clear" the area ahead of you before moving into and through it, somewhat like a military operation.

If you do become involved in a high-profile escort, manpower and weaponry are important elements of safety. One option is for at least two officers to provide the actual escort, staying with the protected person all the time he or she is in transit. An additional officer, in communications contact, remains in a separate vehicle to provide the reactionary observation, staying back far enough to avoid the probable kill zone. The escorting officers should be armed and well-trained with at least shot-guns. They should carry them in the port arms, "ready" position with a fully loaded magazine...round chambered, safety on, finger off the trigger until some sign of a threat is detected.

Even this may be inadequate. Remember, robbers willing to take on a visibly escorted money run *know* they are going to encounter police or security personnel. They are likely to be prepared with strategy, fire-power, manpower and deadly determination.

Even short escorts are dangerous and require constant vigilance. A sergeant with 30 years' experience in Massachusetts was escorting a bank employee who was making a transaction between two institutions directly across the street from each other. They had to travel only a few feet...but the distance was far enough for a team of robbers to fatally wound the sergeant with six shots from a .223 cal. rifle.

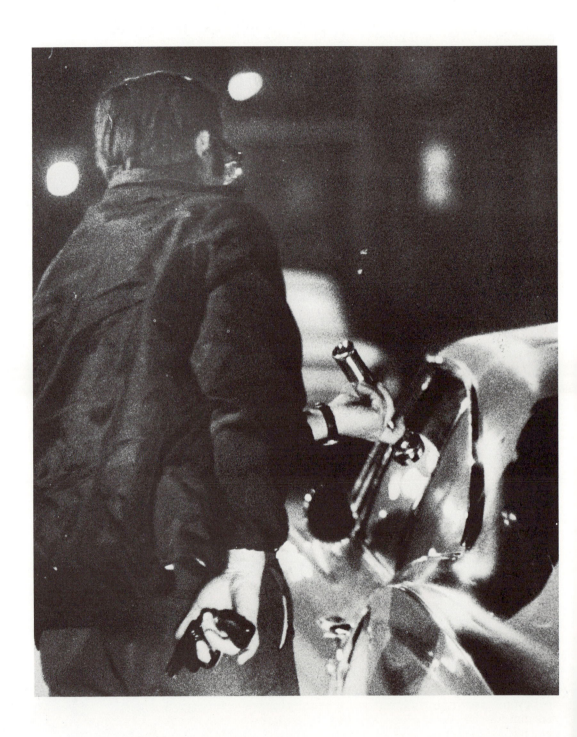

6

VEHICLE STOPS

When it comes to vehicle stops, terminology sets a lot of officers up for injury or death.

Most likely, you've been taught to appraise the stops you make as either "misdemeanor" or "felony" or, in more current terms, as either "low-risk" or "high-risk." The implication is that only when you're stopping an individual you *know* to have committed a serious crime or to be dangerous are you going to be exposed to much threat. It's natural, then, to lower your level of alertness when dealing with common or relatively minor infractions, and this "misdemeanor mind-set" *encourages* you to overlook or misinterpret important danger cues. For instance, a West Coast sergeant who stopped a drunk driver *automatically assumed* the man was hiding an *open bottle* when he made furtive moves under the front seat. The sergeant approached the car, held an extended close-up conversation with the violator, learned he was an ex-convict on parole, watched his mood change from "whining cooperation to tense agitation," returned to the patrol car without inspecting under the driver's front seat and buried his nose in paper work without visually monitoring the violator or vehicle or apparently sensing any need for extra caution. Only after another officer was called to help with field sobriety tests was the "open bottle" found to be a sawed-off shotgun. With his misdemeanor mind-set, the sergeant had also failed to notice in the violator car an unrestrained, full-grown, male bulldog, its face covered with scars from pit fighting.

The fact is that of officers who die making vehicle stops, *MOST die making so-called LOW-RISK stops for MISDEMEANOR violations.* What the professional terminology minimizes *really* turns out to produce the *highest* incidence of *ultimate* threat to you.

To sharpen your vehicle stop tactics, you should first change the terms you think in. Where you have some *reason* to believe there's a potential for danger, you should accurately consider yourself making a HIGH-risk stop. *EVERY other stop should be thought of as an UNKNOWN-risk stop.* When you actively acknowledge to yourself that the level of threat is *uncertain* and may prove to be *much different* than it initially appears, then staying alert to *assess the risk more precisely* becomes a logical part of your procedure.

In truth, you cannot *reliably* draw conclusions about the threat level of most stops until the stop is *over* and the occupant(s) of the vehicle are beyond assault range. Usually you'll have no prior knowledge of the personal history, personality or current state of mind of the violator or passengers. The infraction that catches your attention may be inconsequential compared to what else is going on in their lives at that moment.

Officers by the hundreds every day stop motorists for minor traffic violations and discover at some point during the stop that they are dealing with an individual who has just committed murder or robbery, who is transporting contraband or weapons, who is bent on committing suicide, who is fearful that the stop will mean a parole violation, who is in a homicidal rage over a fight with a spouse, who is abducting a rape victim or who has vowed to "kill the next cop who pulls me over."

The *violation* itself is no indicator of what you are dealing with. One NCIC on a driver stopped for speeding in Georgia produced a *10-foot-long* computer printout of felony wants and warrants from 13 states and two federal agencies. The *appearances* of the driver and vehicle may offer no warnings. One get-away driver for bank robbers in California dressed like a businessman and drove a Mercedes. Nor will the extent to which you have been able to *progress* with a stop without resistance necessarily mean anything. One study of officers killed on vehicle stops indicates that 17% are assaulted while their vehicles are still moving, before they effect the stop…28% after their vehicles are stopped but before they exit…22% while exiting or approaching the violator…and 43% after making initial contact, while interrogating, citing, seeking radio intelligence or returning to their vehicles.

In short, a stop can suddenly turn ugly at *any* stage.

Once you accept vehicle stop terminology as it should be, you then want to maintain the *flexibility* to adapt the tactics you use to *match the level of threat you're facing*. In this regard, officers tend to go wrong in two major ways. Either:

1. they approach *every* stop essentially the same way, even if they *know going in* that there's good reason to presume unusual risk. In other words, they don't accept that where potentially high risk can be *presumed*, you use special tactics *from the outset*. Or:

2. where there's no initial indication of danger, they fail to perceive *new and more ominous information* that is revealed during the stop as a signal to *alter and intensify their tactics*. They stay *locked in* to their initial approach, either because they don't read danger cues or they don't know what to do differently when they do.

Typical of the first problem, a Louisiana officer at about 2 o'clock one morning recognized a pickup truck that had been reported stolen a few hours earlier. Any vehicle or subject believed involved in a crime is prima facia evidence of unusual risk. Yet without waiting for backup or adopting any special caution, the officer started up toward the lone male visible behind the wheel, just as he would have on an ordinary traffic violation. As he entered the kill zone, two teen-agers who'd been hiding in the rear of the truck suddenly ambushed him with a 12 ga. shotgun and a large caliber pistol. Their close-range fire to his face shredded parts of his tongue and nearly blinded him. Similarly, a sergeant in California walked up to a car he *knew* to be the suspected getaway vehicle in an armed robbery, and a detective on stake-out in Washington rushed up to a car believed to contain a suspect in an illegal arms transaction. Both were shot in the head and died.

The second problem was fatally illustrated in a Southern state when a highway patrolman stopped a driver with four passengers for operating a sedan erratically. As the stop progressed, a multitude of danger cues arose: the occupants became verbally abusive…illegal drugs were confiscated from the driver's shirt pocket…a long knife was recovered from his boot…the passengers attempted to interfere with the officer's procedures…and everyone refused to obey commands. These unforeseen developments undeniably changed the stop from one of *unknown* risk to one with strong overtones of *high* risk. Yet the trooper did not alter his orientation. He did not call for backup...did not handcuff and arrest the driver...did not secure the knife (just left it easily accessible on top of his patrol car)...did not attempt to physically control the passengers...did not hesitate to turn his back on the driver and a passenger who were standing near the knife...and, apparently, did not see anything wrong with putting his entire upper body into the car to search it while two of the passengers remained inside. Not surprisingly, he was stabbed in the back while conducting this search, and murdered.

Operating more flexibly was a sheriff's deputy in California who began what he thought was going to be an ordinary traffic stop. As the violator car came to a halt, however, the driver and two passengers got out and came back toward the deputy as if they intended to flank his patrol car. He ordered everyone back in the car. The passengers hesitantly complied, but the driver, a huge "biker type," kept walking forward, demanding to know, "Who the fuck are you?" The deputy drew his firearm into a ready position and repeated his command. The driver grudgingly complied. When backup arrived, this appropriate escalation of tactics continued into a full-fledged high-risk stop—with no injuries.

An average of 13% of officer deaths over the last 10 years have occurred on vehicle stops, a somber indication that these patrol events are by no means as simple as they are common. Whether you are conducting high-risk or unknown-risk stops, they require strategy built on observation...distance...cover...timing...and physical placement. As where a building is involved, here you must deal with a *structure* as well as with a human being. It isolates the violator from you and offers him the opportunity to conceal activity. Plus, this structure has the capability of *moving* on you. *How* you deal with the *structure* may be as important to your safety as how you deal with the *violator* and other occupants.

A detective points his revolver at a male drug dealer following verbal commands to stop his car. How do you feel about his vehicle stop approach and arrest?

Your best hope for coping safely with this complex situation rests with your:

1. Seeking and assimilating INFORMATION *throughout the stop* that will help you evaluate your level of risk at any given moment;

2. Understanding that on any stop your PHYSICAL POSITIONING is of utmost importance in both discouraging and overcoming an assault;

3. Knowing WHEN to use TACTICAL OPTIONS for dealing with a higher level of threat than you normally encounter or originally anticipated...and,

4. Knowing WHAT those special options should be.

Assessing Risk

Your assessment of the risk you're facing should begin as soon as you contemplate making any stop. Training experiments indicate that if you don't begin preparing mentally and physically for a potential threat *within 5 seconds* of deciding to stop a violator, you may be forfeiting a tactical advantage and be forced to play "catch up" from then on. An early evaluation will guide you on whether to attempt the stop at all and, if so, how best to engineer it tactically.

Seven interrelated survival questions form the core of your **threat assessment:**

1. *What is the **NATURE** of the offense involved?* Think in terms of *threat potential*, not just penal code categories. The offense that prompted the infamous stop at Newhall, where four California Highway Patrolmen were killed, was "brandishing a firearm;" two subjects had waved a gun at a young couple on an interstate highway—a misdemeanor.

Some of the firearms left behind by the Newhall offenders.

But if the officers who initiated the stop had truly considered the *implications* of that offense—that there must be at least one gun in the violator vehicle and thus the known capacity for a deadly assault—their maneuvers might have been more tactically sound than stopping close behind the car and approaching it without benefit of cover and without waiting for backup.

The stated offense meant that there was at least one gun—and thus the known capacity for deadly force—in the violator car. In fact, there were six guns—and two hardened ex-cons hellbent on bank robbery to go with them. Consider what you *suspect* about the offense as well as what you see or have been advised. Visual clues and intelligence from your dispatcher may not reflect the full situation. *Respect your sixth sense.*

2. *How many **OCCUPANTS** are readily visible?* The number of people represent the number of Problem Areas you'll potentially have to deal with. Their size, sex, age, mood and chemical condition all are important factors in measuring your control capability. Regardless of the offense or any visible danger cues, *numbers alone* may make backup prudent. That should have been the case in Arkansas when a sergeant decided to stop a car with four rough-looking men, all of whom got out immediately and confronted him. The sergeant stood his ground and tried to handle the situation alone. In a moment of distraction, the driver was able to draw a .45 cal. semi-automatic and gun down the sergeant with shots to the neck, abdomen and leg that left him partially paralyzed. Count the occupants visible and every time you look at the vehicle thereafter, *recount*. With high-risk stops, especially, remember the *"plus one" rule:* think that there is always at least one more occupant present than you can see.

3. *What is the **BEHAVIOR** of the occupant(s)?* Abusive language ...obscene gestures...furtive movements (particularly to the glove box, under the front seat, beneath the instrument console, to the sun visors or to cut-out door panels, the favorite hiding places for guns)...attempts to change places inside the vehicle...and refusals to obey your instructions or requests all are *danger signs* any time they occur. They challenge your objective of maintaining control. Be careful not to *stereotype* behavior. Training exercises have shown that one way in which suspects can almost always succeed in attacking officers is to prepare themselves for the assault by making *slow* and *casual* movements. Most officers are conditioned to associate danger with sudden, violent moves and do not consider the possibility of risk coming in any other form. Be alert also to how the driver *positions* his vehicle. Street-wise offenders may turn their cars at a 45° angle to your patrol car when they're stopped. This gives them a direct field of fire at you as you exit your vehicle, without having to turn in their seats. If an "ordinary" violator acts as if he is in a high-risk situation—such as putting his hands up after you stop him—don't dismiss it automatically as nervousness or confusion. Remember, he knows a lot more about who he is and what he has done prior to the stop than you do, but he may *think* that you know, too, and be responding accordingly.

4. *What **WEAPONS** are involved?* Don't fail to consider the long guns commonly carried in rear window racks in some parts of the country. These may not be "criminal"-type firearms, but they are readily accessible, usable weapons and should be tactically acknowledged, not automatically ignored as they often are by officers given to the "good ol' boy" syndrome. On stops known to be high-risk, you may receive intelligence on weapons that have been used in the crime that is

prompting the stop. Compare the number and nature of these firearms *realistically* to what *you* have available. There's a "plus-one" rule here, too: always assume there is one more firearm of the next largest caliber within the violator's reach than what you know about.

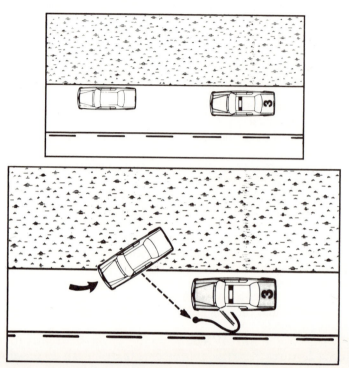

One version of the 45° angle maneuver which has been pulled off successfully by sharp offenders.

5. *What type of **VEHICLE** is involved?* Certain vehicles carry more threat potential than others. Their construction may offer superior cover for whomever is inside...or superior concealment for hidden occupants or firearms...or an Area of Responsibility you can't keep under surveillance if you approach. A vehicle that's unusually high or low may place you at a disadvantage for checking the interior or for maneuvering physically at the driver's door. Accessories, such as parabolic mirrors, may limit your use of surprise.

6. *What **ENVIRONMENTAL HAZARDS** exist?* Two Southern officers chose a parking lot for ticketing a driver with expired plates. The driver was compliant, but two of his brothers, attracted by the stop, emerged from a nearby bar and interceded. In a fight that broke out, one officer was disarmed, and his young partner shot dead. Drinking establishments, housing projects, public parks, fast-food hangouts and similar locations are loaded with ambulatory Problem Areas (people) who may be drawn by the sound, lights and action of your stop like bugs to a beacon. Hostile, they can present more threat than the driver or his vehicle. At some locations in some neighborhoods, *nobody* gets stopped by prudent officers. Besides crowds, consider trees, hydrants, rocks and other cover options that may be available both to you and the violator, and also terrain features, such as curves and hills, that may add to your risk from other traffic.

7. *What are my **STRENGTHS** in this situation?* Your evaluation is like a poker game. You're weighing the cards you know you hold—your backup, your firearms, your ammunition, your cover, your strategy—against what you can see or surmise that your opponent has to play with.

In a matter of seconds, this checklist can help you peg the initial level of threat and and select the tactical strategy you feel is appropriate. Once you've decided to proceed with the stop, keep asking yourself an eighth question *throughout:*

ARE THINGS STILL THE SAME AS I THOUGHT THEY WERE WHEN THIS STARTED?

If at any point, circumstances change and the threat escalates, then *adapt your procedures.* Don't remain trapped inflexibly in an approach that is no longer valid.

Threat Zones

Most officers would agree that when the threat potential seems *low,* you want the occupant(s) of the car you've stopped to remain *inside* while you approach the vehicle on foot. This allows you to better perform certain important duties, such as visually checking the interior for contraband and suspicious activity, and to establish a strong position in case of attempted assault.

If you stay seated behind your wheel and let the driver come back to your window, it's true that you separate him from his vehicle and any weapons concealed there and that you'll be able to further assess him as he walks toward you. But if he presents a threat after he reaches your patrol car, he has the high-ground advantage…your possible reactions are limited because you won't be able to use physical force against him from your position…and your ability to maneuver your sidearm to deliver deadly force is greatly inhibited or impossible.

To maximize the safety of your approach, first *park your patrol car to give yourself an edge*. Some trainers advocate parking no more than 6 feet to the rear of the violator vehicle on the theory that this will thwart him from ramming you backwards at a forceful speed. But by getting back about 15 feet, the extra distance gives you more time for assessment and threat reaction initially. Your position should allow you to fully illuminate the other vehicle's interior and occupants and to read the license plate without having to redeploy your patrol car. Some officers in one-officer units like to angle their vehicle to the left to gain more protection from the engine block. Actually, the engine provides only minimal cover, because of its relatively small size, and by angling the car you lose effective use of your high beams. At night, the concealment offered by a good curtain of light may be more important to you. *Offset your car* (or at least the left front fender, if you do angle it) about 3 feet to create a walking lane.

A good example of how little protection is provided for you when you sit behind the wheel during a stop. If an offender were to shoot at you at window height, there is no protection at all. Even below that, the engine block position may permit bullet penetration.

From the beginning, *throw a blinding flood of light inside* the violator vehicle. This illuminates the visible occupants and also prevents the driver from using his mirror(s) to observe you. To try to see you, he may turn in his seat, providing a more noticeable warning sign. If you've angled your car and have lost full use of your high beams, your spotlight(s) at least can be directed to your advantage. Officers on some agencies are permitted to mount halogen "take-down" spotlights or airplane landing lights on their light bars. These project a dazzling light that does not produce the obscuring bounce-back effect from sheetmetal and bumpers that your high beams may. From the violator's viewpoint, these high-intensity lights cause your windshield to turn black. If your vehicle has a four-headlight system, your high beams can be made more effective by tightening their top adjustment screws so these lights will point into the rear windows of most cars. In winter, be sure during your shift to wipe off *all* your light lenses periodically, including your lightbar and take-down lights. Otherwise a film buildup will cut your candlepower by half or more.

Before exiting, you want the ignition of the violator car turned off, and before moving past the limited cover of your open car door, you want a *visual on the violator's hands.* If they're hidden, consider asking him to rest them on the steering wheel where you can monitor them. On a growing number of departments, this is now standard procedure on all stops; public service announcements are broadcast on radio and television to condition motorists to expect it.

If indications so far suggest it's safe to walk up, you can casually put your hand on your gun butt as you begin, as if arranging or protecting your sidearm. This is called *"Gun Location,"* and prepares you to draw in minimum time. Another option when you want extra caution is to have your gun out beside your leg. The driver won't see it as you approach, and if you perceive no threat you can reholster while he's looking for his driver's license.

Your goal in approaching is to reach a position that looks non-threatening to the ordinary "good" citizen, but appears unchallengeable to would-be assailants. This requires a seemingly casual approach that, in fact, has a foundation of strong defensive placement.

Thinking tactically about your approach, consider the area immediately to the left of the violator vehicle as being divided into four contiguous **Threat Zones.** These are geographic areas where you are vulnerable to attack when you approach on the driver's side. Each harbors special hazards for you, based on the principles of physics and physiology that are involved in launching an assault from inside a vehicle. Some of these areas you should avoid altogether. Others require a good grounding in tactical options to maneuver safely.

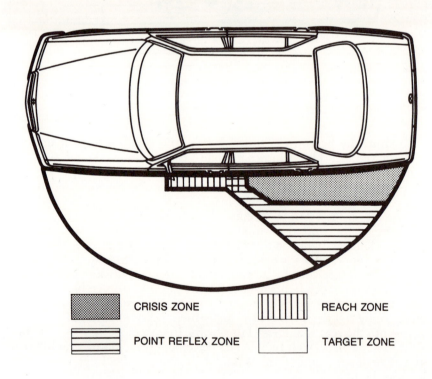

CRISIS ZONE   REACH ZONE

POINT REFLEX ZONE   TARGET ZONE

The Threat Zones are:

The **Crisis Zone,** a strip about 20 inches wide (approximately the typical width of the human body) that starts at the violator's rear bumper and usually ends about 10 inches away from the driver's window. If passengers are in the back seat, however, it ends about 10 inches from the passenger window;

The **Reach Zone,** which extends forward an arm's length or so from where the Crisis Zone ends;

The **Point Reflex** Zone, which fans out from the back corner of the driver's (or passenger's) window at about a 45° angle to the Crisis Zone and fades into...

The **Target Zone,** which arcs from where it overlaps the Point Reflex Zone around to the front fender of the vehicle.

If you approach or stand in the Point Reflex or Target Zones, you make yourself extremely easy to attack with a firearm from the front seat of the violator vehicle. Little movement is required of an assailant other than to point the gun and squeeze the trigger. If his window is down or if he opens his door, he has no physical barriers to deal with. He can take action against you in a fraction of a second. This was evident in Virginia when a trooper stopped his patrol car *ahead* of a speeding violator's vehicle and walked back right into the Target Zone. The driver, who turned out to be a fugitive burglar, said later, "He gave me the field advantage. It just seemed like he took things for granted. When he got right close, about 10 feet away, I just pulled my gun out and put it on the window and shot him. I fired once and then as he was falling, I fired again. He fell down (dead) right alongside the car."

If you avoid the most vulnerable areas and approach *through* the Crisis Zone, you at least will force an offender to *work*—and take longer—to get you. Biomechanically, a left-handed assailant will find shooting very awkward. Even for a right-hander, major upper body twisting, arm movement and joint action will be required to achieve the proper angle. In addition, the offender will be under stress, subject to a high adrenalin surge that will probably warp his timing and judgment. Tests have shown that in his hurried effort to strike you in the Crisis Zone, his first shots are *most* likely to hit the door post or to discharge prematurely into the Point Reflex region. If you're in close to the vehicle, that gives you some protected time in which to react.

Still, the Crisis Zone *is* a high-risk area for you, as the name implies. If a driver or passenger *does* manage to move as necessary to present a threat, you have only limited opportunity for protective movement. Moving out from the car thrusts you into a more hazardous threat zone. The farther out you move, the less body effort is required to shoot at you. In addition, you are vulnerable to being hit by traffic (and, in terms of threat, more officers are injured and killed each year by *accidents* during vehicle stops than by felonious assaults from violators). If you are alongside the rear fender when the assault begins, you can leap onto the trunk and roll to the other side of the car. But if you're beyond that point, the solid mass of the car will prevent you from moving to the right. If you drop down, the assailant has only to make a minor adjustment to keep you in his line of fire. If you turn and try to run away, his car and yours on one side and the flow of traffic on the other may keep you from running properly. Unless there is no traffic, only in the gap between the two vehicles will you be able to make a major change in direction that will force him to shift his point of aim.

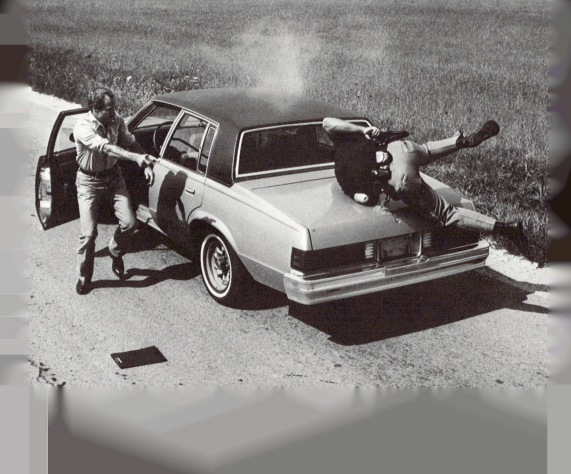

Probably your best option is to try to exit the kill zone with your sidearm in hand and with your soft body armor in position to provide some defense. Even at best, this affords you only limited protection.

Against these odds, some officers try to *creep* through the Crisis Zone, equating slowness with caution. But given your limitations so long as you are in this zone, a better tactic is to *hurry* through it, especially once you are past the trunk area. Once you arrive at the Reach Zone you have better defense options. That is *not* a *safety* zone, but it is a region in which you have more control. Of course, hurrying should not preclude your visually checking the back seat before you are abreast of the passenger door, to determine just where you want to stop advancing.

(above left) The proper body positioning on an unknown-risk stop. (top right) This Target Zone positioning used to be popular. Some officers still use it so oncoming traffic can be watched. (lower right) Here both officers also are easy targets. Only one officer should approach her on the driver's side

Assuming there are no rear passengers, you want to stop just before you reach the center doorpost. Stand *slightly away* from the car (so your clothing won't get caught by the bumper if the vehicle rolls forward suddenly) and parallel to it; that is, with your front toward the side of the car, if you're right-handed. Twist your upper body *slightly* to the left. Your gun should be away from the driver. This positioning is preferable to standing "squared off" at a 90° angle to the car and obviously better than standing parallel abreast of the driver's window. In either of those positions, little effort is required to shoot you; the driver does not even have to move his gun outside the window. In fact, a Kansas offender was able to assault an officer in this position so easily that the officer did not even see the gun until *after* he was shot—and the gun was a full-size *rifle*. (In this case, the officer had already made two other serious tactical errors. Initiating the stop, he noticed the violator reach under the front seat, "but never thought about a gun until I was shot." On approaching the car, he at first shined his flashlight on the driver's face, but then kindly lowered the beam because the violator "flinched." One of several bullets striking the officer just missed his heart.)

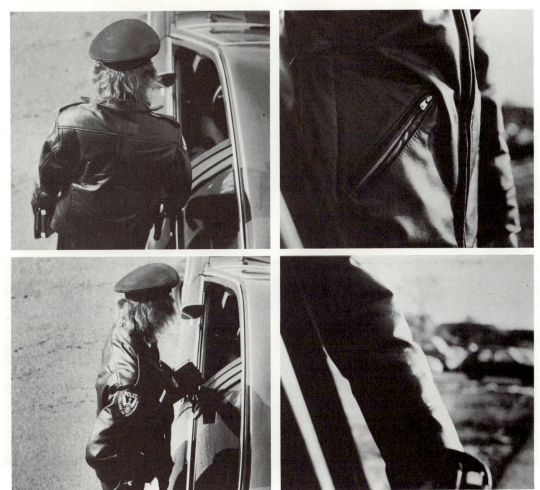

In the top two photos you have the traditional stance at a 90° angle to the vehicle. One disadvantage of this stance is having your sidearm too close to the violator. (bottom two photos) Here there is a marked decrease in torso exposure by altering your stance.

Standing basically parallel to the vehicle and *back* from the window, you do not present as broad a target, and your body is outside the highest risk zones. From the driver's perspective, he *cannot* easily move even to shoot *side-to-side* through your body. Although it seems as if he could, you'll see in role-playing that because of the particular angles involved and the obstruction provided by the car, he will not naturally be able to point a firearm directly at your side. Thus, you still get the protection of your soft body armor, while being harder to target than when you are squared off.

Correct positioning for a left-handed officer
when approaching on the driver's side.

Once you're in position, immediately tell the driver *why* you've stopped him. This usually will ease the tension somewhat with an ordinary citizen and *may* forestall an attack by a criminal. A person who has just committed a crime or is wanted may think he has been stopped because he has been identified, whereas you may in fact know only that he has violated a traffic law. If you *do* know or suspect something more serious, you should *not* be approaching the car. High-risk procedures should be in effect.

Maintaining Gun Location, ask the driver *where* his license is located before asking him to hand it to you. This will give you a better chance to assess his movements, for his reaching toward any *other* location would be a behavioral danger cue. Use your *off hand* to accept his identification when it's presented. You can reach out with your cite book resting on the fingers of that hand and simply clamp his license down on top of the book with your thumb as he offers it.

To use additional caution with a female violator, consider this: Command that both hands be placed on the wheel. Then have her place the purse on her lap using her left hand. Finally, have her withdraw the license using her left hand. This will slow down her reaction time if she tries to pull a weapon.

Now your off hand is in an excellent position to dart forward and block any assault with physical force. It's a barrier an attacker must get past. If you see a firearm come up, let the cite book, license and flashlight fall and thrust your hand out to intercept the gun. Do this *all in one motion.* If you let the items fall and *then* thrust your hand, your response will be too slow. Coming up from underneath with your palm up, you can hook the barrel in the web of your hand and slam the assailant's hand *hard* against the top window frame or roof line. You'll drive the barrel up and deflect it away before it targets your body mass or face. This will be a very natural reaction, for you have been taught since childhood to catch with your off hand, and this is a "catching" move. As the offender's hand and gun strike the car, the pain and force will tend to relax his grip. Now jerk the weapon down sharply with your fingers clamped around it and tear it out of the assailant's hand. With your other hand, you can physically reinforce your disarming movements, then "introduce" the attacker to *your* gun.

Practiced physically and through Crisis Rehearsal, this maneuver can give you much faster and surer control than simply trying to draw against his moving gun or even dropping to the ground. While attempting to get below his line of fire *is* an option, training tests indicate that most officers can't move fast enough to get their *heads* as well as their center mass below range before shots are fired. Also trying to shoot back from that position is chancy. Once you drop below window level, you'll have difficulty seeing the driver as a target if he moves away from the door. And there's less than a 50% chance at *best* that your ammunition will be able to effectively penetrate the metal.

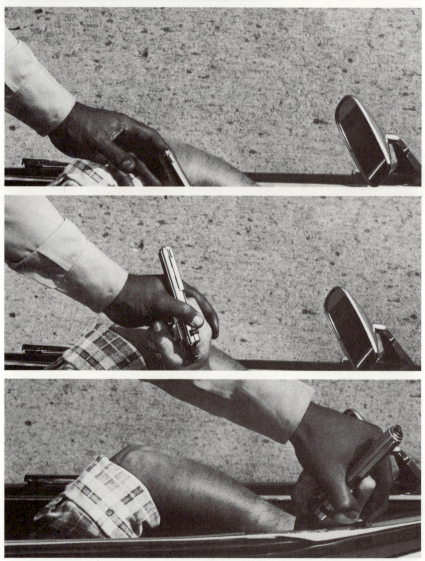

In progressing through the Crisis Zone, there are other considerations to keep in mind.

Because of your vulnerability in that zone, it's to your advantage if the driver does not know exactly when you enter it. Daytime, you can instruct him to turn his outside mirror in before you leave your patrol car and at night shine your high-intensity flashlight or spotlight into it to blind him so he cannot watch you without turning in his seat. Instead of pulling up or pushing down on the trunk lid to be sure it's closed and won't pop up to produce a hidden assailant, just visually inspect the crack or brush your fingertips over it to confirm that both sides are aligned. If you touch the car forcefully, the movement will reveal your location not only to occupants up front but also to anyone lurking inside the trunk. Once you are Located, an assailant hiding in the trunk can easily shoot out through the car's side and hit you.

If your inspection of the back seat reveals a *hidden* passenger you assess as a potential threat, don't stop and conduct a challenge in the Crisis Zone. *Back off,* either by retreating backwards to your vehicle or moving to another cover position. *Then* command the passenger to make himself and his hands visible to you. Under these circumstances, you may choose to *quickly* run *between* the two vehicles to a safer spot. The relative risk of the driver being able to start his engine, back up and pin you before you clear the bumpers is probably less than that of an assault from someone who hides in a back seat.

Where a back-seat passenger is *visible* and you stop your approach just short of the rear window, have the driver relay his license back to you via that person. That way you are not moving to where the passenger has an easy angle of attack.

Some officers like to walk all the way forward to the front windshield post and turn and face the driver to converse with him. They argue that they can see his hands better, can read the VIN and can also watch out for approaching traffic. Bear in mind, however, that this puts you squarely in the Target Zone. Depending on the design of the violator vehicle, hands actually are not always as visible as you may imagine from this position, especially those of back-seat passengers. If an occupant does succeed in making a hidden threat action, your options for cover and movement again are very limited.

As a use of surprise and a means of avoiding the Crisis Zone, you may want to approach from the *passenger* side on some stops, circling around the rear of your patrol car as the most cover-conscious means of getting there. Numerous officers have saved their lives with selective use of this approach, especially in high-traffic areas. A patrol supervisor in New Mexico chose it when he noticed that his spotlight in the side mirror seemed to make a driver he'd stopped for drag racing unduly nervous and fidgety. With the driver's attention focused on the mirror, the officer came up undetected on the right side—and saw the violator holding a .32 cal. semi-automatic in wait for a conventional approach. The supervisor drew his revolver, ordered the driver to take the pistol by the barrel with his left hand and put it on the dash; in stunned compliance, he did. In Illinois, an officer discovered from the passenger side, that a *submachine gun* was levelled for a driver's side approach. He had unknowingly stopped a drug dealer who was transporting 20,000 illegal Quaaludes.

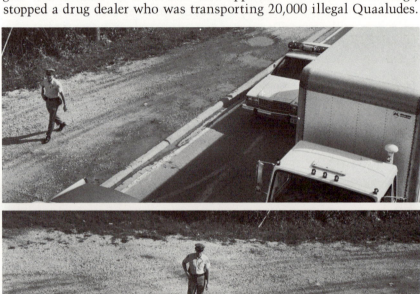

A passenger-side approach requires EXTRA CAUTION on your part not to give away your position. Remember, from inside the car, the passenger side constitutes broad Target and Point Reflex Zones that, with anticipation, are easier for a driver to shoot into with *either* hand than the same zones on his side.

If you are working with a partner, only one of you should approach the car initially to keep both from being drawn into the kill zone simultaneously. One option is for you to go up while your partner stands behind the passenger door of your patrol car, with access to the radio and shotgun. Have a means of communicating, via code words or sign language, that can't be understood by occupants of the vehicle. Two Maryland officers, for instance, arranged that calling out to each other by the wrong first name meant something was amiss. Once you've established that there's no detectable threat, your partner then can move to the right rear of the violator car, where he can keep an eye on any occupants and provide a different field of view of the interior.

An alternative, especially at night, is for the passenger officer to approach first on his side and attempt to clear visually as much of the car as possible without being detected. He then signals you, as driver officer, to approach on your side. Just as you are about to enter the Crisis Zone, the passenger officer knocks on the side of the car, attracting the occupants' attention. You then quickly advance through the zone to the position where you want to contact the driver. After that, your partner stays by the violator's right rear fender, returns to your patrol car or flanks out to cover or concealment on the right to monitor the stop.

Having an officer on each side of the vehicle offers obvious visual superiority. The officer watching the passenger side of a small pick-up truck in Virginia was able to see a violator reach toward a cocked semi-automatic lying beside him on the seat and push off the safety. When the officer yelled out a warning to his partner, the offender realized there were more officers deployed than he'd thought. He quickly pulled his hand away and surrendered without resistance.

Proper approach for two officers in making an unknown-risk stop.

Besides the Threat Zones grouped around the violator vehicle, there's also a **Cite Zone,** where you write your citation. This satellite zone is moveable at your option, but some locations are better than others.

In your front passenger seat, for instance, you are less likely to be in a direct line of fire from the violator vehicle than behind your steering wheel. By keeping your ticket book up at eye level as you write, rather than resting it on your lap so you have to lower your head, you can maintain good peripheral vision on your principal Problem Area and Areas of Responsibility. Keep the passenger door open to facilitate a fast exit, if necessary. If someone approaches and tries to slam that door while you're in the passenger seat, you can repel them by drawing your knees toward your chest and kicking out on the door hard enough to knock them down.

You'll have more physical mobility and more of your patrol car as cover if you stand near your right rear fender, with your front passenger door open. Here the violator will have to make a major, detectable movement to Locate and Attack you. Don't stand directly behind your patrol car but slightly to the side so you're likelier to be clear of the crash if you are rear-ended by a drunk or reckless driver. This is not an uncommon problem, especially on nighttime stops, because drunks sometimes perceive stationary tail lights, hazard lights or flashing emergency lights as highway markers they should try to drive *between*. From this location, you may be able to look under, over or through your emergency light bar to maintain your visual on the violator vehicle. If shooting starts, you can drop down beside the wheel and right rear quarter-panel out of sight. If you are a motor officer, you can use the right rear of the *violator* vehicle as your Cite Zone with the same advantage, provided the driver is the vehicle's only occupant. This tactic should never be bastardized as it was recently in the Midwest, however. The officer was on the passenger side of the vehicle writing the ticket with his book on top of the car—and with the violator standing directly *behind* him.

Locations that may be convenient, but are also dangerous.

What they see (left) and what you see from inside using the front right passenger seat. The cite book is held up against the dash so you can periodically glance at the subject vehicle to maintain visual contact.

Standing to the right rear and slightly to the side affords the best concealment (left). Above right, you see how this location also allows you to surveil the violator between the roof and the light bar.

Above all, DO NOT PLACE THE VIOLATOR INSIDE YOUR PATROL CAR BESIDE YOU while you write the citation. There he has ready access to everything you have that he can reach, probably including your *sidearm*, and to any radio intelligence you receive about him at the same instant you hear it. Violators and their passengers are unpredictable. While a speeder sat inside a trooper's car on the West Coast, listening to him run a warrants check, a passenger who'd been left behind in the violator's car suddenly drove off at a high rate of speed. Keeping the violator beside him, the trooper gave chase. The pursuit lasted for 13 miles at speeds up to 100 m.p.h. and ended when the suspect lost control and struck a fire hydrant. Later the trooper discovered what an incredibly close call he'd had: both subjects were wanted for robbery and in their car was a ski mask, a sawed-off shotgun and other contraband. There also was a big dog which, when the trooper ran past the wrecked car to catch the driver, attacked the officer, knocked him down and chewed his face. Despite a legion of horror stories, highway patrol officers, especially, persist in sharing their front seats with violators, usually without even searching the persons they're allowing to enter their "sanctuary." In some cases, officers even put *prisoners* in the front passenger seat, handcuffed *in front.*

As you walk from the violator vehicle to the Cite Zone you've selected, do not lose visual contact with your principal Problem Area, the violator vehicle. By twisting slightly, you can keep looking behind you to observe the vehicle, while appearing just to be checking it over for possible safety violations.

When you return to present the citation, be alert to changes that may have occurred in your absence. A passenger who was asleep may now be awake or a weapon may be newly visible. Returning a violator's license, one Wisconsin officer again shined his flashlight into the rear seat, as he'd done before. Only this time, he saw the barrel of a sawed-off shotgun sticking out on the floor. He'd missed it earlier—when it had been concealed between the driver's legs.

Each new approach to the vehicle is like a new stop. Don't be lulled into a false sense of security by the initial encounter. Your threat assessment should be just as active the second time up as the first, attuned for even subtle signals that your risk has changed.

Your return to your vehicle should be survival-oriented, as well. One California motor officer maintained the tactical edge throughout the stop of a young driver and his female companion. But as the officer headed back to his bike after handing the driver a citation, he turned his back on the car. Several shots rang out from that unmonitored Problem Area. The officer was hit three times, and then was disarmed as he lay dying.

Searches

There will be times during some vehicle stops when you develop probable cause to search the interior, without sufficient evidence yet to make an arrest or to initiate full high-risk procedures. NEVER TRY TO SEARCH AN OCCUPIED VEHICLE.

If you are alone and dealing with a lone driver, you can place him in your patrol car (if it's partitioned) after searching him first. At night, turn off your headlights, turn on your interior lights and turn your lighted spotlight around so it shines into the back seat. This will sharply reduce his vision, but leave him clearly visible to you as you check on him periodically from the violator vehicle.

Prior to including this tactic in the book, it was important to test it. What you see to the left is what the suspect sees if he looks ahead. This tactic can also be used with prisoners on high-risk stops.

With multiple suspects, *wait for backup*. Then before you "toss" the car, ask all occupants, for their "own safety," to step out to the curb. Here you can search them; unless they exhibit threatening behavior, you may not choose to handcuff them in lieu of an arrest at this point, depending on your departmental policy. Do get them seated, though, to decrease their mobility, and group them together to keep your Problem Areas as confined as possible. Try to get them to spread their legs and place their palms on the pavement as a further precaution. While you or your backup conduct a search of the vehicle, the other officer maintains surveillance over these individuals.

As searching officer, beware of possible booby traps. Some offenders position razor blades or dirty narcotics syringes in seat cushion cracks to injure "snoopers." Several officers have been killed by infections caused by needles they jabbed against on car searches. Before sticking your hand into a crack, first "clear" it by running a pen or mini-baton along the inside.

Before permitting the occupants to return, check areas commonly used to hide weapons. Such as: the glove box...armrests...door panels...the sides of the seats next to the doors...under the seats, including up in the springs...inside torn upholstery...inside heater and air conditioning vents, especially if loose...under headrests...on the shelf-like lip under the instrument panel...in ash trays and litter bags...under floor mats...behind or in center arm rests...behind visors...inside the gasoline cap...under the spare tire, etc.

Rather than just search "blindly" with your hands, try actually to *look* in all these places. Sometimes firearms and other contraband are wedged in place or suspended on strings and not easily detected by feel. You can use the same kind of small mirror here for looking into tight spaces that is so handy on building searches.

Two-shot derringer concealed in a Bible and discovered on a vehicle stop. Driver had exited and asked the officer if he could go back inside to shut off his ignition. The request was denied and the alert officer immediately secured the Bible. An additional gun was found in the trunk.

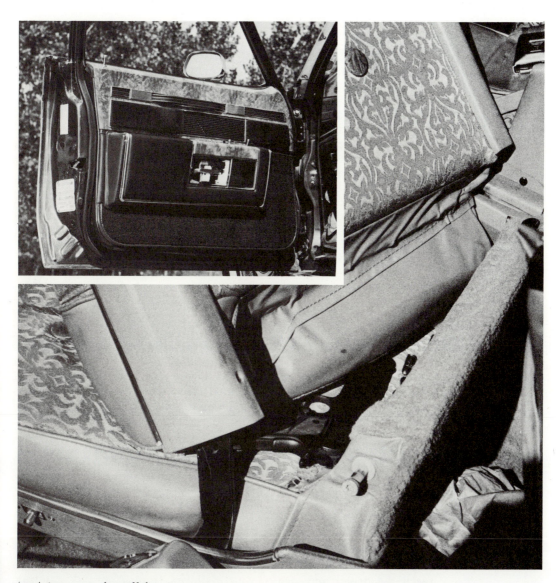

(top) An array of small firearms can
be hidden almost anywhere in a
passenger car. Popular places today
include under the hood and in door
recesses and pockets. (middle)
Propping the front seat forward may
also produce a few surprises. (right) In
more rural areas and border towns,
drug traffickers can be found with
custom cases behind the front seat for
fully-auto machine pistols, etc.

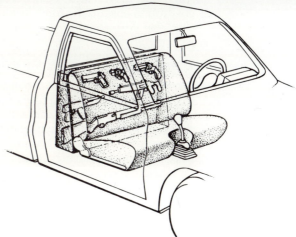

Extractions

Occasionally you'll encounter drivers on seemingly low-risk stops whom you *do* instruct to leave their cars but who refuse to cooperate. Most often they're chemical-abuse suspects who won't get out of the vehicle for your field sobriety tests. Or they may be irate citizens who refuse to sign a citation...mentally disturbed individuals...subjects wanted on misdemeanor warrants who panic...accident victims who freeze up...or persons experiencing a diabetic coma, an epileptic seizure or some other medical emergency. For their safety or to effect an arrest, you'll need to extract them from the vehicle—while still minimizing your vulnerability to attack.

First, of course, try your verbal skills: simple, direct commands for the subject to exit the vehicle. Avoid unnecessary dialogue that may be misunderstood or offer opportunity for argument, avoid racial epithets or other abuse that will likely add fuel to already overheated emotions, but also avoid coming across as fearful or indecisive, in case the driver or some other occupant is weighing the odds of taking you on. If he flips you off or yells back obscenities, you at least know that he heard you and that he's uncooperative. Then, unless you're prepared to call a tow truck and have the car dragged off with him still inside, you'll consider *physical* extraction.

Reevaluate the threat at this point. *Be aware that you are moving higher on the risk spectrum.* At the very least you can reasonably anticipate that the driver will attempt to struggle. What are his size and strength compared to yours? Does he show symptoms of being influenced by pain-deadening, violence-enhancing drugs? If there are passengers, is their mood such that they seem likely to be passive observers...or will they aid him in resisting you? How about a dog inside? Does the design of the vehicle place you at a disadvantage? Pick-up trucks, vans, semitrailer tractors, some four-wheel-drives and other high-riding rigs put you at the driver's leg level and may necessitate your climbing up to reach him. He maintains the high-ground advantage, your visibility and physical agility are drastically compromised and your risk of being knocked down into traffic with a kick or by a door suddenly opened is great. Physical extractions from such vehicles are virtually impossible to pull off with any degree of safety. By the same token, low-riding sports cars add to your hazard because you have to reach *down* abnormally to reach the driver and, again, your visibility from a normal standing position is obscured. *Don't become so caught up in getting compliance that you fail to monitor your hazard level and adjust your tactics accordingly.*

Where you are outsized or outnumbered, you will want to get *backup* before you get physical. Any cooperative passengers then can be ordered out to sit on the curb or the ground, while your backup watches to prevent them from interfering. *Un*cooperative passengers change the complexion of the stop and should cue you to *initiate high-risk procedures immediately.* If the driver is alone (or if a third officer is available to monitor passengers), you can use backup to distract the driver from the passenger side of the vehicle or as a second set of eyes from that location. Or you can have backup stand behind you in the Crisis Zone to assist or cover you during the extraction. According to the circumstances, *you* determine where your backup best serves your purposes.

As the extractor, you want to take action through the driver's open door, primarily from the Reach Zone. Trying to pull a resisting violator out through his window is not only awkward and time-consuming but usually unsuccessful; he's more likely to pull you *in* before you pull him out. Likewise, trying to extract him from the passenger side is risky because he's well-positioned then to assault you with the most powerful parts of his body, his legs.

If he has, in effect, barricaded himself by locking the doors and rolling up the windows and you cannot persuade him to open up, you may have to consider breaking in in order to reach him. Legally, you have the right to order him out of the car and he is obligated to comply. But by the same token, some courts have held that if you smash his window for the extraction, you are liable for damaging his property. You should know your departmental policy on this issue.

If that *is* an option and you choose it, the best technique will be with a hard, jamming thrust of the pointed end of a crowbar or tire iron, or with the release of a spring-loaded set punch, which you may carry with you on patrol as a rescue tool for working accidents. Flashlights and batons do not work as well because they are too blunt to deliver shattering pressure to safety-sealed windows. The blow should hit about 1 inch up and 1 inch in from the corner of the window nearest the driver's doorlock. You deliver it from just to the rear of the center doorpost. An alternative is to penetrate the window just *behind* the driver as a precaution against him being cut by flying glass or injured by the tool. Either way, the instant the window disintegrates, you drop the ram and simultaneously pop the lock with your right hand and swing the door open with your left.

A female who was driving this car refused to exit. Police smashed the side window to force her out. Location: A gate near the White House.

All your moves now should be fast...decisive...efficient. Some that seem good in theory are likely to fall short in practice. Trying to pry the driver's hands off the steering wheel leaves you open to being grabbed, punched or bitten, as does trying to seize his groin or inner thigh for pain compliance or trying to wrestle him with a headlock. Trying to yank him loose of the wheel with a bear hug around the chest is next to impossible, unless you're a lot bigger and stronger than he is. Trying to pull him out by his ear may leave you holding a ripped off ear—and the nasty end of a lawsuit for injuries.

More realistically, your Focus Point should be the driver's *left wrist* or his *head*. (This assumes, of course, that he has not produced a weapon, in which case you would Focus on controlling the weapon first and foremost.) You are now in the arrest process, so *control is your top priority*. You want to use methods that are keyed to *nerve control* and *leverage*, not strength. Your best options include:

The **Wrist Clamp.** This is particularly suitable if the driver is clenching the steering wheel, but it can work when he's in any position that allows you to reach his left wrist, preferably. Without thrusting your head or upper body into the car, *quickly* clutch his wrist between your left thumb and a hard instrument (flashlight, mini-baton, pen) clenched in the fingers of your left hand, if you are right-handed. Your thumb should hook against the outer edge of his wrist. The instrument should lie across the opposite edge, in the little groove between the base of his thumb and his wrist bone. By tightening your hand you create a "pain vise" by pressing the instrument down against his radial nerve. You can make the pressure even more intense by also using your other hand, although this adds somewhat to your risk because it ties up both your hands. Just thrust your right hand up under his arm, clutch the end of the instrument in your fingers and place your right thumb beside your left one on the edge of his wrist for leverage as you tighten down.

Simultaneous to applying pressure, you sharply pull his wrist down and back toward you. This hyperextends his arm, pushes his shoulder and head forward and gives you the torque necessary to pull him right out of his seat. Your pressure on his radial nerve tends to promote motor dysfunction as well as pain, which can make it effective against subjects whose pain sensititivy has been dulled by drugs or alcohol.

Keep the suspect low and off-center as you bring him out. Once he is clear of the vehicle, you can direct him to the side of the vehicle or into a prone position for handcuffing and searching. If he struggles at any point, simply bring his wrist up higher behind his back for compliance. You even have the capability of breaking his arm by suddenly jamming down on his flattened elbow with your right palm while yanking up on his wrist with the pain vise. If he still comes after you, you've at least robbed him of one useable arm.

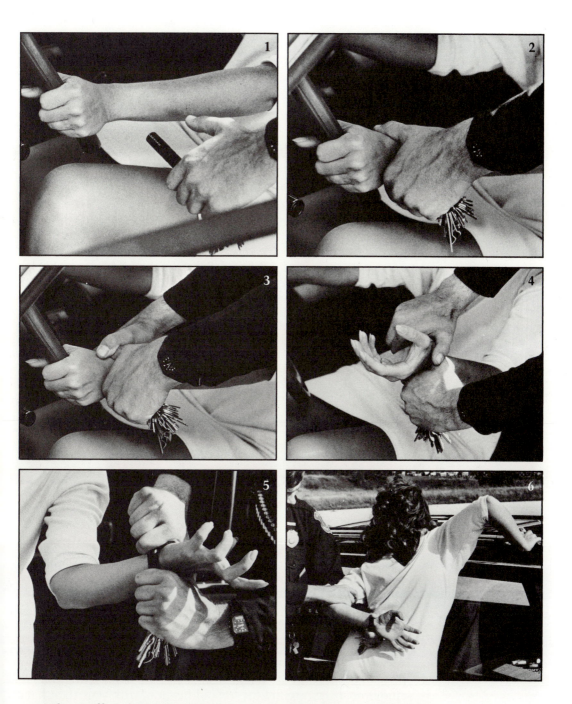

The **Cuff-and-Torque.** Similar in principle, this is particularly effective if you use hinged handcuffs. You quickly apply and *tighten* one handcuff on his left wrist. Yank down and back to hyperextend his arm and inflict pain. For maximum effect, handcuff between his wrist bones and his hand so that when you twist the handcuff to bring his hand back you are hitting the radial nerve.

As with the Wrist Clamp, be careful not to telegraph your intentions. You want to move for his wrist without warning and pull it into the torque position *immediately* before he realizes what's happened.

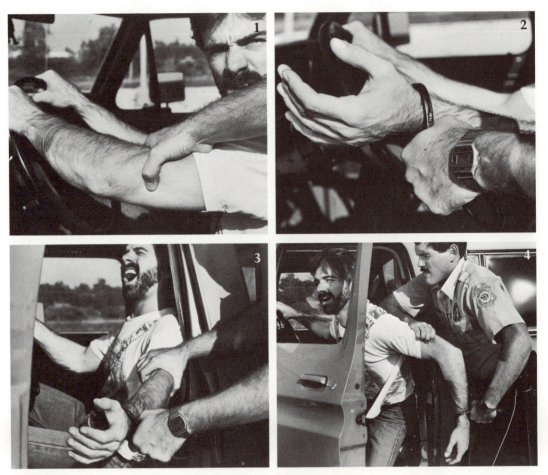

The Cuff-and-Torque.

The **Head Press.** This "empty-hand" technique starts with a diversion. Standing behind the driver and parallel to his vehicle, gently pat him on the hand or arm with your left hand and, if he's clutching the steering wheel, say: "Come on, pal, let go and come on out." This separates his focus and also sets up your hand to move into his face. Keep your voice *calm and friendly* so you don't hint at the aggressive move you're about to make.

Now quickly thrust your left hand up under his nose, palm up, so that the blade side of your hand hits right at the juncture of his nose and face. (Keeping your palm up, you minimize the risk of his biting you.) At the same time, reach around the back of his head with your right hand and put your index finger on a Pressure Point called the mandibular angle, located along the jawbone just behind the ear lobe. Your right hand can keep his head from moving backward to jerk free.

Pressing in and up hard and steady with your left hand and in firmly with your right index finger, you create painful nerve disruption. As you press, twist his head down and toward the open doorway. Lead with his nose where you want him to go, and he'll be inclined to follow it right out of the car. Continue pressure, if necessary, until you have him in a good handcuffing position.

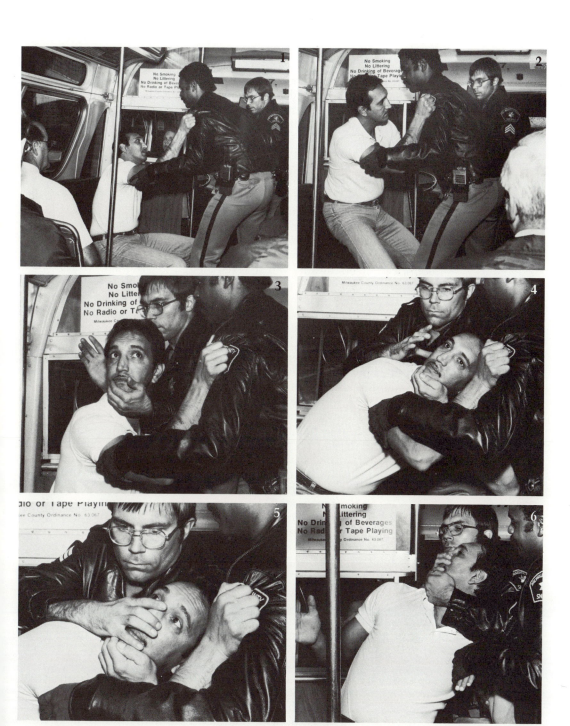

Whatever technique you use, be sure to give the violator instructions in a firm command voice *all the time you're applying pressure.* Just as your creativity and clear thinking are diminished under high stress, his are shut down by the pain and dysfunction you're inflicting. He needs you to tell him what to do. If you just silently apply pressure, he's likely to think you're maliciously assaulting him. His panic, fear and rage reactions then will skyrocket, and his belief that he needs to fight for his life may be enough to overcome the messages for compliance his brain is receiving.

Remember, once you lay hands on a violator, keep hold of him until he has been handcuffed and searched. Only then should you break physical contact with him. The only exception would be if you decide to disengage from him and retreat to a better tactical position as a defensive measure.

Some strong "don'ts" pertain whenever you consider or attempt an extraction:

DO NOT reach into the vehicle except to control and remove the driver. And under no circumstances should you put your *head* inside. One common mistake that injures and kills officers every year is to reach through the driver's window to try to turn off or take out the ignition key. When a sergeant in Phoenix did that, the violator jerked the car into gear and floored the accelerator. The sergeant's watchband caught on the doorlock button, and he was dragged along the pavement. In Canada, a violator grabbed an officer's wrist and sped off. The officer was dragged for nearly a block before he managed to pull his arm away. Even if you reach for the keys through the open door, you're vulnerable to being grabbed or disarmed. A California deputy was shot in the head by a violator who easily took his gun while the deputy was leaning across him reaching for the ignition. Forget the keys. Concentrate on the driver. Positioned properly and working through the open door, you can release him and jump clear if the car does move forward.

DO NOT enter the vehicle. Suppose you climb into the back seat thinking you can extract the driver by yanking him over the seatback. If he manages to resist and drives off, you become a semi-hostage, at least temporarily. If you *do* pull him back with you, you have cramped mobility and limited space in which to subdue him. If you climb into the front seat, you'll necessarily be low and slow there, too. You may not be able to react fast enough if he produces a weapon.

DO NOT ignore dogs. Dogs riding with a person you want to extract are unpredictable: potential distractions at best, potential attackers at worst. Some breeds, with the capability of biting with more than a half ton of pressure, can present you more danger than the violator. When the dog is small and seems friendly, your backup may be able to distract him while you perform the extraction. In other cases, if you have a K-9 officer available, call him to the scene to evaluate the dog's threat potential and advise on his handling. He'll also have equipment, such as protective sleeves, that your backup can use during the distraction. Where hard-core attack dogs are involved, definitely consider firing chemical agents into the car to motivate a "voluntary" exit by the uncooperative violator.

DO NOT use excessive force. Overreaction in these situations can be as much a problem as underreaction. If you're excited and unnecessarily rough, you'll only further agitate the subject and any bystanders who may be sympathetic to him. *Avoid* trying to scare him into compliance with gunplay, such as shooting out his tires or firing your shotgun under his car as a bluff. Your using deadly force in a non-threat, misdemeanor situation can have serious legal ramifications for you in the event of a mishap.

DO NOT discount medical factors. A driver's motivations may not be what they appear. A young Arizona trooper working an accident met resistance from a driver who was gripping the steering wheel, shaking and shouting: "Fuck you! Fuck you! Fuck you!" A veteran sergeant blamed the refusal to cooperate on drugs. As the trooper extracted and handcuffed the subject, however, he was bothered by the look and feel of the man's skin and insisted that paramedics be called. Their diagnosis: the driver was heading into a diabetic coma that could have been fatal had it gone unattended. Moments after they gave him an injection, he was calm and apologetic for his behavior.

Problem Vehicles

Some vehicles, because of their design, require you to alter the stop tactics you'd normally use in dealing with ordinary passenger cars. Even in situations with no evident threat, approaching these vehicles for conversation or extraction involves special risks that most officers don't want to incur.

With rigs such as vans...cars with tinted windows...semi-trailer trucks...or others like campers and motor homes where visibility and height are against you, your ability to Locate and Identify potential threats in time to React effectively is seriously hamstrung if not eliminated. Besides mirrors that may make a surprise approach on the passenger side impossible, thick carpeting in some vehicles may make it difficult for you to detect noise or movement inside. With a motorcycle or similar two-wheeled vehicle, your "visibility" problem may be one of disguised weapons subtly customized into the machine. Plus the possibility that a violent subject may try to use the bike itself or other riding equipment to assault you. In addition, there are some conventional vehicles that you may feel a "pucker factor" about and be leery of approaching for reasons you can't logically explain. Perhaps you decide that rack of guns visible in the rear window is something you'd just as soon not get near.

With *unknown*-risk stops of such problem vehicles, *you want the driver to separate voluntarily from his vehicle.* If he refuses, one option is to call backup and shift into high-risk stop procedures. Or you can still decide to approach. Just be sure *you* are making the decision on the basis of *your* threat assessment and not being lured into complying with *his* strategy. And if you *do* approach, understand that your hazard potential is undeniably greater than normal.

Assuming the driver is willing to obey your commands to exit, here are some considerations for your tactical positioning. THESE DO *NOT* APPLY TO *HIGH*-RISK STOPS. THEY'RE VALID *ONLY* WHEN THE VIOLATOR YOU'RE HANDLING IS STILL OF *UNKNOWN* RISK.

VANS. Vans are among the most treacherous vehicles you stop. Generally they have at least four possible points of exit: two front doors, the rear door(s) and a sliding side door, all but one of which are completely hidden from your view once you enter the Crisis Zone on the driver's side. The interior, of course, is hidden then, too, plus some vans also have sun roofs and customized escape hatches in the floor. With that many Areas of Responsibility out of your sight, you're rarely on sound tactical ground approaching, especially if you're alone. It's almost impossible to "sneak up" on a van. But by parking farther back than usual (20 to 25 feet) and maneuvering the driver properly, you can improve your control.

One option is to open your front passenger door and move around the rear of your vehicle to the passenger side before issuing your initial command to the driver. Then with your P.A., instruct him to turn on his interior lights, to bring his keys and license and to come back toward you. In this position, you lose a visual on him as he's exiting, but you'll be able to see him before he reaches the rear of his van and be able to check his hands.

When he reaches his rear bumper, ask him to turn and open the rear doors of the van. With the help of your high beams and spotlight, even at night you can now get at least a rough view inside. If occupants are visible, tell them to remain in the van...immediately summon back-up...and order the driver to close the door(s) *tight.* This will retard their exiting from the rear. Advise the driver that he is responsible for the actions of his passengers, then wait for backup. If no better cover is available, you do have some protection behind your passenger door, if shooting starts. If the door is open to the first catch, bullets have a chance of ricocheting off, and if you've rolled the window down, penetration is even less likely.

If the van appears empty, ask the driver to close the door(s) and come to the center front of your patrol car. *Keep his hands visible.* Tell him he can rest them on the hood if the metal is cool enough.

Depending upon your assessment of him, you can have him hand you his license across the hood while you stand behind the open door or after you've advanced to the front fender, still keeping the hood as a barrier. Or you can direct him to a spot where you both can stand off the roadway, ideally near something you could use for cover in case of trouble. Of course, you always keep him between you and the van. If your patrol car is equipped with a computer console and you need to operate it, you can direct him back to the front of your vehicle and use the computer from your passenger seat. This gives you the quickest access to your sidearm if you are right-handed. Even if he has not brought his license back with him, remember that you do not need to send him back to the van or accompany him to get it. You can run a check with just his name and DOB.

A van which was stopped and searched following a fatal shootout nearby. A total control position for any hidden offender. Fortunately, this was not the offender van.

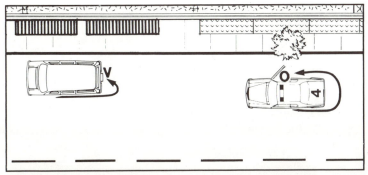

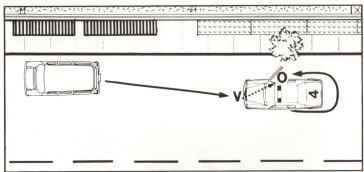

Handing over the license allows you to put the driver at a disadvantage and also observe his vehicle.

Among the van stop lore that has developed in recent years is the claim that you can safely prevent rear doors from being opened from inside by driving your patrol car smack up against the van's bumper. This not only puts you dangerously close to the violator vehicle and cuts your visibility on both sides but also fails to achieve the stated goal. The doors *still* can be opened far enough for shots to be fired, or offenders can shoot through the windows in the doors.

A "tactic" that isn't tactical.

Most passenger and cargo vans have a side door—a real potential hazard if you don't have the driver come back to you.

TINTED GLASS. In a growing number of states, smoky vehicle windows have been outlawed, but even in those jurisdictions you may run across out-of-state drivers who inadvertently are violating the law; you have difficulty seeing into those cars. Even with clear glass, your view may be obscured by dirt, glare, condensation, snow, ice, stickers, sun shades, etc. Again, you can increase your safety by parking back farther than normal and by relying initially on voice commands rather than a direct approach.

Dealing with tinted glass at night, you may be able to use the violator's inside dome light to your advantage. Try to conduct the stop where the violator vehicle is exposed to little ambient light. Turn off your headlights and spotlight, then ask the driver to turn on his interior light(s). Often this will reverse the effect of the tinted glass, allowing you to see in but barring occupants from seeing out. You then can get a reading on who is in the car besides the driver.

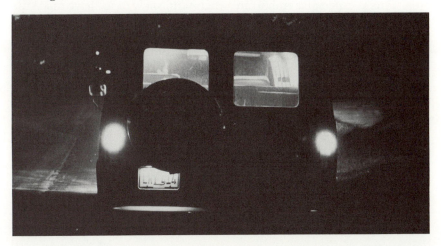

If that's not possible, ask all occupants to position themselves as close to the side windows as possible. Instruct them to lower the windows. You can then get a better perspective on who's inside. As an extra precaution, have them stick their hands out where you can see them... to separate their fingers... and to slowly rotate their hands while you check for any palmed weapons.

While they keep their hands outside, ask the driver to exit the vehicle with his license and come back to you, along the lines explained for van stops. Your vehicle should be off-set to provide him a walking lane. His failure to cooperate with any of this may well indicate a heightened risk. *Don't proceed further without summoning backup and considering high-risk procedures.*

If, after conferring with the driver, you want a better look inside the car or at the passengers, ask the driver to accompany you to the vehicle. You can tell him that you need to check his front license plate or that you think one of his headlights is out or use some other ruse. Approach on the passenger side, maintaining Gun Location and keeping the driver between you and the vehicle at all times. Keep in mind, though, that if you approach without having backup to help monitor the Areas of Responsibility, you are increasing your potential hazard. If you think you need a look, you probably need a backup.

If you choose to leave the driver in the car and approach as you would an ordinary vehicle, remember that your flashlight generally will *not* penetrate the densely tinted glass—but it *will* give away *your* position. By understanding this and using a flashlight judiciously, one California trooper saved his life. An oily film obscured the rear windows of the car he stopped. Making a passenger-side approach, he kept his light off until he neared the front window, which was open. Staying back a bit, he extended his light away from his body, directed it into the open window—and saw the driver pointing a rifle at the opening.

The driver fired and so did the officer, followed by his partner who was positioned back behind the open passenger door of their patrol car. The driver was fatally injured and the officers escaped with no injuries.

SEMI-TRAILERS. Your first concern in stopping an 18-wheeler, a bus, a car hauling a large house trailer or other heavy equipment is the *location*. Select a level stretch of roadway or slight downgrade—*not* an upgrade—so that a roll backward into your vehicle is avoided and the violator can resume forward motion without undue difficulty after the stop. This is especially important when rain, snow or ice have made the pavement slippery. Where a truck is hauling livestock, avoiding the use of your siren so as not to startle the animals is another courtesy that may help keep the driver's hostility toward you in check.

If you elect to approach, be sure your patrol car is offset to the left of the semi-trailer to provide a safety lane. Other truckers may try to harass you during the stop by driving so close that they blow your hat off, etc., and this offset will make that harder for them to do. By parking 40 feet or so to the rear, you will get a better visual on the driver's side. Watch his side mirror as you approach. If the driver is not visible in it, that's a warning that he is not in a normal position and may be preparing a surprise.

The safest way to roll underneath is by cupping your face with your hands as you roll. This helps protect you against metal edges that you will pass on your way to the far side of the rig.

Be aware, though, that an approach may be your riskiest option. In the cabs of most trucks, there is no place that is not within easy reach of the driver, and the height and physical obstructions of the rig make it difficult for you to track his movements. In approaching, the full length of the trailer is your Crisis Zone—and you never do really reach a Reach Zone. About your only hope of protection in case of shooting is to duck *under* the trailer and particularly to seek cover in the area between the back wheels of the cab. There's more steel there to deflect bullets than anywhere else on the truck. If he tries to drive off, his acceleration will be slow enough that you can safely dodge the tires.

Never stand in front of the driver's door or climb up on the side of the truck to talk to him. He can easily open the door against you or if the truck has a sleeping bunk, a passenger hidden there can shoot you.

Instead of approaching, you may prefer to call the driver back, as with vans and tinted-glass vehicles. He may not be able to hear voice commands if you have no P.A. because of noise from his rig, but if you have a CB in your patrol car, you may be able to contact him on that. Or you can advance to the left rear corner of his trailer and gesture to him from there. That location provides you some cover protection while he is disembarking from his cab. As he starts back, you can move to a position behind your passenger door or to a spot near cover off the roadway.

Don't take your eyes off the truck while you move. You may be able to follow his legs below the trailer bottom. That becomes an Area of Responsibility because he'll have to duck below there to shoot you, until he reaches the trailer tail.

At night, consider flanking out and approaching on the passenger side. The lights of oncoming vehicles in the opposing lane will light up his cab and enable you to observe the occupants before you move closer.

The driver is commanded back to your position. If you offset your patrol car like this and then move to the front passenger side, he cannot see you until he reaches the rear of the truck. The manifest is placed on the hood of your car or handed to you while he remains in front of your bumper.

MOTORCYCLES. Just as a passenger-side approach to some vehicles can often throw off the violator's normal anticipation and let surprise work for you, so can asking a motorcyclist to dismount on the *right* side of his bike. This is a completely unnatural act. Instead of easily swinging off to the left without even using his hands, the rider now has to *work* in order to keep his balance. This tends to break his concentration on you and, because of the way he'll likely turn to touch ground, you'll get a full front view of his body and hands, if he's cooperative.

You can conduct your conversation with the violator across the hood of your patrol car or near cover, as with other special stops. If he is wearing a helmet, ask him to leave it on his head or behind on the seat so he does not have it in hand to throw or swing at you.

Ask any passenger or traveling companion who's on another bike to remain on their bike(s) with the kick stand(s) up, their hands on their thighs. They'll need to balance the bike(s) with their legs and this will lessen their mobility. To assault, they'll have to turn to Locate you. On the other hand, if you have them dismount and sit on the curb or stand at the roadside where you can watch them peripherally as you deal with the violator, they'll then be in a better position to watch *you* and choose the best time to assault. As you talk to the violator, keep him between you and his companions to afford some possible protection.

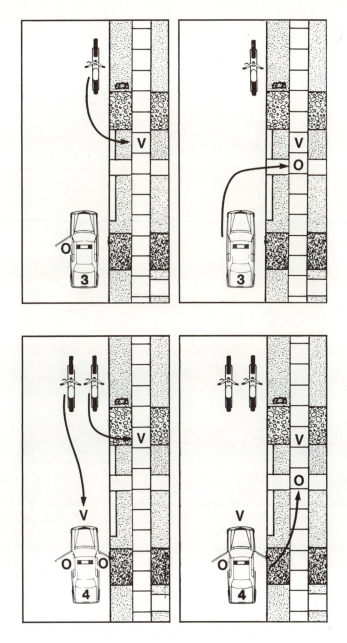

Independent of full-fledged "run" situations, which are considered as high-risk stops, you may occasionally stop a lone or paired cyclist who is "flying colors" of an outlaw biker gang. Increasingly, gang members are forsaking motorcycles in favor of vans, expensive sports cars and other vehicles for their day-to-day transportation, in part to lessen their visibility to police. Even those on bikes may not display the usual obvious insignia or jackets or vests. But if the violator looks like a biker, smells like a biker and acts like a biker, he probably *is*.

Generally, bikers will acknowledge their club affiliations if asked, "Are you a lone rider or do you belong to a club?" Biker gang members often carry printed calling cards, bearing important indicators like "1%er" and "F.T.W." (Fuck the World, the universal outlaw slogan). Similar danger signs may be conveyed by tattoos or by logos on the bike.

Such intelligence is important in assessing your risk and the need to summon backup for conducting the stop. More information can be gleaned by "reading" the patches sewn to the biker's colors. For instance,

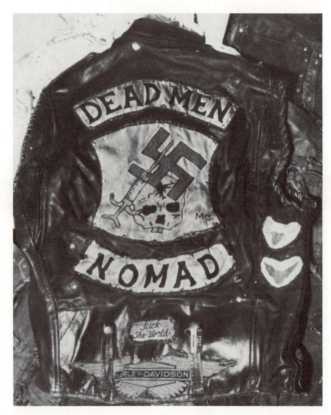

the word "Nomad" appearing below the club insignia on the back indicates a roving troubleshooter dispatched by the group's national headquarters ("mother club"); his duties may include those of an enforcer and hit man. A shoulder patch from a police agency sewn upside down on the jacket indicates a previous assault on an officer from that department. A set of blue wings signifies that the wearer has performed oral sex on a female law enforcement officer, presumably against her will. And so on.

Female officers, in particular, should exercise extreme caution in dealing with bikers, as their chauvinistic, anti-authority philosophy breeds enormous hostility toward this combination of gender and power.

Whatever your sex, always stay to the *right* of a motorcycle during your stop. If a shotgun has been jerryrigged into the handlebars, a custom feature favored by some bikers and other criminals, it will almost certainly be in the left grip of the bar, because that area is normally left empty by motorcycle manufacturers.

Right and below, you see how easy it would be to assault an officer who approaches from the driver's side. The crosshairs line up with the approaching officer for a devastating shotgun blast from the handlebar.

One strong motive for separating an outlaw biker, especially, from his motorcycle is the possibility that he has equipped the machine as a rolling cache for hidden weapons. What at a distance may look to you like a road flare tied to the frame may in fact be a crude shotgun made from two pieces of pipe and painted red. Some bikers weld a hunting knife blade to the inside of their gas cap, which can be quickly twisted off and brandished. On some bikes, the sissy bar can be jerked loose quickly and the ends have been filed to a point to create a lethal double lance. There's an escape consideration, also. Most bikers at least carry extra (hidden) keys and often they have a special switch installed to by-pass the ignition, requiring no key to start up and take off.

High-Risk Stops

So far we've discussed only stops of unknown risk, where there is no initial evidence of threat. Where there *is* presumption of risk, you are a lot more *high-profile* with your tactics. That includes cases where your NCIC check indicates the car you're about to stop is stolen...or where the driver or a passenger fits the description of a suspect who is reported to have displayed firearms or is wanted for a serious crime...or where a traffic violator suddenly rabbits into a high-speed chase...or where your intuition and experience warn you that something's hinky. Here you want to give *yourself*, not the driver, the benefit of the doubt.

To effect an arrest under such circumstances, suspects must be *removed from their vehicle* while *you* remain at a *distance*, with your sidearm or shotgun in position. One of the few absolutes in officer survival applies to high-risk stops: *never* EVER approach an occupied vehicle.

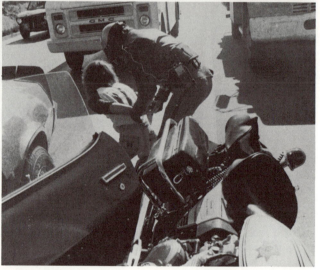

An incredible set of photos of a motor officer conducting a high-risk stop by himself. Although the officer survived and made the arrest, look at his vulnerability if the driver had decided to start shooting (above).

There's a *near*-absolute, too: except in *rare* cases, DO NOT attempt one of these stops ALONE. There may be some occasions in which your threat assessment indicates that you have hope of controlling the Problem Areas and Areas of Responsibility you're faced with by yourself. For example, you may stop a robbery suspect who's riding a motorcycle, and you can see he has no backup support and no effective cover opportunity. Or you may stop someone who moments earlier beat his wife in a domestic row and then fled in the family car. You can be reasonably certain he has no hidden passengers and that you're confronting him one-on-one. Even then, you're incurring certain risks you should be aware of; it's extremely difficult, if not impossible, for you as a single officer to give commands, make arrests and provide firearms control when you may be up against violent resistance. But for certain in any case where you're outnumbered or for any other reason feel you may be stretching beyond the point where you can protect yourself, *hold back* until you get support there, regardless of how long it takes.

Resist the kind of impulsive *action orientation* that could have easily proved tragic for a West Coast trooper. During a high-speed chase, a small pickup truck, later found to be stolen, spun out of control and landed against a fence along a freeway ramp. As the teen-age driver struggled with the gear shift, the officer drove his patrol car *directly up against the front bumper* of the truck to block its escape. The officer then exited into the open with his sidearm drawn. The suspect lowered his hands out of sight for a moment, but finally surrendered. Within his reach was a .30-30 rifle lying on the seat beside him. During the chase, he had fully loaded it and put a round in the chamber, intending to shoot the trooper. He changed his mind at the last moment.

Here an officer pulled up alongside this pick-up camper, which he knew was stolen, exited and was shot and killed. He had called for back-up but didn't wait.

Restraining yourself may mean following the suspect to another location or jurisdiction where backup is available. Or radioing ahead to arrange a roadblock. Or you may *initiate* the stop by halting the suspect vehicle and then *freeze the process* by attempting a bluff containment until help arrives. That is, you:

• *locate the stop to your advantage.* Halting the vehicle on a high bridge or pulled so close to parked cars that the right doors can't be opened, for example, limits escape opportunities. In bad weather, you may be able to position yourself under an overpass, with the suspect car exposed to the elements. (If the suspect vehicle stops suddenly before you intend it to, consider accelerating *around* it. Offenders may try this, especially just around a blind corner or by using their hand brake so as not to flash their tail lights, in hopes of startling you into stopping cold where you are powerless to defend yourself. *Keep going past the vehicle until you are in a protected position.* Don't make the mistake of two Canadian constables, who stopped close in front of a vehicle that braked suddenly. They then got out and approached the driver. In effect, they placed themselves in a "free fire" zone. The driver, a commando fanatic, opened up with a volley of rifle shots and killed one of the officers.) Stopping to the rear, you should be back about 30 to 40 feet to buy time and distance. At night, ideally, you want yourself concealed in darkness, the suspects exposed in light.

• *illuminate the suspect vehicle.* Even in daylight, your high beams, spotlight(s) and an ultra-powerful auxiliary light mounted on your light bar can enhance your vision and hamper the suspects'. Before you go on patrol, either an auxiliary light or your spotlight can be set at a level to hit directly in the eyes of a driver of average height exiting a vehicle.

• *get behind cover.* If better cover than your patrol car is available, *leave your vehicle.* You may still be able to use your outside speaker to broadcast commands to the suspects. If radio traffic can be fed into your P.A. system and you have a secondary, low-traffic channel available, set your radio to that frequency. You can now relay your commands through your speaker from a remote location via your portable. The suspects will likely believe you are still in your patrol car. In addressing the suspects, always use the term "we" when referring to yourself, to imply the presence of other officers. And if you do leave your vehicle in cold weather, be sure to take your *gloves* along.

• *announce your purpose.* You want to eliminate all doubt as to your identity, intent and ability. After identifying your agency, state the reason for the stop. Example: "You are under arrest. You are robbery suspects. We believe you are armed and dangerous." This informs true suspects, as well as mistaken ones, that this is serious business and adds a degree of reasonableness to your demeanor. This may later prove helpful in court.

If your announcement is in English and the suspects don't speak that language, your initial dialogue and subsequent instructions may not be comprehended. This may be true with intoxicated subjects, too. Under these circumstances, offenders may get out of the car and come back toward you to see why you've stopped them. Be prepared to make a tactical retreat if they attempt to approach your position. Above all, don't let their supposed inability to understand you lure you into attempting to approach them.

• *order the suspect vehicle immobilized.* If it has been hot-wired, there may be no ignition key. A command simply to "shut off your engine" rather than "turn off your key" will cover all circumstances. When the engine's off, have the driver place the keys, if any, on the roof or drop them on the ground. Throwing them out the window may rocket them into a snowbank, a field, heavy traffic or some other place where recovery will be tough.

• *command the occupant(s) to stay inside.* So long as everyone is inside, your Problem Areas are consolidated. If you order the suspects to prone out on the pavement while you're alone, as some observers recommend, you expand your Problem Areas—and their mobility—beyond what even your trained mind may be able to deal with. A rural Illinois officer one night allowed seven occupants of a car he'd stopped on a drug arrest to get out while he waited for backup. They quickly spread out all over the highway and into the ditches. One slipped on wet grass and broke a leg. Had they turned violent, the officer would have had little hope.

Some officers order all occupants to roll down the window nearest them and stick their *hands outside,* with fingers spread and palms turned so these Areas of Responsibility can be kept under surveillance. With this option, cold can be used to your advantage in winter by having the suspects remove gloves. After a bit their hands may be cold enough to affect their shooting accuracy. The hands-out tactic can work well on vehicles with tinted glass and other barriers to seeing inside. But keep in mind that having a suspect lower a window gets his hand out of sight temporarily and puts it in the vicinity of where firearms are often hidden. With the glass lowered, it's easier for him to suddenly stick a gun out and shoot you.

A better option where visibility inside permits is for the suspects to interlace their fingers behind their heads, elbows out to the side. If the car is well-illuminated, you have a good chance of seeing an early warning of movement. Unless a nearby window was already down when you initiated the stop, a suspect in order to shoot will have to open a door, lower a window or shoot through glass. The latter constitutes a strong psychological barrier to most people. If one or more suspects do fire, the sound of the gun going off inside the vehicle will be so deafening it may seriously disorient them in terms of their immediate follow-through ability.

• *maintain surveillance with a shotgun or rifle trained on the suspect(s)*. With the prospect of having to fire at assailants inside a car, a long gun with good penetrating power is highly desirable. So is their *knowing* that they are in your cone of fire. In California, one suspect said the only reason he decided to launch a fatal attack during a vehicle stop was because he knew no one had a gun on him.

• *stabilize the situation until you have enough manpower to proceed*. Finish the stop ONLY when the balance of power is in *your* favor. Meantime, creativity may buttress your bluff. Some officers patrolling remote areas alone secure a spare helmet on their passenger headrest to simulate a partner. One carries a tape recording of a German shepherd, snarling and barking, that he can activate over his P.A. periodically on a portable recorder to make it appear he has a K-9 with him. In any case, *tell* the suspects they are under control. If you sound convincing, they'll be encouraged to act accordingly.

Display cases in police department lobbies are filled with the badges of dead officers who didn't have the patience or confidence to wait...or who bought into the lethal philosophy that "if backup is an hour away, you *have* to go it alone." A 12-year officer in New York stopped a vehicle suspected of being used in a series of neighborhood robberies. Without waiting for backup, he approached and was shot by the driver with a .38. Although the officer returned fire and wounded his assailant, the suspect backed the vehicle over him, snagged him on the undercarriage, then roared down the street for seven blocks, dragging and mutilating his body. In Alabama, a single trooper approached *two* vehicles he knew to be occupied by robbery suspects. One subject partly opened a door and shot the trooper down with a .44 Magnum, then exited and finished him off with rounds to his chest.

With persistence and insistence, backup often is more available than you may imagine, even in rural areas. An officer who radioed that he was being fired on in a remote farm hamlet in Michigan drew an estimated 60 officers to the scene, some riding three or four to a car from 80 miles away! If you really cannot get help, *you can always let the suspects go*. The law does not demand that you complete *any* arrest at the sacrifice of your own life.

With help on hand, the placement of officers and additional patrol cars is the first step in avoiding the unorganized, free-for-all "clusterfuck" approach so common—and so hazardous—on high-risk stops. *Each officer at the scene should have an assigned responsibility.* Other-

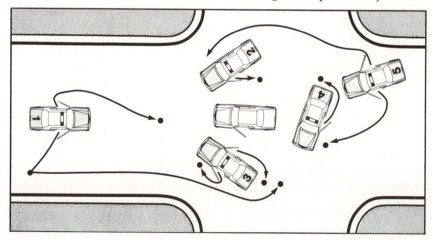

wise, too many officers may be as much a threat to your safety as too few, for one or more are bound to try to force themselves into the action inappropriately. *Don't try to impose one rigid format on every situation, however.* Specific settings and circumstances will change on practically every high-risk stop you make. You want *flexibility* to adapt your positioning to the nature of the threat, to the manpower available and to the surrounding environment—while still respecting sound tactical principles.

Good placement always promotes:

1. *cover* for the officers involved;
2. *separation* of officers, so they are not bunched in a single line of fire from the suspect vehicle;
3. *surveillance* of the Problem Area and all Areas of Responsibility;
4. *fields of fire* from your side that encompass the vehicle and all suspects without endangering any officers or innocent onlookers;
5. *light control* to your advantage;
6. *maneuverability;*
7. *efficient arrest procedures,* and
8. *perimeter control,* if possible.

These principles apply regardless of the number of officers involved.

As illustration for how ignoring or observing these considerations can impact the tactical integrity of a stop, assume you respond as a single backup on a two-officer stop. If you pull up behind the first officer with your lights on and he is still in his patrol car, you silhouette his position, making him an easier target. If you park bumper-to-bumper with him, you eliminate his chance of a tactical retreat. If you park exactly parallel to him, you lose the maximum effectiveness of your headlights in illuminating the suspect vehicle. If you run from your patrol car and position yourself behind his right rear fender, a spot some officers favor, you limit your visibility and make yourself vulnerable to ricochet fire off the side of the car. Also, you'll likely prove distracting to the primary officer, because officers tend to glance around any time someone is behind them to check on their actions, etc.

On the other hand, if you pull along the left side of his patrol car and *angle* your car toward the suspect vehicle about 15°, you maximize your light capability. Also you provide a good angle of fire for yourself if you have to remain in the driver's seat because of inadequate cover elsewhere. You'll have some cover protection from the engine block and the windshield post. Because you are laterally separated from the primary officer, it will be difficult for a single gunman to pin you both down. Both patrol cars can back up, if necessary. If manpower permits an additional officer to deploy to the front passenger seat of the primary vehicle (or flank out to suitable cover nearby), your combined visual expands to include the Areas of Responsibility on both sides of the suspect car. You have good fields of fire on anyone exiting that vehicle from any door or the trunk. As the stop progresses, you can move to an arrest position without creating or entering a cross fire, and so on.

The primary officer alone should issue commands to the suspect(s), regardless of the number of officers deployed. This minimizes confusion and contradiction. As primary officer, keep your sidearm at firing level. Visually and verbally focus on each suspect who exits as your Problem Area, until that individual is in a controlled position.

If there are only two of you, your partner can initially keep a shotgun trained on the suspect vehicle and later serve as control-and-arrest officer. If you're partners in the same car, he can occupy your passenger seat; if he's backup, he can initially stay in his front seat, unless better cover is available nearby.

Various options are available for deploying additional patrol cars and officers. If a third patrol car arrives, one possibility is for it to pull into a crosswise position a distance behind the first two cars. This angle eliminates a lasting silhouetting from that car's headlights and also provides something of a blockade for traffic coming from the rear. The officer from this patrol car can deploy to the passenger side of your backup's vehicle and help in guarding the Areas of Responsibility on the left side of the suspect car. This support will be important, because as primary officer you are bound to experience some separation of focus in trying to give commands, monitor each exiting suspect and maintain firearms readiness. The third officer may also become the control-and-arrest officer, depending on your stop procedure. However, this third car should be positioned far enough back that the first two cars can swing out around it in reverse if a sudden retreat is necessary.

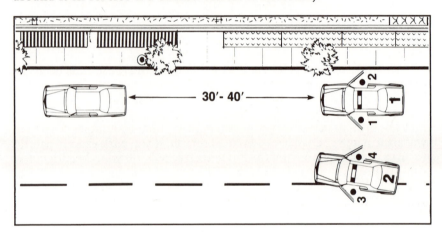

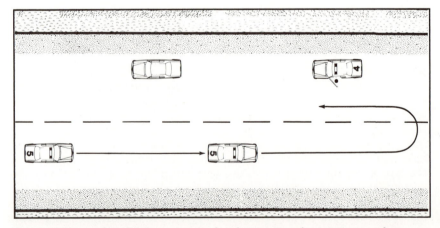

(bottom) If your first back-up approaches by passing the suspect car, he's heading into the kill zone. Better that he approach from your rear. If that is not possible, give him a perimeter position ahead of the suspect vehicle.

What you see is a patrol car–to–suspect vehicle distance of twelve feet...and look at the surprise! At a distance of 30-40 feet, the trunk suspect would have a harder time getting on target, especially at night.

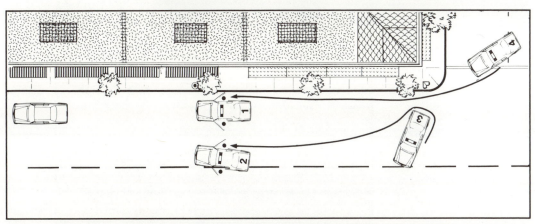

Positioning for the two primary units as well as additional principal units. Both Units 1 and 2 have room to back up quickly if escape is necessary. The driver of Unit 3 moves forward to Unit 2 and takes a cover position on its passenger side. The driver of Unit 4 parks where his vehicle blocks off side-street traffic. He then moves forward to become the passenger officer in Unit 1. He and the driver in Unit 2 are armed with shotguns.

A fourth patrol car approaching from the rear can make a U-turn before reaching the third unit and park facing back into traffic, with headlights and flashers on as a warning. That officer can move to the passenger seat of your primary unit (or flank out to better cover), to

323

provide shotgun surveillance of the right side of the suspect vehicle. If he's able to flank out, his intelligence-gathering from that unexpected angle can be very important.

Additional officers, if any, can help in securing prisoners away from the primary and secondary patrol cars, can serve as forward observers or can establish outer perimeter control to block off traffic flow headed toward the stop.

Generally, the primary officer, regardless of rank, controls the response deployment as well as dialogue with the suspect(s). A superior officer can direct arriving officers to the positions requested by the primary officer, or according to your department's written policy, if one exists. As with tactical deployment in other high-risk situations, however, *positioning for a high-risk vehicle stop MUST be rehearsed on a regular basis*, or it will deteriorate under stress, with participants who have not practiced.

There are *other* possibilities for how to position vehicles on a high-risk stop. These, too, have to be rehearsed. Certainly some are safer than others, and some are nothing more than the technique shown on the previous page being adapted to existing road and environmental conditions. For your analysis we share with you six alternative stop positions. All are currently being used in the field and are being taught to officers. To evaluate each one, list what you see as the strong points and weak points for each positioning. Some observations appear following the last illustration in the series. You can compare your reactions to those of fellow officers who have studied these configurations and experimented with their strengths and weaknesses.

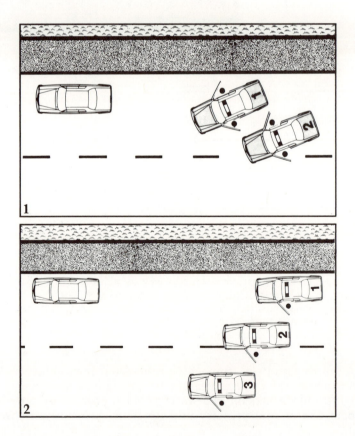

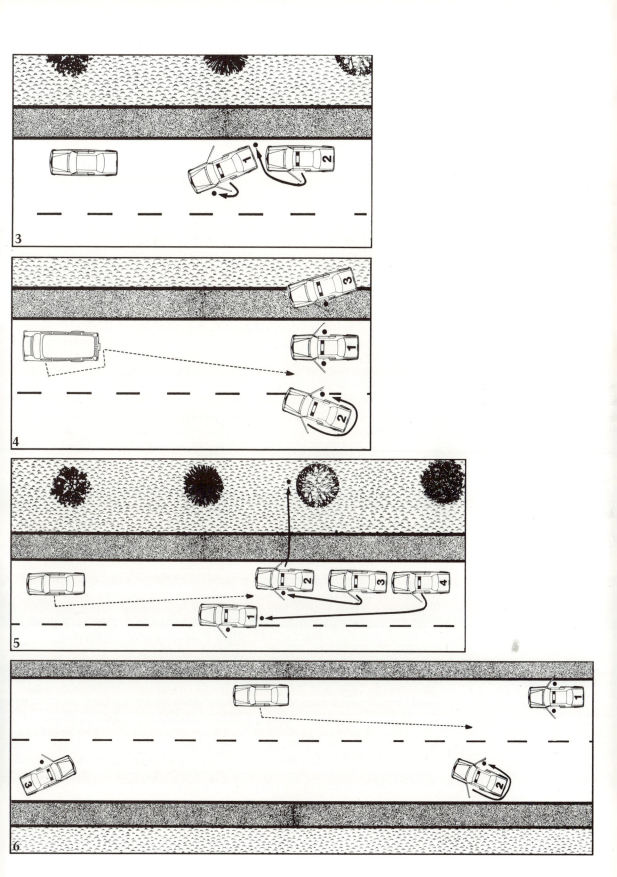

Position 1. This has been a popular two-vehicle positioning. However, today many regard it as obsolete for these reasons:

1. Both patrol cars are parked too close to the suspect car.
2. A 45° angular parking position reduces or eliminates high beam effectiveness.
3. Passenger officer in Unit 2 presents a cross-fire problem for the driver of Unit 1.
4. Passenger officer in Unit 1 is highly vulnerable to attack from the suspect vehicle, especially from its passenger side.
5. A tactical retreat by Unit 1 would be difficult if not impossible unless the shoulder of the road permitted such an exit.

Position 2. This procedure has some very positive features:

1. An effective distance exists between the suspect vehicle and Units 1-3.
2. Officers are well separated, minimizing the bunching effect.
3. Officers are able to maintain good illumination of the suspect car.
4. Unit 3's position shuts down traffic coming up from the rear.
5. All three patrol cars could exit the scene if necessary.

There are some considerations to this stop positioning which must also be considered:

1. Officers in Unit 2 and Unit 3 have to be careful not to park too far forward or they become back lit by Unit 1's lights.
2. On a busy road at night, Unit 3 would probably emit blinding light at civilian vehicles heading toward the suspect vehicle. This problem could be reduced by parking Unit 2 and Unit 3 at a slight angle to the suspect car. Better yet, have perimeter control shut down traffic totally.

Position 3. This positioning has some major problems to deal with:

1. Unit 1 is parked too close to the suspect car.
2. Because of positioning, Unit 1 and Unit 2 are denied the opportunity to aim their highbeams at the suspect car for general illumination and visual tracking of suspects should they flee on foot.
3. If Unit 2 has lights left on, the Unit 1 officer will be silhouetted.
4. Unit 2 officer has a poor visual on the suspect car, especially the driver's side.
5. Officer in Unit 1 has the luxury of a back-up officer. However, Officer 2's position makes his value limited. Officer 2 is also standing to the rear of Officer 1 which can be dangerous.
6. Unit 1 could not make a tactical retreat.

Position 4. This one has advantages outweighing disadvantages and could be effective even with van stops. Advantages include:

1. Excellent distance kept between officers and suspect vehicle.
2. All highbeams are aimed at the suspect vehicle for a solid bath of light.
3. All officers are separated, yet they are in visual contact with each other. This separation would probably be a real obstacle to a hostile occupant of the suspect car.
4. Both sides and the rear of the van are covered.
5. All three patrol cars could retreat if they had to.

When applying this position, realize that there may be limitations due to the type of road.

Position 5. Good points here include:
1. Passenger officer from Unit 2 flanking out to cover (should be behind tree) to observe movement inside the suspect car.
2. Good distance between suspect vehicle and patrol cars.

There are some problems, however, with this positioning to consider:
1. Single file positioning (with Units 2-4 blacked out) is really more appropriate on a narrow street. Given that environment, this positioning might have more validity.
2. A tactical retreat for Unit 2 and Unit 3 would be difficult or impossible.

Position 6. Another stop positioning with some strengths and some weaknesses. Strengths include:
1. Deployment of Unit 3 for perimeter control. Might be better to park even further back from the suspect car and still be out of cross-fire range of Unit 1 and Unit 2.
2. Good lighting on the suspect car.
3. Good escape routes for all patrol cars.

But there are a few problems here to consider. Did you notice:
1. Unit 1 is probably parked too far from the suspect car to detect subtle movement inside.
2. Units 1 and 2 are parked too far apart from each other, which may result in verbal communication between officers being overheard by suspects.

What you should consider now are ways in which the best features of these examples can be adapted to your current high-risk stop positioning. Then role-playing will help give you the crisis rehearsal you need to perform that revision under the stress of an actual stop.

Picture yourself as the primary officer here. You are starting to give verbal commands. One back-up unit is parked to your left and you are waiting for other officers. Suddenly this is what you see of your high-risk occupants. In a split-second they will both take off on foot. What do you do?

In this situation, one option that you and your back-up have is a tactical retreat. Then a re-evaluation of the situation. But you also have a golden opportunity to apply Tactical Thinking in another way to solve the problem of high-risk suspects who won't cooperate and flee on foot. Let's explore for a moment the thinking behind your other option.

As the two visible suspects leave, the male is running laterally away to the left, maybe to a tree. The female runs laterally into the cornfield and has an excellent opportunity, like her partner, to double-back and come around to the rear of the patrol cars and open fire (a proven terrorist tactic). If you and your partner maintain your original positions inside your vehicles because you assume you have good cover and concealment, you made a poor judgment. It would be nearly impossible for you two to defend yourselves from your present position.

Think back to the offenders' Thought Processes necessary for an assault. They have already Located you prior to their exit. Once they run, you temporarily lose the ability to Locate them. The offenders at this

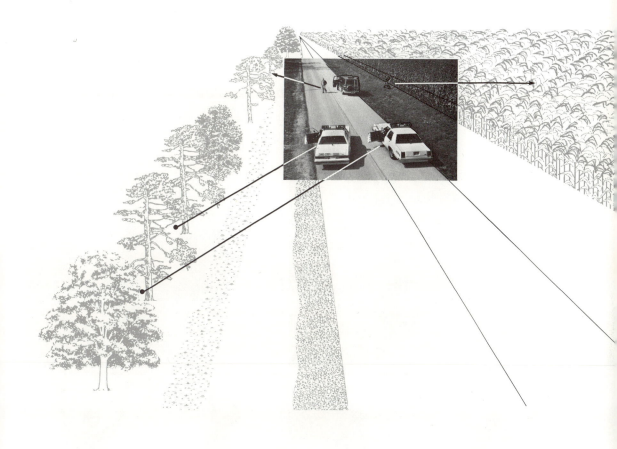

point have four Problem Areas (two officers, two patrol cars). But you and your back-up have a total of five Problem Areas (two suspects, the van which may still contain additional hazards, the tree area and the cornfield). The way to compensate for this limitation is to *increase* the offenders' Problem Areas and eliminate their first Thought Process, their ability to Locate you.

When you and your back-up stay low and quickly move to cover behind trees (not too close together) when the offenders run, you have achieved your goal of increasing the number of offender Problem Areas because you now have added the row of trees and the cornfield to their Problem Areas for a total of six. The cornfield is added because they may think you have headed into that area to arrest the female. Now you have far better odds of Locating them before they locate you two. If they come around from behind to assault the patrol cars because they think you both are inside, you are in a good position to challenge and defend.

Once the stop has been stabilized with everyone in position, your commands to the suspect(s) as primary officer should be loud, clear, brief and specific. Tell them: "Do exactly as we say and no one will get hurt. Do not move suddenly or unless you are told to do so. *Always* move VERY…SLOWLY. We will tell you what we want you to do. But *do not move* until we say, 'Do it now…'" After a suspect complies with an order, tell him: "Don't move now!" before issuing your next command.

Remember: *the most dangerous time in an apprehension is immediately after a suspect has complied with an order.* Your natural tendency then is to relax. The suspect may know that and exploit it for attack.

Where the environment permits, you'll probably want to bring the

suspect(s) out on the driver's side. It's usually further from immediate cover opportunities, such as buildings, parked cars, trees and ditches, and this will help discourage escape attempts.

If a K-9 is available, the dog, placed on full alert and probably barking, will add dramatically to your command presence. Advise the suspects in advance that the dog will be used to stop any occupant who tries to escape or act aggressively against an officer. If someone does run, the dog can be sent after him without an officer having to leave cover and be exposed to risks from the vehicle. In fact, officers should *not* give chase immediately in that case because the dog is likely trained to key on the nearest moving target, in uniform or not. Escape attempts, incidentally, are most likely either immediately after you stop the vehicle or as you begin to remove the suspects. The favored flight paths tend to be to the front and right of the vehicle.)

Beginning with the driver, clear the front seat of occupants first, then the back. If back passengers come out first, then those in front may use the rear doors for cover. First command the driver's hands out the window, then tell him to open the door from the outside and *follow it* as he swings it fully open, keeping his hands through the window frame. This automatically brings him out of the car *facing away* from you and the other officers. Now, command him to raise his hands *high* in the air ("Reach for the stars! *Higher!*") and sidestep away from the car. Consider having him kick the door shut to hamper an exit by another occupant. If he's wearing a hat, tell him to knock it off, to eliminate one hiding place for weapons.

Have him make a *slow* 360° turn while you scrutinize his waistband and other locations for weapons. If you see a weapon in his hand or in his clothing, immediately command him to *face away* from you, in order to maximize his Thought Processes and hamper his ability to attack. *Do not permit him to keep possession of the weapon.* While you and other officers are behind cover with multiple firearms directed toward him and the vehicle in bright light, you have the best opportunity to get him disarmed safely. If the weapon is not already in his hand, instruct him to kneel down, *slowly* withdraw it with his weak hand and lay it down. Have him slide it as far as possible to his left so it will be out of immediate reach of any additional suspects who exit the vehicle. Then instruct him to stand and back away from it. The weapon remains there until it can be recovered later during a search of the interior and trunk.

When ordering occupants out of a two-door vehicle, be especially alert when back-seat passengers tip the seat back forward to reach the door. Shotguns and other firearms are sometimes secreted in the area where the seat breaks to go forward. Because the suspect will naturally be hunched over as he crawls out, these weapons can easily be reached without officers detecting furtive moves.

Where the suspect goes once you command him to leave the "exit arena" immediately outside the vehicle is open to two popular schools of thought.

SCHOOL NO. 1 says you *"bring him back."* If there are two patrol cars positioned side by side with their doors open to the rear of the stopped vehicle, for instance, you can command the suspect to walk backward with his hands up high, and you guide him between the two cars.

Just as he passes the front bumpers, order him to stop, then to drop to his knees. This not only helps immobilize him, but gets him below your eye level so he doesn't block your view past him to the suspect car.

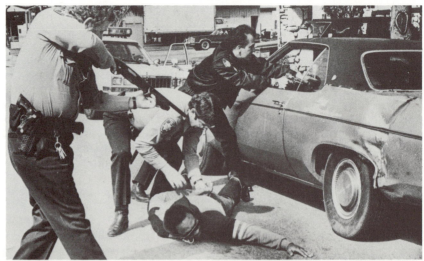

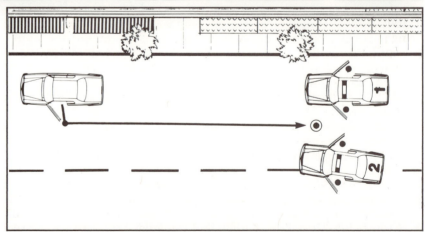

What it looks like when you fail to control distance and forego safety. (top)
Officers rush a bank robber as other suspects are ordered out of the car. (middle)
Officer rushes toward one robbery suspect who is wounded. No cover, no plan.
(bottom) One proper technique, bringing each suspect out one at a time.

You want him down before he's close enough to throw himself against one of the open doors, squashing you or a fellow officer positioned behind it. Tell him: "*Slowly*...bring your arms behind you. Do it now! Palms up! Bring your hands back toward us! *Farther!*" This gets his arms back into a swept-wing position, which will hamper his movement and set him up for handcuffing.

The control-and-arrest officer now moves from his position of cover (ideally, the front passenger seat of the second patrol car). He handcuffs the suspect, searches him and places him in the back seat of his vehicle or, better, in a third patrol car a distance away. The farther prisoners are kept from you, the primary officer, the less chance they'll disrupt your concentration on other suspects. Also at a distance, they have more trouble seeing the action and shouting out advice or intelligence to the suspects you're still trying to control.

A variation in movement can be used if there are only two of you and your partner is positioned on the passenger side of your patrol car. Here you can instruct the suspect to back up to the hood of your vehicle, with his hands back in a handcuffing position. Your partner moves up behind the fender and handcuffs him across the hood. In order to physically attack your partner, the suspect will have to go around or climb over the front of your car. While your partner controls and arrests, you keep the suspect car and any other occupants under continual surveillance.

Once the driver is handcuffed, secured and questioned about other occupants and possible weapons in the suspect vehicle, the next subject is ordered out and controlled in the same fashion. The process is repeated until the vehicle appears to be empty and there is no response to your bluff command for the "passenger hidden inside" to "sit up and put your hands out the window where we can see them." After that, the interior of the vehicle and the trunk are searched.

Some officers like to lay the groundwork for that search by having the last suspect removed leave the door(s) on the exit side open, so that an officer deployed at a distance to that side may be able to see inside from behind cover. This also facilitates a K-9 being sent up to search the interior. The last suspect also can take the keys from the roof and open the trunk. He is then told to place the keys in his teeth or hold them in his raised hand as he completes his movement back to the control-and-arrest officer. Of course, if the suspect vehicle is a van, you'll want the last visible occupant out to open the rear doors.

If you plan to conduct a high-risk arrest and search by a vehicle, you better have a better tactic in mind than this one. You cannot assume suspects will cooperate.

SCHOOL NO. 2 says you *"prone out"* the suspect(s) who are removed. Here you want to get them laid down in an *echelon pattern* to the left of their vehicle. After the driver exits and is visually searched, tell him to keep his hands up as he takes four or so giant steps away from the car, then four or so backward toward you. Exactly how far he should move depends on the number of suspects visible in the vehicle and your estimate of how much space they will take up together on the ground.

At the place you want the driver down, order him to turn *toward* you and prone out, belly down. If space permits, his arms should be back in a swept-wing position, palms up; otherwise order them stretched out in front of his head. Either way makes it much harder for him to do a fast pushup back to his feet than if his arms are straight out to his side. Order him to spread his legs, which will hamper his mobility more than having him cross his ankles. With the top of his head toward you, if he does try to get up, his center mass will be automatically exposed to you and fellow officers and you'll have the 1-to-8-inch ricochet rule working in your

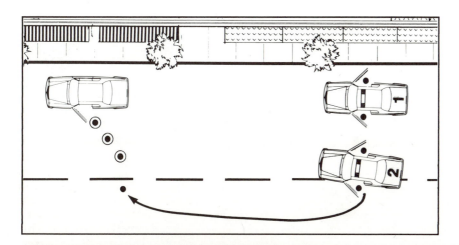

favor. Finally, have him turn his face toward the suspect vehicle.

Additional suspects are arranged similarly in a staggered line, so that the driver ends up being *farthest from the car and farthest forward*. None should be within touching distance of another, and you want the last suspect far enough away from the vehicle that he is not tempted to dive back inside.

Before a control-and-arrest approach is made with this procedure, THE INTERIOR OF THE VEHICLE MUST BE CLEARED and eliminated as a Problem Area. Otherwise the officer who approaches for handcuffing and searching is vulnerable to ambush. The *trunk* is not cleared until later, but it *is* covered by one of your backup officers as a specific Area of Responsibility during the rest of the procedure. Some departments advocate ordering the last suspect to lie on top of the trunk rather than on the ground. He's an easy target there and the lid can't open.

The control-and-arrest officer (coming preferably from the driver's seat of the second patrol car or another cover position nearby), approaches from the suspects' right, with his sidearm in the ready position. Just before he makes physical contact with the driver he holsters his sidearm *quietly* so that the suspects cannot hear this movement.

One at a time, he handcuffs and searches the suspects. Then, one at

Notice that all visible suspects are removed, *then* the search of this vehicle is conducted using extreme caution and thoroughness.

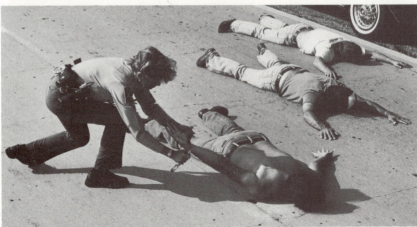

(middle) The control and arrest officer makes her approach *after* the vehicle search has been completed. She positions herself to avoid a cross-fire and further separates the suspect's gun (on the ground) from the driver prior to handcuffing. (bottom) The officer moves in to handcuff. Cover is provided for her as she handcuffs using a wrist lock.

a time, he "peels" them off from the echelon and removes them to a patrol car. Because each is positioned farther back from the other, the control-and-arrest officer can keep the whole line in sight while handcuffing. And if a suspect downline starts to get up or attack, the officer is not in a cross-fire position relative to his fellow officers back at the patrol cars.

Again, if a K-9 is available, it should be readied to intercede if needed when the control-and-arrest officer is making his physical contacts. If manpower permits, two officers may be assigned for control and arrest. One handcuffs and searches while the second covers with a shotgun.

There is also a third school for handling suspects on high-risk stops, widely practiced on the street but tactically unsound. This is to position the suspects against their vehicle essentially in a wall-search position, then attempt to handcuff and search them. In terms of control and immobilization, this is far inferior to the approaches described above because of the ease with which suspects can spin out of this position to attack.

The weaknesses of even the acceptable approaches should not be overlooked, of course. In evaluating them for use, you need to weigh their potential problems against their very definite strengths in determining which options best suit the situation you face.

The bring-'em-back concept probably will be less anticipated by offenders...allows you to deal with one suspect (Problem Area) at a time...tends to destroy suspect unity...gives you maximum protection from a problem vehicle...and offers you excellent control up to the point where the suspect reaches your front bumper—all strong pluses.

However, you are bringing the offender out of a control zone to your cover area. This could create hazardous dilemmas. Suppose he tries to escape by diving in front of your car or your backup vehicle. Shooting him without leaving cover will be difficult, if not impossible. If you drive backward to expose him, you are breaking your established line of defense. If you drive *forward* (as some departments mandate by policy), you may hit and incapacitate him, but you are driving into the kill zone (from the suspect car).

Or suppose he starts fighting when the control-and-arrest officer lays hands on him. You may need to assist and will have to leave cover to do so. Officers who are supposed to be maintaining shotgun control of the suspect car will undoubtedly be tempted to join in. There are, after all, at least two firearms (yours and the arrest officer's) at risk in the struggle. Unless the other officers have the awesome self-discipline to resist, the car may be left unguarded—and all of you subject to a pre-planned attack.

Even if all goes smoothly, bringing them back involves considerable movement. This takes time, increasing the time you're exposed to risk.

Some officers using this approach complicate things even more by ordering the suspects to come back *on their knees.* This takes even longer and, considering the pain involved, will almost guarantee that any suspects who are able to make it to your front bumper will be enraged animals when they get there.

Proning the suspects out has drawbacks, too. It may not be practical under some weather and road conditions. You'll need to shut down oncoming traffic to forestall some citizen running over the suspects proned in the roadway. Also, in order to effect the arrest with any degree of safety, the suspect vehicle must be cleared while the suspects still are nearby not handcuffed and not searched. When the control-and-arrest officer does move up, he not only must leave cover but he also proceeds to the vicinity of a lot of Problem Areas.

Where only one control-and-arrest officer is used, only his or her safety is compromised with this approach. That can be considered a strength, especially when you are dealing with agitated, aggressive subjects. If things go sour, all other officers can have target acquisition without leaving cover, an impressive assemblage of firepower. Also, proning out is easy even for the dumbest offenders to understand. Little movement and little decision-making is required of them.

This method, like bringing 'em back, can be carried to bizarre extremes, though. One Southern agency favors a version of proning that requires all suspects to exit through the driver's window and "dog pile" one on top of another beside the car. Only pregnant women are excused from this procedure. Aside from the question of what you do *next* with any degree of safety, verification of pregnancy may also present a challenging field problem!

Based on what you know of the proper "prone out" method, name at least three things that could be improved upon here for greater control.

Done properly, either mainstream approach gives you an organized, tactical edge over flying by the seat of your pants. The first option, especially, can be streamlined when you're working a hostile neighborhood and perceive that the threat from a crowd that may form during a prolonged stop could be greater than that from the high-risk subjects you're arresting.

Whatever your approach, the suspect vehicle will need to be cleared after all visible occupants have been removed. In the past, it has been recommended that a handcuffed suspect be brought up to the vehicle to "witness" the search while, in fact, serving as a shield for the searching officer. Because of legal interpretations that this is a "hostage" situation, this practice is *no longer acceptable* on most agencies. Of course, suspects can—and should—be questioned about hidden occupants and a bluff command addressed to "occupants hidden in the car," but in the end it usually is officer eyes that will verify the vehicle's status.

On some departments, K-9s have been trained to approach the exterior of a vehicle and detect if anyone is hiding inside, especially if a door has been left open. (It is considered inappropriate by most trainers for a dog to try to enter the vehicle through a window.) If a dog does not "alert" while sniffing the car or K-9 service is not available, an officer will need to cautiously approach the car (assuming the interior can't be checked adequately through doors left open by the last suspect out). In a multiple-officer stop, the approaching officer generally will be the one deployed with a shotgun on the passenger side of the primary patrol car.

If you are the officer selected, leave your shotgun behind and *be certain you are wearing body armor.* With your sidearm pointed at the suspect car in a ready position, move in a circuitous arc *around* (not straight past) the right side to a point diagonally out from the right front windshield post. This is a route of approach a hidden passenger is not likely to expect. Try to use cover—trees, mailboxes, light poles, parked cars—along the way.

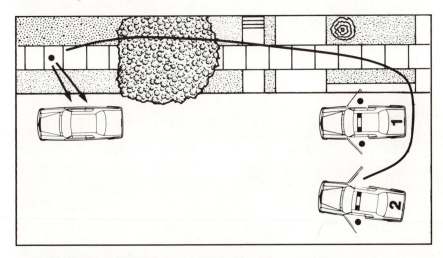

Walking with your gun still in the ready position, "seeing" what your eyes see, approach the vehicle at about a 30° angle, focusing on your Areas of Responsibility. Because of the cross-fire risk, other officers still in position behind the suspect vehicle should concentrate their firearms only on the opposite side of the vehicle and on the trunk. You are responsible for defending yourself on the passenger side.

As you get close, you can stretch up for quick peeks inside. From your angle, you'll be able to see anyone hiding on a seat or floor before they can see you; the dash or seatbacks will interfere with their view up and out. If you do see someone, back off to cover and issue appropriate commands. If a threat's presented, you can defend yourself immediately.

Another option is to approach on the *driver's* side. Here you use a patrol car as moveable cover. You walk in a low crouch behind its front left fender with your sidearm ready as a second officer slowly drives it at an angle in toward the side of the suspect vehicle. He leans low across his front seat, just peering over the dash to steer. When the patrol car stops, you can quick peek from behind it to check the interior of the suspect vehicle. This approach eliminates the cross-fire risk and also the risk that your visibility will be hampered by having to look into the head-lights of patrol cars parked to the rear.

A controlled trunk search requires the teamwork of two officers, one approaching from the driver's side of the suspect vehicle, the other from the passenger side. If you are one of them, move to position from the front or side of that car, not from the rear, which is more predictable and puts you in a direct field of fire from the trunk. As you move in, *no*

Proper tactics (above) for clearing a vehicle are simple to do and so important. Suspects *do* hide in trunks (right). Here three bank robbers are being arrested. Two were in the trunk!

340

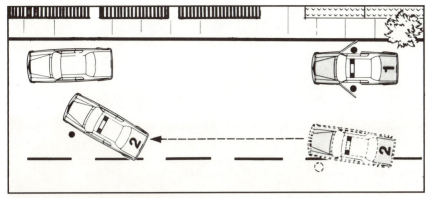

Using the patrol car as portable cover.

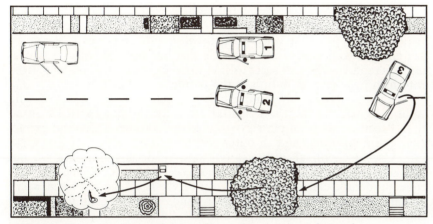

If the suspect cooperates with open doors, this tactic might work.

officers to the rear should attempt to maintain firearms control because of the cross-fire problem. The officer approaching on the *passenger* side provides it exclusively, until the trunk is unlocked.

If you're the officer on the driver's side, you retrieve the keys from the roof or ground, if the suspect hasn't brought them back with him. As the other officer stands on the passenger side at the rear windshield, his gun pointed at the trunk, you crawl around *low*, lie on your back or side behind the car, reach up and unlock the trunk. The other officer keeps pressure on the lid with his off hand so it stays closed while you back off into similar position on the driver's side of the car. Once your sidearm is pointed at the trunk, the other officer releases the lid to see inside.

To dramatically limit the field of view of anyone in the compartment, consider adding this step before the lid is released: at a distance, raise the hood of a patrol car and just before the trunk lid is allowed to rise, have this unmanned car pushed against the rear bumper of the suspect vehicle. When the trunk lid goes up, all a suspect will see will be the raised hood. His disorientation can be heightened if you activate the patrol car's siren before pushing it forward. By the time the suspect becomes oriented to what's happening, you can have him under control. And if he does fire in surprise or frustration, he's unlikely to do any human damage.

(above) What you would observe if you were a hidden offender and popped open the trunk lid. Surprise!

After your search is complete, the suspect vehicle should be locked. *No vehicle should be towed until its trunk is cleared.* One detective lieutenant in the East was killed because this rule was violated. In searching a suspected robbery vehicle that had been towed to a substation, he removed the rear seat cushion to check under it. Shots were fired into him by a suspect hiding in the trunk.

During or before the final search, you may encounter a suspect who refuses to exit the vehicle. Essentially you then have a barricade situation. Because this is a high-risk stop, do *not* consider a physical extraction. Build an inner- and an outer-perimeter, and *wait.*

Use of chemical agents is one option. Because vehicles are not airtight, tear gas used outside may be successful; a CS grenade might be rolled under the car, for example. But if this fails, a 12 ga. chemical agent round might be shot through the rear windshield, although the angle of the glass may make penetration difficult. Because firing any projectile has potentially lethal force, it should not be done until repeated efforts have been made to talk the suspect out. Before firing, he should be warned: "If you do not exit immediately, we will fire tear gas projectiles into your vehicle. You have 30 seconds before we begin! These projectiles can kill or injure you if they strike you directly."

One suburban department in Minnesota tried a more radical approach. During negotiations on a high-risk stop with an intoxicated suspect who refused to exit his car, the subject asked for beer. An officer wearing body armor approached the vehicle with a six-pack, while a special weapons officer crawled next to the car to cover him. The suspect would only open the wing window enough for one can to be handed in at a time. The third can in was a triple-blast CS grenade. The resistance ended soon after.

Another possibility is to summon a firetruck to the scene. Pump about 200 gallons of water into the vehicle—and let the uncooperative suspect float out!

Biker Runs

Stopping a large group of outlaw bikers on a ceremonial "run" to a funeral, a swap meet or a party is a special form of high risk. Even when no known or suspected felony or outwardly aggressive behavior is involved, the threat *potential* is extraordinary.

Here you have a minimum of perhaps 10 motorcycles in two-by-two formation. Many participants have warrants outstanding and/or have past felony convictions and/or are currently engaged in illegal activities like drug trafficking, gunrunning or Mafia violence. Firearms almost certainly are present, in anticipation of a confrontation with a rival gang or other adversaries en route or for use in sport or ritual at the destination. Guaranteed to be present is a pervasive hatred of law enforcement and a perception that any stop is "harassment." And coming along a mile or two behind the main group, possibly indistinguishable from normal traffic, will be one or more "crash trucks" (a van, U-Haul, semitrailer or old school bus), carrying broken bikes, broken bikers, supplies, police scanners, perhaps contraband and heavy weapons and probably some probationary recruits hot for action and a chance to make their marks as macho men.

If you take on that entourage by yourself, you're only asking to be challenged.

In contrast to the terror rides of *The Wild Ones* era, the rare runs still conducted today usually try to avoid police contact by being consciously law-abiding in regards to road behavior. But if a stop is deemed necessary—for intelligence-gathering...because of a strong suspicion that contraband is being transported...to serve an arrest warrant...or to prevent a violent clash down-road with another gang—not only common sense but also the biker mentality *mandates* ample backup.

Outlaw bikers respect a *controlled* show of force. To their thinking, this shows respect for them by law enforcement, which they regard as another gang, of sorts. So you want to display an organized, high-profile, military-style, *cool-headed,* tactical presence. *Numbers are important here.* In Colorado, nearly a dozen federal and local officers joined forces to stop a small run of the Sons of Silence gang for questioning. Even then, the bikers tried to provoke trouble during the interrogation by such behavior as urinating at the roadside so that the officers' shoes were splattered.

Ideally, the stop should be effected at a *roadblock.* Trying to stop a large run from the rear will be futile if the lead riders can't hear your siren over the roar of their bikes, and pulling alongside while they're still

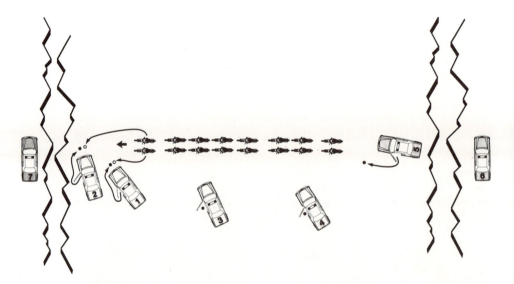

moving exposes you to obvious added risks. At the blockade, officers should be ready to take positions near the front of the run, while others who are following in line behind the bikes are ready to move to the rear and left side when the group halts.

You want to give the bikers the feeling of being *penned in.* With five patrol cars, say, you can have two take positions off to the side, angled in toward the front of the run...two angled perpendicular to the formation's left side...and one about 20 feet back facing the rear of the group. Two other cars should lay off about a quarter-mile to the front and rear to shut down oncoming traffic, and a final unit, carrying at least two officers, should be detailed to intercept and monitor the crash truck.

Understanding and observing biker protocol is vital in fostering as much cooperation as possible. Only the club president and the road captain, who is responsible for the logistics of the run, have any decision-making capacity, and one or both of them should be dealt with exclusively by the highest-ranking officer present. Preferably this will be a lieutenant or above to capitalize on the group's regard for authority.

The club president may be "buried" back amidst the bikers, but the road captain customarily will be one of the two front riders. He at least can be easily summoned to the front of one of the forward patrol cars for conversation with the highest-ranking officer and a backup. The officers are not behind cover but try to stand just a jump away from their vehicles in case trouble starts.

The side officers and rear guard are on their feet, acting as spotters. They have quick access to, if not actual possession of, shotguns. If a biker presents a threat that demands a deadly force response, keep in mind that many these days wear soft body armor under their colors and that shots to the head or pelvic girdle may be your best option for bringing him down.

With his P.A. or command voice, the rear-guard officer gives directions to the group as a whole. You want the bikers and any passengers standing straddling the bikes, kick stands up, their hands on their legs. With the bike at the top of their cultural value scale, they won't let it fall without first engaging the kick stand, which may give you some warning of imminent aggression. With their hands on their legs, you lessen their chances of covertly reaching or transferring weapons.

Common biker tools of the trade.

Because any women in the group are most likely to be the weapons carriers, some officers believe they should be separated to the side or rear. But by doing so, you splinter your Problem Areas and also risk igniting a super macho resistance from the bikers who "don't want our women fucked with."

Back down the road, the crash truck(s) will require at least the tactics you'd normally use on problem vehicles and may warrant high-risk procedures, depending upon the cause for the run being stopped and your evaluation of the threat potential. Naturally, you want to look inside, if possible, once the occupants are out and in a controlled position.

In checking the exterior, something that will help you build probable cause for a more thorough search is the presence of a "dump box." This is a trap-door device under the vehicle that can be released from inside. Narcotics often are carried there so that the door can be opened and the goods scattered on the highway at high speed if a police approach seems imminent. Even if the contents have already been spilled when you find the box, a K-9 may be able to detect lingering odors of drugs and establish grounds for your searching the interior.

Be aware throughout the stop that bikers jealously defend their legal rights. Lawyers are now asked to travel along on some runs. The bikers keep track of how often and why they are stopped, and pounce on any evidence of harassment. Some clubs have sued police agencies and, in at least one case, won an injunction against further stops.

Don't be surprised if they ask for your name and badge number. They may tape record your conversation with them, so be careful what you say and how you say it. In some regions, they use police-like field interrogation cards, filling in your vehicle license number, time they were detained, reason for the stop, your disposition, etc. At their club-houses, they may keep intelligence files on officers' home addresses, make and model of personal car, children's names, spouse's place of employment and so on.

These people are not to be taken lightly, no matter how bizarre or comical their lifestyle may seem. *Above all, do not do or say anything in your contact with them that can be interpreted as belittling or befouling their colors.* These are considered sacred raiment, worth dying for. Some officers, as a prank, have laundered or dry-cleaned bikers' filthy jackets or vests while the owners were in custody, in violation of the custom that colors are never cleaned once awarded. Such acts are declarations of war. You can count on vengeance.

Off-Duty Considerations

Because you're likely to be armed whenever you're off-duty, you may either present a special problem or be able to render special assistance to a working officer on a vehicle stop. You can be a problem if you're stopped as a violator and the officer detects that you have a gun *before* he understands you're in law enforcement. You can be an aide if he has stopped someone else and you volunteer as impromptu backup.

If you're stopped for a violation, turn on your dome light at night and consider immediately placing your badge case open on your dash so it will be in plain view of the approaching officer. Then rest both hands high on your steering wheel and look ahead.

When the officer arrives, tell him: "I'm an officer with (name your agency). I am armed with a (describe your handgun). It's located (wherever you're carrying it). What do you want me to do?"

As the working officer in such a case, this statement should put you in Condition Orange. Until you have checked the violator's credentials and verified his identity, he should be treated like any other violator under those circumstances. More than just that dialogue should be required to reassure you.

Even then, remain conscious of the subject's hands and movements, maintain ready access to your sidearm and follow through faithfully with survival-conscious positioning and procedures. As always, *do not assume there is no risk until the violator is back in traffic and out of assault range.* Under the wrong personal pressures, police officers can become assailants, too.

Helping with a vehicle stop when you're *off-duty* is best done with prior planning.

To compensate for scarce or frequently delayed backup, officers in some locales use a stopgap "buddy system" approach. Here, if you drive by off-duty and notice an officer working a stop, you park nearby and keep a watchful eye on the situation, ready to offer assistance if needed. One version works like this:

To identify yourself, signal with your lights. Daytime, put on your headlights and hazard flashers; at night, activate the flashers and flick your headlights twice. Then wait in your car, hands atop the steering wheel or resting out of the window to confirm that you're not a threat, until the officer motions you over or waves you on, depending on how he feels about the stop he's making.

If you are on the same side of the street as the officer, park behind his unit and wait until he notices you before making your signal, so as to minimize the distraction. In an opposing lane, signal as you pull over, then stop almost opposite his unit and wait there, to get you past the Target Zone.

An alternative, in well-lighted areas, is to use coded hand signals. In one department, for example, a hitchhiker's thumb signal by an off-duty officer means, "I'm a police officer. Do you need help?" If the working officer returns a signal with two fingers raised, he's saying,

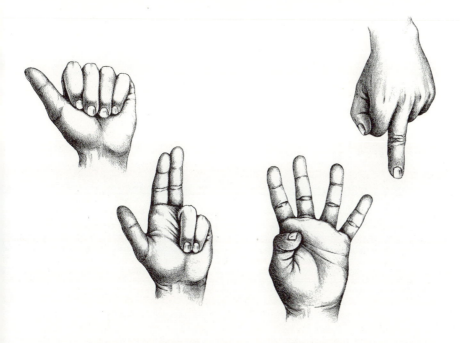

"Show me your badge" for verification. If he flashes four fingers, it means everything's okay and he needs no assistance. If his middle finger is extended in any direction, he's signaling, "The situation is very dangerous/explosive. Use extreme caution."

At the very least, your presence should make the violator think

twice before he attacks the officer, because there is now a witness to his actions.

To maximize the effect of this system, all enforcement agencies in an area should be briefed on the recommended procedures. Of course, confidentiality is important to keep the working officer from being deceived by an imposter who is, in fact, backup for the violator.

7

DOMESTIC DISTURBANCES

In a mountain county of North Carolina, a deputy sheriff and his captain responded to a family fight at a rural residence. A mother and her daughter had gotten into a row with the husband over how much vodka to pour into the punch for a high school graduation party. The husband, who'd consumed a six-pack of beer, began beating the women, and the daughter called for help.

The officers drove up and stopped directly in front of the house at the end of a long dirt driveway. The husband came out, carrying a .30-06 rifle. The officers paid it no mind. Both knew him...had dealt with him nonviolently in the past...and apparently felt they could deal with him again.

He raised the rifle and killed the captain before that officer made it to the front porch. Then he fatally gunned down the deputy by the passenger door of their vehicle. Later he ambushed a state trooper around a blind curve on a winding mountain road and killed him, too.

The first officers forgot the single most important thing to remember in handling domestic disturbance calls: *what happened before is not a reliable measure of what will happen this time;* what is happening *right now* is no predictor of what will happen hours, minutes, even *seconds* from now.

Even highly experienced mental health professionals have an unimpressive record in predicting which individuals will exhibit violent behavior at any given time. One study shows them accurate in no more than one-third of their attempts, even though they have full psychological data and years of behavioral observations on the subjects they're evaluating. With far less to go on, you invite tremendous risks relying on *your* guesses. Circumstances change...pressures change...people change. Fifty times officers responded to domestic disturbances at a certain address in the Midwest. There were never any weapons or serious violence involved. The 51st time, one of the disputants without warning fired through the door and killed two officers as they walked up from their patrol car parked in front.

The only thing more *unpredictable* than a human being is a human being in *crisis.* And a domestic disturbance in many ways is a crisis that inflicts uniquely heavy stresses. The parties are in a conflict they do not know how to resolve peacefully. They generally are battling with someone of great emotional value to them, which exaggerates their intensity and volatility. They frequently are intoxicated. They are likely to be angry, frustrated, hostile, defensive and out of control—all at the same time. And they may each view you as a threatening intruder into their private realm. Their confusion, distorted perceptions, impulsive urges, instability, distrust and other symptoms of crisis behavior all conspire to put you in a particularly perilous position. One-third of all officer assaults occur on disturbance calls.[1] Nearly one in five officers killed on duty die on these calls, which are among the fastest-growing, as well as the most hazardous, in law enforcement.

Even the rawest recruit these days knows the core considerations of safely approaching disturbance calls: roll in quiet and dark...park a few doors away...approach the location at an angle (from the knob side of the door, if at all possible), walking apart and somewhat behind your partner...avoid silhouetting yourself against lighted areas...stay alert to windows, including those on upper floors...don't stand in front of the door you're knocking on...and don't barge in if someone inside yells, "Come on in!"

Yet more than half the officers slain on domestics are killed making their initial approach—and generally when violating these common sense basics. Inside, officers often make themselves vulnerable by breaching other fundamentals, in the way they position the disputants ...or manage potential weapons...or try to calm the crisis or conduct their departure. Too often, officers seem to approach these calls focused more on why they *dislike* them ("I'm not a marriage counselor"..."I don't want to meddle in, in someone else's home"..."I want to be out fighting *real* crime"..."It's the same old thing every Friday night"... "Shit marries shit. There ain't no one here worth savin'") than on their *great potential danger.*

As with other high-risk assignments, controlling disturbances

[1]FBI Uniform Crime Reports.

Officers and emergency medical personnel desperately try to save two officers who were shot while responding to a call which started out as an argument between two neighbors over a rosebush. Both officers and offender died.

safely begins with a mental attitude that *respects* the call. Considering that *weapons* are used in about 30% of family violence cases...that *injuries* are inflicted on someone by the participants more than half the time...that in about one-third of the cases, *force* is used by responding officers...and that *always* these calls are *unpredictable,* they warrant your *full attention* to your best psychological and physical skills.

Handling disturbances *tactically* involves a *control process* that includes:

1. Developing a tentative plan of action en route to the call;
2. Initially approaching and deploying tactically at the scene;
3. Assessing the status of the disturbance and the level of immediate threat it presents;
4. Making entry safely into the location;
5. Physically positioning the disputants;
6. Calming the disputants;
7. Exploring the reasons for the dispute;
8. Determining and conducting the police action most likely to prevent further violence;
9. Departing safely from the scene.
10. Evaluating your performance.

The steps of this process build progressively upon each other. If you eliminate or slight any one of them, the outcome may be shatteringly different than it should be.

Cycle of Violence

The disputants involved in domestic disturbances tend to operate on a repetitious *cycle of behavior.* Comprehending that cycle and knowing where they are in it when you arrive will strengthen your control process. This knowledge can help you select the tactics you need to safely manage their conflict. The cycle was originally defined to explain *violent* spouse abuse, but some of the same factors are at work in *nonviolent* disputes, too. And they can apply whether the participants are actually married or not.

With physical violence, males by tradition are most often the aggressive subjects, with females perhaps fighting back in defense and resorting to weapons to compensate for their relative size and weakness. When the aggressor is not a male spouse, ex-spouse or boyfriend, he's likely to be a son. But do not be trapped by stereotypes. *Women* are becoming increasingly violent as *aggressors.* In one study among university students, more than half the persons surveyed admitted using physical violence in a major personal relationship, and half of those were women. Shelters for battered women are reporting seeing a significant increase in women who have been abused by *other women,* in roommate or lesbian situations. So you should not assume if you're met by a woman at a disturbance location that she is necessarily the *victim,* even though she may bear injuries.

Before the violence erupts, as researchers chart the cycle, there's a period in which the eventual disputants experience *tension building* between them. This Phase I period may last hours or months or even years. The soon-to-be-aggressor is edgy, irritable, possessive, demanding. Minor outbursts may betray his or her mounting anger and aggression.

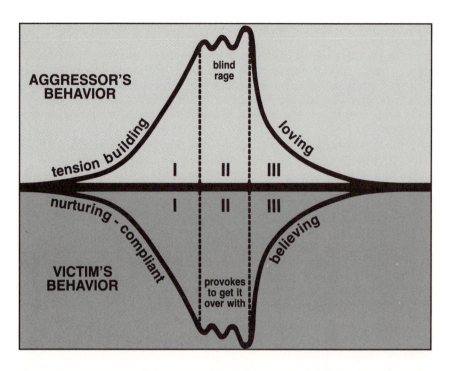

The victim may withdraw or deny the stress of this period, or be especially nurturing or compliant in hopes of defusing it. But that proves futile; the victim cannot please the aggressor, because the demands are unrealistic. In one Wisconsin case, a husband insisted that his wife have sex with other men according to his explicit directions while he watched. But her performance never satisfied him. Either she unhooked her bra too soon or too late or she moaned too loud or too soft or she writhed too vigorously or not enough. Whatever she did, he ended up furious with her.

In Phase II of the cycle, the aggressor *explodes* in a blind rage, having convinced him- or herself that aggression is justified. Out of control, his (or her) actions may range from shoving, slapping or punching through sexual abuse, torture or murder. The victim may reciprocate violently, but be consistently "outpointed." Even if physical contact is not actually made, the victim may be threatened with death or menaced with a gun or knife. Property and pets, too, may suffer the full force of the aggressor's fury. Indeed, as you approach a scene, take a close look at pets that appear to be sleeping. They may, in fact, have been killed—a clear danger sign for you of more potential violence.

Ironically, the victim may do something consciously or unconsciously to *provoke* the explosion in order to get it over with and move the cycle into Phase III. This is a contrite, *loving* period when the aggressor expresses regret about the damage and injuries, charmingly comforts and pampers the victim and earnestly promises better treatment in the future. In a sense, these are the victim's "rewards" for being abused. Though it all may have been heard a hundred times before, the victim *believes*, and is loving, trusting, accepting. This may be the only period in which the couple has sexual relations, and it generally fades quickly.

In time, of course, the cycle repeats. The longer the disputants maintain a relationship, the shorter Phase III becomes. And as the violent encounters occur more frequently, they also become more *severe*. The suicide or homicide of one disputant or the other is not unusual.

You're generally called during Phase II, the most volatile and dangerous point in the cycle. When you arrive, you typically will find an aggressor who is very angry and a victim who is very fearful. *At least* one will not want you there. While your arrival may *appear* to stop whatever violence is taking place, the fires are often only thinly banked, capable of rekindling at any moment without warning. Indeed, *inappropriate officer response* is often the cause of violence and other abuse *reescalating* into Phase II instead of being resolved.

Drugs are commonly involved in this cycle, alcohol somewhat more often with married disputants, other drugs more with unmarried. Disputants often convince themselves that booze *causes* an aggressor to be abnormally violent by lowering his inhibitions and self-control. But some psychologists believe that many times the aggressor drinks with the *intention* of beating the victim, knowing that responsibility then can be ducked because the alcohol can be blamed. In about a third of the cases, *both* parties will be drunk or drugged or both. That means you'll frequently be dealing with two people who may be difficult to communicate with, who are not capable of full rationality, who may be resistant to following orders and who thus are even more unpredictable and prone to violence.

Whatever the dispute seems to be about on the surface, underlying it are bound to be intense feelings about highly emotional subjects. Love, honor or property are generally the true roots of domestics, according to one authority; another says they are sex, money, drugs or alcohol or family and acquaintances. The disputants may not admit the *real* issues even to themselves, much less to you. But if you're sensitive to these potential unspoken forces, you'll be better prepared to manipulate the situation to your advantage and avoid "hot buttons" that can provoke an attack.

Males who are habitually abusive, for example, are believed by some authorities to feel mind-bending insecurity and profound sexual inadequacy, even though they often seem glib, personable, self-assured and "macho" in their everyday lives. They're desperately afraid their women will leave them, and upon real or imagined provocations they use violence to dominate and control them. With that in mind, you should avoid saying anything that such a subject might interpret as a sexual slur. You may even want to avoid speaking privately with the victim where the aggressor might imagine that sexual overtures are being made.

Victims in a cycle of violence may appear masochistic, for all the repeated abuse they endure. But in fact they often feel *trapped* by fear, shame, guilt, financial dependence, children, marital loyalty, a sense of worthlessness and the naive hope of reform. They are generally looking to you for the restoration of peace and some sense that their plight is believed and cared about at that moment. *But they are not necessarily looking for the punishment of their attacker.*

Occasionally a domestic has *mutual* combatants, where each party participates equally in initiating and inflicting violence. Here a neighbor or relative is often the complainant, and neither participant may welcome your arrival. These calls can be especially dangerous.

By the time you arrive at any domestic, the situation will generally have escalated to a crisis point where the participants cannot resolve it rationally by themselves. They now are under an enormous amount of stress and frustration. As emotions rise, control drops. *Be prepared to deal with any type of behavior that can be sparked by a stress overload,* including the most bizarre.

Keep your limitations in mind. You are not likely to work any marvels here. *Your objectives are modest* measured against the true problems the disputants probably have...but *vitally important* to you and to them, nonetheless. Guarding your *own* safety first and foremost, you want to:

1. stop any violence that is underway;
2. get treatment for any injuries that have been inflicted;
3. assess the advisability of arrest, and
4. take whatever action you think is most likely to forestall the recycling of potentially violent conflict.

You will probably have very little control over the *cause* of the disputants' problems. But you have a *great deal* of control over *your* behavior. DO NOT GET CONFUSED ABOUT WHAT YOU CAN MANAGE TO YOUR ADVANTAGE.

Unexpected Approach

As you approach the scene, the right intelligence from your dispatcher helps you begin to formulate a *survival plan* as part of your tactical process. With coaching you can help your dispatcher see his or her importance in your protection. Besides the address and phone number of the disturbance location, the names of the parties involved and a brief description of the problem, you want to encourage your dispatcher to find out:

• *what is the relationship of the complainant?* About half the time, the female in the disturbance calls the police. If the caller is a *disputant*, then at least *one* of them will know you're coming. If it's a *neighbor*, which it is about 20% of the time, *neither* disputant may be expecting you. This will increase your chances of using *surprise* in your approach, but may mean you'll be greeted with greater resentment for "interfering" uninvited.

• *is anyone injured?* This may clue you to the *violence level* you'll have to deal with, but bear in mind that some victims may not know they are injured or may deny or minimize it out of fear. The injuries may also indicate which disputant is the more violent.

• *has anyone there had previous contact with the police?* This may alert you not only to habitual combatants but also to disputants with other criminal records who may harbor hostility toward law enforcement or be unusually attuned to police tactics. One study indicates that nearly 60% of the suspects in domestic violence cases have prior arrest records and that more than 30% have been arrested for violent offenses.[2]

• *are weapons involved?* If so, *what kind* (particularly get as many specifics as possible regarding firearms) and *who has them?* Remember, the *victim* may be armed, too, perhaps holding his or her attacker at bay. Although subjects sometimes falsely report weapons only to hurry the police response, assume that any mention of them is valid. But do *not* assume that you will confront *only* the type of weapon mentioned. A woman complained to a Texas department that her estranged husband was threatening her and a friend with a knife, but when officers arrived at

---

[2]*Centurion*, publication of the San Antonio (TX) Police Officers Association, February, 1985.

the apartment complex, the offender met them as they rounded a corner and opened fire on them with a .22 cal. rifle. One city officer was killed with a bullet to the forehead and a security officer was wounded in the arm.

• *are there [other] firearms on the premises?* If so, *where* (in a cabinet, hidden in chairs, tucked under mattresses?) and *who has access to them?* At least one functional firearm is kept in nearly half of U.S. residences; in rural areas, a shotgun or rifle on hand for killing varmints or hunting is almost a certainty. Do not assume there aren't any available just because the complainant says there aren't. A Minnesota sergeant responding to a woman's complaint that her son was causing a disturbance in their apartment in a wealthy suburb was assured no guns were in the residence. Yet the instant the door opened, a bullet from a .357 Magnum tore into the officer's stomach from a gun in the son's hand. The officer was then shot in the back as he spun away and twice more after he had fallen. The last round penetrated both lungs and his heart. The assailant later wounded three other people, including a policeman, before shooting himself in the head with the dead sergeant's revolver.

• *has anyone been drinking or using drugs?* Even legitimate medication may affect a disputant's temperament and lucidity.

• *is the dispute still in progress?* If not, *has any participant left the scene?* If he has, you'll want a description, and you'll want to be especially alert to the risk of ambush as you approach.

• *who else is there?* You may have a crowd to deal with.

Regardless of the image this intelligence conjures up, ALWAYS regard the call as *high-risk.* "Reassuring" information may be inaccurate or have been misinterpreted by the dispatcher. The situation may change drastically between the time the call is logged and you arrive. Or your arrival and actions in themselves may affect what takes place.

As with other high-risk calls, A MINIMUM OF TWO OFFICERS SHOULD BE DISPATCHED, *even if previous calls to that location have been nonviolent.* Most departments with written policies now require this. Inside a residence with two or more potentially violent disputants and possibly emotional onlookers to control, there are far too many Problem Areas and Areas of Responsibility for one officer to cope with safely. If you're assigned as backup, continue to respond even if the first officer says the situation is under control. *New developments can occur quickly and affect the situation greatly.*

If, despite the risks, you accept a domestic assignment alone, at least arrange for extra support from your *dispatcher.* Ask him or her to telephone you at the residence or call you on your portable soon after the time you expect to be inside, and also to check back with you periodically. You can then respond with a prearranged code if you are in trouble. But understand that by deciding to "lone wolf" *any* aspect of your response, *you are taking on hazards that have often proven fatal to other officers.* In New York state, a trooper was shot and killed with a .30-30 rifle when he went in alone to talk to a disputant, even though he took his K-9 with him and *four other officers* were surrounding the house outside. Completely alone, a potential assailant will likely perceive you as even more vulnerable.

Officers average just under four minutes between dispatch and arrival at domestics. In this time, you and your partner can refresh your memories of the scene if you've been there before, recalling the floor plan and possible hazard areas. You should also decide who's to be *"contact man."* Initially one of you should have primary responsibility for establishing contact with the disputants and handling most of the talking. The partner acts primarily as *observer*, watching for potential hazards. This reduces confusion for the subjects and allows each of you to concentrate more thoroughly on your assigned role. You also agree en route to a *tentative* plan of action. Be ready, however, to stay open-minded and flexible, understanding that your planning may need to change as you get more information. If either of you has drifted into Condition White, this on-run discussion will help jerk you back where you should be, in Condition Yellow.

Your goal in approaching is "*star-trekking*"—to suddenly material-ize at the door without being seen by either disputant. You can anticipate the address and stop short of it by watching house numbers, illuminating them if necessary on the *opposite* side of the street. In rural areas, consider stopping short on the road that passes the property rather than driving in. You may then be able to follow a tree line on foot or use other concealment to allow you to approach from the side that gives you the

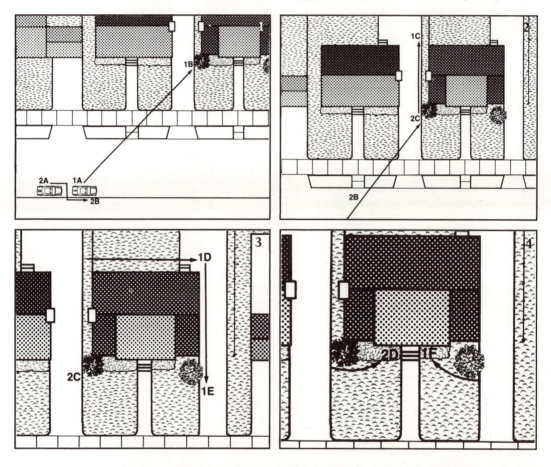

least visibility from the house. You're trying to avoid the kind of approach used by a Maryland officer, who pulled his marked unit into the driveway and within *6 feet* of the back door of a house where a retired oyster shucker had just killed his son-in-law. The suspect appeared in the doorway and riddled the officer "from head to toe" with a shotgun as he stepped out of his patrol car...Or of the two Alaska officers who responded to a man-with-a-gun call (frequently how violent domestics are dispatched) and pulled directly in front of the house. Both were shot dead before they could exit their vehicle by a suspect who easily targeted them. If for some reason you feel you *must* drive onto the property in a rural area, say, continue on past the end of the driveway or cut across a yard—whatever it takes to avoid stopping where you're "supposed" to if you're a "polite" visitor...and where you'll be expected. Always watch that you park where you're not *blocked* from leaving. You may need to get out fast.

A *back* door is generally a more surprising contact point than the front. Would-be assailants inside will seldom be as geared to attack there as toward the front of their location. Also, especially in country areas, going to the back may produce a subtle psychological benefit, because that's where "friends" call. Where apartment houses have back doors, approaching there can be preferable because you can often come in off an alley and avoid having to cross an open courtyard "trap" in front.

Even if you don't plan to enter at the back, one option is for you and

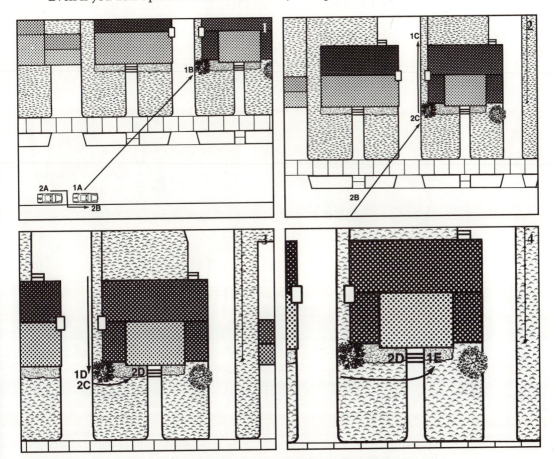

Above and left, two different approaches to the disturbance location.

your partner to split up temporarily and one of you circle around the rear of the house and come up on the other side as a means of getting on opposite sides of the front door. The disadvantages, of course, are your momentary separation and the risk of running into dogs in the back yard. But this quick circuit may allow you to hear things or see things (through

357

quick peeks at windows) that you'd otherwise miss and that will give you a different perspective on what's happening inside. It also *assures* that you don't approach so close together that you invite fire as a single target.

During your approach, be alert to gun racks in the cabs of trucks, pens of hunting dogs, decals indicating gun club membership, signs or symbols of extremist group affiliation and other clues to suggest that you may be facing an armed combatant. Watch for toys in the yard that will indicate you may have children to deal with (most violent disturbances involve families with young children).[3] Also be aware that an aggressive disputant may have moved outside and could be lying in wait for you. Watch shadows, bushes, even unlikely locations. Virginia officers responding to the fourth fight in a week at one residence were fired upon by a middle-aged man with a .22 cal. revolver who crouched inside a back-yard doghouse with his German shepherd after killing his grand-nephew and wounding his nephew. *Get an emergency escape route in mind in case you come under attack.*

As contact officer, you stand on the *knob side* of the door to shield yourself from an immediate field of view from inside once the door is opened. The person answering will have to move the door farther in order to see you, thus exposing more of the interior to your view. Ideally, your partner can be positioned several feet away from the *hinged* side, close to the building, if architecture and landscaping permit.

At those angles an assailant can't shoot either of you *through* the door itself. If he's armed with a .308 semi-automatic rifle or some other heavy weapon, he may be able to fire through the door jamb and walls. But to fire on you with a more conventional weapon immediately upon opening the door, he'd have to expose himself past the jamb to target you. If a screen or storm door is in place, he may have to open that, too, to find you. From your contact position, you may be close enough to grab or deflect his gun or get enough visual warning to drop down, dive for the nearest corner of the building and shout, "Gun!" to warn your partner. Your partner can drop down, too, below the assailant's natural line of

---

[3]Loving, *Responding to Spouse Abuse and Wife Beating,* Police Executive Research Forum, 1980.

3

Initial deployment (left) affords officers flexibility in case of attack. Officer on right stands so the porch support is aligned between the front doorway and himself if a shooting erupts. (top photo) Here he yells, "Knife" but doesn't give away his partner's position.

4

5

6

fire. Return fire from either side will then be angled up toward the attacker, minimizing the cross-fire threat. (This position can be adapted to hotel and apartment house hallways, too. There, instead of heading for a corner if there's trouble, you or your partner may be able to duck into a nearby stairwell or alcove.)

You must be ready to move FAST and be certain to drop LOW in case of threat. Of course, you exit the kill zone as quickly as possible, *backing away* ready to fire, not turning and running. A deputy in Idaho, using a modified version of the doorway positioning described with a city officer, reacted too slowly and forgot to drop when an elderly disputant suddenly presented himself with a shotgun. The deputy was shot in the back in a natural line of fire, still trying to reach a protective corner.

From your knob-side position, if the person who answers the door stays behind it and presents a threat, you may be able to kick it hard with your nearest foot, driving the assailant back and off balance. On the other hand, if the door is opened and a subject presents himself apparently unarmed and nonthreatening, you can get a broader visual on the interior by moving slightly. In fact, as soon as the door begins to open you can start looking through the crack on the hinged side. Before you begin moving into the doorway, though, be sure you can see *both* of the subject's hands. A disturbance suspect who opened an apartment door for two officers in Minnesota stood so his hand holding a gun was hidden behind the door. In this case, a neighbor who had called in the complaint was peeking in a patio door behind the suspect and saw the weapon. She ran through her apartment and into the hallway screaming a warning. The officers shoved the door back hard enough to knock the suspect down and force him to drop the gun.

One alternative positioning is for both you and your partner to stay on the knob side. Then neither of you risks being in an immediate field of view when the door opens. Here a concern will be bunching, though, so strive for some separation, such as your partner perhaps staying down off the porch.

Another option is for your partner to deploy behind a tree, a pillar, a car or other cover or concealment, away from the dwelling where he can watch you and also see into the interior when the door is swung open. You should be out of his line of fire, of course, so he's free to shoot if a threat presents itself. Still another possibility is both of you staying well clear of the door. Here you can announce your presence by knocking on the *side* of the structure, rather than on the door or its frame. This can work especially well with mobile homes, where the sound will easily carry inside. Keep in mind, though, that there is *no* truly safe area along a mobile home because of its penetrability.

Don't be in a hurry to knock. LISTEN FIRST. In 10 to 30 seconds you can tell from voices how many people are involved...the level of their intensity and sobriety...who's the more aggressive...where that person is located...and possibly whether any weapons are involved (through comments like, "Stop pointin' that gun at me!"). *Communicate what you learn to your partner.* Don't assume he picks up on everything you do. The sequence you want to follow between you is: *Analyze ... Advise...Act.*

Avoid a "raid-type" knock that conveys an unmistakable police presence. You want to delay being made as long as possible. If someone inside yells, "Who's there?" one officer who patrols housing projects in California likes to answer in an urgent voice, "Hey, bro', lemme in!" That gets the door opened faster than bellowing, "Police! Open up!" In other environments, try: "Mr. Jones, I'm here to *help* you. What's going on? ...I'm with the police department. Can I talk to you for a minute? ... Let me *help* you." That strategy, leading off and ending your dialogue with potentially "good" news (that you're a possible source of help) and burying the "bad" (your police affiliation) in the middle, is one you can use throughout your contact. It helps minimize resistance and keeps your presence seeming as positive as possible.

You want the door opened *for* you, as a hedge against walking into an instant ambush. Insistence that you "just come on in" can usually be countered successfully with a bluff: "It's locked" ...or, "I'm sorry, but the law says you have to escort me into your home."

If the subjects refuse to open the door or refuse to admit you, perhaps denying there's a problem, try: "Look, we got a call that there's a problem here. We just have to be sure everyone's okay and that things are safe in there. Once we see that, we can leave and be out of your life. You *want* us to *leave*, don't you?" (Always, Yes.) "Well, we have to *come in* first." If necessary, cite your legal authority to enter, including your right to enter *forcibly* if you have reasonable cause to believe a felony (like assault) is taking place or that the reported victim is in danger. Evidence of such danger would include cries of distress or for help, signs of a struggle, display of weapons, etc. If you do enter by force, consider coming through a *different* door to capitalize on the unexpected. And if even that seems too hazardous, call the nearest special weapons team and treat the situation as a barricade.

When an apparent *victim* of a violent dispute answers the door, as is most common, make low-tone inquiries to verify or supplement the intelligence already conveyed by your dispatcher. If the other disputant is not visible, your *first* question should regard his or her whereabouts. Hidden, that person probably constitutes your greatest potential hazard.

Usually your next best question is, "Are you all right" or "Do you need medical attention?" This may give you a quick assessment of violence and can also show concern and begin your rapport-building with one of the disputants. Yet one study indicates that only 3% of officers ever ask this. Even if the victim *looks* okay, ask; some injuries are not readily visible, particularly those from blows to the back of the head or breasts or kicks to the stomach or genital areas. Pregnant women often are assaulted in these latter areas.

Ask also about weapons ("Has he threatened you with any weapons? How about your children? Does he keep any weapons around here?" etc.). *Do not neglect this important area of concern, even if you already know a weapon is involved.* Officers responding to an altercation between a merchant seaman and his fiancee in a Southern port knew he'd threatened her with a knife, but they did not probe her about *other* weapons on the premises. After they made entry, the aggressor grabbed a revolver from an end table drawer and got the drop on a patrolman trying to arrest him. He marched the officer through the house with the gun to his head, cocked, and threatened to "cut up" the other officers. Going up a stairway, the hostage officer fortunately managed to duck around a corner and draw his gun. Before the offender could react, the officer ended this close call by shooting the gunman in the heart.

It takes only seconds to ask these questions, but they can measurably affect your next moves. Press for *precise* answers. At a call in Michigan, the young person who answered the door told officers, "My dad is sick." They entered expecting a medical problem. What the kid meant was *mentally* sick—as the officers realized when the father leaped out of a room in front of them with a shotgun.

It's safest not to enter until all reported disputants are visible to you and apparently unarmed. You also want to ascertain who else is on the premises...and where. If the aggressor is not in sight and refuses to come forward himself, consider asking the victim to step outside to be interviewed. You may be able to prompt a hidden disputant to appear by announcing that you are taking the victim *away* with you. If you do bring a victim outside, be sure to conduct any subsequent conversation from a *cover* position, to avoid the fate of a Mississippi officer who stood out in the open on the front lawn to interview a victim. With no protection, he provided an easy—and lethal—shot to the suspect hiding inside.

If you're working solo and are in an area where crowds are unlikely to form, consider getting *both* disputants outside and deal with their conflict there. They'll probably have less access to potential weapons and you'll have fewer Problem Areas and Areas of Responsibility to monitor. Try to get them out of their own yard, if possible. Psychologically, that will lessen their territorial instincts to protect their domain from your "intrusion."

Above all, if your initial "threshold evaluation" indicates a known high-risk to you inside, *do not go in.* To help any one else at the scene, you must stay alive yourself. Tombstone courage is *yesterday's* version of police professionalism. Still, many of today's officers persist in trying it. Like the detective lieutenant from a Michigan sheriff's department who responded to a trailer where a husband was beating his wife and was reported to be "armed, intoxicated and in an extremely violent state of mind." When the offender opened the door, he held a rifle and threatened to shoot both the lieutenant and his deputy partner. Nevertheless, the

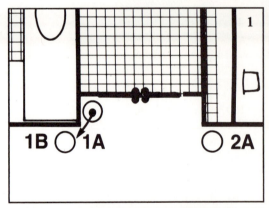

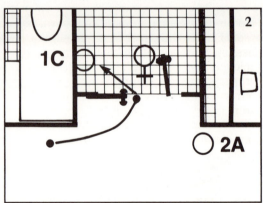

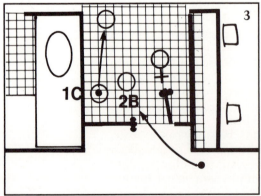

To parallel the text's description of how you and back-up conduct an entry on a non-violent domestic, you see (upper left) that each officer takes a position on either side of the door with Officer 1 knocking, then moving to position B. (above) Officer 1 has the initial contact with the female disputant as Officer 2 stays back momentarily. Officer 1 does enter after he has assessed that it is safe. (left) Now Officer 2 makes entry and conducts conversation with the female disputant as Officer 1 advances to observe what he can. (The male disputant is out of view at this time).

lieutenant still *went inside alone,* thinking he could talk the suspect into surrendering the gun. Moments later, a shot rang out and the lieutenant staggered out, mortally wounded.

If it does seem safe to enter, ask that any dogs be shut in a bedroom or basement *first.* Keep the door answerer ahead of you. As contact officer, you probably can see more of the room from your position and thus should enter first. Your partner should wait three or four seconds before entering. (This tactic paid off for one team when the first officer was surprised and taken hostage by an offender with a shotgun when he stepped in. Because his partner was still outside, he was able to take cover and radio for help, getting enough superior firepower to the scene to eventually free the captive officer.) If you can engage the more aggressive disputant while your partner is still watching from outside, start moving around him as you talk. He'll likely turn to keep facing you, and this will give your partner a "360° visual frisk" of him without anyone having to touch him.

Some officers like to enter with a hand in a jacket pocket, gripping a concealed backup gun. On particularly intense calls, others hold a drawn gun in front of them, hiding it by holding their hat over it in the same hand. This looks relaxed; indeed, some authorities believe that taking your hat off will help defuse the tension. However, both these tactics have serious drawbacks. You practice drawing from your holster and getting accurate shots, but when do you practice shooting from your pocket with a backup gun? And if you *draw* from your pocket and shoot, you'll be even slower than drawing from your holster. Also if a shooting does occur, you may have difficulty in court justifying the use of a backup gun as your primary weapon.

As for holding your sidearm behind your hat, this can hamper your response if you need your hands to defend against a physical attack. Also at *some* angle, the weapon may become visible to one or more disputants, possibly causing them to panic and escalate the situation. Certainly, any accidental discharge of a firearm held in this manner would be difficult to defend in court. You are probably better off to enter with your hand on your gun butt, prepared to draw, if you perceive the situation to be intense enough for that...or to come in with your baton out and ready.

In any case, once inside, stand apart from your partner. Close the door after you're both in to slow down a surprise entry behind you by anyone else.

Keep your demeanor *non-hostile* (friendly but cautious) as long as you can. This will help in defusing the tensions that greet you. If you do make a tactical blunder, a cordial attitude may help you recover control before it's too late. Two California officers called to a hotel about a disturbance made the mistake of walking right into the suspect's room when a voice inside told them to enter. The subject was sitting on a bed with his hands in a warmup jacket. "Something told me the guy wasn't true," one of the officers recalled later. But the officer came on friendly: "Hey, man, how's it going? Is that a comfortable bed?"

With that he suddenly grabbed the subject's right hand and gripped it through the jacket. The subject held a cocked .32 semi-automatic.

At that point the officer was able to control the situation physically. "But if I had approached this guy *hardline* from the beginning, my partner and I would have gotten it. By staying friendly until I could afford to get tough, I caught him off guard. He thought I hadn't attached any seriousness to the problem yet. How do you shoot a cop who's saying, 'Is your bed comfortable?'"

Tactical Calming

Once inside, *think C-A-L-M.* After you've approached and entered, your process requires that you:

establish **C**ontrol
get the disputants **A**part
Look for weapons
Moderate the mood.

The faster you can get the participants calmed down and order restored, the faster you diminish your risk. So long as they're distraught, one or both will be highly tempted to switch the fury they've been directing at each other to *you* as a convenient scapegoat. Especially if you're alone, outnumbered against two or more hostile subjects, *calming becomes an urgent tactical priority.* It doesn't *solve* the problem; it just creates a *lull* so you can strengthen your control.

Some of your best survival maneuvers now will be *verbal and psychological.* These are still survival oriented. Your mouth and your mind in this situation are critical tactical tools. Don't make the macho mistake of ignoring them as only for "pussies."

In establishing **CONTROL,** *first* control *yourself.* Above all, do not get "hooked" into joining the dispute itself; *if you become part of the conflict, you cannot help with the solution,* and the potential for violence and injury increase. Also, do not act impulsively or emotionally in trying to deal with the disputants. You can avoid these traps by *staying acutely aware of your own frame of mind* as you are bombarded with stimuli in this tense environment.

As early as possible, tap into your Survival Awareness Wheel, which actually works on *any* high-risk call, not just domestics:

Keying initially on any segment of the Wheel and quickly moving around in either direction, you can assess where you're "at" in this situation and *consider how that may be impacting your tactical decisions and performance.* Ask yourself, for example:

1. What am I *feeling?* Anger? Frustration? Sympathy? Revulsion? Embarrassment? Fear? You don't have to *report* your feelings, just be *aware* of them. When you *deny* what they are, you're more likely to lose

control over them. Like the Oregon officer who was nearly disarmed as he struggled to restrain a violent husband. When he finally fought the man off, he did not consider how angry he was. Acting from that feeling rather than thinking tactically, he *handed his gun to the offender's wife* and proceeded to "thump and bump" him to a fare-thee-well. Luckily, the wife had more restraint and didn't shoot the officer.

2. What do I *believe?* Do you think women who get beaten up "ask for it?" Do you think blacks automatically are "career assholes?" Or that *all* conflicts can be *talked* out if you're glib enough? Or that your presence is a welcome development for a victim? Unacknowledged, your personal beliefs can subconsciously direct your actions in ways that *escalate* rather than calm the confrontation or that make you *unnecessarily vulnerable.* A chief in Tennessee, for instance, evidently believed that a show of good faith was adequate protection against an enraged, armed disputant who'd held two females hostage. After the women were safe, the chief took off his shirt and approached the suspect with his hands in the air. As he turned to prove conclusively that he wasn't armed, the suspect shot and killed him.

3. What are my *senses* telling me? Your sight, hearing, smell, touch and taste all feed you a wealth of information in any situation. *Monitor them closely.* Too often officers draw conclusions and act inappropriately in high-risk encounters because they don't consciously intercept important messages that their senses are sending, due to their stress overload. In one training exercise, two seasoned officers "responding" to a domestic failed to give any indication that they *saw* a sawed-off shotgun lying on a table in plain view and within reach of an angry subject throughout a 20-minute confrontation! An officer in Virginia didn't attach enough importance to what he *heard.* A woman disputant warned him a dozen times, "Don't come any closer. I have a knife in my apron." He closed in anyway—and got stabbed to death.

4. What do I *want?* Maybe you want to get out of there so you can have a cup of coffee. Or you want to bust the chops of the guy who's in your face. Or you'd like to bed the female disputant who's standing there in lace bra and panties. Being aware of your unspoken desires for yourself and other people in the situation helps you prevent taking actions or displaying attitudes that may promote those wants *but* that are *detrimental to your safety.*

5. What am I *doing?* Your words and actions, even your tone of voice and unspoken body language, can heavily influence the reactions you get from disputants. Closely watch *their* behavior, of course. But remember that *yours* will probably be the single greatest ingredient in shaping events once you're on the scene.

Staying aware of these five factors keeps you alert to what's going on and how you're reacting to it. You'll better control yourself because you'll understand the *reasons* for the decisions you make. Rather than being driven by "hidden forces" within you, awareness enables you to *choose* your behavior. The more awareness, the more choices you're likely to have. And the more choices you have, the more effective you'll be.

With practice, you'll learn to check your Awareness Wheel as quickly and as automatically as you check your Problem Areas and Areas of Responsibility.

To begin controlling the *disputants*, you may first have to get their *attention.* They may continue their battle despite your presence. Or the disturbance may be a crowded, noisy party where no one's even aware you're there.

Do not wait for a "logical pause" in the conflict. There rarely is one in a heated argument. Create your own interruption that distracts them from each other and forces them to acknowledge you. One officer blows a traffic whistle at full blast and yells, "Everybody out of the pool!" Sometimes this gets a laugh, easing tension a bit; always it gets attention. Others have shouted: "What's burning? I smell something on fire!" Or they flick the room lights on and off several times or whack a baton loudly against a door jamb or against the floor. Still others just enter and watch, mute. Their *lack* of words or action becomes a startling attention-getter as the disputants wonder what the officers are going to do. Your goal is to get their momentary *eye contact,* which will make separating them easier.

If the disputants are fighting *physically* and won't separate on command, consider using a baton...a mini-baton...hair-pulling or the pain compliance, stunning or neck restraint techniques described in chapter 8. You and your partner each take a different fighter, not both focus on just one, which leaves you vulnerable if the other keeps fighting. In pulling hair, incidentally, don't just yank randomly wherever you

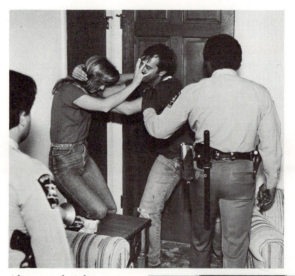

Above and right, note how officers move in so they do not get in each other's way. As they get closer, the officer on the right uses the hair pulling technique as well as a proper arm restraint. The other officer controls the female, rather than both officers attempting to control the male.

366

The disputants are separated as quickly as possible. During this time verbal communication should be occurring between officers, especially if visual contact is not possible. This gives each of you feedback on the stability of the situation. Note how the disputant on the carpet is still being controlled with the hair pulling technique prior to handcuffing.

happen to grab. You want *physical leverage* working for you as well as pain. Grasp the subject's hair close to the roots and as near the base of his skull as possible. If you slide your fingers into the hair so tufts are between them, you can usually get a closer, tighter grip. Now pull back and down *hard*. The leverage will force his chin up and you'll pull him off balance, away from the fight.

To the extent circumstances permit, avoid brusquely ordering people around, automatically coming on authoritarian. Start with the *least* aggressive technique that seems practical and work toward the *most* aggressive, *if that becomes necessary*. Your entering someone's *home* has highly emotional connotations for them. Their primal instinct to "protect" their territory will be intensified by the emotion of their dispute. In a sense, you'll be like two dogs, sniffing each other out to determine who's in charge.

Subconsciously, the disputants may *want* your control for the stability it provides, and of course, if you let them manipulate you and *don't* assert yourself when appropriate, you risk greater hazard. Physical assaults often begin with disputants being allowed indefinitely to continue verbal assaults. If you then let a verbally abusive subject get away with shoving or punching you, the next move may be to *really* go for you. *Don't let any disputant be in charge*. But usually you can do this subtly, so they aren't consciously confronted with just how much power you actually are exerting. Learning to control while *reducing resentment* is especially important if you're alone and thus lack a partner to back up a more traditional show of authority.

A male disputant who's super-conscious of his manhood, for example, may violently resist being *ordered* around, but may grudgingly comply to being *asked* to do something, because it protects his ego. This can be especially true in Hispanic cultures, where a heavy emphasis is often placed on machismo. Try phrasing your commands in the form of *requests* that the average person would find hard to refuse: "You don't mind doing so and so, do you?" If the disputants are left with the impression that every move they're making is because *they've* decided to, rather than because *you're* directing it, you stand a much greater chance of accomplishing what you want. Your precise words are not the most important thing...your MANNER is. Normally if you're being effective with your calming, you'll see the disputants begin to settle down within 30 to 60 seconds.

Don't make assumptions about how readily a disputant can be controlled based on his *size.* A team of California housing officers responded to a disturbance scene and found six large men and one small man sitting in a room. The female complainant was upstairs hiding. The small man looked innocuous, but when one of the others started to leave, he snapped: "Sit down, motherfucker." The man sat. The little guy, it turned out, was an ex-convict and violent mental patient who needed to be hospitalized for more treatment. When everyone's afraid of someone, that's your cue to be apprehensive of him, too, regardless of size or appearance.

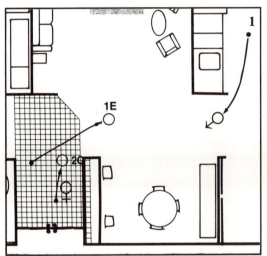

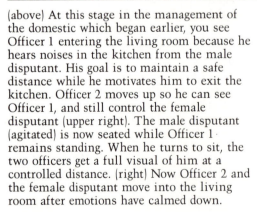

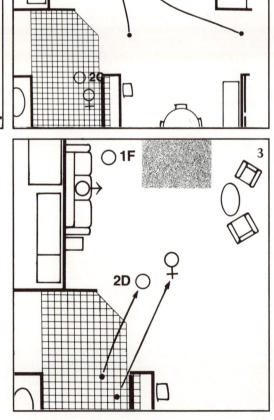

(above) At this stage in the management of the domestic which began earlier, you see Officer 1 entering the living room because he hears noises in the kitchen from the male disputant. His goal is to maintain a safe distance while he motivates him to exit the kitchen. Officer 2 moves up so he can see Officer 1, and still control the female disputant (upper right). The male disputant (agitated) is now seated while Officer 1 remains standing. When he turns to sit, the two officers get a full visual of him at a controlled distance. (right) Now Officer 2 and the female disputant move into the living room after emotions have calmed down.

Getting disputants **APART** involves *quickly* separating them *visually*, as well as *physically*, if possible. So long as they maintain eye contact, just the powerful *looks* they exchange can keep the fires fanned, even if they say or do nothing. However, *you and your partner ALWAYS want to stay where you can see and hear each other.*

One option is to get the disputants back-to-back, separated by several feet. Usually you can deftly maneuver this when you walk in. With each of you engaging a different subject, one of you starts moving around the room to the right, the other to the left. Keep your backs toward the wall. The disputants will turn to face you and by the time you reach opposite sides of the room, they'll be back-to-back. However, you and your partner are positioned where you can watch each other. Because the disputants are between you, if they start fighting again, you can separate them without getting caught in the middle.

An alternative is to move one disputant around a corner or partition so they're even better separated visually , but you stay where you can see each other. Either way promotes calming them by forcing their visual and verbal attention away from each other and onto you.

Be sure you and your partner each concentrate on calming a *different* disputant. Don't both of you zero in on the aggressor (or on the loudest and most profane subject) and ignore the victim (or the quietest), who may become a sudden and surprising threat. Stay aware of *all* combatants—and witnesses—and don't lose sight of *any.* If you're alone, *do* work primarily at calming the more aggressive party. Instruct the other to remain quiet and get that person as far away from you as possible, while still within your peripheral vision.

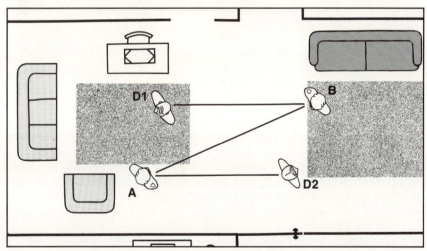

A variation of the conventional back-to-back positioning of disputants. Disputants (D1 and D2) cannot see each other, yet you can see your partner.

Angry people need more "personal space" than normal in order not to feel threatened, and you buy yourself more reaction time by giving it. Try to avoid touching either subject, unless they require physical control. If they try to move where you don't want them, consider blocking their way by spreading your arms in a "cow-herding" gesture. This suggests a barrier without actually invading their space. People will be reluctant to run into your arms to get past you. Remember, though, to keep your gun side turned slightly away.

Avoid positioning the disputants in a kitchen, a bedroom or a bathroom. A kitchen usually contains more tools for attack than any other room, ranging from knives and bottles to hot grease and boiling water. The bedroom is the most common storage spot for firearms in the home (usually near the bed); that room also may symbolize the most intimate (and volatile) part of the disputants' relationship. A bathroom, besides being too small for safe distancing, harbors dangerous implements, too (razors, curling irons, glass, etc.) and is another "private" area. Generally the *living room* or family room is safer, more neutral ground.

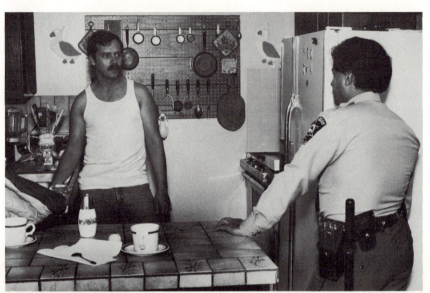

There are over ten categories of potential weapons within easy reach of the male disputant. Take a moment and observe. Did you notice the handgun on top of the refrigerator? What about the officer's own weapons?

Be alert for a trick some aggressors use: gradually back away from you into another room. In Oklahoma, a "good ol' boy" slowly backed toward a bedroom while angrily cussing his wife and a responding officer. He'd never offered trouble on a call before. But this time, as soon as he hit the bedroom doorway, he grabbed a .45 semi-automatic hidden inside and took the officer hostage.

LOOK around any room you enter for *potential* weapons as well as obvious ones. Don't tunnel in just on the disputants and miss what's accessible to them. Avoid positioning a subject near anything that can be swung or thrown (a heavy ashtray or metal trophy on a coffee table)...or move the object out of reach...or position yourself between it and the subject. If he's holding a drink, ask him to set it down, so it doesn't end up in your face. An officer handling a domestic in Wisconsin where drug paraphernalia was around was stabbed in the hand when an angry subject suddenly grabbed a hypodermic syringe and attacked him.

Take IMMEDIATE control of any obvious weapon, even if it's not in a disputant's hand. If you do not, you are BETTING YOUR LIFE you can get to it before an opponent can. A knife can be clipped on your clipboard, if you have one. It should be secured by the officer dealing with the seemingly least aggressive disputant, so it is farthest away from someone likeliest to fight for it. Even safer is to *hide* it in another room—under a sink, in a drawer, in the freezer or the oven or dropped behind the stove or refrigerator.

With guns, *unload them* and pocket the ammunition. Simply explain: "We don't want anyone hurt out of this deal." If someone objects, *pick up on it.* That person is more agitated or more hostile to police than you may think. *Still secure the gun.* It's better that he be mad *but unarmed.*

Even consider taking obvious weapons with you when you leave the premises and book them for safekeeping at least overnight, where that's permitted. Or, in rural areas, you might tell the disputant you'll put the weapon in his roadside mailbox as you leave, if it's a gun he legally owns. One California officer returns knives at the end of disturbance calls only by placing them on the hood of his patrol car. The owner then retrieves the weapon while the officer watches at a safe position. Never *hand* a knife back. Some skilled offenders can open a folding buck knife on you so fast you'd think it was a switchblade.

Officers who regularly work high-violence neighborhoods generally insist on *patting down* disputants, if weapons are not evident. A light-hearted comment can usually ease the way and win legal cooperation: "You don't have any machine guns or submarines on you, do you? I know you don't, so you don't mind if I pat you down, do you?" Or: "My dispatcher said someone had a gun here. Mind if I look?" Have the subject stick his arms out to his sides or interlace his fingers behind his head, and you quick-pat him from behind. Keep your thumb hooked in his pants so if he starts moving, you can move with him. If you're concerned about a female disputant being armed but don't want to touch her directly, run a mini-baton or your pen over high-risk concealment areas. Or have her pull loose clothing tight across her breasts and between her legs to reveal any suspicious bulges.

One "visual frisk" can be performed unobtrusively when you persuade a disputant to sit down. Stand so he has to cross in front of you to reach the chair. You can check one side of him as he approaches. He'll present the other as he turns to sit. Be careful, though, that you do not stand in front of your partner so that one shot could take out both of you or where a cross fire would prevent a good defense in case a weapon is drawn.

You're safest to check for weapons hidden in any furniture with cushions *before* a subject occupies it. Again, a light remark can keep your rapport intact. Or apologize for your action as "department policy," which may take some of the edge off it. Some officers insist that subjects sit on hard, straightback chairs as "safer" than overstuffed furniture. But an assailant can roll or spring out of them faster and can also swing them as a weapon. When you're concerned about a violent person, having him sit on the *floor* is better.

Safely *seating* the disputants will help you **MODERATE** their mood, sitting being more physically relaxing and therefore more mentally calming than standing. It's harder for a subject to attack from a seated position, especially if he's in a low, soft chair or sofa; he loses much of his ability to act quickly, and his range of motion becomes much more limited. You'll see him start to get up (scooting to the edge of the seat, leaning forward or gripping his hands on the arms or on his knees are common cues) and have more time to react. Generally a fast, firm shove will put him back down. Getting the parties to the point they *will* sit as a prelude to discussing the conflict, however, may take some skillful manipulation. They'll want to be up and mobile because they're hyper.

Confusing, loud statements from you will just feed the turmoil. Use *repeated...calm...simple...direct* communication that implies *you* are not emotionally upset by the situation ("Sir, please calm down. I need you to sit down."). If for no other reason, the subjects may obey because after a while they'll get tired of hearing the same instructions. Some officers speak almost in a whisper (sometimes feigning laryngitis) so disputants will *have* to quiet down to hear what's being said. And usually they *do* want to hear what you have to say to find out what you're going to do about the situation.

A disputant's body language while seated can tell you a great deal about a possible assault attempt. If you remain standing you have a tactical advantage. A subject on the edge of his seat can spring up quicker than one who is sitting back and relaxed. Signs of real tension include clenched fists and focused eye contact.

Eliminate distractions that inhibit calming and *introduce* ones that promote it. Small children can be sent to another room (perhaps to keep the family dog company) or to a neighbor's. Segregate older kids from the disputants, but keep them where you can watch them. Or ask them to leave the house until things are settled. Be cautious about just sending them to another room, out of sight. Officers on one domestic sent a 14-year-old to his bedroom. He came back with a gun and shot one of them. He could handle Mom and Dad arguing; he'd lived with that all his life. What he couldn't handle was "cops pushing Mom and Dad around." If a party's going on or other uninvolved onlookers are present, ask them to leave ("We need to handle this privately. You can come back when we leave"), or move the disputants where you have privacy. Otherwise, you risk the bystanders taking sides, interfering and threatening your control. Also, with an audience, disputants are more likely to remain angry, deceitful and resistant to avoid losing face.

Get rid of noise, too, like a blaring television set or stereo. Noise itself is arousing, plus it forces people to raise their voices, keeping emotions even higher. It may also keep you from hearing threatening sounds from other quarters of the house. If you encounter a female disputant who is only partially clothed, ask her to cover herself, to minimize your distraction.

By introducing *calculated distractions,* you divert attention to something noncontroversial and nonthreatening. One tactic is to ask a small favor, something most people would grant even when they're upset. Examples: "Can you call the station for me? I need to let my dispatcher know I'm here"...or: "Could I have a Kleenex? My nose is runny." At one disturbance involving multiple family members who wouldn't calm down, one creative officer put his finger to his eye, cupped his other hand under it and said, "Oh, Jeez, I think I've lost my contact lens." Within two minutes, all the disputants were on their hands and knees looking for it and had even taken off their shoes to avoid crushing it. One request often recommended, asking for a drink of water, is *not* advisable, however, because it may encourage a disputant going into the kitchen.

Some officers successfully distract by commenting on the disputants' personal interests. Hunting is a good area to talk about, as it may offer information about weapons in the house. Usually *visual cues* tell you what a person's interests are; people's deepest interests are usually reflected by what's on their walls, shelves and tabletops. "Fairy-tale" them into thinking you have something in common with small falsehoods: "Hey, that's a neat velvet painting. I've been looking for one like that. Where'd you get it?" Or: "Is that your daughter's picture? I've got a daughter about that age." (But be careful trying to talk about their kids as a calming distractor *if* the kids are the subject of their argument.) Compliments distract, build rapport and help restore self-esteem, which may have been badly damaged in the dispute. After you've praised and gotten a disputant to talk about his arrowhead collection for awhile, it may be easier to slip calmly into a discussion of the reason you're there: "You seem like a nice enough guy. What's going on here?"

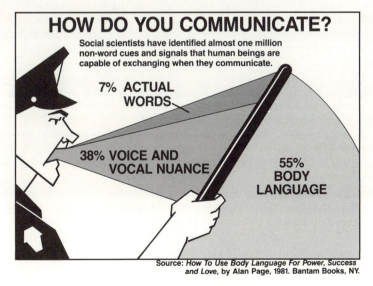

HOW DO YOU COMMUNICATE?

Social scientists have identified almost one million non-word cues and signals that human beings are capable of exchanging when they communicate.

7% ACTUAL WORDS

38% VOICE AND VOCAL NUANCE

55% BODY LANGUAGE

Source: *How To Use Body Language For Power, Success and Love,* by Alan Page, 1981. Bantam Books, NY.

Another distractor is to just start asking routine informational questions: name, address, phone number, date of birth. Even non sequiturs: "When did you buy this house?" Playing the Columbo role, purposefully misunderstanding or not comprehending, can sometimes be effective, *in moderation* ("Your name is Smith? Is that S-m-i-t-h or S-m-y-t-h-e?") because it gets them speaking more slowly and clearly. Improvise: "Is that your car with the lights on out front?"

When a subject is antagonistic, you can sometimes moderate his mood by first asking him a series of questions that are likely to prompt a "No" answer: "You're not the one who called me here, are you?"... "You're not happy with my being here, are you?"..."Your brother doesn't live here, does he?"..."You don't work for the city, do you?" His negative responses, which he'll usually elaborate on, give him a chance to vent some of his hostile feelings. Then start to ask him questions that are likely to have "Yes" answers: "You're going to be happy when I leave here, aren't you?" etc. This helps bring him into a more positive frame of mind.

Your objective is to provide the disputants a *mental break* from their argument, something new to occupy their minds. This gives you a toehold for building *rationality.* Angry, their thoughts probably surpass reality; they may not care about consequences. But as you get them settled down, you get them less dangerous because they're then more likely to use rational *"if/then" thinking:* If I attack this cop, then he'll attack me back, *harder.*

When you've calmed them enough to seat them, indicate where you'd like them, perhaps just by gesturing to keep things low-key. If someone wants to go to a seat other than the one you're indicating, ask yourself: *why?* It may be a danger sign. You want the more aggressive subject in the softest, lowest seat available *(provided* you've checked it for weapons), so it'll be harder for him to get up. Seat *both* disputants...and far enough apart so that you and your partner could restrain them before they could get to each other again. Don't stand right on top of them, a bad but common police habit. Back off. The effect will put you closer to being on the same eye level (less threatening and offensive) and also give you better visual control.

In some situations, you may be willing to sit while the disputants are sitting (never when they're standing) to bring yourself closer to their eye level. (Most officers prefer not to, however, unless they have a partner who remains standing.) Do *not* sit or squat *below* eye level. This puts you in a demeaned position and may psychologically encourage attack. Also, *always be ready to move.*

One option for sitting is with your legs crossed, your elbow resting on your upper knee. If someone attacks, you can raise your knee up and duck your head. Your leg will protect your rib cage and your arm will block an attack coming toward your face.

An alternative is to sit on the edge of a chair (or arm of a couch), on the tip of your buttocks or turned on just one flank. Pull your feet back under you. (If you can put your feet under the chair, you don't have to sit out so far.) Now if you have to stand fast, you can quickly get the proper tension and balance in your legs to spring up.

Even if you remain standing, be conscious of your *positioning.* Don't get boxed into a corner, against a wall, between furniture or in a doorway. Try to stand where you can quickly exit, through a window, a door or into another room. Avoid standing at the top or the bottom of stairs. At the top, you risk being pushed down or being shot from downstairs by someone you can't see. At the bottom, you can be secretly targeted from above or something may be dropped on you. Don't stand with your hands stuck in your pockets, as officers tend to do when things get calmed. Don't rock back and forth from your toe to heel, which can leave you off-balance and very vulnerable in case of attack. And don't trust your partner *too much.* If he lets his guard down, he compromises you. But if you let yours down by placing too much reliance on him, then you've compromised yourself.

Remember: *calming doesn't always stick.* Tempers that simmer down can boil up again. This time *you* may be the subject of attack, without warning. STAY PREPARED.

Arrest Strategy

Preliminary calming is good tactical strategy even if you intend an arrest. This is especially so if you're alone. Embarrassment, anger, hostility all increase markedly with arrest, particularly in middle- and upper-class environments or in any setting where an image must be preserved in front of family, friends or neighbors.

Do not rush your arrest moves unless a threat is imminent. You'll most likely be making arrests only in cases where assaults and/or injuries have occurred, so you *know* you are dealing with someone who has a *proven capacity* for violence. *You do not have to take action precipitously where it is prudent to wait.* Justice can generally stand a slight delay. Talk longer. Distant backup may arrive...you may be able to build enough rapport to win the offender's cooperation...or you may discover things about him or the setting that will change your tactical selections.

The most common mistake officers make with arrests at domestics is *discounting* a very important Problem Area: the *victim.* The last miscalculation that a lot of dead officers have made is to assume that the victim *supports* their arrest effort. Of course that assumption is valid with most crimes, but not necessarily with domestics, where a *special relationship* exists between the offender and the victim.

The instant it becomes clear that an abusive husband is to be handcuffed and transported, his injured wife often undergoes a rapid and startling transformation. Just as the offender knows the "hot buttons" with which to abuse her, he also knows the ones that will tap her *sympathy.* The same is true, of course, when roles are reversed and the arrestee is a woman. With the right coaxing—and often with none at all—the victim switches from possibly pleading for your intervention to *attacking* you—often with any weapon in sight. One East Coast officer was hit in the head with a *telephone,* causing him permanent eye damage and eventually ending his career. Loyalty...fear for the future...humiliation over the fact that you've "caught" the couple being their true selves may all be involved. But the bottom line is that you now have *two* to fight. And the victim, because she's the *unexpected* assailant, may well pose the greater threat.

A typical example occurred when Kentucky officers walked in on a man who had his woman by her hair and was punching her face. Every time he hit her, blood flew; "she looked like she'd been hit with a meat cleaver." An officer grabbed him and freed the woman. But she then snatched a frying pan and clobbered the officer on the back of his head.

Much grimmer was another Southern case, in which a man was hacking his wife with a hatchet. Officers pulled him off and saved her life. She seemed almost in shock, with a deep gash in her shoulder. Yet in a matter of moments, she fatally stabbed one of her rescuers in the back with an ice pick. In some cases, officers have been hurt by victims accidentally. Two Detroit officers saved a woman from being drowned in a bathtub by her husband. After he was handcuffed, she suddenly picked up a 7-inch knife and came at him. An officer tried to restrain her, but she was naked and dripping wet, hard to hold. Twice the officer was slashed with the knife—but protected by his soft body armor. *Never underestimate the aggression and fighting ability of females, including female victims.*

Having you or your partner take responsibility for monitoring the victim while the other arrests the offender is probably your most practical option. Move fast and get it over with.

Another possibility is to send the victim to another room or next door on a fabricated errand (checking on the kids, for example). You then effect the arrest while that disputant's gone. Here you must judge whether you feel safer letting that person out of your sight or having him or her present to see you take action against the abuser. Historically, women have not come back with guns from other locations as commonly as men do. They're more likely to assault with a knife or go for *your* sidearm as they remain close by.

At the very least, explain the situation to the victim *and* the offender. Indicate you are "just acting as an agent of the law," not from personal preference. Some disputants may not be aware that they can be arrested for "private" behavior in their own home, so brief them on your legal authority. Explain that you have certain procedures you must follow; one of these is to handcuff the offender. Try to *minimize* the effect of the arrest—the arrestee's not going to Leavenworth, the victim can provide bail, etc. The victim will probably be dealing with a lot of fear, and offering an understanding of what's going to happen procedurally and what the victim can do about it if he or she chooses may help the arrest be accepted better and perhaps temper an impulse to interfere.

Remember, even at the point of arrest, *backing off* can still be a tactical option. For example, if there are more people in the house than you thought and they start coming downstairs to intervene, *back out* (with your gun drawn, if necessary) to a safe location and summon help. Don't let your ego trap you where it's dangerous to be.

Once you've arrested, *don't linger.* The longer you stay there, the more dangerous the situation becomes for you. Remain alert for people who may attempt a rescue at your expense.

In some jurisdictions now, you are *told* when an arrest must be made by legislative mandate or departmental policy. But where you still have flexibility and discretion, don't *forget* arrest as an option where circumstances permit it. Too often, officers think they have *failed* if they make an arrest at a domestic, and, in fact, are even instructed that arrest should be considered *only* as a last resort. Yet in reality not every dispute can or should be resolved by other means. To under-enforce the law can be as dangerous as over-enforcing it. What message is being conveyed to a violent offender like the one in Massachusetts, where officers responded to domestic disturbances at his home *51 times* without even making out a report? Maybe the message is that *family* violence is okay.

Far more than one officer has been killed going back to a disturbance location where an arrest *should* have been made the *first* time. Indeed, one of the arguments advanced for mandatory arrest requirements is that some limited documentation suggests arrests *do* reduce callbacks, *even when a conviction does not ultimately occur.*

"Getting Through the Night"

The most accepted alternative to arrest is *mediation,* where you try essentially to help the disputants "make it through the night" non-violently...and perhaps sow a few seeds for long-term change. You are not a marriage counselor...nor a psychiatrist...nor a miracle worker. Accept that when you leave, their lives are probably *not* going to experience a major turn-around. Your hope is simply to create in perhaps 20 minutes or so enough of a truce to prevent coming back for as long as possible—because it's on return calls that you run the greatest risk of being injured or killed. Think of mediation as a means of further controlling people. It's as much—if not more—for *your* benefit as for theirs.

When you bring the disputants together to resolve their conflict, either you or your partner should be in charge. This should *not* be a democratic forum. A sure way to escalate a delicate situation is for *both* of you to actively pursue the discussion and then get into a battle between yourselves over differing opinions about the "right" way to handle matters. If you disagree, hash it out later. Of course, if the mediator feels he is not being effective, you can always switch. The one who does not guide the discussion listens and watches (particularly the disputants' hands) for threats. During mediation, there will likely be fresh outbursts of anger—and a need for constant vigilance.

As mediator, do your *ABCs:*

Acquire information about the *immediate* issue(s) that touched off *this* particular dispute (not about all the deep-seated grievances of long standing regarding their whole relationship)...

Boil it down and repeat it back in one statement so everyone agrees in simple terms what the fight is about...and then help the disputants find ways to

Cope with the symptom(s) they've identified.

Your tone should be one of: "We've got a problem here that we've got to work on together." Not: "I'm going to tell you how it is." It's the *"collective problem-solving approach"* of hostage negotiation, really. However...before getting the discussion underway, indicate you have some limit on your time to give them an urgency about moving things along. And spell out certain *ground rules* for them, to preserve the calm you've established:

1. NO VIOLENCE. Offer some motivation for cooperation ("When we get this worked out, then I'm going to get out of your life and leave you alone"). But explain: "We're all going to stay calm and talk like adults. But if anyone tries to hurt me or my partner or each other, then you leave me no choice." This is "if/then" positioning that puts the responsibility on *them.* How well they do when together will help you assess how much of the anger and violence has drained out of them. Whatever you promise, follow through if there's trouble, or you'll create hazardous credibility problems for yourself or other officers the next time.

2. No insults, including name-calling. And no yelling.

3. Only one person talks at a time. Emphasize: "You will each get a

chance to tell your side of things, but we can't be interrupting each other." Verbal interjections will counter the calm and foster violence.

Establishing rules helps generate cooperation because it underscores that you are in control. Rules have a calming effect; few people really enjoy chaos. Try to cement these ground rules by getting a verbal agreement from both disputants that they'll abide by them.

Keep in mind important *private* rules for yourself and your partner:

1. Do not get personally caught up in their problems. Don't let *them* interview *you*. If a disputant demands to know, "How would *you* like it if *you* came home and found *your* wife in bed with *your* dog?", just reply that *your* problems and your feelings are not important here...and get back on track. *Your control depends on your not getting emotionally "hooked in."*

2. Do not ask for a fight by ridiculing, demeaning or insulting any disputant. Also don't talk *formally* with people who don't understand formality. "Hey, man, what's going on?" will get you farther in many settings than a stiff "I'm Officer Jones of the First Precinct, and I'm here to deal with your domestic disturbance." Use your own first name...but *ask* the disputants if it's okay before you use theirs.

3. Hear both sides. Show *empathy* ("I can understand how you feel") for both points of view, but not *sympathy* ("He's right, you're wrong") for either. Your perspective may change with more information. Remember the old adage: "There is the truth of the field mouse cornered by the black snake. And then there is the black snake's truth." One officer dealing with a husband who'd slapped his wife because she never got out of bed to fix meals, clean house or tend the kids thought the man's claim that she was "lazy" seemed right on—until the wife's side of the story revealed that she *couldn't* do those things. She was dying, of an illness her husband was psychologically unwilling to accept.

4. "Honor" the problem. The reason for the dispute may not seem important to you, but to relieve the stress of it you must regard it with the same level of importance that the disputants do. They may perceive it as being of great threat to their lives, to their social status, to their self-esteem, etc. Minimizing the impotance of the problem is something disputants say officers often do that makes the situation worse.

5. Be sensitive to cultural differences. You can easily be unintentionally insulting if you don't understand whom you're dealing with. Officers who work with Eskimos, as an extreme example, know that any reference to their faces must be very subtle. A question like, "How did you get that scar on your face?" is an insult, for an Eskimo regards the face as the most esteemed part of his body, representative of his inner self. To call attention to a scar there is the same as saying his inner self is scarred or flawed.

6. Remember what people in crisis need: to ventilate their feelings...to understand what has happened...to feel they are regaining control of themselves...and *no* surprises. Because of the stress effect, they may not hear clearly, so use simple statements and confirm that you are understood. They may have a hard time making decisions and want you to do it for them. But be leery of giving emphatic advice ("You ought to divorce him"). If they take it and things turn out badly, you'll be blamed.

7. Stay calm. Your screaming and yelling as if you've lost control will only cut your tactical edge and increase the risk of violence. Psychologically, your being loud and excited so occupies your mind with the thought of your forceful verbal delivery that you cannot stay fully

aware of your surroundings and potential threats. By staying low-key, you encourage the disputants to follow suit...and if you do need to react with physical force, your move will be much less expected and thus more likely effective.

8. Listen *attentively* to what's being said. A disputant's voice may seem calm, but his words may contain danger cues of an imminent attack.

9. Don't let *talk* replace *tactics.* Sacrificing your safety in hopes of building rapport is always a foolish sacrifice.

Use the Survival Awareness Wheel, if need be, as a means of drawing out information: what they're feeling, what they want, what action they're willing to take to get what they want, etc. Their answers will help you assess the options for resolution. Some of the same listening and creative communication skills crucial in dealing with barricaders or hostage-takers will help you be effective here. If you're *lacking* in these skills, *that may prove to be your greatest hazard,* just as it may at other high-risk calls.

After you have their stories, you'll move fastest toward a positive solution if you start with something both parties can *agree* on. Maybe they'll agree that "it got a little loud tonight" or that they want you to leave. Build the discussion from there into the management of their differences.

As with calming, try *subtly* to point the way toward the short-term solution you think best to prevent more violence...but let the disputants think *they* are the ones making the ultimate decision. People tend to carry out only those decisions they have helped formulate. Suppose you think a couple should separate for the night to cool off. One way to manipulate cooperation is to pose matter-of-fact questions so they see the potential consequences of *not* cooperating. Start with getting the more aggressive disputant to imagine what might happen if they stay together ("If my partner and I leave here now and this starts up again, what could happen?"). Then encourage him or her to voice what *that* might lead to ("If you do hit her, she might take out a warrant. You'd have to go to jail and to court. Do you have anyone to come up with your bond? If you have to stay in jail, are you going to have to miss work, or do you have some vacation time coming?"). Paint a step-by-step scenario, then say something like: "From what you're telling me, if you stay here tonight and this thing breaks down, it sounds like the whole system is going to come down on your head. If you've got anywhere else you can spend the night, it looks like you should. What do you think?" With any capacity for logic, your subject will probably conclude it's in his best interest to leave, without your having created a potentially violent resistance.

A "cooling off" *separation* is used in more than 20% of disturbances. One option is to *suggest* (you can't *order*) that one disputant leave and that they meet at a specified time later in some public place, where their conflict is less likely to regenerate. A restaurant where they can have coffee together or a shopping mall where they'll be distracted by merchandise and activity are possibilities. Suggest they avoid bars ("People there just like a free look at other people's problems. You don't want to give 'em a free show"). Going to relatives is often inadvisable, too, because they may egg on the conflict. If one of the parties is concerned about future safety, suggest a phone conversation first, instead of a face-to-face meeting.

If a party is drunk, he or she usually should *not* be encouraged to leave, except to be transported to a detox center, a woman's shelter or other supervisory institution. Otherwise, the risk of drunk driving is too high. Where possible, consider making an arrest. Or suggest that the *other* disputant leave and the intoxicated one cool down by watching tv (and probably drinking more and passing out). When drunks are involved, rational mediation may be difficult or impossible and more forceful measures may be necessary. But if you leave one behind, convince yourself he does not have ready access to weapons. An intoxicated man in Arkansas agreed to an officer's suggestion that he stay alone in his house. But before the patrolman stepped off the front porch, the man grabbed a .22 rifle and reappeared. In a struggle for the gun, the officer was shot, fatally, three times in the chest and the offender, too, was killed.

In some cases, *compromises* can be worked out on the spot. So long as they satisfy both disputants, *they do not have to make logical sense.* A compromise has to be what *they* can live with, not what *you* can live with. A screaming-and-punching match broke out in North Carolina, for example, when an ex-wife came to her former husband's home, claiming she'd been gyped in their property settlement. During mediation, an officer asked her, "What do you want?" She looked around the room and, seemingly on impulse, decided: "That candy dish." The husband agreed, and she left, peacefully. Aggressors often have a strong need to *dominate,* so you need to leave them with a feeling of having *won* something to better assure the peace.

Also consider suggesting *referral agencies* where the disputants can get longer-term help like alcoholism treatment, sheltering from a violent spouse, marriage counseling, legal aid, etc. Officers often ignore such referrals because of the traditionally poor follow-through by disputants. But many of these people do not know specifically what help is available or how to reach it. If you carry a notebook with you with referral names, numbers and hours, you can dispense this information faster and thus be able to leave this potentially dangerous scene sooner.

Your expressing concern about the disputants' future may have an effect that will not be immediately apparent. Many battered women, for instance, report that their first step in leaving an abusive relationship was a support statement (but *not* pressure) from a law enforcement officer to the effect that they did not have to continue to take such treatment, that it was morally wrong, illegal and not their fault.

During your mediation or in preparation for a temporary separation, NEVER let either disputant leave the room alone. You don't want the fate of two California officers who permitted a seemingly calm aircraft worker to go to his bedroom to get some overnight things together. He came back with a .357 Magnum and killed them both. Again, "department policy" can be your excuse. Let the disputant lead the way. As you follow, your partner should move where he can keep a visual on your back for as long as possible, while continuing also to monitor his disputant. When you're out of sight, you can still reassure him you're okay by talking louder in conversation with your subject so your partner can hear you. (If a disputant has darted out of the room before you could stop him, do not pursue him. You and your partner take new positions, so you won't be where he expects if he reappears...and watch and listen for him. Consider leaving with the other disputant, if that seems feasible.) If the subject is gathering a jacket or other clothing, give it a "crimp search" (squeezing it in your hands, a better way to detect weapons than just patting it) before he takes possession of it.

Accompany either disputant even to the *bathroom.* An Illinois woman who'd been disarmed of a butcher knife during a domestic was allowed to go to the bathroom—and returned with a jagged piece of broken mirror, which she slashed across the chest of an officer who moved to control her. With either sex, make a quick check of the bathroom for potential weapons before they enter and inform them that you will need to stay outside with your foot in the door until they are finished. With these ground rules, they'll usually decide they can wait.

Difficult as it may be at times, *don't lose touch with why you are there.* You are *expected* to bring some semblance of peace to the scene before you leave.

Time, of course, is an issue. But with the right skills, you can accomplish a great deal at many domestics in just 20 minutes or so. And that can represent a lot *less* of your time in the long run. To answer officers who argue that even *that* much time is *too* much, one instructor offers this comparison:

TIME SPENT ON CALL

Mediation	vs. *"I Ain't Got Time for This Shit"*	
20-30 mins. at scene	Act like bull in china shop	5 mins.
20-30 mins. writing report	Arrest/resisting	5 mins.
(if necessary)	Time at hospital	2 hrs. 30 mins.
	Report writing	2 hrs. 30 mins.
_____	Booking	30 mins.
40 mins.-1 hr. maximum	Warrant application	2 hrs.
	Court (on day off)	4 hrs.
	_____	
	11 hrs. 40 mins. minimum	

And, he adds, this does not include time off if you are injured or time you will spend with internal affairs or with the FBI answering complaints.

Safe Departure

The next step in your process is leaving the scene safely. When you've calmed the situation enough to depart, *the officer exposed to the greater risk should withdraw first.* Generally that's the one of you farthest away from the door. If you're in that position, your partner can watch your back as you start out, and there's less chance you'll be isolated deep inside the dwelling and cut off from escape should the disputants attack by surprise at the last minute. Try to get the subject who instigated the trouble to open the door for you. Then you don't have to turn your back on him to exit. Once you're outside, stand to the side of the door and watch the interior until your partner is clear and has pulled the door firmly shut behind him.

Consider advising the complainant that if there are any more problems during your shift to call and ask for you or your partner *personally.* If other officers have to go to the scene, they may be starting from ground zero, not knowing the subjects involved, the layout of the residence, the background of the dispute, special hazards, etc. Thus, they're likely to be in greater danger. You can also request dispatch to assign any call-backs to you during your shift. *Do not directly threaten that a disputant will be arrested if you have to return.* If an offender thinks that's a certainty, he may prepare for your next visit...tactically.

Before leaving, you may be able to note whether the disputants have a scanner in the location. If so and if you have a portable, consider keying your mike on the various channels you can access and note which channels are received by the scanner. If one of your channels is *not* received, mentally note it. The next time you're called to that location, you may be able to use that channel during your approach, thus better assuring an element of surprise.

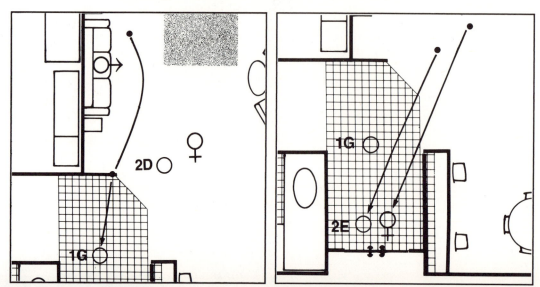

Here the male offender (unarmed) remains seated and has been calmed to a point where the officers begin to leave. Officer 1 maintains limited visual contact on the male complainant as he moves. Officer 2 and the female complainant move toward the foyer.

Outside, officers in some communities write in pencil up high on a porch pillar or door jamb the date, the type of call (by penal code number) and whether a weapon was involved, as ready reference to fellow officers who may be called there later. (In some communities, the initial knock at a domestic is done with a baton or flashlight handle on the upper door jamb, which also leaves an imprint, although this approach may not promote good officer positioning.)

Stay alert for trouble as you walk away. Listen near the residence for 10 to 30 seconds to be sure the dispute isn't reescalating. Avoid walking away side by side like a dual target. Rather use a "leap frog" style where one moves at a time while the other watches. If you've confiscated a weapon, don't assume that's a guarantee of safe departure. As one Maryland officer walked away with a 12 ga. shotgun he'd persuaded an elderly disputant to give him for safekeeping, the suspect produced a .38 cal. revolver and shot him, then finished him off with a .30-06 rifle.

Back in your patrol car, away from the scene, take a moment to *unwind.* These calls are emotionally draining. More than 45% of officers say they emerge from domestics "concerned" (worried) about what will happen. Nearly 40% feel "frustrated," nearly 17% "sad" and nearly 15% "angry." Many are churning with a combination of these negative emotions. Use your breathing exercises and other stress fighters to restore your equilibrium.

As your final step, *critique your performance,* as you would with other high-risk calls. Mentally reinforce what you did that seemed to work well and analyze your mistakes. These calls can teach valuable lessons, if you take time to identify them, as a young patrolman learned after he was stopped about 3 o'clock one morning in a small Louisiana town by a muscular male who wanted an escort to his residence. The subject said he'd had an argument with his wife and wanted "to get some clothes" so he could leave.

The officer complied and approached the front door with the subject trailing behind him. He cautiously stayed to the side when he knocked. But when a woman's voice called out, "Who is it?", he moved in front of a curtained glass panel in the door so she could see his uniform.

Suddenly the door swung in and a shot burst out of the darkened interior, passing so close it burned the officer's skin. He tried to draw and fire back, but he couldn't move. The male had seized him by the elbows and was using him as a shield against the woman, who now loomed in the doorway, cursing and waving a pistol in the officer's face.

The male dragged him backward to a corner of the house. Together they dove behind it and escaped. Only later, the officer learned that the couple had fought physically before he was hailed. The man already had his clothes and was going back for his shotgun. The woman, nine months pregnant, had warned him she'd kill him if he returned, and her shot was intended for him.

Reflecting on the incident, the officer made a long list, headed:

MY MISTAKES WERE:

They began:

"1. *My frame of mind* was that this was one of those average family disturbances that occurs in a small town and that nothing serious ever happens in a small town...."

"The mistakes I made during that 20-minute time have haunted me to this day," the officer says. *But his experience and his analysis of it changed forever his handling of these calls.*

Officer Disputants

Domestic violence occurs as often in police families as among the general population...even *more* often, according to some researchers. Chances are that sooner or later you'll take a disturbance call where one of the disputants is a fellow officer. Here, you *know* the subject probably has access to at least one gun. *He'll* know that if he's charged with a crime because of the dispute, he could be fired and possibly ruin his career.

Your mental condition approaching these calls should be on the borderline between Condition Yellow and Condition Orange. *They can be extremely deceptive.*

Officers deal with stress every day, and most develop the ability to conceal tension and emotion better than the average citizen. The best are skilled at using the element of surprise to their tactical advantage. An officer in a dispute may *appear* relaxed when in fact he's at the explosion point. The gross warnings you normally look for may be hidden—up to the moment he draws his weapon.

Listen closely for subtle indicators of the depth of his emotional upset. If you hear things like, "I don't care any more" or other hints that his internal controls are weakened, *believe them*. They may not be *said* with emotion, but they can still be a prelude to emotional *action*.

Note if he has his sidearm or backup gun...and where it is. Is he carrying it in an unusual place for an off-duty officer? If it seems unusually accessible and visible, he may be planning to use it.

Getting him to surrender the gun during your call is desirable, of course—*provided* you can win his compliance without worsening the situation. Many officers will view this request as demeaning. Pushed, they may push back harder. Especially in a crisis, officers are geared not to back down...nor to surrender their weapons. You'll be aided in separating him from his firearm if your department has a *written policy* that this is required when officers are involved as disputants. With that to fall back on, you can more easily depersonalize this touchy situation. Otherwise, consider getting a supervisor at the scene immediately. Calling in an officer one rank higher than the subject can be a good first step toward establishing control.

Remember that *trust*, which normally is the key to successful interaction between officers, may work *against* you in this situation. On the street, officers build up trust for each other to act predictably under stress. But here, predictability cannot be counted on. Regard the officer disputant as you would a civilian: *expect the unexpected*.

Two California patrolmen learned one indelible midnight the price that can be paid for regarding an officer disputant as "safer" than others.

They were dispatched to the apartment of a young woman who said she was being harassed by a former boyfriend, a fellow officer of theirs. He showed up, off duty, as they interviewed her. When she wouldn't let him in, he asked one of the responding officers to hand her a paper bag, which the officer did without looking inside.

The officers talked to him outside. His shirt was stained where she'd thrown coffee on him earlier. His tone of voice was even and cool, but when the officers mentioned that she might seek a restraining order, he replied: "She's not going to need it. Go ahead and arrest me if you want to. Call the supervisor. I don't give a fuck." Several times he repeated, "I don't care about anything—the job, her, nothing."

After a few moments, he walked into the apartment and started "ragging" the woman as she sat on a couch across the room. One officer moved between them and tried to establish eye contact with the man to distract him, but he avoided it. His voice got louder, but his body still seemed relaxed.

"Have me arrested!" he shouted at the woman.

She smiled at him.

"You think this is funny, bitch? You think I care? *Watch this!*"

"We'd never noticed the gun," the officer nearest him softly recalls. "Never looked for it. He had it tucked in his pants, under the tail of his shirt, a .38. He had it up to his shoulder before I realized what was happening.

"I dove to the right trying to get my gun out. My partner rolled around a corner, trying to get his out.

"The officer put his gun against the left side of his head, just behind his ear, and popped a cap. He went back about 2 feet and hit the wall. Like slow motion, he slid down until his butt hit the floor. Blood gushed out of his nose and mouth like someone turned a tap on full blast."

Later, someone looked inside the paper bag. There was a note in there—"I have nothing to live for any more"—and a brown teddy bear the girlfriend had given him. He'd cut the bear open and torn its guts out.

"If he hadn't been an officer, we would have opened the bag," one of the responding officers believes. "We would have looked for weapons. We wouldn't have let him go inside the apartment. We would have been more forceful in the way we talked to him. We wouldn't have let him carry the show as much as he did.

"But we'd all worked together, and you trust your fellow officers so much....

"He could have taken my partner and me with him if he'd wanted to. I was just 3 feet away, my partner was just 5. He could have killed us both, and we couldn't have done a thing. Too much lag time...and no cover."

Bar Fights

Sometimes domestic disturbances take place in drinking establishments, but most often bar fights are brawls without domestic overtones that may escalate to near riots. Whatever the cause, the same basic tactics apply here, plus some special considerations.

Some officers argue that you should respond high profile to bars, with lights and siren going, in hopes that the noise of your approach will intimidate the fighters into stopping. In reality, the racket inside the place is likely to be so loud they won't hear you. And if they do, they then have forewarning to set up an assault when you walk in. Remember, there may be other patrons in the bar besides the combatants who have reason to respond violently to your presence. You want the element of surprise working for *you*.

Avoid pulling up in the parking lot to further your low profile and also to lessen the chance of being penned in if resistance develops to your taking one or more prisoners away.

NEVER ENTER THE BAR ALONE. As you wait for backup, you may be able to quick peek in a window to assess what's going on and particularly to get a fix on exactly where the fight is. The larger the fray, the more backup you'll likely need to bring things under control safely.

Also avoid taking in your shotgun. In close quarters, it'll be more hazard to you than protection. One officer carried his into a bar fight thinking that by racking a round into the chamber he'd scare the battlers into submission, like he sometimes does on the street. As soon as he racked a round, though, he realized that the country-western music was blaring so loud even *he* couldn't hear the slide move. Nobody stopped anything...and now he had a charged gun that he wasn't sure how to render safe!

One piece of equipment to consider taking in, though, is a boxer's mouthpiece, one whose design will protect your *jaw* as well as your teeth from serious injury. One officer who uses this device likes to wait to insert it until the combatants have caught sight of him. The implication that he has "been there before" and knows what he is doing often proves intimidating.

One option for entering if multiple officers are available is an organized approach called the "M" formation.

The three officers on the front line have batons at the ready position. As they enter the bar, the team leader signals which offender he wants arrested, by yelling out his description. As the group confronts him, the arrest team moves between the front officers like linebackers and grabs him. The other officers then position themselves protectively around the arrest team as the group moves toward an exit.

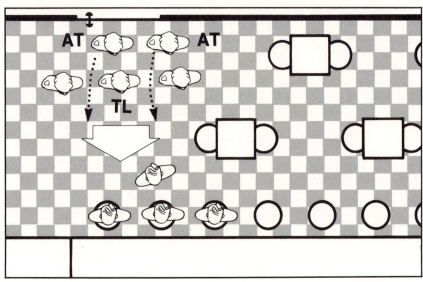

The "M" formation. Team leader in front, arrest team behind.

With fewer numbers available, some officers like to split up, so they and their partners go in different entrances. There are obvious risks with this: you temporarily lose visual contact with each other and may end up inside in cross-fire positions. However, it does separate your firepower, can enhance surprise (everyone's expecting you to come in the front door but may not expect your partner coming in the back), can yield a faster perspective on what's going on and may give the combatants a greater feeling of being hopelessly "surrounded." This approach tends to work best when more than two officers are available.

Pause a moment inside to *assess the situation*. This takes discipline, because your instinct will be to wade in immediately. But even if the circumstances seem serious, hang back for a few seconds to size up what you have. Check the number of people involved in the fight-...whether more than one fight is going on...the mood and size of the crowd...the possibility that weapons are present. Even in a dark bar you sometimes can catch a bright glint from a crowd scene, which may betray that someone has a knife or gun.

Before you push through the crowd, be sure your sidearm is secure. If your gunbelt has a Velcro fastening, check it, too. If it's loose, a quick yank from the crowd can lose you the belt and everything on it.

Often you can avoid the crowd altogether by going *behind* the bar and walking the full length of it to get closer to the action. The bar provides a barrier between you and the crowd; behind it you have only the bartender to contend with and it will offer some cover if shooting starts. Back there may also be switches that turn on bright lights used by the bar's cleanup crew. Use them to light up the scene. Also, by using this route you can check for handguns and shotguns often concealed by many bartenders.

Don't just grab the first person you spot who seems to be a combatant. He may be trying to break up the fight and could be an ally you can use later. Know whom you're touching and why. If possible, check with someone on the outskirts to see who started the skirmish.

He's your prime objective. The sooner you can control him, the sooner you'll get the fight stopped.

Try to view the action from the *side*. This will give you a better visual of the combatants' hands and also place you where you're less likely to step into a wild punch. If a knife or a broken bottle is involved (probably the most common weapons in bar fights), having your baton in hand is important as you approach. Your gun may not provide you practical defense in a crowded bar, but by swinging your baton you may be able to knock a knife or bottle from an assailant's hand or strike him on a pressure point so that he is temporarily immobilized. DO NOT ATTEMPT *HAND-TO-HAND* CONTROL AGAINST A WEAPON.

A physical response of some kind is almost certain to be required, as words alone rarely have much impact in a bar fight, even if they can be heard.

However, that does not mean that *you* necessarily have to get physical. Ask the crowd: "Does anyone know these people?" Usually some friends of the combatants are around. If so, suggest: "Let's get this thing broken up. We don't want anyone to go to jail." *They'll* probably work then to pull their buddies off each other... and take any blows in the process. *Make the situation work for you.*

If you *must* intercede, either you or your partner—*not both*—should take responsibility for breaking up the fight. The other of you stands by, watches your back and makes sure no one interferes. When you are physically dealing with the fighters is when their buddies are most likely to leap in to help them resist. Although you view the fight initially from the side, *try to move against the instigator from his rear* for the best and quickest control. Communication between you and your partner should be *short*; one-word cues, if possible... like "Knife!" if one of you sees one. With all the noise that'll probably be present, you'll never hear whole phrases.

Once the situation is under control, again use the walkway behind the bar for leaving... or go out exit doors, which are usually quicker. If that's not possible, try to get the other bar patrons back to their stools and tables before attempting to remove any arrestee. If you try to push through a crowd, there's too much opportunity for a friend of your prisoner to attack from close range, and you'll soon have people on you like gnats on a pear. One option is for your partner to go first to clear back anyone who approaches; shining his high-intensity flashlight in their eyes will help incapacitate them. If additional backup is unavailable, you may be able to recruit a "friend" on the premises to follow behind you and your prisoner to watch your back. This might be the bartender, who usually will not want trouble with the police. An alternative is for you to guide your *prisoner* ahead of you while your partner follows behind, walking backwards if necessary, to deflect thrown bottles, chairs, sucker punches, etc.

Again, it may be safer for you to let a combatant's buddies drag him outside for you. That saves you having to handcuff him and take him through a hostile crowd. They'll likely cooperate if they get the impression you just want to talk to the fighters to "find out what happened." Once you're in a safer environment, you can invent jobs for the friends ("Go call his wife and see if she'll come down and get him"... or "Go get his car and bring it around"... or "Go back in and get some ice and a towel.") Then if you do intend arrest, handcuff him while they're gone, put him in your unit and leave.

If you moonlight as security in a bar, you may be in even more danger from fights than responding officers because you will be there, possibly alone, at the outset. Besides watching for argumentative individuals and separating them before violence erupts, perhaps your most important protective tactic is to arrange in advance a *visual* coded signal with the bartender or some other employee who is likely to be within sight of you. Example: your raising your closed fist high over your head. When he sees that code, he knows to call the police immediately and tell the dispatcher that an officer needs help to assure the fastest possible response.

8

HOSTAGE OFFICERS

One winter afternoon in Arkansas, a forest ranger stopped at a little country store to buy gasoline for his duty truck. He left his sidearm in the cab as he serviced the vehicle, and he did not bother to retrieve it when he headed inside to pay the bill. Weaponless, the officer walked right in on an armed robbery-in-progress.

Along with the store's elderly owner, he was quickly taken captive and forced into the robber's car. The officer was ordered to drive to an isolated wooded area. There, the storekeeper was shot and left for dead when he tried to escape. The officer offered no resistance whatever. In compliance with the gunman's demand, he lay down on the ground at gunpoint and let a hole be blown in his head at close range with a .38 cal. revolver.

During the time inside the store, on the drive to the woods and while the action at the execution site unfolded, there *must* have been moments when the captor was physically close…when he was distracted…when (with two people to control) he experienced a separation of focus. Yet amidst the thoughts of terror that undoubtedly bombarded the officer as his life raced toward its end, apparently not a single concept for how he might save himself that he thought worth trying entered his mind.

In officer-hostage situations, which are relatively rare but increasing in frequency, this paralysis of hopelessness is probably the single greatest barrier to survival you'll need to overcome. Whether you're the victim officer or an officer responding to the situation, the temptation is strong to immediately feel *resigned* to the predicament. The attitude that "I'm going to die…my life is in his hands…there's nothing I can do" may leap to the surface and dominate your thoughts and behavior.

True, there *are* no-win situations. In the infamous Memphis case where a patrolman was seized by a cult of religious zealots, tortured and killed inside a residence where he'd been lured by a questionable complaint, the odds were so heavily stacked against him once he was inside the building that he didn't stand a prayer. The same is often true where greatly outnumbered correctional officers are taken hostage during prison uprisings. Martyrs, psychos and others who are willing—or actively *want*—to die also can create situations extremely difficult to manipulate, where the hostage-taking is just part of the planned sacrifice dedicated to their "cause."

But the more common occurrences are not carefully orchestrated seizures with multiple or fanatical offenders involved. They are *unplanned* and *spontaneous*. Because you happen to be in the wrong place at the wrong time or are caught by surprise, you suddenly become a hostage of opportunity, *one-on-one* with your captor. Like the federal agent who ended up with a gun to his head when he tried to serve a warrant at a used car lot in Virginia. Or the Illinois patrolman who was surprised by a hostage-taker when he responded to a man-with-a-gun call at a hospital. Or the Utah officer who was disarmed during a scuffle with a mental patient and taken on a high-speed ride across two states. Or the Connecticut correctional officer who was jumped and held captive by a single disgruntled inmate with a razor.

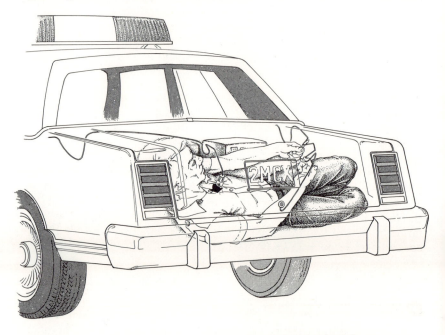

What if you're held hostage in the trunk of your patrol car? If your vehicle has an automatic trunk release, here is an escape trick. Reach up and bend the trunk light assembly down until the light is tipped at the angle that activates it. Use this as a work light. Isolate the trunk light wire, then find the wire that connects to the trunk lock. Scrape away enough insulation to lay your pen knife across both bare wires to create a live contact. This will automatically release the trunk lid!

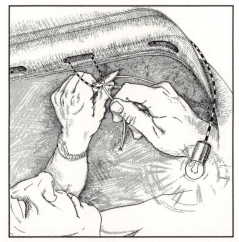

Frightening and volatile as such events surely are, some officers perceive their chances of surviving them as being virtually non-existent.

Yet in fact, with the right responses, a spontaneous officer hostage-taking is more likely to prove no-win for the hostage-*taker* than for the hostage.

A captor may overpower you or a fellow officer physically, but you have the capability of overpowering him *psychologically,* and using that springboard to turn the tables on him physically, as well. What's necessary is to:

1. *remain as calm as possible.* Especially early in the incident, the hostage-taker will have an extremely high anxiety level, regardless of whether he is psychologically unbalanced or a trapped criminal. Hysteria on your part will only increase his chances of using violence.

2. *free yourself from deadly misconceptions and illusions* about this type of armed encounter. This, in turn, will enable you to overcome the grip of "frozen fright" and play a decisive role in resolving the incident.

What *seems* obvious in these situations "ain't necessarily so." The hostage-taker *appears* to have *total* control, but *rarely* is that really the case. Once you understand his vulnerabilities—the TRUE dynamics of an officer hostage-taking—you can exploit them against his will to your advantage, either as a responding officer or as the officer victim.

In managing these events, as with other tactical challenges, knowledge and preplanning are *power.* They can help you lay the groundwork for that one galvanizing moment when you can overcome the threat …They can help you recognize when that moment is at hand…And they can help you make the moves to make the most of it.

As a patrolman who was taken hostage while serving misdemeanor warrants in Colorado puts it: "Don't waste time thinking over and over, 'God, I really screwed up,' which is a common reaction, or 'God, what are the other guys going to think of me!' You have to live *with* the past, but not *in* it. Your psychological focus *must* be in the here-and-now. *Seconds count.* Use them to make a plan for how you're going to get free."

Dynamics of Confrontation

It should go without saying that you never *voluntarily* put yourself in a hostage position. Yet the annals of law enforcement are replete with cases where officers do just that, by exchanging themselves for civilians who are under a captor's control.

Predictably, the outcome of such misdirected heroism is often tragic. Just seconds after a Mississippi sheriff exchanged himself, unarmed, for a woman and three children being held hostage in a car by a manslaughter suspect, the offender shot the lawman point-blank in the chest and killed him. In Wisconsin, a combination of darkness, sudden movement and target confusion got a small-town police chief accidentally killed by an officer who was his best friend, after the chief defied his hostage negotiation training and switched himself for a teen-aged robber's two hostages.

When an officer agrees to become a hostage in a situation where tensions already are sky-high, the added emotional impact on everyone involved—the hostage-taker, other officers, the victim officer himself—is like a lighted primer cord to disaster. A hostage-taker will likely watch an officer more closely than a civilian hostage, while fellow officers are more likely to lose their perspective on the situation. When multiple officers are present, especially, some ill-advised, regrettable action by someone at the scene is almost a certainty. At best, there's heightened risk of the officer being accidentally shot. At worst, the exchange plays directly into the suspect's plans. He may have had previous beefs with the police and may now want a sacrificial lamb. He may have had no intention of harming his original hostage(s) but uses them as a ploy to get a cop...and revenge. Also by becoming a hostage, you *add* to his "prestige" as a hostage-taker through your stature. He might not have intended to kill the original hostage(s), but with some psychotic types you may now become a murder candidate because of your special status.

Of course, the actions you can take to free yourself or a fellow officer can work regardless of how the hostage status occurs. But anyone who *deliberately* puts himself in a position where these maneuvers are necessary to save his life is asking for more risk than any reasonable person ever should solicit.

More typically, an officer becomes a hostage when he intervenes in a domestic or some other crisis assignment that gets out of hand or he interrupts a crime-in-progress and is seized as a shield for escape. For now, let's assume you are the victim's partner or a responding backup

A negotiator stands near a police vehicle with the hostage officer on the passenger side. The offender is armed and behind the wheel. The incident was successfully negotiated.

officer. As you approach the scene, you confront the suspect, his gun to your fellow officer's head. He may scream at you something like: "Gimme your gun, motherfucker, or I'll blow his shit in the street!"

If your firearm is NOT already in your hand, trying to draw against his drawn weapon may very well be a losing proposition. Your more viable options probably are to:

1. dive for the nearest cover, while drawing your sidearm. If his gun is pointed at you initially, ideally wait until he is distracted, then move

down and to the outside of his arm. If he fires, it will most likely be to where you *were* and his muscle contraction and recoil will tend to bring his weapon up and in. If his gun is pointed at the hostage officer, he'll likely move it to shoot at you, possibly opening an opportunity for that officer to take physical action against him. As a moving target, you'll be hard to hit.

2. try persuasion and other negotiating gambits in an effort to defuse the situation and change his mind. Talking calmly and *slowly* backing toward cover may be possible.

3. as an absolute *last resort*, consider relinquishing your weapon and pray that because he hasn't killed the first officer he won't kill you, either. Keep in mind, though, that if you do surrender your firearm, you

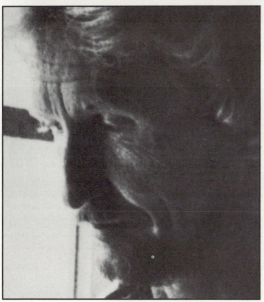

Greg Powell (lower left) and Jimmy Lee Smith (lower right) were stopped one night by officers Ian Campbell and Karl Hettinger. They disarmed the officers and forced them to drive to an onion field. There, Powell shot Campbell in the face. Then Campbell was shot four more times in the chest. (top) Recreation shows where Campbell stood (hands raised). Pierce Brooks, chief investigator on the case, stands with revolver pointed just as Smith did. The real Smith observes on far left.

are then totally at the suspect's mercy. You've given up any chance of negotiating "with teeth" or of shooting back if you are fired upon. Also, if for some reason he has not already taken the hostage officer's gun, you have armed the suspect with a gun that you *know* works; his may not. (Some officers with extensive experience in recovering suspect weapons estimate that about 40% are unloaded or not loaded properly, have defective ammunition, are non-functional or are just toys.) Even though your sidearm is holstered, he still may perceive you as a threat and not elect to take you on so long as you retain your firearm. On the other hand, you may feel that cooperating with him is your only hope of staying alive. A Texas captain involved in a hostage-taking by an armed robber recalls: "I knew from his eyes he meant business. I had no doubt at all that if I didn't give up my gun, I'd be dead on the spot." Adds a sheriff's lieutenant who surrendered his weapon during a hostage incident at an Illinois jail: "I felt that resistance would only make a bad situation worse." The decision is a *personal choice*, but should be talked over between partners before it happens, so each can anticipate the probable reaction of the other.

If you DO have your gun in hand when you respond and are able to draw down into a stand-off, you then have different—and more favorable—dynamics to consider. In that case, STEADFASTLY REFUSING TO SURRENDER YOUR FIREARM IS ESSENTIAL. Despite the suspect's threats to kill your partner if you don't comply, the fact is that the victim officer's life—and yours—may well be in *greater* danger if you are disarmed. Because then instead of at least holding "half a deck," you have *no cards* at all (unless, of course, you have a backup gun you are confident you can reach).

With you *still armed*, the "typical" hostage-taker has strong motivation to keep his hostage alive. If he doesn't, you will shoot *him*. Yet if you give up your firearm, he now has a *second* hostage: you. And, aside from conscience and possible fear of future punishment, he may have no real reason to keep either of you alive. In fact, killing you both might hasten his escape at that point.

You have the dual priority of protecting yourself and protecting the hostage officer. If you surrender a drawn firearm, you give up your best ability to fulfill both those responsibilities. By keeping your capacity to deliver deadly force, you keep the offender somewhat boxed in by limiting his options.

So long as you are armed, the hostage-taker is in probably the second most dangerous position. Perhaps surprisingly, *you*, as responding officer—*not* the hostage officer—are very likely in the *most* danger. In over 200 realistic simulations of officer hostage-takings conducted by a department in Maryland, *responding* officers ended up getting "killed" about five times more frequently than *hostage* officers. Killing a responding officer can *eliminate* an immediate problem for the hostage-taker, whereas killing the hostage only *creates* one. Moreover, responding officers often increase their own risks by not understanding the power principles involved and thus not knowing the proper moves to make.

After the first few moments in a hostage-taking, the person in the *least* danger is likely the *hostage* officer (unless, of course, you surrender your firearm, thereby leaving the *offender* facing the least threat). Working in the hostage officer's favor is the suspect's state of mind.

The suspect, in most cases, has no emotional ties to the victim officer. This contrasts to many civilian hostage-takings where the hos-

One option to keep in mind when an offender has the drop on you is to *appear* to be surrendering your sidearm. If it's already drawn, put your hands up and let the weapon dangle down against your open palm with your trigger finger inside the trigger guard. Or you can hook your little finger inside the guard if you're able to cock the hammer first. At the last minute, quickly swing your arm down and close your hand on the gun butt. Your gun will be upside down as it comes down, but you can still squeeze the trigger and get off rounds. If your sidearm is holstered, you can pull the same trick by reaching for it with your non-gun hand, to put the hostage-taker most at ease. Then as you withdraw it and bring it around, fire it upside down as explained. Like all other tactics mentioned in this chapter, this takes extensive practice, not only to fire the weapon but to hit what you're shooting at.

tage is a family member, say, toward whom the suspect feels intense, even homicidal hostility. The hostage officer is in a more coldly practical position. If the offender really intended to kill him, he would probably have done so before you arrived. The hostage's value, really, is that he's breathing and therefore can still be killed. Keeping the officer alive as a ticket out is now the suspect's only rational alternative. That doesn't mean he isn't *capable* of killing; it's currently just not his top priority.

By seizing the hostage, the offender has given himself more mental demands than any one person can possibly accommodate. At least five concerns are battling for his attention: 1) his escape; 2) the hostage; 3) you and your threat of deadly force; 4) any dialogue you start with him, and 5) bystanders and other stimuli from the surrounding environment.

No one can adequately deal with that many problems at one time, especially under high stress. One or more of these concerns is going to have to go on his back burner. And the most likely candidate is the hostage officer.

The *only* thing the offender physically controls at the moment is his hostage. Because of that domination, the hostage will seem to require less attention. Hard as it may be to believe, numerous real-life encounters have proven that the hostage may be virtually *forgotten* as the hostage-taker attempts to cope with his other pressing concerns.

If you and the hostage officer understand the dynamics at play here, *you can banish the illusion of hopelessness and work together to effect a rescue.*

Creating and *anticipating* the right moment for action is critical. An ill-timed, impetuous move on your part can be disastrous. For instance, if you shoot the suspect while he has a gun pointed at the hostage, particularly if it's cocked, a startle reaction from being shot or involuntary movements even after he technically is dead may cause him to pull the trigger and shoot the officer. It's claimed that if you plant a sniper-like shot in his head (as described in Chapter 4), you can paralyze him instantly and forestall any movement, even ambulation after death. But realistically, especially considering the stress you'll be under and the fact that you'll probably be shooting your *sidearm* (not a rifle), your chances of doing that are pitifully slim, compared to your chances of missing your intended precise placement or of the bullet ricocheting off his skull or teeth or following an erratic, less effective penetration path. Thus your shooting may do more to *endanger* the hostage than save him.

Line up a sight picture on the hostage-taker or at least get your gun into a good return-fire position. But what you want to fire at him initially instead of bullets are *words*.

Dialogue

As the responding officer, initiate dialogue with the hostage-taker ASAP. Not only will this help distract him from the hostage officer, but it also can help guide him to the behavior you desire.

Under the enormous stress of the situation, the offender will be experiencing a "restricted option capacity;" that is, his tensed mind will not be able to register the full range of alternatives to his predicament. He may think his only option is to shoot. You want to offer him other avenues so that he does not lock in on undesirable action, believing it's his only choice. In a sense, you want to sell him on the choices *you* would like to see him make.

Avoid a shouting match. You may have to fight a temptation to repeat back to him the same commands he's giving you. The tendency to uncontrollably parrot words spoken by another is called "echolalia" and is especially powerful under stress. But nothing is gained by screaming back and forth, "Drop your gun, pig!"..."No, *you* drop *your* gun, asshole!" ad infinitum. This will only fuel his already-volatile anxiety level. You don't want to *challenge* him. You want to *calm* him and then *manipulate* him. The more relaxed you can get him, the more rational he's likely to be. That will make him easier to deal with psychologically and also tend to increase his lag time in responding to any surprising physical moves you or the hostage officer might make.

If he wants to escape from a crime scene, in a sense his motivation in keeping his hostage is one of *power.* He wants to prevent officers from doing what they want to do (arrest him). If you anger him, you may push his motivation into a more dangerous category, one of *revenge.* He may shoot his hostage—or you—as an expression of his ire, for spite.

Officers often are conditioned to issue "parent-like" authoritarian demands, with the expectation that people will obey. But now you are up against an individual whose life may also be structured around getting people (his victims) to do what he wants. *Don't promote this clash.* Whether you're the responding officer or the hostage, don't antagonize him with insults, profanity or belittling language. *Use psychology.* By trying to out-intimidate him, you will only increase the danger.

As the responding officer, make it look to him as if your options are limited, while his are open. If he's yelling at you to drop your gun, tell him, as *calmly* as possible: "I can't do that. My department won't let me. *You're* the only one with that choice." If he tries to impose time limits or escalates the intensity of his threats, reinforce: "Look, pal, I *can't* drop my gun. *It's the rules.*" Once he understands this, you can then work to develop a situation *you* can control.

As a key part of your thinking for him, you want to establish in his mind not only what *your* priorities are but also what *his* should be. Remind him of his goal: "Do yourself a favor...Let the officer go and *get out of here!*" By emphasizing the possibility of escape, you will help him focus on *why* he seized the officer hostage in the first place. If he loses touch with that, his desperation and irrationality will only increase—and so will your problems. For if he is allowed to contemplate shooting as a serious option, he will then begin thinking about whom to take out first. And you can bet he's not going to start with his *cover*, the hostage officer!

Show him that he can still achieve his initial goal and that *you will help resolve his predicament.* Paint a word picture of *easy* gratification: "Just let the officer go, and you can get out of here...You haven't killed anybody...You don't have to hurt anybody to get away...All I want is that officer...You let him go and you can walk...Nobody'll hurt you...Just let the officer go and get away..."

If you can get him talking, perhaps by asking questions ("What do you want?...What can I help you with?") if he doesn't voice demands, you will widen his distraction from the hostage officer. The second he speaks, he'll slacken his control over the hostage, because any individual tends to concentrate his primary attention on the person he's talking to. Keep him focused on you and the positive options you're suggesting. The more you can get him to respond to what you are saying, rather than vice versa, the more you are establishing dominance over him.

Sometimes your quick assessment of the suspect's mental state and alertness may convince you to try an unorthodox ploy. In Vermont, an emotionally disturbed individual invaded a municipal building and seized a meter maid, then took the responding police chief as a second hostage. Both were held at gunpoint in a dark locker room. Sensing that the suspect could best be managed by a calm, "rational" approach, the chief first quietly told him, "I'm going to take my hat off and turn around so I can see who I'm talking to." When that was permitted, he said: "I can't see you to talk to you in the dark. I'm going to turn on the lights." With this kind of verbal "inching forward," he gradually adjusted the environment to his advantage and eventually positioned himself where he was able to grab the suspect's gun and bring him under control, saving his own life and that of the frightened meter maid as well.

As the responding officer, you want to strive for a cover position when talking with the hostage-taker.

Another unstable offender took a deputy hostage in Ohio and was holding a gun to his head when a fellow officer responded. "What's the problem?" the officer asked. The suspect replied: "I don't like this guy!"

"I don't either," the cop snarled. Then disgustedly to the hostage deputy: "Get the hell out of here!"

The deputy broke and ran, leaving the dumbfounded suspect exposed without cover to the officer's sidearm.

Remember during your dialogue that you MUST closely monitor your primary Area of Responsibility—his hand holding the gun—at least in your peripheral vision. Do not get lured into establishing eye contact with him to the extent that you are delayed in perceiving even subtle movement of that threat location.

Also DO NOT GET LOCKED INTO DIALOGUE AS YOUR ONLY OPTION. A female officer was held hostage down on the ground for about 15 minutes by an armed suspect who repeatedly threatened to kill her. Responding officers had excellent cover positions and several opportunities for clear shots when the offender moved his gun away from her head. However, command personnel reportedly refused to okay their firing because of a single-minded commitment to negotiate. As the incident dragged on, the hostage-taker yanked the officer's hair and made her scream out, "I don't want to die!" Then he put down his gun, grabbed her .38 special and killed her. Resolving an incident with *everybody* unharmed is a desirable goal, but the hostage officer's safety *always* should have priority. So long as deadly force is justified and can be delivered without endangering innocent parties, it should not be eliminated as an option.

If you're the *hostage*, rather than the responding officer, you're generally best off to *keep quiet* during the dialogue phase, if possible. Don't address remarks either to your fellow officer or the suspect. This not only reminds the hostage-taker of your presence but may confuse him, thereby increasing his anxiety level. Letting the two of them do the talking while you fade into the background will hasten the moment when you may be able to act physically to gain your release.

Suppose the hostage-taker *does* give up the officer and tries to escape. As the responding officer, you then have a whole new ball game. *With the hostage safe,* you can reevaluate any promises you've made and intervene in any way you decide is appropriate, given the environment and new circumstances. Or you can reason as a New York detective did who responded to the hostage-taking of a uniformed officer. The detective persuaded the hostage-taker to shove the hostage aside and run away. Why didn't the detective shoot as the suspect fled? "I got my top priority," he explained. "I didn't want to do anything that might jeopardize anyone else's safety." The offender, incidentally, was caught just eight minutes later.

Should the suspect try to escape with the officer still a hostage, be aware that the risk to you and your fellow officer may be escalating to a new plane. Blocking the escape route may be hard without making yourself vulnerable. Even following may require you to leave cover. Indeed, based on the experience of other responding officers, when you emerge from cover and attempt to pursue is when you are most likely to be assaulted.

Yet, if you do not maintain the offender in your field of view and range of fire, the threat to the officer hostage increases substantially. If the suspect gets far enough away from you so that he thinks his escape is in the bag, his focus then will shift from you to his hostage. At that point, it may fully dawn on him what it means to have a cop as a captive: the officer is a trained professional. If he's released, he may be able to thwart the suspect's escape—or even kill him. The officer, consequently, is now at great risk of being shot rather than freed.

If you cannot safely pursue by moving from cover to cover and you are about to lose sight of the suspect, you know that you may also be about to lose the hostage. Actions then must be more immediate and extreme. The hostage may need to try physically to liberate himself. This may be easier now that the hostage-taker is moving away from you. To avoid turning his back on you, he'll have to move backwards or sideways. His focus is likely to be on where he is going, on maintaining his footing and balance and on keeping control of the hostage. This can make him easier for the hostage officer to take.

If the hostage fails to take action, you may need to play some long shot in hopes of successfully concluding the incident. One option if you feel yourself losing control is to appear to be helping him actually *plan* his escape. From behind cover, tell him, "Okay, okay, I just want my buddy back. You've got nothing to worry about from me. I want you to just move slowly toward that car (building, corner, door, etc.). When you get by that garbage can, I'm going to lower my gun. When I do, let my buddy go and haul ass. *You won't be hurt."* Even if he doesn't comply, you may now have a basis for re-instituting dialogue. ("Okay, you don't want to do that. What do you suggest?")

If you can't negotiate a prompt release, you may be able to control the incident long enough, through dialogue and by maintaining your capacity for deadly force, to convert it into a tactical operation, with adequate backup officers to seal off the area and a trained hostage negotiator to take over. Remember: as a rule, the longer a hostage event lasts, the less likely it is to turn violent. However, it is often tough to contain a spontaneous officer hostage-taking longer than 4 to 6 minutes.

Escape

Now say that you are the *hostage officer*. With a responding officer handling dialogue, what's needed from you generally is not talk. The hostage-taker has the dominant role, you have the subordinate role. If you try to negotiate, you have nothing to negotiate *with*. He can easily convince you to shut up by applying pain. Also, if you are talking, he's less likely to shift his attention away from you.

Even if you're alone, you may decide you're better off to stay quiet and let the suspect possibly be diverted by stimuli from the environment—noise, barriers he needs to traverse, other people. Of course, if he asks you questions, respond, lest your silence anger him and increase his irrationality. Otherwise, consider remaining passive until you can initiate meaningful *movement*. Like a North Carolina deputy who was taken hostage by a man with a rifle who'd just shot another man in the back. The deputy was able to draw his sidearm but was afraid to raise it. However, when the offender turned his head at the sound of backup arriving, the deputy dove behind a tree and then safely brought his gun up. The suspect surrendered.

Moving to free yourself is not an impossibility in most situations. Again, the hostage-taker likely will have less control over you than you may fantasize. Even if he's holding you with his arm around your neck and his gun to your head, he'll rarely use a *strangle* hold. Occasionally there may be restraints that make your physical movement impossible. One Rhode Island officer searching a residential neighborhood for bank robbery suspects, for example, was surprised when he rounded a garage corner and was taken hostage. Initially, his captor held him in a tight bearhug with a gun pointed to each side of the officer's head. But more likely you *will* have flexibility. Even in the Rhode Island incident, as time passed, the hostage-taker released his grip and pointed his guns away from the hostage officer. If you know how to move—and *when*—the odds are overwhelming that you can get free...and survive.

A key is to make your movement *purposeful*, designed to help you reestablish control. *Not* like that of a Midwestern security officer who was taken hostage during the robbery of a savings and loan. When the robber shoved a 9mm pistol at him, the officer reflexively put his hand up to shield his face. This did nothing to change the balance of power. The gunman shot him in the arm, then, as a group of horrified bank patrons and employees watched, threw him to the floor, straddled his waist and shot him fatally in the chest.

Ironically, your captor is likely unwittingly to give you the right opening *himself* for you to break loose. Your alert monitoring of his physical and mental states—watching for gross or subtle changes in his voice, muscle tension, breathing patterns, posture, anxiety level, focus—will clue you to the moment. You're best off making your move at one of these times:

1. *When he eases his grip.* If he has hold of you, he'll probably not be able to maintain a consistently tight grip, even for a few moments. Tension quickly produces muscle fatigue and, especially as he feels you are securely under his control, he will tend to relax from time to time. You can feel the relaxation or shift of grip taking place.

2. *When he's talking.* If he talks, you can "own" him. Dialogue initiated by the responding officer (or later by a hostage negotiator, if the incident becomes long-term) will necessarily create a separation of focus for the hostage-taker. He can't concentrate equally on you, on what the

The typical arm and gun positioning is similar in both officer and civilian hostage-takings. Note how the gun-hand relaxes as time passes.

responding officer says and on the verbal responses he makes. When he is talking, his attention is likely to be diverted most from you. This often is accompanied by an easing of his grip, as the dialogue tends to defuse his anxiety.

3. *When he takes his gun away from you.* He may start out with his gun to your head or back, but experience shows a high probability that over time he will point it at another person or place, if only momentarily. This may reflect a high-stress reaction, a dilemma of not really knowing what to do with the weapon, or the perception of another threat, such as from a responding officer. If your responding officer is in the open without cover but has his sidearm pointed at the hostage-taker, he can encourage this movement by starting to move in a circle around the offender toward the outside of the offender's gun hand. The suspect will most likely point the gun at the responding officer, letting you act. In some cases, hostage-takers start "talking" with the gun, gesturing with it as they would an open hand or pointed finger to emphasize their remarks. Once the weapon is pointing away from you, your risk diminishes markedly.

4. *When he moves.* For reasons of escape or protection from responding officers, the hostage-taker will probably try to change locations at some point, taking you along. As he starts to move, he's bound to be thinking about where he's going, and he inevitably will have to adjust his body weight, the position of his weapon and his grip on you. These adjustments make him vulnerable to unexpected reactions.

At any one of these four moments, your use of surprise will have maximum impact. He's not expecting you, whom he "controls," to do anything; you're on the back burner of his thoughts. From your point of view, you're in the position usually enjoyed by offenders: you can initiate action and decide when and how to do it, while he can only react. In this case, *he'll* be stuck with the lag time (about 3/10 to 1/2 second) it takes for his brain to register your action. By the time he realizes what's happening and can react, you can be in a position of strong advantage, if not full control.

With good mental conditioning, physical practice and full concentration, you can move with incredible speed. In fact, the human hand can actually move faster than a rattlesnake can strike. If you exploit his distraction and vulnerable posturing and DO NOT *telegraph* your intentions by what you say, where you look or how you tense your muscles, *you can break free before he can shoot you.*

Just what move you make will be determined by the circumstances. Some require the presence of a responding officer to help you with the follow-through. Some require the use of your hands, so they won't work if you are handcuffed in back. Some require certain "set-up" actions on the part of the hostage-taker.

All require that you know where the suspect's weapon is located to shape your action. If he surprises you from behind initially, he'll probably order you not to turn around. If you can feel his gun touching you, then you have it located. If not, try immediately to jerk your head around to look over your shoulder for just a fraction of a second (simultaneously shouting, "What the hell?!"), as if that is part of your startle response. In your peripheral vision, you may be able to pick up his gun position. Or try to see its position reflected in nearby car and store windows, in mirrors or in other shiny objects.

When a responding officer is present, *both* of you need to anticipate the moment for action and react with coordination. Both of you need to be in Condition Orange from the moment the incident begins. Two federal agents working undercover narcotics set up a hotel room heroin buy that abruptly changed flavor when the suspect jammed a gun to one agent's head. The officer's partner immediately grabbed a gun she had hidden under a pillow and pointed it at the suspect. "Drop your gun or I'll blow your fucking head right off your shoulders!" she commanded. Initially, the suspect ignored her, but when she repeated the order, he turned his head slightly to look at her. The hostage was ready. At the instant of distraction, he knocked the gun out of his captor's hand and freed himself, then both officers joined in subduing the suspect.

It's best, of course, if you've practiced hostage escape moves together so that you can work confidently with unity. However, *don't* practice the moves once, then expect to use them effectively 18 months later. Like all physical skills, they need *regular*, repeated reinforcement to master. And both you and your partner should be willing to risk cuts, bruises, etc., so that you can practice with realistic speed and impact.

MOVE DECISIVELY...fast and forceful. GO FOR IT WITH EVERYTHING YOU'VE GOT. *Hesitant, half-hearted measures won't work.* Nor will "trying it out a little bit" and changing your mind in mid-move. If you aren't resolute and unequivocal, the hostage-taker may regain control over you, or the responding officer may end up shooting *you* instead of the offender.

Assuming your captor is *behind* you with an arm around your neck to position you as a shield, your options include:

GUN GRAB. This can free you when his gun is to your head. It's an escape move you can make either with or without the presence of a responding officer.

With your hands up at about chest level, palms out (as if you are urging the suspect or your partner to "stay cool"), wait until the suspect's grip relaxes or his focus separates. Then swiftly swing up your hand nearest the gun and clamp it over the top of the weapon. With a revolver, try to grab near the hammer so that your fingers and palm can lock the cylinder tight and your hand won't slide off the barrel as you move the gun or the suspect reacts.

The instant you grip the gun, *twist it out from your head* and try to force it down, so if it does go off (*expect* that it will), it won't shoot you or the responding officer. As you make your move, turn your head away from the weapon and close your eyes for protection from flying particles. The reach, grab and twist should be all one fast, fluid motion.

Simultaneous to yanking the gun out and down, twist your lower body and pop your hip back *hard* into his gut or groin. Bend your knees and crouch for this move, if necessary, to adjust for his height and steady your footing. Your thrust back will automatically knock him off balance and may inflict pain.

With both hands now on the weapon to overcome his strength, you'll have great torque capability. Pull his arm out straight and twist the gun so his wrist bends backward. The pressure will pry his grip open. If his finger is still inside the trigger guard, it will probably break or be ripped off as you throw your full force into the move.

As he releases the gun, just pivot away from him and take the weapon with you.

With practice, the Grab can be made even if you are handcuffed, provided your hands are in front of you. In preparation for that possibility, be sure to practice firing a gun while handcuffed.

Once you complete the move, try to get *your* gun on the suspect as

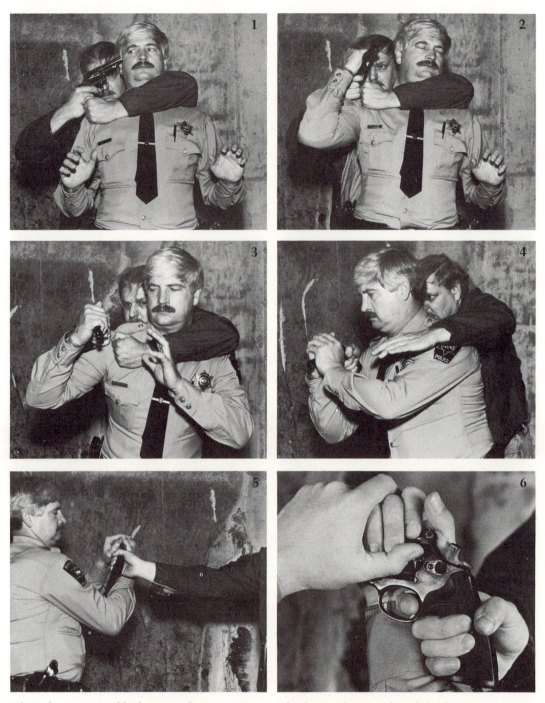

When the gun is grabbed, try to close your eyes in the event of an accidental discharge.

quickly as possible, if you still have it. Relying on his firearm for your defense is risky. You probably won't know for sure *if* it works and, if it's a model you're unfamiliar with, you may not know *how* it works, either. (This may especially be true if his gun is a semi-automatic and you're accustomed to a revolver. Participants in one study took an average of 17 seconds to successfully operate a semi-automatic after picking it up, compared to 2 or 3 seconds for a revolver.)

Also, create distance at once. Otherwise, he may jump back on you and fight you for the gun. Avoid the temptation of wanting to "give him a receipt" for what he has done to you, and concentrate on your safety.

WRIST SLAP. This move is appropriate when the hostage-taker for some reason—either to threaten a responding officer, to direct you where to move or as a startle reaction to some other stimulus—sticks his gun out from behind you, past your head. The direct threat to you is obviously diminished. Yet if he kills your fellow officer, your survival chances will probably evaporate. The Wrist Slap can let you become the primary force for controlling the scene and save you both. Like the Gun Grab, it can be done even if you are cuffed in front, but may be slower and harder that way.

Both your hands *simultaneously* should move up fast. Assuming the hostage-taker is right-handed, strike the weapon with your left hand, hitting your palm against the cylinder and coming over the top with your fingers. At the same time, your right hand hits his wrist, just past the back of his hand. Hit *hard* with the heel of your hand, letting your fingers curl over the top.

As you act, *think* "SLAP!" Thinking "grab" may cause you to telegraph your intent and move more slowly.

As you connect, thrust your hip nearest the gun back into his groin to knock him off balance.

The force of your hands hitting from opposite directions can numb his hand, break his grip and give you control of the gun. As you destroy his balance and cause his grip on you to be further loosened, you can slide out of his grasp and pull the weapon with you. Then tactically retreat (run for cover) or defend yourself, whichever seems your better option.

The Wrist Slap technique was used to successfully disarm the man lying against the trunk.

STEP-OUT. This maneuver was designed for the hostage officer who is handcuffed, particularly in back, but it can be done uncuffed, also. It requires the least amount of training and practice, so even if you have not spent much time honing your survival skills it offers you hope for escape. However, it should be used *only* when there is another officer present who has drawn down on the suspect.

Again, with your captor's non-gun arm holding you as a shield, you wait until he points his gun out straight from behind you. Then suddenly lunge and dip toward his gun arm, driving your neck or head with all your strength against his arm. Throw your full body weight and energy into the move so you strike his arm with a real *whack*. This will knock his gun out of line so he can't shoot the responding officer, and also knock him off balance.

If you are handcuffed, now lurch back in the opposite direction to further break the hold he has on you with his non-gun arm. As you come upright, pivot outward and then either spin farther away from him or drop to the ground. This leaves him exposed to the responding officer without you as his shield. (If there are multiple officers present, you're probably safest to hit the dirt, because lead is bound to start flying from someone as soon as he is in the open.)

If you are not handcuffed, you can do even more. Here, as you pivot out, grab the wrist of the arm he has around you. Anchor his hand to your chest, and as you spin you will pull his arm straight. If you put your other hand behind his elbow and yank forward, you now have leverage to throw him down, thrust him toward the responding officer or push him away, then run or drop.

Some officers may argue that once the hostage-taker realizes what's happened, you're vulnerable to being shot. Technically true. *But*, the dynamics are such that once the suspect sees that his cover (you) is gone, his natural reaction *most* likely will be to point his weapon toward the responding officer. That's where his threat is now, and he'll move to defend himself from it. He may *look* at you to confirm what has happened, but he won't instinctively point his gun at you. It will go *out* in self-defense, *not* down to shoot you. If he has emotional ties to you, he might behave differently. But you are more likely just a practical opportunity whose practicality no longer exists.

With you out of the way, the responding officer, of course, has a clear field to take him out.

CAUTION: There is risk to you in this maneuver. With your first move against the suspect's gun arm, you duck out of the responding officer's line of fire. Then as you move back to step out, you reenter it. A responding officer who does not anticipate the full extent of your movement may fire prematurely and catch you just as you line up with his gun on your way back. This is one of many reasons it is important for *all* officers with your agency to be familiar with the various methods of hostage escape.

Another version of the Step-out can be done when you are hand-cuffed behind your back and the offender is holding you either by the handcuffs or by your belt. Here you make a sudden jolting pivot away from his gun hand. This locks his other arm and crimps that hand. With jarring movement, you can whip him around and thrust him off balance toward the responding officer. Moving *hard*, you'll force him to lose control.

As a last-ditch desperation move (as most escape tactics are), this can be done even if you are alone, especially if you are near a pole, a wall or some other solid object that you can throw him against with stunning effect. However, it is best done with another officer present and primed to take appropriate action.

If you must act alone, *run* for protective cover the instant he releases you. Even handcuffed, you may be able quickly to reach a speed of 10 to 15 miles per hour and sustain it for 40 to 50 feet. Especially if you are running, lateral to his position, you'll be hard for him to shoot. If he does hit you, it may very well be in a non-vital area.

The Step-out. Unhandcuffed and handcuffed.

DROP. This move capitalizes on the fact that a suspect who has relaxed somewhat, and is not anticipating any action from you, will not be able to react fast enough to hold up your suddenly dropping weight. Like the Step-out, the Drop requires the presence and anticipation of a responding officer for thorough follow-through. It can be accomplished whether you are handcuffed or not. It also works when you are held by the handcuffs rather than in the classic manner.

Basically, it consists of your waiting (with the hostage-taker holding you from behind) for the right moment for movement, then abruptly *squatting* below the level of his gun.

As you plunge down, be sure to turn your head to the side so your chin will clear the arm he's holding you with. You can turn either way, but facing into his bent elbow and closing your eyes lessens the chance of facial injury or blindness should his gun discharge when you make the move.

Once you're down, spin out and get away. Again, you've created a "sniper opening" for an alert responding officer.

The Drop is a valid option ONLY when your captor has his gun to your HEAD. If you drop with his gun to your *back*, he may be able to pull the trigger before your head gets below the barrel.

(A stylized version of the Drop that's sometimes cited as an option is the fake heart attack, where the hostage officer clutches his chest, then lets his weight fall. This is not likely to prove as successful as a straightforward drop. The "heart attack" movements will attract the hostage-taker's attention back to you and probably cause him to tighten his grip. Then when you drop you'll be relying not on surprise but only on your strength and physical capabilities to break free. If he's stronger, probably the best you can hope for will be to pull him down with you and to fight him on the ground.)

Some trainers argue that it is "absolutely essential" for the hostage officer and the responding officer to have code words or gestures worked out in advance to assure the proper timing and reaction for escape moves. One code, for example, calls for the hostage officer just before he's ready to move to alert the responding officer by saying a prearranged phrase like, "Please…please don't hurt him." Or the hostage signals with exaggerated eye blinks: one blink means he's planning to do something; two blinks mean he's going to do it *now*.

In another coded communication taught on one department, the hostage officer who's being held from behind is supposed to indicate with a subtle show of fingers at his waistline (out of the hostage-taker's view) whether the suspect is wearing a vest. The officer may be able to detect this if his back is pulled close to his captor's chest. One finger means no vest, two means he's armored. This then guides where the responding officer shoots after the hostage moves.

Keep in mind that codes in hostage situations, like codes for silent alarm verifications, are more likely to work in training sessions (or in theory) than on the street. Obviously, they need to be understood by both officers involved, and they require constant reinforcement to prevent them being forgotten, garbled or missed under stress. If they involve movement or talking by the hostage officer, they'll shift the suspect's attention to him at a time when that is least desirable and may, as a consequence, actually work *against* the move that's about to be made. At best, they tend to be one more thing to think about when your mind's already overloaded.

If both officers confront the situation in Condition Orange…if they both understand the dynamics of a hostage-taking…and if the hostage officer's escape moves are well-timed and decisively executed, codes usually won't be necessary.

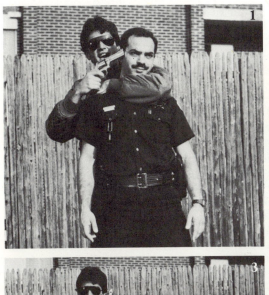

Sometimes at the start of a hostage incident or during its progression, the hostage-taker does not actually have a physical hold on you as his hostage. He may be standing a distance in front of you or behind you, keeping you at gunpoint. Either he has disarmed you and is using your gun or he has gotten the drop on you and you have not been able to draw.

If he's close enough that his gun is *within your reach*, escape is still possible. In fact, it may be *easier* because your moves won't be complicated by his physical restraint. Yet many officers apparently are unfamiliar with their options in these circumstances.

Psychological confidence is a major factor. Officers who get disarmed or out-drawn generally expect to get shot and often just give up. But if you understand how incredibly fast your hands can move…how surprising a move can be if you establish the gun's location *only* in your peripheral vision and *do not look at it directly* to telegraph your intent …and how mental and physical practice will hone your skills, then you can believe in—and *execute*—a successful gun take-away.

Your options include:

FRONTAL SLAP. Assume you are facing the suspect, either with your hands raised or at your sides, and that the gun is in his right hand.

Take a quick step to your left to pull yourself out of the line of fire. At the same time, swiftly lower or raise your hands. With a sweeping motion, slap the outside of his gun with the knife edge of your right hand, knocking it further off target. As your hand slides along the gun barrel, it will be easy and natural for your fingers to curl over the top and grip the gun tightly. Twist the gun so the barrel points in toward the suspect's center mass.

Simultaneously, bring your cupped left hand up under the suspect's wrist. As you push toward him with your right hand, slap his wrist and yank toward you with the fingers of your left hand. The opposing tensions should pry his finger out of the trigger guard and loosen his hold on the gun. If it does go off, the round will discharge toward him.

By the time your move registers on the suspect, you should already have his wrist bent and the gun pointing toward him. His natural reaction will likely be to yank his arm back, trying to free his gun. But you have his wrist bent, this movement will only loosen his grip more and help you take the weapon away, the mark of a good tactic.

Concentrate on controlling your Area of Responsibility (the weapon) first, then step out further to your left as you pull the gun out of his hand.

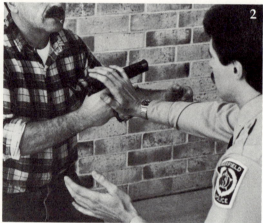
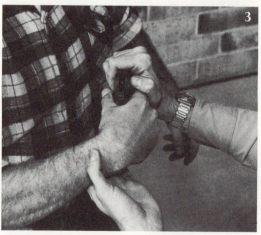

The Frontal Slap.

410

DOWNEY-ROTH HOOK. If you have no background in street fighting or the martial arts, this take-away, named for the two West Coast trainers who've popularized it, may be easier for you to master than some others. That does not mean, however, that it does not require practice—or that it's a preferred technique.

Here the gun is at your back and you've confirmed its exact location either through feel or a sneaked quick peek behind you.

With your hands raised, suddenly pivot out toward the back of the suspect's hand that holds the gun. At the same time swing your arm on his gun side down sharply. You want to strike the back of his gun hand with your elbow or your arm to thrust the weapon away from your back.

As you complete your pivot, swing your striking arm up under his gun arm and hook your hand over the top from the inside. Your hand should be positioned near his elbow. Instantly cup that hand with your other hand and yank down *hard.*

As you drive down with all your strength and weight, his gun barrel will point toward the sky and he'll be twisted off balance and fall onto his back. At that point, his arm will be extended and with your non-hooking hand, you may be able to yank his gun away.

If he's exceptionally strong, he may retain his grip on his gun. He may clutch it tightly as the only solid thing he has left to hold onto. Or he may be able to grab the gun with his free hand, since you really are controlling his arm and hand, not the weapon. Then consider dropping

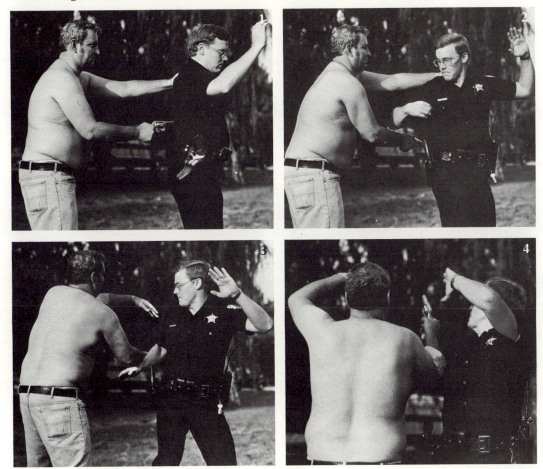

full force with your knees onto his face or neck to stun or distract him.

HAND CLAMP. This alternative to the Downey-Roth technique is as easy or easier to conduct initially but may require a higher level of skill for follow-through.

Again, with the suspect behind you and the gun close enough to touch, you pivot toward his non-gun hand. As you turn toward him, thrust your elbow over his gun arm and clamp your upper arm down *tight* on his gun hand. Simultaneously, cup his forearm underneath with your hand. With his hand and gun butt locked against your ribs, the barrel will point out and away behind you. His wrist should be cradled in your inner elbow.

Now if you lean your weight back and pull up slightly, you'll stretch his arm taut. All that's needed to lift him right off the ground and break his elbow in the process is to cup your other hand on top of your first under his forearm and yank up sharply while his arm is hyperextended.

Your potential follow-through problems occur because he's still facing you, essentially in a good fighting position. If surprise, pain and distraction have not overcome him, he can still attack you. To discourage that, you may need to "blitz" his chest (described in the next chapter).

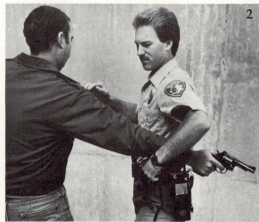

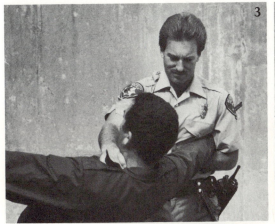

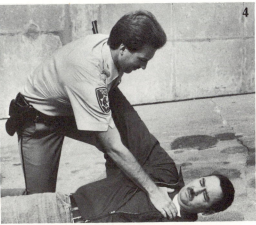

The Hand Clamp.

With any take-away, remember these key tenets:

1. Deflect the muzzle away from your body and head...and *hang onto it* to continue controlling it.
2. Expect the weapon to discharge. If it doesn't, that's a bonus.
3. Avoid a pushing or shoving match. You are *fighting for your life*, so take measures that *establish decisive control*.

Handcuff Defeat

Fortunately, your chances are slim of being handcuffed during a spontaneous hostage-taking. The suspect is likely to be under such stress he may not remember even to disarm you, much less restrain your hands. But still anticipating the possibility, you can lay the groundwork in advance for breaking free when he least expects it.

One precaution is to routinely carry an extra key taped down inside your handcuff case, under your wristwatch or to the inside back of your pants belt or concealed in a small pocket sewn into the back of your uniform pants. At a point when time and the suspect's distraction are in your favor, you may be able to reach and use it. That is, *if you've practiced*. Uncuffing yourself with a key takes *polished* agility.

An alternative is to carry an extra key on the end of your whistle neck chain, if you carry the whistle tucked out of sight in your uniform shirt pocket. Handcuffed, you can pull the chain from your pocket with your mouth and swing it around over your shoulder. It should be long enough to reach the handcuffs.

Your captor may order you to handcuff yourself, because this would be hard for him to do with a gun in his hand. Then you can rig the handcuffs for easy defeat, assuming he is not scrutinizing you closely. As you apply the first handcuff, instead of inserting the ratchet blade into its receiver, place the tip to the *side* of the opening. Then squeeze the handcuff as if you are closing it; it will "close" with the two pieces overlapping rather than engaged. At the same time, you should be holding the other handcuff loosely in the hand you are cuffing. Squeeze this handcuff to create the sound of a ratchet tightening. The suspect, will think that this is the rigged handcuff closing and will be reassured by the noise. Then apply the second handcuff normally. At quick glance, the rigged handcuff will look okay. But in fact, you can easily rip out of it.

Before handcuffing yourself, try to convince your captor that you need to apply the handcuffs in front. This will give you quicker and easier mobility for your escape move and also puts your hands where you can defend yourself somewhat even while handcuffed. But if he insists that you handcuff yourself in back, the defeat trick can still work.

Either way, be sure you *follow through* once you make your move. A half-hearted effort may not separate the handcuffs fully and may allow the offender to react against you.

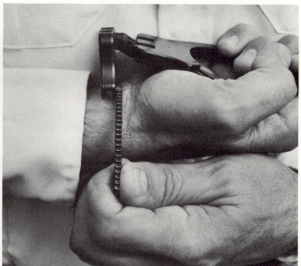

(left) As you can see from the hostage-taker's point of view it is difficult for him to see what you are doing as you manipulate the handcuffs. The sounds that you create provide the suggestion that he is in control. (above) The overlapping effect.

"Hideout" Weapons

On a major Eastern department, some officers reportedly are so concerned about being disarmed and taken hostage that they carry their service revolvers *empty* and rely on hidden handguns for any and all defensive shooting.

Few would endorse this extreme position. In fact, some departments prohibit backup guns altogether. But where permitted, having a concealed handgun (or knife) that evades detection by a hostage-taker can obviously give you an edge at certain critical moments. If you're disarmed of your primary firearm, having a second weapon (called the "principle of redundancy" or "Onion Field insurance") translates into having a second chance.

This point was unforgettably impressed on two Midwestern state troopers who were disarmed and forced into a car trunk by two prison escapees. As one of the offenders struggled to get the trunk lid closed, one of the troopers noticed "he was wide open for a belly shot if either of us had had another gun, since he could no longer see what we were doing in there." Fortunately, a third trooper who then arrived at the scene stuck a backup gun into his hip pocket before exiting his patrol car. He appeared to be surrendering, too, by handing over his service revolver on the offenders' demands. Then at a crucial moment, he whipped his spare .38 out of his pocket, shoved the muzzle into one convict's neck and quickly brought the incident to an end.

In size and placement, a concealed handgun should be able to withstand discovery during an eyeballing or a quick frisk by the suspect, while still allowing you to make a blink-of-the-eye draw and deliver reasonably effective stopping power. Most derringers, while highly concealable, pack too few rounds for some officers' satisfaction. Small caliber semi-automatics, sometimes carried in an extra handcuff case, are notorious for feeding problems, for unintentional discharges and for failing to stop adversaries even with head shots. In 300 fatalities studied in California, researchers found that most persons shot with .22 or .25 cal. ammunition were ambulatory and coherent—able to return fire or take other retaliatory action—for 10 to 60 seconds after being hit, even when the bullets struck the heart itself.[1] If you do carry such a weapon, try for a *contact shot*, if possible. Besides the bullet damage, gases expanding inside the body cavity will add to the impact of the hit.

A scaled-down version of what you carry as your duty weapon is probably your best bet. The compatability of ammunition and your familiarity with the mechanical operation will be strengths you'll appreciate under stress. If your duty sidearm is a .38 revolver, you're fortunate, because your "natural" backup choice will be the highly reliable and concealable small-frame, 2-inch barrel .38 snub-nose. This is widely regarded as probably the most desirable all-around hideout handgun.

Any hidden wheel gun generally is likely to give you faster first shots than a semi-automatic, unless the latter is a double-action model. A revolver can be fired instantly with either hand, and you won't be slowed down by having to activate a slide or release a safety when you draw. But if you carry a semi-automatic as your regulation weapon, it's probably still advisable to stick with the "family feel" for your secondary firearm rather than to "mix species" and try in the heat of a hostage-taking to adjust to a handgun that feels and functions differently. That may slow

---

[1]Clede, "Off-Duty Gun/Backup Gun," *Texas Police Journal*, December, 1983.

you down even more because it will require you to think about something that should not be an issue.

With fast accessibility possibly being a life-saving necessity, the ideal carrying location is one you can reach with either hand, handcuffed or not, with minimal delay. Here compromises and trade-offs are inevitable, and you have no choice but to decide which of the various imperfect options you're most comfortable with, given the environment you work in, the way you wear your uniform and carry your body and the dangers you're most likely to confront.

A hostage-taker attuned to the popularity of backup weapons among police may order you to pull up your pants legs so he can look for an ankle holster. Also, these rigs tend to be awkward, slow and difficult to reach without telegraphing your intent when you're standing. If you patrol deep-snow country, that's another potential problem several months a year. In certain uncommon circumstances, though, they may work to your advantage. Say you're being transported in a car as a hostage. It will probably not appear threatening to your captor(s) if you shift in your seat to tuck your holster leg up under you, especially if you're turning to talk to someone in the back seat. That can put your handgun where you can reach it quickly, even if you're handcuffed in front. The same is true when you're forced to kneel in an "execution" position (although hopefully you've reacted long before reaching this desperation point).

Detection of an ankle holster can definitely give the offender the opportunity to disarm you. However, the trick of putting your stocking *over* the holster and gun might prevent detection, especially under low light level conditions. Certainly no guarantee against a patdown, but something to consider.

A handgun hidden in the small of your back or in your hip pocket usually can be reached whether your hands are restrained or not and may be missed in a cursory pat-down. But it's uncomfortable to sit on, it may work its way up and out during your normal activities and unless the hammer spur is shrouded or ground off it may snag on your clothing when you try to draw. Also if you are knocked down and fall on it, you may severely damage your spine.

Carrying it in a jacket or front pants pocket is more vulnerable to a frisk and may be difficult to reach without alarming the suspect, because a move to those locations, if seen, will almost certainly be interpreted as threatening. But some officers, any time they're out of their cars on a call, keep their off hand in a jacket pocket, holding a hidden handgun and surreptitiously pointing it at anyone who might be a potential adversary. If you're already in that position when the hostage-taking is attempted, you can probably abort it then and there.

A special holster is available that lets you carry a hideout handgun in a cross-draw position on your upper torso, anchored under your arm to the webbing on your soft body armor. This offers excellent concealment and, because this area is usually poorly frisked, relatively slight chance of

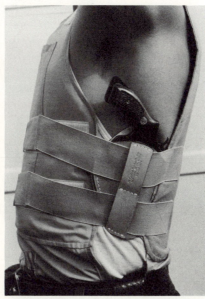

detection. With practice, it can be in your hand and pointing toward your captor in less than two seconds. It takes only a basic gross movement to draw. But getting to it involves ripping open your shirt. Handcuffed in back, forget it.

The carrying location many officers favor in the final analysis is the front waistband area, despite the fact that it may be felt by the suspect (or seen, if he notices a bulge or commands you to raise your shirt) and that it will be out of reach if you are handcuffed in back. These objections are weighed against the speed of easy accessibility, even in contorted physical positions. One option is to carry the handgun inside your shirt to the left in a holster clipped to your shorts. Leave one or two buttons above your belt undone to speed your counterstrike. If you wear a necktie, it will cover the gap. By positioning the handgun near your belt buckle, you can minimize the chance of it being discovered during a frisk.

Instead of or in addition to hideaway handguns, some officers carry hidden knives as last-ditch survival weapons. Here a practical carrying location is in a scabbard that can be strapped or taped to your arm, inside

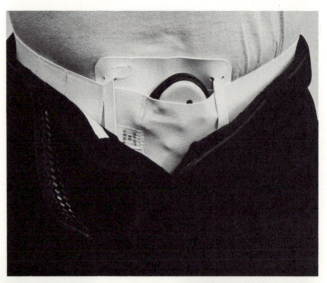

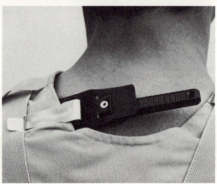

your sleeve. With the blade tip pointed toward your elbow, the knife can be pulled out discreetly even in most handcuffing configurations. Some officers who wear soft body armor with a back panel clip a scabbard with a thin knife to the top of their vests below the back of their necks. If you are told to place your hands behind your head or can pretend to be scratching there, you can quickly reach the knife. With practice you can learn to throw it accurately up to 10 feet in less than half a second. For comfort, keep the blade to 5 inches maximum. Some officers also carry an ice pick-like, push-button probe that retracts into what looks like the cap of a ballpoint pen. These can be "hidden in plain sight," clipped to a shirt pocket. Movement to that area is probably least likely to seem threatening to a suspect.

These devices, like knives or even extra handguns, are prohibited by some agencies. Officers who carry them anyway argue that they'd "rather risk a ride downtown to the trial board than a ride downtown to the morgue" because they didn't have any fallback equipment once disarmed. But understand that the use of unauthorized weapons can have serious disciplinary or civil liability implications for you.

Whatever your secondary weapon or its hiding place, practice drawing and using it until you can bring it into action by unconscious reflex, just as you can your duty sidearm. Above all, of course, you don't want to *forget* where your backup gun is, as some officers have done under stress. Carrying it as close as practical to your duty weapon may aid your memory. *ALWAYS qualify with your hideout handgun at the same time you qualify with your service weapon.* This not only will groom you for surviving on the street but also in *court*, as well, in case you're accused of using excessive force with a handgun with which you have not been trained.

On duty or off, when you're packing a hidden weapon, weigh its value against other options for your escape. It may not always be your best way out. As an off-duty Chicago K-9 officer was pulling into a filling station one day, a fleeing armed robber ran up to his car, shoved a handgun in his face and crowded in behind the wheel. He viciously pistol-whipped the officer, then ordered him to put his head under the dashboard, with his hands up near the windshield. The officer had a concealed handgun strapped to his leg, but under the circumstances he considered going for it a riskier option than trying to disarm the suspect physically. At a moment of distraction, he knocked the hostage-taker's handgun to the floor, pushed his head against the driver's window and successfully held him under control until help arrived.

In some cases, what you're up against will be the sole deciding factor. A few years ago, a federal agent, carrying a concealed handgun, was on an airplane that was hijacked. Asked later, after the incident had been successfully negotiated, why he didn't start shooting when he had the chance, he replied. "There were seven offenders. I had six bullets."

Persuasion

If a physical escape move seems impossible...or you are outnumbered...or your hostage-taking drags into a lengthy affair with no other officer present to pose a tactical threat to your captor, persuasive conversation may eventually become your best hope for getting free. Here, rather than remain silent so the hostage-taker forgets you, you actively shift gears in an effort to create a relationship with him.

On however tentative a level, you want him to begin to regard you as a human being he *likes*, not as just a "uniform" or a symbol of what he hates. You want to project a calming, reassuring image, keeping your voice low and steady. *Strictly avoid threats, abuse and scorn.* Try to demonstrate respect and understanding for him, without grovelling. And, most important, LISTEN to what *he* wants to talk about. DO NOT ARGUE with him. Two detectives who were held hostage for more than an hour by an armed robber and his doper girlfriend in a Florida pharmacy built such a level of trust with the suspect by listening sympathetically to his complaints about the criminal justice system that he finally decided it was unnecessary to keep his gun on them. After he lowered the weapon, he was readily disarmed.

One study of officers who survived extended hostage-takings suggests that there's about a 50-50 chance that you can develop enough rapport to get the suspect to start relying on you for *advice*. You may then be able to offer "problem-solving" ideas for resolving the incident in your favor.[2] About 20% of the hostage officers in this study, for instance, talked the hostage-taker into giving up.

If the suspect has moved you away from the original crime scene so he is clear of any immediate threat from responding officers, work to convince him that he can free you alive and complete his escape unimpeded. If he shows a willingness to do this, he may also be good for additional important favors.

A California trooper, for instance, was disarmed, handcuffed and tied up with his belt in broad daylight after being suddenly drawn down on by a motorist he'd stopped for speeding on a freeway. As the suspect started to flee, the officer asked if he'd please leave behind the gun he'd grabbed from the officer's holster ("my personal weapon.") The suspect obligingly wiped the gun with his handkerchief and tossed it under a bush, where the trooper later recovered it.

In Florida, an officer detected a load of marijuana in a pickup truck he chased and stopped for running through an agricultural inspection station. As he questioned the two occupants, one feigned illness and, as he bent over, pulled a revolver from his boot. The lawman was disarmed and for several hours bounced at gunpoint in the bed of the truck as the offenders tried to find their way along unfamiliar back roads. As his captivity dragged on, he not only persuaded them not to kill him, but talked them out of leaving him tied to a tree where he had little likelihood of being found by convincing them he might be "eaten by a bear." At his suggestion, they ended up leaving him comfortably stretched out on a pew in a rural church, handcuffed to a post, a pillow under his head and a jug of water by his side. Like the California trooper, he persuaded them to leave his service revolver nearby, pleading that he'd have to replace it "out of my own pocket." In exchange, he drew them an escape map to Georgia.

If you're convincing, you may also be able to use persuasion of sorts to bluff your way out of a hostage-taking. A Virginia investigator made the mistake of rushing in on a silent alarm response and, along with a uniformed sergeant, was taken prisoner by the armed robber. The suspect disarmed the sergeant, but the investigator was glib enough to convince him that he was carrying no gun. Moments later as the robber proned the hostages out on the floor, the investigator drew his hidden weapon and plugged the suspect with five .357 rounds. The hostage-taker fired back four shots and stumbled outside, where a sixth police round brought him down, fatally.

Throughout your persuasion effort, of course, remain alert for any escape opportunity. A motor officer was kidnapped at gunpoint in Arkansas by two offenders on a traffic stop and driven to an isolated rural area where it seemed certain he would be killed. His hostage-takers ordered him to take off his uniform and then fired a round across his abdomen so close it left powder burns. Then they turned to put the officer's uniform and radio in their trunk. At that moment of distraction, the officer, clad only in his underwear, broke and ran for the woods and successfully escaped without further physical harm.

The key to his survival proved to be his unwillingness, ultimately, to submit hopelessly to the fatal intentions of his captors.

---

[2]Crews, "An Empiracle Study of Law Enforcement Officers Held Hostage," 1983.

III

THE
FORCE
EDGE

9

PHYSICAL CONTROL

In a physical confrontation, your body is your ally for just so long. Initially, it draws on energy reserves to fuel your fighting, boosted by an "adrenal dump" of natural chemicals into your blood stream to enhance your strength and staying power. But if you're the average officer in average shape, your ability to exert maximum effort will last no more than *20 to 45 seconds.*

After that, if the struggle continues, it's as if a plug is pulled. Quickly your strength level drops...by as much as *50%* below normal. This is accelerated in many cases because a large number of officers in this country are in worse shape physically than the average offenders they're up against. Feeling your strength waning, you may "overreact" with excessive force in a desperate effort to regain control. Or, against a stronger opponent, you may now be savagely beaten. Or, in the twisting and turning of a wrestling match, your adversary may suddenly be presented with your sidearm...and the opportunity to turn it against you.

The longer a fight for control goes on, the greater your chances of injury or death. So the message is clear: *any physical encounter to gain compliance from a resistant subject or defend yourself against attack needs to be won FAST*—before your inevitable energy loss kicks in and sets you up for defeat.

The problem is that just as many officers truthfully lack confidence in their firearms proficiency, even more are inadequate in *physical* control skills. They cannot reliably establish control over offenders when their verbal commands are ignored or when force instruments (like their baton or sidearm) are not legal or practical options.

Resistance is commonplace among today's offenders. About half the people arrested challenge police authority at least verbally. At least 12% are violent or aggressive, requiring "coercive contact."[1] Today's average officer, however, is smaller, weaker in upper-body strength and more middle class-rooted than ever before. Lacking the rough and tumble experience of contact sports or military service, many have never even been *punched* hard, certainly never have been in a fight for their lives. Yet they're expected to subdue people who grew up watching their mothers'

---

[1]Sykes and Brent, *Policing: A Social Behaviorist Perspective,* Rutgers University Press, 1983.

friends bite each other's ears off, who were accomplished street fighters by age 6 and who've pumped iron to physical perfection in prison.

At the very least, officers without sharp physical skills work much harder—and at greater risk—than they really have to in order to gain control. Their apprehension and lack of self-assurance cause their internal stress systems to accelerate faster than they should, prematurely exhausting their strength reserves and dangerously straining their hearts. (One test in Missouri measured the heart rates of officers not trained in efficient combat skills during simulated street fights. When told they were going to fight, the officers' average heart rate leaped from 72 beats per minute to 85. Placed on mats and given the fight rules, the average rate surged to 120. After actually struggling with partners for just 30 seconds, their rates ranged from 185 to 235 bpm. The average human heart starts coming apart when 220 beats or more per minute overload it over a period of time. In short, if you can't conclude an encounter quickly, you risk not only severe assault but a heart attack as well.) Some officers, struck hard or knocked down in real fights, are so startled and shaken they simply *give up*, just as those without an understanding of survival frequently do when wounded in nonvital areas by hostile fire.

The results are written in the surgical thread it takes to sew up many of the 60,000-plus officers who suffer batteries—and worse—each year. As with: the Florida officer who suffered spine, head, arm and back injuries during a fight with a burglar that left him with severe back pains, frequent headaches and a virtually useless right arm even after surgery...the Nebraska chief who tried to control a violent, mentally disturbed, 360-pound suspect with his bare hands and ended up disarmed of his service revolver, which the offender then used to kill one citizen and wound another...the two California security officers who were bitten and clawed "like crazy" by a shoplifter they caught stuffing maternity clothes inside her girdle...

There's no denying that physical control is a formidable challenge. Nearly 75% of subjects who assault you will be under the influence of alcohol or drugs. They'll likeliest be construction workers or other manual laborers...young (19-23)...angry or otherwise emotionally distraught. They may already be engaged in violent activity when you arrive and simply extend their sphere of violence to include you. Or your uniformed presence may precipitate attack.

The most common officer reaction is to grapple or brawl with the resistant or assaultive suspect catch-as-catch-can, with no regard to tactical maneuvering, praying he'll give up before you give out. Some bad techniques are made to work because the officer is able to muscle them through. One officer admits that after seven years on the street for a large municipal agency, he has yet to learn an effective wrist lock; he just *tackles* anyone who gives him trouble.

Some officers skip physical efforts altogether; they leap directly from verbal commands to their baton or gun to meet any resistance. Rarely is that reaction an appropriate use of force...nor does it often represent *true control*. An off-duty officer in the Midwest, for example, witnessed a vehement dispute over 20 cents between a customer and a service station attendant. The customer angrily rammed his car into the cashier's booth, and the officer, anxious to restore order, flashed his badge and pulled his gun. Instead of calming down, the customer grabbed him. The officer ineptly struggled back and ended up accidentally shooting the customer in the neck.

Even if you're proficient with up-to-date physical control tech-

Two different control choices in the absence of a better evaluation of the situation. (left) A suspected looter is knocked through a plate-glass window of a cafeteria. (below) Officer draws down on unarmed man who had been acting in an erratic manner. Notice the distance between them, the officer's stance and his one-hand hold with the revolver.

niques, you may still be at risk. Untrained fellow officers who jump in to "help" you may actually work against you with what they try, enabling your adversary to break free or overcome you. Part of your success with physical control tactics, as with others we've discussed, will depend on your missionary ability in getting them adopted in your agency and at the very least in getting your partner proficient with them.

Again as with firearms, an officer's deficiencies are likelier an outgrowth of improper training than of personal indifference. What most defensive tactics instructors teach is really a mishmash of ad hoc procedures. They may demonstrate 15 different come-along holds, for instance, along with other isolated "combat" techniques they've picked up here and there. But these are seldom integrated into a *tactical system* for control—nor do they generally reflect the *realities* of suspect resis-

426

tance. Sometimes what's taught is so complicated and specialized that instructors themselves can't master it. One trainer, wanting to demonstrate his favorite takedown maneuver to a visitor, said: "Go ahead, hit me!" The visitor cocked his right arm. "No, no," interrupted the trainer, "use your left." After detailed instruction on how to swing "correctly," the trainer spent another four minutes struggling to position his "attacker" so the pet procedure (which the trainer had taught for *five years*) would indeed bring him down. Some techniques that are taught defy physiological principles. One Eastern academy promotes an elaborate crescent kick as a means of disarming knife attackers—despite the fact that most officers are unable even to *lift* their legs high, much less kick with them accurately.

Scarce wonder that much of what is "learned" in traditional training is quickly forgotten on the street, or tried once and then abandoned because it fails to work or gets the officer injured.

Similarly, officers on the whole have shown little enthusiasm for—or patrol application of—martial arts training, again with good reason. Martial arts maneuvers tend to be too complicated, take too long to develop and require too much practice to retain to be practical for most cops. Moreover, they usually aren't *control* techniques; they're moves to crush and destroy.

To be considered realistic...tactically sound...and workable, a physical control or "suspect management" technique should meet certain criteria:

1. It should be *simple* to learn...retainable under severe stress... *rapid* to apply...and *immediate* in its consequences (techniques do not have to be difficult to master or complicated to use in order to be sophisticated);

2. It should be *effective* regardless of your size, strength or sex (if the technique works well for a small officer, it should work even better for a larger one) and regardless of the environment in which you need to use it (you should be able to defend yourself and defeat resistance whether it erupts in a toilet stall, in a hallway, over the hood of your patrol car, around a desk or a couch or hanging upside down from monkey bars);

3. It should be grounded in an accurate understanding of *anatomical processes* and *body mechanics* (yours and the suspect's), and

4. It should be part of a *broad, versatile system*. That system, in turn, should allow you to:

- *adapt* your response to the type of resistance you meet (the passive, dead-weight noncompliance of a social demonstrator; the defensive, uncoordinated flailings of a drunk; the spontaneous, unpredictable assault of a psycho; the calculated, practiced attack of a dangerous criminal, etc.);
- smoothly *escalate* your force or safely *disengage* from the encounter if you don't quickly gain control of the situation, and
- *justify* your actions later in court as reasonable for the level of threat you faced.

The volume of lawsuits lodged against officers and agencies for excessive use of force is expected by some experts soon to exceed even the epidemic flood filed against physicians for malpractice. These days, any time you place hands on someone, you realistically incur the potential for a lawsuit. And under current court rulings, you personally, rather than your agency, can be held liable for punitive damages. Thus, court defensibility has become a major issue in physical control. Your moves now should be oriented toward *two* outcomes: paramount, of course, toward the outcome of the threat against you that necessitates a forceful physical response…but also toward the "postscript" outcome when what you did is put to a legal test. In other words, you have to defend yourself twice—once on the street and again in court.

Anticipating this defense, you need to distinguish between "*can do*" techniques and "*may do*" techniques.

"Can do" are those you're physically capable of performing. You *can*, for example, jam your fingers inside an uncooperative suspect's mouth and pull out sharply on his cheek. The pain and pressure are so intense his head will likely follow wherever you yank, even if he has a high pain tolerance. If he tries to kick or slug you, you can quickly jerk him to the ground. So long as your fingers are pulling, he can't bite you. But you can literally rip his cheek apart if he continues to resist. Or you *can* block a suspect who's trying to stab you, twist his wrist and plunge his knife into his own stomach. Or you *can* choke a suspect out with an arm bar across his throat that may crush his windpipe. In one treatise on "realistic" police fighting techniques, one patrolman suggested that officers in desperate situations consider poking out a suspect's eyes with a ballpoint pen…hooking his eyes out of their sockets with fingers ("Don't get sick")…rupturing his eardrums…kicking his temple "with the toe of your shoe as if you are returning a punt in the last seconds of a football game"…ripping his windpipe from his throat…and biting through the neck arteries that carry oxygenated blood to his brain.

All these moves may do the trick, and you may argue that it's better to be judged by 12 than carried by six. But do understand that to a civilian jury or review board, such measures are likely to seem *startlingly savage*. In some jurisdictions, something as conventional and accepted in police practice as smashing a threatening suspect's kneecap with your baton as a means of collapsing him is now said to be regarded as *deadly force*, because it inflicts significant "permanent or disfiguring injury; i.e., great bodily harm." You'd better be awfully convincing when you insist that you *had* to use techniques like these as your *only* hope of saving your life or limb.

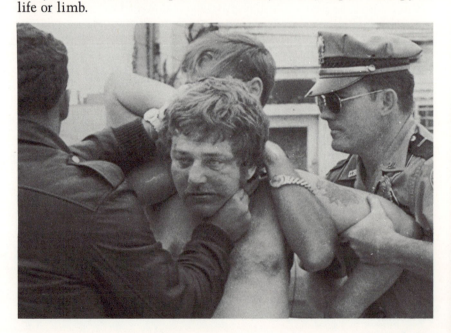

"May do" tactics are also practical and effective. Some recently refined ones, in fact, are far superior to old-fashioned brutal tricks in terms of fast, reliable control. They are not necessarily "soft." Some are "hard" enough in terms of impact to cause severe injury to a suspect. But if you apply them correctly under the proper circumstances, they are *court defensible*. In other words, they work on the street *and* in court. That's why, as an officer operating in the current social and judicial climate, you "may" use them as force resources.

About 75% of the time, assaults on law enforcement personnel are by *unarmed* assailants. More often than not, you'll be expected to respond with unarmed force of your own. All things being equal, physical encounters are won by the bigger, stronger participant. As an officer who will not always be superior in stature, you can't live with that. Physical control tactics are what you can use in many situations to make up the difference—to make the confrontation *unequal* in your favor and to help you do what you otherwise might not be able to.

The focus that follows is on some of the latest, fastest "may do" techniques, which give you maximum control through minimum effort...and on the tactical and legal framework into which they fit. The techniques pertain to *physical* control, the force option concentrated on here. Control through the use of deadly force from firearms is referenced in previous chapters and is developed in detail in the *Street Survival* book.

Keep in mind that the techniques described here are best learned through structured, *hands-on* training, conducted by persons certified in the skills they are instructing. You should gain experience through more than just static, stationary training. Learn the basic moves "by the numbers" with that. Polish them with "fluid" training, where you improve speed, form and precision. Then continue beyond into street simulations, where you learn to apply these techniques with full speed and power under stressful, varied, realistic circumstances. If you live where there's cold weather, be sure to practice in full winter clothing, too. Reinforce everything with mental exercises of Crisis Rehearsal.

The Force Continuum

On patrol, you need to be a "confrontational generalist." You are not permitted just one or two specialized responses for any time a subject resists your attempt to enforce the law or physically assaults you. You cannot, for instance, automatically *shoot* everyone who fails to comply with what you want them to do. Resistance and attack come in *many* forms, with varying degrees of intensity and at different levels of threat to you. And you're expected to tailor your reaction from a *range* of options so it is *adequate* to stop the suspect's hostile behavior and establish your ability to command and direct him...but no more.

With the right training and experience, you can suitably manage *whatever* action the suspect presents, selecting from among tactics that range from your mere presence to center-mass gunfire. In a sense, *he* decides what he wants from you and justifies a certain level of force in the way he behaves. You deliver just enough force to accommodate his decision. He may be *violent;* you must *only* be *forceful*. Violence connotes a loss of control, whereas *force* implies a *conscious decision* and a *controlled action* to direct a person. Contrary to how it seems some-

A few moments after this picture was taken, the deputy shot the man holding a club and a Bible.

times, you *are* permitted by law to *injure* a subject in the process of performing your duty. But you have to be able to *justify* it later as *reasonable and appropriate* considering the specific circumstances.

In this regard, officers often are their own worst enemies. Some don't understand—or stop to think—what *appropriate* force is. One sergeant responded to a domestic disturbance and confronted a man standing on his front porch with a baseball bat. The subject yelled at the sergeant to stay on the lawn and swung the bat to emphasize the warning. The sergeant shot him.

That degree of force far exceeded the provoking threat. The sergeant failed to consider that for any attack to occur a suspect must have 1) **intent,** 2) a **weapon** (this can include body parts like fists and feet) and 3) a **delivery system.** If any one of these three is missing, an assault cannot take place. The man with the bat appeared to have intent and did have a weapon. But he had no delivery system that would have allowed him to harm the sergeant at that distance. The sergeant could not have been facing the ultimate threat, yet he used the ultimate force option. He reacted *emotionally,* not *tactically.* So did a California motor officer who choked a middle-aged woman into unconsciousness while she was handcuffed behind her back because she refused to offer identification, refused to sign a citation and refused to submit to a patdown in the presence of male officers after he arrested her for *jaywalking.* And so did a sheriff's deputy who shoved a female traffic violator against his patrol car because she threw his ticket book down. He broke her arm, which cost the county $40,000 and him 15 days' suspension.

Other officers use questionable force (like a baton or flashlight to the head) because they think nothing else can possibly work—or they don't know other options.

Some use it as a bluff. At first sight of a difficult subject, they unholster their sidearm and try to coerce cooperation at gunpoint. But if the suspect just laughs and deadly force is not actually justified, what then?

Still others use force appropriately, but then don't know how to defend their actions when challenged later. Up against attorneys who can skillfully manipulate words and images, they easily fall victim to "self-

430

inflicted wounds" when they try falteringly to make a jury understand their actions. If a few shopworn, subjective phrases (like, "I was in fear of my life") don't prove persuasive, they're lost.

To select effective force options in a physical encounter and *be able to justify them later as reasonable,* you must weigh many variables. Unfortunately, you cannot evaluate these according to any rigid formula. They are subject to different interpretations with each encounter. Sometimes their relative influence changes even *during* an encounter. What's appropriate for a given officer against a given offender in a given set of circumstances can be totally *in*appropriate when the players and the setup are changed.

Included in the factors that are important for you to evaluate are your:

- **age**
- **size,** and
- **sex**

—plus the age, size and sex of the *offender.* How you *compare* to the offender in these areas and what that implies may be important in determining the level of force that's appropriate to use in controlling him. All other things being equal, if you're a young, 6-foot, 210-pound male trying to subdue a combative, unarmed, short, middle-aged woman weighing 105 pounds, you'll likely be able to justify using less force than the 120-pound female officer in Illinois who recently was attacked by a 206-pound weightlifter wielding a steel bar. A judge and jury would normally regard her risk of suffering serious harm (broken bones, gaping wounds, damage to internal organs) as being much greater (in fact, she did suffer a concussion, a broken collar bone, a split lip, two black eyes and multiple bruises.) Therefore, her using greater force is easier to accept as being reasonable; higher risk permits higher force.

On the other hand, officers in the real world often are attacked and seriously injured by people *smaller* than they are. Say you're a male officer trying to subdue an older, smaller female whose exceptional fury and adrenalized strength have already permitted her to overpower other officers. You can justify more powerful force than might normally seem reasonable because of *special circumstances.* But where special circumstances require something more than "normal" force, be ready to *identify* them—not only to yourself so you can make better force decisions, but to those who may later evaluate your actions legally to see if they were "appropriate."

Special circumstances that can influence your force choices and their "reasonableness" include:

- **the suspect's skill level** (does he show evidence of knowing martial arts, for instance? Or is he a professional combatant, like the two heavyweight wrestlers who took on some 15 municipal, county and state officers in a suburban motel room, broke one deputy's leg and knocked out several of his teeth and repeatedly slammed his female partner against a wall, fractured her skull, broke seven of her teeth, knocked her unconscious with a knee drop and left her with a permanent loss of feeling in most of her face—before finally being stopped by threat of gunfire?);
- **your training** (are you competent in the most appropriate technique?);
- **your prior knowledge about the offender** (does he have a reputation or history of attacking and beating officers? One West Coast deputy who

stopped a motorcyclist for a seemingly routine violation wisely handcuffed him immediately for better control when he recognized him as one of a trio who had been relieved of two knives, a revolver, five rifles, more than 400 rounds of ammunition and a throwing star during another arrest 10 days earlier);

• **the suspect's ability to rapidly escalate his force** (is he near a firearm; either yours or some other one?);

• **your physical condition** (are you injured or near exhaustion from having struggled with him?);

• **your physical position** (are you on the ground...or closed off from an escape route?);

• **your perceptions** (federal agents thoroughly creamed an offender who pointed a gun at a presidential candidate along a rope line. That the "weapon" later proved to be a harmless squirt gun was deemed immaterial because they logically *perceived* it as real when they took action);

• **the surrounding environment** (are there other people nearby who are sympathetic to the suspect and who seem inclined to interfere against you?)

Where these factors tend to increase your jeopardy and make control more difficult, you are justified in increasing your force beyond what might otherwise be regarded as appropriate. Just be prepared later to *anchor your actions to relevant FACTS* about yourself, the suspect and the circumstances to confirm that what you did was *reasonable*. By evaluating the situation you face against this checklist, rather than just knee-jerking to turbo-charged emotions, both your force decisions and your explanations of them will be sounder.

With all these variables to consider, your mental computer has to quickly process a *lot* of information to keep you from underreacting (an important survival consideration) or overreacting (which impacts court defensibility). In high stress, your mind may be groping desperately for what to do—unless you have a practical *framework* that can help you organize your options.

One useful approach is to think of force as a flexible *continuum*, on which the various means of exerting control are positioned.

Building up from bottom to top, each mode represents force of greater intensity. That is, the continuum moves from those options that are *most reversible* to those that are *least reversible*...from those offering the *least certainty of control* to the *greatest certainty*...and from those with the *least expectancy for tissue damage* to the *greatest*. Thus as you go up the scale, you need greater justification.

Within each of these broad categories there are also identifiable, escalating gradations of intensity.* These indicate that even within a given type of response, you have options of lesser or greater force. (Unfamiliar terms used below are explained later in this chapter.)

---

*Some officers view the baton more as a leverage tool than as an impact weapon. Used as such, it would rank in this Force Continuum with pain/pressure compliance. Likewise, a mini-baton could fall into several categories, depending on how it is used. The designers of this force scale have omitted chemical agents, arguing that those available in aerosol canisters for duty use generally are too limited in application to be ranked. Also omitted are electronic stunning devices, on grounds that more medical testing regarding their safety is needed to place them precisely in the force spectrum. The use of K-9 has also been omitted because of special applications involving dogs and handler training which do not involve the average officer on patrol.

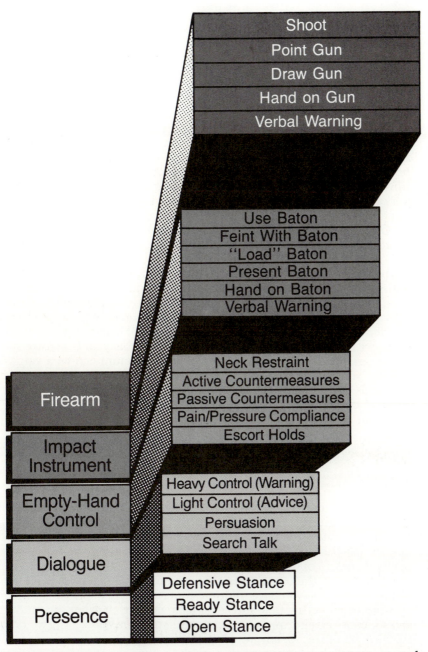

	Shoot
	Point Gun
	Draw Gun
	Hand on Gun
	Verbal Warning

	Use Baton
	Feint With Baton
	"Load" Baton
	Present Baton
	Hand on Baton
	Verbal Warning

	Neck Restraint
	Active Countermeasures
	Passive Countermeasures
	Pain/Pressure Compliance
	Escort Holds

	Heavy Control (Warning)
	Light Control (Advice)
	Persuasion
	Search Talk

	Defensive Stance
	Ready Stance
	Open Stance

Firearm

Impact Instrument

Empty-Hand Control

Dialogue

Presence

By understanding the relative force behind your various control options and also by knowing how they potentially affect an adversary, you are better equipped to select the one(s) best suited to the physical resistance that you face. And if you have *confidence and skill* in the verbal and physical components of the Force Continuum, you will be less likely to resort to your firearm prematurely.

Confronting a suspect who's trying to crush your skull, of course you do not actually have to progress step by step up the force ladder until you hit on something that stops him. Juries strongly prefer that you *talk* first and use force only if your verbal skills fail. Chances are you will say *something*, if nothing more than *"Stop!"* But with any subject, you can

433

mentally run through the full Force Continuum in about a quarter-second and choose what seems most likely to work relative to the threat he presents. If your maneuver fails or circumstances change, you can escalate your force on the basis of a new conscious decision, rather than from fear or anger. This option-evaluation approach helps keep your decision *tactical*.

In court, you then have a framework to hang your hat on. You can cite the Force Continuum...point out where the procedure you used ranks relative to others in intensity...describe your relative strengths in the encounter versus those of the suspect...and then explain why, based on your training and experience, you considered the option you chose to be the *minimum* force you could use to control the confrontation. In other words, you explain why less forceful options would not have worked—or actually did not work—in that situation.

With this kind of *structure* to refer to, you take a lot of vagueness out of your testimony, you sound more professional and you give the jurors a framework for judgment that they, too, can understand.

A growing number of departments are incorporating the Force Continuum into their use-of-force policies. One in Wisconsin has begun coding officers' reports according to the Continuum's various segments. A computer can then analyze all of an officer's physical encounters and determine how frequently he uses each type of force. With this system, if an offender you've severely injured accuses you of habitually resorting to excessive force, the data will readily document what your *true* pattern is.

Keep in mind that while the Force Continuum can be a valuable tool *for* you, it can also be used *against* you. As police performance standards are raised, you will increasingly be expected to apply it to physical control situations—and *to be competent in the various force options it reflects.*

Yes/Maybe/No People

Some officers walk into a bar brawl, and the action stops cold. Others seem always to end up in a fight, even when the subject they're handling is initially nonviolent, the prototype white-haired grandmother who has run a stop sign. It's estimated that just 10% of officers are involved in 90% of the instances of physical resistance or assault, as well as with 90% of the complaints alleging excessive use of force. During any of your shifts, you have multiple contacts where physical conflict is *possible*—conducting field interrogations, issuing citations and making arrests, controlling crowds, breaking up disturbances, rescuing would-be suicides, handling social protesters. Whether resistance and/or assault actually *result* has to do not only with the nature of subjects you confront but also in large part with how they read you...how you read them...and how you use the signals you pick up.

Basically, people you deal with fall into three categories:

YES PEOPLE are *cooperative.* You can get them to do what you want by *words alone.* If you must arrest them, they can be handcuffed in a voluntary *free-standing* position. In color code terms, you're in Condition *Yellow* dealing with them.

MAYBE PEOPLE are *undecided.* They may comply because they're not sure whether you have the upper hand, but they're likely to be *"passively uncooperative:"* moving slowly in response to your directions, looking around for an avenue of flight, asking you to repeat instructions or asking a lot of procedural questions, maybe even tentatively pulling away a time or two. In short, they *frustrate the process* while trying to make up their mind what they really want to do. You'll probably need *some* level of physical force with them. Handcuffing with aid of a *wrist lock*, at least. With them, you stay in Condition *Orange.*

NO PEOPLE are *actively uncooperative.* They may *run* from you, repeatedly *jerk away* when you try to control them or violently flail, swing, kick, bite, scratch, spit or otherwise *assault* you. Your goal is not to spar with them, but to get them *on the ground* as quickly as possible for handcuffing. You're in Condition *Red* with them.

Examples of Yes/Maybe/No People. (upper left) Drug dealer captured in a motel room during a multi-million dollar cocaine bust (Yes person). (above) Man reacts to being maced by holding his ground for a moment (Maybe person). (left) A terrorist sympathizer gives a fight before entering a jail bus (No person).

Obviously, you're safer if you can avoid a physical contest; it's usually easier to *stay* out of trouble than to *get* out after you're in it. Thus you want to keep suspects from escalating into a higher-force category. In other words, you want to convert a Maybe subject into a Yes subject, rather than allowing him to explode into the No mode. And you want to *stabilize* a Yes subject at the level he's at. Some suspects you will *have* to deal with physically; that's the only thing they'll accept from you. But a great many can be influenced mightily—*either* way—by the *body language* and *verbal personality* with which you confront them. Studies of sales encounters show that in the first 10 minutes of conversation between a salesperson and a customer, the customer's feelings can change *10 times* or more. The same is true on the street when suspects are confronted by you.

People, including suspects, tend to be overridingly concerned in life with their *egos*. When we interact with others, we all are sensitive to protecting our self-esteem and will sometimes go to great extremes to defend it. A sense of personal dignity and worth may not always seem deserved, but it is always deeply *needed* by everyone. When you confront a wrongdoer, you threaten not only his freedom but also his ego, his most precious psychological component. Your authority to command him—to force him to obey *your* will, not his own—automatically diminishes it. If you couple that with a manner that is domineering, insulting, abrasive or belittling and with actions that back him into a corner or make him look cowardly in front of people who are important to him, he may feel that the only thing he has left with which to defend his ego is his capacity for violence. *Violence oftentimes is an expression of feeling powerless*, of being backed into a corner. It can often be avoided if you understand and shrewdly manipulate human dynamics.

The stereotyped police confrontation pose *invites* violence. That's when you stand with your feet planted apart, your hands on your hips or your arms folded across your chest, square on to the suspect, up close "in his face." Maybe you're rocking back and forth, lording it over the person you're dealing with. This is a "nonstance for nonsense." It makes you slow and physically vulnerable because you can easily be knocked off balance and/or disarmed. In addition, it comes across as *very threatening* to the suspect. (If *you're* met with this stance in a suspect, consider yourself facing a *very hostile* individual.)

Standing like this implies harshness, arrogance, challenge, antagonism, narrow-mindedness, rigidity, and insensitivity to the person you're confronting with it. When a suspect sees you in a pose he perceives as aggressive (dangerous), he may himself assume an aggressive stance to counter it; in confrontations, people tend to mimic the behavior of their antagonist. Also, in our culture moving any closer than about 18 inches to someone invades his "personal space." That close is reserved psychologically only for intimates who are *wanted* there. As a definite non-intimate, your being so near is likely to provoke in the suspect a strong desire to draw back, run or defend against your "invasion." Whatever you actually say to him when you are that close, it will be *heard* as aggressive. One survey of assaults on police in California reveals that they occur *most often* because the suspect perceives the officer as "tampering" with him either verbally or physically. That is, "intruding into this personal domain" in some offensive way.

Of course you'll need to move in close if you're going to break up a fight or control someone for handcuffing and searching. Distance gives the suspect too much latitude at that point. But many unarmed encounters can initially be defused and stabilized (i.e., maneuvered to the way you want them to be) from a more comfortable distance for both of you.

One of your verbal options is to try to *persuade* the suspect to cooperate voluntarily. Some subjects are Maybe people because they are stressed, scared or confused rather than intending you harm. Psychologically, the most effective distance for persuasion is roughly 10 feet back from the suspect. This creates a buffer zone of "public space" in which most people tend to be more at ease with strangers, and it provides a *"reactionary gap"* to your advantage. That is, you're back far enough that you can scan the suspect's entire body (your Problem Area) for nonverbal clues to his intent. Plus you're out of *immediate* range of his hands, feet and head (your Areas of Responsibility). By the time he can cross that distance to attack physically, you (in Condition Yellow or Orange) have a higher probability of being able to *perceive* the threat...*evaluate* it...and *react*. (There will be times when you want to widen the gap, especially if you know your lag time tends to be slow. Remember that the time you

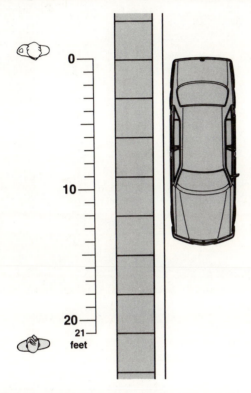

A nearby sidewalk or parked car provide handy landmarks to gauge where you are within the danger zone (0–21 ft.).

need to *react* will *always* be longer than the time he needs to *act*. If he's holding a knife or other weapon that extends his reach, like a club, expand your reactionary gap to *21 feet* or more. Have your sidearm pointed at him while you're dealing with him. *Don't rely only on verbal persuasion against potentially deadly weapons.* If he has a gun or has one or both of his hands in his pockets, *get and stay behind cover;* distance and dialogue then are strictly secondary. Don't move out until you can clearly see his *palms,* your primary Areas of Responsibility.)

To reinforce a "persuasive" approach in the absence of known weapons, your body language should convey openness, fairness and lack of hostility, so there are no nonverbal signals to conflict with your conciliatory, calming tone of voice. A persuasive or *"open" stance* is one where your hands are below your waist, elbows loosely against your ribs, palms toward the suspect, fingers down. This signifies that you are receptive and presenting no tools of aggression, not even a closed fist (one of your silent signals that can fastest escalate a confrontation) or the backs of your hands. You appear at ease, unafraid, noncombative. Yet if you stay mentally alert, you can still move quickly to defend yourself. This stance may seem uncomfortable and awkward, but it is not one you maintain for long. If persuasion does not work *quickly* as a control measure where control is important, consider escalating to higher force.

The Open Stance.

The open stance MUST change if you choose to move closer to impose more authority. Closing the gap cuts down the time you have for reacting, so you must then sacrifice some appearance of openness for protection. Any time you are within a suspect's "striking fringe" (generally from about 10 feet to 5 feet), you should be in a *ready stance.* This is true no matter how cooperative the subject appears; you can't rely on *any* individual staying a Yes person. Your hands should be up at your shoulder level, palms toward the offender to still suggest no aggressive violence, your gun side angled away from his reach. You can appear to be "talking with your hands" when really you are in an emergency defense position. With your hands up, you will *reflexively* react with minimum lag time to block or deflect any grab or punch he may try while you continue dialogue with him. Your forearm will instinctively fly up to block high assaults, drop down for low. And you can quickly jerk your forward knee up across your gun leg to interrupt attempted kicks and protect your groin. At that distance, you even still have a good chance of *stepping away* from many aggressive moves.

Approaching still closer—crowding in on his personal space, prepared to take physical control—raise your hands up in front of your face. In effect, you assume a high guard without closed fists. This *defensive stance* shortens your lag time for protecting your head as you shorten the distance between you. It also puts you in a prime position to move against the suspect with the control techniques described later. Yet with your palms still out and away from your sidearm, you continue to somewhat soften your aggressive image. Also because you're close to him, his range of vision is not likely to pick up that your feet are in a more poised stance. This allows your dialogue its maximum chance of still preventing physical conflict.

The Ready Stance.

The Defensive Stance.

Moving into the reactionary gap is something *you* do, by conscious decision, with purpose. DO NOT PERMIT THE *SUSPECT* TO CLOSE THE DISTANCE BETWEEN YOU AT HIS DISCRETION. Understand that *as you move closer, you reduce your options.* Do not move in if you feel you cannot control the subject with *empty-hand* tactics. Contrary to what some firearms "experts" claim, you *will not have time* to draw your sidearm and get off two center-mass shots to defend yourself against a suspect who suddenly attacks when you are close in to him. Even with the fastest reflexes, it is physically impossible. Officers who say "I'd shoot him" when asked what they'd do to control a subject who unexpectedly lunges at them with a knife at short range, for instance, are depending on a reaction they *can't possibly* perform.

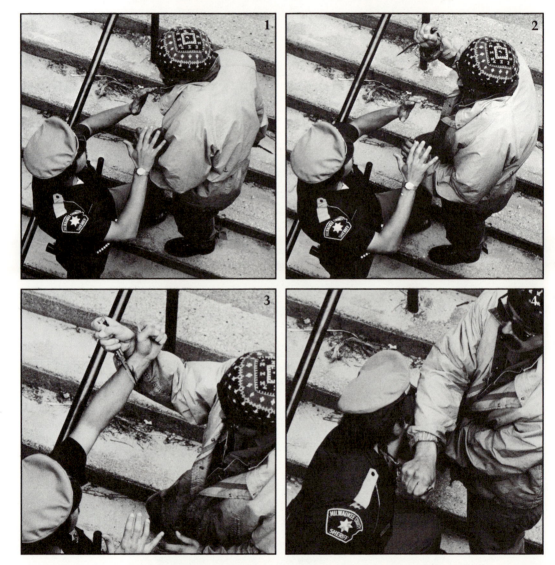

At left, a State trooper is confronted with a knife-wielding (left hand) resident of a housing project. The trooper believes he has control because of his pointing response. Below, you see an alternative approach in which the officer quickly backs off (disengages) and prepares to escalate his level of force if it becomes appropriate.

True, empty-hand tehniques are NOT the preferred force against knives. In skilled hands, knives can inflict as much or more damage than a bullet, and many officers fail to appreciate how very dangerous they are. If you see a knife and have time and distance, your sidearm should be out; you are facing deadly force. *But* at a *short* distance you may have to perform an intermediate step in order to draw. *Unless your sidearm is already out and ready,* you'll *first* have to *block* or evade the suspect's threatening move in order to buy yourself time to *then* get your sidearm in hand and get on target. Even if your hand is on your holstered sidearm, trying to get it out at close range *without first interrupting the assault* is a good way to get yourself killed or seriously injured. By keeping your hands up in a ready or defensive stance, you are in the best position to react properly with a block and parry until you can control the attacker at gunpoint.

Just *looking* alert and ready (though not *threatening*) is one of your best defenses against assault. If you assume a prepared posture, you automatically assume the tactical mental attitude to go with it. Officers who get taken tend to be those who look as if they *can* be taken: sloppy in personal appearance, untactical in positioning and distracted, bored and either hesitant or overconfident in manner. Often they stand with their hands in their pockets or thumbs hooked in their gunbelts.

A ramrod military bearing isn't right, either. Posture that's too erect makes you look like a rigid, heavy-handed authoritarian. And it's *weaker* and *less stable* than being relaxed. If you are stiff and tense, a suspect needs less power to knock you off balance because the impact of any force he delivers is conducted throughout your entire body. Think of the ease of pushing over a concrete block (rigid) compared to a sandbag (relaxed). With the block, you move one particle you move the whole thing.

To find the position that not only looks best but also is actually the most powerful one for you, tense your abdomen. About 1 to 4 inches below your waist, you'll find a spot that doesn't really tense up. That is your *"center."* Shift your body weight until muscle tension in your back and neck is at a minimum...gently pull your shoulders up and back-...and elevate your head slightly until you feel your upper body is arranged *comfortably* over your center. Now with your feet about shoulder width apart, imagine a straight line from your center to the ground, touching equidistant between your feet. You want to maintain this *same relative alignment* whether you are standing open or ready or actually applying physical control techniques against a suspect. In short, *always keep your top over your center, your center in the middle of your stance,* with everything lined up with the ground. Keep your knees slightly flexed, your weight mostly on the balls of your feet. All this gives you your *best balance base* and allows you to deliver force most efficiently.

Being centered (balanced) is crucial; where your center is, is where *you* are—either balanced or off-balance. Without balance, you can't do anything else, especially if you are smaller and less physically strong than the offender. Indeed, one of the best ways to increase your power if you don't have upper body strength is to improve your ability to stay centered. Yet a centered posture looks—and is—relaxed and calming.

As you work to manipulate the suspect, be conscious of your *voice tone* and *words* as additional elements influencing his response. You have various potential *levels of intensity or insistence* you can use in your dialogue with suspects. These range from *"search talk"* (the low-key, matter-of-fact, conversational tone for gathering information) to *"persuasion"* (asking for cooperation), to *"light control talk"* (directly telling a suspect what to do in a more insistent tone) to *"heavy control talk"* (commanding a suspect to comply and warning him of immediate physical consequences if he doesn't; in other words, "either/or" dialogue). The level you choose must be *consistent with your purpose* for addressing the suspect. Unsureness of purpose or inconsistency between your goal and your tone can lead to erratic or confused behavior by the person you're trying to control.

At *all* levels, it's to your advantage to keep your tone and content *purely professional.* Your talk is an important part of how a subject evaluates you. Don't play games (taunting, teasing, one-upmanship) with strong or violent people. The violence-prone are likely to be better game-players. Profanity, racial epithets, name-calling and graphic threats may very well intimidate some suspects. But verbal barbs (especially *personal* comments, including references to "you people...") can just as easily ignite resentment and retaliation—often in ones you *least* want to become No People. As one officer puts it: "Never let your mouth write a check your body can't cash."

If you're at a point where "control talk" is needed, it's not: "Awright, asshole! Get movin' or I'll knock yer fuckin' head off!" More

often than not, this betrays an officer trying to compensate for weak verbal and physical skills. Appropriate light control talk is on the order of: "Sir, you are under arrest. You're going to have to come with me...Now calm down! I can see you're getting tense. But it'll be easier if you just stay calm." Heavy control is: "SIR!! Come with me NOW or I'll have to take you down to the ground! *If you don't want to be injured, COME NOW!! Come NOW, sir!"* (Or a smaller officer might tell him, truthfully: "You're too big for me to fool with. If you don't come now, *I'll have to hit you with my baton!"*)

Part of the suspect's strategy may be to "hook" you into reacting emotionally so he can better manipulate you. When he is jibing you with ridicule, suggestive personal comments or profane abuse or building your frustration by pointedly ignoring you, it becomes all the more important that you remain *emotionally* detached. Otherwise you risk the kind of fiasco that developed in Ohio. Two officers were called to a restaurant where two subjects were trading insults over a girlfriend. As the officers tried to talk to the instigator, he just kept eating and refused to acknowledge them. One officer angrily yanked him out of the booth by his shirt—and the fight was on. The first officers were knocked cold. Reinforcements rolled in from three municipalities and the county—and one by one were stacked up like cordwood on the restaurant floor. Finally a veteran officer walked in, looked at the offender and declared matter-of-factly, "You're under arrest." After some 20 attempts at controlling the situation, this was the first nonemotional effort at subduing the offender with something less than physical force. "Okay," said the brawler—and meekly put his hands up in surrender.

In many cases the mini-drama of your confrontation will be played out before an audience of witnesses. Even if talking to the suspect appears useless, *talk for the audience,* because when it's all over they are going to talk about *you.* If you do have to use force, you're best off if they hear you issue a clear, direct, *unemotional, nonabusive* warning first. Their statements then can substantiate that you politely offered the suspect an opportunity to cooperate; he refused to take it. You're still delivering a forceful message. You're still telling the offender that you have the capacity and willingness to inflict injury, if necessary. And because your restrained-but-pointed dialogue suggests you are in control of *yourself,* he's encouraged to believe that you are in control of *him.*

Do you see anything wrong in this picture? Among other things to consider: deputy has his sidearm within easy reach of the subject, subject's hands are not visible, the deputy is too relaxed with his hand in his pocket, he stands too close to the subject, and the deputy could become a sudden assault victim.

Be aware that a significant percentage of criminals have *learning disabilities*. In some cases, this may interfere with their comprehending your instructions, as may alcohol and drugs. Keep your directives simple and to the point...speak slowly...use visual cues (hand gestures)...and *repeat* what you say for reinforcement.

Above all, avoid emphasizing your words with the *"chest jab"* or the *"parental finger."* If you poke a suspect's chest with your forefinger or thrust your finger in his face while ordering him around or telling him off, you are making highly aggressive gestures that frequently touch off violent responses. In psychological terms, you're more likely to encourage cooperation by keeping your comments, commands and gestures *adult-to-adult* (in the tone and content of one grown-up speaking respectfully and unemotionally to another), not *parent-to-child* (critical superior to inferior). The latter tends to evoke the "rebellious child" in the suspect. Your respecting a subject's ego is not the same as mollycoddling or fearing him; it projects *strength*, not weakness. And in many cases, it will increase his respect for your authority.

While managing the verbal and nonverbal messages you're sending, you want also to monitor the suspect for signals *he* is emitting. Reading *"behavior indicators"* is far from an exact science. Yet subjects who are contemplating or actually heading toward the No mode often do unconsciously telegraph their bent.

Warning signs include a suspect who:

• conspicuously *ignores* you. By not responding to your questions, refusing to look at you, talking to companions as if you're not there, starting to leave, etc., he's showing contempt for your ability to enforce your authority.

• gives you excessive *emotional attention*, as by talking to you too loudly, arguing belligerently, staring angrily. There's a high correlation between emotional distress and physical conflict, especially when he starts identifying *you* as a problem to him or alleging that you want to use violence against him. If he's shouting, "You wanna kick my ass," he may be projecting onto you what *he'd* really like to do to *you.*

• displays *exaggerated movement* that invades your reactionary gap. Through generalized, agitated motion, suspects often "gear up," physically and mentally, for directed violence.

• abruptly *stops* all movement. This may be "the calm before the storm."

• has a known *violent background.* The more violence a suspect has experienced in his life, either as a perpetrator or a victim, the higher the probability that he will use violence as a tool in your confrontation.

These, of course, are only *cautions*, not *certainties.* Don't automatically assume they mean attack is imminent and become overtly aggressive yourself, thereby *provoking* assault from a suspect who now feels he's endangered by you. Just use them as a means of adjusting your awareness level.

Understand also that some body language varies among ethnic groups. Hispanics who avoid eye contact may be perceived by Anglo officers as deceitful or guilty. Yet in their culture, not looking an authority figure in the eye actually is a show of respect. Ghetto blacks tend to move around more than whites in the presence of police ("shuckin' and jivin'") and may be more given to touching. Their behaving normally or "cool" in this regard may be misread by white officers as threatening. Likewise, two blacks hurling vicious insults back and forth and appearing close to homicidal combat may only be "playing the dozens" or "selling woof tickets." According to its cultural rules, this "put-down game" almost always ends nonviolently when one participant abruptly walks away—unless a white officer unfamiliar with what's happening physically intervenes and escalates the encounter.

The answer is not to assume that everything unfamiliar is safe. That's crazy. But in dealing with ethnic groups, take extra care to *explicitly* direct the *specific behavior* you want. Suspects sometimes fail to be Yes people because they don't understand what's expected.

Don't waste time closely scrutinizing a suspect's body believing it is a mirror of his mind. Some pop psychologists make sweeping claims, insisting you can tell whether a suspect is lying by how he positions his eyes, whether he is likely to strike you by how he places his thumbs relative to his pants pockets or belt, and so on. Much of this is highly speculative. At best, single indicators taken out of context are almost always meaningless and can easily lead you to faulty conclusions. And to try to analyze "behavior clusters" (multiple detailed body cues that add up to a consistent pattern) is likely to prove more distracting for you than revealing.

In the few seconds you may have to size up a volatile situation, the body language you most want to watch for are a few precise, subtle but *significant moves.* These are often associated physiologically with a human being's preparation to attack. They include:

1. **The Boxer Stance.** The suspect may begin by *shifting his weight* from foot to foot. Then he drops *one foot back* or steps forward; if he's right handed, his right foot will go back, his left forward. This instinctively balances his weight better for striking from his strong side: it's hard to throw an effective punch or karate kick from an "at ease" position. Simultaneously or separately, his *elbow crooks* and starts to bring his hand up from his side. He may be preparing to grab you, someone else or some object, like a hidden weapon. A *clenched fist* (or one

that closes and opens nervously), especially above the waist, adds danger, even if the suspect is across the room using his fist to wipe his brow. His final move before assaulting may be to *turn sideways* to you ("blading" himself), to protect his vital areas.

The Boxer Stance.   The Hand Set.

2. **The Hand Set.** The suspect *positions his hands* 2-3 inches out from his body, one at chest level, the other away from his abdomen. His fingers may be together in a *"chopping" style.* Especially a subject with martial arts training can get very aggressive very fast from this pose. Unobservant officers sometimes confuse it with the more benign "Who, me?" gesture meant to convey a suspect's shock and innocence at being hailed by the police. But there the subject usually presses both palms against his upper chest, fingers spread.

3. **The Shoulder Shift.** The suspect's body in general will *tighten* just before he moves, to provide the necessary tension for his action; his mind is communicating to his muscles the preparation that's needed. If he's going to try to hit you, you may be able to see the shoulder of his striking hand *move forward* and dip slightly as the trapezius muscles tighten to stabilize the shoulder for the punch. If his shoulders *drop down*, he may be moving into a leg-grabbing, tackling or wrestling position, an attack mode often used by subjects with wrestling or football backgrounds. Where heavy clothing obscures the shoulders, watch his *neck* for tightening muscles.

4. **The Target Glance.** Unless a subject is highly trained, he will *instinctively look* where he intends to strike. He may scope you out in a general way to pick what he thinks is your vulnerable spot, then main-

tain steady eye contact for seconds or minutes. But at the last instant, immediately before he acts, he'll *glance at his target point* about 95% of the time. If he glances at your groin, get ready for a kick...at your throat, a choke.

5. **The 'Thousand-Yard' Stare.** Here the suspect experiences a *radical facial change* from the time you started talking with him. His expression goes *absolutely blank*. Even if you're just 2 feet away, he *looks right through you* as if nothing is in his line of sight for a thousand yards. His *eyes go "dead,"* as if suddenly covered by a dry-ash film. He may remain verbally and physically animated. But often he becomes *ominously silent*. In his mind, he may be justifying his urge to attack you. Once decided, he can explode with startling suddenness.

If you see any of these potential indicators, either back off and give the subject more room, possibly reinforcing that he still has options ("I can see you're getting upset. You'll be okay if you just calm down. I don't want to take you down, but I will if I have to.")...or consider immediate physical measures to attempt control. If the body signals seem to conflict with a suspect's nonthreatening words, your safest strategy is to believe his *nonverbal* messages. *Don't just stand and wait*. Some of these indicators will precede by only a fraction of a second an actual attack.

If he's too fast or you're too slow to avoid his first hit, even having that slight anticipation of it will help you withstand the blow psychologically. Sensing something's coming, rather than being assaulted completely by surprise, will lessen your shock, tighten your reaction time and allow you to come back stronger.

The Shoulder Shift.

The Target Glance.

447

The Thousand-Yard Stare.

Three D's

Some of these considerations change when you're dealing with the *"Three D's"*—subjects who are drunk...drugged... and/or deranged. Controlling them with rational dialogue may be extremely difficult or impossible. The verbal and nonverbal cues they send you and the messages you try to send them are more likely to be meaningless and unreliable because their communication and interpretation abilities are garbled. Faster than "normal" subjects, they seem able to escalate without warning into verbal intimidation, physical bullying, even sadistic assault.

These people are *colossally unpredictable.* You don't know where their heads are at...and they don't, either!

Drunks are rarely Yes people, more often Maybe, but in many officers' view overwhelmingly No. Take a stab at verbal tactics, but if you don't connect with some lingering element of rationality in the subject, *act.* The faster you establish physical control over an offender who's that far gone (incoherent, weaving, stumbling, falling down) usually the better. The longer he's unrestrained, the greater his danger to himself and to you, especially if he's a "mean" drunk. Some will have quick reflexes, but usually their physical movements are slower than normal; if your subject gets aggressive as you move in, you stand a good chance of sidestepping or blocking his assault. But by the same token, your moves (especially pain compliance) will take longer to register because his senses are dulled. With drunks, as with other individuals, don't automatically accept what you see at face value. Some martial arts schools are now teaching a means of feigning drunkenness as a ruse to gain the edge of surprise in a sudden, clear-headed assault.

Users actively under the influence of certain *drugs*—marijuana, heroin, various downers—are considered unlikely to offer much physical resistance, while the strength, endurance, aggressiveness and super confidence of those wired on uppers, cocaine, PCP and hallucinogens are legendary. With the latter group, pain compliance will probably have no effect whatever. Only measures that cause the subject an actual *physical dysfunction*, thus preventing him from further resistance or attack, offer much hope. Even then, your success with physical control may ultimately depend on whether you can overwhelm your adversary with sheer numbers. Try to stay behind cover (even if the subject is unarmed) and avoid contact until you have sufficient backup at hand. Officers' most common mistake with violent drug users is overextending themselves while alone. If you are alone and cornered against someone made superhumanly powerful by chemicals, deadly force may be your only practical defense option.

That's sometimes the case with *mentally ill* subjects, too. Like the lunatic in Georgia whom two officers tried to arrest. He knocked the first officer cold with a single punch. The partner whacked him "up side the head" as hard as he could with his nightstick. The offender just wiped the blood off with his hand and licked it—and kept on coming.

The handling of an intoxicated subject (above) and someone who is emotionally disturbed (right) can be mistaken to be a routine contact. What could the officer above have done to give *herself* the benefit of the doubt rather than the drunk? At the right, a woman climbed on the front of the bus because it would not stop for her. How would you approach her knowing she has a weapon in her right hand?

449

Often, though, dealing with the deranged is a more complex matter. You may not be able to reach these subjects on all levels, but more often than many officers realize they can be reached on *some* level of rationality, assuming they are sober. By using sharp psychological tactics, you often can avoid premature or unnecessary physical conflict.

Your ability to manipulate the mentally ill is more important today because of changes in society and in psychiatric treatment programs. Many who in the past were routinely institutionalized are now free to be anywhere. Unsupervised, they often fail to take the medication that's supposed to keep them placid. And when they start wreaking havoc that no one around can handle, you get called. It can prove to be one of your most dangerous assignments.

Try to gather intelligence en route, to guide your tactical strategy. If a known mental patient is creating a disturbance, for example, your dispatcher can ask the complainant:
• Does the subject have any known hostility toward law enforcement officers or toward strangers generally?
• What tends to agitate him or make him violent?
• Is he under the influence of any drugs or alcohol?
• Does he have access to any weapons—knife, gun, club, pipe, anything else that could do physical harm?
• Does he ever hide any weapon on his person?
• Has he ever done bodily harm to anyone in the past?
Survival-conscious deputies with one Southern sheriff's department have gotten similar questions incorporated as an official part of the sworn affidavit that's signed to initiate commitment pickups for mental illness, alcoholism and drug dependency.

At the scene, unless there's violence underway that you must immediately subdue, *patience* and *timing* are your watchwords. Anticipating that eventually you may need to use physical measures, set the stage for moving *to your advantage.*

First, remove any family or friends of the subject immediately, as you would on a domestic disturbance call. They are certain only to make matters worse. With you there to protect them, they may start scolding or berating the subject. Or if you have to get physical, they may intervene "to keep you from hurting my baby." Or the suspect may be defiant and aggressive to show off for them. Get them next door or into the next room with polite but firm instructions: "Don't interfere." If you're in a location where a crowd forms and can't be removed, stay aware that an attack from someone in the crowd who decides to rescue or protect the suspect from you is a common risk.

If you have a partner, one of you should act as an *"initiator,"* the other primarily as a *"distractor."* The initiator—the more outgoing, cooler-headed, better actor of the two—does most or all of the talking. Depending on the circumstances, he may also make the first physical move to subdue the subject. If the initiator cannot create a diversion of his own, the distractor does so at an opportune moment to take the suspect's attention away from this move. This division of labor, however, should not be an excuse to take foolish chances. Three officers in Virginia were trying to subdue a mentally disturbed young woman who was wielding a knife. As two distracted her with calming dialogue, the third started to sneak up from behind to disarm her, despite the inappropriateness of voluntarily trying to use empty-hand techniques against a knife. She whirled on him and stabbed through one of his major arteries. He died before he could be removed from the scene.

Let the suspect rant and rave if he wants to. His venting his feelings will help calm and deenergize him; "acting out helps burn him out." If he's tearing up his own room or house, so what? Moving in or even leaning on him verbally when he's fired up—pacing around, perhaps flailing his arms or kicking furniture, slamming walls—is the worst timing from a safety standpoint. Be ready to act in case he turns *physically* assaultive toward you, but otherwise *wait,* if you can afford to do so. One deputy who has handled over 3,000 lunacy cases says he once stood in a subject's presence for more than 15 minutes without saying a word. Some officers, on the other hand, react to mere *verbal* abuse as if they were physically attacked—and end up in a lot more fights than necessary. Watched and waited out, the suspect may settle down rather quickly. Sometimes the emotionally disturbed carry on just to goad a reaction from you.

Gradually try to calm him. Speak quietly and conversationally, even if he's boisterous and loud. Avoid teasing, criticizing, laughing at him or asking, *"Why* did you do that?" If there's something in the room that suggests his hobbies or special interests, try to get him talking about that. Offer him a cigaret; smoking reduces most people's agitation. Emphasize that you're there to help, not hassle. Keep any commands simple (though not patronizing), with a tone of respect. Some officers try to solicit a promise of nonviolence, saying, for example: "I don't want to hurt you... You don't want to hurt me, do you?" A "no" answer may help commit him psychologically. Stay ready, though. Aggressive subjects lull some officers just by smiling, although a smile is the most common unfelt expression.

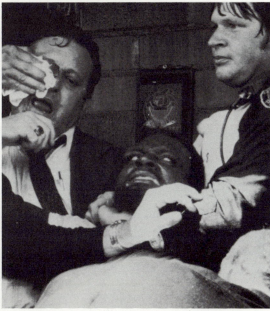

Officers use a water hose on a mental hospital escapee who threatens police with a sharpened screwdriver. To the subject's right (above) is a lieutenant whose eye was cut in the struggle.

Listening attentively, even if the subject makes no sense, is an important part of calming him. The people that mentally disturbed individuals ordinarily come in contact with do not receive the messages these subjects think they are sending. This frustrates and angers them. Pretend to understand whatever they say. Don't argue; you won't persuade them they're illogical anyway. Look for opportunities to use their fantasies to your advantage. One prisoner in a Georgia jail ripped a sink from the wall barehanded while hallucinating that a giant crawdad was trying to kill him. A deputy calmed him not by saying he was nuts or trying to physically overpower him but by pretending to see the fearsome creature himself and helping the subject "escape" it by sneaking quietly to another cell. You may not understand a subject's fear, but you can understand fear...and you can see in his eyes that it is very real to him. Use that to build rapport.

Some bluffs should be attempted *only* if you have the background to pull them off, however. One Missouri officer was facing resistance from a mental patient who believed himself to be a CIA agent on a top-secret mission. He thought police and paramedics sent to deal with him were "commies" out to stop him. By using several military terms and engaging in "spy-type" conversation, the officer gained the subject's confidence and convinced him that he (the officer) was an undercover agent from Naval Intelligence. If the subject went with the paramedics peacefully, the officer promised, "I'll see to it the CIA is informed of your whereabouts, and you'll be able to maintain your security clearance." The bluff worked, but if the officer hadn't spent time in a military intelligence unit, he might have inadvertently given away his trick and escalated the situation.

The *religiously deranged* are potentially among the most dangerous offenders you'll confront, particularly if they perceive that you are standing in the way of their mission from God. One officer has found that he can sometimes persuade these subjects to cooperate by playing on their (usually) literal interpretation of the Bible. He quotes Romans 13:1,2:

> Let every person be subject to the governing authorities. For...those that exist have been instituted by God. Therefore, he who resists the authorities resists what God has appointed, and those who resist will incur judgment....

Don't make sudden moves, unless it's a control move. Remember, the subject's perceptions are not normal. The highly paranoid, especially, may interpret a simple but abrupt movement as something threatening and explode into violence. However, you should make *deliberately slow* movements with your hands (scratch your head, reach into a shirt pocket, etc.) or even walk around slowly. Getting him used to seeing you move will tend to relax his guard and set him up for a fast surprise action that brings him under control before he realizes what's happened. As you move, however, still try to keep yourself between your adversary and the doorway or some other escape route.

A *distraction* just a split-second before your control move will help you get the edge. Something simple—kicking dirt or scraping the floor with your shoe, your partner shouting to get the subject to turn his head—is usually sufficient. Be prepared to move *immediately* with your control technique. Move without hesitation and with a technique you know you're proficient at; this isn't the time for practice or experimentation.

Expect to feel some fear; it's nature's way of giving you "fore-warning to be forearmed." But don't let fear take you over. It's hard not to show nervousness or fright when you're facing a maniac who's dipping a Bible in blood, making his mother kiss it and having intercourse with the family dog, as happened with one deputy. But the emotionally disturbed, like animals, seem exceptionally keen at sensing fear and are more likely to challenge you if they detect it. Stay out of reach until you're ready to invade his personal space; with these subjects, especially, be careful of crowding close. But staying too far beyond a reasonable reactionary gap can cause problems, too. The subject may interpret this as fear on your part.

Act confident, but don't ever let a suspect's apparent compliance or your honed skills lead you to believe you can't be taken. When a suspect is complying, it does not necessarily mean he's surrendering. It just means he's not doing anything negative *at the moment.* Moods can change fast. DON'T RELAX TOO SOON. An officer in Illinois stopped a teen-ager for riding a motorbike after drinking. Through the interview and arrest, the kid was politely compliant. Then his bike happened to topple over. The officer stooped to pick it up—and *POW!* Without warning, the youth socked him in the head, started wrestling with him and tried to grab his sidearm. He almost made it, but the officer was able to execute a weapon retention technique that saved him.

If you do get punched in the face, smashed in the ribs, kicked in the groin, bitten or thrown to the ground, by a mentally impaired subject or anyone else, *know that you can keep going…YOU WILL SURVIVE.*

Tactical Positioning

Once you've closed the reactionary gap and invaded a subject's personal space, how you physically position yourself to deal with him will determine how *vulnerable* you are to his attack versus how *capable* you are to *control* his actions.

Try to AVOID what's called his **"Inside" Position.** That's where you're in *front* of him within the area that would be *inside his open arms* were he to extend them. THIS IS THE MOST DANGEROUS PLACE YOU CAN BE WITH ANY SUSPECT. Human beings are built to attack and fight *forward*, so when you're there you are where he can exert the greatest force against you—punching, kicking, grabbing, choking, bit-ing—with the greatest ease.

If you *must* fight from his Inside, your counterforce will have to be *hard and penetrating* to be effective, like the Active Countermeasures discussed later.

Given a choice, you want to control him from *Outside*. It's easier and generally safer. However, you want to keep *your* Inside toward him, so he is susceptible to *your* strongest fighting position. As he shifts his body, you'll need to move, too, to keep him at that disadvantage, until you can apply the appropriate physical control measures to stop him.

Outside, there are various positions you can occupy, each with different tactical considerations.

Ideally, you'd like to take control of a subject's strong side first. (If he's wearing a wristwatch, his strong side will be opposite his watch side.) But realistically, you should be able to operate from these positions on either side of him:

INSIDE

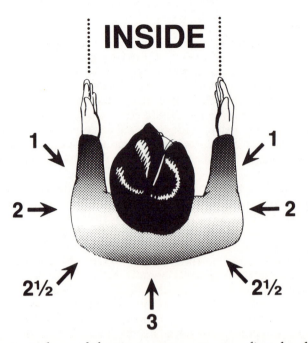

From a ready or defensive stance, you can first lay hands on effectively from any of these locations. But normally, you'll want to *get to* **Position 2½** *as quickly as possible.* Move yourself or turn the suspect. This *"escort position"* is safest for you because it gives you an *"advantage of angle."* You're hardest for the suspect to hit, kick or grab here because he has to pivot or twist to connect well. You can turn before he can do so. You can most easily *maintain* control for an extended period from this position once you've established it, through come-along holds, pain compliance, etc. And, if necessary, you can *disengage* from physical contact with him more readily at this location. *Handcuffing* should be done from here, also. *For control standing up, as with Yes or Maybe subjects, 2½ is overall the best position.* If you can make your initial contact from here, fine. But many suspects will not let you get behind them until they are restrained.

To approach a suspect from the front, **Position 1** *is best.* Coming toward his Outside at an angle, you appear to be invading less of his personal space, so he may let you get closer without resistance. He probably will not understand your *tactical advantages:* 1) you can keep your gun side angled away; 2) you significantly reduce his threat potential (If he tries to swing from his opposite side, for instance, you can deflect or *parry* the blow if you're alert to that possibility; as soon as he starts moving, you'll *reflexively* spin away); 3) although you're Outside in a more protected position, you can still readily reach his Inside with your *elbows* and *knees* for control if he becomes a No person. Remember, though, with Yes or Maybe suspects, you want to *move to 2½* once you've established physical contact.

Position 2 is closer to that goal. It's a good location for *moving in from the side.* Your strongest fighting position (your Inside) is toward a position of relative weakness for the suspect. You can readily grab his nearest arm, pivot away from action from his far side, and elbow or knee his Inside if he becomes assaultive.

If you can get to it (or turn the suspect to it), **Position 3** is the *best location for taking control of a highly violent No person.* Neck restraint, some Pressure Point techniques and the stunning Countermeasures described later all can be effectively initiated from here. If the suspect is fighting forward with a civilian or with your partner, you can move in from behind for what amounts to a "free shot." He may be able to kick, elbow or grab backwards or throw you over his head, however, so *don't stay here long.* Take him to the ground immediately or move to the escort position at 2½.

When you approach to take control from any position, keep your hands up in a ready stance...and *"step and drag."* That's the foot movement you use in crowd control and boxing where you step forward with one foot and pull the other one after it. *NEVER WALK in a confrontational setting.* Your balance is tenuous then, and you're vulnerable to being knocked over.

Partners can use the position numbering as a code when communicating in a subject's presence. For instance: "Joe, you take 1, I'll take 2½" or "Jane, watch Inside" (if you think there may be a weapon in the suspect's waistband). This allows you to coordinate movement or alert a partner to danger without tipping your hand.

Escort Control

At the moment you touch someone you create a "crisis of decision" for that individual. He's forced to decide whether to *flee* you...fight you...or *follow* your directions. That's when you're most likely to get resistance. And because your hands are on him, you are intertwined with him, at least to some degree.

Man who walked into a convenience store because he needed cigarettes. Poor positioning on the part of the officer. Her sidearm is accessible. Handcuffing from the front can be extremely dangerous. Notice her gaze. She was not hurt during this arrest.

Don't touch until you have to. When you do, intend to be effective from the first. And understand that you may have to go the whole way.

If you can't control a subject properly the first time, some other officer might inherit an even worse threat.

 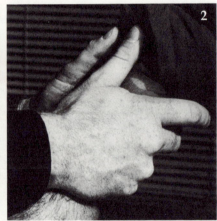

The "blanket."

One hold to consider for initially touching Yes and Maybe subjects from any of the tactical positions is *"the blanket"* (so called because it's soft like a blanket). Just lightly place your hands on either side of the suspect's arm at the elbow, as if you were going to clap them gently. If his arms are in motion, it'll be easier to grab his elbow than his wrist because it can move only half as fast. One of your hands goes in front, the other behind so that the tips of your thumb and longest finger are positioned approximately where the ends of his elbow crease would be if he were to bend his arm. With this *pincer grip*, you can squeeze on a nerve there to apply Pressure Point pain, if necessary.

Accompanied by soothing dialogue, the blanket without pain presents probably the lowest possible amount of threat to the suspect. You can easily guide him with it from the 2½ position if he's compliant. Yet it gives you versatility for quickly escalating to greater control if necessary.

From there, you can quickly establish, among other things, the:

"GOOSENECK." This "common wrist lock" technique, combines both pain and leverage to your advantage. From the suspect's right side, run your right hand down his arm to his wrist and clamp it so your first two fingers are on top of his wrist bone, your thumb is wrapped tightly

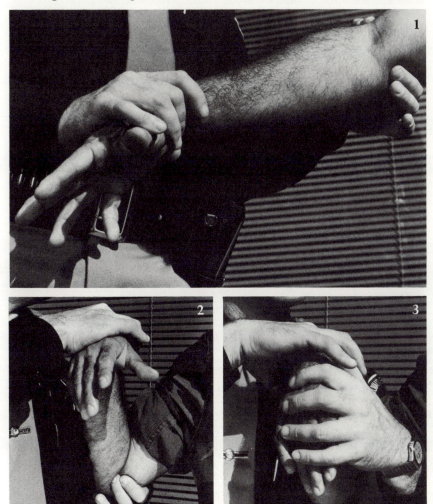

Above and on previous page, "The Gooseneck." (right) This technique can be effective for two officers when controlling a passively resistant person with a minimum use of force. Based on the subject's behavior you can either disengage or escalate your force control. (below) Further application of the technique for prisoner movement into a cell where there is resistance to cooperate.

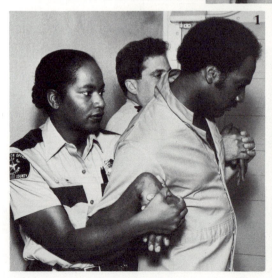

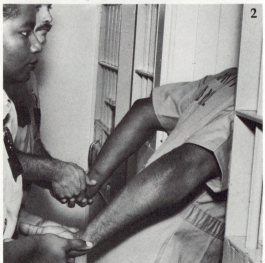

under his wrist and your palm is tight against the back of his hand, with your fingers curled over his thumb. (Just reverse your hands and movements if you are on his left side.) Now sharply push his hand under, bending his wrist, and raise it up, bending his elbow. Pull his elbow in to the center of your chest for this maneuver and keep his wrist bent under pressure so his arm folds into the gooseneck configuration. Be sure his hand ends up well above his elbow. Now come up under his arm with your left hand and clamp it over the back of his hand. Keep his elbow tucked in against your chest, holding it in place with your elbow. Release your right fingers and lay them over your left hand to secure the hold. By applying pressure down on the suspect's hand and into your body, you can exert intense pain and can readily bring him up on his toes and off balance for compliance. You can add even more pain by twisting the knife edge of his palm up toward your nose. Many officers consider the gooseneck to be the simplest wrist lock come-along hold with the highest chance of success, but be aware that a suspect may try to defeat this hold by stomping on your feet. If the suspect does resist, drop your center a bit. This can force him down.

One option if you can't get the suspect's elbow bent is:

"THE ARM BAR." Grasp his wrist as you would to start a gooseneck. But instead of bending it, pull his arm taut to take out its slack. At the same time maintain your pincer grip at his elbow with your left hand so your palm is firmly against his elbow. Now at once twist the back of his hand in, pull back on his wrist and push against his elbow to pitch him forward off balance and to exert pain. From this position, he cannot attack without telegraphing his intentions. If he continues to resist, you can shove hard against his elbow to bring him down (possibly breaking the elbow in the process). Or you can "roll" the blade of your left arm against his upper arm just above the elbow, twisting it to pitch him forward and down more. Either way, the more he tries to come after you, the more you can take him down. To take him down with the least chance of him regaining balance, whip him around in a spiral fashion as

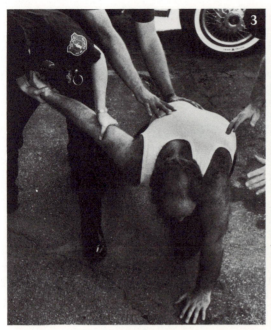 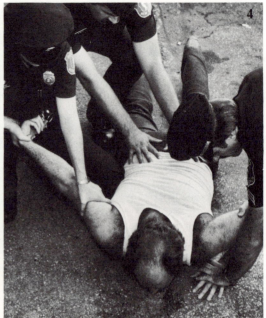

you push him to the ground. This takes his feet out from under him and makes him fall so that he lands in a more manageable position for you.

From these and other escort controls, you can move into the handcuffing holds described shortly...If higher force is needed against a suspect who becomes resistant, you can deliver Pressure Point control, Countermeasures, neck restraints, etc...Or, if he becomes too violent for you to control, you can disengage from contact by pushing him away. This allows you to move (run) to a safer position or draw a weapon. In other words, these techniques *flow easily* to others either higher or lower on the Force Continuum.

Remember, though, ESCORT HOLDS ARE *NOT* APPROPRIATE TO USE FOR MAKING *INITIAL* CONTACT WITH SOMEONE WHO IS *ALREADY* ACTIVELY RESISTING OR ASSAULTING YOU (i.e., a No person). And, like any control measure, they may not always work. If a Yes or Maybe suspect successfully resists them, he automatically places himself in the No-person category. Then only harsher measures are appropriate or are likely to be effective.

Escort holds can often be successful, however, in gaining compliance from *passive* resisters, such as demonstrators who may try to sit in place and not budge. These fairly discreet holds, applied from a well-balanced kneeling position, can motivate such individuals to move on their own, so you are spared the hard work and bad press of having to drag them. (Incidentally, if you're confronting demonstrators whose arms are interlocked, don't try to move the whole row simultaneously. Instruct the subject you're dealing with that *he* is responsible for making whomever is connected to him let go.)

With any of these maneuvers, one of the suspect's hands is free. You always want this important Area of Responsibility behind his head or out to his side, palm up. *Control his free hand* with verbal commands or pain compliance. Otherwise, you're vulnerable to an unexpected sucker punch. If another officer is available, he or she can simultaneously apply the same escort hold you have on the other side of the suspect's body. This "double pain compliance" can be very effective.

As with other physical control measures, you're bound to develop favorites as you practice the escort possibilities. Stick with what works for you. Rather than trying to master a vast repertoire of escort holds, learn to quickly apply the hold(s) you like *best* under as many different circumstances as you can think of. And always be ready to disengage from contact or to escalate to higher force if the suspect increases his resistance.

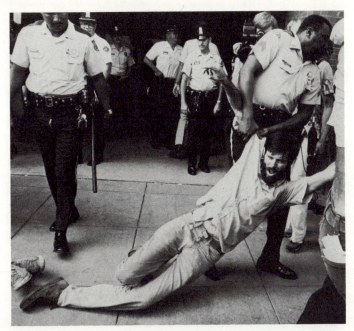

See something strange in this situation? The officer is doing all the work! Perfect application for a quick, decisive escort hold.

Whatever you use, your goal is always the same: to *decentralize the suspect*. If he is off balance (not centered), he cannot fight you effectively. You must move *decisively*, putting 110% into your effort, without hesitation. Deliver with *power*, understanding that power is not just strength alone. It is constituted from six other components, as well: balance, endurance, flexibility, mind-body coordination, speed and simplicity. All these can be improved dramatically with practice and conditioning. With proper workouts, you can double your strength, for example, is less than six months.

Getting these moves started may be difficult, particularly with a well-conditioned subject. If you're trying to bend his wrist and he's focused on resisting, you might not be able to overcome his strength if you tried all day. *Use distraction.* If you can shift his concentration to something else, you will sap his strength momentarily.

One option from the "blanket" hold is to squeeze your hands at his elbow and without warning yank straight down *hard* on his arm to take out the slack. This disrupts his balance, and as he's focused on regaining it you can quickly get his wrist bent and pull off the gooseneck move. Because it's unexpected, it usually works even if the suspect is bigger than you are. It's akin to a streetwise arm-wrestling trick: so long as your

461

opponent is concentrating solely on exerting strength against you, you may not be able to overcome him, but if you reach under the table with your free hand and suddenly pinch his leg, his focus will abruptly shift there and the strength in his arm will evaporate for an instant. In that moment of distraction, you can smash his arm to the tabletop with ease.

Whenever you're using compliance pain on a subject, train yourself to accompany it with verbal direction. This enhances the chance that the technique will work. Under such sudden, intense, stressful stimulation, his brain will be confused, and he may not be able to think on his own what to do to stop it. In this state, he'll be more suggestible, more likely to follow directions. With short, direct, explosive commands, tell him precisely what you want ("Sir! Put your hand down! Put your hand down!"). Keep repeating it so your words penetrate the pain. Remind him that by resisting, *he is causing the pain himself* ("Sir! Stop it! You're hurting yourself, sir! Stop it!!"). The more pain you're inflicting, the louder your commands should be yelled, as he may be experiencing auditory blocking from the high stress.

When the subject starts to comply, you'll feel the *"resistive tension"* ease in his body. Reward him by lightening up...but *don't abandon control.* Get him handcuffed ASAP, before he changes his mind again. If he resists, reimpose your sanctions.

Talk to your partner, too, to coordinate your moves. Short key words are enough. This helps intimidate the suspect, who may think, "I can't beat them. They've got their act together!" And, by telling each other your intentions, you can avoid techniques that work against each other.

Pressure Points

Resistance by any subject begins in his brain, with the *thought* of not cooperating. His nerves act like gas lines to carry this intent to his muscles. At various locations, the "gas lines" that feed the major muscle groups most involved in resistant or assaultive action run close to the surface of the skin. With your fingers, your palm or your baton, you can easily reach them, and with the right pressure you can shut off their instruction for action. In its place, you can send back along the nerves a strong motivational message for cooperation to change the suspect's thinking.

Some officers are frankly skeptical of attempting control through "Pressure Points;" they claim this technique is merely pain compliance...that pain compliance is notoriously unreliable...and that you can't tell by looking at a subject whether it is going to work. Well, *no* control system is effective against 100% of the suspects you confront. In fact, one tactical shortcoming of many officers is that they are always looking for *the perfect solution to every problem in one package.* Anything less than that they reject as "useless." Some individuals are able to survive even *shotgun* blasts, probably your ultimate force option. But that doesn't mean shotguns are "useless" as police tools. Nor does the inability of any one system of physical control to subdue *everyone* it is attempted on make it useless. The fact that *nothing* is sure-fire is why you always want a "Plan B" in mind, regardless of your tactical approach.

If you master a system of Pressure Points, its advocates claim you can reasonably expect that it will help you establish or maintain control over at least 80% of the subjects you use it on. Pressure at some locations on the body does *much more* than just inflict pain. It actually disrupts the suspect's *functioning,* whether he feels pain or not. When you strike a nerve, it compresses and spasms. Less "fuel" can pass through it, so the muscle action it feeds is temporarily paralyzed or weakened. At the very least, because nerve pressure can help you distract a suspect or destroy his balance, Pressure Points comprise a valuable tool that complements and supplements your other control measures. Among other things, they can help you control subjects during a fight or an attempted assault …while you are recovering from energy loss after a foot chase or struggle…when you are trying to separate a subject from other combatants…and while handcuffing and searching. When you have no handcuffs or their use is inappropriate, some Pressure Points can assist in come-alongs. And because some can be applied so discreetly that they are virtually unrecognizable to the untrained eye, they are ideal for forcing cooperation from such offenders as sit-down protesters.

Some 370 potential Pressure Points exist in the human body, but fewer than a dozen are considered practical for use by law enforcement. Here we'll describe the seven that are *most likely* to be effective for your purposes. At least one of these is almost certain to be accessible to you in any physical conflict.

You do not have to locate these nerve sites with pinpoint accuracy, nor is extensive training necessary to learn how to use them. The nerves involved are large enough and accessible enough that with practice you'll be able, even under stress and while struggling with an offender, to apply the right amount of pressure within an allowable radius for effectiveness. As you read the descriptions here, you'll be able to locate most of these points on yourself and, by applying *mild* pressure, get a feel for the sensations you can transmit.

Your size, strength and energy are relatively inconsequential. This is a system based on technique rather than brute strength. Just *touching* these spots with about ½ to 2 pounds of pressure—less than it takes to pull a trigger—can produce medium- to high-intensity pain. *Quick penetration* at certain sites (that is, jabbing your finger in deep and hard after you've made contact with the Pressure Point) can deliver a low-level stun, scrambling the "computer impulses" of the subject's brain and leaving him momentarily disoriented and immobilized. And *striking* some Pressure Points can actually disrupt the suspect's motor capabilities temporarily. Any one of these pressure levels may at least buy you enough time to get one handcuff on him and bring him under control.

For touch pressure and quick penetration, use the *tips,* not the pads, of your fingers. Pads diffuse the pressure over a wider area and weaken it. The smaller an area force is concentrated in, the greater effect it has on the part of the body receiving it. Apply pressure *decisively* and with *immediacy.* If you build up your pressure gradually, the suspect can adapt to it and possibly overpower you before he's affected. It must be *abrupt and significant* to cross his pain threshold with meaningful impact. He'll then likely feel as if he's being subjected to destructive or crippling force. Yet according to research and street experience with this system, he'll suffer *no permanent or disfiguring injury.* Even striking certain of the Pressure Points with a baton leaves only a bruise.

You can reach four of the most popular Pressure Points by hand in or near the suspect's *head.* In physical conflict, wherever your hand happens to land on a suspect's head or neck, you are no more than a slight movement away from one of these points. It is possible to activate more than one simultaneously, using either one hand or both together.

Their locations are:

BASE OF THE NOSE. Your target is under the suspect's nose, right where it joins his upper lip. Sharp touch pressure or a strike with either blade side of your hand will impact on the infra-orbital nerve that feeds this area. The pain from touch pressure can force a passive resister to his feet, for example, while a strike can recoil an attacker or prompt him to release you in a fight. Or you might use this Pressure Point to knock an offender off balance or distract him preparatory to moving in with other control measures. Drive your force up at about a 45° angle toward the top center of the suspect's head for the greatest pain. A strike will probably water his eyes, making it harder for him to see you, and also will likely stun him. With your hand angled above his mouth, he can't bite you.

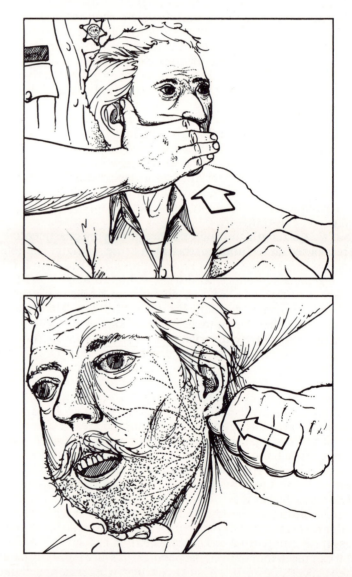

UNDER THE EAR. Three major nerves run together behind the lower jaw bone. Touch pressure at this site, called the mandibular angle, can produce such severe pain that many suspects will submit immediately. Pressing hard with your thumbtip or fingertip on this super-sensitive spot offers you a high probability of stopping all the suspect's intentional motor activity for valuable milliseconds, besides distracting and unbalancing him. For best results, press sharply at the base of the ear lobe between the lower jaw and the mastoid (the bony prominence that runs up behind the ear). Direct your force toward the center of the suspect's head, with a slight angle toward his nose.

UNDER THE JAW. Here you want to apply pressure to the sensitive part of the suspect's hypoglossal nerve, where it enters the back of his tongue. The Pressure Point is about an inch forward of the bend in the lower jaw and about an inch in under the jaw. Push toward the top center of the suspect's skull with either firm touch pressure or quick penetration. Besides pain, distraction and balance displacement, the right touch pressure delivered from the Inside Position will force the suspect to involuntarily throw his arms out to his sides. With quick penetration, you also get an immediate shutting down of motor activity and mental stunning that can last from 3 to 7 seconds.

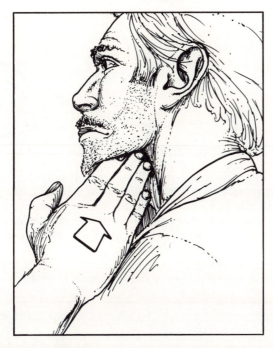

BASE OF THE THROAT. This is another Pressure Point that can save you if you're caught in the suspect's Inside position. With touch pressure or quick penetration, drive one or two of your fingers into his jugular notch, the bony U-shaped dent at the base of the throat. Direct your pressure down toward the center of his body at about a 45° angle. This will stimulate his gag reflex. He'll involuntarily reflex away from you, shift off balance and probably experience some mental stunning and motor impairment. He may perceive that his breathing apparatus is threatened, and that can prove a major distraction. One example of effective distraction occurred when a burly suspect grabbed a Midwestern officer by the shirt with both his hands and "curled" him into his Inside. This is one of the most powerful upper body moves someone can make. The officer could not pry the offender's hands apart—until he jabbed the jugular notch. The sudden distraction weakened the suspect's grip for an instant, and the officer then easily peeled himself loose.

If the suspect responds to the pain, you can use these Pressure Points to direct him to the ground—or bring him off the ground—with minimal force and with much less skill than most of the martial arts-type control techniques require. With *loud* verbal commands and directional pressure, you can guide him wherever you want him to go, making sure to keep him off-center. Some trainers refer to this as *"power steering."* To prevent him jerking away from the pain and breaking contact, keep your free hand on his head opposite the Pressure Point to serve as a counterforce.

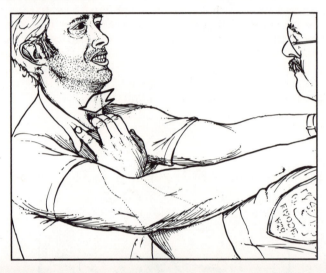

Three other of the most-used Pressure Points are located where you can strike them with your baton, one of the newest concepts in police defensive tactics. If that's not available (and depending on your position), then try hitting with your fist or the heel of your open hand... or kicking. With these points, pain and distraction are strictly secondary benefits. The main payoff is *motor dysfunction:*

TOP OF THE FOREARM. About 2 inches below the elbow joint atop the forearm, the radial nerve runs where it is readily reached. If you

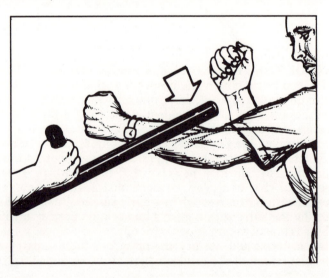

strike this spot *hard,* with the force driven toward the center of the suspect's arm, you can take out the use of his arm and hand. In particular, he'll find it difficult or impossible to control his index finger, his middle finger and his thumb. This Pressure Point, then, may be an appropriate target when you're trying to disarm a suspect with physical measures or when you are acting to keep him from disarming you. If you're at close quarters and don't have time to draw your gun to counter an assault with a knife, for example, going for the assailiant's radial may be an option to make the subject drop the knife.

ON THE LEG. Hit correctly with your baton, this Pressure Point not only will collapse and temporarily immobilize the leg you strike, but can also set off a sympathetic reflex in the other leg, tumbling the suspect to the ground. You also can inflict intense pain and befuddling mental stunning. The point of impact should be on the outside rear quadrant of the upper leg about 4 inches above the knee. That's where the common peroneal nerve branches off from the sciatic nerve. Do not strike for the knee joint, which can produce permanent damage to cartilage, ligaments, tendons, bones, etc. Keep your baton parallel to the ground as it hits to keep it from glancing off. Don't snap it back immediately after impact. Let the blow *sink in* a bit to deliver the most force. An alternative is to kick so that your hard shin strikes this Pressure Point.

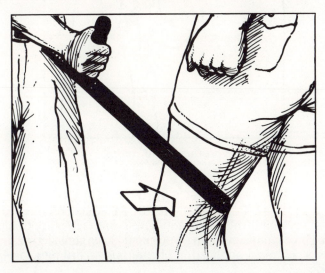

ON THE CALF. Roughly the same pain, stunning, immobilization, dysfunction and sympathetic response can be inflicted by striking the suspect's calf with your baton. Deliver your blows directly into the calf, preferably at the top. You'll connect with the tibial nerve (the lower branch of the sciatic nerve), which starts just above the back of the knee and runs down through the back of the leg muscle.

To aid in training, some officers paste small orange dots on each Pressure Point location in the arms and legs of a partner. Using foam rubber batons, they then practice striking the dots as the partner moves. Soon they are able to strike the correct location, despite fast, unpredictable movement. In street encounters, some officers have reported being able to visualize these dots on a combative suspect, helping them Focus mentally on their intended target areas.

For your safety, in no case should Pressure Point control be applied for a sustained period of time. Subjected to prolonged pain, some suspects could pass out...but, more important, others will experience a rush of adrenalin and anger that will super-energize them into more violent behavior, increasing your risk of injury and death. As soon as a suspect complies with your commands, or his resistive tension subsides to a level you can control with less force, ease off on your pressure. *Reward compliance.* This is important from the legal standpoint of not employing "excessive" force, also. If the technique doesn't end his resistance *quickly,* disengage or escalate to higher force.

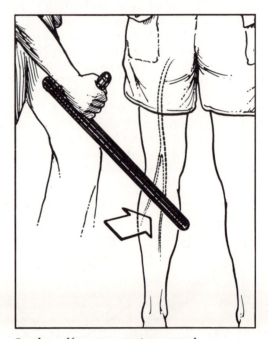

On the calf pressure point control.

Stay flexible. DON'T BECOME FIXATED ON THIS OR ANY OTHER PHYSICAL CONTROL MEASURE. You don't *have* to hang in and *make* any *one* thing work. You have *other* tactical options, up and down the Force Continuum, that you should keep considering. Indeed, in some cases the rapid application of *multiple* techniques may be what works best.

When Pressure Points do lead to control, a major advantage is that they don't drain your energy. In one experiment, Missouri officers discovered that by using Pressure Points they could cut the average length of physical conflicts to only *10 seconds.* Their stamina stayed higher and their heart rates lower than when they used random control techniques.

Also the Pressure Point system can *sound* as impressive in the courtroom as it *works* impressively on the street. Imagine how your credibility is enhanced if you are able to testify: "The strike from my impact weapon was delivered to the common peroneal nerve, which caused a motor dysfunction, a temporary weakening of the affected muscle group. The strike also produced a flex-reflex response—that is, an involuntary flexing and relaxation of the knee joint—which caused the offender to fall. Once the offender was down, I had the opportunity to gain control and apply handcuffs."

If you try Pressure Point control unsuccessfully and then have to escalate your force, you can testify that you attempted a lower level of force before going higher, again strengthening your image of cool, tactical professionalism.

Countermeasures

Countermeasures are techniques for forcefully using your hands, arms, elbows, legs, knees and/or feet to gain control over a No person...or regain it if you've lost it. Your goal with any Countermeasure is to *get the suspect to the ground* for handcuffing...or get him away from you long enough to disengage from the encounter or to *draw your weapon*. These tactics employ *gross movements* (that is, large and simple ones) rather than delicate or complex actions.

Some Countermeasures are considered "passive" (sometimes called "soft"), because they produce a low-level stun or take an assailant off his center and direct him to the ground with relatively little risk of serious injury. Others are "active" (or "hard"). When you use some of them, you'd *like* to be using your baton or firearm, but for one reason or another (time, distance, circumstances) you can't. Active Countermeasures may inflict serious injury. They're not nice, but when you have to use them you're at risk of suffering "not nice" consequences if you don't. Aside from the neck restraint perhaps, they are the surest means of stopping a violent assailant with your empty hands.

One example of **Passive Countermeasures** is the:

BRACHIAL STUN. Your target here is a spot at the base of your assailant's neck about halfway between the side and the front—*not on his throat*. This spot is where many nerve fibers radiating from the neck vertebrae meet to form the brachial plexus group. To stop a fighter, swing your arm against this site so that the meaty muscle mass of your inside forearm impacts it *hard*. Direct your force toward the center of his neck. Your strike is likely to cause high-intensity pain and mental stunning for

Emotionally disturbed subject presents a brachial stun opportunity.

In (4) the deputy rolls the subject's head to protect his larynx. Then in (5) he applies the brachial stun. In (6) the subject is directed to the ground and manuevered to a handcuffing position. During this response no guns were drawn. An excellent example of two deputies working as a team to control a potentially dangerous subject.

up to 7 seconds. It may also temporarily impair movement of his arm on that side, and in some cases will knock him into a low level of unconsciousness. By the time his mental faculties are back in gear, you can have him down and handcuffed.

A low-level stun can also be delivered with the:

HEAD SLAP. With your palm open, swing your arm in hard and fast and hit the side of your attacker's head with the part of your palm that is at the base of your fingers. If you can strike his side cheekbone area, you'll produce the severest jarring.

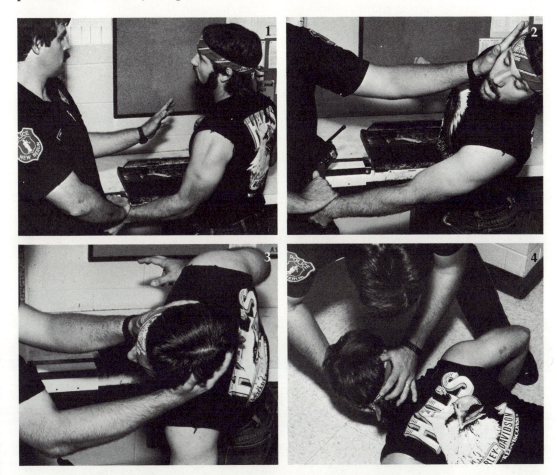

Active Countermeasures, representing higher force options done in close to a suspect, consist of high-level stuns...strikes or kicks...and "blitzes."

HIGH-LEVEL STUNNING not only disorients a No suspect's mental processes by giving his brain more sudden stimulation than it can accommodate, but also interferes with his respiratory system to help you get control. Yet, because it spreads the trauma of impact over a wider area, it is not as likely to do as much damage to the subject's body as a more concentrated strike or kick. Thus, it's generally easier to defend in court and, in some respects, tends to be more effective on the street, too. Some officers find it to be the most realistic option for handling maniacs, martial artists and other subjects who present unusual difficulty.

Sudden assaults can often be countered successfully with the startling *"wall stun."* If a suspect grabs you, tries to push or strike you or lunges for you, he'll expect you to react "naturally" by jerking away or stepping back. Doing so keeps you at the distance *he* wants. Instead, abruptly move *forward.* Move from your "center" so that you move with all your power. With your hands already up in the defensive stance, strike his chest (or his arms if they're in the way) *hard* with your forearms, and with your *full body force* drive him backwards into a wall, a tree, a utility pole, your squad car or some other solid surface. *This may be one of your best options if you are smaller than he is.* Turn your body slightly as you go into him to protect your sidearm. If the nearest object is a few feet away, move quickly and forcefully with a step-and-drag and propel

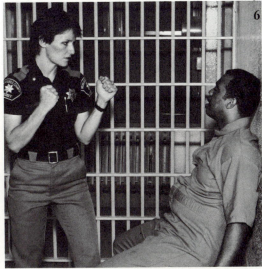

In this series, the "wall stun" was applied after a prisoner attempted to assault the deputy. (3) She assumes the high guard positioning to protect herself from the oncoming hold. (4) Notice how the stun is diffused. She doesn't actually strike him. (6) Now the deputy can follow-through by disengaging until assistance arrives.

him back rapidly. Just as he strikes the obstruction, twist your upper body and thrust your chest (pectoral muscle) hard at a slight angle into his chest.

This "double tap" adds to the force of the impact. The larger your attacker is than you are, the more important this tap is. The suspect experiences diffused trauma along his spine. The jarring collision disrupts the synapses of his brain ("disconnects his personal computer system") and knocks the wind out of him. However, his skull is unlikely to crack against the wall because your pushing him thrusts his head forward. To the extent he's able to think at all now, his consuming focus will be on breathing again. He is distracted from all else. You should be able to get him to the ground, perhaps by simple guidance alone, without having to hit him again. It'll help if you yell, "Get down!" as you stun him. In the suggestible state induced by stunning, he may at least drop to his knees.

Any time you can get an assailant bent over, either with a wall stun, a knee to the stomach or some other method, you're in a good position then to "ground stun" him to thwart further resistance. Standing with your knees flexed at Position 1 or 2, hook your hands behind his neck with the fingers of one hand firmly gripping the knife edge of the other. Pull your elbows toward each other to secure his head. As you yell, "Kneel!" or "Get down!", step-and-drag backward to pull him forward off-center. As he starts to fall, you can disengage by pushing down on him sharply with your clasped hands, then stepping back to draw your gun or baton as he goes on down. If you are smaller than he is, this might be your best choice. But if you feel you are capable of physically controlling him, you can give him the final push and follow him on down, tactically.

The *body stun* may be effective if the subject tries to get back up. Just as your assailant starts to rise, throw your feet out and fall full-weight on top of him. You want to land either angled across his back or

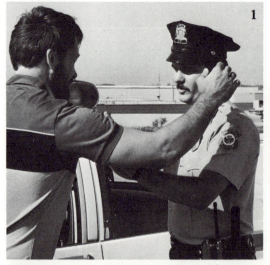

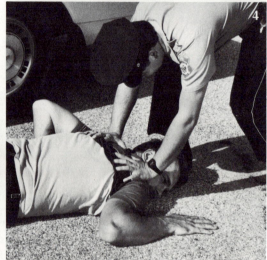

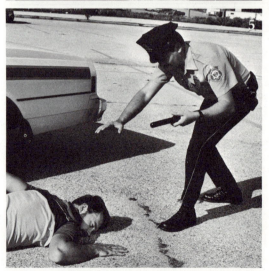

The "ground stun." (5) Now you can escalate with your baton or move onto a ground handcuffing procedure. Notice the officer's control of distance and the fact that he did not pull out his sidearm, thinking this was the only follow-through consideration.

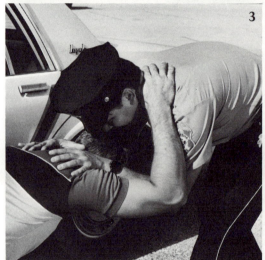

with your head toward his buttocks to avoid being hit in the face by his head. Land on his upper back with your forearms, then immediately double tap with your pectoral. This won't knock the wind out of you because you don't hit him with your stomach, but it will empty his lungs. As he's gasping and dazed, scoop his arm up and handcuff him. You can also do a body stun from the *ground*, in case a suspect has you in a wrestling match there. Try to break free enough just to push up over him, then collapse on him and double tap. Even if you're small (120 pounds or less), falling from 3 or 4 feet will give you significant force on impact. Stunning a subject just *once* is generally all it takes. You thus avoid any drawn-out confrontation.

(below) A rowdy, intoxicated subject eventually requires Countermeasures. The officer on the right separates the less resistant participant.

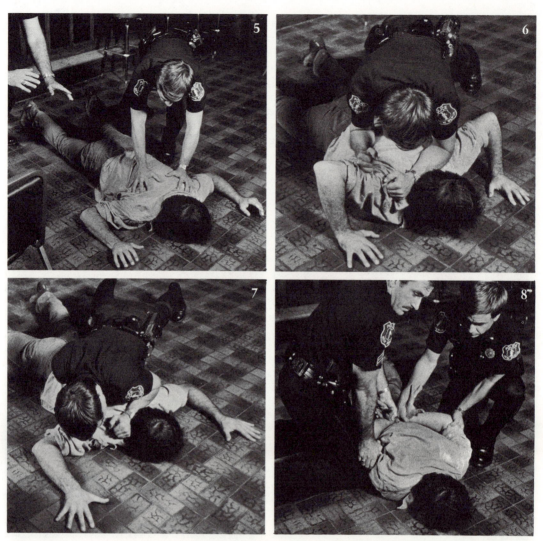

The "body stun" is applied when the subject attempts to get up off the floor. The application of the technique is with the body, not the hands.

Unarmed **STRIKES** or **KICKS** may be more difficult to perform successfully, especially if you are a smaller officer with limited strength. These are not pushes, shoves or taps. You *smash* him with your *total power* ("give him all your love," as one trainer puts it), keeping in mind what's called the *"fluid shock wave"* concept. That is, you don't throw a punch and immediately snap your hand back. Nor do you try to drive it *through* your target, as is often taught. Neither style delivers the greatest impact from your blow. Instead, you should connect to your target with full power and *let the blow sink in* a bit. This detonates a ripple effect through the assailant's tissues and body fluids that spreads your energy force deep and wide within him. It is somewhat akin to the damaging hydrostatic pressure caused by bullet penetration. Don't leave your hand there indefinitely, of course, or you give the subject an important part of you to grab.

The most effective strikes or kicks are paired with "set-up" hits that distract or disorient your attacker and open him up for your primary strike, whose purpose is to decentralize him.

One combination, for example, starts with a *jab* by your off hand to his jaw from a high-guard, defensive position. Don't try to seriously hurt him or knock him out. You just want to divert his attention, stop his forward movement and hopefully get his hands up to his face to clear his abdominal area. Keep your fist *vertical* and *clenched*. There's less risk of jamming your wrist this way, and if he should block your punch there's less chance of breaking or spraining your fingers than if they are open.

Follow your jab with a hard punch *downward* into his stomach with your strong hand. Aim for his *belly button*. The blow will knock the wind out of him, moderately stun him and help drive him down. If you're so close to him you can't throw a punch well, then "shorten the stick" (bend your arm) and strike him in the stomach with a hard blow from your *forearm and elbow*. Pivot your hips and keep your fist doubled, palm down, for maximum power. Another alternative, after your jab, is to drive your *knee* up into his stomach.

Do not count on just one strike doing the job, no matter how strong you are. Be prepared to "*overload*" the subject with multiple hits to the same location...or to escalate to a higher-force technique...or to disengage if the technique is not effective.

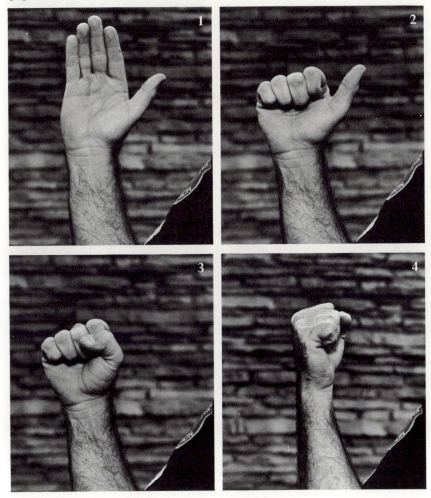

How to form a proper fist for a jab that's powerful.

What makes the tactic work is proper hand positioning. The subject who assaults is a No person. (3) The one-two punch combination. Once the technique works, the subject is brought to the ground for handcuffing.

For a Countermeasures *kick*, a good set-up is a jab with your *foot* to his knee. Hit the *front* of his knee with the *ball* of your foot. This may shake his center and start him off balance or at least stop his forward assault. Then with your other leg, deliver an *"angle kick"* to his leg. Bring your knee up toward his leg at about a 45° angle and drive your shin into the outside rear quadrant of his leg, about 4 inches above his knee, then complete your step. If you can do this in one continuous, fluid motion it will be hard for him to grab your leg and easier for you to maintain your balance. Your strike should affect his common peroneal nerve. A full strike will likely knock him down or so weaken his leg that he will have difficulty standing. This kick will also work to the *inside* of his thigh if he is standing with one leg forward. And you can impact with your *knee* rather than your shin if that works better for you. Your shin is like a big baseball bat and is capable of delivering about three times more power than your baton.

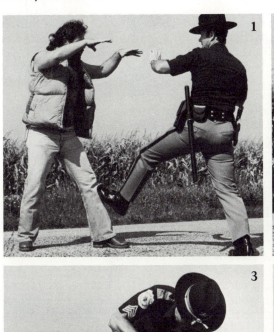

Rather than the foot jab, you sometimes can use a baton as a diversion. Cock your baton and warn the suspect that you're about to use it. When his attention goes there, then step in and deliver an angle kick. Some officers are agile enough they can kick an offender in the *stomach*, which also produces dramatic and immediate results. But remember, the higher your foot goes, the greater the risk that he will grab it.

A **BLITZ** is like playing a fourth-down-and-goal defense: you pull out all the stops. When other Countermeasures fail or when you are unable to disengage from other physical control efforts, this offers you strong probability of either gaining control of the subject or being able to disengage safely.

It consists of multiple strikes with your elbows and knees until you can break loose or your assailant goes down. This can deliver devastating force. In some states, blitzing could be considered deadly force because of its propensity for great bodily harm, so it's appropriate *only* when you're *desperate.*

When you're facing an attacker Inside, you can *elbow blitz* three ways:

1. thrusting your elbows out as fast and as hard as you can from a ready or defensive stance *horizontally.* In other words, you tighten your fists palms down, keep your forearms parallel to the ground and blast straight into the suspect's chest or midsection. Pivot your hips to strengthen the blows. The striking surfaces should be 1-2½ inches forward from your elbows on the hard, bony edges of your forearms; 2) striking *up* at about a 45° angle. Here you're smashing your elbows into your assailant's face; 3) striking *down* at 45°. If your attacker is bent over at all, you can blitz his head and shoulders this way to help bring him to the ground.

Knee blitzes, of course, can jackhammer his legs or stomach. Or in extreme circumstances you can hook behind his head with your hands, pull it down and repeatedly drive your knees up into his face. Just think of yourself as a pompon cheerleader doing a high, fast, can-can dance—but with devastating results. *Any blitz should definitely be considered capable of inflicting serious bodily harm on the subject.* Don't do it unless you can justify that level of force.

Blitzing is a close-range option. The only time you can use it is when you are within 18 inches or so of your assailant. If you try to reach a suspect who's out of range, your impact will be minimal. As a rule of thumb, you're close enough to blitz if you're close enough to rub shoulders with the subject.

The power of these strikes must come from your body, not just from your limbs. Torque your hips and upper body the same direction as the striking limb is moving for fast, explosive, maximum force.

Blitzing can get you out of at least 90% of otherwise no-win physical conflicts, its developers estimate. It can be done regardless of what position you are in. An elbow blitz can even work against what many officers consider a tough hold to break—a bear hug from behind. With whatever force and range of movement you can manage, start driving your elbows repeatedly back into your attacker's ribs and stomach. Try to blast him with their *points* as much as possible. A few good impacts will probably prompt him to relax his arms somewhat, allowing you to deliver even greater force, until you can strike to the subject's face and break free. An alternative, if you're about the same height as your attacker, is to butt your head back hard into his face.

Blitzing might have helped two West Coast troopers who were attacked by two suspects during the search of a car they'd stopped for a traffic violation. One officer was grabbed around the neck from the rear and the other was knocked to the ground because he was too close to his attacker to swing his baton effectively. Without a close-quarters technique that worked, the first officer was disarmed, the second surrendered his sidearm and the suspects fled the scene. During a high-speed chase that followed, one of the officers was shot, four vehicles were damaged or disabled by gunfire and two others were wrecked when they collided.

Any time you're confronted alone by *multiple attackers* who assault suddenly from in close, your tactical strategy will probably favor Countermeasures as your best initial option. Concentrate on defeating and

The Knee Blitz.

controlling *one assailant at a time.* Try to keep him positioned between you and the others as you "adjust his attitude." This provides a buffer to keep them away from you. Throw the subjects against each other if you can, or use one as a "wall" to stun another. Such Countermeasures may buy you the ability eventually to reach your baton or sidearm.

On the other hand, if there are two officers and one assailant, one effective tactic is for you or your partner to fight the subject while the other moves to Position 2½ or 3 and applies a neck twist (where the head goes, the body goes)...Pressure Point control (bring your hand up sharply under his nose from behind and simultaneously press your thumb into the mandibular angle under his ear, for example)...a brachial stun...Countermeasures...or neck restraint.

Working from behind is often an effective role for a *female* partner. Suspects commonly let female officers preliminarily position themselves to advantage because the suspects fail to perceive these officers as threats. This may allow partners to strategically "bracket" a subject between them. Usually if a male officer is present, he will be the target of attack and a female, with effective control skills, can provide a surprising counterattack.

As with other physical controls, Countermeasures should *cease* when the subject complies with your verbal commands or ends his resistive tension. Your purpose is not to brutalize him. However, do not stop *thinking* of him as a No person. *Once someone goes No, he should stay No in your mind.* You should never leave him uncontrolled, no matter how subdued you get him to appear.

Any time you're assaulted, *drop any nondefense items that you have in your hands.* These are no longer important; therefore in terms of your concerns they should *cease to exist.* Too often officers behave like a Wisconsin patrolman, who was taking notes during a field interview with a suspected prowler when the subject suddenly grabbed the officer's throat. While the assailant was trying to choke him out, the officer was busy trying to tuck his flashlight into his belt! Another officer was assaulted and shot five times at contact range with a .22. All the time the offender was attacking, the officer was trying to get his radio functional. He didn't realize that when bullets were ripping into him it was too late to call for help...too late even to try to use his own firearm. Where his attention should have been focused then was on his only true option: physical force.

Your tools are valuable *only* so long as they are appropriate to your needs. You may have to *train* yourself specifically to get rid of them under stress. For this, you can use a piece of 2 x 4 cut to simulate your portable radio, a large dowel as your flashlight, etc. When you're attacked, don't even take time and effort to throw what you're holding in your assailant's face or throw it down. Just *let it fall*...and fight back with Countermeasures until you can disengage or escalate to your baton or firearm.

Neck Restraint

Neck restraints have fallen into disrepute with many police administrators and officers—not because they're ineffective, but because their use (or misuse) has created severe civil liability problems. Deaths from so-called "choke holds" have sparked vehement protests from offender sympathizers. And at least one influential medical association has categorized neck restraints as deadly force.

Nevertheless, *proper* neck force should be among your tactical capabilities. You should use it only *selectively,* generally as an unarmed technique of *last resort.* The more violent an attacker is and the bigger and stronger he is than you, the more valuable this control option becomes. In trying to subdue actively resistant subjects whose rage, pain tolerance and strength are extraordinarily high, it may be the *only* unarmed technique that works.

In practical terms, it can save you in summer when an offender's wrists and arms are sweaty, making him difficult to control with other holds, and in winter when bulky clothing may interfere with effective

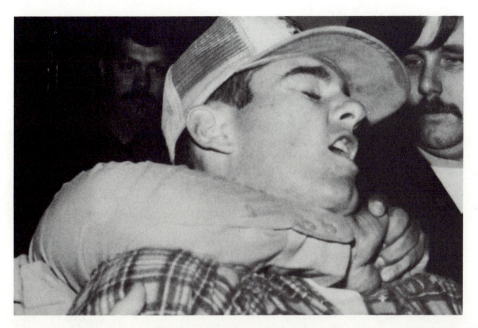

Bar Arm Choke Hold is obsolete and dangerous. Pressure is applied across the throat by the arm pushing backward and the hand behind pushing forward. The effect is to slowly shut off the air supply. DO NOT USE THIS PROCEDURE. (below right) An unacceptable procedure to control blood circulation in the head. With the improper application shown here, there is no control of backward movement nor neck protection. Remember: NO TECHNIQUE SHOWN ON THIS PAGE SHOULD BE USED.

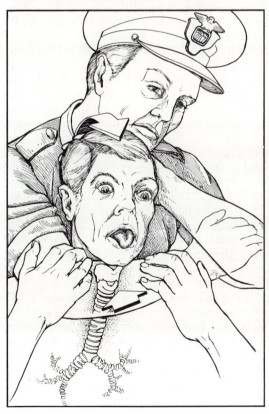

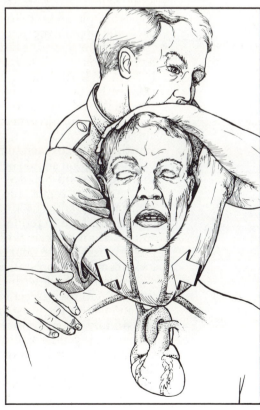

pain compliance. The truth is that if you get into a battle royal and feel yourself losing, you'll probably try to choke your opponent. That's a natural human response to desperation. With a proper neck restraint, you can apply force roughly to the same area of his body that is even more effective than choking, which realistically may only fuel a more violent, panicked reaction against suffocation and excruciating pain from a suspect who's already out of control.

In short, the right neck force is safer for him—and for you. Yet it has a power that is inescapable.

The safest and fastest neck hold is the **lateral vascular neck restraint.** Sometimes called "the sleeper hold," it involves your applying pressure to the sides of a violent subject's neck in such a way that if he continues to resist he literally knocks himself out. It can be adapted to work from an assailant's front, side or back, while you are standing, kneeling or lying down.

To apply this restraint from Position 3:

Quickly encircle the suspect's neck with one of your arms, preferably your left if you shoot right-handed. (You should be proficient with both arms, though.) Turn sideways to him with your knees braced and bent as you make contact to get your sidearm away and to position yourself for the steadiest balance if he tries to react backward. Your staying back to the side makes it harder for him to resist by grabbing your groin, blitzing with his elbows or pitching you over his head.

Your left palm should be down and your elbow should form a "V" directly in front of the offender's throat. In this position, the bicep of your upper arm touches one side of his neck and the inside of your forearm the other side, keeping his neck from moving sideways. Raise your right hand, palm up, and grasp your left hand so your palms are together. Now you can apply pressure to the suspect's neck by drawing your right hand back and up, closing your left arm in a pincer effect.

Be sure that your elbow stays in FRONT of his THROAT and the palms of your hands BEHIND his SHOULDERS. It's a *"neck brace"* hold, NOT A CHOKE HOLD. The pressure you apply should be only to the *sides* of his neck, leaving his windpipe unaffected. Otherwise you are potentially delivering deadly force. If your hands are not behind him, you risk having your forearm across his throat in a bar-arm choke hold where, among other damage, it can crush his trachea, instantly and fatally shutting off all oxygen to his lungs. Also, in that position you are closer to him than you should be, and he has a greater chance of using leverage to knock you off balance.

As you're establishing your hold, place the side of your head above your ear against the back of the subject's head. This creates some forward counterpressure to reinforce the pull of your arm…helps hold his head so it is aligned safely with his spine…helps keep his neck positioned properly relative to your arm…prevents him from butting you…and locks him in to forestall escape.

Simultaneous with these actions, step-and-drag back sharply so that you pull the suspect backward onto his heels and off-balance. Then he can't use his leg, waist or shoulder strength to continue resisting. He'll remain under your control so long as you continue to break his balance backward. If you have difficulty getting him off-center, pull back and at the same time step down hard on his calf with the ball of your foot, driving in against the back of his knee. His leg will buckle and he'll lean back. This is especially helpful in dealing with a suspect taller than you.

Should he manage to get you on the ground, you can still control him so long as you keep your arm around his neck. If you're on your back with him above, wrap your legs around him and pull them down to straighten out his body as much as possible and increase your arm pressure against the sides of his neck.

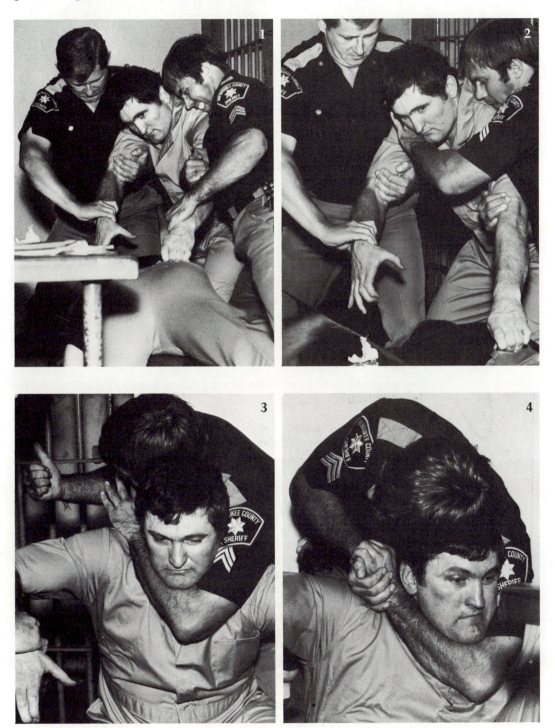

The proper technique with a No person. (1) The deputies encounter one deputy down and attempt to pull the subject off. (2) The neck is encircled. (3) Level 1 restraint applied. (4) Level 2 restraint. ➤

(5) Level 3 restraint applied. (6) Subject is lowered to the ground to be handcuffed and searched. Under control, he can be monitored.

In any position, you can apply three distinct levels of force, depending on his resistance. This allows you to use what's necessary to control him and to relax to lesser force as you gain cooperation. Again, applying this force *properly* is very important. Done wrong, it can be extremely dangerous.

For **mild restraint,** just hold his neck loosely with his balance broken to the rear. This is often enough to break up fights, keep belligerents from getting at each other or to convince an uncooperative subject that he can be easily controlled.

For **medium restraint**, hold him firmly by the neck with his balance broken. If he continues to resist, raise your rear elbow about 20° and apply more pressure. This increases his pain by pressing on his nerves and begins to compress major blood vessels that are associated with the brain's supply of oxygenated blood. (The conventional view holds that the carotid arteries are affected, but some medical authorities lately have theorized that certain important *veins* are really what's affected.) Usually this controls all but the most violent subject, as it proves he is firmly restrained and can't resist at will.

Extreme resistance with refusal to submit gets **maximum restraint.** Keep his balance broken, raise your rear elbow about 45° and increase pressure to the sides of his neck until all movement and resistance stops. This should occur within 4 to 7 seconds as the neck restraint produces unconsciousness if the suspect persists in resisting. Then ease off your pressure *immediately.*

In some cases, the use of maximum restraint may involve several officers—against PCP users, for example, or other suspects exhibiting superhuman strength who cannot be controlled by just you and your partner. One technique here is the *"pile on."* Four officers surround the offender, each takes an arm or a leg to control as they literally pile on him and a fifth applies the lateral vascular neck restraint. Good communication and *coordination* among the officers is important to minimize the risk of injury. Of course this technique is *not* designed as an option of choice for dealing with suspects who are *armed.*

With any level of restraint, give *loud verbal directions* all along in an effort to stop the suspect's resisting. Emphasize: "Sir! Stop! Relax! You're making it worse!" Indeed, the more he resists, the more efficient this hold *does* become. His struggling accelerates the effect. By exerting himself, he is consuming an abnormal quantity of oxygen. Yet at the same time, he's shutting off his oxygen supply. Just having your arm around his neck prompts him psychologically to hold his breath or to hyperventilate. As you bring him back off center, it tightens up his diaphragm, making breathing more difficult. The pressure on his neck constricts major vessels involving the blood needed by his brain. With enough struggling under these circumstances, he'll become weaker and eventually become unconscious.

If this happens, lower him carefully to the ground, protecting his head and handcuff him immediately. Lay him on his side so he won't choke if he vomits. As his muscles relax, anticipate that he may also defecate or urinate involuntarily. He should revive in 5 to 20 seconds without assistance. Be sure to loosen any tight clothing around his neck which may hamper his breathing. If he doesn't revive within 30 seconds, immediately begin medical procedures to revive him as a precaution. When he comes around, advise him that medical attention is available. Some authorities recommend that the suspect should then be closely monitored for about an hour, with a means of cardiopulmonary resuscitation at hand, if needed. Indeed, some agencies require that *any* time a neck restraint is used, the subject must be examined by a physician afterwards.

CAUTION: A baton should *never* be used in applying a neck restraint. In California, Pennsylvania and elsewhere, baton choke holds have broken suspects' necks. Also you should resist applying the lateral vascular restraint repeatedly to the same subject, if at all possible. Even though this is the safest neck force known, it is remotely possible that its use can affect nerves that will cause the suspect's heart to slow down. This can be dangerous to an already unhealthy heart, perhaps leading to cardiac arrest. Each additional application increases the risk of such injury.

Tactical Handcuffing

The first step in survival-conscious handcuffing is to *stabilize* the suspect once you feel he's under control. That is, you get him in a position where your reactionary gap is spaced to your advantage...his ability to move is modified...and handcuffs can be applied with fast, efficient, fluid motions. He can then remain essentially in this position while you search him. If he is still fighting and is not stabilized, you should not be attempting to handcuff him, for there are very few suspects whose arms you can simply muscle behind them. *It's control first, then handcuffing.*

If you are smaller and weaker than the offender and have a legitimate fear that he could overpower you, don't be in a hurry to handcuff.

Back off with your sidearm on him, verbally get him proned out—arms out, palms up, head turned…and *wait for backup.* If he gets up and tries to attack you, you may have cause to consider deadly force. If he runs, you may decide to let him go and figure he'll be dealt with later under more favorable circumstances. DON'T CHARGE IN AND TRY TO HAND-CUFF IF YOU KNOW YOU CAN'T CONTROL HIM. *It is no longer considered necessary for proper police action that you knowingly expose yourself to probable injury.* You have options for how deeply you feel it is appropriate to get involved. If you can't establish control, given what you have to work with and what the suspect has to resist with, *disengage.*

Some traditional stabilization poses are now considered far *too risky* to use any more. One is the *"wall search"* position, where the suspect spreads his legs and leans or braces against the side of a building, a patrol car or some other more-or-less vertical surface. Besides encouraging the potentially deadly mistake of searching before handcuffing, this position can easily become a booby trap for you. At the very least, an offender braced against a wall can quickly drop down to one knee and assault from that position, possibly with a concealed weapon you have not yet detected. Prison inmates and some other seasoned offenders are known to spend hours practicing ways to spin off walls or to trip, overcome and disarm arresting officers from such positions. The flat surface merely serves them as a platform from which to attack you, as a young officer in Massachusetts discovered after making a vehicle stop and finding a stolen tv set in the car's back seat. He had the driver and a passenger "spread-eagled" on the trunk when the driver suddenly bounced back and began scuffling with him. The officer was disarmed and shot in the neck at point-blank range as he radioed for help. He died later in the arms of his new bride, also an officer and one of the first who responded to try to save his life.

Obsolete and potentially dangerous control and arrest positions. Why?

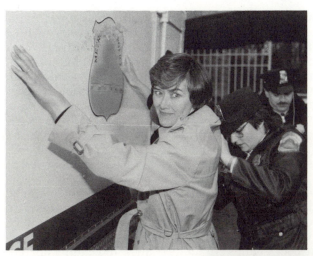

(above and right) The classic problem of searching before handcuffing. A real failure to operate in Condition Yellow. (below) In a multiple arrest situation such as this drug bust, commanding the arrestees to this prone positioning can be effective. Of course, you want to avoid walking amongst them like this tactical officer is doing.

Also increasingly disfavored is kneeling where the suspect, facing away from you, interlaces his fingers behind his head and you grip them in a pain-compliance hold to control his hands for handcuffing. Street-wise offenders practice with this position, too. Many now know how to lock you in at the moment you grasp their fingers, duck forward and flip you overhead. Some academies no longer teach this technique because smaller officers, especially, tend to lose control when using it.

And blatantly unsatisfactory is a prone technique seriously recommended at a national training session by one instructor. According to his tactics, you order the suspect down on the ground, put a .357 Magnum in his mouth, toss a pair of handcuffs onto his back and say, "'Cuff yourself!"

What's better is a combination of tactical positioning and a version of newly-developed *"speed 'cuffing"* that gives you surer control faster with less risk. It offers a handcuffing *plan,* in contrast to the most common procedure among officers: fumbling for control...trying to manage both the suspect's hands simultaneously...and ending up making different moves every time.

To stabilize and handcuff a seemingly cooperative, nonviolent **YES SUSPECT:**

Tell him to raise his hands high over his head with his fingers spread and turn around 360°. This pulls his clothing tighter and may help you spot hidden weapons.

As he faces away, have him spread his feet wide with his toes pointed out, bend slightly forward but keep his head raised back as far as he can. This prevents him from watching you through his legs. Even a karate expert can't kick from this position. Now tell him: "Stretch your arms out to the side...thumbs down. Now *slowly* bring your hands back toward me. Make like a jet fighter. Keep your thumbs down." Now he's ready for fast handcuffing.

To improve your speed, *always keep your handcuffs "loaded"* or "cocked;" i.e., with each toothed single strand pushed through its spring receiver to the *last* click. With chain-linked handcuffs, grip them in your right hand so that the top handcuff is vertical, with the single strand toward the suspect. The bottom handcuff is held between your little finger and palm so that one of its flat surfaces is facing out. (Hinged handcuffs work slightly slower because you can't twist them into this configuration, but some officers believe they are more secure once they're on, because they give the offender less mobility.)

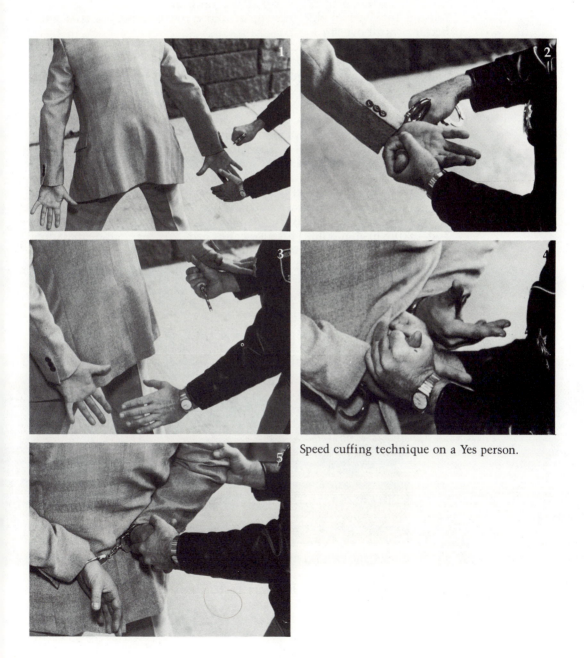

Speed cuffing technique on a Yes person.

491

Approaching from the rear with your gun side turned slightly away, reach for the subject's right hand with your left hand as if you were going to shake it. Grip his thumb in a lock. At the same time, bring the loaded single strand of the top handcuff firmly against the outer edge of his wrist. You want it to contact *between his wrist bone and his hand* (not *behind* his wrist bone, as is often taught.) This will give you the greatest leverage and roughly doubles your pain compliance capability once the handcuff is closed. Firm pressure as the handcuff touches his wrist will pop the strand through its receiver and swing it around on its rivet. Just reach over with your right index finger and push the tip back into the receiver and ratchet the handcuff closed until it is snug. Now with your thumb lock, twist or "flip" his hand, palm up and out. The grip and tension involved in this movement allow you to establish somewhat better control over him.

As you pull this hand toward the small of his back with the closed handcuff, grab his other thumb with your left hand. Turn that palm up and out and bring his hands together so they are back-to-back. Depending on how the single strand of your second handcuff is positioned, make contact from above or below his wrist. "Fire" the loaded strand around his wrist between the bone and hand and tighten its tip back through the receiver with the fingers of your left hand.

Some officers object to thumb locks. If hands are sweaty, they may be hard to control. And if the suspect is stronger than you, he can grab *your* thumb and twist you under his power. An alternative is to have him spread his fingers as he brings his arms back initially. You then control his hand by grabbing his two middle fingers instead of his thumb. If he starts struggling, you can inflict pain by sharply bending his fingers back and jerking his hand up. This also bends him over for Countermeasures like your knee to his stomach or chest, if necessary, or allows you more easily to power-drive him down to the ground.

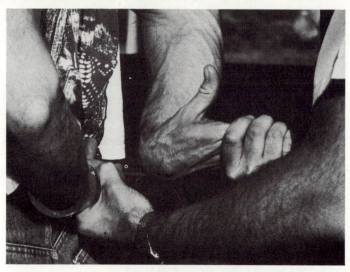

Compliance with control of the two middle fingers.

Either way, with this basic speed-'cuffing technique, you can have a subject securely "hooked up" in about *2½ seconds*.

This method has great versatility. The cooperative subject can also position his arms properly for you while kneeling or proned out (to

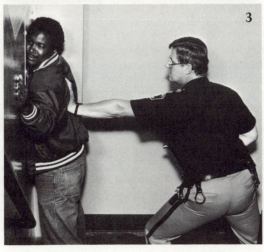

A SWAT application of the Yes person speed cuffing technique when a suspect is caught on a search warrant and you want top speed. Sequence 1–4 can be mastered with minimum role-playing.

⟶

further reduce his mobility) or while sitting in a chair (so you get him handcuffed and under control before he's on his feet). If the suspect is in a room that you're leery of entering, remain outside in a covered position and order him to put his left hand behind his head, his right arm back in the "jet wing" position. Have him walk backward to your position, handcuff his right hand first, then his left. You never have to enter the room. If you're alone, you can keep your sidearm on him until he's close, if that's appropriate, or your partner can cover.

A drunk you may want to arrest on a vehicle stop can be bluffed into the jet wing position. Get his arms back step by step by telling him those movements are part of his field sobriety test. You can then move in and speed handcuff him before he realizes he has been duped. It's a good way to keep him Yes without a fight. If you're dealing with a muscle man or

With a **MAYBE PERSON,** one option is to:

Begin handcuffing with a gooseneck hold on his right hand, his left hand behind his head. Maintain the gooseneck with your left hand, handcuff him with your right with the loaded handcuff maneuver. You can get easiest access to his wrist if you rotate his hand toward his body so his fingers point toward his chest. Keep the gooseneck effective by always keeping his wrist above his elbow.

When the handcuff is snug, grab his bicep with your right hand. Let the other handcuff just dangle. With your left hand, bring his hand down and roll it behind his back. *Keep his elbow into your stomach or chest under pressure at all times to reinforce the hold* and keep pulling back on his hand for pain compliance. Your hand on his bicep will help prevent him from twisting out.

When his hand is behind him, slip your right hand through his arm and lay it on top of his right hand to take control. Still keep his elbow wedged into your stomach. This is the point at which Maybe subjects seem most likely to try to spin away. You can often discourage this by firmly hooking his left shoulder with your left hand and telling him to stay still. When you feel he is stabilized, then release your grip and open the free handcuff with your left hand. Hook your thumb on the single strand so the handcuff stays open like a "W". Now order him to bring his left hand down and back slowly into the handcuff, then close it snug. Your left hand does the work; your right hand's only function is pain compliance.

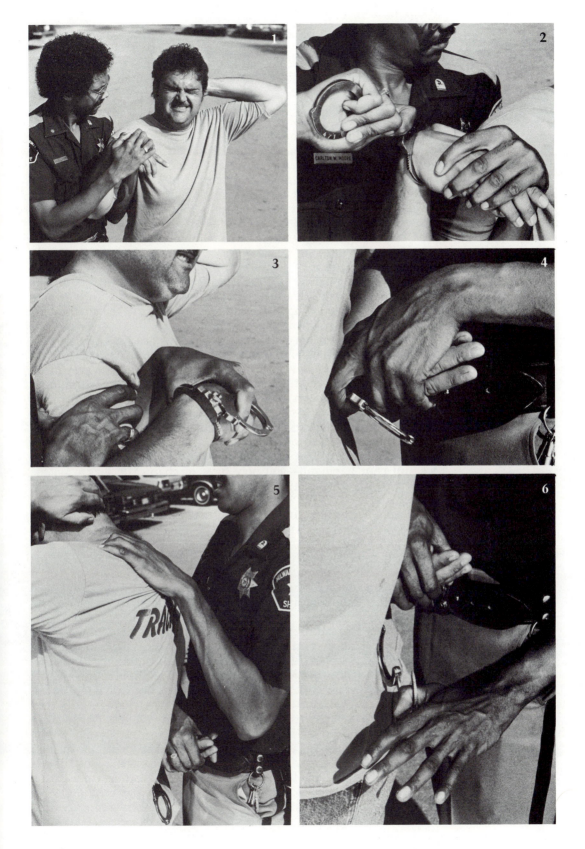

As with any subject, lead him in the escort position with your right hand gripping just above his elbow, your gun side away. *You want to AVOID letting a handcuffed suspect walk free, just as you want to AVOID handcuffing a subject in front* except with a belly chain. Any time you violate these rules you are significantly increasing your risk of assault. To escort him, keep your left hand on his right hand. If he starts struggling, you can bend his arm into a gooseneck, in which case the handcuff will add to his pain—or push him away.

A **NO SUSPECT** is stabilized *on the ground*, because that's where he ends up from your Countermeasures or other control tactics. You want him on his stomach, facing away from you. Not only does this facilitate proper handcuffing, but it also is likely to hamper his drawing a concealed weapon, because suspects generally hide weapons on the *front* of their bodies. If he's on his back, use Pressure Points and order him to turn over. Or if he's fighting, ground stun him and roll him over. Once he's on his stomach, no matter how crazy it was getting him there, you now have good options for control.

One is what's called *"the three-point landing."* Working from his right side and applying Pressure Point control to his head with your right hand if necessary, scoop up his right hand and get it in the small of his back. Apply a wrist lock to help you control it.

Move your right foot within 4 inches of his head as he faces away. Kneel so your lower leg is diagonally across his upper shoulders, with your right knee on his left shoulder. Leaning on this knee keeps him pinned down. However, *stay off his neck so there is NO pressure there.* Staying on the ball of your foot will help with that. Move your left knee in tight against his side to trap his elbow. Keep this knee on the ground— not on his body—to enhance your own stability. Continuing to bend his wrist, pull his arm up toward his neck slightly to tighten the wrist lock and his elbow. With three coordinated points—your right leg, your left knee and your left hand—you now have mechanically locked up the whole right side of his body. If he tries to move out, he will dislocate his shoulder.

Now order his left hand out to the side, palm up, so you can see he holds no weapons there. It's important that you *always* know where this hand is and what's in it.

Lift his hand slightly with your left hand, further tightening his shoulders, and handcuff it from under his wrist with your right hand. For fastest movement, hold the chain links with your palm up, the single strands pointing up your right arm. Then order his left hand back and handcuff it.

With any handcuffing situation, *don't get hung up about where the keyholes are.* That is *not* an important consideration, in light of your *true* priorities. But do DOUBLE LOCK the handcuffs. If they're double-locked, your prisoner has less chance of picking or slipping the locking mechanism. Also he can't tighten them as a way to set you up for attack by luring you into readjusting them. Nor, if he struggles, will they tighten inadvertently, cutting into his wrists and providing injuries for evidence of "police brutality." If you squeeze the single strand and the handcuff becomes tighter, it is not double-locked; if it doesn't move, it is.

To get him up, bring him first to a sitting position. Hook his left shoulder with your right hand and roll him toward you, while giving verbal direction and while continuing pain compliance with the wrist lock. From the sitting position, get him kneeling, then standing. Continue the wrist lock as he gets to his feet with you at the escort position

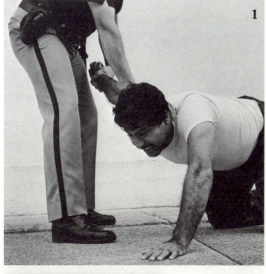

1

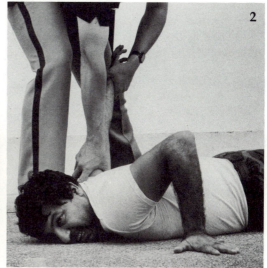

2

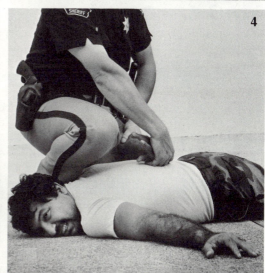

3

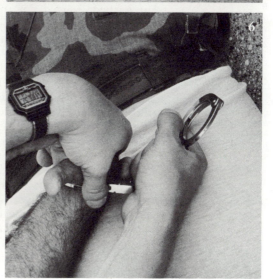

4

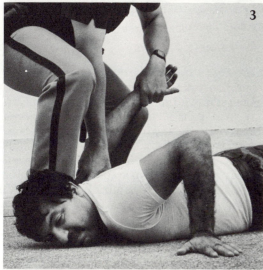

5

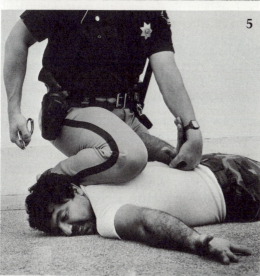

6

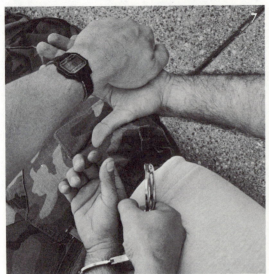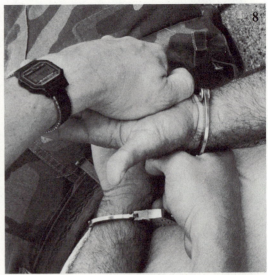

Arresting a No person. Notice how in (5) the deputy does not apply undue pressure to the arrestee's neck.

and as you lead him away. Never step in front of the offender, even though he is handcuffed. Stay at 2½ or 3 so you never turn your back to him.

For extra restraint, consider using a rappeller's D ring (which you can carry in your pocket) to secure the handcuffs' chain to the subject's belt. This is faster than trying to loop the chain itself through the belt. Also consider pulling the suspect's coat or shirt down below his shoulders so that his arms are pinned. Or bind him with a braided nylon restraining "rope," which can easily be carried in an old Mace holder or folded inside a semi-automatic magazine carrier. Some officers have also found the larger hinged handcuffs fast and effective for restraining suspects' ankles.

Remember: EVERY arrestee should be handcuffed with hands *behind* him—and *stay* handcuffed—regardless of how cooperative he appears to be. One officer was starting to hook up a drunk driver when the suspect begged not to be handcuffed. Because the man identified himself as a county employee and seemed nonviolent, the officer gave in. As he was returning his handcuffs to their case, the offender, who had no previous criminal record, whipped a small handgun from his waistband and shot the officer. Another officer took another drunk driver in handcuffs to a hospital emergency room after a traffic accident. The arrestee said the handcuffs embarrassed him, so the officer took them off. Immediately, the suspect grabbed them from the officer's hands and struck him in the face with them. The officer lost several teeth and suffered severe slashes on his face and head.

Even if an attacker is shot and appears to have been killed, handcuff him. Rather than being dead, he may still be deadly. Consider the ramifications of this California incident: swept with a suicide urge, a subject put a .22 between his eyes and shot himself. All officers at the scene thought he was dead. As they chatted, awaiting the coroner and ignoring the body, the victim sat up, put his hand over his face and mumbled, "That hurts." The bullet had glanced off his skull and angled down behind his right eye. Needless to say, those standing around complacently thinking he was out of the game and they were out of danger were given a moment they'll never forget.

Remember that any handcuffing or restraining device is *temporary.* Permanent control, from your standpoint, does not begin until a cell door clangs shut behind the suspect.

The first step is to accept the fact that you have made an arrest. (left) Drug dealer being taken into custody. (bottom left) Man who had just murdered a five year old being taken into custody—neither handcuffed! (below right) Interesting control and arrest problem here. This derelict, covered with maggots, was refused transport by two hospitals and the city jail. What would you do to transport?

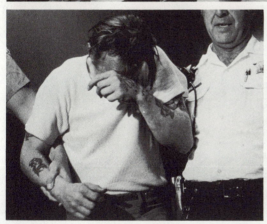

Q: Why spoil this section of the book by reminding me for the millionth time to handcuff prisoners from behind? I know that. Nobody handcuffs in front anymore.

A: If they don't do it anymore then how come...

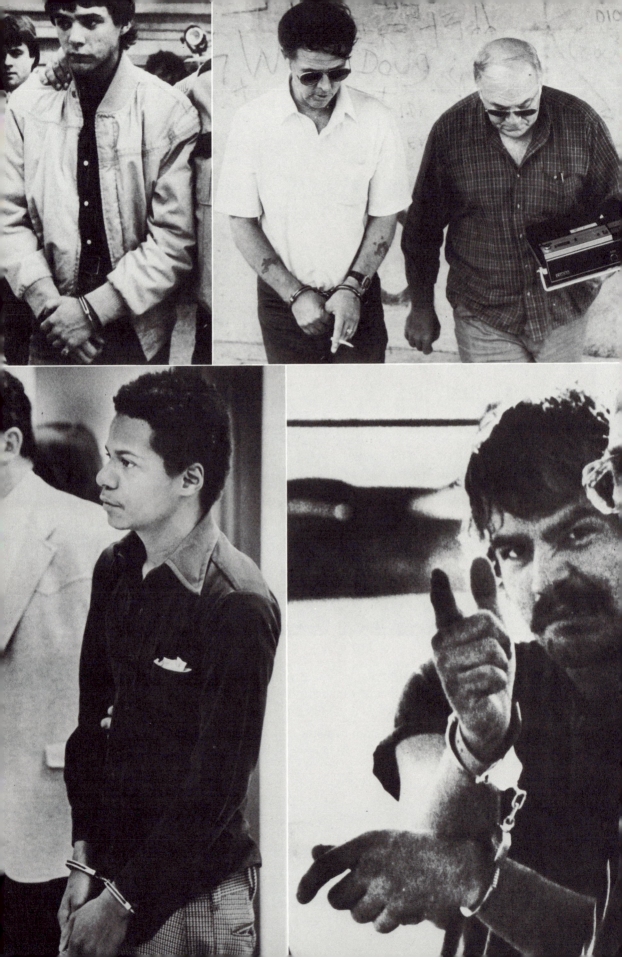

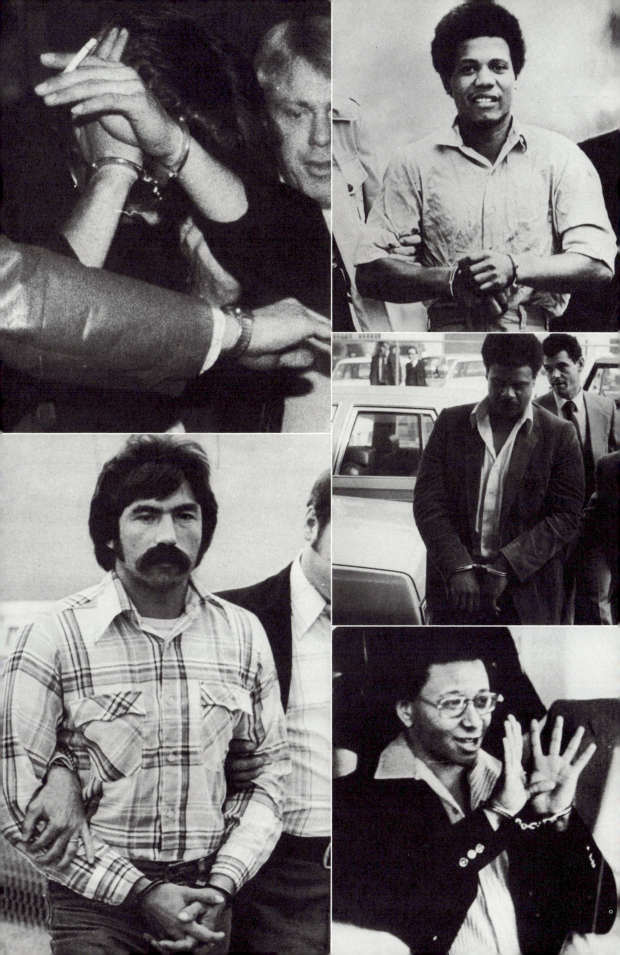

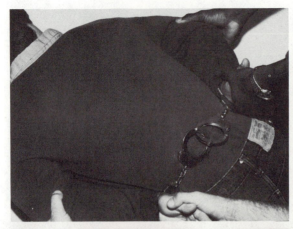

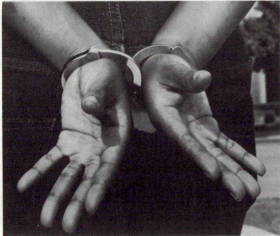

(top left) If you're dealing with a large individual who can't bring his wrists close enough together behind him, you can link two sets of handcuffs together. (above) In handcuffing small wrists, put both wrists inside one handcuff and loop the other inside the waistband. This works only with the hinged-style cuffs. The older-style handcuffs can be interlocked, making sure the ratchets don't cut the wrists.

This suspect was shot after a hostage-taking that led to the killing of an officer and three other people. Afterwards, he was handcuffed as an added precaution. Here the handcuff has been released after confirmation that he is dead.

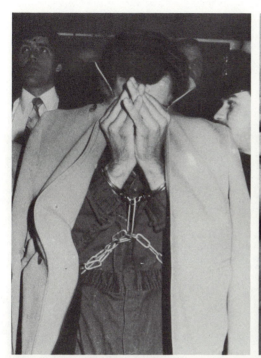

When belly chains are applied properly, they fit snug around the waist for your protection.

Eleven members of the Outlaws motorcycle gang are about to be transported to jail. High-risk prisoners with poor security procedures. They should at least be handcuffed behind and secured with leg irons.

(top left) Hard-core inmates practice defeating leg irons by tying string between their legs and hopping around. One way to defeat their mobility when transporting is to decrease the distance between feet by tying a knot in the chain. (top right) For added security, use duct tape over the key holes aimed downward. (above) Be on the alert for hidden handcuff keys. This one was made from a ballpoint pen refill. (right) Your prisoner should be stabilized and moved. Keep people away who might pass along weapons.

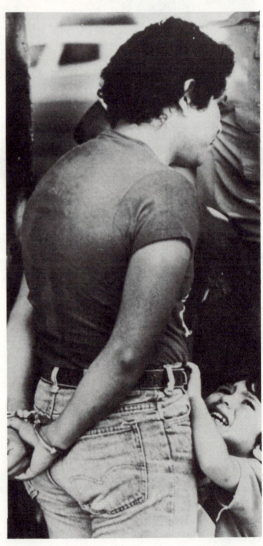

(above) Good control of a prisoner prior to transport. Officer is all alone. Yet she has a good compliance hold on her prisoner, and radios with control.
(below) The officer simply applies the same handcuffing procedure used on a Maybe person for placing a subject in the rear of the patrol car.

⟶

The prisoner's head is cupped so he does not bang his head when entering. This positioning allows you to use pressure point control and prevents you from being kicked. (above) A heavy-duty nylon cord wrapped around a No person's feet and hung outside the closed door provides excellent security against violent feet.

Mopping Up

Once the suspect is subdued and handcuffed, calm yourself, then calm him. You may be gasping for breath and unable to communicate. This weakens your control capabilities and suggests to your adversary that you're out of shape and still might be vulnerable to attack.

To help clear your thoughts, ease your emotions, restore your speech and revive your strength, *use your stress-fighting breathing exercise.* Control your exhaling; *don't pant.* Repeat until you've established a slow, rhythmic breathing pattern, which will help restore your body to its normal equilibrium.

As you gain control over your respiration, you'll find your grip on your *feelings* strengthening, too. You'll lessen the risk of a chargeable violent outburst, such as a rookie California officer experienced after he chased and grounded a suspect he was trying to arrest for driving with a revoked license. While the subject lay face down in surrender on a beach, the officer "without provocation" allegedly attacked him with his baton in the presence of more than a dozen witnesses. Their testimony earned him a five-day suspension without pay.

A better approach is to calm the subject verbally...check him for *injuries,* again talking to the audience as well as the subject ("Are you hurt, sir? Do you need medical attention?")...then stand him up promptly. This offers less temptation for abusive force than if you leave him lying on the ground.

To reduce the chance of his flaring up again, *reassure* him that nothing more will happen so long as he complies peacefully. This reinforces that *he* is the one who decides whether you use force. Take a moment to *rehab his self-image.* This is especially important if you've bested him in front of family, friends or relatives. Consider *discreetly* telling him something like, "Boy! You were really tough to take down! I really thought I was going to have to use my baton or my gun on you—you were *that* bad!" (Avoid saying you were *lucky* to subdue him, however.) If you've just put his face in the mud, this little ritual will be a welcome massage to his bruised ego. Subtly, you're indicating that the fight's over with no hard feelings...that he's tough but you're tougher...that you still have some options you didn't use. Keep your tone conversational, at the search-talk level. You don't have to rub his face in your power. Then chances are he won't feel the need to test you further. If he believes you really were impressed with him, he may spread the word on the street that "that cop can take *anybody*...he knows what he's doin'."

Many officers, once they've used force, stop talking to the suspect. This only fuels resentment and a desire to get even. Officers who reestablish rapport as soon as they can tend not to get excessive force complaints or lawsuits filed against them.

After you've searched and transported a subject, *unhandcuffing* him in a booking area or jail presents additional risks. In fact, it might be argued that more officers are injured unhandcuffing uncooperative suspects than in getting them handcuffed initially.

Maximum control for taking off handcuffs involves *three officers.*

The suspect should be positioned with his front side up flat against a wall, head turned, legs apart. The insides of his feet should be against the wall, too. One officer stands on each side of him, maintaining a "double compression" hold; that is, each officer's inside hand applies a wrist lock while the outside hand grips an elbow. The third officer, approaching from Position 3, removes the handcuffs.

As the left handcuff is released, the officer controlling that hand moves it up into a gooseneck. When the key is removed and the handcuff closed, the officer controlling the right hand rolls it up into a gooseneck. Then that handcuff is unlocked. With the suspect in a double gooseneck, he can be led into a cell or any other location you desire, with little risk that he's going to punch anyone in the face.

If just one officer knows this procedure, he can talk the others through it. Just hearing this communication helps control the suspect psychologically.

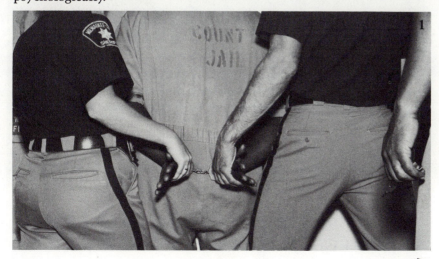

507

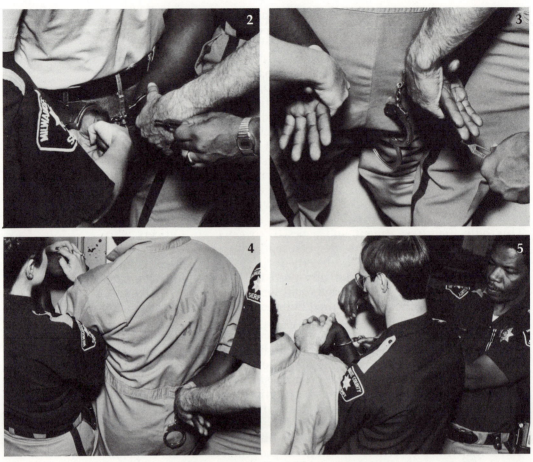

An effective technique for using extra caution when taking off handcuffs with a combative prisoner. After they are removed, a compliance hold can be used to move prisoner to his cell.

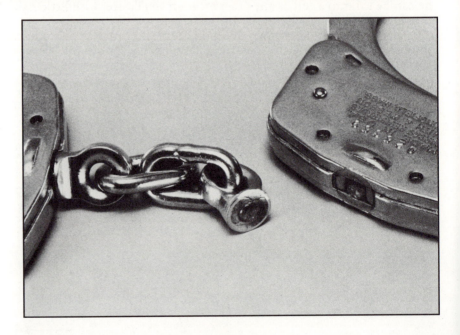

Remember, handcuffs are only a temporary restraining device. Those at the bottom of the previous page were snapped in two by an inmate who mastered the technique inside prison. The photograph above symbolizes today's offender capacity and the true need for keeping your tactical edge. As you study what is left of these handcuffs, realize that they were opened by a mentally deranged man who gripped them in his teeth and pulled. What look like marks from the jaws of a vise were made by the man's teeth.